Highly Parallel Computing

Highly Parallel Computing

SECOND EDITION

George S. Almasi
IBM Thomas J. Watson Research Center

Allan Gottlieb
NYU Courant Institute of Mathematical Sciences

The Benjamin/Cummings Publishing Company, Inc.
Redwood City, California • Menlo Park, California
Reading, Massachusetts • New York • Don Mills, Ontario
Wokingham, U.K. • Amsterdam • Bonn • Sydney
Singapore • Tokyo • Madrid • San Juan

Executive editor: Dan Joraanstad
Sponsoring editor: Jennifer Young
Editorial assistant: Laura Cheu
Production manager: Gwen Larson
Production editor: Merrill Peterson, Matrix Productions
Cover designer: Yvo Riezebos Design
Illustrations: George M. Almasi, Max Illustration
Copyeditor: Nick Murray
Proofreader: Cheryl Smith

This book was designed and set in ITC Garamond by George S. Almasi and Allan Gottlieb using the IBM Document Composition Facility (SCRIPT) and the DCF Generalized Markup Language (with extensions added by the authors and the Yorktown text consultants). Some portions of the book were written first in TROFF and then translated to SCRIPT using a program developed by the authors. The figures were created on IBM and Apple personal computers and imported as Encapsulated Postscript. The final document was processed into a (17 MByte) Postscript file on an IBM ES/9000, and camera-ready output was then printed on a Linotronic 1200DPI Photocomposer.

In using quotation marks, we follow the American Chemical Society Style Guide's recommendation for "logical placement", and place punctuation inside quotation marks only if the punctuation is part of the quotation.

Many of the designations used by manufacturers and sellers to distinguish their products are claimed as trademarks. Where those designations appear in this book, and the publisher was aware of a trademark claim, the designations have been printed in initial caps or all caps.

Library of Congress Cataloging-in-Publication Data:

Almasi, George S., 1938 -
    Highly Parallel Computing / George S. Almasi, Allan Gottlieb. --
2nd ed.
        p. cm. -- (The Benjamin/Cummings series in computer science
and engineering)
    Includes bibliographical references and index.
    ISBN 0-8053-0443-6
    1. Parallel processing (Electronic computers) 2. Parallel
programming (Computer science) I. Gottlieb, Allan. II. Title
III. Series
QA76.642.A46 1994
004'.35--dc20   93-34231
                                                          CIP

1 2 3 4 5 6 7 8 9 10-DOC-98 97 96 95 94

Preface

Over 40 years ago, before transistors replaced vacuum tubes, David Slotnick, who later became the father of the Illiac IV, proposed a parallel computer to the great John von Neumann himself. The master reflected a moment and replied in his charming Hungarian accent: "too many toobs" ... and he was right. It took technology forty more years to produce microprocessor chips with enough "toobs" to make a parallel computer practical. But now it has happened – the "attack of the killer micros" has indeed occurred, at least ten highly parallel computers are commercially available, and "it's an exciting time" is even truer than it was when our first edition appeared five years ago.

Some of the hot topics of the 80's are now settled. There is no longer any question that there are significant parallel applications. Instead, one asks how best should they be described and what hardware/software design is most cost-effective for their solutions. And there is also no longer any question that large-scale parallel-processing hardware can be built. Indeed, if your checkbook is in good shape, you can have proof delivered to your doorstep. System software for these new architectures is, however, still immature—perhaps *the* key problem to be solved. Alan Karp's 1987 paper was subtitled "The State of the Art of Parallel Programming and What a Sorry State that Art Is In". A similar remark could still be made today. For one thing, job scheduling is now complicated by a desire to have processes within a job in some sense scheduled together. In addition, it is still not clear what the appropriate programming language(s) should be, programming environments need much improvement, and difficult compiling questions remain to be solved. Also still not settled are the debates about SIMD vs. MIMD and shared memory vs. message passing, although in the latter case significant convergence has occurred at the level of hardware architecture.

What sets this book apart?

- Unlike more specialized works, we discuss the full range of inter-related decisions that go into designing a parallel computer, and bring the reader up to date on the entire field.
- We do discuss the evolution from uniprocessors to machines exhibiting small-scale parallelism, but we concentrate on HIGHLY parallel computing: designs scaling to thousands (and perhaps millions) of processing elements.
- We treat fundamental issues and software as well as specific hardware.

- Unlike reprint collections, conference proceedings, or multi-author special issues, we give the reader a unified and consistent viewpoint and terminology for this complex subject.
- We have both led parallel processor projects, one in an industrial and the other in a university environment, and we have both worked and taught in both settings.
- We think the reader's time is valuable. We think what we didn't put in the book is as important as what we did. This is not a "describe everything and get a complete catalogue" approach. We concentrated on distilling the essence of the big picture, and on UNDERSTANDING the key problems, solutions, and their interrelationships.

What's new in the second edition?

A full summary of each chapter is given further below, but here we highlight various improvements in this edition for those familiar with our first edition. By popular request, there are now EXERCISES for each chapter! And of course much material was added and updated to reflect the developments of the last five years.

Specific modifications include a quantitative treatment of speedup introduced in Chapter 1 and expanded upon in Chapter 4. A new application, seismic migration, has been added to Chapter 2, as well as a discussion of the pros and cons of using a network of workstations as a parallel computer. Chapter 3 has tracked the (large) changes in technology, including the rise in importance of disk arrays and optical fibers, and we have expanded the discussion of the impact of technology. We have consolidated the material on computational models in Chapter 4 and clarified its relationship to the programming languages we discuss in Chapter 5, which has been completely rewritten to include Fortran 90, Fortran D, HPF, Occam, remote procedure calls, Express, PVM, Linda, and other near-term parallel programming approaches, and to compare these with the work in new languages based on functional, dataflow, and logic programming approaches. Although the fundamentals of parallel compilers and operating systems have not changed, there has been considerable research and development, which we have tracked in Chapters 6 and 7. Fat trees, as used in CM-5, and cut-through (wormhole) switching have been added to Chapter 8. Chapter 9 includes treatments of three new commercial SIMD offerings: the MasPar MP-1 and MP-2, the Cray Y-MP C90, and the NEC SX-3. In addition, the section on CM-2 has been expanded. Six new commercial MIMD offerings have been added to Chapter 10: the Thinking Machines CM-5, the Kendall Square Research KSR1, the Intel Paragon, the IBM SP1, the NCUBE Corp. NCUBE-2, and the Cray Research T3D. Information is also included on an expected machine from Tera Computer as well as the recently popular idea of assembling a cluster of workstations as an MIMD system. Although commercially the battle still rages between shared memory and message passing, some convergence can be seen, especially in research machines like the Stanford Dash and the Alewife and J machines from MIT. These three prototypes are described and the convergence issue is discussed. Many of the newer MIMD machines feature directory based caches and this important memory organization is explained.

Ways to Use this Book

Although the book is an organic whole, it is also divided into three meaningful parts—Part I: Foundations, Part II: Software, and Part III: Architectures. Readers with a particular interest in architectures can proceed directly to Part III. Readers who have somewhat broader interests can read the Overview chapter and then proceed to the Part of their choice. And readers interested in the full breadth of parallel computing can proceed through the chapters in order.

It is tempting to begin with parallel architectures ("the fun stuff"), and those who succumb to this temptation are referred to page 377 where the third and largest part of our book begins. Four chapters there cover interconnection schemes, parallel computers whose processing elements do not have their own programs, those that do, and hybrids of these two.

However, parallel computing is a much broader subject. Its major software components form the subject of the second part of this book, which starts on page 223. The three chapters involved discuss parallel languages, compilers, and operating systems.

But we are dealing here with a fundamental expansion in the possible ways of thinking about and doing computations, one that re-opens many questions that arose during the forty years that electronic computers have been with us and were answered under technological constraints that no longer exist. To put into perspective the opportunity and adventure that parallel processing represents, we begin this book with a four-chapter first part entitled "Foundations". It provides a preview of the whole book and a perspective on potential parallelism in applications, technological limitations and opportunities, and formulation of parallel solutions.

Chapter Summaries

Chapter 1 (Overview)   establishes a hardware/software theme that runs through the book: the driving forces for parallel processing come from both areas. Hardware technology (chiefly VLSI) has led to a repeal of "Grosch's law", which held that the best price/performance was obtained with the most powerful uniprocessor. This repeal makes it reasonable to propose super-computers made up of a collection of processors, and a number of such machines exists. From the software side, there is a strong argument for new languages to increase programmer productivity, which creates a demand for new architectures to execute these new languages efficiently. This chapter also serves as an overview of things to come; a number of the key concepts are introduced here and expanded upon in subsequent chapters.

Chapter 2 (Applications) focuses on the applications that offer sufficient parallelism to keep many processing elements busy simultaneously. These applications fall into two broad categories, numeric processing and symbolic processing, distinguished by the ratio of calculation to data motion among the processing elements. Scientific and engineering applications offer some very large numeric computation problems such as particle calculations (plasmas, QCD), fluid dynamics (weather modeling, aircraft design), seismic migration, computer-aided design, and others. Symbolic processing applications include database systems and artificial intelligence. We discuss Production Systems, Expert Systems, and projects in the more distant future, such as perception/planning systems.

Chapter 3 (Technology) discusses hardware technology as it limits the speedup of uniprocessors and also as it constrains and encourages the development of parallel processors. VLSI is a prime factor, providing powerful and cheap microprocessors for assembly into an ensemble, and enabling more unconventional and customized approaches to building a parallel machine. We also discuss (RAM) memory and (I/O) storage technologies including disk arrays and communication media such as optical fibers. But technology alone is not a panacea; wiring, packaging, and power dissipation still exert strong influences on a feasible design.

Chapter 4 (Computational Models and Algorithms) describes the most prominent parallel computational models, and terms like speedup are defined both informally and quite rigorously. We consider what language features and constructs are needed to express what one wants done in parallel, and discuss the communication and synchronization functions that ANY computational model has to perform. We then turn to the first step in getting an application solved on a parallel computer: choosing the algorithms to be used. We give examples, and discuss how a good algorithm is a necessary but not always sufficient condition for speeding up execution of the entire problem.

Chapter 5 (Languages) separates and compares imperative languages, including implicit and explicit parallelism, and declarative languages, including functional and logic programming. Some languages, like Occam, Id and Sisal, are comparatively new and were designed with parallel execution in mind.

Others, like HPF and Fortran 90, are parallel versions of existing serial languages. A third class, including PVM, Express, and Linda represent "aftermarket" parallelism in the sense that the user adds them to an existing serial language. We discuss how this all impacts the programmer's world.

Chapter 6 (Compilers) treats the problem of compiling high-level language programs to run on parallel processors. We discuss vectorization vs. parallelization and show the importance of program flow and dependency graph techniques. Examples are drawn from Parafrase, PFC, PTRAN, MIMDizer, and Bulldog, which all accept FORTRAN. We also discuss an APL and a Sisal compiler.

Chapter 7 (Operating Systems) deals with operating systems for a highly parallel computer. They will have features in common with operating systems for serial processors, but also have critical additional functions to perform. We distinguish between systems that support parallel applications and systems that are themselves parallel, and then give examples of systems having different degrees of internal parallelism.

Chapter 8 (Interconnection Networks) examines the variety of networks that can be used to interconnect the processing elements. We present the topologies and routing methods used including those found on the newest commercial offerings. We also compare alternative switching strategies including, circuit switching, store-and-forward, cut-through, and wormhole routing. We also discuss the engineering costs and limitations of the various networks.

Chapter 9 (SIMD Architectures) treats the class of parallel computers known as SIMD, or Single Instruction, Multiple Data stream designs. These machines are used mostly for problems having high degrees of small-grain parallelism. We discuss the essentials of pipelined SIMD vector and array processors such as the Cray series from the original Cray-I to the C90, the NEC SX series, the Cyber 205, and FPS machines, as well as parallel SIMD designs such as systolic arrays, the Connection Machine, the MasPar MP-1 and MP-2, the MPP, the DAP, and GF11, and we discuss tradeoffs between SIMD and MIMD.

Chapter 10 (MIMD Architectures) shifts to the class of parallel architectures known as the MIMD, or Multiple Instruction, Multiple Data stream category. Most of these designs are intended to take advantage of medium- and large-grain parallelism. We distinguish between private-memory and shared-memory designs, and between machines built from thousands of microprocessors and machines made up of tens of larger processors. We also discuss why MIMD is harder but probably more generally applicable than SIMD. We describe many MIMD designs and commercial offerings including both shared- and private-memory configurations, and discuss the tradeoffs involved. In particular, the new CM-5, KSR1, SP1, T3D, NCUBE-2, and Paragon are described as well as several research prototypes. The partial convergence of shared and private memory is noted, workstation clusters are discussed, and the key issue of consistent caches is explained.

Chapter 11 (Hybrid Architectures) concludes the book with a description of some interesting parallel machines that do not fit neatly into either the SIMD or MIMD category, namely, VLIW (Very Long Instruction Word) and MSIMD (Multiple SIMD) designs.

Acknowledgements

We are most grateful for the generosity and encouragement of our families and of our many friends at IBM, NYU, and the rest of the parallel processing community, including the reviewers of this book. Allan Gottlieb was supported in part by grants from the National Science Foundation and the Applied Mathematical Sciences program of the Department of Energy.

George S. Almasi
almasi@watson.ibm.com

Allan Gottlieb
gottlieb@nyu.edu

Table of Contents

Part III: Parallel Architectures   377

List of Illustrations

Part I: Foundations

2

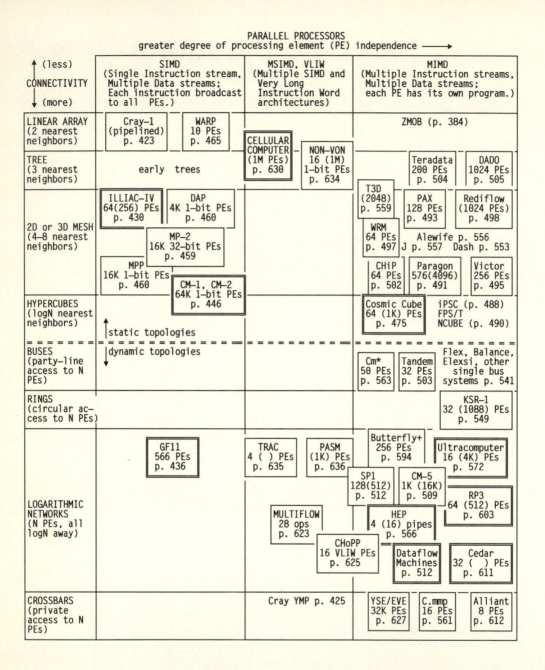

Figure 1.1 *Parallel architecture projects* grouped according to the independence and connectivity of the processing elements (PEs). Heavy boxes denote projects that we treat as detailed case studies, light boxes denote less detailed descriptions, and names without boxes correspond to brief summaries. The page numbers indicate where they appear. The nominal number of PEs is given in parentheses, preceded by the number built so far. MIMD designs before page 540 use message passing to communicate; those after use shared memory.

1

Overview

Anew era in computer architecture is dawning. It is becoming increasingly difficult to obtain more performance from the time-honored von Neumann model, and many of the technological constraints that influenced its design over thirty years ago have changed drastically. Many of the arguments for processing a single instruction at a time no longer apply, and both commercial and research parallel processors are now available (Figure 1.1), allowing many processors to cooperate on a single problem. However, we still have a Pandora's box of questions about how computation should be done, a box closed four decades ago by the von Neumann model. Some of the strengths of this model become especially apparent when one tries to replace it. The field is at an interesting juncture. Much work has been done, and significant speedups have been obtained with real programs. But John Hopcroft's 1986 Turing Award speech still rings true: "People [don't] have a good understanding yet of parallelism and what it is going to buy us. We have to develop ways of thinking about parallelism and languages for expressing parallel algorithms. There will be major activity in that area for 5 or 10 years to develop the science base that's needed to exploit it."

This chapter presents a fairly substantial overview of parallel processing and of this book. It is written at such a level that readers not interested in nitty-gritty details should still be able to derive from this chapter a knowledge of what the main problems are and what solutions have been and are being pursued.   However, sufficient annotation and examples are provided so that this chapter can also be used as a road map to the more detailed treatment of these topics in subsequent chapters.

This chapter is organized as follows: "Definition and Driving Forces" begins to define what we mean by parallel processing and why the interest in it is growing so rapidly. "Questions Raised" shows that, on reflection, our definition raises a number of additional questions. "Emerging Answers" starts to answer some of these questions, weaving in a bird's-eye preview of projects that are providing some of the answers and that are treated in detail later in the book. Finally, in "Previous Attempts: Why Success Now?", we discuss why parallel processing is successful now as compared to, say, fifteen years ago.

1.1   Overview and Scope of This Book

As we said in the Preface, this book is organized into three parts called "Foundations", "Parallel Software", and "Parallel Architectures", each with several chapters.

It is tempting to begin with parallel architectures (the fun stuff), and those who succumb to this temptation may begin with the third and largest part of our book. Four chapters there cover interconnection schemes, parallel computers whose processing elements each have their own programs, those that do not, and hybrids of these two.

However, parallel computing is a much broader subject. Its major software components form the subject of the second part of this book. The three chapters involved discuss parallel languages, compilers, and operating systems.

But we are dealing here with a fundamental expansion in the possible ways of thinking about and doing computations that reopens many questions that arose during the forty years that electronic computers have been with us, questions that were answered under technological constraints that no longer exist. To put into perspective the opportunity and adventure that parallel processing represents, we begin this book with a four-chapter first part titled "Foundations". It provides a preview of the whole book and a perspective on potential parallelism in applications, technological limitations and opportunities, and formulation of parallel solutions.

Some important topics that are absent from this book help to clarify its focus. We are interested in computers that use a high degree of parallelism to speed the computation required to solve a single large problem. This leaves out much of the world of business programs, where I/O rather than computing power is typically the bottleneck. It leaves out most commercial multiprocessors, whose added processing units are used to increase the *number* of jobs that can be handled at a time, rather than to speed up a single job (in other words, to improve *throughput* rather than *turnaround time*). Strictly speaking, it also leaves out distributed systems [286][108] such as a network of personal workstations, because, although the number of processing units can be quite large, the communication in such systems is currently so slow that it prevents large speedups on one job. However, we have added a case study of a parallel cluster of workstations to illustrate the additional features that a parallel supercomputer needs in order to achieve highly parallel computing.

1.2   Definition and Driving Forces

The following definition describes many highly parallel processor designs:[1]

> **A large collection of processing elements that can communicate and cooperate to solve large problems fast.**

One could include other important factors such as reliability and ease of programming. However, we shall soon see that even this simple definition raises more questions than it answers.

1.2.1   Driving Forces and Enabling Factors

The basic driving force for parallel processing is the desire and prospect for greater performance: users have ever bigger problems, and designers have

---

[1] Some terminology: A *functional unit* is a logic circuit like an adder, multiplier, or shifter. A *processing element* (PE) is the same as a CPU; it contains functional units, registers, clock circuits, and processor and bus control circuits. In some cases (MIMD computers) the PE contains an instruction decoder and program counter. A *computer* contains PE(s), memory, I/O, and control for all. Hence, the definition of *parallel processor* given in the text leaves out computers whose only parallelism consists of multiple, pipelined functional units, like the CRAY-1. These are interesting but are not the main emphasis of this book.

ever more gates. Historically, most of the impetus has come from people with three different kinds of concerns:

1. How to solve large problems that run too slowly even on the fastest contemporary supercomputer. Typical examples have been weather modeling, design automation, and other scientific/engineering applications. More recently, artificial intelligence has become a source of such problems.
2. How to obtain solutions to problems that *could* be done on one of today's supercomputers when one's budget is limited.
3. How to increase programmer productivity. One proposed solution is the use of higher-level languages (functional programming, for example). These languages often require more performance, but also have features that make it easier to exploit parallelism.

In short, parallel processing is perceived as having the potential to improve *performance, cost/performance,* and *productivity.* (There are other factors as well, including reliability/availability and reduced part numbers.)

The key enabling factors have been hardware technology improvements (chiefly VLSI) that have led to a repeal of Grosch's law [353], a long-valid observation that the best price/performance was obtained with the most powerful uniprocessor. Thus it is no longer automatically true that a collection of smaller processors will always have less performance than a single large processor of the same total cost. At the same time, physical effects such as the finite speed of light are making it increasingly difficult for technology alone to speed up the fastest serial processors (Chapter 3 on technology discusses this). In these circumstances, a parallel computer made up of a number of small cooperating processing elements becomes an attractive proposition for many problems. Chapter 2 on applications gives some examples of such problems.

From the software side, John Backus, the inventor of FORTRAN, argues strongly that programmer productivity is declining due to the anachronistic "von Neumann bottleneck" [48] and that new languages and new architectures to support them are needed. We discuss this in Chapter 5.

1.3 Questions Raised

Let us return now to the definition we gave for a parallel processor. We said it was a collection of processing elements that can communicate and cooperate to solve large problems fast. Two of the implementations we might con-

Figure 1.2   Generalized parallel processor showing two ways to arrange the processing elements (P) and memory modules (M). The "dancehall" configuration at left is used primarily for designs with a shared-memory model of computation in which every P has equal access to every M. The "boudoir" configuration at right was used primarily for message-passing designs in which the processing elements each have their own memory and communicate by exchanging messages, but now is often used in shared-memory designs as well. Shared memory is a more powerful communication mechanism, but costs more to implement.

ceive for this definition are sketched in Figure 1.2. However, a few minutes spent thinking about this definition in a very commonsense sort of way shows that it raises quite a list of fundamental questions. In fact, readers are encouraged to pause here, make their own lists of questions, compare them with the following list, and then keep these questions in mind while reading the rest of the book. Some of the key questions raised by the different parts of our definition are as follows:

1.   *A collection of processing elements...*

   - How many?
   - How powerful is each?
   - What operations do they perform? What technology do they use?
   - How much memory do they need?
   - How much secondary (disk) storage do they need, and how do they perform I/O access to it?

2.   *...that can communicate...*

   - How will they communicate? What protocol will they use?
   - What sort of interconnection network will they need?

3.   *...and cooperate...*

   - How will they coordinate (synchronize) their efforts?
   - How large should each processor's task be?
   - How autonomous should each processor be?
   - How will the operating system coordinate these efforts?

4. *...to solve large problems fast.*

- Which problems (applications) are amenable to parallel processing?
- How? That is, what computational model will be used?
- How general-purpose vs. special-purpose should our approach be?
- What algorithm is best now?
- How much speedup can be expected?
- What is the programmer's view of the machine?
    - What programming language and software tools will be available?
    - How is a problem decomposed?
    - How is concurrent execution specified?
    - Who does each of the above? The user or a compiler?
    - What about reliability, availability, serviceability (RAS)?

Almost as interesting as the questions themselves is the high degree to which they are intertwined. The answers are far from independent of each other. If one divides the world into architecture issues and software issues, then item 1 in the list above can be thought of as a set of questions related primarily to architecture and technology, whereas item 4 relates mostly to software. However, items 2 and 3 fall under both umbrellas, and the umbrellas themselves interact. Is computer design driven by problems looking for solutions, or by solutions looking for problems? The answer is, by both. This is nicely illustrated by the deceptively simple diagram in Figure 1.3 on page 9, which shows how the key elements of a computing system are related. This relationship is discussed in more detail in Chapter 4 on computational models, but it is interesting to note that both the problem and the technology appear as driving forces.

These key elements are also reflected in the flow of this book: the two driving forces of progress, namely, the problem to be solved (i.e., the application) and the technology (i.e., what is possible to build) are discussed in chapters 2 and 3. At a higher level of abstraction, computational models (or rules of the game) available for problem solving are treated in Chapter 4 along with parallel algorithms (or recipes) for selected problems. Chapter 5 on languages describes how the programmer can choreograph the dance that the hardware elements of the computing system are supposed to perform. Chapter 6 on compilers describes how the programmer's instructions are translated into terms the dancers can understand, and Chapter 7 on operating systems discusses the issue of directing the dancers during the performance. Chapter 8 on interconnections describes how the elements stay in touch while they perform the dance, and chapters 9, 10, and 11 on architectures give examples

Figure 1.3   Key elements of a computing system and their interrelationships
(after [76]). Numbers in parentheses are the chapters treating each element.

of real dancers and real dances. The emphasis is on the new elements introduced by the decision to do things in parallel.

The rest of the present chapter is intended to provide a brief summary of
the emerging answers to the questions listed above, and also a glimpse of the
parallel processing projects and activities that are providing these answers.

1.4   Emerging Answers

We will discuss briefly the answers that are emerging to the questions posed
above, particularly as represented by some of the projects shown in Figure 1.1
on page 2. The discussion here follows the order in which the questions were
listed.

1.4.1   Processing Elements: Their Number, Power, and Nature

A glance at Figure 1.1 on page 2 shows that parallel processor designs tend to
cluster into three groups: those with tens of processing elements, those having

on the order of a thousand, and those approaching a million. This statement should not be taken in a strict sense: *tens* may mean as low as 4 to 8 and as high as 32, *order of a thousand* covers at least 256 to 4096, and there are designs that fall in between these ranges. Nevertheless, there is such a trend, and the reason is that there are several different philosophies when it comes to choosing processing element size.

First of all there are designs like the Cray Y-MP C90 and IBM ES/9000, which consist of a few very powerful processors. They represent the design approach of making as fast a computer as possible (normally a pipelined vector machine; see page 413) and then combining as many of them as is practical. This group contains the bulk of today's high-end computers. They tend to use high-speed, high-power bipolar transistor technology (page 104) requiring sophisticated cooling techniques (page 109 ff.). By and large, however, the parallelism of these designs has not been applied to speed up a single job,[2] but rather to increase the *throughput* of the system, that is, to allow it to handle *more* jobs each day. As we explained earlier, this book is about parallelism used for *speedup* rather than for throughput, and so we say relatively little about such systems despite their commercial importance and high absolute performance.

The other designs in the "tens of PEs" category contain *bus based* machines that emphasize cost/performance (rather than raw performance). The hardware is built from slightly slower but smaller, lower-power, and more easily cooled NMOS or CMOS transistors (page 102). Although the bus is economical and allows all PEs to communicate directly, its fixed bandwidth limits the number of PEs.

Computers with hundreds to thousands of PEs are mostly designed to take advantage of available *microprocessors* or other VLSI computing engines. The bandwidth required for the larger number of processors is obtained by using more powerful networks, which are discussed in Chapter 8. At least one design (page 603) uses bipolar technology for this network.

At the other extreme from the "most powerful PE possible" approach are the architectures with up to a million processing elements. They emphasize obtaining the maximum *number* of PEs allowed by current technology. The PEs are "minimalist", often bit-serial computers, implemented as custom VLSI designs in which multiple PEs are fabricated on a single chip. The interconnection scheme is necessarily sparse.

---

[2] Here we are referring to the high-level hardware parallelism arising from the multiple processors. Certainly the lower levels of hardware parallelism arising from multiple, pipelined functional units concurrently operating on wide data items is applied to a single job.

In summary, PEs used for parallel computers to date include powerful stand-alone computers, commercial microprocessors, and tiny computing engines grouped on custom VLSI chips. The trade-off between number and power of the PEs is still very much an active research area, and is discussed further in the representative case studies that come later in this book (Figure 1.1 on page 2 provides a map to their locations).

1.4.2　Memory and I/O

Two architectural questions strongly influence the details of a parallel computer's memory system. The first is whether each PE should store its own program (rather than have the instructions from a common program broadcast to all the processors by a central controller). The second is whether each processor should have exclusive access to its part of the data (rather than pooling all the data and adopting a Turkish bath philosophy of letting everyone see what everyone else has got). The three answers given (no, yes-yes, and yes-no)[3] map to the left half, right upper quadrant, and right lower quadrant of Figure 1.1, and are discussed in detail in chapters 9 and 10. In the much briefer but nearer discussion on page 18, we explain that these three possibilities are named SIMD, MIMD with private memory, and MIMD with shared memory. These three possibilities represent three progressively greater degrees of autonomy and interactivity for the PEs.

Here, we are going to talk about the *gross* memory and I/O requirements of the entire parallel system. For want of a better way, the relationships between memory capacity, disk I/O bandwidth, and processing rate are being extrapolated from rules of thumb established for serial processors (one current example is "about one MByte of memory and one MByte/sec I/O rate per MIPS"). Chapter 3 discusses these briefly. The memory and I/O structure will be influenced by a number of factors, including:

1. The power of the processors
2. The ratio of processing to communication
3. The frequency and nature of the I/O (sequential, random, paging, etc.)

---

[3] Although four answers are theoretically possible, a design with pooled data and a single copy of a program (shared-memory SIMD) has not been implemented to date. With a shared memory, the tight synchronization favored by SIMD enthusiasts becomes difficult because the possibility of memory access conflicts leads to unpredictable instruction execution times [360].

The last two items will depend strongly on the application, and can be expected to be quite different for problems in, say, numeric computation, symbolic computation, and database operations. Chapter 2 treats these applications.

1.4.3 How Do the Processors Communicate?

The interconnection networks that allow communication among the PEs have ranged from the elaborate to the simple, representing a trade-off between communication power and cost. At one end of this spectrum is the crossbar network, which allows complete connectivity and minimum delay among the processors, but costs a great deal to implement. At the other end are easy-to-build tree networks in which the PEs are connected to only their three nearest neighbors. Intermediate trade-offs, such as mesh, cube, and multistage networks, are shown along the left edge of Figure 1.1 on page 2 and discussed in more detail in Chapter 8.

The *mode* of communication in the network must also be specified. In *circuit switching*, a connection is established that lasts at least until the entire message has been transmitted. The classic example is the telephone system, in which a circuit is established when a call is made and remains until the call is terminated. The lines and switches being used are unavailable to anyone else in the interim. In a *packet-switched* network, the message is broken up into packets, each bearing a destination address (and often a source address). These packets then steer their way through the network releasing resources just after they are used (see Figure 8.8 on page 400). This process avoids the overhead of setting up individual connections and is more economical if the communication consists mostly of short messages scattered to different destinations. Both modes are represented among the projects in Figure 1.1.

These communication *mechanisms* (networks and protocols) can be used to build either a shared-memory or a message-passing communication *system*. Page 572, for example, describes a MIMD shared-memory system using a packet-switched omega network, page 436 describes a SIMD system using a circuit-switched Benes network, and page 475 describes a MIMD private memory system using a (static-topology) cube network. In the shared-memory case, PEs communicate via common access to a shared global memory. On the other hand, if each PE has access to only its own private memory, a separate message mechanism is needed to communicate with the other PEs. (The shared memory can, of course, also be used for message passing.) Message passing and shared memory are compared briefly on pages 29 and 470, and in much more detail on pages 474 ff. and 540 ff., respectively. Communication is discussed further in Chapter 4 on computational models, Chapter 8 on interconnection networks, and chapters 9, 10, and 11 on specific architectures.

1.4.4   How Do the Processors Cooperate?

Synchronization

Things must happen in a certain sequence if our parallel computer's cooperating processors are to produce the desired results. This requirement introduces the need for *synchronization*. An interesting example of this was given in the *New York Times* in an article [456] describing how lions seem to use a calculated team approach when hunting a herd of wildebeests, as shown in Figure 1.4 on page 14. One lion slinks, unseen by the herd, along the bottom of a ditch into a position of ambush. Two lions then climb a hill close enough to the herd to insert themselves into the herd's consciousness and make it nervous, but not close enough to panic the herd yet. Then a fourth lion charges the herd. Remembering the other two lions, the herd charges away from the new lion *and* away from the hill and toward the lion waiting in ambush. All four lions then share the kill.

The success of this plan depends strongly on the exact *order* in which the lions perform their tasks. Analogous situations exist in many programs, which is why the language used to write such programs must be able to *express* such synchronization requirements,[4] and why hardware and/or software means are needed to *implement* them. There are many ways of doing this, as discussed primarily in Chapter 5 on languages and touched on also in chapters 4–9 (the *synchronization* entry in the index may be useful, too). The choice among synchronization methods depends on the size and nature of the subtasks, which is discussed next.

The Size of Each Processor's Subtask—Granularity

This answer section is longer than the others and was the most difficult to write. It took us a long time to understand why. It is because the size of each processor's subtask[5] is in many ways the *central* question in parallel comput-

---

[4] Dataflow language programs (page 271) are an example of an exception.

[5] We use this term loosely here. The precise definition of *task* in languages like PL/1 and Ada is treated later.

Lions, when hunting, have been observed using a calculated team approach. Two lions (L's in the diagram at left) let themselves be seen on a hilltop, as a ploy. Another suddenly appears and drives unsuspecting wildebeests toward a fourth lion waiting in ambush.

Figure 1.4   *An illustration of the need for synchronization* *during a cooperative task. The plan succeeds only if the tasks are performed in the right sequence. In writing parallel programs, incorrect synchronization also results in failure, but even "correct" but poorly designed synchronization can cripple parallel performance.*

ing. Now the art of designing parallel architectures and the art of writing programs meet for the first time on our list of questions. This is still very much an active area, and it is surely not the first time that the meeting of two different cultures has generated both exciting work and confusing terminology.

We first point out the role played by the *communication* needs of the subtasks. After a brief pause to discuss jargon and synonyms, we compare different methods of parallelizing the same problem by examining a common program example that can be divided into large or small subtasks and executed using several different computational models, in ways treated more extensively in later chapters. We list some of the other subtask sizes and their sources, and conclude with a small parallelism map (Figure 1.5 on page 19) that depicts the supply of parallelism that several of these program constructs represent.

Choosing and Partitioning the Problem

Problems can sometimes be divided into almost completely independent, non-communicating pieces (see "easy parallelism" on page 21), but in general the subtasks need to communicate in order to exchange data and coordinate their activities. For good efficiency, the time spent on such communication and on such overheads as starting up the subtasks should be small compared to the time spent executing the subtasks. For example, a problem that has been divided into a few large subtasks may be well matched to a parallel computer consisting of a few powerful processors, and can afford the overhead of the Ada language's "rendezvous" mechanism (see Chapter 5) to control the interaction of these tasks. However, this combination of architecture and language would be a very poor way to obtain speedup for a problem divided into a much larger number of much smaller pieces. Although there are some simple, useful theoretical models (page 179), the general topic of finding the best workload for a given parallel computer is a complex subject occupying much of the rest of this book.

To probe the question of subtask size further, let us examine what is available. We can start constructing a parallelism map by analyzing existing (serial) programs to see what sort of pieces they naturally break into. First, some terminology:

* The *granularity* or *grain size* is the average subtask *size*, measured in instructions executed (on some agreed-on serial computer).
* The *degree* or *extent* of parallelism is the *number* of subtasks available.
* *Level* (as in *procedure-level parallelism, expression-level parallelism,* etc.) refers to the *source* of the parallelism in what was originally a serial program.

The last term reflects the view that a program consists of certain characteristic building blocks, themselves made from other blocks, and so on, as in the following hierarchy for a serial program [11]:

* Program
* Subroutines and blocks
* Statements
* Expressions
* Operators and data references

Procedures and *subroutines* perform specific computations needed by the program. They may contain *program loops,* a very popular source of parallelism (see the NASA weather code example on page 48).

The program and its substructures (above) are static quantities — always there. Executing the program creates for the computer a chunk of work called a *job*, a <u>dynamic</u> quantity that comes and goes. As candidates for parallel workloads go, jobs are the largest and least communicative units of work on a computer. There is no shared memory and perhaps not even shared disk space among jobs, and any communication among them is limited to exchanging messages or perhaps only files. Such loose coupling corresponds more to distributed processing or throughput-oriented parallelism, whereas this book concerns the use of parallelism to speed up a single job, like the computation of tomorrow's weather, which takes a significant amount of time when performed at the precision desired.

To utilize the multiple processors found on an MIMD computer, a job is broken into a number of pieces called *processes* or *tasks*, terms that are used interchangeably in this book to mean executions of a program or multiple parts of a program.[6] An important distinction that we *do* make is that programs and subprograms are static; that is, once written they exist forever. Jobs and tasks/processes, however, are dynamic quantities that come and go. In some systems, tasks and jobs have the same lifetime, so a job has a fixed number of tasks; in others, tasks are more dynamic, with their number varying during the job's execution. This topic is discussed further in Chapter 7 on operating systems.

Four Ways to Do Matrix Multiplication in Parallel

The best-known source of parallel workloads may be the loops in FORTRAN scientific programs. As an example, consider the matrix multiplication

$$C(i,j) = \sum_{k=1}^{N} A(i,k) \times B(k,j)$$

which is often coded as

---

[6] Many efforts have been made to give these two terms different definitions that distinguish between the resources needed for execution (i.e., a *protection domain*) and the execution itself (the thread of control) or, more loosely, between the ability to do something and the actual doing of it. Unfortunately, different authors have used different definitions, and none is accepted universally. Instead, we take *process* and *task* to be synonyms that mean an execution of a (sub)program. Where finer distinctions are needed, we discuss them explicitly.

```
      DO 100 I=1,N
        DO 100 J=1,N
          DO 100 K=1,N
              C(I,J) = C(I,J) + A(I,K)*B(K,J)
100  CONTINUE
```

(the Cs are initialized to 0). The two outer loops (the ones in which I and J vary) generate N^2 independent computations, which is as it should be since each one computes a different element of C. These N^2 iterations of the outer loops could *each* be a task for a PE that has the equipment to store and execute the program represented by the inner (K) loop, as is true for the PEs in an MIMD parallel computer. In practice, however, a larger task consisting of several iterations may be more favorable due to communication overheads and other factors. For example, in a 400×400 matrix multiplication on the 256-PE Butterfly (page 601), assigning each PE a different iteration created too much traffic in the network leading to the memory, and 6×6 subsets of the matrix were parceled out instead. Thus each PE produced 36 elements at the cost of fetching 6 rows and 6 columns from memory. By contrast, computing 36 elements one at a time requires fetching 1 row and 1 column *each time*, or six times more memory traffic.

The foregoing partitioning is appropriate for an ensemble of reasonably powerful, more or less conventional (serial, von Neumann) processing elements — microprocessors or larger — able to operate in asynchronous MIMD mode, that is, having provisions for the likelihood that some of the subtasks will take longer than others. In some of the designs in Chapter 10 that fit this description, these subtasks are scheduled at the time the program is executed, while in others it is done earlier. A simple, useful theoretical model for the maximum useful parallelism in such machines appears on page 179.

This same problem can also be sliced to yield a much finer granularity of parallelism, that is, into much smaller parallel tasks. The most thoroughly explored of these levels is that of machine instructions. We describe three approaches that use this fine-grained parallelism: dataflow, vector processors, and systolic arrays. The thinking behind all three is that surely at most moments of a program's execution there is a huge backlog of instructions that could be done in parallel, even though the von Neumann model does them one at a time. Dataflow computers are in a sense an extreme effort to capitalize on this.

As described on page 512, dataflow computers are MIMD, but use a radically different computational model in which instructions may execute as soon as their input data are ready. (This is the synchronization mechanism in this model.) Figure 5.8 on page 272 shows a dataflow method for solving the matrix multiplication example above.

SIMD, a more modest approach to exploiting parallelism at the instruction level, has had more commercial success to date in the form of the vector processor, which is the basis of the present generation of supercomputers. As discussed on page 415, a vector processor has some extra computing units and fast memory designed for efficient execution of long sequences of identical operations. An added restriction in a vector processor is that the identical operations are performed on data stored in a highly regular manner (i.e., the data can be considered as a vector). Thus ILLIAC IV (page 430) is a parallel vector machine, the CRAY-1 (page 423) is a pipelined vector machine,[7] but GF11 (page 436) and CM1 (page 446) are more general SIMD parallel computers. All use instruction-level parallelism. By moving the K loop to the outside, the iterations of the inner loops become independent, as explained on page 307, and the program above is then ideal for a vector processor. Vectorizable and nonvectorizable loops from a weather code are shown in Figure 2.5 on page 48.

The type of VLSI-oriented systolic array shown in Figure 9.13 on page 462 can be regarded as a low-cost vector processor designed to perform one particular algorithm, in this case the matrix multiplication above. Subtasks must still be independent, as with a more general-purpose vector processor, but are now scheduled at hardware design time instead of at compile time.

Vector machines can afford to use subtasks as small as an instruction because the synchronization is performed by the hardware automatically. The cost is the necessity to cast algorithms in vectorizable form. Pure dataflow hopes to be able to afford instruction-level parallelism for essentially the same reason: the machine is self-synchronized, in this case by the arrival of data. The key is a large supply of other subtasks that can execute while one communicates.

How Autonomous Should Each Processor Be?

Should each processing element execute its own program, or should they all receive the same instructions from a central source? These two possibilities (robots or puppets?) are called MIMD and SIMD, respectively, from a classification originally made by Flynn [176] and still widely used. The idea is that the von Neumann model of computation (page 142) can be viewed as a stream of instructions and a stream of data being knitted together, one instruction at

---

[7] Pipelining may be considered SIMD by viewing the stages of the pipeline as the multiple PEs.

Figure 1.5   Parallelism map *showing degree of parallelism available at a given granularity. The total parallelism can be multiplicative: 16 tasks could be running, each with 1000 independent iterations of a loop, and so on. Open areas denote sources of parallelism in a program; shaded areas denote hardware parallelism. ILLIAC IV had 64 PEs, a pipelined vector processor might have 16 independent functional units, and so on. "CIRCUIT" area refers to horizontal microcode and multiple-bit logic circuits. Speedup is bounded by the degree of parallelism and determined by the size of the overhead. Several examples of such overhead are shown on the top edge of this map. Chapter 5 treats these parallel coordination constructs in more detail.*

a time, to produce a useful result. Since there is a Single Instruction stream and a Single Data stream, its category receives the name SISD. One can take a step into the world of parallel execution by having this Single Instruction stream manipulate Multiple Data streams (SIMD), and a further step by adding Multiple Instruction streams (MIMD).

SIMD/MIMD debates are sometimes heated. This book devotes a chapter to each of these architectures. SIMD processors have been around for a while in the form of vector processors and array processors (see page 415), and even though there is more research on MIMD designs these days, there is still a substantial amount of work being done on SIMD designs.

SIMD offers simpler synchronization: the processors are kept in lockstep by the broadcast instructions. Therefore, the processors need not talk to *each other* for synchronization purposes. Since they need not store their own programs, the processors can also be smaller and more numerous.

MIMD is seen as a more general design capable of performing well over a broader range of applications. However, in an MIMD machine each processor needs enough memory to store its own copy of at least part of the program and enough logic to decode instructions and manage its program counter; this makes designs with more than a few thousand processors seem difficult to achieve. But some researchers are inherently interested in machines with millions of processors, because of the nature of their applications or because of perceived analogies with the brain; SIMD is their only alternative, given the technologies that are available now. SIMD designs tend to be associated with smaller-grain parallelism than MIMD, since the overhead costs per task are lower.[8] Examples are given in chapters 9 and 10.

How Will the Operating System Coordinate These Efforts?

We discuss operating systems for parallel processors in Chapter 7. To paraphrase the "beautification principle" from that chapter, an operating system provides a thin veneer of civilization between the machine hardware and the programmers who wish to use it.[9] Key functions include the creation and scheduling of tasks, and the management of resources such as memory, I/O devices, and file systems, with an eye toward various kinds of system load balancing and protection. As pointed out in the introduction to Chapter 7, even an operating system for a uniprocessor has parallel aspects to the extent that it allows multiple programs to timeshare the machine or allows, say, computing, I/O, and printing to go on concurrently. Now, however, we contemplate a vast increase in the number of parallel activities. In addition, the operating system itself is being asked to run on a parallel machine and take advantage of its multiple computing resources.

---

[8]   But there are MIMD designs, such as dataflow, that are aimed at fine-grain parallelism.

[9]   Working with one of the unfriendlier operating systems, a friend said, "You ask it to do something, and it replies 'Let's arm-wrestle', and two out of three times, you lose."

Not surprisingly, this increased activity creates new difficulties. For example, a common way to prevent unconstrained accesses to a shared resource in a multiprogrammed uniprocessor is to serialize the accesses by making each a critical section (see Figure 4.10 on page 157). But in a parallel computer, critical sections become more and more of a problem as the degree of parallelism increases (see page 371). Chapter 7 talks about the critical sections in the Hydra operating system developed for the early, 16-processor C.mmp parallel computer (see also page 561). As an example of a more recent approach that anticipates much higher degrees of parallelism, the discussion of the NYU Ultracomputer starting on page 572 describes parallel task queues, and so forth, based on an atomic "fetch-and-add" memory operation developed specially to eliminate critical sections. Such constructs are also being implemented in the RP3 (page 603). For a contrasting approach, the Rediflow section (page 498) sketches an interesting but still-untried distributed control scheme in which a pressure-like mechanism rather than a central task queue is used to balance the load among processors.

1.4.5   Choosing and Attacking the Problem

Applications Amenable to Parallel Processing

Which applications will provide enough parallelism to keep all these processors busy? In other words, "Where's the parallelism?"

Easy Parallelism

There are many examples of easy parallelism in which the work to be done can be divided into subtasks that have negligible communication with each other. One trivial example is ADP preparing the payroll for several independent companies; another is a group of people independently keeping track of the time. In both cases, the overall task can be assigned to multiple hardware entities (computers or watches) without worrying about communication among the entities. A more serious (scientific) application is some Monte Carlo application in which a large calculation is to be performed many times using different random inputs, and the outputs are to be accumulated in a simple manner. Some database applications have the flavor of multiple, largely independent transactions, applied to a central database, which could be performed in parallel.[10] In general, however, problems are not so easily divided into independent pieces,[11] and the communication requirements between the subtasks play a key role. In these cases more care is needed to recast applications in parallel form. Chapter 2 discusses several representative application areas in which this has been done.

Scientific and Engineering Calculations

Other application areas are scientific and engineering calculations, including flow dynamics (incompressible fluid), particle behavior, weather prediction (compressible fluid), and seismic modeling. Analysis at NYU [292] has shown that levels of parallelism in the thousands are available from the first three types of these calculations. The Cosmic Cube project at Caltech (page 475) and the users of the DAP machine at Queen Mary College (page 460) offer encouraging analytical and experimental results in this area. The 576-processor GF11 (page 436) at IBM Yorktown uses a parallel approach for a problem in this area (quantum chromo-dynamics, or QCD; see QCD in the index).

VLSI Design Automation

Another application area is VLSI design automation, including logic simulation, circuit simulation, shape checking, placement and wiring, logic synthesis (silicon compilation), and test generation, fault simulation, timing analysis, and logic equivalency analysis. The YSE experience (page 627) demonstrates that at least 256-way parallelism is available in logic simulation, with a corresponding speedup that can approach 150 [361]. The degree of available parallelism is estimated to be in the thousands for this application as well as for circuit simulation, shape checking, and wiring (the WRM discussed on page 497 demonstrated 64-way parallelism in chip wiring). Logic synthesis, with a higher degree of interdependencies, is felt to offer parallelism in the hundreds.

Database Operations

Database operations also offer opportunities, including parallelism among as well as within transactions. Teradata and Tandem are two parallel machines associated with this application.

---

10 Obtaining the necessary I/O bandwidth may limit the number of concurrent transactions that can be processed, as may the coordination required to ensure that each transaction is atomic.

11 A favorite example, from Bob Newhart's old television show: Bob staggers home from a night with the boys and finds he forgot to defrost the turkey. "Put it in the oven at 2,000 degrees," suggests one friend, but the dial only goes up to 500. "OK, then use four ovens!"

Near-Term Artificial Intelligence

A fourth group of applications involves near-term artificial intelligence. The search procedures employed in expert (production) systems and other logic programming applications are expected by some to yield on the order of thousandfold parallelism. Present programs contain much lower degrees of parallelism [209], but this lower degree is said to be an artifact of their being written for a serial computer (see page 83). DADO (page 505) is one project aimed at this application.

Long-Term Artificial Intelligence

A final group is formed by long-term artificial intelligence applications, including perception/planning systems, visual recognition, natural language processing, motor control (robotics), and learning. These are all problems that appear suitable for a highly parallel computational model called "Computing with Connections" (page 87); parallelism on the order of tens of thousands appears to be available.

What Parallel Computational Models Are Available?

As discussed in Chapter 4, a computational model describes, at a level removed from hardware or software details, what a computer can do, that is, which primitive actions can be performed, when these actions are performed, and by which methods data can be accessed and stored. In other words, a computational model gives the essential rules of the game for performing computations. As Tanenbaum [427] points out, a modern computer system consists of up to six levels of abstraction (including the machine hardware, operating system, and programming language), each representing a virtual computer with its own computational model. Thus, one must consider not only the model at each level, but also how well it can represent the actions of its neighbor in the hierarchy (see page 140).

SIMD and MIMD (Figure 1.1 and page 18) represent two major parallel computational models. In the MIMD case, in which a PE gets its instructions from its own stored program rather than from a central broadcast source, there is a further division into private-memory and shared-memory models, depending on whether each PE has exclusive access to a separate chunk of memory and must therefore communicate with other PEs via message passing,[12] or whether there is a memory to which *all* the PEs have direct access.

---

[12] Fahlman [164] further subdivides message passers according to the size of the message.

However, we have addressed only the data mechanism; there is also a control mechanism to be considered. Treleaven [441] breaks the latter down into control-driven, pattern-driven, demand-driven, and data-driven approaches, representing progressively less explicit control. The von Neumann model (page 138), for example, is control-driven, and instructions are executed exactly on schedule ("Fire on command!"), whereas in dataflow (page 136), a data-driven model, instructions may execute as soon as their data are ready ("Fire at will!").

These two data mechanisms and four control mechanisms can be used to classify most parallel architectures (see Figure 1.6 on page 25). The advantages of the various models are discussed in chapters 9, 10, and 11 in the context of specific embodiments. Shared- and private-memory designs are compared briefly in the box on page 29.

What Algorithms Should Be Used?

As in the serial case, the choice of a parallel algorithm depends on the computational model to be used and the problem to be solved. As pointed out on page 137, the computational model gives the costs associated with algorithms, including the *time* required for primitive operations and the *space* used for data objects. For parallel processing, there are additional charges that depend on the number of processors and the required interprocessor communication.

A parallel algorithm is a recipe for solving a given problem using a given computational model, and hence parallel algorithms too come in SIMD and MIMD varieties. In the MIMD case, there are further subdivisions: the distinction between shared-memory vs. message-passing communication that we discussed above, and another distinction between synchronous vs. asynchronous algorithms that is discussed in Chapter 4 on page 201.[13]

A fair amount of analysis has been published on parallel algorithms. Given N processors, the choice of algorithm can determine whether the speedup is a discouraging $\log N$ or a very encouraging N. The still-acceptable $N/\log N$ is frequently the best that one can do. Most of the analysis is for SIMD (Sameh [381], Heller [226], Gottlieb and Kruskal [203]). MIMD algorithms are discussed in an excellent paper by Kung [309].

How Much Speedup Can Be Expected?

As important as the algorithm is, it is only one of the factors that determine the actual program's running time. As Amdahl noted, the compute time can be

---

[13] These represent two different methods of handling communication among parallel processes, given that the process execution times are not predictable.

CONTROL MECHANISM	DATA MECHANISM	
	SHARED MEMORY	PRIVATE MEMORY (message passing)
Control driven	von Neumann	Communicating processes
Pattern driven	Logic	Actors
Demand driven	Graph reduction	String reduction
Data driven	Dataflow with I-structure	Dataflow

Less explicit control

Figure 1.6   Classification of computational models, with examples.

divided into the *parallel portion* and the *serial portion*, and no matter how high the degree of parallelism in the former, the speedup will be asymptotically limited by the latter, which must be performed on a single processing element. Consider, for example, a sequence of 100 operations, 80 of which can be done in parallel, but 20 of which must be done in sequence. Compared to a single processing element, an 80-PE machine would attain a speedup of not 80 but somewhat under 5, even though the PE cost is 80 times higher.

Pfister [360] subdivides the serial portion into an *algorithmic* part, which refers to serialization intrinsic to the algorithm, and a *hardware-induced* part, which refers to serialization not required by the algorithm but induced by the hardware. Figure 1.7 on page 26 shows these relationships in a diagrammatic way for a shared-memory computational model; also listed is one set of solutions, namely, those used for the NYU Ultracomputer. However, these observations are quite general, and all computational models must supply some such set of solutions. A speedup of 1000 demands that the *total* serial portion be less than 0.1%. Evidence that this speedup is achievable for important applications has been reported by several groups.

We discuss speedup quantitatively at some length later in our book, (page 170). Here we present a shorter summary. Three limiters on speedup are communication overheads, serial sections of code that cannot be parallelized, and the degree of parallelism. If we assume that the parallel processes doing the work cannot compute and communicate at the same time, then T_P, the total time for the parallel job with P workers, can be written

Figure 1.7 *The serial portion of a parallel program's compute time.* *The program's speedup due to parallelism is limited by the serial portion, which is influenced by both the algorithm and the hardware design. This example shows the contributions in a shared-memory environment, and lists the set of solutions used by the NYU Ultracomputer design.*

$$T_P = TCOMP_P + TCOMM_P + other \; terms$$

If the serial computation time is T_S, then

$$TCOMP_P = T_S(1 - A) /P,$$

where A is the fraction of the work (the serial or Amdahl portion) that must be done by a single worker. For the special case of a manager-worker parallel program described in more detail on page 170, the total communication time grows in proportion to the number of workers; that is,

$$TCOMM_P = P \times TCOMM_1$$

and the speedup $S_P = T_S /T_P$ becomes

$$S_P = \frac{1}{A + (1 - A)/P + P/r_1}$$

Figure 1.8 **Speedup limited by communication**, *serial sections and finite divisibility.*

where the quantity r_1 is given by

$$r_1 = T_S / TCOMM_1$$

and is the ratio of computation time to communication time in a system with one worker. It is a useful quantity because, for $A << 1$, the maximum speedup is approximately $0.5\sqrt{r_1}$ and occurs near $P = \sqrt{r_1}$. Figure 1.8 shows the behavior of the speedup for $A = 0.005$ and $r_1 = 100$, 10^4, and 10^6 (r_1 can increase due to a larger problem or faster communication). The figure also shows the divisibility limit that results when the degree of parallelism is 1000. The first two curves ($r_1 = 100$ and $r_1 = 10,000$) correspond to speedup limited by communication. By the time r_1 reaches 10^6 (third curve), the Amdahl limit predominates at 1000 processes.

The computation to communication ratio depends on the parallel system's communication parameters, and we illustrate this by means of another example, an FFT algorithm that we discuss on page 177. This is not a manager-worker program, but uses parallel communication instead. If we assume that

Figure 1.9 **Effect of communication bandwidth and latency on speedup** of 2D FFT algorithm (N = 10,000, P = 1000). For comparison purposes, some representative hardware bandwidth-latency values are added as small shaded circles: P = Paragon (page 491), C = CM-5 (page 509), V = PVM (page 252, but note values are for 32 processors), W = workstations on a LAN (one would not use 1000 for this problem). Note that the bandwidth for the point W is the total system bandwidth, whereas the other points are positioned according to the bandwidth per processor. The latency in all cases is from user space to user space.

sending a message of x words between any two processors takes $L + x/B$ seconds, where L is the latency and B is the hardware bitstream rate in words/sec, then if L is large, the communication time is proportional to P, the number of workers, but if L is small compared to the delay caused by finite B, the communication time varies as $1/P$.

The results of the analysis are plotted in Figure 1.9 as lines of constant speedup on a bandwidth-latency grid. The speedup depends on how L and $1/B$ compare with the time needed to perform a floating point operation, that is, with 1/FLOPS, which we call a, and the figure shows speedup vs L/a and $(1/B)/a$. A second set of axes at the top and right of the figure show L in seconds and B in MBytes/second for $a = 10$nSec, corresponding to 100 MFLOPS

The Pros and Cons of Shared Memory

The contrast between running a modest-size program on the Cosmic Cube and simulating a larger program on the NYU Ultracomputer gives (highly anecdotal) evidence for the relative advantages and shortcomings of shared memory. In designs like the Cosmic Cube without shared memory, interprocessor communication is accomplished via message passing. The Ultracomputer can use its shared-memory machine to support message passing efficiently and also permits the common store to be used directly to hold shared state information for the cooperating tasks. We thus see that the Ultracomputer is the more flexible design, especially when trying to program algorithms that use shared state information heavily. Indeed, we believe that shared memory often eases the task of converting existing large serial programs with arbitrary data dependencies (such as the weather code) into parallel programs.

The flexibility available in shared-memory machines does not come for free. A severe disadvantage is the difficulty of hardware implementation. The Ultracomputer design in particular includes a sophisticated processor-to-memory interconnection network. Since this network was not yet available, all the large-scale parallelism results on the weather code were from a software simulator. In comparing the NYU and Caltech situations, one of the Ultracomputer designers was heard to say, "We're smart, they're smart, but while we're still designing chips, they're doing real science."

One must also note that even when the designs are complete, the Cosmic Cube will retain an advantage. For a given size configuration (i.e., for a given cost or component count) the shared memory will offer noticeably less peak computational power since a considerable number of its components will be devoted to the network. (The designs differed in other respects as well. For example, the Cosmic Cube's original microprocessor, an INTEL 8086, did not support large programs as easily as the Ultracomputer's original Motorola 68000. On the other hand, the 8086 had a floating-point coprocessor well before the 68000.)

In summary, shared memory offers increased flexibility and programming ease at the cost of additional hardware complexity and thus lower peak performance for a given machine cost. Software implementation is easier, and hardware implementation is harder.

processing elements. The figure quickly shows that a parallel machine with a thousand 100 MFLOPS processors needs latency below 10 microseconds and bandwidth above 40 MByte/sec to reach a speedup of 900 on this problem. If the latency exceeds 1 millisecond or the bandwidth drops below 0.4 MBytes/sec, the speedup is limited to 50.

1.4.6   What Will Be the Programmer's View of the Machine?

Finding and Specifying Parallelism

At least three different views of the programmer's role are represented among the parallel processing projects surveyed here:

1. At one extreme is the "dusty FORTRAN deck" approach, in which a translator attempts to convert existing programs for parallel execution and allows the programmer to continue using FORTRAN.   Chapter 6 discusses compilers for parallel processors.
2. At the other extreme, the programmer would use an entirely new language, as in the approach advocated by Backus and other supporters of Functional Programming. This approach has some influence on the Cellular Computer, Rediflow, and Dataflow projects. The chapters on language and architectures discuss this topic further.
3. Somewhere in the middle are the performance-starved physicists, say, who are willing to rework their programs for a machine like the Connection Machine, the Delta, or the GF11.

Program decomposition and synchronization are performed automatically in the first two of these approaches, and the programmer need not be aware of them.   In the last approach, however, some specific language constructs or synchronization primitives will be needed to specify how the computer is to apply parallel processing to our problem. Chapter 5 treats this matter in some detail.

What About Reliability, Availability, Serviceability?

A fair amount of work has been done on fault-tolerant interconnection networks, and we show one example (the extra-stage cube) in Figure 8.13 on page 408. But this is only part of what is needed. A parallel system introduces two new elements: it can fail in new ways, and potentially, at least, the multiple processors permit it to keep running (at degraded performance) in the face of many failures that would cripple a uniprocessor. Both of these new factors pose significant new challenges to the system software. We discuss some of these points further in our section on the Tandem system (page 503).   However, a great deal of work is needed in this area.

1.5　Previous Attempts; Why Success Now?

Parallel computers have been built before without really taking over the world. For example, when "The First Supercomputer" [246], the 64-processor ILLIAC IV, was retired after several years by NASA, it was replaced by a CRAY-1, a very fast one-processor machine.   Other early examples of parallel processors that worked but did not turn into commercial products are the Cm* and the WRM, discussed below.   What has changed to improve the commercial prospects of parallel computers?   The answer boils down to one word: *technology*.   In one way or another, the shortcomings of these early machines can be identified with technology that was inadequate for the architectural concepts involved. The thesis is that in the time that has passed since ILLIAC IV was designed in 1967, technology (especially the VLSI chip) has made such great strides that it no longer limits the successful implementation of a parallel computer.   Let us examine this argument.

One strong lesson from experience is the importance of raw processing power; in order to attract users, a parallel processor must offer substantially better performance than is otherwise available *at the time it appears*.[14] This is similar to the "moving target" problem faced by most new technologies: like the task of unseating a boxing champion, a new technology must not only catch but also *surpass* an entrenched technology in order to replace it, which is very difficult while the entrenched technology is still making good progress. The von Neumann computer will probably always be with us, but at the high-performance end, the rate of progress has slowed down as physical effects like the speed of light have become more and more of a problem.   Also, the designer of a parallel computer has ammunition now that wasn't available before.

The designer has a choice between off-the-shelf and custom-built processing elements.   In the past, commercially available microprocessors were so slow that a huge number would have been needed for high performance.   On the other hand, a smaller assemblage suffered not only in raw performance but also in the interconnection technology that could be justified with this lower performance, a sort of double whammy.   This dilemma affected both the Cm*, a collection of 50 16-bit microcomputers, and the WRM, a collection of 64 8-bit microprocessors.   The Cm* also suffered from the high communication overhead of its microprogrammed hierarchical network, and from the small memory space of its processors (16 address bits, 64KB); the latter condition meant

---

14　This remark does not apply to a system on which existing application programs can be run
　　without modification.

that programs too large to fit into the memory had to be loaded in and out in pieces using overlay techniques. The WRM suffered from the inflexible communications imposed by a two-dimensional mesh interconnection as well as from the fact that only Z80 assembly language was available for programming it, a consequence of the fact that its performance did not surpass the best serial computers of its day. A compiler to a high-level language would have degraded the performance further, and hence the work required to write one was hard to justify.

These two computers were built primarily for experimental purposes. The ILLIAC IV, on the other hand, was designed to be a computing workhorse, a true supercomputer. It actually preceded the other two, and the arguments above called for a custom processor design to get the necessary performance. Both the processor and the memory used very aggressive technology for the day. The processor was able to perform a floating-point addition in 250 nanoseconds, corresponding to a peak instantaneous processing rate of 4 million floating point operations per second (MFLOPS). Theoretically, the full 256-processor machine would have had a peak instantaneous performance over 1000 MFLOPS. (The *sustained* performance, of course, was much less.) The processor was built from discrete components; in that pre-VLSI era, the designers did not have to consider the alternate choice of a VLSI design and the extra delays associated with early VLSI design systems. The large number of discrete components, however, resulted in a serious reliability problem. Today, microprocessors are so powerful that many fewer are required to achieve high performance, and better interconnection networks are more justified (as well as more affordable).

To keep pace with the processors, the ILLIAC IV memory had to be much faster than the predominant core memories of the day; magnetic films were planned first, but the emerging semiconductor memory technology was eventually chosen. The amount of memory was amazingly small by today's standards: each processor had only 16KB, giving the whole machine just 1 MB. To put this into perspective, the NEC SX (page 428) has roughly 10 times the peak performance of ILLIAC IV, but has 256 times as much memory, a testimony to the progress in memory technology over the last fifteen years.[15]

Another lesson from experience is the importance of flexible, general, fast communications. Past parallel processors either assumed more regularity

---

[15] One might expect this to lead to a substantially better ratio of sustained to peak performance. Interestingly enough, this is not so in this case. SX obtains about 290 MFLOPS on the "Livermore loops" benchmark, or about 22% of peak, in the same range as ILLIAC IV. The *size* of the problem that can be handled, of course, is much larger.

(two-dimensional mesh) than there really is in most problems (ILLIAC IV, WRM), or provided global communication that was too slow (Cm*). Today, the communications problem is easier to solve because a much smaller number of processors is needed for a given performance. Better communications networks with functions like buffering and combining of messages at reasonable cost have been made possible by VLSI. And communications concepts not previously applied to computers are now available (binary N-cube, omega network, etc.).

It seems, therefore, that hardware no longer represents a major stumbling block to parallel processing and that the question becomes how practical is a parallel model of computation? How much parallelism is there in applications, and how well can software exploit it? These questions are explored in the next several chapters.

1.6   Conclusions and Future Directions

To summarize the foregoing discussion, we need a new way to think about computing. The sequential architecture devised by von Neumann was a brilliantly successful match to the technology of the 1940s and several decades thereafter, when the processor and memory were both expensive, precious resources. By now, however, there have been millionfold improvements in the speed, cost, and power dissipation of processors as well as a millionfold improvement in the cost of memories, and these two technologies no longer stand in the way of a many-processor parallel computer. The networks needed to provide adequate connections between the elements of such a computer are still a formidable undertaking, but this situation, too, is rapidly being improved by the progress in technology. Now we have to learn the best way to capitalize on all this.

Parallel processing is essentially a divide-and-conquer approach to problem solving, and there are many ways to divide up a problem. Each has its own overhead costs. Put another way, parallelism can be perceived at a number of levels of program execution. An important consideration is the *cost of achieving this parallelism*, which will set the lower bound on the size of the code segment that is profitable to run on a given system. As Lorin [327] points out, it is manifestly unprofitable to execute 50 microseconds of task establishment code to enable the execution of a 3-microsecond sequence in parallel with a 5-microsecond sequence in a multiple processor system. A subtask profitably done in parallel on an MIMD multiprocessor like the Butterfly comprises a reasonably large number of instructions. In a parallel SIMD vector processor, on the other hand, the unit of work is considerably smaller (an instruction stage) because there is essentially no cost of parallelism, no overhead involved in starting up a successor instruction. The cost here is the expense of designing and implementing the capability. In between these extremes lie a number of potential subtask sizes, some not previously seen in existing serial computers.

To make a choice among these possible task sizes, or levels of granularity, we need to determine the best ways to detect their existence and then express and control their parallel execution. Translated into computer terminology, major work is required in compilers, languages, and operating systems. The state of the art in parallel software is far behind the hardware. There *are* compilers that take existing serial programs and achieve modest parallelism, but to go beyond this to parallel programs that have high performance currently takes considerable programmer effort. These are areas of active research, and significant improvements are hoped for. The outlines of some of these critical research areas were sketched in the last sections, and our next chapter provides a better sense of the current state of things. Meaningful progress will require bringing together significantly large programs and significantly powerful parallel processors. This is the challenge facing the search for the best way to do parallel processing.

1.7 Exercises

1. Define each of the following terms:

Amdahl's law	Message passing
Computer	Parallel processor
Degree of parallelism	Parallelism for increased throughput
Dusty deck	Parallelism for reduced turnaround time
Easy parallelism	Process
Functional unit	Processing element
Granularity of parallelism	SIMD
Grosch's Law	Shared memory
Job	Speedup
Level of parallelism	Task
MIMD	

2. Match each of the terms on the left with its definition on the right

    a. Boudoir configuration
    b. Circuit switching
    c. Dancehall configuration
    d. Dataflow model
    e. Degree of parallelism
    f. Granularity of parallel-ism
    g. ILLIAC IV
    h. Level of parallelism
    i. Packet switching

    1) Average subtask size
    2) Communication maintained throughout message transmission
    3) Each processor paired with its memory
    4) First parallel supercomputer
    5) Instructions may execute as soon as data is available
    6) Message portions routed separately
    7) Number of subtasks
    8) Processors and memories on opposite sides of network
    9) Source of parallelism

3. Read Backus's 1982 paper and explain his main objection to the Von Neumann architecture. What does Backus mean by the "Von Neumann Bottleneck"?

4. Read Flynn's classic 1972 paper and write short paragraphs defining and contrasting SISD, SIMD, MISD, and MIMD. Which are popular today?

5. We defined a highly parallel processor as "a large collection of processing elements that can communicate and cooperate to solve large problems fast". On p. 7 ff. we also noted several questions raised by this definition. Raise others. (*Note to instructor: This has worked well as an in-class assignment with the class broken into four teams, one for each set of questions.*)

6. The annual Gordon Bell Awards are given for achievements in supercomputing. The three categories are performance, price/performance, and compiler parallelization. The winning entries are described each year in the May issue of

IEEE Software. Plot the values attained by the winning entries for the last five years. What class of computer holds the current "land speed record"?

7. An increasingly popular method for parallel computing is to use multiple workstations connected by a local area network (LAN). What are typical communication latencies on your LAN? (Hint: investigate the ping command). Approximately how many instructions could your workstation have executed in the same time? What does this suggest about granularity of parallelism?

8. How do you expect the answers to the previous question would change for a shared-memory machine, where communication involves writing and then reading the shared memory?

9. Workstations on a LAN and machines like the Intel Touchstone both use message passing for communication. Why can the Touchstone communication be orders of magnitude faster?

10. What are the advantages of building a parallel computer out of very powerful processors? Very weak processors?

11. How can a system with enormously high I/O bandwidth still have an I/O problem?

12. Give real-life examples of the need for coordination when multiple agents cooperate on achieving an objective.

13. Recall the matrix multiplication example given on page 17. Why did BBN use 6x6 blocks instead of 36 entries in one row or column?

14. Within the next few years, nearly every automobile produced will contain a microprocessor in excess of 10 MIPS. Estimate how many MIPS will be traveling on Interstate 80 (a 5000 km highway connecting New York and San Francisco) at one time. Why would this distributed computing resource not be suitable for modeling global warming?

15. Give five examples of "easy parallelism" .

16. Figure 1.6 on page 25 classifies eight computational models. For each one mention a specific parallel computer that supports it.

17. Consider a problem with a 1% serial portion. What is the maximum speedup possible with 5 processors? With 5000 processors?

18. Would you prefer to use a system with ten 10-MIPS processors or one 100-MIPS processor?

19. What are the pros and cons of using custom-built vs. off-the-shelf microprocessors when designing and building a parallel system?

20. What problems is the rapid increase in the speed of microprocessors causing for designers of parallel systems?

2

Sample Applications

Many applications that offer sufficient parallelism to keep many processing elements busy simultaneously fall into two broad categories, numerical processing and symbolic processing, distinguished by the ratio of calculation to data motion among the processing elements. The more traditional scientific and engineering applications offer some very large numeric computation problems in particle calculations (plasmas), fluid dynamics (weather, aircraft design), computer-aided design, and many others. The symbolic processing applications include database systems, applied artificial intelligence (expert systems, the Fifth Generation project), and longer-range artificial intelligence projects like perception/planning systems. In this chapter we present a small sample of both numerical and symbolic applications.

2.1   Scientific and Engineering Applications

Since the earliest days of computers, the most powerful machines have been used for large scientific and engineering computations. Although supercomputers have also been used for large-scale symbolic processing, there is little doubt that an increasing proportion of future scientific investigations will rely on the use of high-performance computers. In this section, we present as a case study a program used by NASA to predict global atmospheric circulation (and hence the weather). Next we look at seismic migration (done in parallel on a network of workstations), and finally we discuss computer-aided VLSI design.

2.1.1   Parallel Solutions to Significant Scientific Problems

A great effort has been expended in writing scientific programs that vectorize, (i.e., that perform most operations on vectors) and hence attain high performance when executed on vector processors. For some algorithms, it is reasonably straightforward to cast efficient programs in this form. For others, the task is considerably more difficult. Since there is much literature on the use of vector processors for scientific problems, we shall focus on the more recently developed area of scientific programming for large-scale MIMD machines.

We shall further limit our discussion to the solution of entire problems, as opposed to parallelizing individual algorithms. Having parts of a problem solution fully parallelized may still yield a very ineffective utilization of highly parallel machines. Many algorithms have been studied extensively, none more so than the basic linear algebra routines. The reader should see Heller [226] and the work on isolating BLAS (Basic Linear Algebra Subroutines) so that they can be optimized for each parallel architecture (see box on page 39).

A number of significant scientific computations have been executed or simulated on various real and proposed parallel architectures. The problems studied include:

The BLAS—An Effort to Achieve Portable High Performance

Most problems in scientific computation rely at some point on the basic operations in linear algebra: solving linear equations, finding eigenvalues and eigenvectors, etc. It is therefore not surprising that carefully written linear algebra software packages have been developed. One widely used package, LINPACK, has been the subject of a recent research effort aimed at achieving high performance on a wide range of computer architectures. The subroutines comprising LINPACK have been rewritten so that the bulk of the computation is done by a lower level of routines (the BLAS, or Basic Linear Algebra Subroutines), which operate only on one-dimensional arrays. These BLAS are then hand-coded (in assembler) for each computer. When run with these "coded BLAS", LINPACK runs significantly faster (*Computer Architecture News,* March 1985). For example, the measured megaflops (Millions of FLOating Point operations per Second) increased 57% on a Cray X-MP, 197% on a Cyber 205, and 100% on an FPS 164.

- Global atmospheric circulation (the "3D weather code")
- QCD (quantum chromodynamics)
- Blood flow in the heart
- Molecular dynamics
- Evolution of galaxies

In this section we will give a detailed discussion of one solution to the first problem. The weather code was parallelized and run under simulation on the NYU Ultracomputer by David Korn and Norman Rushfield [292]. On page 487 an example of an n-body problem on the Cosmic Cube is discussed, in which this private-memory MIMD implementation is compared with a shared-memory MIMD approach. An SIMD solution of the QCD problem as formulated for the GF11 parallel computer is described on page 444.

The next two pages have a brief primer on the Navier-Stokes equations used in the weather computation. Readers who are not particularly curious about these equations may safely skip those two pages and just read the discussion of the weather code.

2.1.2 *The Weather Code*

Considering the great benefit of accurate weather forecasts to both the economy and the quality of life, it is not surprising that considerable effort has been

Navier-Stokes Fluid Equations

This box is a bit of optional reading on the source of four of the equations used for the NASA weather model (see Figure 2.1 on page 41). The Navier-Stokes equations of motion for a viscous fluid are a special case of the Boltzmann transport equation[†], and can be written

$$\frac{d\vec{V}}{dt} = \frac{\partial \vec{V}}{\partial t} + (\vec{V} \cdot \nabla)\vec{V} = -\frac{1}{\rho}\nabla P + \vec{F} + \nu(\nabla \cdot \nabla)\vec{V} + \frac{\nu}{3}\nabla\nabla \cdot \vec{V}$$

where (x,y,z) is the position of a particle of the fluid, $\vec{V}(x,y,x,t)$ is the corrresponding fluid velocity, with components V_x, V_y, and V_z ($= dx/dt$, etc.), t is time, ∇ is the del operator (see below), ρ is density, P is the pressure, F is the force, and ν is the viscosity.

This equation reduces to three scalar equations that can be obtained by successively replacing V by V_x, V_y, and V_z in the above equation. These, in turn, lead to the motion ("momentum") equation, the two continuity equations, and the energy balance equation ("first law of thermodynamics") in Figure 2.1 on page 41.

Del operator refresher:

$$\nabla \cdot \vec{V} = \text{div}\,\vec{V} = \frac{\partial V_x}{\partial x} + \frac{\partial V_y}{\partial y} + \frac{\partial V_z}{\partial z} \quad (=0 \text{ for incompressible fluid})$$

$$\nabla\vec{V} = \text{grad}\,\vec{V} = \frac{\partial \vec{V}}{\partial x} + \frac{\partial \vec{V}}{\partial y} + \frac{\partial \vec{V}}{\partial z}$$

$$(\vec{V} \cdot \nabla)\vec{V} = V_x\frac{\partial \vec{V}}{\partial x} + V_y\frac{\partial \vec{V}}{\partial y} + V_z\frac{\partial \vec{V}}{\partial z}$$

$$(\nabla \cdot \nabla)\vec{V} = \frac{\partial^2 \vec{V}}{\partial x^2} + \frac{\partial^2 \vec{V}}{\partial y^2} + \frac{\partial^2 \vec{V}}{\partial z^2}$$

[†] The Boltzmann equation also leads to the equations for the flow of electrons in a semiconductor. Charge density replaces velocity as the dependent variable, its time derivative gives the electrical current, the force includes electric and magnetic field terms, and the "viscosity" becomes the electron mobility that makes a cameo appearance on page 101 when we discuss the speed advantage of gallium arsenide transistors.

II.　Primitive Equations of Motion

1. & 2.　Horizontal momentum equations

$$\mathbb{V}\frac{d\pi}{dt} + \pi\frac{d\mathbb{V}}{dt} = \frac{\partial \pi \mathbb{V}}{\partial t} + \nabla \cdot (\pi \mathbb{V}\mathbb{V}) + \frac{\partial}{\partial \sigma}(\pi \dot{\sigma}\mathbb{V})$$

$$= -\pi\nabla\phi - \pi\sigma\frac{RT}{p}\nabla\pi - \left(f + u\frac{\tan\phi}{a}\right)\mathsf{K}x\pi\mathbb{V} + \pi\mathsf{F}$$

3.　Continuity equation

(3.1)　$\dfrac{\partial \pi}{\partial t} + \nabla \cdot (\pi \mathbb{V}) + \dfrac{\partial}{\partial \sigma}(\pi\dot{\sigma}) = 0,$　or

(3.2)　$\dfrac{\partial \pi}{\partial t} = -\displaystyle\int_0^1 \nabla \cdot (\pi\mathbb{V})d\sigma = -\nabla \cdot \displaystyle\int_0^1 \pi\mathbb{V}d\sigma$

4.　Equation of state

$$\alpha = \frac{RT}{p}$$

5.　First law of thermodynamics

$$\frac{\partial \pi T}{\partial t} + \nabla \cdot (\pi \mathbb{V}T) + \frac{\partial}{\partial \sigma}(\pi\dot{\sigma}T) = \frac{\pi\omega\alpha}{C_p} + \frac{\pi Q}{C_p} \qquad\qquad \left(\omega = \frac{dp}{dt}\right)$$

From $\theta = T/p^k$, $p = p_T + \sigma\pi$, $\omega = \dot{\sigma}\pi + \dot{\pi}\sigma$, $\dot{\pi} = \dfrac{\partial \pi}{\partial t} + \mathbb{V}\cdot\nabla\pi$, $k = R/C_p$　　　we get

$$\frac{\partial \pi\dot{\sigma}T}{\partial \sigma} = p^k\frac{\partial \pi\dot{\sigma}\theta}{\partial \sigma} + \pi\frac{\dot{\sigma}\alpha\pi}{C_p} \qquad \text{Replacing in 5,}$$

$$\frac{\partial \pi T}{\partial t} + \nabla(\pi\mathbb{V}T) + p^k\frac{\partial \pi\dot{\sigma}\theta}{\partial \sigma} = \frac{\pi\sigma kT}{p}\left(\frac{\partial \pi}{\partial t} + \mathbb{V}\cdot\nabla\pi\right) + \frac{\pi Q}{C_p}$$

6.　Humidity equation

$$\frac{\partial \pi q}{\partial t} + \nabla \cdot (\pi\mathbb{V}q) = 0$$

7.　Hydrostatic equation

$$\frac{\partial \phi}{\partial_p k} = -C_p\theta \qquad\qquad \left(\text{from } \frac{\partial p}{\partial \phi} = -\rho = -\frac{1}{\alpha}\right)$$

Figure 2.1　The Flow Equations used in writing the weather code

expended in "perfecting" this task. Although the *Farmer's Almanac* and mid-western rain dances are fascinating subjects, we are interested only in *numerical weather predictions*. Simply put, this technique attempts to solve the following problem: Given the current *state* of the atmosphere (i.e., the values of certain specified meteorological quantities), calculate the state at various times in the future. Computer programs that perform this calculation are frequently referred to as *weather codes*.[16] The specific program that was parallelized is the NASA GLAS/GISS fourth-order general circulation model of a three-dimensional atmosphere [273]. For another parallelization effort directed at the same program, but this time using the dataflow computational model, the reader is referred to [138].

Before we can discuss the parallelization effort undertaken by Korn and Rushfield [292], we must describe the mathematical development that underlies the serial program. We will first define the meteorological quantities that characterize the state of the atmosphere and give the hydrodynamic equations relating these quantities. Then we *discretize* both the variables and equations. That is, we divide the atmosphere into subregions, associate a gridpoint with each subregion, and replace the partial differential equations relating the meteorological variables (defined at infinitely many points of space) with difference equations relating the discretized variables (defined on only the finitely many gridpoints). Finally, we give the procedure by which values of the discretized variables at time t can be used to calculate these same values at time $t + \Delta t$.

In the GLAS/GISS model, the atmosphere has two horizontal dimensions representing the surface of the earth and one vertical dimension representing altitude. The state of the atmosphere is characterized by the following eight quantities:

$\vec{V} = (u,v)$ The two horizontal components of the wind velocity.

T   The temperature.

q   The specific humidity.

π The "shifted surface pressure" (i.e., the pressure at the surface minus the pressure at the top of the atmosphere). The latter quantity is fixed at 10 mb.

ϕ The *geopotential,* which corresponds to gravitational effects.

$\dot{\sigma}$ The vertical component of the wind velocity.

p   The pressure.

---

[16] It is common to refer to scientific application programs as *codes* (even when the programmers have worked hard to ensure that their result is highly readable!).

As we shall see, the first five components, u, v, T, q, and π, called *primary variables* by Kalney-Rivas and Hoitsma, are of particular importance to the computation because, starting with values at time t, the time derivatives of the primary are first approximated, and then these values are used to compute the primary variables at time $t + \Delta t$; the remaining three, called *secondary variables,* are updated directly (i.e., without using derivatives).

Perhaps the most interesting observation to make about this list is that according to the weather code, the meteorological state of the atmosphere does *not* include precipitation and cloud cover. Although one might use this observation to explain the prevalence of the forecast "partly cloudy and a chance of rain", it is indeed reasonable that these (let's call them *tertiary*) variables are not included: They can be calculated from the primary and secondary variables (particularly from the humidity and the vertical component of the wind velocity) and are not themselves needed to calculate other variables. Thus the weather code simulates changes in the atmosphere by updating the primary and secondary variables to reflect their values at a succession of times in the future, specifically at times t, $t + \Delta t$, $t + 2\Delta t$, and so on. The tertiary variables can be calculated once, at the final timestep.

The heart of the model consists of the relevant laws of nature expressed as (partial differential) equations involving the meteorological quantities and the procedure used to calculate the state at time $t + \Delta t$ from the state at time t. As one might expect, the equations used are formidable, and their full exposition would take us quite far from the issue of parallel processing. We will instead write down the equations (see Figure 2.1 on page 41), discretize one of them, and then give portions of both the serial and parallel codes used to implement this equation. We will ignore one (really two) significant complications: the north and south poles.[17]

The atmosphere simulated by the NASA model has the geometry of a region located between two concentric spheres, one representing the surface of the earth and the other the "top" of the atmosphere.[18] Since the meteorological quantities are defined on this three-dimensional region and also vary with time, the problem to be solved is inherently four-dimensional.

---

[17] Of course the poles were *not* ignored by either Kalney-Rivas and Hoitsma or Korn and Rushfield. Anecdote: Early flight simulators, when used to simulate over-the-pole flights, would turn the aircraft upside down when the north pole was crossed in a desperate attempt to keep east out the starboard window.

[18] Actually, the NASA program does not assume the earth is spherical: mountain ranges are modeled, for example.

Figure 2.2   *A subdivided rectangle with gridpoints.*

The computational method chosen for this and many other scientific applications divides the region into a number of subregions and restricts its attention to only one point in each subregion. To understand this process of subdivision and choosing gridpoints, let us begin with a simpler geometry, namely a rectangle of length a and width b, and form subregions by subdividing the length into M pieces and the width into N (see Figure 2.2). The dashed lines are called a *grid,* and the points of intersection are called *gridpoints*. The point chosen to represent a subregion is normally one of the bounding gridpoints (often the lower left) or the center of the region. Occasionally, as in the weather code, a mixture is used in which one coordinate is a gridpoint, and the other is centered between gridpoints. For example, the shaded subregion could be represented by p1 (the lower left gridpoint), p2 (the center), or p3 (length at left gridpoint, height at midpoint).

Next consider placing a grid on the surface of the earth (but staying away from the poles). The idea is to take the previous rectangular diagram, glue together the left and right edges, place the resulting cylinder over the earth, and view the configuration perpendicular to the axis of the cylinder. With this interpretation the gridlines have simply become lines of longitude and latitude. To be more specific, we number the vertical lines from 1 to $M + 1$, with the line numbered i representing longitude $i\Delta\lambda$, where $\Delta\lambda = 2\pi/M$ and lines 1 and $M + 1$ are identified. Similarly, the horizontal lines are numbered from 1 to $N + 1$, with line j representing latitude $j\Delta\phi$, where $\Delta\phi = \pi/N$ and lines 1 and $N + 1$ represent the south and north poles, respectively.[19] Later we will need the distance between adjacent lines. For lines of latitude, this constant, denoted by n, is simply $a\Delta\phi$, where a is the radius of the earth. The correspond-

---

[19]   Of course, it is strange to see the poles represented as lines rather than points. This is one
of the ways in which our description is not adequate for the poles.

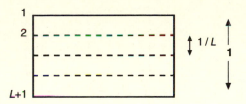

Figure 2.3   A vertical slice of the atmosphere.

ing distance between lines of longitude varies with latitude. At latitude $j\Delta\phi$, the distance is denoted n_j and equals $a \cos \phi_j \Delta\lambda$.

Figure 2.3 depicts a vertical slice of the atmosphere, that is, one vertical dimension corresponding to altitude and one horizontal dimension corresponding to a line of longitude or latitude. The altitude lines are numbered from 1 to $L+1$, with lower numbers higher in the atmosphere. Altitude is scaled so that the top of the atmosphere is zero and the surface of the earth is unity, and thus the distance between altitude lines, denoted $\Delta\sigma$, is equal to $1/L$. The L altitudes used in the weather code are the midpoints between the lines. Although our diagrams will not indicate these midpoints, our formulas will reflect the fact that altitude k is located at position $(k - \frac{1}{2})\Delta\sigma$.

Extending the vertical slice of Figure 2.3 to include the two horizontal dimensions shown in Figure 2.2 on page 44 yields the three-dimensional grid used in the weather code. The result is illustrated in Figure 2.4 on page 46, in which each line of longitude and latitude has become a vertical slice. In particular, the left and right faces, corresponding to longitudes 1 and $M+1$, must be identified, and the front and back faces, corresponding to latitudes 1 and $N+1$, represent vertical rays emanating from the south and north poles. Similarly, the top and bottom faces, corresponding to altitudes 1 and $L+1$, represent the top of the atmosphere and the surface of the earth. This completes our program of subdividing the atmosphere into MNL subregions and associating a gridpoint with each.

Having defined a grid, we now proceed to discretize the primary and secondary variables discussed above. This process is accomplished by replacing each such variable A, which is defined on all the (infinitely many) points constituting the three-dimensional atmosphere, by MNL variables, each defined at only one gridpoint. The original variables, defined on an entire region of space, are often called *continuous*. These new variables are called *discrete* since they are defined at only a finite number of discrete points. For example,

Figure 2.4   The three-dimensional grid used in the weather code.

we replace the humidity, q, by q_{ijk}, where q_{ijk} is defined on the gridpoint having latitude, longitude, and altitude equal to

$$(i\Delta\lambda, j\Delta\phi,(k - \frac{1}{2})\Delta\sigma).$$

At this point some reasonably advanced applied mathematics is brought to bear, and the equations of state given above are rewritten in terms of the *discretized* variables just introduced. We shall consider just the humidity equations, which fairly represent the difficulties involved.

We begin with three definitions:

$$u_{ijk}^{*} = n\pi_{ij}u_{ijk}$$

$$v_{ijk}^{*} = m_j\pi_{ij}v_{ijk}$$

$$\dot{\Sigma}_{ijk} = \pi_{ij}\dot{\sigma}_{ij}$$

A mathematical analysis shows that D, the time derivative of the product of the pressure π and the humidity q at the gridpoint (i,j,k), is well approximated by the following formula:

$$D = \{\ 4.\times[(U^*_{ijk} + U^*_{i-1jk})(q_{ijk} + q_{i-1jk}) - (U^*_{ijk} + U^*_{i+1jk})(q_{ijk} + q_{i+1jk})]$$

$$-.5\times[(U^*_{ijk} + U^*_{i+2jk})(q_{ijk} + q_{i-2jk}) - (U^*_{ijk} + U^*_{i+2jk})(q_{ijk} + q_{i+2jk})]$$

$$+4.\times[(V^*_{ijk} + V^*_{ij-1k})(q_{ijk} + q_{ij-1k}) - (V^*_{ijk} + V^*_{ij+1k})(q_{ijk} + q_{ij+1k})]$$

$$-.5\times[(V^*_{ijk} + V^*_{ij-2k})(q_{ijk} + q_{ij-2k}) - (V^*_{ijk} + V^*_{ij+2k})(q_{ijk} + q_{ij+2k})]$$

$$+.5\times[\dot{S}_{ijk-1}(q_{ijk} + q_{ijk-1}) - \dot{S}_{ijk}(q_{ijk} + q_{ijk+1})]/\Delta\sigma_k\ \}$$

From the approximation

$$\frac{\partial f}{\partial t} \simeq \frac{\Delta f}{\Delta t}$$

we can approximate $\pi q_{ijk}^{t+\delta t}$, the value of πq_{ijk} at time $t + \delta t$, by $\pi q_{ijk}^{t+\Delta t}$. Analogous procedures are used to obtain $\pi u_{ijk}^{t+\Delta t}$, $\pi v_{ijk}^{t+\Delta t}$, $\pi T_{ijk}^{t+\Delta t}$, and $\pi_{ijk}^{t+\Delta t}$. Finally, dividing by π gives q, u, v, and T.[20]

From this description, the serial program nearly writes itself, yielding a multilevel loop structure in which the outer three loops are used to increment the longitude, latitude, and altitude during the computation for each time step. As a convenience in writing these loops, we use the compact notation

Using this notation, we would write the serial program as shown in Figure 2.5 on page 48. Note that it is not possible to combine the loops shown in this figure: several elements of the ustar and u arrays are needed to calculate D.

---

[20] The NASA program does not use this simple first-order time scheme but instead permits the selection of either the Matsuno (Euler-backward) predictor-corrector or smooth leapfrog scheme. Each of these can be roughly described as applying the first-order scheme twice.

Foreach longitude, latitude, altitude
    ustar[i,j,k] = n * pi[i,j] * u[i,j,k]
    vstar[i,j,k] = m[j] * pi[i,j] * v[i,j,k]
    sdot[i,j,k] = pi[i,j] * sigmadot[i,j]
End

Foreach longitude, latitude, altitude
    D = 4 * ((ustar[i,j,k] + ustar[i-1,j,k]) * (q[i,j,k] +q[i-1,j,k])
      + terms involving indices i±1, i±2, j±1,j±2, and k±1)
    (this is the equation for D from p. 47)
    piq[i,j,k] = piq[i,j,k] + D * deltat
    Four similar pairs of statements for piu, piv, piT, *and* pi
End

Foreach longitude, latitude, altitude
    q[i,j,k] = piq[i,j,k]/pi[i,j,k]
    u[i,j,k] = piu[i,j,k]/pi[i,j,k]
    v[i,j,k] = piv[i,j,k]/pi[i,j,k]
    T[i,j,k] = piT[i,j,k]/pi[i,j,k]
End

Figure 2.5   The original serial version of the NASA weather code. *This is repeated for each time step Δt. The first and third* **Foreach** *loops are vectorizable, since the iterations are all independent of each other, unlike the second loop, in which iteration [i] depends on iteration [i-1] and others.*

Parallelization of the Weather Code

Observe that for each of the three loops in Figure 2.5, all its iterates are independent and may, therefore, be executed concurrently. However, we want to ensure that all the iterates of one loop terminate before the subsequent loop begins.[21]

---

[21] This is a stronger synchronization than necessary. An individual iterate of the subsequent loop cannot start until specific (but not all) iterates of the preceding loop complete. Thus, the minimal precedent constraints are weaker than the ones we give. Indeed, there is no need to consider each iterate in its entirety. Carried to the extreme, one could give constraints of the form "operation x of iterate y of loop z must precede operation a of iterate b of loop c". This extreme approach, which exposes the maximum possible parallelism by imposing the minimum possible constraints, typifies the dataflow approach to parallelism described in Chapter 5.

Constant deltat
Shared ustar, vstar, sdot, u, m, pi, v, sigmadot, piq, piu, piv, piT
Private D, i, j, k

Forall longitude, latitude, altitude **in parallel**
     ustar[i,j,k] = n * pi[i,j] * u[i,j,k]
     vstar[i,j,k] = m[j] * pi[i,j] * v[i,j,k]
     sdot[i,j,k] = pi[i,j] * sigmadot[i,j]
End Sync

Forall longitude, latitude, altitude **in parallel**
     D = 4 * ((ustar[i,j,k] + ustar[i-1,j,k]) * (q[i,j,k] +q[i-1,j,k]) ...)
     piq[i,j,k] = piq[i,j,k] + D * deltat

     Four similar pairs of statements for piu, piv, piT, and pi

End Sync

Forall longitude, latitude, altitude **in parallel**
     q[i,j,k] = piq[i,j,k]/pi[i,j,k]
     u[i,j,k] = piu[i,j,k]/pi[i,j,k]
     v[i,j,k] = piv[i,j,k]/pi[i,j,k]
     T[i,j,k] = piT[i,j,k]/pi[i,j,k]
End Sync

Figure 2.6   *The parallelized version of the NASA weather code of Figure 2.5.*

With a shared-memory design such as that of the Ultracomputer used by Korn and Rushfield, the parallelization of this code segment is reasonably straightforward.[22] Referring to Figure 2.6, we see that the code looks seductively similar to the serial version. But there are differences! The **Forall ... in parallel** notation, like the **Foreach** construct introduced earlier, abbre-

---

[22] But it was not so easy in real life. For example, there are the north and south poles and the more sophisticated time-differencing schemes that were mentioned above. Moreover, the code was banded to save memory, and a filtering technique was applied to alleviate high-frequency errors known to be introduced by the numerical method we have described. Another point is that there are various common subcomputations occurring in the calculations for u, v, q, T, and π. The code calculates each one only once.

viates a triply nested loop, but in the new construct all the iterates are to be executed concurrently, each on a separate processor.[23] We end the construct with **End Sync**, rather than just **End** to indicate that the end of the loop represents a synchronization point. This approach has been called *barrier synchronization* by Harry Jordan [271] to indicate that the tasks encounter a barrier through which none can pass until they all arrive. That is, no statement following a loop is begun until all iterates of the loop have completed. Barriers are discussed further on p. 160.

The **Shared** and **Private** constructs determine whether the variables specified are unique to each task created or are shared among them. For example, D is declared private so that the values calculated by tasks created to execute iterates involving different (i,j,k) tuples will be kept separate, whereas q is declared shared so that all tasks will refer to and update the same humidity array.

For the parts of the code shown, the parallelism obtained is *NML*, which would exceed a million for fine meshes. Other large parts of the code have parallelism *NM*, still very large. Some (fortunately) smaller parts have parallelism equal to only N, M, or L, and there are some tiny serial sections. A careful analysis, performed by Korn and Rushfield, showed that for fine meshes, the entire code exhibits enough parallelism to yield extremely high efficiency on an ideal shared-memory parallel computer (a PRAM augmented with Fetch-and-add; the index indicates where these terms are defined) containing thousands of processors. For an actual Ultracomputer (p. 572), network delays would lower the efficiency somewhat, but the speedup would still be in the thousands.

For a message-passing machine the situation is more involved. The usual technique is to perform a domain decomposition; that is, we partition the gridpoints and assign one partition to each processor. For example, assume that the topology of the parallel computer is itself a three-dimensional grid of size (a,b,c). Then a natural procedure would be to partition the latitude into a intervals, the longitude into b intervals, and the altitude into c intervals and then assign a gridpoint to the processor whose position in the topology of the computer corresponds to the latitude, longitude, and altitude intervals of the gridpoint. For the most part each processor can work on its gridpoints separately from the other processors. However, when updating the values at a

---

[23] More precisely, all the iterates *may* be executed concurrently. That is, the programmer (or the compiler) has guaranteed that there are no inter-iterate dependencies. Correct execution will thus result if the iterates are executed in any serial order or, depending upon the available hardware resources, if many are executed concurrently.

gridpoint located very near the boundary of the region assigned to the processor, values are needed from gridpoints in other regions. Messages need to be passed. It is not hard to see that the difficulty in writing such a program depends upon how closely the topology of the computer matches the topology of the problem being solved. Moreover, the amount of communication needed is determined by the number of gridpoints that are near region boundaries. If the ratio of boundary to interior gridpoints is low, the communication will be dominated by (useful) computation, and thus the efficiency will be high.

2.1.3 Molecular Dynamics

On page 487, we treat an n-body problem as programmed for the Cosmic Cube, and then we compare this private-memory MIMD implementation with a shared-memory MIMD approach.

2.1.4 Quantum Chromodynamics

An SIMD solution of the QCD problem as formulated for the GF11 parallel computer is described on page 444.

2.1.5 Seismic Migration

Seismic migration is a key step in obtaining an undistorted subsurface image from seismic echo data (see Figure 2.7 on page 52), and is of great importance to the petroleum industry. A major difficulty in seismic migration as compared to other image processing techniques (for example, those used in the medical field) is that the propagation velocity of the seismic signals can vary by a factor of ten from one part of the seismic image to the other. The seismologist starts with a rough velocity profile and uses a cut-and-try iterative procedure to converge on an output image that is physically feasible and consistent with other measurements. The process is computationally intensive and can take several weeks. Even a parallel program that achieves only single-digit speedup is useful in such a situation, and we describe such a program for 2D depth migration [20], [21] on a network of workstations. (In geophysics, *time* extrapolation or migration assumes that the velocity varies only vertically, whereas *depth* migration is able to handle horizontal velocity variations as

Time section to be Depth Migrated on IBM RISC System/6000

Depth Migration on IBM RISC System/6000

Figure 2.7 Seismic stack section before and after migration. *This is a 467-trace x 400 time sample subsection of a survey from the Gulf of Mexico. Feature at left is a salt dome. Several of the basic effects of migration are shown in this before and after comparison, including removal of diffraction artifacts and steepening of dipping features like the edge of the salt dome.*

well.) Highly parallel computing was not achieved, but the reasons are instructive.

The technique used here involves a solution of the sonic wave equation that is run *backward in time*. That is, in atmospheric modeling we are interested in what the weather will be a day from now, given what the weather is now. In seismic migration we are given echo signals that were recorded at the

Figure 2.8   The computation cube for seismic migration

surface, and are interested in going back to the moment in time when these echoes were generated by whatever geological discontinuities lie beneath the surface. If we can deduce the wave pattern at this "time zero", we are on our way to generating an accurate subsurface map.

The Serial Program

The starting (serial) program used in this case study is described in "Stable Explicit Depth Extrapolation of Seismic Wavefields" [218]. It uses finite difference techniques to solve the wave equation that governs the propagation of seismic signals and to extrapolate the signals recorded at the surface downward into the desired region; that is, it solves the wave equation to find out what subsurface features gave rise to the echo pattern recorded at the surface. To be more specific, if we define ∇ as on page 40 and take z as the depth dimension, x as the lateral dimension, t as time, and v as propagation velocity, then we can say that the program finds the subsurface pressure pattern (image) $P(x,z,t=0)$ from the recorded pressure pattern $P(x,z=0,t)$ by solving the wave equation

$$\nabla^2 P = \frac{1}{v^2(x,z)} \frac{\partial^2 P}{\partial t^2}$$

via a Fourier transform from the time domain to the frequency (ω) domain, followed by step-by-step downward extrapolation at each frequency using a convolution-like filtering with filter coefficients that vary with both ω and v (see Figure 2.8). The output is an array in which each (x,z) entry is the sum over all ωs of the computed (x,z, ω) values.

Several different legal evaluation orders are possible, as discussed in reference [20]. The serial program used here was structured as a nested loop with ω as the outermost variable, followed by z and x. The inner x loop is shown in

```
for (ix=0; ix<nx; ix++) {
  ...
      /* extrapolate with focusing term */
      spr = pr[ix];   spi = pi[ix];
      er = e[iwdxov][0].r;   ei = e[iwdxov][0].i;
      qr = er*spr-ei*spi;   qi = er*spi+ei*spr;
      for (je=1; je<ne; ++je) {
          spr = (double)pr[ix+je]+(double)pr[ix-je];
          spi = (double)pi[ix+je]+(double)pi[ix-je];
          er = (double)e[iwdxov][je].r;
          ei = (double)e[iwdxov][je].i;
          qr += er*spr-ei*spi;
          qi += er*spi+ei*spr;
      }
  ...
}
```

Figure 2.9   Seismic migration inner loop *(untuned; see* [20]*).*

Figure 2.9.   Each pass through this loop, that is, computing each point in $P(x, \omega, z)$, represents about 200 floating-point operations.   For a 1000×1000 input array (a survey with 1000 traces along a survey line, each trace having 1000 time-sample points), this code fragment is executed a billion times.   For large, 3D seismic surveys, a trillion iterations of this inner loop might be required.

With ω as the outer variable, the iterations of the outermost loop are independent and may be evaluated in any order.   A random order is useful in enabling the seismologist to inspect the partly developed image and decide whether the computation is worth completing with the velocity profile that has been chosen.   (Deterministic orders of evaluation, such as low-to-high frequencies, tend to produce artifacts in the partial image, artifacts that disappear at completion.)   For parallel processing, of course, this independence is a bonanza: the iterations of the outer loop become a pool of tasks that can be performed in parallel.   For the 1000×1000 array mentioned above, for example, there are 1000 tasks each consisting of 200 million floating-point operations.   In terms of the parallelism map in Figure 1.5 on page 19, the degree

Figure 2.10　Parallel seismic depth migration program. *The MANAGER starts a number of WORKERs on different workstations, which then use remote procedure calls (RPC) to communicate with three procedures in Manager (init, nextFreq, and reportWork) to obtain needed parameters, obtain the next chunk of work, and report intermediate and/or final results. (The two big arrays are the velocity profile V and the seismic section P, which is transformed into the seismic image q. The parameter mw controls how often an intermediate image is displayed; mw is also a handy "knob" to vary the degree of communication.) This self-service paradigm provides a useful combination of performance, load balancing, and fault tolerance.*

of parallelism is 1000, and the granularity, or grain size, of parallelism is so large that it is far off the scale to the right.

The Parallel Program

The parallel implementation (Figure 2.10) uses a manager-worker organization, similar to a master-slave arrangement except that the workers request assignments. Another way to look at it (for readers familiar with client-server programs) is that the manager starts out as a client activating a group of servers

to perform computation, but then the roles are switched, and the manager becomes a server sending data in response to requests from the clients who are
performing the computation (see page 170 for a little more detail). The manager (the main process) spawns remote workers on the various processors.
The workers repeatedly request assignments from the manager and process
the work they are given, which consists of computing the x-by-z array
$P(x,z,\omega = \omega_o)$ for a particular value of ω. The desired quantity is the inverse
Fourier transform

$$P(x,z,t = 0) = \sum_{\omega} P(x,z, \omega)e^{-j\omega t}$$

but since we want the result at $t = 0$, only the sum of the arrays computed by
the workers is needed.

The parallel program was first implemented using remote procedure calls
(see page 166) provided by NCS (Network Computing System), and was tested
using IBM RISC/6000 workstations connected by ethernet, token ring, and SLA
fiber optic communication with hardware transmission rates of 10, 16, and 220
Mbit/sec, respectively. Reference [21] describes experiments with up to a
dozen workstations. The effective datarate (bandwidth) of the remote procedure calls was measured first, followed by measurements of the parallel program's performance. The good news was that the parallel performance could
be predicted from the effective datarate quite well, using a simple analytical
model (page 61). The bad news was that the effective data rates were far below the hardware speeds, due to software overheads, and only single-digit
speedups were obtained. Nevertheless, useful speedup was obtained for
small numbers of workstations, and a speedup of 3.3 for 4 ethernet-connected
workstations received special mention in the 1990 Gordon Bell prize competition for achieving a cost-performance ratio of $625/MFLOPS, a four-fold im-
provement over the previous year's winner, the CM-2 performing a reservoir
modeling problem.

Subsequent efforts were aimed at improving portability and performance.
Reimplementation of the RPC-based program using PVM and Linda (page 252
ff.) meant that the program was no longer limited to systems that supported
NCS. However, speedups remained the same, a consequence of the fact that
NCS, PVM, and Linda were all implemented using Internet Protocol (IP), which
entails substantial software overhead. One attempt to improve performance
was to bypass IP and to rewrite the parallel program using low-level send-
receive routines provided by IMCS, the proprietary native protocol for the SLA

fiber optic adapter. Effective datarate and speedup did increase, but the new program was less reliable and, of course, less portable than the NCS version.

PVMe and SP1 Results

A useful combination of performance and portability is represented by PVMe, a version of PVM implemented in IMCS, not IP. PVM programs ran unmodified and with higher datarates and better speedup. The trade-off is that one loses the heterogeneity of PVM, since PVMe works only on hardware equipped with the SLA fiber optic adapter. Also, the SLA is a point-to-point device, not a LAN adapter, which made it necessary to use a special interconnection switch for clusters of more than three RISC/6000 workstations.[24] On the plus side, the PVMe-based seismic program achieved a speedup of 6.85 for 7 workstations (98% efficiency) and made a speedup of 20 seem achievable if enough workstations were available. In fact, as shown in Figure 2.11, a speedup of 23 for 29 worker processors was obtained later in the improved communication environment provided by the IBM SP1, whose computational elements are repackaged RISC/6570 workstations.

Projections for Higher Communication Speed

What if communication can be made still faster? The speedup derivation on page 57 shows that the megaflops achieved by the parallel program scale as $(F \times nz \times B^*)^{1/2}$ where

> F is the floating-point rate achieved by a single processor (MFLOPS)
> nz is the linear dimension of the input seismic array
> B^* is the effective datarate between two processors

and where we have assumed that we have just enough processors to give peak speedup[25] for our choice of F, nz, and B^*. The projected results are displayed in Figure 2.12 on page 59. As can be seen, 30 workstations that can each perform the seismic migration program at 65 MFLOPS and that can exchange data at an effective 2 MByte/sec should achieve almost 1 GFLOPS for a 1000-by-1000 array (and in fact do better than that for the 8 MB/s available in the SP1, as shown in Figure 2.11 on page 58).[26] The next fiber optic adapter for the RISC/6000 will use Fiber Channel Standard (FCS) protocol and will have

---

[24] Larger clusters with a ring topology can be formed without a switch, since the SLA has two bi-directional ports. Rings are useful for some problems, such as matrix multiplication.

[25] Since the efficiency at peak speedup is only 50%, one would probably choose fewer processors, e.g., half the optimum number chosen above gives 0.8 times the peak speedup.

[26] It is amusing for one of us (GSA) to remember the skepticism generated by Figure 2.12 during some of his presentations in 1991.

Figure 2.11 ***Early parallel seismic migration results on the IBM SP1*** *(page 512). The curves are from the analytical model in the text, and are seen to agree well with the measurements (triangles and stars). The lowest curve is for the original PVM program using ethernet communication on the SP1, and represents the best that can be obtained with a LAN-connected cluster of workstations [21]. The middle curve shows the same program using SP1 switch communication and benefiting from the higher bandwidth, but limited in speedup by the loop of sends and receives in the original PVM program, which accrue communication costs linear with the number of processors P. For the upper curve, the loops were replaced by broadcast and reduce operations from the SP1 collective communication library, resulting in a log(P) growth in communication overhead and significantly better speedup for large P. This is an example of the combination of hardware and software needed to support a shift from the serial access paradigm to the concurrent access paradigm (SAP to CAP), as we discuss further on page 176.*

a hardware speed of 100 MByte/sec (1 Gbit/sec). The challenge will be to devise communication software with appropriate lightweight protocols and overheads and hence obtain a comparably high datarate.

Figure 2.12 *Projected maximum megaflops for increased datarates. The horizontal axis is B*, the effective RPC bandwidth that one actually measures. The upper line is for a 65 MFLOPS serial program (43 MHz workstation and a program that achieves 1.5 floating-point operations per cycle). The lower line is for an 18 MFLOPS serial program (20 MHz, 0.9 FLOP/cycle). Numbers along the lines tell how many workstations are needed.*

Lessons for Highly Parallel Computing

As we say elsewhere (page 170 ff.), the manager-worker model is a handy way to achieve modest parallelism, but the bottleneck at the manager prevents highly parallel computing. Unless much higher datarate links and protocols are developed, the solution has to be to remove some of the burden of communication from the manager and spread it among the workers, using a different algorithm in conjunction with a richer connection topology. Some remedies of this type are discussed on page 170 ff. and also in references [20] and [21]. The other remedy, of course, is an algorithm that does less communication altogether.

Applications Related to Seismic Processing

Reverse and Forward Modeling

Geophysicists make extensive use of both reverse modeling (seismic migration) and forward modeling (cross-borehole tomography). Reservoir modeling and global basin modeling are two other computationally intensive geoscience applications. In both cases one is interested in establishing the extent of a reservoir and then modeling its fluid dynamics, possibly including chemical reactions among the fluids. The difference is in the time scales—reservoir modeling deals in decades and is of interest to, say, petroleum engineers in charge of extracting a certain find and who want to know "how can I get it out?". Basin modeling deals in eons, and interests a geologist asking "how did it get there?". Both are relevant for toxic waste disposal planning, an increasingly important computer application.

Image vs. graphics processing (computer graphics)

Image processing starts with a bitmap (measured image with noise, distortion, geometry effects) and creates another bitmap (corrected "true" image). In other words, image processing starts with an image and tries to figure out "what's really in it", using a model of the process that created the image. (If this model includes not only measurement geometry and signal propagation but also includes a catalogue of possible objects, then we have crossed from image processing to *image recognition,* which is treated later in this chapter on page 88.)

Graphics processing is just the opposite. An object is specified, and the program is supposed to figure out "how it will look" when viewed from a certain point in certain surroundings and under certain illumination. The image-forming model is the same as for image processing, but it is now run "forward", using techniques such as ray tracing, hidden surface removal, shading, and so forth. These graphics operations are the source of parallelism that can be exploited by computers like the Power Visualization System (page 252), among others. In image processing, much of the parallelism comes from matrix operations.

With regard to obtaining faster communication, it is worth pointing out that we showed that it is the *latency* more than the hardware bitstream rate that is currently the villain in preventing more speedup for this application, and it is also the latency that must be improved in order to obtain useful speedup for applications with a finer grain of parallelism. The villain behind latency, in turn, is a combination of software and (multi-) user environment. A workstation cluster on a LAN provides many features and protection mechanisms that are not essential in the more specialized environment of a parallel supercomputer, and, as usual, there is a price. All that the parallel processes in our program want to achieve with their inter-processor communications is to transfer some data from the user space of one processor's memory to the user

Seismic Program Speedup Derivation

Assume that sending a message of x bytes between any two processors takes L + x/B seconds, where L is the latency and B is the hardware bitstream rate. Let B^* = effective bandwidth (defined below), P = number of processors, f = time for a floating point operation $(FLOP/\,sec)^{-1}$, and w = packet size. Assume a square input array, i.e., nx=nz=nt=nω=N. Then the time for the original sequential computation is

$$T_S = 200fN^3.$$

The time to send an N-by-N velocity array to each of P workers is

$$P\left(L + 4N^2/B\right) + L \times \lfloor 2P \times 4N^2/w \rfloor$$

where the last term exists only if non-pipelined packet communication is used, as in a LAN, and accounts for the extra latency from data that take more than one packet to send. ($\lfloor x \rfloor$ means the smallest integer in x.) If we drop the $\lfloor\,\rfloor$ and make a continuous approximation instead, the time to send the velocity arrays can be written

$$P\left(L + 4N^2/B^*\right)$$

where the effective bandwidth B^* is

$$B^* = B/(1 + BL/w).$$

For an ethernet, B = 10^6 bytes/sec, and the user data w in a maximum packet or frame is somewhat below 1400 bytes. A typical value of L for an NCS RPC is 0.01 sec, which leads to

$$B^* = B/7,$$

which mostly explains why the measured RPC datarate B^* can be ten times less than the hardware speed.

The time to send rows of P(x,z=0,ω) for each ω to the workers is

$$N(L + 4N/B^*),$$

and the time to receive an N-by-N partial image from each worker is

$$P\left(L + 4N^2/B^*\right).$$

Neglecting the time needed for other operations in the serial program, the time needed by the parallel program becomes

$$T_P = 200f\frac{N^3}{P} + 2P(L + \frac{4N^2}{B^*}) + N(L + \frac{4N}{B^*})$$

Let us assume that $N >> 2P >> 1$. Let us also assume that $LB^* << 8NP$, since, for L=0.01, $B^* = 100{,}000$, and N=1000, $LB^* = 1000$ while 8NP is 8000P. The equation above then simplifies to

$$T_P = 200fN^3/P + 8N^2P/B^*$$

and the equation for speedup $S_P = T_S/T_P$ becomes

$$1/S_P = 1/P + 2P/(200fNB^*/4),$$

which is in the same form as the equation we derive in chapter 4 for a generic manager-worker program, namely,

$$1/S_P = 1/P + P/r_1,$$

where r_1 is the ratio of computation to communication times for a system with a single worker and in the present case becomes

$$r_1 = 25fNB^*.$$

A more detailed derivation shows that N is really nz, the depth dimension. By then setting $d(S_P)/dP = 0$ we find that $P_{opt} = 5\sqrt{f \cdot nz \cdot B^*}$, $S_{max} = 2.5\sqrt{f \cdot nz \cdot B^*}$.

space of another processor's memory while staying in user mode, where the cost of doing things is much cheaper than in supervisor mode (kernel mode), with its larger protection boundaries and higher software overheads. But an ordinary system of workstations on a LAN does not allow this direct communication between user spaces. Instead, as in the example of the remote procedure call illustrated in Figure 4.13 on page 168, the only mechanism for communication is from kernel space to kernel space, which means that the services of the operating system must be invoked on each workstation, data must be copied from user space to system space and back, and latencies below one millisecond are very difficult to achieve.[27] This is why a highly parallel message-passing supercomputer cannot simply be put together from existing workstations and software, but instead requires the development of special hardware and software in order to achieve the latency that is needed, which is in the range of microseconds (see Figure 4.17 on page 178).

2.1.6 Computer-Aided VLSI Design

The topic of parallelism in design automation (DA) is well treated by Pfister [361]; much of this section is based on that paper. Interesting results on this topic continue to appear at the annual conference on design automation; see, for example, the paper by Jacob et al. [263], and the references therein.

In the days when computers were built from individual transistors, the effects of a design error like a wrong connection (like the one in Figure 2.13 on page 63) could be fixed fairly quickly. The design time and manufacturing time were both less than in this VLSI era. The building block in question would fail to give the correct output for one of the inputs in a fairly small set of tests, and the errant input-to-output path could be probed point-by-point to locate the problem.

This method of debugging a design is no longer practical now that many computer circuits are contained on VLSI chips. First of all, much more time is needed to design and "assemble" a building block (the chip) before it can be tested (see Chapter 3 for more discussion of this topic). Second, many of the internal points are inaccessible for probing because the chip's inputs and outputs are limited in number. The net effect is to increase the pressure to make VLSI chips correct before any actual hardware is created.

---

[27] There are interesting efforts to develop more convenient and faster remote procedure calls implemented in a high-level language [468] and in a shared-memory environment [62], but these are not yet commercially available.

Figure 2.13   *Example of a design error in a logic circuit* (*see text*).

Thorough verification of design correctness becomes critical, which explains the need for the design and checking tools shown in Figure 3.16 on
page 118.   One such tool is extensive *simulation* of the logic design.   This
simulation represents a probabilistic search for errors, and the design of a large
new computer can easily consume tens of thousands of CPU hours for simulation of the design with a simulation program running on a large existing
computer.   Fortunately, the application is ripe for parallel processing.

The parallelism comes about because of the finite number of *levels of logic*
in the hundreds of thousands of circuits in the computer's processing unit.   As
is discussed in connection with Figure 3.8 through Figure 3.10, an operation
performed during one execution cycle sends a set of input bits cascading from
one logic gate to the next until the set of output bits is created; but this cascade
seldom spans more than 10 logic gates.   In other words, the levels of logic seldom exceed 10 and never exceed 30, which results in an average of about
10,000 gates per level, all of which can be simulated in parallel.

To understand this discussion better, consider what it is that identifies one
of the logic gates of a big design:

1.   The function that it performs (AND, OR, NAND, ...).
2.   The gates that it is connected to, that is, the gates that it gets its inputs
     from and sends its output(s) to.

Beyond the above, a gate has no individuality or uniqueness.   To set up a
simulation, it is necessary to keep track of

•   Where the inputs come from

- What each input is (1 or 0) .
- What the gate does in response to an input pattern (truth table)
- Where the output goes
- What the output is (1 or 0)

Assuming that each gate delay is equal (called *unit delay mode* and a necessary though not sufficient test for correct operation), all gates that are the same number of steps down the cascade from the input to the chip are *independent of each other* and are influenced only by the outputs of the immediately preceding level of logic. Hence, the simulation can proceed from level to level, with each gate on a level being simulated in parallel.

Several special-purpose parallel processors have been built to do such logic simulation much more rapidly than present methods allow. In particular, the Yorktown Simulation Engine that is described on page 627 has demonstrated at least 256-way parallelism [297], and yet higher degrees of parallelism have been achieved by its successors. A number of other steps involved in VLSI design also exhibit substantial parallelism, as discussed in the following sections.

Circuit Simulation

Circuit simulation is the detailed simulation of the electrical characteristics of circuits. New techniques in this area [318] use points of low coupling in the circuit to break the task into a multitude of smaller ones, in blocks that roughly correspond to logic blocks. Thus parallelism on the order of that achieved in logic simulation should be possible.

Shape Checking

Shape checking verifies that the area chosen for deposition of metal, polysilicon, and so forth in integrated circuits meets manufacturing criteria. For example, elements on the same plane, such as two metal wires, must be a minimum distance from each other. Interelement comparisons are completely independent and so can be done in parallel. With hundreds of thousands of elements on today's chips, the average degree of available parallelism is large—on the order of thousands. In essence we have an image-processing problem, so large degrees of parallelism are not surprising.

Placement

Placement refers to the automatic positioning of blocks (gates or higher-level entities) on a chip. Current techniques typically use some form of random block motion and/or pairwise block swap, attempting to minimize an objective function such as total wire length. Except when identical blocks are chosen (unlikely with a large chip, and avoidable), individual random moves interact with each other only through their effect on the objective function. Thus very large degrees of parallelism should be feasible, again in the range of thousands.

Wiring

Automatic wiring forms the desired connections between blocks once they have been placed. The 64-processor Wire Routing Machine has been employed effectively to execute the universally used Lee-Moore maze-routing algorithm [245] and higher levels of parallelism have been proposed. The Lee-Moore algorithm is a wave-propagation technique whose computation load grows roughly as the square of the length of each wire. Wires in nonoverlapping sections of the chip do not interact. Hence it should be possible, with suitable wire choice, to route many wires simultaneously, and this ability should increase with chip size, assuming most wires are local (desirable for performance).

Logic Synthesis

Logic synthesis is the generation of detailed logic from higher level specifications. Recent successful attempts in this area [127] use local pattern-match and substitution techniques on the network of blocks being synthesized, rather than using classical global minimization. The pattern search potentially has a very great degree of parallelism, since tens of thousands of gates may have to be examined. Since the substitutions performed are generally independent of each other, parallelism is available in this process also, but to a lesser extent (e.g., hundreds). So this technique can potentially benefit from highly parallel processing also.

2.1.7   Other Areas

CAD is only one engineering application amenable to parallel processing. Other prominent examples are signal processing, image processing, fluid flow (airplane design) and reservoir modeling and seismic exploration (oil wells). These applications are amply described in the literature.

2.2   Database Systems

A database [128] is a collection of data representing facts that is organized to facilitate access and maintenance. Typically, the database is much too large[28] to fit into the computer's memory, and so interactions with the database involve the magnetic disk devices on which the database is stored. Opportunities for fairly high degrees of parallelism exist at several stages of the operation of a database management system, but the overall speedup attainable was a matter of controversy until recently.

A database transaction consists of query processing (deciphering what data are wanted) and I/O (getting the data). The time required for these two operations is often comparable in present systems. Parallelism looks promising for reducing the query-processing time, but less so for reducing the I/O time. Thus, the amount of *useful* (vs. available) parallelism in the former depends on technological trends in the latter. Two factors have helped: more experience in partitioning databases and the availability of cheap memory for disk buffers that reduce the apparent I/O time.

The next section discusses opportunities for parallelism in query processing. The I/O situation is discussed in the section after that. (The substantial contribution of Dr. Anil Nigam to these sections is gratefully acknowledged.)

2.2.1   Sources of Parallelism in Query Processing

Parallelism Within and Among Transactions

A multiuser shared database system affords two main sources of parallelism: *among* the user transactions (as in on-line transaction processing) and *within* a single complex transaction (also called *decision support*). Put another way, one can try to increase the number of simultaneous transactions as well as to decrease the time that they take.[29] Which one is more important depends on the application. Figure 2.14 on page 67 gives a brief summary of database applications.

The simple transactions of a commercial database are often independent of each other (for example, two bank customers asking about the balances in

---

[28]   For instance a large airline reservations system uses a database of over 100 gigabytes (100 billion bytes!).

[29]   The shouting match of the well-known beer commercial would change from "less filling/tastes great!" to "high transaction rate/complex queries!"

CLASS	CHARACTERISTICS
Commercial (Banking, airlines, sales, manufacturing)	• Short simple transactions • High traffic (100–1000 trans/sec) • Moderate update rates
Engineering/CAD (VLSI design, aircraft assembly)	• Long transactions • Many versions of design • Hierarchically structured
Statistical (Census, weather)	• Relatively stable • Statistical queries
Text (Library databases)	• Complex pattern matches on text-oriented data
A. I. & Expert Systems	• Complex queries • Some deductive capability

Figure 2.14   Characteristics of various database applications [342].

two different accounts), and in principle the degree of parallelism available among such transactions is in the thousands for a large system. The Tandem computer (page 503) is one parallel machine being used this way. An implementation of the Oracle relational database system atop a 64-node nCUBE parallel computer was the first system to demonstrate more than 1000 transactions per second on the industry-standard TPC-B benchmark [143].

Within a single complex transaction, the degree of parallelism is probably in the range of tens to hundreds. An example of a complex transaction is a query for "All the suppliers in Paris who have a certain part in stock." The majority of recent database research has been in this second area. The Teradata computer (page 504) is a commercial database machine that employs parallelism in processing large complex queries.

The Relational Database Model

The remaining discussion is more easily carried out in terms of a specific database model. From the user's viewpoint, three alternate models exist for database management systems [128]:

- *Hierarchical*, like IBM's IMS, in which the data are organized in a tree-like structure.
- *Network*, like Honeywell's IDS, in which the user (application program) is viewed as a navigator who guides a sequential thread of computation through the database [64].
- *Relational*, like IBM's SQL or U.C. Berkeley's INGRES, in which data are organized into *tables*, and data retrieval is viewed as table construction (see Figure 2.15 on page 69).

The relational model will be used herein, because its modular nature makes it a more obvious candidate for parallel processing.

Figure 2.15 on page 69 offers a quick review of the relational model by showing a small database and an example query, "Find the part names (PNAME) for parts supplied by supplier S1." Given the starting information shown there, you and I would first make a list of the part *numbers* shipped by S1 and then look up the *name* of each. The relational database system is shown doing the same thing, using its three most basic operations [128]:

- **SELECT,** which constructs a new table by selecting a *horizontal* subset, namely all tuples (rows) satisfying some condition (S#=S1 in the example).
- **JOIN,** which forms a wider table from two (or more) other tables. The example shows a Natural JOIN in which tuples having *identical* entries in the P# column are concatenated.
- **PROJECT,** which forms a vertical subset by extracting specified column(s) (PNAME) and removing duplicate rows.[30]

Parallelizing Relational Database Operations (an Example of Parallelism Within a Transaction)

Each step of the algorithm representing the example transaction above has a potential for parallel processing. Assume that the job is to be divided among p processors and consider single-relation operations first. SELECT can be performed by horizontally decomposing a relation (table) into p fragments of one or more tuples. Each processor can then independently test the qualification predicate on its fragment of the relation.

---

[30] For example, if the query had been, "What colors does supplier S1 use?", the procedure shown would have yielded "red, green, red", and an extra step would be needed to eliminate the redundant "red".

Figure 2.15   Relational database refresher. *The heavy boxes hold the database. The example shows the three basic primitive operations SELECT, JOIN, and PROJECT being used to answer the query, "What different part names have been shipped by supplier S1?" The answer: "Nuts, bolts, and screws."*

However, the PROJECT operation involves two steps—discard certain columns and remove duplicate tuples from the resulting table. Each processor can perform these steps on its fragment independently, but then a global duplicate elimination must be done. This requires cooperation among the processors.

In general, the operations are processed in a local phase (processors work independently) followed by a global phase (processors cooperate). The relative length of each phase is a design trade-off determined by the granularity of the decomposition. A large number of small fragments results in a short local phase but a longer, more complex global phase (more processors need to cooperate). The choice depends on the machine architecture to be used as well as on the application. Similar considerations apply for vertical decompositions.

Horizontal decomposition can also be used for parallel execution of a two-relation operation like JOIN. But first, some background. Conceptually, the simplest joining procedure is the *inner-outer loop join*. In terms of the example of Figure 2.15 on page 69, this join works as follows. For each tuple in the first relation (TEMP 1), all tuples in the second relation (PART) are inspected, and if the join attributes (P#) match, an output tuple is constructed. The result is a new relation (TEMP 2).

Suppose a different query were put to the database in Figure 2.15, namely, a request for a table listing what the dealers have access to in their own home cities. The procedure can be done by performing a join between the SUPPLIER and PART tables (relations) for tuples with equal entries in the CITY attribute column. With the data shown in Figure 2.15, the result would be:

```
┌─────────────────────────────────────────────────────────┐
│ TEMP 3: Parts accessible to dealers in own city         │
│                                                          │
│ S#   SNAME   STATUS   CITY     P#   PNAME   COLOR   WT   │
│ ──   ─────   ──────   ────     ──   ─────   ─────   ──   │
│ S1   Smith     20     London   P1   Nut     Red     12   │
│ S1   Smith     20     London   P4   Screw   Blue    14   │
│ S2   Jones     10     Paris    P2   Bolt    Green   17   │
│ S3   Blake     30     Paris    P2   Bolt    Green   17   │
└─────────────────────────────────────────────────────────┘
```

Suppose the data were different; suppose the cities listed in both SUPPLIER and PART were Antwerp, London, Paris, and Rome. Suppose also that two processors were available. A straightforward parallelization would be to split the smaller relation horizontally, give one half to each processor, and have each perform the inner-outer loop join with all tuples of the other relation. The problem would be solved approximately twice as fast as with a single processor. However, since the total number of steps required for an inner-outer loop join is the product of the relation sizes (in tuples), the solution could still take a long time.

The situation can be improved if the relations are already in some sequence for the join attribute—for example, if the cities were listed alphabetically in both tables. One could divide *each* table into a part with cities in the first half of the alphabet (A–L) and a part with cities in the second half (M–Z) and give both first parts to the first processor and both second parts to the second processor. The first processor need no longer compare its tuples with those of the *entire* relation, because we *know* that there are no matches in the second part. We have managed to put the tuples into two disjoint "buckets" and thus create two smaller independent subproblems. If there are equally many tuples for each CITY, the join gets done approximately four times faster, or, in general, in $1/n^2$ as much time with n processors as with one (assuming the merge at the end comes for free).

Very often, however, the tuples are *clustered* rather than uniformly distributed on the join attribute. For example, suppose the PART table contained 2 entries each for Antwerp and London, but 50 each for Paris and Rome (suppose the parts were, say, red wine). The partitioning above would be disastrous! The processor assigned the second half of the alphabet would do most of the work, the first would do almost none, and the speedup would be a few percent at most. Clearly, a better partitioning would be to put the Antwerp and Paris tuples in one bucket and the London and Rome tuples in another.

One method for attaining a more uniform distribution of processor workload is to use a hashing scheme [392][31] . A meaningful problem will have a large number of join attribute values, and the range of these values will be divided into n buckets corresponding to n processors. But instead of assigning the first $(1/n)$th of the attribute values to the first bucket and so on, as in the scheme above, the attribute values are assigned to buckets using a hashing scheme (the GRACE database machine [283] uses this approach). The advantage is not only that the processing time is reduced to that of the largest bucket, but also that the randomizing property of the hashing scheme gives a good chance that the largest bucket is almost as small as possible.

This approach can be applied to the PROJECT operation as well. Duplicate elimination can now be done in each bucket independently, with no need for inter-bucket comparisons, since the buckets are disjoint. Thus, the global phase of computation (in which the processors must communicate with each

---

31 Note the similarity to the solution of the accidental memory-access conflict problem in RP3 (page 603).

Parallel Database Machine Terminology

In the terminology of papers on the subject [249], a database machine consists of three parts:

1. A *Front-end* (communications) *Processor* that, for example, handles requests from the terminals of a banking system and passes them to
2. A *Host Machine* that runs the application program and passes database interactions to
3. A *Back-end* machine that provides database management functions and returns the results to the host. (Sometimes the back end alone is called a database machine.)

Back-end processor architectures can be grouped into two broad categories—*search engines* and *multiprocessor architectures*. Search engines are designed to process data as close to the secondary store (disks) as possible, with the intent of minimizing the data sent to the host. In the case of a SELECT operation, for example, only the tuples that satisfy the qualification predicate are sent to the host. Logic-per-track, logic-per-head, and logic-per-disk architectures have been proposed. There are several reasons why they failed to prosper for a long time [69]:

1. They were poor at complex operations like JOIN and SORT.
2. Some were based on technologies that did not live up to their promise, like charge-coupled devices and magnetic bubbles.
3. Others require expensive modifications to present disk systems.

The progress in semiconductor technology has been very beneficial in this area, however, making large amounts of memory and simple controllers available. Search engines are now able to perform the complex operations mentioned above, and disk latency can be largely masked by semiconductor buffer memories. These two developments make the speedup from multiprocessor architectures worthwhile. Two database machines that capitalize on these developments are described on pages 503 and 504.

---

other) can be eliminated. Optimum hashing schemes are still a subject of research.

So far we have been discussing the parallelism that comes from breaking a relational operation like JOIN into many smaller identical operations. Another level of parallelism comes from the way these operations are implemented. Sorting, for example, is a key building block for both join and duplicate elimination. Many parallel sorting algorithms exist (see [66] and page 203), but one must choose among these carefully, since many assume that the data (e.g., the operand relations) all fit into memory. This assumption is not usually true with current database systems and architectures.

2.2.2 The I/O Situation

In spite of the opportunities for parallelism discussed above, the prospects for a parallel database machine have had an up-and-down history [143]. A 1979 paper titled "Database Machines are Coming, Database Machines are Coming!"[249] was followed four years later by another paper *almost* titled "Database Machines are Dead, Database Machines are Dead"[69] . The reason for this fluctuating optimism has to do with I/O.

As mentioned, the time required to complete a transaction is made up of the query-processing time, discussed above, and the I/O (data fetch) time, which involves getting the data into the central memory from the hardware storing the database, usually a set of moving-head disks. Until recently, the difference between these two times was small enough that the application of a relatively low degree of parallelism to query processing merely uncovered the I/O time as the new bottleneck.[32] The speed of the disks themselves is strongly limited by electromechanical effects (see page 129), and the technological trend is toward disks with greater storage capacity rather than shorter access times.

What has improved this situation is cheap memory. The continuing dramatic improvement in the cost per bit of silicon random access memory (page 125) has made disk buffers or disk caches practical—large silicon memories used to mask the disk access time in much the same way that the cache serving the CPU masks the access time of the main memory. In both cases, the key to success is having the right data in the cache at the right time, and this is the second area in which improvements have been made—the distribution of data among the components of the disk storage system. Taken together, these two developments result in a considerably shorter apparent I/O access time, which means that there is more room for improving the query-processing time via parallelism. Hardware for doing this is discussed further in the box on page 72, and on pages 503 and 504.

---

[32] In one set of experiments [69], for example, joining a 10,000-tuple relation to a 1000-tuple relation took between 13 and 22 milliseconds (mS) of VAX 11/750 CPU time per disk access. The time to access a page on a disk averaged 30 mS.

2.3   Artificial Intelligence Systems

Parallelism ranging from the thousands to the millions beckons from many artificial intelligence (AI) applications, largely because *search* techniques play such a central role.   There is no universally accepted definition of AI, but one that is useful for present purposes is that it is an area of computer science research that is trying to advance the border between what computers can do well and what people can do well.   This moving frontier is now at the point at which commercial program products are appearing for problems characterized by a concise body of well-defined knowledge (certain areas of medical diagnosis, for example).   These *expert systems* perform useful reasoning based on a set of built-in rules obtained from a human expert and accepted as *givens*.   Present systems contain up to 10,000 rules and represent an equal degree of potential parallelism.   Other, different AI approaches still in the experimental stage represent much higher degrees of potential parallelism.

This section begins with a brief review of artificial intelligence and search techniques (Nilsson [343] provides a good background and perspective on these topics) and then discusses some practical aspects of the parallelism to be found in AI applications like the production systems being used for medical diagnosis (Kuo and Moldovan [312] present a good review of the state of the art).   This discussion is followed by a description of an AI visual perception system that uses a connectionist rather than a rules-based approach and that represents potential parallelism in the millions.

2.3.1   Artificial Intelligence

Two components of intelligence are *knowledge* and *reasoning*.   There are various ways to represent knowledge and various methods of reasoning from it to create more knowledge.   Computer programs that do this are said to exhibit *artificial intelligence*.   The main activities in this field at the present time are shown in Figure 2.16 on page 75.

2.3.2   Production Systems and Expert Systems

One category of knowledge being exploited by AI is called *expert knowledge*.   It turns out that much of the knowledge of some experts such as medical specialists or computer system configurators can be expressed as a set of perhaps

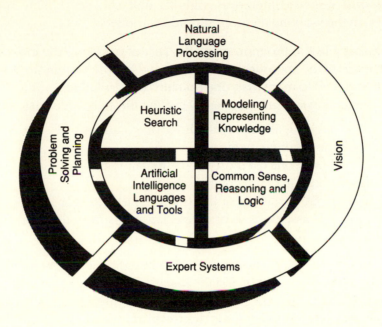

Figure 2.16   *The elements of artificial intelligence* (after Gevarter [192]).

several hundred *rules* of the form "If such-and-so is true, then it follows that ..." or "... then do the following ...".

production system is a program that has provisions for storing such rules, or *productions*, and for applying these rules to perform reasoning on the input facts the system is presented with. When the set of rules corresponds to a domain of expert knowledge, the result is called an *expert system.*[33]

Production systems have three parts:

1. A *working memory* that stores the *global database* (various facts or data about the world).
2. A *production memory* that stores the *knowledge base* (set of production rules, i.e., what the production system knows how to do). Each rule has a precondition (if ...); when the precondition is satisfied by any one of the facts in the global database, the rule itself (then ...) can be applied. Note that this often changes the global database.

----

[33] A fine point: Production system rules are forward-chaining of the type "if A then B". There are other expert systems with backward-chaining rules of the type "A if B".

3.   A *control system* ("inference engine") that chooses which applicable rule(s) in the working memory should be applied.

This modularity in the program eases the task of updating the expert knowledge (changes in the tax code, for instance) and lets the system serve as a shell that can be applied to more than one domain of knowledge.

The production system operates by cycling through three basic steps:

1.   MATCH—Filter out all the rules whose preconditions (if ...) don't match the facts in the working memory.
2.   SELECT—Choose one (or more) of the remaining rules according to some predefined criterion of the control scheme.
3.   ACT—Carry out the action of the rule's right-hand side (then ...). This action can add assertions to or delete assertions from the working memory.

Control schemes for production systems are based on a variety of techniques for searching state spaces. Since state-space searching is very widely used in AI, it is reviewed briefly in the next section and the three examples that follow. Parallelism in production systems is discussed after that. Reference [312] is a good review of the state of the art in parallel production systems.

State-Space Searching

The great sculptor Michelangelo is said to have approached his work with the idea that the finished statue was already present, imprisoned, in the block of marble, and that his task was to remove the excess marble and free it. Many problem-solving techniques in artificial intelligence are based on a similar notion that the solution is already "in there" and that the task at hand is an intelligent *search* technique for finding it. The potential benefit of parallel processing is the same as that of a search party looking for a lost child: the more searchers, the greater the probability of finding the child quickly.

The search is considered to take place in the *state space* of the problem (Nilsson's book [343] treats this very nicely). In chess, for example, a state would be one configuration of pieces on the board, and a transition to another state is governed by a set of rules, the rules of chess. The complete space of allowable states is generated by repeatedly applying a rule to an allowed state, starting with the initial board position. Thus, each state is "connected" to at least one other successor state via one of the rules or allowed moves. The *goal* of the search in this space is a path from the initial state to some state corresponding to victory, that is, checkmate of the opponent's king. The portion of the state space that was explored in searching for this path is called the *search tree* because at any one state the search may branch out to several possible successor states. Just as in real life, the search must be properly organized if it is to succeed in an acceptable time. Since an unguided exhaustive search may lead to near-endless computation called a "combinatorial explosion", the search procedure must be carefully controlled.

So far this discussion is pretty general. Let's get specific again and get back to production systems. Instead of chess-board configurations, the states are now *assertions,* and a goal might be finding a path (chain of rules) from an initial set of assertions in the working memory such as "The child has red spots, a fever, and a cough", to a diagnosis or assertion such as "The child has measles." The control mechanism should apply the rules in a way that causes motion through the state space and stops when the termination condition is met. Some simple examples help to illustrate the concepts involved.

Example 1: Heuristic Search

Nilsson [343] puts the eight-puzzle to elegant use as an example of a miniature production system. The eight-puzzle consists of eight numbered, movable tiles set in a 3×3 frame (see Figure 2.17 on page 78). The problem is to find a sequence of moves that changes a given initial configuration into a given goal configuration, using an appropriate sequence of moves. Each of the 362,880 (9!) possible configurations can be thought of as a state in a problem space. This set of configurations is the global database, or working memory. The production memory contains four rules:

1. If the empty space is not at a left edge, then move it left.
2. If the empty space is not at an upper edge, then move it up.
3. If the empty space is not at a right edge, then move it right.
4. If the empty space is not at a lower edge, then move it down.

The control strategy is a (one hopes) "clever" search process in which rules are tried until some sequence is found that solves the problem. (In most AI applications, the information available to the control strategy is not sufficient to guarantee that the most appropriate rule is selected each time; one tries to maximize the probability.)

One way to organize the search is to simply cycle through the four rules repeatedly, with two provisos:

1. A list is kept of the states visited; they are not revisited.
2. The rule applied to state n is one that least increases the evaluation function. The evaluation function is $f(n) = W(n) + d(n)$, where $W(n)$ is the

Figure 2.17   A heuristic search tree *corresponding to a solution of the eight-puzzle. The search is directed using a simple heuristic, or "rule-of-thumb", evaluation function f(n) (see text). For each state (large box) of the puzzle, all applicable rules (moves) are contemplated, f(n) for the resulting states is evaluated (small "price tag" box next to each large box), and the smallest f(n) is chosen. The numbers above each large box show the sequence of states explored.*

number of misplaced tiles (with respect to the goal state) and $d(n)$ is the number of steps made since the initial state.

The resulting search tree is shown in Figure 2.17.

This procedure is an example of a *heuristic* search, guided by the rule-of-thumb proviso 2 above, which works quite well to keep the tree narrow and focus its growth toward the goal. Eliminating the term $W(n)$ gives a much

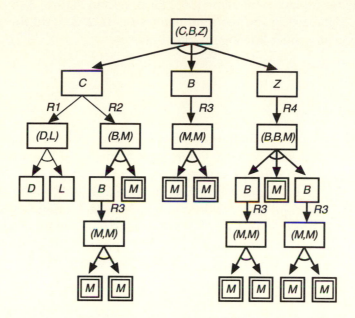

Figure 2.18   **An AND/OR graph** *for the letter-substitution game* [343] *(used with permission).*

wider tree corresponding to a *breadth-first* search of all states that are one move away from the initial state, then all states that are two moves away, and so on. A narrower tree (but wider, in this case, than the heuristic search tree) is produced by *depth-first* search, in which $d(n)$ is increased at each step up to some limit, at which point the search procedure "backtracks" to the last decision point and starts again. (This procedure is illustrated in the Prolog example that follows.) Nilsson [343] gives a good discussion of trade-offs among search-control strategies.

Note that this example starts at the initial state and uses *forward* or *data-driven* search. Since there is a single initial state and a single goal state, one could also start at the goal state and use *backward* or *goal-driven* search. The production system language OPS-5 does the former, while Prolog, another language used for production systems, does the latter. The strategy yielding the highest efficiency is problem dependent.

Example 2: AND/OR Graphs

Two other notions important to parallelism are those of a *decomposable* production system and its associated AND/OR graph. An example is provided by a simple letter-replacement game [343] illustrated in Figure 2.18 on page 79. The initial database in the working memory is (*C*,*B*,*Z*), and the production memory contains the following rewrite rules:

R1: C → D,L
R2: C → B,M
R3: B → M,M
R4: Z → B,B,M,

and the termination condition (goal) is a database containing only $\dot{M}$s. The procedure used here is shown in Figure 2.18 on page 79. The initial database is decomposed into separate components that can be processed independently, and the global termination condition is expressed as the conjunction (ANDing) of the same termination condition for each component database. The AND nodes in Figure 2.18, indicated by a circular mark linking their incoming arcs, are so called because in order to process those nodes to termination, *all* of their successor nodes must be processed to termination. For the OR nodes, processing one *or* the other of the successor nodes to termination is sufficient.

This example sets the stage for the third example, which illustrates potential AND-parallelism and OR-parallelism in Prolog.

Example 3: Resolution and Unification in Prolog

Although not yet a major player in the writing of production systems [312], Prolog (page 279) is an AI language that seems well matched to production systems, and had a prominent role in the launching of the Fifth Generation Computer project [338], [364]. Prolog is based on the branch of mathematics called *logic programming,* which means that its mind-set is that of deriving answers by "proving things", in contrast to a language like Fortran, whose mind-set is to build a little "factory" that "constructs" the desired answer. A brief review of Prolog terms to be used herein is provided starting on page 280, where the reader will also find more discussion of the Prolog language.

Consider a small production system whose working memory contains the following database [324] listing certain people's fathers (f) and mothers (m),

f(curt,elaine).   m(elaine,john).
f(dan,pat).
f(pat,john).   m(marian,elaine).
f(sam,larry).
f(larry,dan).   m(peg,dan).
f(larry,doug).   m(peg,doug).

Figure 2.19   Latent AND and OR parallelism in a Prolog program.

and whose production memory contains two rules defining grandfather (gf):

1. $gf(X,Z) \leftarrow f(X,Y), f(Y,Z).$
2. $gf(X,Z) \leftarrow f(X,Y), m(Y,Z).$

(The first of these rules, for example, says that X is the grandfather of Z if X is the father of Y and Y is the father of Z.)

The processing of the query ← `gf(sam,G).`   , meaning "Sam is the grandfather of whom?", is shown in Figure 2.19.

Unlike the search procedure used in the two previous examples, Prolog proceeds backward from the goal and uses a depth-first, left-to-right search to try to find answers that satisfy the query. In our section on the Prolog language itself, which begins on page 279, we describe the control scheme in a little more detail. It is called a *resolution inference system,* and attempts to solve a query by proving that its *denial* ("Sam has no grandchildren") is logically inconsistent with the set of clauses comprising the program, that is, with the contents of the production and working memories [207]. The sequence of states visited is shown in Figure 2.19, and the result is an AND/OR tree that resembles Figure 2.18 on page 79. An important difference is that the states in the nodes of the present tree contain *variables*, and Prolog tries to assign (bind) values to the variables in both branches below the node that will satisfy the query. It does this binding using a pattern-matching algorithm called *unification* (explained on page 281). The procedure in Figure 2.19 is as follows:

1. Search the rules to find a clause whose head matches the body of the query clause (two such rules are found).
2. The body of the first rule is decomposed into its component clauses, and each of these generates a search for clauses with matching heads in the working memory.
3.–4. The search for a match for f(sam,Y) finds one match, namely f(sam,larry).
5.–6. Traversing back toward the root (goal state) and collecting unmatched graphs leads to the search for a match for f(Y,G) with Y=larry.
7.–8. Two results are produced, namely f(larry,dan) and f(larry,doug). Traversing back to the root encounters no unsatisfied unknowns, so these resultant bindings are solutions.
2. (again) The solutions to 4 and 7 are successfully unified (since Y is assigned to larry in both cases) giving one solution to 2 with G=dan. Another solution to 2, this one with G=doug, is found by a unification of nodes 4 and 8.
1. (again) The two solutions to 2 are the two solutions to the original query.
9.–13. A similar procedure on the right side produces no matches.

The effect is to produce an answer that Dan and Doug are grandchildren of Sam.

2.3.3 Sources of Parallelism in Production Systems

The foregoing glimpses into the operation of production systems suggest several opportunities for parallel processing. Perhaps the most obvious is to assign each rule to its own processing element, which can then search the working memory for pertinent facts in parallel with all the other processing elements, rather than use the sequential methods that were used in the preceding examples. At least one parallel architecture does precisely this (see DADO on page 505). Since production systems can have thousands of rules, this use of parallelism certainly provides employment for many processing elements. How much *speedup* is obtained is a more difficult question. The answer depends (at least partly) on how many of the rules are actually used in a typical transaction.

Experiments on some production systems written in OPS-5 show that only two or three dozen rules are involved in a typical transaction, suggesting that the maximum speedup will be the time to process three dozen rules on a large serial computer divided by the time to process one rule on one of the parallel machine's (presumably) slower processing elements. In other words, the expected speedup is less than three dozen, and in 1992 this was still the case [312]. However, these systems were optimized to run on serial machines, and much effort and cleverness went into making the system as "deterministic" as possible (many choices were pre-eliminated to minimize the searching time). It has been claimed that a production system that was written with parallel processing in mind would yield a higher degree of useful parallelism and would also be easier and faster to write (hence cheaper) than these highly optimized examples. Moreover, there are some serial production systems in which a typical transaction does involve thousands of rules. So the useful parallelism and speedup from this "rule-per-processing-element" approach is yet to be fully established.

Other sources of parallelism in production systems are contained in the last two examples, involving decomposable problems and the matching of expressions containing variables. These sources are:

1. AND-parallelism
2. OR-parallelism
3. Parallel pattern matching

AND-parallelism comes from trying to solve many parts of one problem at once, that is, pursuing solutions to a number of subgoals at the same time. (The main goal is solved if the first subgoal is solved AND the second AND the third, etc.) *OR-parallelism,* on the other hand, involves trying to achieve one goal several ways at once. (The main goal is solved if the first subgoal is solved OR the second OR the third, etc.) There is less optimism today for *parallel pattern matching,* which would correspond to parallel versions of the unification algorithm used by Prolog or of the Rete-match algorithm [177] used by OPS-5 while processing an AND-subtree. Examples of these situations were shown in Figure 2.18 and Figure 2.19.

The application determines which type of parallelism is most profitable. If a program is largely deterministic (has few matching clauses for any subgoal), it may exhibit large AND-parallelism but little OR-parallelism. Some expert systems are like this. OR-parallelism can produce multiple answers for one query, and may therefore be well matched to database systems (discussed earlier in this chapter). Combinations of AND- and OR-parallelism are also possible.

When looking for only one solution, AND-parallelism may provide more speedup than OR-parallelism, since the resources are concentrated on a single potential solution. If it is the right one, we win. However, because the sub-goals are working on the same problem, they share a common set of data and variables, and execution models for AND-parallelism must ensure that these variables have no "binding conflict". This situation leads to interesting trade-offs regarding how much of the available parallelism one actually tries to ex-tract, as discussed further on page 282 and in reference [132].

By contrast, OR-parallelism involves working on *different* problems, each a potential solution to the original query. Because the problems are different, minimal cooperation or communication between the different activities is re-quired, with obvious benefits for parallel processing in cases in which *all* and not just one of the solutions are needed. The greatest challenge is manage-ment of a large, distributed data space. The OR-parallel activities may not *need* communication, but preventing *unwanted* communication (overwriting, etc.) can demand considerable copying of data, which in a practical implementa-tion can be a significant overhead.

Although parallelism at least in the hundreds was thought to be available from the various AND- and OR-approaches being proposed, the work in ob-taining practical implementations has turned out to be decidedly nontrivial (see page 279 ff.), and the actual numbers will depend strongly on the appli-cation (the number of rules per transaction as well as other factors) and are yet to be determined.

2.3.4 Perception and Problem-Solving Systems

Production systems are good for drawing inferences from knowledge that can be expressed as a set of rules, but many activities require a more general problem-solving approach. Examples are commonsense reasoning, visual perception and language understanding (recognizing the contents of visual scenes and the meaning of spoken phrases), motor control (control of motions such as those of robots), and the processes of knowledge representation and learning. The illustrative examples used in this section concern an early par-allel approach to commonsense reasoning about knowledge represented in the form of a semantic network, followed by an application from the field of visual recognition and an approach called *computing with connections*.

Commonsense Reasoning with Semantic Networks—NETL

One area of opportunity for fine-grained parallelism is the retrieval of commonsense knowledge from a semantic network, a data structure frequently used in artificial intelligence to model the human brain's ability to manipulate relatively unstructured data and quickly extract (i.e., infer) facts that were not explicitly put into the database. Fahlman [163] uses the following example:

> Suppose ... that I am describing to you a certain animal named Clyde, and I tell you that Clyde is an elephant. You can store this single fact away with little apparent mental effort, but suddenly you know a great deal about Clyde. You can tell me, with a considerable degree of confidence, what color Clyde is, whether he needs oxygen to breathe, how many eyes he has, what the eyes are for, and what it might mean if they are closed .... It seems obvious that none of this information is stored initially in your description of Clyde, but that you find it by a process of search and deduction.

Furthermore, a serial search process is too slow to be practical, either in the brain or in a computer.

A semantic network is a labeled graph in which each vertex (node) represents a concept and each edge (link, line) represents a relationship between concepts. For example, the fact that Clyde is an elephant is represented by an IS-A link between the specific CLYDE node and the more general ELEPHANT node (see Figure 2.20 on page 86). As a very simple example, consider answering the question, "What color is Clyde?" In terms of the semantic network, the task is to intersect the set of things that Clyde is (the set of nodes to which Clyde is directly or indirectly connected by IS-A links) and the set of things that have a color (the set of nodes connected to a color by a COLOR-OF link). Both of these sets can be quite large. In Fahlman's NETL approach, the intersection is determined by assigning each node and each link to a small processor that can communicate with the other processors via a network (see the right side of Figure 2.20 on page 86). The method proceeds by passing around *markers,* which are very simple (1-bit) messages that do not even need to be stored separately and hence do not have the potential for network conflict that exists in the more general message-passing model of the Connection Machine (page 446). (Markers are always combined if they meet, rather than retaining their individuality like true messages.) Each node processor has a distinct serial number, a few bits of information about the type of the node (whether it represents an individual or a class), and storage for about a dozen marker bits. A link processor has a few type bits and some wires that can be

Figure 2.20   **Example to illustrate parallel search of a semantic network.**   *On the left, a small portion of a semantic net representing knowledge about Clyde the elephant. On the right, a close-up of the CLYDE and ELEPHANT nodes connected, respectively, to the input and output of a node representing an IS-A link (modified figures from Fahlman [163]). The bus provides party-line connections, the IS-A link, private ones. CLYDE's marker bit 1 is on, but the IS-A link has not yet propagated this M1 marker to ELEPHANT. The text describes the parallel search process.*

connected to node processors via the network. All processors communicate with a central processor via a party-line bus.

Answering the query, "What color is Clyde?" proceeds as follows. The system first marks Clyde with an M1 marker (turns its marker bit 1 on) and then broadcasts a command, "Every IS-A link whose subject[34] node (such as Clyde) is marked with an M1, please propagate this mark to your object node (such as elephant); every newly changed node, please acknowledge the change with a signal on the shared bus." This process is repeated until all nodes superior to Clyde (that is, nodes from which Clyde might inherit properties) are marked with M1 and the acknowledgement signals cease. (The assertion is that IS-A trees tend to be short [less than 20 links] and bushy, so this process does not take too long.) The next broadcast instruction tells each COLOR-OF link whose incoming end is connected to a node marked with M1 to mark the

---

[34] *Subject* and *object* here connote parts of a sentence.

node at its output with M2. In the simple case of one color per object, there will be only one such node. In this case, the link between ELEPHANT and GRAY responds. The node marked with M2 is then told to report its identity via the bus. Thus, a single sweep up the hierarchy plus two broadcast commands answer the query and do so no matter where above Clyde the COLOR-OF link is attached. More details and examples may be found in the literature [163].

Visual Recognition Systems

Nilsson [343] introduces AI approaches to perception as follows:

> Attempts have been made to fit computer systems with television inputs to enable them to "see" their surroundings or to fit them with microphones to enable them to "hear" speaking voices. From these experiments, it has been learned that useful processing of complex input data requires "understanding" and that understanding requires a large base of knowledge about the things being perceived.
>
> The process of perception studied in artificial intelligence usually involves a set of operations. A visual scene, say, is encoded by sensors and represented as a matrix of intensity values. These are processed by detectors that search for primitive picture components such as line segments, simple curves, corners, etc. These, in turn, are processed to infer information about the three-dimensional character of the scene in terms of its surface and shapes. The ultimate goal is to represent the scene by some appropriate model. This model might consist of a high-level description such as "A hill with a tree on top with cattle grazing". The point of the whole perception process is to produce a condensed representation to substitute for the unmanageably immense, raw input data.

The basic strategy is that of making hypotheses about various levels of description and then putting these hypotheses to some kind of test.

Computing with Connections

Connectionism is a highly parallel computational model [4], [165] that seems to offer efficient support for vision and some of the other intelligent activities listed above. Connectionism suggests that instead of representing pieces of information as passive patterns that are operated on by a program, they be implemented as simple, active computing elements (often called *units*) that interact in parallel by exchanging simple messages.[35] The elements maintain an internal potential or activation level that is updated on the basis of their input messages. They also generate messages that are transmitted to other units via a pattern of direct links, or *connections,* provided by a switching network. The *pattern of connections* represents the long-term knowledge of the system. The update computation is limited to simple operations like multiplication and thresholding, and messages are usually integers that reflect the potential.

This model was born out of the difficulties in programming von Neumann computers and the recognition that the brain appears to use quite a different computational model. Intelligent activities require the integration and resolution of large numbers of interacting constraints and pieces of knowledge. For example, visual recognition consists of mapping the many bits of information in the image into an internal model of the object, subject to many constraints imposed by knowledge of the world. The difficulty lies in quickly reducing the possibilities to the one that "best" fits the input and constraints, sometimes despite imperfect information.

The developers of the connectionist model felt that the strict sequentiality of the von Neumann model is a bottleneck in evaluating the multiplicity of interactions between input and constraints and that its precision is at odds with the noise of the real world. They were also aware that the brain appears to function in a highly parallel, distributed manner. The computing elements in the brain, the neurons, are relatively simple and slow, and the interconnection patterns are quite complex. The influence of these factors is seen in the parallel approach to visual recognition described in the next section.

2.3.5   *Computing with Connections in Visual Recognition*

The application of AI techniques to the recognition of line drawings of three-dimensional flat-faced shapes called *origami objects* has been described by Sabbah [380].

---

[35] There is a similarity here to *semantic nets,* a knowledge representation consisting not of a list of rules but rather of a large network of linked nodes in which the nodes stand for objects and the links express relationships between objects (see Figure 2.20 on page 86). (The Connection Machine architecture [page 446] is strongly influenced by this idea.) So it may be helpful to think of the connectionist model as a semantic net with computation built in. However, it is important to note that semantic nets are a restricted subset of connectionist nets. More things can be proved about semantic nets, but connectionist nets have a broader set of abilities, including distributed as well as localized knowledge representations.

Simple 3–D Objects		8
Complex Joints	2–D Shapes,Faces	6
L–joints and T–joints		4
Rays	Lines	2–3
Edge Segments		3

Figure 2.21   ***The origami world hierarchy*** *(5 lowest levels) and the number of parameters (dimensionality of the parameter space) associated with each. (From Sabbah [380].)*

Any visual recognition system must have internal models of the world to be recognized and must control the matching process between the scene being analyzed and these internal models. To be genuinely useful, the system must also handle imperfect inputs; that is, it should degrade gracefully in the presence of noisy, incomplete, or partially occluded (hidden) images. It was the desire to give the system this latter set of abilities that motivated the introduction of an AI approach. The problem came down to three key problems:

1. How to represent these objects in a connectionist system.
2. How to control the recognition process to take full advantage of the potentially massive parallelism available in the connectionist approach.
3. How to make this control process robust enough to deal with imperfections in predictable and "pleasing" ways.

(Knowledge representation and reasoning method, again.)

Representing the Origami Objects

The representation of origami objects is actually a hierarchy of representations (see Figure 2.21). This allows the recognition to proceed in stages from raw data up through levels of increasingly useful subobjects [333].

Since three-dimensional origami objects are composed of planar surfaces, their two-dimensional projections are composed of only straight-line segments. The lowest level of representation is in terms of a set of *unit edge segments,* each characterized by three parameters: two for location and one for slope (corresponding, for example, to the output of an optical detector that can report an edge's position and orientation, but not its length).

Edge segments can make *edges* or *lines* (synonymous here); these are infinite in length and have only two parameters: slope and intercept. Edge segments can also make *rays,* which are edges with a known starting point and which therefore have three parameters.

Two rays can define an *L-joint,* which has four parameters (two for position and two for angles); three or more L-joints can define a two-dimensional *face* with six parameters (position, angles, and size); two or more faces can make a *simple three-dimensional object*; and these in turn can be assembled into a *complex three-dimensional object* like a chair, or the child's block duck shown here.

The number of different features on each level is determined by how many parameters the feature has and by the size of the increments chosen for distances and angles. For example, a 10×10 grid and 10-degree angle increments result in

- 1800 unique edge segments (1 of 18 angles per grid point), maximum 100 per scene,
- 3600 different rays on the next level,
- 61,200 different L-joints,
- several hundred thousand faces,

and so on. Each edge segment could be part of 1 of 10 rays (or 1 line), each ray could correspond to 1 of 34 different L-joints, each L-joint could correspond to 1 of up to 100 different-sized faces, and so on. This representation is mapped to a connectionist network as described in the next section.

Mapping to the Connectionist Network

Features in the hierarchy above become nodes, or *units,* in the connectionist model described earlier, and the *correspondences* between features become links, or *connections,* in the network. Three types of connections are allowed among nodes representing features on the same level or directly adjacent levels of the hierarchy:

- *Bottom-up,* corresponding, for example, to the fact that one L-joint can correspond to many faces. For perfect input, this is the only type of connection needed.
- *Top-down,* corresponding, for example, to the fact that one face corresponds to four L-joints. These connections provide feedback for cases with imperfect input.

- *Lateral, inhibitory* connections among mutually antagonistic features on the same level, corresponding to the fact that two features can't occupy any of the same space at the same time. Again, these connections are important for imperfect input.

The essential action takes place over these connections. Even for the small 10×10 grid above, the connection set (the total number of connections) is potentially quite large.[36] The success of the recognition scheme depends on instantiating only a small fraction of these on each level. The next section describes the implementation of one such recognition scheme.

How the Recognition Scheme Works

By a process called *iterative refinement,* the confidence levels of the lowermost features (the edges) are transmitted upward along the connections, in effect "voting" for a feature on the next highest level, and the process is repeated until a winner emerges at the highest level.[37] A key feature of this scheme is the way that the evidence is accumulated, interpreted, and acted on. In order to prevent the system from "leaping to conclusions" prematurely and perhaps incorrectly, each node has associated with it a *threshold* that must be crossed before the node decides in favor of its own existence, and two mechanisms for *losing* as well as gaining confidence that are important in the case of imperfect inputs:

1. Inhibitory or negative votes from mutually exclusive competing features on the same level.
2. A "decay" mechanism for slowly *losing* confidence in the absence of reinforcement. (This mechanism also functions as a noise threshold.)[38]

These mechanisms are embodied in a simple *evidence accumulation formula* [380] for each active feature's activation level (confidence level). When a feature reaches the threshold value, the unit temporarily goes into a saturated state and, for a fixed period of time, the unit's activation level remains at the maximum value regardless of additional input. Local decisions without support from other levels are reversed quickly through decay, inhibition, and/or lack of feedback. This dynamic voting process in the network gradually connects units on the various levels to a stable coalition corresponding to a

---

36 For example, 1100 potential bottom-up connections from the lowest level alone.
37 The actual mechanism for this process involves transforming each feature from "real" space to "parameter space" using a so-called Hough transform. Features in real space become *points* in parameter space, thus making the votes easier to collect.
38 A small negative vote is cast during each pass through the hierarchy.

globally consistent interpretation of the inputs. The largest of these stable co-
alitions eventually suppresses all others and becomes the winning interpretation.

Sources of Parallelism

Several opportunities for parallel processing are present in this approach:

1. Each feature space or level of the hierarchy can be allocated to a (pre-
    sumably large) processor, which then sends messages (votes) to two other
    such processors. The degree of parallelism is in the range of tens.
2. Alternately, each unit or feature can be assigned to its own (presumably
    small) processor. The potential degree of parallelism here can be
    millions.

This has been simulated on a serial processor [380]. The program was split
into several concurrent subprograms, each representing an individual feature
space. Each subprogram included algorithms to compute connection sets and
a scheduler for allocating computing resources to units active in a given scene
presentation. The scheduler received and distributed all messages sent to
units in that feature space. A unit and its connections were generated only after receipt of a message for that unit. The process starts with a maximum-
confidence description at the input level and proceeds in an iterative fashion.
Each unit recomputes its activation level and communicates to its connections
according to the new state. The next iteration starts after all spaces finish.

An illustrative result is shown in Figure 2.22 on page 93. In the figure, the
input is a set of L-joints corresponding to a box with an open top, and the system starts to conclude that it "sees" a closed box and then corrects itself.

Degree of Parallelism, Combinational Implosion, Trade-offs

Both the magnitude of the potential degree of parallelism and the need to
avoid the combinational explosion in the number of actually instantiated units
and connections are brought home when it is pointed out that the numbers
generated for the small 10×10 example above are multiplied by 10,000 for a
real example with 1000×1000B resolution. It is the communication of partial
results built into the above system that keeps the number of units and connections tractable. This method for avoiding combinational explosion is
sometimes called *combinational implosion*.

There are some interesting trade-offs in computing with connections.
Reducing the number of levels in the hierarchy reduces the number of units
but increases the size of the connection set. For the simple 10×10 example

Figure 2.22 Recognition of self-occluded box (top to bottom). The top figure shows a set of L-joints that are presented to the system as input. The clue that the box is open is that the two uppermost L-joints do not have a third companion. In the second figure (after 22 iterations), the system has strong confidence in the existence of the two front faces (represented by the two large dark crosses that correspond to the axes of each face), and is in the process of deciding that the top face exists too (the lighter large cross). Dashed crosses show faces with a lower confidence level. In the third picture (after 30 iterations), the system is sure the top face exists. However, the inconsistencies of this interpretation catch up with it after five more iterations, and the fourth picture shows the correct interpretation: two more dark crosses for the back faces, and a fading cross for the top face.

discussed above, for example, each edge segment is connected to 10 rays, 2 rays are connected to each L-joint, and 4 L-joints are connected to each face. If this four-level hierarchy were reduced to one with only edges and faces, then each edge would be connected to over 100,000 faces, and the existence of a few edge segments would cause activation of a huge number of units on the face level, most with little evidence for existence.

2.4   Summary

Recall our definition of a parallel processor:

> A collection of processing elements that can communicate and cooperate to solve a large problem fast.

As we mentioned previously, this definition raises a number of questions (see page 6) and it is interesting to see what light the sample applications described in this chapter have shed on these questions.

The seismic application runs on just a few processors and communicates fairly infrequently, which is why it can tolerate the slow communication offered by a network of workstations.   In short, the granularity of parallelism is coarse.   The experiments run yielded high efficiency but low absolute speedup, being limited by the small number of processors employed.

The weather code shows parallelism at the inner-loop level, that is, medium granularity.   If the maximum loop indexes, starting with the inner loop, are L, M, and N, then the maximum parallelism case corresponds to LMN processing elements, each doing one iteration of the inner loop.   This weather code can utilize hundreds of processors profitably but (at that level of parallelism) cannot tolerate the millisecond latencies typifying the seismic experiments.   If only a few dozen processors were available, the innermost loop in each loop nest could be run serially (in other words, only the two outer loops would be run in parallel), resulting in a lower degree of parallelism (maximum MN) and coarser granularity (each processor does L iterations of the inner loop).   If the parallelism degree were lowered yet further, so that each processor was responsible for hundreds of grid points, the granularity would be coarser still and perhaps millisecond delays would be acceptable.

For database applications, performance is at least as much dependent on I/O as it is on CPU computation.   In addition to multiple processors, we need multiple I/O devices (disks) that each contain portions of the data needed and that can be accessed concurrently.   See the discussion on disk arrays on page 131 for one possibility.   Sometimes parallel database applications are run on dedicated database machines.   If, instead, the application is run under a general-purpose operating system, it is important that the OS itself does not become a serial bottleneck.   See our classification of parallel operating systems that begins on page 360.

AI applications have been the source of some controversy.   In the mid-1980s questions were raised about the utility of large-scale parallelism for executing production systems.   See our discussion of the Dado parallel computer on page 505 for more information.   Several projects, most notably the

Japanese "Fifth Generation", attempted to show that the logic programming language Prolog (suitably extended) would be effective in describing AI applications for parallel execution. However, as discussed in our languages chapter (see pages 282 and 285), the initial enthusiasm has become tempered as low levels of parallelism were obtained, and most current efforts are directed at "flat" logic programming languages that are rather different from Prolog.

Finally, connectionist approaches suggest a machine architecture having truly massive numbers of very weak processors, that is, extremely fine-grained. This application class was one early motivation for the CM-1 design from Thinking Machines. Later models (CM-2, etc.) have shifted the emphasis more to numerical computations and a less fine granularity (see the discussion of slicewise software on page 458).

2.5 Exercises

1. Define the following terms.

LINPACK	Hierarchial database
BLAS	Network database
QCD	Relational database
Navier-Stokes equations	Database management system (DBMS)
Barrier synchronization	Production system
Domain decomposition	Expert system
Discretizing variables and equations	State space searching
Forall ... in parallel ... End Sync	Combinational implosion

2. Match each of the terms on the left with its attribute on the right:

AND-parallelism	Form a horizontal subtable
Back-end machine	Form a vertical subtable
Front-end processor	Form a wider table
Host machine	Handles terminal requests
Join	Parallel computer for logic simulation
OR-parallelism	Runs DBMS
Private declaration	Runs application
Project	Solving goal by alternative means in parallel
Select	Solving subgoals in parallel
Shared declaration	Variables shared among tasks
YSE	Variables unique to each task

3. Assume each primary and secondary variable in the weather code is an 8-byte quantity. How much memory is needed to store the grid if N=46, M=72, L=9? (these values are referred to as a fine grid in the original NASA GISS documentation). How much memory is needed for NASA's very fine grid, N=72, M=120, L=9? (In 1980, this was considered too large to store in memory at once; a so-called *banded* method was used to shuttle parts of the data back and forth, to and from disk.) More recent weather grids have been based on a 1-degree model (i.e., longitude and latitude lines every one degree) or even a 1/4-degree model. How much memory would be needed for each of these modern problems? Consider a private memory parallel machine in which each node contains 4MB of memory. What would be the smallest parallel machine capable of running each of these modern weather codes?

4. As mentioned at the end of the weather code section, the communication to computation ratio is proportional to the surface to volume ratio of a region. Assume L=9 and M=2N. How big must N be for the latter ratio to be under 1%?

5. An important technique used in VLSI circuit analysis is *waveform relaxation*. Read the key paper [318] and describe the technique and its amenability to parallel processing.

6. Consider a relational database system and describe the parallelism within a single select operation? A join operation? A project operation?

7. Consider the example database in Figure 2.15 on page 69 and form the natural join of the SUPPLIER and SHIPPED relations.

8. Why do AI applications often yield enormous degrees of parallelism?

9. Describe the operation of a production system?

10. Interchange the 2 and the 8 in the Start Node of Figure 2.17 on page 78 and generate the resulting search tree. Where could parallelism be profitably employed?

11. What limits the speedup on the seismic code? The weather code?

12. Is one likely to need more communication with OR- or AND-parallelism? Why?

13. What kinds of connections are commonly used in a connectionist visual recognition system and what is their purpose?

i860™ XP Processor

Figure 3.1 **The Intel i860 XP microprocessor chip** used in the Intel Paragon (page 491). The chip contains 2.5 million transistors and measures 1.04 cm by 1.57 cm. (Photo courtesy of Intel Corporation.)

3

Technological Constraints and Opportunities

The technology used in traditional (serial) computer systems can be grouped into three broad categories:

- *Logic circuits* used in the CPU and its associated computing functions
- *Memory circuits* used by the CPU during calculations
- *Storage devices* for long-term storage of programs and data

For parallel processors, additional major *functions* will be needed, such as inter-processor communication, and some basic relations may change, such as the amount of memory needed to go with a given net processing power. However, the technological building blocks will be the same as those above, at least for the foreseeable future.[39]

This chapter discusses these three areas of hardware technology as they limit the speedup of uniprocessors and also as the technology constrains and encourages the development of parallel processors. VLSI is a prime factor, providing powerful and cheap microprocessors for assembly into an ensemble

---

[39] *Fiber optics* communication is an interesting new technology, and we discuss it briefly, but as we point out, its potential role for parallel computing lies more with physically distributed systems than with compact, massively parallel systems.

and enabling more unconventional and customized approaches to building a parallel machine. But it is not a panacea; wiring, packaging, and power dissipation still exert strong influences on a feasible design.

3.1   Processor and Network Technology

The electronic computer has undergone many changes, but one thing that remains true is that it is a collection of electrical relays (remote-controlled on-off switches). What *has* changed drastically is the technology of these relays. In the Mark-I, a computer built at Harvard in the 1940s, they were electromechanical steel devices wound with spools of copper wire similar to those still used in doorbells. Today, they are silicon transistors too small to see with the naked eye. But they do the same thing—allow one electrical current to turn another current on or off. What has changed is the speed and cost of this operation. Today's transistor is 10 million times faster than the relay of the 1940s and costs a thousand times less.

Nevertheless, there is a big difference between the speed at which events happen at the transistor level and at the user level. For example, the transistors in the Hitachi M200H can switch on and off in a nanosecond (10^{-9} seconds). However, executing an instruction useful to the user takes over 100 nanoseconds on the average. A more recent product, the NEC SX-3, has a 2.9 nanosecond cycle time and gates that switch in 0.07 nanoseconds.[40] Several factors contribute to such large ratios: the *circuit speed* becomes multiplied by the *levels of logic* (about 10), *packaging delays* can double this result, and the *cycles per instruction* can contribute a multiplier of 3 to 5, depending on the architecture and machine design (these are very rough estimates). In other words, the computation speed in millions of instructions per second (MIPS) can be written as follows:

$$
\text{MIPS} = \cfrac{1}{\left\{\begin{bmatrix} \text{circuit} \\ \text{switch} \\ \text{time} \end{bmatrix} \times \begin{bmatrix} \text{levels} \\ \text{of} \\ \text{logic} \end{bmatrix} + \begin{matrix} \text{package} \\ \text{delays} \end{matrix}\right\} \times \begin{matrix} \text{clock cycles} \\ \text{per} \\ \text{instruction} \end{matrix}}
$$

---

[40]   The M200H cycle time is about 20 nSec. The architecture and cycles per instruction are different from those of the SX-3.

Transistor Terminology

Two families of logic circuits using bipolar transistors are TTL (transistor-transistor logic) and ECL (emitter-coupled logic). The current in an ECL cell is always on and is switched back and forth between two output ports; hence, the circuit is also called a *current switch*. A TTL cell has one output, and the current is turned on and off. As might be expected, the ECL cell is faster and consumes more power, typically by a factor of 2.

Since gate electrodes in field-effect transistors were once metal, and since the insulator still is an oxide of silicon, the name MOS device, or MOSFET, is used for the transistor in Figure 3.2 on page 103. Because n-type silicon is created under the gate region of that transistor, it is also called an n-channel, or NMOS, device. Linking three such transistors can make a 2-input NAND logic gate. The book by Mead and Conway [335] describes how VLSI (very large scale integration) technology accomplishes this linking all on the same piece of silicon. High circuit density is the MOSFET's strongest feature.

A CMOS, or *complementary* MOS circuit, like the one in Figure 3.4 on page 104 uses both n-channel and p-channel transistors and achieves lower power dissipation because virtually no current flows in the steady state. This low flow of current translates into longer battery life (watches, calculators), easier cooling, or higher speed. Circuit densities are lower because extra distance must be maintained between the two different transistors. Linking 2.5 million such transistors yields the i860 32-bit processor chip (Figure 3.1) pictured at the beginning of this chapter. The CMOS-bipolar speed gap has narrowed to a factor of 2.

An approach called biCMOS attempts to marry the two technologies and obtain a chip with low power requirements but powerful off-chip drivers, that is, a chip with CMOS circuits for on-chip functions but with bipolar off-chip drivers that are as powerful as those on a bipolar chip. The biCMOS fabrication process is more complex than either a bipolar or a CMOS process alone, and one must guard against obtaining the worst instead of the best of the two worlds.

Gallium arsenide, or GaAs, is a semiconductor with double the electron mobility of silicon (see the footnote in the box on page 40). Thus, GaAs FET and bipolar transistors are faster. Power dissipation is higher, however, and large, defect-free crystals are as yet much harder to obtain than with silicon. Also, CMOS is difficult with GaAs because the "hole" mobility is low. GaAs is widely used in lasers and light-emitting diodes for fiber optic communication, and is starting to be used for special-purpose supercomputers and critical portions of general-purpose computers.

In summary, bipolar transistors are faster than NMOS due to vertical current flow, CMOS transistors have lower power because standby current is eliminated, and GaAs has higher electron mobility than silicon.

The next few sections examine these factors that determine the speed of a serial computer—circuit speed, levels of logic, package delays, and cycles per instruction. In some ways, these sections bear out the old saying, "There's many a slip between the cup and the lip".

3.1.1   VLSI Circuit Speed

Transistors today fall into two categories: field-effect and bipolar.[41] They are both made of the same material, usually silicon. Pure silicon is an insulator, but it can be made into a n-type or a p-type conductor of electricity by introducing small amounts of impurities, or *dopants*. Readers interested in more detail are referred to a semiconductor physics book like the one by Sze [424] or to a technology update like the one by Ning and Tang [344] or Osburn and Reisman [349]. For this discussion, the key points are that there are two types of silicon and that the interesting effects that make transistors work occur at boundaries between n-type and p-type silicon or at boundaries between silicon and another material. Despite all the elegant quantum mechanics that went into the invention of the transistor, the main concern of the sophisticated high-tech processes used to manufacture transistors today is the minimization of unwanted resistance and capacitance.[42]

Field-Effect Transistors

Figure 3.2 on page 103 shows a cross sectional view of the essence of a field-effect transistor, or FET. Application of a voltage to the gate electrode allows a thin layer of electrons to flow from the source to the drain in the silicon channel just below the gate. Lowering the gate voltage blocks this flow of current. The drawing shows an n-channel, or NMOS, device, so named because the channel created under the gate is n-type.

Figure 3.3 on page 103 gives an example of a technological development that improved FET speed. The gate was originally metal. This metal could not withstand the heating that occurred during the manufacture of the drain and source regions, and so the gate had to be put on afterwards. To compensate for possible misalignments in its placement, it had to be made oversized, which increased the electrical capacitance and slowed the transistor. A polycrystalline silicon gate electrode does not conduct electricity as well as

---

[41] The bipolar transistor gets its name from the fact that its action is carried out by *both* electrons and holes [424]. FET's, which operate with one or the other (but not both) ought to be called unipolar transistors to be consistent. Instead, they get their name from the fact that charges in the active region are moved by an electric *field*. The motive mechanism in bipolar transistors is diffusion, and a name consistent with FET would be DET, or diffusion-effect transistor. However, it seems that the names bipolar and FET are here to stay.

[42] Ironically, a large part of silicon's pre-eminence over other semiconductors springs not from the properties of silicon itself but from those of its oxide, which has a very happy combination of properties. Silicon oxide is also the main ingredient of glass, optical fibers—and the sand on the beaches of the world.

Figure 3.2   *Cross-sectional view of the essence of a field-effect transistor.*

metal, but it withstands much higher temperatures. Hence it can be put on the silicon first and actually used as a stencil mask during the manufacture of the source and drain, automatically aligning the three correctly. The resulting gate is smaller, the capacitance is less, and the transistor is faster.

Figure 3.4 on page 104 shows an n-well CMOS (complementary MOS) inverter circuit. The n-channel transistor of Figure 3.2 is combined with its *complement*, a p-channel transistor, to form a circuit in which both steady states have almost zero current because one or the other transistor is off. Average power dissipation is greatly reduced, since significant current flows only while switching from one state to the other. As before, a positive V_{in} puts the NMOS in the low-resistance state, which puts V_{out} in the low-voltage state. Decreasing V_{in} turns the NMOS off and the PMOS on, and brings V_{out} to the

Figure 3.3   *An example of a process improvement resulting in a field-effect transistor with reduced capacitance and higher speed.*

Figure 3.4   Cross-sectional view of a CMOS (complementary MOS) circuit.
*The n-channel transistor of Figure 3.2 on page 103 is combined with its complement,
a p-channel transistor. In either steady state, one transistor is off and current flow
is almost zero; hence, average power dissipation is much lower.*

high-voltage stage. Significant current flows only during these state transitions. The price of CMOS is a more complex process (for example, creating the
n-well for the PMOS takes extra steps) as well as more complex device design
and lower circuit density (undesirable interactions between the two different
kinds of transistors must be prevented, and the transistor count per function is
higher). Nevertheless, this trade-off has proved to be profitable, and CMOS
has become the dominant FET technology. As a point of calibration, the DEC
Alpha RISC chip described at ISSCC '92 achieves a 5-nanosecond cycle time
using a CMOS technology that achieves minimum dimensions of 0.75 microns.
Experimental chips with dimensions as small as 0.3 microns were reported.
Further details on CMOS technology may be found in [241].

Bipolar Transistors

The essence of a bipolar transistor is shown in the cross-sectional drawing of
Figure 3.5 on page 105. Here, the flow of electrons from the emitter to the
collector is turned on and off by a voltage applied to the base electrode. This
controlled emission and collection takes place at the junctions between n-type
and p-type silicon regions. The reason for the bipolar transistor's greater
speed is that the current flows through a short, wide active region (the base),
whereas the current in an FET flows horizontally through an active region (the
channel) that is long and narrow by comparison. An electrical engineer would
call the FET a high-impedance device because it presents more impedance to
the flow of current, just as a long, thin straw is harder to drink through than a
short, fat one.

Figure 3.5   Cross-sectional view of the essence of a bipolar transistor.

Bipolar transistors are usually faster than FETs, at the cost of higher power consumption. But the performance gap is narrowing: the DEC Alpha RISC chip described at ISSCC '92 has a 5-nSec cycle, obtained with CMOS technology. On the bipolar side, the NEC SX-3 operates with a 2.9-nSec cycle, and Cray Computer Inc. is struggling to deliver the Cray-3 with a 2-nSec cycle. Bipolar circuits are used in supercomputers and top-of-the-line commercial models, whereas FETs are used in middle-of-the-line models down through minicomputers, workstations, and PCs. There are also efforts to marry the two technologies (biCMOS, for example).

As was mentioned earlier, the bipolar transistor pays for its greater speed with higher power consumption and heat generation. In addition, bipolar transistors must be surrounded by buffer regions to prevent interference with their neighbors on a VLSI chip, whereas field-effect transistors are basically self-isolating and can be packed more densely on a chip.

Like the speed of an FET transistor, the speed of a bipolar transistor is limited by its resistance-capacitance product. Much technological effort is devoted to reducing this quantity. For example, Figure 3.6 on page 106 shows how the isolation between transistors was originally provided by a surrounding ring of p-type silicon. However, the junction between this p-type ring and the n-type collector gave rise to a large capacitance. With more sophisticated techniques, a ring of insulating oxide can be created instead, and the capacitance can be cut almost in half.

Figure 3.6 An example of bipolar transistor process improvement. *In the early VLSI transistor profile at the top, a p-type trench surrounds the transistor and isolates it from its neighbors. Note the dual contacts to the base and collector for increased speed [226]. Changing to an insulating oxide trench (bottom) cuts the capacitance and increases transistor speed.*

The speed of a transistor, like that of an automobile, is determined by its size and power. Simple analysis shows that if all the dimensions of a transistor were cut in half, the same amount of power should make it switch four times faster, assuming that the voltages have been kept the same (as required by semiconductor physics). The same size chip could now hold four times as many transistors, each switching four times faster. However, the chip would also generate four times as much heat! If the chip package is already dissipating as much power as it can, then each transistor can only be given one-fourth as much power as before. The designer could choose to only half-populate the chip with the smaller transistors and run them twice as fast as before, but economics favors as many transistors per chip as possible. As a consequence, scaling down the size of VLSI devices does not speed up the circuits as much as one might expect.

Within limits, the speed of a transistor increases linearly with its operating power. For example, the bipolar NAND logic circuit in Figure 3.7 on page 107 switches in 2 nanoseconds at 1/2 milliwatt when it is used in the IBM 4341 and

Figure 3.7   A 3-input bipolar NAND logic gate *used in both the IBM 4341 and the IBM 3081. The load resistors were twice as wide in the latter case. Thus the latter had half the resistance and hence used twice the power and ran twice as fast. It also necessitated changing from an air-cooled package in the 4341 to the water-cooled package, shown in Figure 3.11 on page 111, for the 3081.*

in 1 nanosecond at 1 milliwatt when it is used in the IBM 3081. The doubling of power has a profound effect on the cooling package needed (discussed below). But in each case, the product of switching time and power (the speed-power product) is 1 picojoule. This product remains constant over a speed range of about 3 for this typical circuit. The speed-power product is characteristic of a given technology. A technology yielding smaller dimensions has a smaller speed-power product.

Field-effect and bipolar transistors are usually made by different processes, which makes one-to-one comparisons somewhat difficult. Broadly speaking, however, a given set of technology ground rules (for minimum linewidths, etc.) will give on-off bipolar and FET circuits with about the same speed-power product. Because FETs have higher impedance, their speed-power curves are shifted toward lower power and longer switching times. A fictional FET circuit with dimensions corresponding to the bipolar example above might consume 0.1 milliwatt and switch in 10 nanoseconds.

The net of the preceding discussion is that, once the design and technology are chosen, the speed of a transistor circuit depends on how much power it can be given and on how short its connections to its neighbors can be kept. Thus, packaging is very important and is discussed right after the next topic.

a	b	c	s	c
0	0	0	0	0
1	0	0	1	0
0	1	0	1	0
0	0	1	1	0
1	1	0	0	1
1	0	1	0	1
0	1	1	0	1
1	1	1	1	1

Figure 3.8 *A 1-bit full adder* with two levels of logic and six gates per bit.

3.1.2 Levels of Logic

The first factor that multiplies the circuit's switching time has to do with the way that logic gates are interconnected to carry out the computer's instructions. The sequence in Figure 3.8 through Figure 3.10 is an illustrative example. Figure 3.8 shows how logic gates can be combined with others to form a 1-bit adder. Note that an input signal must pass through *two* logic gates

Figure 3.9 *A 4-bit adder* with 4 levels of logic and 7.5 gates per bit.

Figure 3.10   A 16-bit adder with 6 levels of logic and 8.5–10.5 gates per bit.

and is delayed by two switching times. Put another way, even this simple circuit involves two levels of logic.

This small circuit can add two binary numbers of arbitrary size in the same way that we do with pencil, paper, and decimal numbers: add the ones and carry to the tens column, add the tens, and so on. This bit-at-a-time addition is fast enough for electronic pocket calculators, which work in exactly this way. In commercial computers, however, speed is much more important, and, in an early application of parallelism at the circuit level, their circuits were expanded to handle a number of bits (a *word*) at a time. Figure 3.9 and Figure 3.10 show two stages in this progression. By the time a 16-bit adder is reached, the number of logic levels (or circuit delays per operation) has increased to six. (Also note how the number of gates per bit grows.)

The cycle time of the full computer is usually determined by more than just addition (data must be brought to the adder and then put away safely somewhere), and the number of logic levels per cycle varies with the design, but 10 is a reasonable estimate for the expansion of the single-gate delay due to this effect.

3.1.3 Packaging

An additional source of delay occurs when a signal must leave a chip and travel to another chip. This can easily dominate the cycle time. We must pause a moment and define cycle time. A precise, universally accepted definition is surprisingly slippery[43] , but for present purposes, it suffices to regard the CPU (clock) cycle time as the time needed to get information out of and safely back into a register, the fastest part of the computer's memory system (see Figure 3.20 on page 124).

In 1 nanosecond, an electromagnetic signal can travel 15 centimeters and back in free space, but this distance is reduced by a factor of 2 to 3 in many materials used to package computers. Thus, to get a 10-nanosecond cycle time, all the circuits involved in what happens during the cycle must be within roughly half a meter of each other. The central processing unit (CPU) of a modern large computer has several hundred thousand circuits. The packaging technology must place all these circuits close enough to each other and still remove the signals as well as the several kilowatts of heat they generate. Without this cooling, the CPU would literally turn into an oven. Reference [445] is a well-written, comprehensive book on microelectronics packaging.

Two different ways to do this packaging are shown next. Figure 3.11 on page 111 shows the thermal conduction module (TCM) used in the IBM 3090 and ES/9000 series (Figure 3.12 on page 112 shows an exploded view). The chips sit on a multilayered (laminated) ceramic substrate about the size of a bathroom tile, the "wires" connecting the chips run through and between these multiple layers, and a short metal rod pressed against each chip carries its heat away into a water-cooled metal housing. In the ES/9000, each TCM has almost 1800 signal pins on the bottom, and holds about 50,000 ECL circuits on about 120 chips [126]. The TCM can dissipate 2000 watts, or about a hundred times more heat than a typical CMOS microprocessor is allowed to generate (the disparity in power per transistor is more like a thousand).

Figure 3.13 on page 113 shows a different packaging approach, the one used in the CRAY-1 and some of its successors. In this approach, the number of circuits per chip is less, each circuit dissipates more power, and the heat is carried away to a liquid cooling system through metal plates on which the

---

[43] Hayes [221] defines it as well as anyone: "The sequence of operations involved in processing an instruction constitutes an *instruction cycle*, which can be subdivided into ... the *fetch cycle* and the *execution cycle*. The instruction is obtained from main memory during the fetch cycle. The execution cycle typically includes decoding the instruction, fetching any required operands, and performing the operations specified by the instruction's opcode [see Figure 9.1 on page 412]. The behavior of the CPU during an instruction cycle may be defined by a sequence of *microoperations*, each of which involves a register transfer. The time ... required for the shortest well-defined CPU microoperation is defined to be the *CPU cycle time*" [our underlining].

Figure 3.11   *A thermal conduction module (TCM)* – *a high-density, high-power multichip package* [68],[126]. *Upper photo shows chips mounted on the 4" × 4" multilayer ceramic substrate and the cooling structure. Lower photo is a cross section of the ceramic substrate and shows the "wires" running through and between the layers. Figure 3.12 on page 112 provides an exploded view.*

Figure 3.12 *Exploded view of the TCM* of Figure 3.11 on page 111. Seventy-eight TCMs form the guts of the 6-processor IBM 3090-600, plus 3 TCMs for each processor equipped with a Vector Facility (page 427).

chips are mounted directly. The wires are kept short by arranging the circuit boards in a circle.

Both of these approaches are driven by the twin needs of putting the circuits as close together as possible and giving each circuit as much power as possible in order to make the CPU as fast as possible. Further improvements in such CPUs can still to be expected, but at progressively greater expense. This expense provides more and more motivation to explore alternate approaches like parallel processing.

Figure 3.13   Hand-wiring a Cray-2 (photo). The several hundred thousand wires that interconnect the circuit boards are adjusted in length so that the signals between any two points deviate from the desired travel time by less than one nanosecond. Drawing at left shows the central processing unit and central memory of the original Cray-1 model. The benches at the base hold the power supply. (Its appearance has caused this machine to be nicknamed "the world's most expensive love seat") See page 423 for a discussion of architecture and performance. (With permission from Time, Inc., and the Association for Computing Machinery.)

3.1.4   Gate Delays per Cycle

The adder circuit is one of the components of the ALU (arithmetic/logic unit). The ALU and a few registers make up the computer's *E-unit*, the part that exe-

Coaxial Cables vs. Optical Fibers

Coaxial cables and optical fibers both carry signals at the speed of light. The fiber's advantage is that a signal travels much *farther* before it is attenuated so much that it needs amplification at a repeater station. The distance-bandwidth product for a coaxial cable is about 1 km-Mbit/sec; it is at least a thousand times better for optical fibers.

COAX (thick = good)

The coaxial cable suffers from the "skin effect": at high frequencies, all the current flows at the conductor's surface in a thin layer whose thickness or "skin depth" is $\delta = \sqrt{1/\pi f \mu \sigma} = 6.6\mu$m for copper at $f = 100$ MHz (μ is the permittivity of free space and σ is the metal's conductivity). The result is a resistance per unit length proportional to $\sqrt{f}$.

The attenuation grows with the ratio of the transmission line's total resistance divided by its characteristic impedance Z_0. Z_0 grows with the separation $d/2$ between conductors. Thus, thin-wire ethernet (10 Mbit/sec, 50 ohms) can run 185 meters between repeaters, while thick-wire ethernet can run 500 meters (but it is more expensive). But Z_0 is limited to $\sqrt{\mu/\epsilon}$, which is 377 ohms in free space and less in the coaxial cable (ϵ is the insulator's dielectric constant). Cables a few meters long can support bandwidths in excess of 1 Gbit/sec.

FIBER (thin = good)

The communications bandwidth of an optical fiber is much greater than that of a coaxial cable because the frequencies used are much

higher (the frequency of red light is about 500,000 GHz). Exploiting this huge bandwidth was made possible by two developments: inexpensive glass fibers with controlled diameters as small as several micrometers (μm), and affordable controllable GaAs (gallium arsenide) light sources. *Multimode* fibers are 50–60 μm in diameter but operate with either GaAs lasers or with cheaper GaAs LEDs (light emitting diodes). The distance-bandwidth product is about 1000 km-Mbit/sec, leading perhaps to a system with 100 Mbit/sec bandwidth and 10 km between repeaters. *Single-mode* fibers approach a micrometer in diameter (a few wavelengths) and operate with GaAs lasers. The payoff is a distance-bandwidth product of 20–500 km-Gbit/sec, leading perhaps to a system with 1 Gbit/sec bandwidth and 100 km between repeaters.

cutes instructions (once it is clear what they are). Registers are very fast little memories that can transfer data to and from the ALU in only a few gate delays.

A complete addition cycle has to include getting the two numbers from somewhere and putting their sum somewhere. The fastest cycle occurs when the source and destination for these numbers are registers. In a computer like those in the IBM 3090 or ES/9000 series, the adder and the registers are on different chips within the TCM corresponding to the E-unit. So the time for a register-to-register add operation includes the delay of the adder, the access time of the registers, and the packaging delay or time needed to transfer information between the chips. Each of these can be about half a dozen gate delays, and so an 0.5 nanosecond gate delay becomes roughly a 10-nanosecond execution cycle time.

3.1.5 Cycles per Instruction (Beyond Technology)

The preceding discussion assumed that the computer had already *decoded* the instruction it was to perform ("Add the contents of two registers and put the sum into a register"). The time needed to get this instruction and decode it must also be accounted for. In addition, the operands (the numbers) are not always in registers; generally they must be fetched from the memory system. This system is usually organized in a hierarchy according to speed, with the most frequently used information kept in a fast *cache* (see page 546) backed up by successively slower memories, disks, and tapes. Caches are much larger than registers (the IBM 3090 uses a 64 KB cache, for instance) and may have access times equal to two execution cycles.[44] Both the time to fetch and decode instructions and the time to access cache and memory must be included in the instruction execution rate (see Figure 3.14 on page 116).

As shown in Figure 9.1 on page 412, strictly sequential, unembellished von Neumann–style execution of an instruction that involves fetching both the instruction and the operand from a 2-cycle cache requires 8 CPU cycles or more. Overlapping the instruction fetch and execution operations (instruction prefetch) can reduce this time to 4 or 5 cycles, at the cost of more hardware. Allowing several instructions to execute concurrently in overlapped or pipelined fashion (at a further cost in hardware) can reduce the average instruction execution time to about 3 cycles. (See Figure 9.1 for details. For scientific/engineering problems that make heavy use of floating-point computations on large, regular arrays of data, an execution rate of several floating-point operations per cycle can be obtained under ideal conditions in special vector processors and superscalar RISC processors. This topic is discussed on page 415.)

The last step in our odyssey is to consider finite-cache effects and cache misses. The preceding analysis assumed that all the instructions and data of

---

[44] Cache operation is discussed in more detail on page 546.

Figure 3.14   **Performance figures of merit.**

the program are contained in the fast cache memory. This analysis yields the so-called infinite cache performance. Real caches have finite capacity, and occasionally the desired item will not be in such caches. This situation is called a *cache miss*, and the fraction of cache requests for which it happens is called the *cache miss ratio*.[45] In this case, the item has to be fetched from the main memory, a process which is several times slower than accessing the cache. The delay added to the execution time depends on the memory-access time and the misses per instruction, as analyzed in one of the problems at the end of this chapter. For 4% misses per instruction and a memory-access time of 200 nanoseconds, the infinite-cache performance for a 20-nanosecond execution cycle time is degraded by only about 20%, corresponding to about one extra cycle per instruction.

Figure 3.15 on page 117 shows that, as technology is used to improve the cycle time, a higher and higher penalty is incurred unless the misses per instruction and/or memory-access times are also decreased. Such decreases are hard to accomplish because technology improvements are needed in the cache and memory just to keep pace with the processor: the cache must be made faster and the memory must be made larger. To reduce the misses per instruction probably requires a larger cache, which means that one is trying to make both the cache and the memory larger *and* faster at the same time, which is a doubly difficult technological feat. So the 1-nanosecond gate delay in our

---

[45] *Cache misses per instruction*, a term used in calculating processor performance (MIPS), is the *cache miss ratio* multiplied by the number of memory references per instruction ≈ 2).

Figure 3.15   Effect of memory-access time on MIPS.

hypothetical uniprocessor has turned into an average 80-nanosecond instruction execution time. Note that only about 10% of this time is used for the actual addition in this example; the other 90% is used to get the right numbers to the adder and to put the result in the right place, in other words, for bookkeeping and data motion. It is hoped that this treatment illustrates how this time expansion occurs, gives the reader a feel for the technological challenges involved in speeding up uniprocessors, and lays the groundwork for a discussion of the influence of technology on the design of parallel processors.

3.1.6   The Costs of VLSI

A finished VLSI chip is a marvel, but the tremendous value it represents is bought at the cost of a long and expensive design process and fabrication process. To take advantage of VLSI, one must understand its nature, whether one is designing a uni- or a parallel processor.

Figure 3.16 shows the levels through which many designs pass on their way from an initial concept to a final working chip. A commercially successful chip cannot afford to have a single line out of place, must obey technology ground rules, operate over a wide range of temperatures and supply voltages, and be easy to test after manufacture. High-quality design tools are essential for such a complex venture. A good rule of thumb is that a chip design group averages between one and ten good new custom logic circuits per designer per day, depending on the maturity and quality of its design tools.

With good tools, ten designers can custom-design a chip like the Intel i860 (Figure 3.1 on page 98) and get it fully operational in about two years. With-

Figure 3.16 *The levels of a VLSI design and the tools needed to make and check progress. Some of these levels are implicit rather than explicit in various design procedures, but their function must be performed somehow.*

1. *Concept: An idea, like a microprocessor or traffic light controller.*
2. *Architecture: The essential rules or principles of operation, usually in English.*
3. *High-level logic: The design broken into large building blocks like ALUs.*
4. *Detailed logic: A logic-gate-level description of the design, derived from and checked against the high-level design.*
5. *Test patterns: A set of inputs designed to detect defects quickly after manufacture. May be generated automatically from the previous level.*
6. *Circuit level: Electrical simulation (using SPICE, ASTAP, or some other program) to ensure correct behavior over wide temperature and voltage swings.*
7. *Layout: Specification (using CIF, GL/1, or some other language) of the many stencil mask patterns used in fabrication. Graphic entry systems abound, but the unsung heroes are the programs that check for design errors like ground rule violations, calculate circuit performance, and check against the logic design.*
8. *Manufactured chip: First tested for functionality by the designers. Eventually must be tested in seconds.*

Sequence starts at lower left, proceeds clockwise, and illustrates formation of the simple transistor circuit shown in the box in the middle. End result is a computer board that holds several TCMs like the one shown a few pages earlier.

Figure 3.17   **VLSI fabrication** of bipolar circuits in the TCM of Figure 3.11.

out good tools, the project would be doomed. The role of these design and checking tools is shown in Figure 3.16 on page 118. The point is that a large custom VLSI chip that is designed to industrial standards rather than as an academic exercise is an undertaking substantial enough to warrant careful weighing of a custom vs. an off-the-shelf chip.

One alternative is to use gate arrays, which are partially designed chips containing an array of predesigned, unconnected logic gates, like the one in Figure 3.7 on page 107. If the ground rules are obeyed, the designer's task ends when the detailed logic is completed and shipped to the physical design house. Programs will automatically place and wire the detailed logic design's gates onto the chip, the design is fairly well guaranteed to work, and the design is completed in weeks. The price is lower speed and density than a custom design could achieve with the same technology, due to unavoidable waste of some of the gate array's resources. For example, a 2-input NAND in the logic design must still use a 3-input gate if that is all the chip provides, and if the wiring uses less than the maximum space allocated to it, there is no way, in contrast to a custom design, to "cash this space in" for more circuits or higher performance. On the other hand, the chip can be ready in months instead of years.

In addition to taking a long time to design, VLSI chips usually take a long time to manufacture. The equipment used is very expensive, and so production lines are maximized for throughput, not speed of passage. The traffic is deliberately heavy enough to ensure queues at the key pieces of equipment. To show a representative process, Figure 3.17 on page 119 traces the formation of a simple transistor circuit in the technology used for the IBM 3090 and ES/9000 series. The chip alone requires 15 mask-alignment steps, during each of which the pattern being created must register with the previously created patterns within tolerances less than a micrometer. Over 100 other steps are also needed. Each entails a delay.

Chip fabrication times of several months for a custom design are not unusual, and the testing of the first design often results in a second design and manufacturing cycle. A commercial design close to the limits of technology, like the Intel i860 or DEC Alpha, costs millions of dollars before the first chip ever returns. Gate arrays, though less aggressive in density and speed, offer a faster and cheaper design and manufacturing process, but only to those with the right tools and interfaces. These are some of the ways that VLSI influences the design of uni- as well as parallel processors.

3.1.7 *Technology and Parallel Processing*

From the technologist's standpoint, parallel processing offers the chance to solve the "parts-number problem". The parts-number problem has to do with the large variety of chips needed to build a powerful uniprocessor. It is not unusual for large processors (like those in the IBM 3090 and ES/9000 series) to contain hundreds of different chip designs, many of which are used only once or twice. Each additional chip design increases the development cost as well as the manufacturing cost. It would be very attractive to build instead a computer that uses only a few versatile mass-producible building blocks.

Memory and microprocessor chips are two prime examples of such versatile building blocks. Assuming that the other problems of parallel processing (see chapter 1) are solved, the main problem from the technology viewpoint is, "How do you get processors by the ton talking to memories by the ton at a reasonable speed?"[282] . Let us first discuss this question in terms of a tightly coupled, microprocessor-based, shared-memory parallel processor (like the NYU Ultracomputer, page 572) and then consider other architectures. The development of memories with multiple ports for input and output should solve the aggregate bandwidth problem at that interface. The performance-limiting factor then becomes the interconnection network and its associated switching technology.

How fast should the interconnection network be? Microprocessors and memories, interestingly, have roughly the same cycle time (at present, both are made using FET technology). Intuition suggests that the network cycle time should be of the same order, and there are simulation experiments that bear this intuition out (see the RP3 section that starts on page 603). Depending on the functions that the network must perform and the technology assumptions, this intuition can force rather fundamental technology decisions. In the RP3, for example, the multistage network that interconnects the FET processors and memories obtains the speed needed to keep up with them by using bipolar circuits on TCMs. Most of these interconnection networks (see Chapter 8) are made up of many identical chips, and so they also help with the parts-number problem.

What about fiber optics? As we explain in the box on page 114, electrical cables and optical fibers can both carry signals at the speed of light. The advantage of fiber optics is in the much greater *distance* that a high-frequency signal can travel before it needs amplification. So optical fibers are not the key to improving the performance of a *tightly packed* parallel computer, but rather that of a parallel system distributed over a substantial distance, like a local or wide area network.

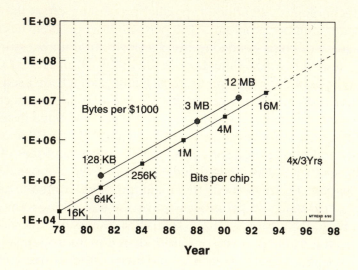

Figure 3.18   Memory density, a barometer of technology trends.

What about other architectures like the Connection Machine (page 446), which also tries to bring processing into the memory but does so with many more, much smaller processors? There are serious questions about setting up problems to be executed efficiently on such an architecture. Strictly from the parts-number viewpoint, however, "homogenizing" the processor, memory, and switch into one chip type is an attractive prospect. Systolic arrays, on the other hand, with a different chip needed for each algorithm, represent the wrong direction from the parts-number viewpoint.

The Headroom Problem

The *rate* at which technology is improving leads to what has been called the *headroom* problem for the developer of a parallel computer: unfortunately, it is not usually possible to pop in the best microprocessor that exists at the end of a parallel computer's design cycle, because manufacturers change interfaces from one chip generation to the next and so forth. As a consequence, the processing element's specifications are frozen near the *beginning* of the design cycle, and a parallel computer becomes a collection of yesterday's processors competing against today's best uniprocessor, whose performance

Figure 3.19   Parallel computer design time window *resulting from continued improvements in technology.*

is still growing rapidly, especially for microprocessors and workstations. The effect of this "moving target" phenomenon is to create a rather narrow time window during which the parallel processor *must* be designed and built quickly.

We illustrate this situation with two figures. The first one, Figure 3.18, shows that memory chip capacity quadruples every three years, while chip cost tends to remain constant and performance tends to improve. The trend curve for microprocessors is similar.

The impact of these technology trends is illustrated in Figure 3.19 using an example of a parallel computer with 64 processing elements. A widely held rule of thumb says that the parallel computer must offer the user an approximately tenfold improvement in performance to make up for more difficult programming and so forth. At the start of its design cycle, the parallel computer exceeds this minimum required performance advantage by a factor of 6.4. After a time window of four years, the uniprocessor performance has improved by a factor of 6.4, and the parallel computer has used up its headroom. If it is not ready at that point, it will not be competitive, as is borne out by a number of real-life examples.

Figure 3.20   *The memory/storage hierarchy* *of a computing system like the IBM 3090 or ES/9000 series comprises devices with a wide speed and capacity range:*

1.   *Registers: Very fast small memories, deliver a word to the CPU in only a few gate delays. The registers characterize an architecture as much as do the number of cylinders in an automobile. S/370 has 16 general-purpose registers.*

2.   *Cache: Larger and slower than registers, but still much faster than main memory and used to hold copies of the memory items being used most frequently by the present job.*

3.   *Main memory: Equally accessible cells in a collection large enough to hold the operating system and perhaps several dozen large programs. Maximum capacity is set by the architecture. For example, ES/9000 instructions have a 31-bit address field, which allows access to 2 billion bytes. The difference in memory and CPU cycle times is handled by organizing the memory into interleaved modules, so that a 128-Byte block (a cache line) is delivered each time the memory is accessed.*

4.   *Secondary storage: An ensemble of moving-head disks (see next section). Contains all programs running in the system and considerably more. Delivers to main memory portions of programs and data in (typically) 4-KB increments called pages.*

5.   *Storage backup: Magnetic tape system used for data storage and disk backup.*

3.2 Memory Technology

Now we treat random-access *main memory* (RAM) technology, which occupies a middle position in the memory/storage hierarchy of a traditional (serial) computer system (Figure 3.20 on page 124). The size and speed of this memory are strongly influenced by its upstairs and downstairs neighbors, as discussed below.

3.2.1 Memory Size: Megabytes/MIPS

Experience with large computers has shown that the memory tends to grow in proportion to the processor's performance at an increment of about 1 to 2 megabytes per MIPS, and this ratio is often used as a rule of thumb to project memory requirements for future large computers.[46] Whether a rule valid for one architecture at 20 MIPS can be used for a very different architecture at 1000 MIPS is an open question. To begin to answer it, one should at least understand what causes the present rule. One explanation is that disk speeds remain constant, CPU speeds increase, and the difference is made up by running more programs at the same time.

The memory must be large enough to hold (the resident portions of) the essential system software, like the operating system, and at least one user program. A memory large enough to hold absolutely everything that the program needs is not practical, and so the program must occasionally access the disk for items of data, and so forth. The disk response time (25–50 milliseconds) is very long by CPU standards, and *not likely to get substantially faster,* for reasons discussed in the "Storage Technology" section of this chapter. In a 10-MIPS machine, then, half a million instruction cycles can go by until the requested information is delivered. Rather than have the processor idle during this time, the program is put on hold; the processor goes on to service other programs, and picks up the original program sometime after the disk delivers the needed item. Having the processor divide its time between several programs is called *multiprogramming.* The number of programs active at the same time is called the *multiprogramming level,* or *mpl* for short; it is bounded from below by the ratio of disk reaction time to the time between disk requests. As the CPU gets faster, the time between disk requests gets shorter, and the mpl increases.

---

[46] For example, the 24-bit addressing of the IBM S/370 architecture limited the main memory to 16 MB (2^{24}). The announcement of the S/370 XA with 31-bit addressing coincided with the development of performance in the 10-MIPS range.

"Dennard's Folly"

The semiconductor memory chip that sells for a few dollars is now taken for granted. Yet such a chip was originally a daring proposal that might have immortalized its inventor's name in the phrase "Dennard's folly". True, semiconductor memory cells had been used in the central processing unit for registers and other small, fast memories, but

these used six-transistor cells [226] whose *current* was on or off to signify a stored 1 or 0. Dennard's proposal [132], requiring much less power and space, was to store the bit as *charge* on a single small capacitor guarded by a single transistor. Squeezing enough bits onto a chip to be economically feasible forced the stored charge to be so small that reliable detection of its signal seemed dubious. Also,

One-device memory cell using field effect transistor of Figure 3.2. WL, BL, PL = word-, bit-, plate line.

the charge leaked away in a few milliseconds. Dennard persisted, however; the rest is history. Today's megabit chips still use his simple design.

In the one-device memory cell, the field-effect transistor of Figure 3.2 is modified as shown above. The source region S is expanded and capped with an extra electrode connected to the plate line PL. The charge is held in the capacitor formed between this electrode and the source region. Actuating the word *and* the bit line charges or discharges (writes or reads) this capacitor.

A memory chip is formed by arranging such cells in a matrix and adding arrays of row decoders, column decoders, and sense amplifiers, as sketched at right. (In a real chip, the single 1000 × 1000 array is replaced by several smaller arrays to reduce the bit-line capacitance; some designs also transfer more than one bit at a

time.) The pin count exemplifies a trade-off: the cell address is sent in two steps, during which the 10 address pins do double duty. Activating the RAS or CAS pin specifies whether a row or column address is being sent. Thus 12 pins do the work of 20, but at the expense of a longer cycle.

(continued next page)

Each program needs its own chunk of memory, and so the necessary total memory capacity grows proportionately, in qualitative agreement with the observed trend. The simple analysis in the box *Megabytes per Mips* below shows that this model makes quantitative sense as well. As shown in the box,

"Dennard's Folly" (continued)

As improved technology produces finer linewidths, one might expect the new, smaller cells to allow faster chips. In reality, each new generation of chips has brought a fourfold increase in memory capacity, but little improvement in speed. Present computer designers place more value on memory capacity than speed. In a large system, the cache makes the performance relatively insensitive to memory speed, while small systems like personal computers are caught between software designers who say "memory is cheap" and customers who say "Fifty dollars is dinner at a restaurant". So the memory designer trades chip capacity for speed.

Insight into this trade-off is provided by the scaling behavior of the memory cell. This cell can be modeled as a simple RC (resistance-capacitance) circuit that discharges with a time constant $\tau = RC$ (R = effective cell resistance, C = capacitance, including the bit line's.) With initial voltage V on the capacitor, the average power during τ is $V^2/2R$. If the chip has N cells, then the product of τ and the chip power P (the speed-power product) is **$P\tau = NV^2C/2$**. If all dimensions are assumed proportional to x, then V and C both scale approximately as x, and **$P\tau$** scales as **Nx^3**. Including the power of the word-line drivers and other circuits increases **$P\tau$** by a multiplicative factor, but leaves its scaling behavior basically unchanged.

This calculation says several interesting things. Since P is limited to less than a watt per chip to allow air cooling, chip response time (τ) ought to be proportional to chip capacity (N) for a given technology (x fixed), which is borne out in practice. Halving the technological dimensions and keeping the chip's capacity and power constant should reduce chip response time eightfold, and there is evidence for this, too. But, for reasons discussed above, the designer usually opts for the maximum chip capacity available under the new ground rules. Thus, a 64-kilobit chip with 2.5-micron linewidths becomes, two generations later, a 1-megabit chip with 1-micron lines and roughly the same access time and power as before, in accord with the derived scaling. Parallel processors may call for rather different design trade-offs. They are available.

the analysis suggests that a 10-MIPS machine will need between 6.4 and 15 MB of memory, which calibrates reasonably well with reality. The analysis also provides a plausibility argument for the "1-2 MB/MIPS" rule of thumb mentioned above.

Does this rule still apply when the processing speed is 100 times higher? The safest assumption is that it does, even if the driving force is different, and most supercomputers (actual and proposed) do not stray far from this ratio.

Megabytes per MIPS

Memory capacity (MB) = a + (b x mpl)

       a = fixed, 2 – 4 MB
       b = working set size, 0.2 – 0.5 MB
     mpl = multiprogramming level

$$mpl = \frac{\text{average disk reaction time (R)}}{\text{average time between disk requests}}$$

$$\frac{\text{time of a transaction}}{\text{P (page faults per transaction)}}$$

time of a transaction = (T + S + PQ) / (u x FMIPS)

            T = transaction (assume 10*6 instructions)
     S + PQ = overhead for multiprogramming and paging
                   (assume 0.4 x 10*5 instr.)
            u = processor utilization (assume 1)
     FMIPS = finite–cache MIPS (see last section)

$$mpl = R \times FMIPS \times \frac{uP}{T + S + MQ} .$$

With the above assumptions,

mpl = 36R x FMIPS = 2.2FMIPS for R = .06 sec.

Memory capacity (MB) = (2 – 4) + (.44 – 1.1)FMIPS

3.2.2 Memory Speed and Bandwidth

The fact that memory is needed in such large amounts has a strong influence on memory chip design. A 16-MB memory made with 64-Kbit chips needs at least 2000 chips; a 1000-MB memory using 1-Mbit chips needs over 8000. The chips need to be cheap to make and to package; that is, they must be small (to get as many as possible from a wafer), have few input/output pins, and dissipate well under a watt (to allow simple packaging and cooling). Memory speed is the chief quantity traded off. The designer achieves these requirements by using a one-device FET memory cell and some clever tricks (see the box on page 126). The computer system tolerates the loss of speed by providing a faster, smaller cache memory with copies of the main memory's most frequently used contents (see "Cycles per Instruction" earlier in this chapter).

It is very interesting to ask how one would design memory differently for a parallel processor. The "von Neumann bottleneck" is of architectural more than technological origin, but present memory designs are strongly influenced by this shielding effect. Memories for parallel processing will almost surely need higher rates of input and output, whether achieved by faster chip cycles, wider chip I/O paths, more ports, or other means. In fact, the distinction between processor and memory technology may fade away entirely. Fortunately, most of this appears feasible at reasonable cost; that is, memory technology does not seem to be up against a hard performance limit nearly as much as does storage technology (next section).

3.3   Storage Technology

If the transistor is a scientific triumph, the magnetic disk is an engineering marvel [458]. The basic principle is the same as that used in everyday audio and video casettes, but in a rigid magnetic disk (also called a *hard disk*) like the IBM 3380, the magnetic medium moves past the read/write head 1000 times faster, and instead of making direct contact with the medium, the head actually *flies* above it at an incredibly low altitude—less than the wavelength of visible light. One trip around a 3380 track is equivalent to flying a Boeing 747 from New York to San Francisco at an altitude of 2 meters. Contact with the medium or with a submicroscopic dust particle generally causes permanent damage and loss of information.

The flying height determines the bit density along the track. Getting more than the present 47KB on a 3380 track requires a lower flying height, which isn't easy. The disk spins at 3600 rpm; if it went much faster, it could fly apart. So these two factors determine the bitstream rate of one head: 47KB every 17 milliseconds, or about 3 MB per second (3 MB/sec).

3.3.1   The Amazing Disappearing I/O Bandwidth

A 180-GB IBM 3390 disk configuration contains 960 read/write heads (see Figure 3.21 on page 130). Each one has 57KB pass beneath it every 14 milliseconds. So if each one were reading data at the same time, the aggregate bitstream rate would be over 3.9 GB/sec. Yet the flow through the channel

Figure 3.21   An IBM 3390-3 disk configuration (180 GB). *Not all the spindles are shown.*

connecting the disk system to the memory is at most 4.5 MB/sec. What happens in between? The aggregate bit rate above gets reduced by the following factors and for the following reasons:

- 15× because only one head per arm is active at a time. When the head assembly is moved to a cylinder (i.e, a seek operation), the read/write heads are not properly aligned on their respective tracks, and servo-mechanical fine adjustment is used to align the head selected for reading/writing. Due to thermal expansion of the arm, alignment must take place continuously (even while the track is being read/written). The other heads will not be optimally aligned and may even be on the wrong track. This alignment problem is one reason that a parallel-readout disk is difficult.

- About 10× because the head spends over 90% of its time seeking data and under 10% transmitting it. The time to read a 4KB page from a 3390 track is only 0.93 milliseconds. The average time to get to that information is at least 13 milliseconds (it takes 7 milliseconds to get halfway around the track, and 40% of the time it is necessary to move to another track, which averages another 15 milliseconds.)

- The remaining factor comes from the contention of several heads trying to use the same storage control unit and several control units trying to share a channel (a classical queueing-theory problem).

The reduced bit rate is reflected (and somewhat "cast in concrete") in the 4.5-MB/sec data rate of the channel, which is actually a complex computer dedicated to ensuring that the I/O operation occurs as intended. The channel interface protocol used to accomplish this involves a great deal of "handshaking" of the following kind:

> I'm going to send you data!
> Are you going to send me data?
> Yes.
> Hang on—OK, I'm ready.
> Took too long—catch you next time.
> OK.
> I'm going to send you data!
> Are you?
> Yes.
> OK, I'm ready.
> OK, here it comes!
> [*data is transferred*]
> Did you get it?
> Yes, I got it.
> Is it OK, or shall I retransmit?
> No, it's OK. See you later.
> OK.

(This description is only slightly fanciful.)

As we mentioned above, with currently available disks, only one head per arm is active at a time, and there are serious difficulties in trying to remove this restriction. But we can exploit parallelism at the next level, namely, having many disks active at once. Of course this is done all the time—file A is read from disk 1 while file B is read from disk 2. A comparatively modern wrinkle is to exploit disk-level parallelism for reading a single file. Taking a cue from interleaved memory modules, consecutive blocks from a file are spread across multiple disks. For example, with two disks this would entail placing odd-numbered blocks on disk 1 and even-numbered blocks on disk 2. Now a disk operation accesses both drives, potentially giving twice the bandwidth. A collection of disks accessed in this manner is called a *disk array*.

To get the largest possible bandwidth from a storage system of fixed total capacity, one wishes to configure the system with many small disks rather than a few huge ones. The good news is that such a configuration actually costs less as well as providing higher performance. However, a reliability question arises: with many more disks, will the mean time between failures (MTBF) be acceptably large? In order to raise the MTBF of the many-small-disks system back to the level of the few-large-disks system, redundancy is used. The simplest but most expensive alternative is to replicate the entire system, so-called mirror disks. Other possibilities employ a parity-like system. Returning to our two-drive disk array, we add a third drive and make block k of drive 3 be the exclusive or of block k from the other two drives. These ideas, adapted from error-detection/correction codes used in memory systems, are incorporated in RAID (Redundant Array of Inexpensive Disks) systems. Considerably more sophisticated redundancy techniques have been devised and analyzed [357], and commercial systems are starting to appear (for example the IBM 9570 Disk Array Subsystem, which can store up to 180 GB and sustain data transfer rates in excess of 50 MB/s).

3.4 Exercises

1. Define the following terms;

transistor	RAM
silicon	cache
gallium arsenide	cache miss ratio
bipolar transistor	page
MOSFET	
CMOS	parts number problem
CPU cycle time	levels of logic

2. Which technological development of the last decade is chiefly responsible for the current practicality of parallel computers? Explain.

3. What are the three main categories of technology used in a traditional serial computer? What additional technology is needed for a parallel computer?

4. What are the two main categories of transistors used for computers? Describe their similarities, differences, and relative advantages and disadvantages.

5. Explain why it can easily take 100 times longer to execute a computer instruction than it does to turn a transistor on or off.

6. Compare silicon and gallium arsenide as technological building blocks for computers. Are the differences all a matter of degree, or can one of these technologies perform a new and qualitatively different function?

7. Why do bipolar transistors need more power than FETs? Why are they faster? Will this always be so?

8. What are the two main functions that a packaging technology must provide?

9. Explain the relationship between the computing speed and physical size of a serial computer. Is this relationship likely to hold for a parallel computer?

10. Approximately how much power can a computer chip dissipate and still be air cooled? What are the consequences of exceeding this chip power limit?

11. How much power does your PC or workstation dissipate? How does this compare with a typical hair dryer? What does this suggest about the degree of parallelism that could be achieved by using stock PCs or workstations as building blocks?

12. Derive the expression that gives the curves of MIPS vs. memory access time in Figure 3.15 on page 117. Your model's parameters should include cache miss ratio and processor cycle time.

13. Discuss the tradeoffs between VLSI gate array and custom chip designs. How does today's prospect for widespread use of custom VLSI chip designs compare with the outlook five or ten years ago? Why?

14. Advances in technology influence the architecture of parallel processors and also of microprocessors. Comment on the statement that "CISC (Complex Instruction Set Computer) was the appropriate architecture for the technology of 1980 and RISC (Reduced Instruction Set Computer) is appropriate for the technology of 1990." One useful reference is Dewar and Smosna [139].

15. What is the "parts number problem"? Will parallel processing make it better or worse? Explain.

16. Give the parameters (capacities and speeds) of some memory/storage hierarchies other than the one in Figure 3.20 on page 124. What trends do you see? Are any of the ratios changing? Why? Consequences?

17. What tends to be the relationship between processor speed and memory capacity of a serial computer? Why?

18. How do you expect the disk storage and I/O capability of a computer to vary with its processing power? Why? Which is the more difficult demand on current disk technology, the need for more storage capacity, speedier data transfer, or lower latency?

19. What tends to limit the access time of computer memory? computer disks? Which limit is more "fundamental"? Compare how the designers of each are addressing the tradeoffs between access time and storage capacity. What are their reasons?

20. Calculate how many electrons correspond to a logical "1" stored in a RAM memory cell in a 16 Mbit chip. Assume that the memory cell is effectively a 30 femtofarad (30×10^{-15} farad) electrical capacitor with 5 volts aplied to it.

21. Assume that the lithographic linewidth in the memory cell above is 0.8 micrometers, and that the charge is stored in a simple parallel plate capacitor with plate area equal to 10 squares each 0.8 micrometers on a side, and that the capacitor's dielectric constant is 3 times that of free space. How great is the effective sepa-

ration between the capacitor plates? Approximately how many atomic layers is this?

22. With reference to the analysis on page 127, prove that the speed-power product of a memory cell scales as the cube of the minimum linewidth if all dimensions are scaled in proportion.

23. What is the reason for the complex I/O communication protocol described (slightly facetiously) on page 131?

24. In 1991, the Gordon Bell prize in the price/performance category was awarded for a sustained performance equivalent to about 2 MFLOP/s per $1000, obtained with RISC/6000 workstations operating in parallel. The *peak* price/performance of the most powerful supercomputers was in the same range. 1991 also saw the definition of the "Grand Challenge" problems that would require a performance equal to 1 TeraFLOPS (a million MFLOPS).

    • At the level of price/performance given above, how much would a TeraFLOPS machine cost in 1991?

    • Assuming that the technology trends given in this chapter will continue, when would you expect that $30,000,000 would pay for a TeraFLOPS machine running in experimental mode? In production mode?

25. What are the tradeoffs between the TCM packaging approach and the hand wiring approach? How is the choice of approach affected by the volume of machines sold?

26. What are the advantages and disadvantages of fiber optic vs. coaxial communication links?

27. The finite speed of light adds about a quarter-second delay to every exchange of conversation between two people situated half-way around the world from each other, so, in terms of carrrying on a normal conversation, the speed of light sets a fairly well-defined cluster size for human social organization, and that cluster size is not much bigger than our planet Earth.

    Computers talk much faster than people, and so the speed of light sets a much smaller size on what we can think of as a cluster of fairly closely to closely cooperating computers. This is why supercomputers surprise some people with their compact size.

    Assume two workstations separated by 20 meters are each executing 25 million instructions per second. Assume that signals travel between them on a cable or fiber at 2/3 the speed of light in free space. How many instructions can be executed during the signal travel delay? What sort of minimum granularity does this set on the parallelism that can be achieved in a typical distributed cluster of workstations?

136

a=(b+1)*(b-c)

Figure 4.1 *Control-, data-, and demand-driven computational models* compared on a simple example [440], the evaluation of a=(b+1)*(b-c).

a.) The von Neumann model, showing sequential execution of instructions and the memory traffic generated by the data fetching and storing operations. (Instruction fetching is not shown.)

b.) Parallel control-driven (shared-memory) computation using the FORK construct to spawn parallel executions and the JOIN construct to synchronize them. FORK acts like a branch command on which both branches are taken. JOIN delays one routine until the other routine arrives (see p. 149). The memory references for data (not shown) are the same as in _a.)_ above.

c.) In the parallel data-driven (dataflow) model, an operation is activated when all its input data (tokens) arrive. Note the absence of "variables" that correspond to cells in a global memory.

d.) Parallel demand-driven (reduction model) computation is triggered by a demand for its result, as when some other instruction containing the function "a" tries to execute; this other instruction might be is suspended until its demand for "a" is satisfied. The definition of "a" inside the box is evaluated in a similar series of steps. In string reduction, each demander gets a copy of the definition for a "do-it-yourself" evaluation. In graph reduction, the evaluation is performed at the time of the first demand, and each demander is given a pointer to the result of the evaluation (a=10).

Advantages and disadvantages of these models are discussed in chapters 5 and 10.

4

Computational Models and Selected Algorithms

At this point, we have sketched the diversity of parallel processing research and looked at some of the details of applications and technology. All these details and diversity may give a rather bewildering picture. In this chapter, we step back from the details and take a more abstract look at the decisions facing the system designer once parallelism is allowed. A systematic way to do this is to ask about the *computational model* to be used.

As reflected in the title of Aho, Hopcroft, and Ullman's *The Design and Analysis of Computer Algorithms,* there are two faces to a computational model. On its operational side, a computational model tells us what algorithms we can *design*. The computational model describes, at a level removed from technology and hardware details, what a computer can do, i.e., which primitive actions can be performed, when these actions are performed, and by which methods can data be accessed and stored. It is like a succinct answer to the newcomer's question, "How do you play this game?" An algorithm is a precise method of solving a problem—A game plan, in other words.

The other, more mathematical, side of a computational model permits one to *analyze* an algorithm, and hence to construct highly efficient algorithms. When viewed this way, a model gives the costs associated with algorithms. Traditionally, these costs include the time required for primitive operations and the space used for data objects. For parallel processing, one needs to make additional charges for the number of processors and the required inter-processor communication.

The next section deals with the operational side of computational models. The analytical side is treated after that, followed by a discussion of several representative parallel algorithms.

4.1 Computational Models—An Operational View

4.1.1 What, Where, and When

As we said, a computational model describes just how the computation will be performed. Browne [75] lists the following five key attributes that must be specified in a computational model that includes parallelism:

Computational Model Attributes

1. The *primitive units* of computation or basic actions of the computer (the data types and operations defined by the instruction set).
2. The *control mechanism* that selects for execution the primitive units into which the problem has been partitioned.
3. The *data mechanism* (how data in memory are accessed); definition of *address spaces* available to the computation.
4. The modes and patterns of *communication* among computers working in parallel, so that they can exchange needed information.
5. *Synchronization* mechanisms to ensure that this information arrives at the right time.

The best-known computational model is the one devised by John von Neumann and his associates forty years ago (see Figure 4.2). The von Neumann model's essential features, listed in the same order used above, follow:

1. A processor that performs instructions such as "Add the contents of these two registers and put the result in that register."

Figure 4.2   *Simple von Neumann computational model.*

2.   A control scheme that fetches one instruction after another from the memory for execution by the processor, and shuttles data between memory and processor one word at a time.

3.   A memory that stores both the instructions and data of a program in cells having unique addresses.[47]

Inter-processor communication and synchronization (items 4 and 5) were solved by outlawing parallelism.[48] Processor and memory hardware were both so bulky and expensive at the time that both were treated as precious resources. The model tries hard to avoid wasting the processor's time and the memory's space. This leads to the "bottleneck" (CPU force feeding) and "side effects" (memory overwriting).[49] Nevertheless, this was the right decision given the available technology, and this model went on to become *the* computer.

The von Neumann model is really a description of the computer at the hardware level, and von Neumann's programs were series of octal numbers decipherable by the machine. Today's user no longer interacts with the com-

---

[47] By contrast, a Harvard architecture has separate memories for data and instructions; see p. 628.

[48] *"We are not going to do any arithmetic operations in parallel with any other arithmetic operations, not only to save equipment, since the adding mechanism is considerably more complicated than a few memory elements, but also to simplify the planning for the machine."* [151]

[49] Von Neumann's IAS computer had 1K 40-bit words of primary memory plus 16K words of secondary (drum) storage.

puter hardware directly but rather through several layers of software. As described by Tanenbaum [427], each of these layers atop the physical computer constitutes a virtual computer with its own language and computational model. Thus, a designer of a parallel computing system faces a more complex computational model on at least *four* levels, corresponding to the key levels that are involved in solving a problem with a computer:

The Hierarchy of Computational Models

1. The *algorithm,* or high-level plan of attack.
2. The *high-level language* in which the user writes a program for the computer.
3. The *operating system,* a program that allocates the resources of the system, using its own abstract picture of the system.
4. The *physical machine* architecture, represented by its instruction set.

The overall efficiency depends on how well the members of this stack of models are matched, that is, on how well the computational model on each level can represent the actions of its neighbor(s). Figure 4.3 sketches their relationships.

In addition to specifying the attributes of the computational models at several different levels, a design embodies a decision about the *binding time,* that is, the time at which the details on all the different levels are completely determined and consistent with each other. The algorithm is mapped to successively lower levels until the action of the hardware is completely specified. For example, one step may be a compiler program that translates a high-level language expression like

A = B + C

into a sequence like

LD 1,B (load B from memory into register 1)

LD 2,C (load C from memory into register 2)

ADD 3,1,2 (add registers 1 and 2 and put result into register 3)

ST 3,A (store register 3's contents into variable A's address in memory).

Nitty-gritty decisions like variable A's memory address are made by the compiler and the loader programs. In other words, the final mapping decisions in this example become *bound* at compile time, before the program is executed. For a systolic array, a VLSI chip that performs one algorithm (matrix multipli-

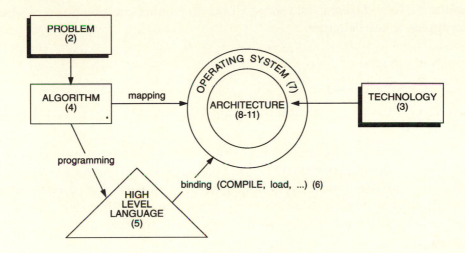

Figure 4.3   Key elements of a computing system and their interrelationships (after [75]). *Algorithm, language, operating system, and hardware architecture each have their computational model. (Numbers in parentheses denote corresponding chapters.)*

cation, say), this binding occurs at design time. The range of times at which binding occurs in the approaches listed in Figure 1.1 follows:

Binding Times

1. Hardware design (systolic arrays)
2. Compilation (Cosmic Cube, GF-11, CEDAR)
3. Program loading
4. Machine reconfiguration (TRAC, CHiP, PASM)
5. Program execution (ULTRA, RP3)

The greatest efficiency is obtained at the top of this list, and the greatest versatility at the bottom.

   The three boxed lists above (computational model, hierarchical levels, binding times) make for a large design space with many choices for a parallel computer. We discussed the key choices in an intuitive way in Chapter 1.

We will now cover some of the same ground in a more formal way, as we tie together several different but related works on parallel computational models that appear in the literature.

4.1.2 Classifications

SIMD/MIMD

The most widely used classification of parallel computational models is the simple one proposed by Flynn [174], who viewed the von Neumann model as a Single stream of Instructions controlling a Single stream of Data (SISD). One can take a step toward parallelism by introducing Multiple Data streams (SIMD), and a second step by adding Multiple Instruction streams (MIMD) (Figure 4.4).

The classic example of a parallel SIMD computer is the ILLIAC-IV, with a number of identical processing elements each receiving the same broadcast instruction to be performed on their own data item. This is the simplest conceptual model of a vector or array processor. It is faster than the SISD model in two ways: it avoids a separate instruction fetch for each data item, and the execution of the data items is done in parallel. However, providing multiple complete processing elements is relatively expensive, and the Cray-1 and many other vector and array processors use a cost-saving engineering approximation to the above model, involving extra registers and special pipelined hardware built into a single serial processor. Fetching a separate instruction for each data item is still avoided, but the data items are executed in overlapped rather than fully parallel fashion (see Figure 9.3 on page 418 and Figure 9.4 on page 419). Examples of such pipelined vector processors are discussed beginning on page 423. The trade-off is that the maximum speedup in such a pipelined design is the number of pipeline stages, which tends to be less than ten, whereas the maximum speedup in a parallel machine is the number of processing elements. At a more abstract level, however, removed from performance considerations, both can be viewed as a single stream of instructions controlling multiple streams of data, and we shall use the terms *parallel SIMD* and *pipelined SIMD* when a distinction is needed.

The majority of current research projects [19] are aimed at MIMD, in which each constituent processor has its own program acting on its own data. As we said in Chapter 1, SIMD designs offer simpler synchronization: the processors are kept in lockstep by the broadcast instructions. Since they need not store their own programs, the processors can be smaller and more numerous. But

		Number of Data Streams	
		Single	Multiple
Number of Instruction Streams	Single	SISD (von Neumann)	SIMD (vector, array)
	Multiple	MISD (pipeline?)	MIMD (multiple micros)

Figure 4.4   First steps beyond serial processing: Flynn's classification [174].

MIMD is seen as a more general design capable of performing well over a broader range of applications. Chapter 10 is devoted to MIMD parallel computers.

Flynn's fourth category is MISD, or Multiple Instruction streams controlling a Single Data stream. The conventional view is that such a machine has not yet appeared, although there is also a view that pipelined vector processors belong in this category, rather than SIMD as we have classified them.

Classification by Execution Streams

Flynn's simple taxonomy has been enlarged in several different ways. As shown in Figure 4.5 on page 144, Kuck [300] replaces data streams with execution streams, and then considers scalar and array instruction streams as well as scalar and array execution streams, for a total of 16 categories vs. Flynn's 4. Multiple data streams could still wind up being executed by hardware with only a single execution stream, say, by multiprogramming, and so Kuck's categorization gives more of a description at the hardware level, whereas Flynn's taxonomy is more at the level of the architecture or the instruction set. In Flynn's view, for example, ILLIAC-IV is classified as SIMD, with multiple streams of scalar data. Kuck, on the other hand, regards ILLIAC-IV as treating a *single* data stream where the data are in the form of arrays, corresponding to the SISSEA category. Although Flynn would categorize both the Ultracomputer and the Cray X-MP as MIMD, Kuck would use separate categories of MISMES and MISMEA, since the Ultracomputer processing elements have scalar instruction sets, whereas the Cray includes array instructions. Kuck's taxonomy is more detailed, but Flynn's is more widely used.

Instruction Stream number and type	Execution Stream number and type			
	Single, Scalar	Single, Array	Multiple, Scalar	Multiple, Array
Single, Scalar	SISSES	SISSEA		
Single, Array		SIASEA		
Multiple, Scalar			MISMES	MISMEA
Multiple, Array				

Figure 4.5   Kuck's classification of parallel architectures [*300*].

Data and Control Mechanisms in MIMD

Treleaven [441] classified MIMD designs further, as shown in Figure 4.6. The data mechanism was divided into shared-memory (von Neumann-like) and private-memory (message-passing) approaches, and four decreasingly explicit control mechanisms were listed; Figure 4.1 on page 136 illustrates three: an operation can be triggered by the arrival of an instruction to do so, a demand for an operation's result, or arrival of the data needed by an operation.

CONTROL MECHANISM	DATA MECHANISM	
	SHARED MEMORY	PRIVATE MEMORY (message passing)
Control driven	von Neumann	Communicating processes
Pattern driven	Logic	Actors
Demand driven	Graph reduction	String reduction
Data driven	Dataflow with I–structure	Dataflow

Less explicit control

Figure 4.6   Treleaven's (slightly modified) classification of MIMD architectures by control and data mechanism [*441*].

```
                           LEVEL, CONTROL MODEL
                          (s = serial, p = parallel)
                        Task     Process    Instruction

        Cray X-MP        s         p           p
        Ultracomputer    p         -           s
        Cedar            p         p           s
```

Figure 4.7　Classification of shared-memory MIMD designs *according to the control mechanism used at several levels of program granularity* [*186*].

In that sense, control-driven designs like the Ultracomputer, RP3, Cosmic Cube, and Cedar are closest to von Neumann's, while dataflow machines are furthest.

One (not universally accepted) comparison of dataflow and reduction holds that these are attempts to improve the computational model at two different levels. Dataflow starts at the machine level and says, "Look at these instructions forever passing data back and forth to the memory. Why can't the data flow directly (and, by the way, in parallel) from instruction to instruction as needed?" (Dataflow *language* work came afterwards.) The reduction model, on the other hand, started at the user (language) level by saying, "Look at this poor programmer's life. How can we improve it? Functional Programming is better, so let's eliminate side effects." It turns out this approach needs lazy evaluation or a demand-driven model, which led to the work on reduction architectures. In this view, then, dataflow was hardware-driven, and reduction was language-driven.

Multiple Levels of Parallelism

Gajski and Peir [186] take Treleaven's shared-memory MIMD category and subdivide it according to the granularity of the parallelism. They consider parallelism at the level of *tasks, processes,* and *instructions.* In their terms, the overall job of executing a program consists of a collection of tasks, which are units of scheduling that can be assigned to one or more PEs. A process is part of a task and is done on only one PE. Their categorization of three different architectures is shown in Figure 4.7.

Summary

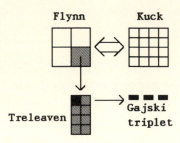

The sketch at left summarizes these four categorizations of parallel computational models: Flynn's and Kuck's both cover the entire design space, with Kuck's being more detailed but Flynn's being more popular. Treleaven's looks at the control and data mechanisms of MIMD in more detail, and Gajski and Peirs's looks in still more detail at the hierarchy of control mechanisms in one of Treleaven's categories, control-driven shared-memory MIMD.

In addition to the computational model parameters that we have covered so far, a number of other decisions are involved in the design of a parallel computer. We have touched on these already in Chapter 1. They include a range of communication hardware (Chapter 8), task scheduling and synchronization mechanisms (Chapter 7), and programming environments (page 30 and chapters 5 and 6). All of these contribute to the diversity of parallel approaches.

4.1.3 Essential Constructs for Parallel Execution

The basic idea behind parallel processing is that some kind of a job is going to be divided up and parceled out to form a cooperative effort. If the workers are intelligent human beings, it may suffice to say as little as, "I'll make the salad while you set the table", or "I'll wash the dishes while one of you dries and the other puts away", or the "Stroke, stroke, stroke, ..." heard by the crew rowing a racing shell.[50] In our case, however, the cooperating participants are computers, and the coordination must be much more carefully planned and programmed. Somehow, the programmer's wishes must be translated into a productive work schedule or script for each participant. Software constructs to fill this need are discussed next. Depending on the scenario, these constructs may be used by the applications programmer (the user), the compiler writer, or the operating system.

To put it more formally [191], in order to execute a parallel program, there must be a way to:

---

[50] These examples correspond, respectively, to MIMD, MISD/pipeline, and SIMD parallelism.

1. *Define* a set of subtasks to be executed in parallel.
2. *Start and stop* their execution.
3. *Coordinate* and specify their interaction while they are executing.

These actions call for certain new constructs, which must either appear in the programmer's language or be inserted into the program automatically by a compiler or other language processor. The constructs used will depend on the nature of the subtasks and the computational model being used. Examples that we shall cover include parbegin, fork/join, doall, process declarations, sequence control and access control, test-and-set, fetch-and-add, semaphores, barriers, blocking vs. nonblocking primitives, send/receive, rendezvous, and remote procedure calls.

In addition to *execution* control, a parallel program's success can depend on how well the *data*[51] is partitioned, especially for a distributed-memory computer, but also for a NUMA (nonuniform memory access) shared-memory design. Tools for data partitioning are beginning to appear in parallel programming environments, and we touch on this subject in the next chapter, "Languages and Programming Environments".

Defining (Identifying and Specifying) Parallel Subtasks

In its simplest form, a program for a von Neumann computer is composed of a number of one-line statements that are executed one after another [367].[52] There are, however, ways to depart from strictly linear sequencing and write more interesting programs. Within the low-level program construct world of statements, the departure can be done with a branch statement, which causes a jump to some other part of the program, either unconditionally, as in the case of goto, or conditionally, as in the case of if...then...else. A looping control statement such as for...do corresponds to the slightly higher-level program concept of the "do loop", which is used as a convenient shorthand notation for the execution of groups of nearly identical statements. And finally there are a variety of ways to define and initiate a subprogram (such as a procedure or subroutine) that may be used more than once by the main program. The behavior and protocol of these subprograms are a large part of what distinguishes one programming language from another [367].

The ideas of sequencing, control flow, repetition, and abstraction that underlie the constructs above are also found in the parallel environment:

---

[51] Wirth did say *Algorithms + Data Structures = Programs* [460].
[52] At this stage of the chapter we ignore other kinds of executable and nonexecutable statements.

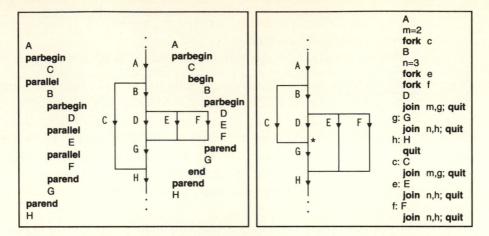

Figure 4.8   Two ways to control parallel execution: parbegin/parend *and* **fork/join.** *A, B, C, etc., are executable statements.*
LEFT: Two slightly different conventions for **parbegin/parend** *accomplishing the same result. In the leftmost code,* **parbegin/parend** *begins/ends concurrent execution of statements separated by the* **parallel** *construct, consistent with Figure 5.7 on page 245. In the other case, all statements between* **parbegin/parend** *pairs are executed concurrently unless* **begin/end** *constructs are used to identify sequential portions.*
RIGHT: A **fork/join** *example. In one indivisible operation,* **join** *m, g subtracts 1 from m and goes to g if the new m=0. The asterisk (*) marks the joining of two processes spawned by different forks;* **parbegin/parend** *cannot do this.* **Fork/join** *is more powerful but less structured and harder to understand. (To see how* **fork/join** *is more powerful, you are invited to implement the left picture with* **fork/join** *and convince yourself that the right picture cannot be implemented with* **parbegin/parend**.)*

- The implicit statement-after-statement regime can be altered by the parbegin/parend pair of control words, which can be used to bracket (precede and follow) a set of statements that are thereby designated for concurrent execution, as shown in Figure 4.8. Parbegin is also called `cobegin` and is written as `and` and comma (`,`) in several languages, including ALGOL68 and CSP.

- The branching to one *or* another part of a program is expanded to allow activation of one *and* another part of a program by the fork half of the fork/join pair of statements [27] (see Figure 4.1 on page 136). Variants of fork and join appear in some versions of the PL/1 language and in the UNIX operating system.

- The doall family, which includes `forall` (page 49) and others, is based on the looping construct of sequential languages and is used as a shorthand notation to designate a block of nearly identical statements to be executed in parallel.

- By relaxing the "copy rule" interpretation (page 152) of sequential sub-programs sufficiently, similar high-level program components known variously as processes, tasks, procedures, subroutines, or subprograms can be declared for parallel execution. They appear in PL/1, Concurrent Pascal, and Ada, among others [367].

These constructs differ in the granularity of the parallelism with which they deal and in the overhead cost that they engender, but all are outgrowths of control and program structures that exist in sequential programs.

A key feature missing from some of the earlier of these constructs, such as fork/join, was the existence of separate mechanisms for *identifying* and *executing* parallel subtasks. It's important to identify the maximum potential parallelism, but we need the freedom to select the amount of parallelism to use based on the specific hardware configuration being used (number of processors available) and on run-time conditions. This subject is discussed further in the next section.

Starting and Stopping Parallel Execution

Computing mirrors other aspects of life in that *starting* parallel tasks is easier than stopping them, and, as we shall see in the next section, coordinating them is yet more demanding. In this section, we elaborate on the four ways introduced in the last section to start and stop parallel activities.

Fork and Join

Although we started our list on page 147 with parbegin/parend, it is the fork/join pair[53] of statements [104] that represents the most primitive of the mechanisms and that may be used to implement parbegin and other higher-level constructs. Fork is conceptually very simple; it is like a goto with the branch both taken and not taken. That is, the original process proceeds to the next instruction and, simultaneously, a new process is created and begins executing at the branch target (some later implementations allow multiple targets). This allows an additional sequence of execution to start anywhere in the program (see Figure 4.8 on page 148). However, creating a new process, requiring hundreds or thousands of instructions, is not cheap.[54]

---

[53] A trio, actually: fork, join, and *quit*. Quit terminates a process. Strictly speaking, when we mention stopping parallel execution with join, we mean join and quit.

[54] For example, a UNIX fork on a Sequent Balance multiprocessor running Dynix required a few tens of thousands of instructions. An implementation in Mach using copy-on-write took

Join is also conceptually simple, but its use is a little more subtle. The meaning of join *m,g* is that, in one indivisible operation, join subtracts 1 from *m* (which is normally a shared variable) and does one of the following:

- Goes to the statement labeled *g* if the new *m*=0.
- Executes the statement that follows join (usually `quit,` which terminates execution), otherwise.

However, making join work in concert with fork as shown in Figure 4.8 is entirely the programmer's responsibility. There is nothing automatic about the way that the three parallel paths spawned at the same time were reunited. The programmer had to ensure that the two forks causing the three-way split were preceded by a statement that assigned the value 3 to the shared variable *n*, and then had to ensure correct placement of the three joins that read *n*. As the example shows, join can be used to join processes formed by (any) different forks.

Since forks can appear in loops and conditionals and thus create arbitrary numbers of parallel activities, and since join can join any of these processes to each other, we have a very flexible and powerful way to (control) start and stop parallel activities. But it is also a very dangerous process, with even more potential than goto for writing unstructured, error-prone, hard-to-understand, "spaghetti" code.

Parbegin

The parbegin/parend statements are sometimes presented as less powerful and versatile versions of fork/join (see Figure 4.8) because they can only represent properly nested process flow graphs—all the children of one spawn must eventually be joined by the same join, or, to put it another way, "What parbegins must parend". However, a more correct view is that these are higher-level constructs that impose some discipline on the wild and wooly fork/join. Even a quick look at Figure 4.8 reveals the greater structure and clarity of parbegin.

Unlike fork/join, parbegin/parend does allow the identification and execution of parallelism to be separated. The meaning of the statements can be interpreted and implemented in several ways. The simplest interpretation is that the execution of every statement enclosed between the parbegin and parend is to start at the same time, but implementations are also possible that

---

about 3000 instructions. Mach also offers "lightweight processes", called *threads,* that do not carry the full state of a UNIX process. Creating a thread costs 375 instructions. Similar costs occur for process termination. (See page 344 for more detail.)

allow the compiler to choose how many of the eligible statements should actually be executed concurrently, based on the hardware configuration and run-time situation. For example, the dataflow language VAL has a construct called FORALL that allows the programmer to identify candidates for parallel execution, but does not *force* such execution. As mentioned, parbegin is also called cobegin, and is written as and and comma (,) in several languages, including ALGOL68 and CSP [27].

Doall

Doall and its clones forall, pardo, doacross,[55] and others can be thought of as a parbegin in which the statements eligible for parallel execution appear inside a loop construct that allows the programmer to use an index mechanism to identify the eligible statements rather than writing each one out explicitly. But note a significant difference between doall and parbegin: the degree of parallelism that comes from a parbegin-parend block, namely, one more than the number of statements between a parbegin and a parend, is a *static* quantity, known before the program is compiled or executed. By contrast, the degree of parallelism in a doall is a *dynamic* quantity known with certainty only at run time, because the number of (parallel) loop executions can depend on some parameter that is computed during program execution. Thus, doall is usually implemented with fork/join, not parbegin/parend.

Put another way, doall does to loop iterations what parbegin does to individual statements. This construct is especially useful for vector and matrix operations and deserves mention because such loops appear so frequently in FORTRAN and other language programs for scientific computation, like the weather code discussed on page 48. A small example is shown pictorially in Figure 5.2 on page 226. Replacing foreach with forall in that figure leads to the parallel execution shown.

In general, it is not an easy task to establish that the parallelization of the loops portrayed in Figure 5.2 is a safe thing to do, especially when trying to convert existing serial programs for parallel execution, that is, when trying to retrofit parallelism into old sequential code. For example, one loop iteration may need a result produced by a previous iteration, in which case their sequence *is* important. The whole program must be examined to see where else and how the variables in the loop are used. This subject of *dependency anal-*

---

55 Sequent's doacross [350] is identical to our doall and is used for completely independent loop iterations. By contrast, the doacross in Cedar (page 611) is somewhat different and allows dependent loop iterations to be executed in "overlapped parallel" (pipelined) fashion. See reference [472] for more details.

ysis is treated in more detail in Chapter 6. For the moment, we assume that somehow the programmer knows that the parallel execution shown in Figure 5.2 is safe.

Subprogram, Task, Process Declarations

Parallel programs can also be constructed using higher-level building blocks than the ones discussed so far, by analogy with the way in which we mentally structure our sequential programs into hierarchies: a main program may call various subprograms, which may in turn call other subprograms, and so on. This procedure saves rewriting frequently used code, and also makes the program easier to construct, understand, and modify/maintain. These advantages are also the motivation for subprograms whose declarations can state that they may be executed concurrently [27], [182]. As with the sequential case, there are questions about the behavior of these subprograms. We shall address these shortly.

Pratt [367] gives a very nice discussion of how progressive relaxation of the constraints on a sequential subprogram's behavior eventually leads to parallel processes (parallel executions of subprograms). The strictest interpretation is the "copy rule", which assumes that the effect of a subprogram CALL statement is to replace itself with the body of the subprogram (with suitable substitutions for parameters and conflicting identifiers). Among the implications of this rule are the following:

1. Subprograms cannot be recursive.
2. Subprograms must execute completely at each call.
3. The called and calling programs do not execute at the same time

A subprogram cannot be *recursive* under this interpretation; that is, it cannot call itself a finite number of times, because the substitution of subprogram body for subprogram call would be unending (think about it). As it happens, COBOL and FORTRAN are the only major languages that use the copy rule view of subprograms. LISP in particular is unthinkable without recursion, partly because the basic LISP operation is list manipulation. FORTRAN is geared toward manipulating arrays.

The copy rule also implies that subprograms must execute completely at each call (at which point the calling program takes back the control that is its prerogative). Relaxing the requirement of complete execution leads to *coroutines,* in which the calling and called program have a *symmetric* relationship and swap control back and forth without either clearly controlling the other. However, *only one can be executing at a time.* Relaxing this "single execution sequence" assumption finally leads to parallel *processes* (sometimes called *tasks*) of the type shown in Figure 4.10 on page 157 and Figure 4.12 on page 167.

The notion of parallel subprograms (Figure 4.9 on page 154) also raises important questions about their behavior. The answers differentiate parallel languages somewhat as in copy-rule interpretations differentiate sequential languages. The first question is whether multiple subprogram instantiations are allowed. If they are not, then a collection of parallel task declarations is equivalent to a single `parbegin` of these tasks. If multiple instantiations *are* allowed, the question is whether the instantiation (task creation) should be static or dynamic, that is, done before or during program execution. Gehani [188] discusses the trade-offs involved and also the details of Ada's mechanisms. Concurrent Pascal and Modula are two languages with static task creation (a fixed number of tasks during program execution), whereas PL/1, Ada, and PLITS allow tasks to be created dynamically (a variable number of tasks during program execution).

In the static case, it is necessary to anticipate the maximum possible number of tasks that will be needed, to create them, and to allocate resources for them at the beginning of the program. This requirement probably creates inefficiencies in CPU and memory usage. On the other hand, dynamic task creation complicates the language and its implementation and requires additional run-time support, such as a more complicated memory-allocation scheme.

Coordinating Parallel Execution

We prefer the word *coordination* rather than *synchronization* because the meaning of the latter has become somewhat fuzzy in the literature. Also, synchronization is needed because of communication, but communication is used for synchronization, and the word *coordination* simply encapsulates all of this without worrying about where the boundaries are. This subject is discussed here and also on page 355 in Chapter 7.

Communication—Shared Memory and Message Passing

In order to make progress, the cooperating activities of a joint effort must in general be able to *communicate* useful results to each other. For example, in the parallelized version of the NASA weather code on page 49, each concurrent activity (originally a loop iterate) accesses some shared variables, computes a value based on them, and assigns this value to another shared variable, thereby making the results of its work available to another concurrent activity. This process is an example of communication via *shared memory*, a natural

Figure 4.9   A tree of parallel subprogram activations *during execution, showing dynamic process creation in PL/1 [367]. The six processes executing at the time indicated by the dashed line could each be an instantiation or activation of the same subprogram, of six different subprograms, or some mixture of multiple and single activations. Recursion is allowed. The problem with PL/1 for parallel programs is that it lacks one of the three essential features we listed on page 146. It has the ability to define and start/stop parallel tasks, but lacks convenient features for their coordination. Semaphores are nearly impossible (test-and-set is not available to the PL/1 programmer), and parallel programs tend to turn into unstructured "spaghetti" code. PL/1 was one of the earliest languages with features for parallel execution, but those are now mainly of historical interest.*

extension of the von Neumann model's globally available memory (see page 189).

The alternative communication mechanism for parallel processes is *message passing*. Languages that support message passing transfer data items from one task to another using some version of the SEND and RECEIVE commands introduced in CSP (page 247). One example, beginning on page 163, is the rendezvous mechanism of Ada, a language that supports both shared memory and message passing.   A parallel language based on CSP message passing is Occam (page 247).

An example written in standard C, which does *not* have special message-passing constructs, is the n-body program for the Cosmic Cube, shown in Figure 10.4 on page 486.   This program uses a custom-written library of routines, some of which handle the sending and receiving of messages from one processor to another.   More systematic/portable ways of adding such inter-processor communication capability to existing serial languages include Remote Procedure Calls (p. 166), Express (page 250), Parallel Virtual Machines (page 252), and Linda (page 253).

Synchronizing Concurrent Activities—Sequence Control, Access Control

Synchronization is often necessary when processes communicate.   As Andrews and Schneider write,

> The time required to execute a process can be unpredictable.   Yet, to communicate, one process must perform some action that the other detects—an action such as setting the value of a variable or sending a message.   This only works if the events "perform an action" and "detect an action" are constrained to happen in that order.   Thus, one can view synchronization as a set of constraints on the ordering of events. [Synchronization mechanisms are used] to delay execution of a process in order to satisfy such constraints [27].

This synchronization is intended to enable *cooperation,* and we shall use the name *sequence control* for this constraining of events to happen in the right order.   Other names for this are *condition synchronization*[27] and *activity synchronization*[188] .

Cooperating activities may also in general *compete* for some shared resource.   Consider, for example, a shared data object that may be manipulated by operations implemented as sequences of statements.   If two processes concurrently perform such operations on the same data object, then one might be exposed to intermediate values produced by the other, and unintended results could occur (see Figure 4.10 on page 157).   This concurrent performance brings about the need for a second type of synchronization that we shall call *access control*.   This type of synchronization is often called *mutual exclusion* [27], although it is more proper to regard mutual exclusion as one (rather severe) example of access control.[56] Figure 4.10 on page 157 shows an example in which Dijkstra's famous "semaphores"[145] [390] are used to implement

---

[56]   Readers/writers is one less severe example.

mutual exclusion in a *critical section* of code, that is, to control the access to a section of code in such a way that only one competing process may enter at a time.[57] This method of access control can introduce extensive delays for large numbers of competing processes, and we shall soon discuss alternate methods. For now, however, let us summarize by saying that *interaction among parallel processes takes the form of cooperation and competition; this situation leads to the need for two kinds of coordination, namely, sequence control and access control.*

This coordination may be achieved by means of hardware or software, depending on the unit or *level* of parallelism. As Woodward [461] puts it, software coordination is required whenever the "unit of parallelism" (what we call the *level of parallelism*) is at a higher level than that at which the hardware operates. With a parallel vector or array processor, the parallelism is achieved at the same level as the operation of the hardware (i.e., arithmetic functions), so software synchronization is not required. In such SIMD machines (like the ILLIAC-IV, MPP, or DAP, discussed in Chapter 9), one has

> many small arithmetic processors attached to a host computer. The arithmetic processors are synchronised by virtue of being clocked by a common timing signal. That is, while parallel operation is being utilised, all the arithmetic processors are performing their steps at the same rate and the host processor is waiting at the hardware level for their operation to cease. Viewed in another way, we may say that synchronisation at the software level is not required since there is only a single program counter (that of the host computer) within the system [461].

On the other hand, a multiprocessor providing parallelism among sections of a program requires software coordination (possibly aided by hardware primitives), since the unit of parallelism consists of many (hardware) instructions. The trade-off is that, whereas SIMD limits the form of concurrency, MIMD pays for its added generality with run-time overhead. We will next discuss the constructs used for these two kinds of coordination.

Synchronization in Shared-Memory Computation

Most of our synchronization constructs and primitives (semaphores, test-and-set, etc.) came from work on operating systems, an area where the von Neumann model's strictly sequential rules were bent a little to allow a small

---

[57] A *critical section* can only be executed by one process at a time; *multiple* critical sections protected by the *same* semaphore may not be interleaved, i.e., they are *atomic* with respect to each other.

Figure 4.10　*Illustration of one need for synchronization*: *access control among two processes competing for a shared resource, namely a bank account record. Bonnie and Clyde go to separate cash-dispensing machines and try to make two withdrawals whose sum exceeds the $1000 balance in their joint account. The scheme is foiled by the use of semaphores to create the mutual exclusion form of access control, which guarantees that only one process at a time may enter the critical cash-dispensing section of the program. This example is discussed in the text.*

amount of concurrency, for example, among computing, printing, and disk access (I/O) operations. The fact that this concurrency existed among a few large operations is reflected in the nature of these synchronization primitives and makes most of them unsuitable for coordinating large numbers of smaller processes, as we shall see.

Access control was most often implemented as mutual exclusion; that is, a critical section of code subject to access by multiple processes was preceded and followed by carefully constructed sections of code that usually used shared variables to implement an "entry protocol" and "exit protocol" that ensured that only one process at a time could use the critical section, as in the example of Figure 4.10. Other properties of interest in access-method protocols are, in order of increasing difficulty, *absence of deadlock* and *fairness*. Deadlock occurs when processes put each other in a state in which they are waiting for events that will never occur; fairness means no process must wait forever.

Test-and-Set: The *coordination* of parallel processes, like their *creation,* can be carried out by low-level primitives at the machine-instruction level. One everyday example in a shared-memory environment is shown in Figure 4.10 on page 157. The example shows the test-and-set instruction being used to implement semaphores that enforce a one-at-a-time *mutual exclusion* rule during that phase of a cash-issuing terminal's program when the bank account record (a shared data object) is being accessed. This procedure is done in order to prevent two (incorrect) simultaneous withdrawals from the same account.

A key feature is the indivisible nature of the test-and-set (TS) instruction. In one indivisible step, TS(S) reads the value of the binary shared variable S and sets its new value to 1. How will this read information be used in a situation with many processes competing? Almost surely to tell one process to go ahead and all the others to halt. Thus, test-and-set is a *blocking* synchronization primitive in the sense that its use is to block every process but one from doing something. Were this primitive not indivisible, the second "test" could begin before the first "set" was made, S could be found to be zero in both cases, and neither machine would branch to L. Then both transactions could be authorized, both would dispense $900, both would say that the final balance should be $100, and the bank would lose $900. With an indivisible TS, however, one of the tests finds that $S = 1$ and, in this implementation, must keep repeating the test or *busy-waiting* at P until the first process leaves the critical section and resets S to zero at V.[58]

There are many other such examples that arise in a program when several processes might asynchronously change the contents of a common data area. Without proper protection, the updated area may not, in general, contain the correct changes. Put another way, a process entering such a critical region of code before a previous process has left it may be exposed to unintended

---

[58] .Note that busy-waiting (also called *spin-waiting* or *spinning*) is like being put on hold—your goal is delayed, *and* you can't do anything else in the meantime. The alternative for delaying a process is task-switching—the process is put on a queue, but at least the processor can do something else in the meantime. The cost is the overhead associated with a task switch. This is like saying that you don't want to hold but rather want the other party to call you back, or that you will call again. You have to spell your name and leave your number, or you have to redial, but you can do your other chores in the meantime. Real task-switching overheads can be substantial, unless special hardware is provided (see page 566).

intermediate results. The important thing is to make the effect of simultaneous accesses be the same as if they had arrived in some unspecified but legitimate sequential order. This requirement is known as the *serialization principle* and is widely used in database management systems [160]. Figure 4.10 shows this serialization being achieved through the use of mutual exclusion and critical sections. As we shall see when we discuss *fetch-and-add,* there are also *parallel* ways to satisfy the serialization principle without using mutual exclusion and critical sections.

Semaphores: The problem with using only low-level primitives like test-and-set, compare-and-swap, and so forth, for mutual exclusion is that their use places a burden on the programmer to create protocols for entering and leaving the critical region in such a way that not only mutual exclusion but also freedom from deadlock and fairness are ensured. Such protocols can be hard to design, understand, and prove correct. Many near misses are described in the literature [390].

To provide a candidate for a versatile, standard protocol, Dijkstra [145] developed the concept of semaphores and a pair of higher-level primitives that come with at least mutual exclusion and freedom from deadlock guaranteed (many implementations also provide fairness). These primitives, designated *P* and *V*, operate on non-negative integer variables called semaphores. Let *S* be a semaphore variable. Then the *P* and *V* operations are defined as follows:

P(S): If $S=0$, the process invoking the *P* operation is delayed[59] until *S* is positive. If, on the other hand, *S* is found positive, it is decreased by 1 and the invoking process is allowed to continue. The successful testing and decrementing of *S* is an indivisible operation.

V(S): *S* is increased by 1 in a single indivisible action.

In other words, *P(S) delays and V(S) resets*. In either case, the fetch, increment or decrement, and store cannot be interrupted, and *S* cannot be accessed by another process during the operation.

A *binary* semaphore results when the variable *S* is allowed to take on only the values 0 and 1. If *S* is initially set at 1, the sequence

$$P(S); \text{ critical section}; V(S)$$

will enforce mutual exclusion on the critical section. This example is shown in Figure 4.10 on page 157. If *S* is allowed to have additional values, then P

---

[59] By using busy-waiting or else by task-switching (see Figure 4.10 on page 157).

and V can be used for condition synchronization as well. For example, allocation of *n* resources can be controlled by setting the initial value of *S* at *n*. Such a semaphore is called a *counting* semaphore and is useful for queues (see pages 586–588 for examples implemented using fetch-and-add).

Barriers: Whereas semaphores are used primarily for access control, that is, to resolve competition among parallel processors, *barrier synchronization* is used for *sequence control,* that is, to ensure correct timing among cooperating processes. An example of this was given in Figure 2.6 on page 49, which shows the weather code broken into three sets of `forall ... in parallel` loops. Although each of the three forall loops performs computations at the same set of grid points, *none* of the parallel computations in the third loop should begin before the last computation in the second loop is completed; the second and first loops are similarly related. This sequencing requirement is why there are three loops instead of just one. A synchronization point of this kind, which no process may pass until it has been reached by all the others, was named a *barrier* by Jordan [269], who also discussed economies of implementation.

A straightforward way to implement the `forall` and `end sync` that begin and end the parallel execution within each set of loops is to use fork and join, as we said before. However, their use results in very time-consuming barriers, since all but one of the processes from the first set of loops must be killed, and then an equal number must be spawned. First of all, fork and join spawn and terminate one process at a time, and second, each fork-join pair takes hundreds or thousands of instructions.

A better method in this case is not to kill any process at the end of the first set of loops, but instead to have it repeatedly check a shared variable that will eventually signal that the last process has completed its first stage, after which any process checking the shared variable may proceed to its next stage of computation; that is, it may pass the barrier.

Jordan's paper gives a set of primitives that, if supported by the proper hardware, allows barrier synchronization to be performed in a time independent of, or at most logarithmically dependent on, the number of processors. An implementation based on fetch-and-add with message combining is given on page 484. Both of these avoid the operating system overhead usually associated with creating and terminating processes (see page 344).

The cost of a barrier (i.e., its effect on a program's execution time) depends on a number of factors, including the variation in how long processes take to execute. In examples like the weather code on page 49 and the n-body problem on page 487, this variation can be expected to be small. However, in barrier synchronization, all the processes must wait for the slowest process, and if the barrier is implemented using busy-waiting rather than task-switching, then each process at a barrier is tying up a PE and keeping it from doing other useful work in the meantime. If the slowest process takes much longer than the average, then most of the PEs are idle most of the time. By contrast, killing a process as with an endall or join does eventually free the PE.

Furthermore, deadlock occurs at a busy-waiting barrier if the number of processes exceeds the number of PEs. A task-switching implementation can prevent this deadlock, but it usually involves the operating system and overheads that are comparable to those of spawning and terminating processes.[60] One solution is a hybrid approach that busy-waits for some period of time and then performs a task-switch.

In summary, barrier synchronization can be advantageous when all the processes being synchronized are short and/or take about the same time to execute. A quantitative estimate of this advantage is complicated and involves many of the issues discussed in Chapter 7.

Blocking vs. Nonblocking primitives: As Andrews and Schneider [27] point out, semaphores are not without their disadvantages. They are rather unstructured, and it is the programmer's responsibility to start each critical section with a P, end it with a V, and make sure that the correct semaphore is being read in each case. Mistakes are easy to make, especially when multiple semaphores are needed. Furthermore, both access control and sequence control are being programmed using the same primitives. Thus, it is hard to identify the purpose of a given P or V. These difficulties have led to higher-level synchronization mechanisms such as *conditional critical regions, monitors* (page 247), and *path expressions* [27]. However, all of these mechanisms are still *blocking* synchronization mechanisms, because the access to the shared variable involved itself involves mutual exclusion: the shared variable that determines whether a process is available can be tested by only one process at a time. Thus, *the test itself constitutes a small critical section.* For few and/or large processes, this critical section may not be a problem, but for a large number of medium-sized processes, it can lead to a situation in which most of the processes are waiting to perform their tests, rather than doing useful work [202]. The significance of the fetch-and-add synchronization primitive discussed below is that it can, in conjunction with an interconnection network that can *combine* requests headed for the same memory location, allow 500 or more processors to access the shared variable simultaneously and quickly

---

60 We are using *task* and *process* as synonyms here.

obtain individualized results; this primitive can be used to obtain critical-section-free, nonblocking coordination among large numbers of parallel processes.

Fetch-and-Add: *Fetch-and-add* is a simple yet very effective multiprocessor coordination operation that permits highly concurrent execution of operating system primitives and application programs.   Superficially, its definition resembles that of test-and-set.   If we adopt the convention that statements enclosed within braces, { and }, are to be executed *indivisibly,* then test-and-set and fetch-and-add may both be written as value-returning procedure (i.e., functions with side effects) acting on a shared variable S (Boolean for test-and-set, integer for fetch-and-add), as shown below.[61]

test-and-set(S)	**fetch-and-add**(S,P)
{ Temp $\leftarrow$ S	{ Temp $\leftarrow$ S
S $\leftarrow$ 1 }	S $\leftarrow$ S + P }
return Temp	return Temp

However, there is a fundamental difference: In response to n multiple simultaneous accesses, test-and-set yields at most one go-ahead; fetch-and-add hands out n different numbers.   If P was the same for each accessing process, the numbers given out would each differ by P.   That is, the effect of n simultaneous accesses is the same as if they had occurred in some (unspecified) serial order.   This effect satisfies the *serialization principle* discussed on page 159.   Hardware has been developed [63] to complete simultaneous fetch-and-adds in essentially the same time as one memory access (see page 572).   Thus, instead of lining up, as in the case of test-and-set, each process is given a unique number and can go on with its business.

   Figure 4.11 on page 164 shows the results of using fetch-and-add to implement parallel access to a queue, a data structure that plays an important role in operating systems and in many algorithms.   In the example shown, the capability to perform concurrent fetch-and-add operations on the shared variable S is provided via the *paracomputer* model,[62] an idealized parallel processor in which every processing element can access a shared-memory cell in one cycle.   In particular, the processors can all gang up on one memory location.   In practice, this capability is approximated by an interconnection network that allows combining of requests to the same memory location [202].

---

[61]   Note that test-and-set(S) is identical to *fetch-and-OR*(S,1).

[62]   More precisely, the concurrent-read, concurrent-write PRAM defined in this chapter.

Naturally, this capability does not come for free. The combining feature in the Ultracomputer switch [143] accounts for a third of the pins and half of the gates.

Synchronization in Message-Passing Computation

As we said in our previous discussion of synchronization, cooperation needs sequence control, and competition necessitates access control. These requirements hold for both the shared-memory and the message-passing models. Message passing is more self-synchronizing than communication via shared variables, since a message cannot be received before it is sent. However, a message can be missed (if you start talking before I start listening, part of the message will be lost) or overwritten by another message, and shared resources other than shared variables may come into play (I/O, buffers, etc.). Message-passing protocols must deal with these problems.

In a shared-memory parallel program, the constituent parallel parts or processes communicate via *shared variables*. In message passing, the shared objects are communication *channels*.[63] A channel provides a communication path between two processes, and can be thought of as an abstraction of a physical communication link. As Andrews [26] points out, *all programming notations based on message passing provide* <u>*channels*</u> *and primitives for* <u>*sending*</u> *to and* <u>*receiving*</u> *from them.*[64]

If a channel can queue messages, that is, if the channel has storage capability, then a process can send a message without having to stop or *block* until the message is received by another process. In this case, the send operation is said to be *non-blocking*,[65] and the communication is said to be *asynchronous*.[66] Examples of asynchronous message passing in this book include Express (page 250), PVM (page 252), Linda (page 253), and the primitives used for the n-body program on page 487.

In synchronous message passing, by contrast, each channel provides a *direct* link between two processes, and the sender process delays (blocks) until the other process has received the message. The exchange of a message

---

[63] The view we take here is similar to that in the book by Gregory Andrews [26].

[64] Channels can be thought of as semaphores that carry data: send and receive are similar to V and P, respectively. In fact, if a channel contains only dataless "null" messages, then send and receive are just like V and P, with the number of queued *messages* being the value of the semaphore [26].

[65] Note that, by its nature, receive is always a blocking primitive.

[66] Sometimes *asynchronous* is reserved for (theoretical) channels with infinite capacity, and *buffered* message passing is used to denote channels with fixed capacity, where send blocks if the channel is full.

Figure 4.11 *Serial vs. concurrent queues*: simulation results showing the efficacy of fetch-and-add in concurrent access in a parallel program for radiation transport, a process in which particles are both spawned and destroyed. A queue is used to represent the pool of particles. During program execution, each processing element (PE) deletes a particle from the pool, performs some physics calculations, and inserts zero or more particles back into the pool. Semaphores were originally used to limit access to the queue to one processor at a time, but the critical sections created by this serial access limited the number of PEs that could profitably be employed to speed up the computation. Use of concurrent queue-access routines based on request-combining plus fetch-and-add (*paracomputer* simulation) restored the originally expected linear speedup [202]. This speedup bodes well for the use of concurrent queues in such critical applications as parallel operating system schedulers.

thus represents a synchronization point between the two processes. Examples are CSP (page 247), Occam (page 247), rendezvous (page 165), and remote procedure call (page 166).

As compared to asynchronous message passing, synchronous message passing has the advantage that it does not need dynamic buffer allocation, but also has the disadvantage that deadlock is more of a concern. Further examples of both types of message passing are found in Andrews [26].

Next, we discuss two synchronous message passing notations geared toward two-way communication, namely, remote procedure call (RPC) and rendezvous. Conceptually, the *send* and *receive* commands of Hoare's CSP language are sufficient to program any type of process interaction using message passing. The *remote procedure call* concept is a structured combination of these commands that provides a clean, convenient way to program client/server interactions. The Ada *rendezvous* shown in Figure 4.12 on page 167 does the same, but in a somewhat different way: the two tasks involved in a rendezvous are co-equal in that either is capable of calling the other, and then continuing onward once the rendezvous is over. By contrast, the calling program and remote procedure in an RPC have a one-sided relationship; the program can call the procedure and continue onward when the procedure returns, but not vice versa.[67] Conceptually, then, a remote procedure call is a subset or special case of rendezvous. However, there are differences in the way the two constructs are implemented and used, as we discuss below.

Rendezvous: Tasks in Ada [188] contain synchronization/communication points called *entries,* which may be *called* by other tasks. An entry call is syntactically similar to a procedure call. Coordination between two tasks occurs when the task *issuing* an entry call and the task *accepting* an entry call establish a rendezvous: For example, if the first task issues an entry call before the corresponding accept is executed by the second task, the first task is blocked. When the second task issues the accept, input parameters are passed from the first to the second, the second executes the body of the accept, output parameters are passed from the second to the first, and then both resume individual execution.[68] If instead the accept is executed before the entry call, the second task is blocked. When the entry call is subsequently executed, the same sequence of parameter passing and accept body execution is performed.[69]

The upper part of Figure 4.12 on page 167 shows such coordination happening in the ideal sequence and with minimum delay. The lower part of the figure shows the more general case, in which the delay may be longer and the order may be reversed; that is, the second task may become ready to accept the entry call before it is issued, and in either sequence there can be a long delay between the events. This delay could block further execution of the task corresponding to the first event. Such blocking is alleviated to a certain extent if the language implementation includes buffering that allows multiple outstanding entry calls and offers of acceptance.

If the first task does not wish to wait for the second task, it has the option of doing something else and trying to establish the rendezvous again later, that

---

[67] This difference is in some ways analogous to the difference between a coroutine and a procedure call on a serial machine (where there is, of course, no parallelism).

[68] By contrast, only one process (or task) continues to execute at the end of an RPC.

[69] Ada tasks can also communicate using global variables; synchronization must then be done explicitly.

is, it can *poll* the other task to see if it is ready to rendezvous. Alternately, the first task can elect to wait a finite period of time before giving up and perhaps trying again, that is, it can *time-out* [188].

Ada was designed for large tasks that involved relatively little cooperation, and the rendezvous mechanism reflects this decision: the primitives involved in entry calls each correspond to many machine instructions, and a rendezvous taking less than 1000 machine instructions was still something to brag about in 1986 [383]. Ada was not designed for fine-grain parallelism.

Remote Procedure Call

As indicated in Figure 4.13 on page 168, a remote procedure call (RPC) allows a procedure to be called on one computer and be executed on another [65]. RPCs have been widely used to implement client-server interactions in distributed computer systems [105]. One example of a client-server system is a collection of (client) workstations accessing a file server in the Network File System (NFS) from Sun Microsystems. A more everyday example is provided by (client) automatic teller machines obtaining service from a bank's central computer.

RPCs have many similarities to rendezvous, and these two synchronous, two-way message-passing constructs were compared in the text preceding the description of rendezvous. One significant difference is that rendezvous is specific to a particular language (Ada), whereas RPC is language-independent, and "programmer kits" for FORTRAN, C, and Pascal are included in several packages. One such package makes available the Sun RPCs used to implement the above-mentioned NFS. The Apollo/Hewlett-Packard RPCs are available in a package called Network Computing System (NCS). Both of these packages run on Unix.[70] A third RPC package is available with the Mach operating system from CMU. Although these packages differ in details,[71] they all provide three essential components that a programmer uses to obtain the RPC operation shown in Figure 4.13:

- An interface generator (a kind of compiler) that creates the stub files
- A run-time library that handles data exchanges and other communication
- A location broker (typically a daemon process) that finds the server

---

[70] Some versions of Unix also have their own RPC system, with more limited programmer support than these two packages.

[71] For example, the Sun RPC location broker determines the server's address and supplies it to the client, so that the client can subsequently contact the server directly. By contrast, in Apollo RPC, the location broker obtains the server's address but continues to act as an intermediary between client and server, like a doctor's answering service.

Figure 4.12   Ada rendezvous [191]. See text.

The RPC model is similar to the (local) procedure-call model [252]. In the local model, the caller places arguments to a procedure in a set of registers. Then, the caller transfers control to the procedure. The caller eventually regains control, extracts the result of the procedure, and continues execution.

This notion of a single thread of control winding through a caller and a callee is also present in an RPC. The program structure that is used is based on the concept of *stubs*[65] and involves the five pieces of program shown in Figure 4.13. The calling program, the client stub, and one instance of the run-time library execute in the client machine. The called procedure, the server stub, and another instance of the run-time library execute on the server machine. When the calling program wishes to make a remote call, it actually makes a local call to the client stub, which contains a procedure designed to communicate with the desired procedure on the other machine (via the stub on the other machine).[72] The client stub places a specification of the target procedure and the arguments into one or more packets and asks the run-time library to transmit this information reliably to the server machine. The run-time library on the server machine receives these packets and delivers them to the server stub, which unpacks them and then makes a local call to the desired procedure in the server machine. Meanwhile, the calling process in the client machine is suspended awaiting a result packet. When the call in the server completes, it returns to the server stub and the results are passed back to the suspended process in the client machine. There they are unpacked and the client stub returns them to the calling program, as if they were the result of a local call. Indeed, if the calling program and called procedure were brought into a single machine and bound directly together without the stubs, the program should still work.

How did these magical stubs get there? They are automatically created by the interface generator. The programmer first writes the calling program and the called procedure, and then places their names and the names and types of their arguments and results into a file, which is then used by the interface generator to create the stub files (in source code). The stubs are then compiled

Figure 4.13   Remote Procedure Call flow and components.

---

[72] To put it another way, the client stub acts as the local representative of the called procedure, organizing the data into a format that can be transmitted to the server and using the RPC run-time library routines to communicate with the server, where similar activities occur [252].

and linked with the rest of the program. The majority of the calls to the RPC run-time library are made by the stubs. A few such calls may have to be made directly from the calling program and called procedure in order to obtain parallel operation, since current interface generators were not designed with parallel operation in mind. This is discussed further on page 51.

What about performance? Ah, there's the rub. With current implementations, RPCs take milliseconds[73][385] , [105]. This is not simply a matter of network latency. In Unix, for example, the flow shown in Figure 4.13 on page 168 involves considerable memory-to-memory *copying,* from calling program to stub, from stub to kernel, from kernel to network buffer, and then a similar number of copies on the other side [105]. In comparing and analyzing RPC performances, Schroeder and Burrows [385] found that even their own highly tuned RPC took almost a millisecond to send and receive a 74-byte packet, of which only 60 microseconds was ethernet transmission time. The 13 other delays that they list provide an object lesson to illustrate the improvements in software overhead that are needed in a massively parallel system, where communication delays must not exceed a few microseconds. Mere improvements in processor speed will not suffice. Of course, the distributed applications for which these RPC packages were developed have much more lenient delay requirements, and even with millisecond response times, there are parallel applications that can obtain good speedup on a network of several tens of workstations (see page 51).

What about ease of use? Now we are in the realm of opinion, so let the reader beware during the rest of this paragraph. In our opinion, the RPC packages mentioned above are fine for writing distributed applications, where multiple independent clients access one server that runs in serial mode. These are the applications for which these packages were developed, and then indeed the interface generators painlessly produce code that runs smoothly and gives the convenience and illusion of a local procedure call. However, parallelizing the seismic code described on page 51 was *much* easier using PVM (page 252) than RPCs, which are as yet an immature technology for parallelization, and require the writer of true parallel programs to become involved with many low-level details (sockets, ports, binding, limits on data size, etc.) that are hidden more effectively by PVM, which was written specifically for parallel applications.

---

[73] There are interesting efforts to develop more convenient and faster remote procedure calls implemented in a high-level language [468] and in a shared-memory environment [62], but these are not yet commercially available.

Finer Granularities: Message passing at finer granularities of parallelism is discussed by Fahlman [162], who describes *marker-passing, value-passing,* and *message-passing* systems (see page 456). The item being passed in these systems ranges from a single bit on upward. The Connection Machine (page 446) is an example of a message-passing system. These systems are mostly SIMD designs, with coordination provided by hardware rather than software primitives.

The Cosmic Cube (page 475) is an example of an MIMD message-passing architecture designed for medium-grained parallelism (RP3 in message-pass mode is another). Programs for these machines use constructs similar to the CSP send and receive, without the additional layer of software imposed by the remote procedure call/rendezvous protocol and the additional delays that this protocol imposes. The trade-off is that the programmer is working with low-level primitives and assumes the responsibility for providing correct protocols and programs.

4.1.4 Quantitative Speedup Discussion

For a more quantitative discussion of the things that limit parallel speedup, let us go through some simple examples and identify the parameters involved. To see the effect of communication overheads, we start with a simple model of communication and show how the computation-to-communication ratio limits the speedup. Next we add the effects of finite divisibility (minimum grain size) and of serial sections of code that cannot be parallelized. Then we show how a better communication scheme can improve speedup, and after that we show how the bandwidth and latency of communication influence the speedup. We examine what happens when the problem size remains constant as well as when it is allowed to grow. Reference [399] discusses several different strategies for scaling the problem size.

Since the discussion that follows moves from the general to the specific, the word *worker* evolves in meaning. At the beginning, the word applies equally well to teams of people and to teams of computers. Eventually, one of the examples that we use is a *manager-worker* parallel program, in which a manager program running on one processor spawns multiple instances of a worker program running on remote processors. These worker processes request assignments from the manager, return their work product to the manager, and ask for more work until the manager runs out.[74]

General Assumption

For all the cases that follow, we assume that the workers cannot compute and communicate at the same time. As a consequence, T_P, the total time for the parallel job with P workers, can be written

$$T_P = TCOMP_P + TCOMM_P + other \ terms$$

where the first term is the time needed for computation during the parallel job, and the second term is the total time needed for communication. The other terms and additional assumptions are spelled out as we go along.

Communications Overhead–Simple Model

For the time being, we make the additional assumption that the original work (the original serial computation) is completely parallelizable; that is, it can be completely parceled out to P workers in equal-sized chunks. Then, if the serial computation time is T_S,

$$TCOMP_P = T_S /P$$

and the other terms in the equation above are eliminated. The speedup S_P for P workers is defined as T_S /T_P, and hence

$$\frac{1}{S_P} = \frac{T_P}{T_S} = \frac{1}{P} + \frac{TCOMM_P}{T_S}$$

The last term is the "ratio of the time you don't compute to the time it took you previously to compute", as a friend put it, and represents the communication overhead. The smaller it is, the better. As we will soon show, it is convenient to define the *inverse* of this ratio, namely,

$$r_P = T_S / TCOMM_P,$$

which is a form of computation-to-communication ratio. The larger it is, the better. The equation for speedup can then be written as

---

[74] The manager-worker arrangement is similar to a master-slave organization (page 360) except for the fact that the workers request assignments. Another way to look at it (for readers familiar with client-server programs) is that the manager starts out as a client activating a group of servers to perform computation, but then the roles are switched and the manager becomes a server sending data in response to requests from the clients who are performing the computation.

Figure 4.14   Speedup as limited by overhead of simple communication model.

$$\frac{1}{S_P} = \frac{1}{P} + \frac{1}{r_P}$$

We begin with the example shown in Figure 4.14, where it is assumed that the total time needed for communication grows in direct proportion to the number of workers in the pool (we treat less drastic cases later). Thus, with P workers, the computation time is cut by $1/P$, but the time needed for communication grows as P, and so there is an optimum value of P that minimizes the time needed by the parallel program. Beyond this point, adding more workers makes things worse. Note that we are not just saying that the efficiency gets worse with more workers, but instead that the job takes longer to run as more processors are added.[75]

---

[75] Similar effects are observed in human endeavors; see *The Mythical Man-Month*[74], in which Fred Brooks reports that adding more people to a late project makes it later. A computer program that gives rise to such behavior is the manager-workers seismic program illustrated in Figure 2.10 on page 55. In that example, all the worker computers exchange

Since the communication time is simply proportional to P in this example, the optimum value of P is easy to find. We have

$$TCOMM_P = P \times TCOMM_1$$

and so the speedup equation becomes

$$\frac{1}{S_P} = \frac{1}{P} + P \times \frac{TCOMM_1}{T_S} = \frac{1}{P} + \frac{P}{r_1} .$$

where

$$r_1 = T_S / TCOMM_1 .$$

To find the value of P that maximizes S_P, we set the derivative $d(1/S_P)/dP = 0$ and find that $P = \sqrt{r_1}$ and $S_P = 0.5\sqrt{r_1}$. The quantity r_1 is the ratio of computation time to communication time in a system with one worker, and is obviously a useful parameter in this special case where the communication overhead is proportional to P. We picked $r_1 = 100$ for the example in Figure 4.14, with the result that the maximum speedup is 5 and occurs for 10 workers. These predictions are consistent with the experimental results in the seismic section on page 51.

Serial Sections and Divisibility Limits

In general, the problem will *not* be completely and arbitrarily parallelizable. There will be some fraction A of the work (the serial portion) that must be done by a single worker (see Figure 4.15 on page 174), and there will be some "divisibility limit" on the number of parallel chunks that the work can be divided into.[76] Below this divisibility limit, the speedup S_P for the example in the previous section becomes

---

data with a single manager computer, which becomes a communication bottleneck. Speedups that grow and then decline are also exhibited by some programs that do *not* use a manager-workers model. One example is the 2D FFT (Fast Fourier Transform) parallel algorithm that we discuss later. Two other examples, discussed on page 179, are the Serial Access Paradigm (SAP) and Concurrent Access Paradigm (CAP), where the communication overhead grows as a result of the need to *synchronize* (in the previous two examples, the communication overhead grew as a result of the need to *move data*). In the SAP, the overhead grows as P, whereas the overhead for the CAP grows more slowly, as $\log P$, resembling the behavior of many parallel programs (see the table on page 217 and its companions for some examples).

[76] For example, the seismic program on page 51 contained a Fourier transform that took 0.5% of the serial computation time for a 1000×1000 array, and was not deemed worth parallelizing for the modest degree of parallelism expected from a cluster of workstations.

Figure 4.15 **Speedup limited by serial sections and finite divisibility** in addition to communication.

$$S_P = \frac{1}{A + (1 - A)/P + P/r_1}$$

where $1/A$ = Amdahl limit on speedup as P grows large

and r_1 / P = limit imposed by communication as P grows large.

For $A << 1$, the maximum speedup is still approximately $0.5\sqrt{r_1}$ and occurs near $P = \sqrt{r_1}$. Figure 4.15 shows the behavior of the speedup for $A = 0.005$ and $r_1 = 100$, 10^4, and 10^6 (r_1 can increase due to a larger problem or faster communication). The first curve ($r_1 = 100$) is the case shown in Figure 4.14 and corresponds to speedup limited by communication. By the time r_1 reaches 10^6 (third curve), the Amdahl limit predominates at 1000 processes.

This Fourier transform thus represents an A of 0.005, and limits the speedup to $1/A = 200$. The divisibility limit or *degree of parallelism* is 1000, corresponding to an independent computation for each row of the array, which is the minimum practical *granularity*.

Figure 4.16   *Effect on speedup of improved communication model.*

Improved Communication Scheme

Figure 4.16 shows the improved speedups that result if the communications cost of added workers can be made to grow as log *PE* rather than as *P*, specifically, if

$$TCOMM_P = (1 + \log P) \times TCOMM_1$$

This can be achieved, for example, by changing a manager-workers program to use a treelike communication scheme (see page 205). Instead of each worker sending its output directly to the manager to be combined into the final result, pairs of results are combined by several stages of workers on the way to the manager. In essence, we create a management hierarchy and promote some of the workers to be submanagers, so we no longer have a simple manager-workers algorithm.[77] The speedup equation becomes

---

[77] In the terminology of the analysis on page 179, we switched from a Serial Access Paradigm (SAP) to a Concurrent Access Paradigm (CAP).

$$\frac{1}{S_P} = \frac{1}{P} + \frac{\log(1 + P)}{r_1}$$

Under the assumption that $P \gg 1$, the optimum values are $P_{opt} = r_1$ and $S_{opt} = r_1/(1 + \log r_1)$. Once again, r_1 is seen to be a useful quantity.

A note of caution, however: this improved algorithm is possible only if the right hardware is in place, in this case, a tree network.[78] Merely implementing a treelike communication scheme on a cluster of workstations connected by a single LAN (local area network) does not improve things, since there is more *total* traffic on the LAN with the treelike scheme, and a LAN, like a bus, has a fixed total bandwidth independent of the number of nodes it connects. To obtain the logarithmic behavior of the CAP model, extra hardware is needed. The workstations would have to be connected into a treelike configuration using multiple LAN adaptors per workstation, multi-ported, point-to-point fiber optic adapters, or some other hardware that provides a higher degree of connectivity than a LAN. For example, the interconnection network of the IBM SP1 enables the CAP speedup results shown in Figure 2.11 on page 58 for a parallel seismic migration program.

In Figure 4.16, we took the liberty to ease the Amdahl limit to $A = 5 \times 10^{-5}$ so we could better illustrate the difference between the previous and new communication limits. Note that for $r_1 = 10^4$ (achievable for large seismic arrays and fiber optic communication among workstations), the improved method (with tree topology) has not yet peaked when it achieves a speedup close to 500 for 1000 workers, whereas the former method (Figure 4.15) peaks at a speedup of 50 for 100 workers. It is easy to see that the simple manager-workers method, with the manager talking to each worker separately, is useful as a quick way to obtain modest parallelism, but is not suitable for massive parallelism. Massive parallelism requires algorithms whose speedup is limited by communication in a less drastic way than the r_1 / P ceiling of the manager-workers model. An example is the method we just described, with its tree-structured communication and $r_1 / \log P$ speedup limit. The table on page 217 and its companions list a number of other algorithms whose speedups behave like $P/\log P$.

Influence of Bandwidth and Latency on r and Speedup

We have shown examples of how the computation-to-communication ratio r_P determines the speedup. But what determines r_P? In a way, r_P depends on *two* computation-to-communication ratios, that of the computer (hardware and

---

[78] As a friend pointed out, "If you want to get a log, you've gotta have a tree".

software), and that of the algorithm. The computer's portion depends on the computing speed of the nodes (MFLOPS) and on the communication speed of the connections (bandwidth and latency). The algorithm's portion depends on how much data must be moved for a given amount of computation.

Let us continue by means of another example, one provided by our colleague Ramesh Natarajan for the case of a 2D FFT (Fast Fourier Transform). Assume that sending a message of x words between any two processors takes $L + x/B$ seconds, where L is the latency and B is the hardware bitstream rate in words/sec. Also let P = number of processors, and a = time for a floating-point operation on a processor $(FLOP/ sec)^{-1}$, Then, as shown in the box below, the parallel time for an N-by-N array is

$$T_P = (10aN^2 \log N)/P + 2(P-1)[L + (N^2/P^2)/B]$$

and, identifying the first term with T_S/P and the second with $TCOMM_P$, we see that

$$r_P = \frac{5aN^2 \log N}{(P-1)\{L + (\dfrac{N^2}{P^2})/B\}}$$

We see that if the latency term is dominant over the bandwidth term, r_P contains a factor a/L, whereas if latency is negligible, r_P contains a factor $a/(1/B)$; both are the computer's computation-to-communication ratios.

The algorithm's portion is a little harder to see. Instead, let us illustrate the situation by using the expression for speedup to plot *lines of constant speedup* in the latency-bandwidth plane (actually, in the $L - B^{-1}$ plane). The speedup S_P is just T_S / T_P, and if we assume that P = 1000 and N = 10,000, then the iso-speedup lines are given by

$$\frac{100}{Ba} = 6.66 \times 10^6 (\frac{1}{S_P} - .001) - \frac{L}{a}$$

The results are plotted in Figure 4.17 on page 178 for 100 MFLOPS processors (a = 10 nS) and also in normalized form allowing evaluation for other values of a. The figure quickly shows that, for example, a parallel machine with a thousand 100 MFLOPS processors needs latency below 10 microseconds and bandwidth above 40 MByte/sec to reach a speedup of 900 on this problem. If the latency exceeds 1 millisecond or the bandwidth drops below 0.4 MBytes/sec, the speedup is limited to 50. For calibration purposes, we have added to this figure the bandwidth and latency values of some of the computers we describe in our architecture chapters.

Figure 4.17 *Effect of communication bandwidth and latency on speedup of 2D FFT algorithm (N=10,000, P=1000). For comparison with the iso-speedup lines, some representative hardware bandwidth-latency values are shown as small shaded circles: P = Paragon (page 491), C = CM-5 (page 509), V = PVS (page 611, but note values are for 32 processors), W = workstations on a LAN (one would not use 1000 for this problem). Note that the bandwidth for the point W is the total system bandwidth, whereas the other points are positioned according to the bandwidth per processor. The latency in all cases is from user space to user space.*

Most parallel programs have more complex communication than that treated here, but the key parameters that determine speedup are still the ones we identified: the bandwidth and latency of communication as compared to the computing power of the nodes, and the amount of communication that the algorithm requires for a given computation. The speedup curves may not be exactly like our simple example, but they will tell the same story.

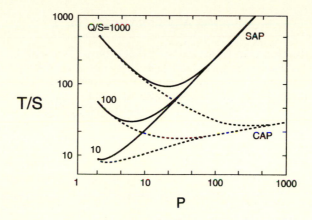

Figure 4.18   ***Normalized task computation time*** *T* *vs. number of processors* *P* *for several ratios of computation work load* *Q* *to processor-processor communication time* *S* *and for two models of access to shared resources, SAP (serial access paradigm) and CAP (concurrent access paradigm). Adding more processors beyond the minimum of each curve causes the interprocessor communication time to dominate the computation time. Basis: equations derived by Cytron [110].*

4.1.5   *Maximum Useful Parallelism*

The question might arise during compiling as to how many processors should be assigned to a given task, or else how much parallelism the target machine needs for efficient operation (which is also an important issue at design time). Cytron [110] tackles this question with a simple analytical treatment of an MIMD collection of scalar processors.[79] His assumptions model an idealized program using the fork and join primitives (page 149). The computation proper executes with perfect speedup, and communication is necessary only to initiate the computation and to determine that the computation has terminated. (Note that on a SIMD or SEA architecture (page 143), in which a single instruction appears to perform an arithmetic operation on multiple operands concurrently, the initialization and termination phases are accomplished trivially because such machines synchronize at each instruction. This synchronization is one difference between a vectorizer (page 301) and a more general parallelizing compiler.) It is hoped that the increased overhead of processor

---

[79] Also called MISMES, or MES for short, to designate multiple scalar execution streams; see page 143.

Parallel Algorithm for 2D FFT

The following speedup analysis for a 2D FFT (Fast Fourier Transform) of an N-by-N array is from our colleague Ramesh Natarajan. Assume that sending a message of x words between any two processors takes $L + x/B$ seconds, where L is the latency, and B is the hardware bitstream rate in words/sec. Also let $P =$ number of processors, and $a =$ time for a floating-point operation on a processor $(MFLOP/ sec)^{-1}$. Assume that we perform N-point FFTs in each direction, using the following algorithm:

STEP 1: Perform $\dfrac{N}{P}$ one-dimensional N-point FFTs on each processor.

$$Time = a\left(\frac{N}{P}\right)(5N \log N)$$

STEP 2: Data transposition. For each processor *in parallel*

(i) send $(P-1)$ blocks of length $\left(\dfrac{N^2}{P^2}\right)$

(ii) receive $(P-1)$ blocks of length $\left(\dfrac{N^2}{P^2}\right)$

$$Time = 2(P-1)\left[L + \left(\frac{N^2}{P^2}\right)/B\right]$$

STEP 3: Perform $\dfrac{N}{P}$ one-dimensional N-point FFTs on each processor.

$$Time = a\left(\frac{N}{P}\right)(5N \log N)$$

Therefore,

$$T_{FFT} = (10aN^2 \log N)/P + 2(P-1)[L + (N^2/P^2)/B]$$

communication in an MIMD architecture is eclipsed by increased performance that comes from greater flexibility in programming and scheduling complex programs.

The initialization phase consists of preparing a collection of P processors for executing a task. The task is assumed to consist of some quantity of work Q that can be scheduled on P processors in such a way that the time for performing the computation proper is $Q \div P$ (perfect speedup assumption). After initialization, a processor moves from the active to the passive state when it completes its component of the task. It can move back to the active state again, but only by persuasion from an active processor. (This persuasion might happen, for example, if the system performs load balancing, which causes an excessively busy processor to transmit some of its work —instantaneously, in this model—to a passive processor. Load balancing is discussed more thoroughly in Chapter 7.) The computation phase ceases when all processors are in a passive phase. The termination phase is completed when all the processors have detected the passivity of the entire system.

The time required to complete all three phases depends on the time S needed to transmit a fact from one processor to another, and on the way in which processors access a shared resource, that is, on the communication topology. Two cases are considered: for the serial access paradigm (SAP), the time taken for all P processors to access a shared resource is proportional to P. A corresponding hardware example would be a ring or bus network (see Chapter 8). For the concurrent access paradigm (CAP), all P processors can access a shared resource in time proportional to $\log_2 P$. Hardware examples include a tree network and an omega network. Cytron shows that the time T for performing all three phases is given by

$$T_{SAP} = S\{ \frac{5}{2} P + \frac{Q/S - 1}{P} - \frac{3}{2} \}$$

$$T_{CAP} = S\{ \frac{Q/S}{P} + 3 \log_2 P \}$$

These equations are plotted in Figure 4.18 on page 179. The values of P that minimize T are given by

$$P_{SAP} = \sqrt{0.4(\frac{Q}{S} - 1)}$$

$$P_{CAP} = \frac{\ln 2}{3} \frac{Q}{S}$$

As expected, the number of processors that should be allocated to a task is determined by the ratio of the computation load Q to the communication time S. Note the following points with regard to Figure 4.18:

1. The task size needed for a given efficiency is approximately $P/ \log P$ times larger for the SAP case than for the CAP case.
2. For a given value of Q/S, the CAP model achieves a lower minimum value of T, but with a more than proportionately larger number of processors (to

a good approximation, the optimum P_{CAP} is the *square* of the optimum P_{SAP}). Thus, the efficiency[80] is lower in the CAP case.

3.　More significantly, for a fixed number of processors, CAP is always better.

4.　For negligible communication overhead, namely $Q >> SP$ (i.e., $Q/S >> P$), the difference between the SAP and CAP cases disappears, as it should, and T/S approaches Q/SP, or $T \rightarrow Q/P$, the perfect speedup situation.

5.　When the communication cost becomes dominant $(P >> Q/S$, i.e., $Q << PS)$, T/S becomes independent of Q in both cases.

6.　The functions for the optimum P_{SAP} and P_{CAP} can easily be generated by the compiler for run-time evaluation and used by the operating system in its scheduling activities. (The actual number of useful processors may be lower than predicted by this idealized model.)

The interested reader should consult [110] for more details.

4.2　Computational Models—An Analytical View

For the remainder of this chapter (but *not* for the remainder of this book), we take a more mathematical approach to the study of computational models. We have previously used these models to tell us, at an abstract level, what a computer can do. Now we wish to determine the costs incurred when a given parallel algorithm is executed. By comparing the cost, or *computational complexity,* of various algorithms for the same problem, one is able to choose among them in an intelligent manner. There need not be a clear winner. For example, it may happen that one algorithm is superior for shared-memory machines but does not do so well when message-passing is employed. Another possibility is that the algorithm to choose depends on the degree of parallelism and the size of the problem.

　　Naturally, before we can consider these questions in detail we must give a precise definition of the cost of a parallel algorithm. We begin with a review of the computational complexity of serial algorithms, which leads immediately to the notion of asymptotics.[81] We next consider the standard RAM model of

---

80　The efficiency E of a task on a multiprocessor is the ratio of the speedup of the computation to the number of processors dedicated to the task: $E = Q/(PT)$. See Chapter 4 for a detailed discussion.

81　Readers unfamiliar with this subject, or wishing a more extensive treatment, are encouraged to consult, for example, the excellent text by Aho, Hopcroft, and Ullman [10].

a serial computer and then extend it in two ways to give models suitable for parallel computation. The first extension, called a PRAM, models shared-memory machines, and the second models message-passing architectures. We then turn to the issue of parallel complexity. As mentioned previously, the size of the parallel processor, as well as the size of the problem to be solved, must be considered. The one-variable asymptotic limits of serial complexity become two-variable limits in this new setting, which adds a considerable complication. We discuss some of the issues involved and then present a possible simplification that considers an asymmetric limit in which one variable is much larger than the other.

4.2.1 Serial Computational Complexity

The efficiency of an algorithm is most often measured by the rate of growth of the time and memory required to solve problems of larger and larger size. We now proceed to make this notion more precise. Associated with each instance of a problem is a number n, giving the size of that instance.[82] For example, the size of an instance of the sorting problem is the number of items to be sorted.[83] It is customary to refer to n as the size of the problem (rather than the size of an instance of the problem), and we shall follow this custom. Now consider an algorithm for the problem at hand and let $T(n)$ be the largest number of computation steps[84] used by the algorithm when solving a problem of size n. This function is called the *time complexity* of the algorithm, and the function $S(n)$, the largest number of memory words used in solving a problem of size n, is called the *space complexity* of the algorithm. When it is clear from context whether time or space is under discussion, either T or S is called the *complexity*. We now wish to consider the limiting behavior of T and S as the problem size gets larger in order to define the *asymptotic time complexity* and *asymptotic space complexity*.[85]

---

[82] For some problems, the size is not characterized by a single number, and one must use ordered pairs, or triples, or yet more complicated parameters. In this section, however, we shall restrict our attention to problems whose size is measured by a single number.

[83] Assume each item fits in a single computer word.

[84] Exactly what is permitted during a single computation step depends on the computational model being studied. We consider several models below.

[85] It would probably be of greater practical value to consider the average rather than the largest number of steps. However, the analysis required is more difficult, and it is thus common to define a *worst-case* complexity as we have done.

Three Hyperopic Greek Analysts—Omega, Omicron, and Theta—and Their Two Children

It is rarely possible to obtain the limiting behavior exactly. Instead, one often needs to consider two functions equivalent if, for large values of their parameters, each is within a multiplicative constant of the other. For example, the two functions

$$f(x) = 2x^2 + 5$$

and

$$g(x) = x^2 + 30$$

will be considered equivalent since, for all $x \geq 3$, we have both $f(x) \leq 2g(x)$ and $g(x) \leq 2f(x)$. We denote this equivalence by Θ and write $f = \Theta(g)$ or $g = \Theta(f)$. In fact, it is more common to write

$$f, g = \Theta(x^2)$$

asserting that both f and g are equivalent to x^2, the "simplest" function in this class. The *asymptotic time complexity* of an algorithm is the set of functions equivalent to the time complexity defined above. Similarly, the functions equivalent to the space complexity are called the *asymptotic space complexity*. For example, an algorithm that solves problems of size n in time

$$2n^2 + 5$$

using space

$$n^2 + 30$$

has asymptotic time complexity and asymptotic space complexity of $\Theta(n^2)$. Since it is implied by the uppercase theta notation, one often omits the word *asymptotic* in these situations and says that the time and space complexity are $\Theta(n^2)$.

Frequently, one can obtain only an upper or lower bound on the values attained by a given function. If, for large x, $f(x)$ does not exceed a constant times $g(x)$, we write $f = O(g)$ or $g = \Omega(f)$. Ignoring both small values of the parameter and multiplicative constants, one may read O as "at most", Ω as "at least", and Θ as "equals". As expected, f equals g if it is at least g and at most g. Symbolically, $f = \Theta(g)$, if, and only if, both $f = O(g)$ and $f = \Omega(g)$. Finally, the lowercase Greek letters are used to denote strict comparison, that is, $f = o(g)$ and $f = w(g)$ may be read, respectively, as "f is (strictly) less than g", and "f exceeds g".

It should be noted that we calculate asymptotic orders because we are unable to determine the values exactly. With asymptotic orders we need only consider the behavior of the function for large parameter values, and even then we are required only to get the answer right within a multiplicative constant. So our Greek friends are really hyperopic;[86] their vision is imperfect, especially at close distances.

We now take the gloves off and give precise definition to these five asymptotic orders, following Knuth [287]. In these definitions we let f and g be positive real-valued functions of a positive integer parameter.[87] Then:

$o(g)$ is the set of f such that f/g approaches 0; that is, the set of f having the property that for each $\epsilon > 0$, there exists an integer N such that for all $n \geq N$, $f(n) < \epsilon g(n)$.

$O(g)$ is the set of f such that f/g is bounded above; that is, there exists C such that for all positive n, $f(n) < Cg(n)$.

$\Theta(g)$ is the set of f such that f/g is bounded above and bounded away from zero; that is, there exist C_1, C_2 such that for all n, $0 < C_1 g(n) < f(n) < C_2 g(n)$.

$\Omega(g)$ is the set of f such that f/g is bounded away from 0; that is, there exists C such that for all n, $0 < Cg(n) < f(n)$.

$w(g)$ is the set of f such that f/g approaches infinity; that is, for all C there exists N such that for all $n \geq N$, $Cg(n) < f(n)$.

Again following Knuth, we often write $f = o(g)$ to mean f is an element of the set of $o(g)$ and similarly for O, Θ, Ω, and w.

This notation is often used to express upper or lower bounds on the asymptotic complexity of an algorithm. If, for example, it is known that T, the (time) complexity of a given algorithm, satisfies $T = \Omega(f)$, we say that the algorithm has asymptotic complexity $\Omega(f)$. As before, the word *asymptotic* is often elided. Similarly, we speak of complexity $o(f)$, $O(f)$, $\Theta(f)$, and $w(f)$.

The Complexity of a Problem

Having defined the (asymptotic) complexity of an algorithm, we extend the notion to problems themselves by defining the complexity of a problem to be

---

[86] "Hyperopia: A condition of the eye in which vision for distant objects is better than for near objects so that the individual is said to be farsighted". *Webster's New Collegiate Dictionary.*

[87] Knuth considers real-valued functions of real variables. We restrict the domains and ranges, since the definitions become slightly easier, and all the functions we consider satisfy these restrictions.

the minimum complexity among all algorithms for solving the problem.[88] For example, since the (time) complexity for bubble sorting n values is $\Theta(n^2)$, we see that the complexity of sorting is $O(n^2)$. By considering the better algorithm heapsort, we reduce our estimate of the complexity of sorting to $O(n \log n)$. Thus by analyzing an algorithm, we get an upper bound on the complexity of the problem. In order to obtain a lower bound, one must either analyze each possible algorithm (a gruesome possibility) or else show that for all algorithms, the lower bound is valid. For example, it is not hard to show that any sorting algorithm *based on comparisons* requires $\Omega(n \log n)$ steps (see [10] for a proof) and thus (comparison-based) sorting has complexity $\Omega(n \log n)$.[89] When combined with the matching upper bound obtained from heapsort (a comparison-based algorithm), this last result shows that the complexity of comparison-based sorting is $\Theta(n \log n)$.

4.2.2 Random Access Machines (RAMs)

One standard computational model for serial computers is the RAM, or Random Access Machine,[90] introduced in [10], which captures the behavior of real machines quite well. A RAM contains five components:

1. An unalterable program consisting of optionally labeled instructions; possible instruction sets are discussed below.
2. A memory composed of a sequence of words, each capable of containing an arbitrary integer.
3. An accumulator referenced implicitly by most instructions. This component has many of the properties of the general-purpose registers found in modern computers.
4. A read-only input tape.
5. A write-only output tape.

---

[88] More precisely, the complexity of a problem is $O(f)$ if there is an algorithm for the problem having complexity $O(f)$.

[89] The restriction that the algorithm be based on comparisons is significant and excludes such algorithms as radix sort. The restriction is enforced by defining the computation model so that the operation of extracting the ith bit is not permitted. See Aho, Hopcroft, and Ullman [10] for details.

[90] One should not confuse this definition of RAM with the more common random access memory.

During one computation step, a RAM executes a single instruction of its program. Instructions are executed sequentially, unless control flow is altered by the execution of a branch, in which case the next instruction executed is the one whose label is referenced by the branch.[91] Since we are considering only asymptotic and not exact complexity, that is, we are ignoring multiplicative constants and small problems, many instruction sets are equivalent.   One possible set is the following, in which all instructions except Branch and Halt reference the accumulator implicitly:

Write
Read
Load   Operand
Store   Operand
Add   Operand
Sub   Operand
Mul   Operand
Div   Operand
BrPos   Label
BrNeg   Label
Branch Label
Halt

Write and Read transfer an integer to and from the next location on the output tape and input tape, respectively. The Load, Store, and arithmetic instructions each include one *operand,* which may be specified in one of the three following forms:

1.   The operand $=i$, often called an *immediate* operand, represents the integer i itself. For example,

Mul $=$-5

multiplies the accumulator by -5.
2.   The operand i (a *non-negative* integer) indicates the contents of memory word i. For example,

Sub 3

subtracts the contents of word 3 from the accumulator.

---

[91] Readers familiar with Turing Machines should note that the primary difference between this model and the RAM just introduced is that the latter is capable of arbitrary memory reference patterns; whereas, the former must access memory sequentially. More colloquially, for memory, a TM uses a tape, but a RAM uses a RAM.

3.   Finally, the operand *i* (often called *indirect* addressing) indicates the contents of word *j*, where *j* is the contents of word *i*. For example, if word 82 contains a 3,

        Sub *82

has the same effect as the previous example.

The arithmetic instructions each replace the contents of the accumulator by

        accumulator op operand.

The BrPos (resp. BrNeg) instruction transfers control to the instruction having the appropriate label if the accumulator is positive (resp. negative), whereas Branch transfers control unconditionally.

Recall that the program to be executed is part of the RAM in which it resides. In this sense a RAM abstracts a special-purpose computer that is intended to solve a single problem. Such special-purpose machines are finding increased use, especially in the area of signal processing. Of particular interest to us are *systolic arrays:* special-purpose parallel processors, pioneered by H.T. Kung [308], which are discussed in Chapter 9. Of course, an abstract RAM, unlike a concrete systolic array, can contain a program of unbounded complexity; thus, the single problem that it can solve may be arbitrarily complex.

One way in which the RAM is not realistic is the assumption that all instructions take the same time to execute. The problem is not that a divide might take 10 times longer than an add, or even that a write may take 10,000 times longer. For any machine, we could find the slowest instruction, slow the others down to this speed, and observe that the hyperopic Greeks would never notice the difference. The real problem is that, since RAMs operate on arbitrary integers, it is unreasonable to assume that operations require time that is *independent of the size of their operands.* Moreover, when computing the space complexity, it is unreasonable to assume that an arbitrarily large integer can fit into a single memory word.[92] A consequence of the constant-time assumption, when extended to multiple RAM systems in the next subsection, is that the resulting configuration is automatically synchronous; that is, all the RAMs will run at the same rate, even during MIMD execution.

---

[92]   Aho, Hopcroft, and Ullman [10] address these problems with their *logarithm cost criterion,* in which the time required by an operation is essentially the number of digits needed to represent the integers used, and the space required for a memory word is essentially the number of digits in the largest integer ever stored in that word. We have used their (admittedly less realistic) *uniform cost criterion* for simplicity.

4.2.3　From RAMs to PRAMs

In this section we extend the (uniform cost) RAM model to a PRAM, or parallel random access machine, which abstracts a shared-memory parallel computer much as a RAM abstracts a conventional uniprocessor. The next section discusses a model that abstracts many private-memory, message-passing parallel architectures.

A PRAM is essentially a collection of RAMs all accessing the same memory. More formally, a *P-processor PRAM,* or a *PRAM of size P,* consists of:

1. *P* unmodifiable programs, each composed of optionally labeled instructions.
2. A *single* memory composed of a sequence of words, each capable of containing an arbitrary integer.
3. *P* accumulators, one associated with each program.
4. A read-only input tape.
5. A write-only output tape.

During one computation step, a *P*-processor PRAM executes *P* instructions, one from each of its programs. Within each program, instructions are executed sequentially unless control flow is altered by a branch, in which case the next instruction executed is the branch target. Note that this is an MIMD model, with each of the programs constituting an instruction stream. Unlike the MIMD computers actually constructed (see Chapter 10), a PRAM is a synchronous model; that is, all the processors proceed at exactly the same rate.

An important distinction between various definitions of PRAMs is whether one permits simultaneous accesses to a single memory cell, especially simultaneous stores. The original PRAM of Fortune and Wyllie [177] adopted a standard readers/writers protocol in which a cell may be read by multiple instruction streams simultaneously, but if one stream is writing the cell, then no other stream may access it. Snir [405] classifies this machine as a CREW PRAM (concurrent read exclusive write PRAM). The most restrictive model, an EREW PRAM, does not permit any simultaneous accessing of a single cell; a CRCW PRAM, on the other hand, permits arbitrary access patterns. This last model was termed a *paracomputer* by Schwartz [386] and a WRAM by Borodin and Hopcroft [70]. The fourth possibility, an ERCW PRAM, has generated little interest (cf. MISD).

When concurrent writes are permitted, one must define the effect of simultaneous accesses. This problem had been considered previously in the database literature, and the concept adopted is the *serialization principle* of

Eswaran et al. [160], which states that the effect of simultaneous actions is as if the actions occurred in some (unspecified) serial order. Thus, for example, a load simultaneous with two stores directed at the same memory cell will return either the original value or one of the two stored values, possibly different from the value that the cell finally comes to contain. Note that, in all PRAM models, simultaneous memory accesses (when permitted) are accomplished in one computation step; the serialization principle speaks only of the effect of simultaneous actions and not of their implementation.

We mentioned previously that the RAM model includes the unrealistic assumption that each operation takes constant time, independent of the size of the operands. The PRAM model suffers from the additional unrealistic assumption that the time required for an operation is independent of P, the size of the PRAM. In particular, the model assumes that P processors can access the shared memory in time that does not grow with P. This access rate is not possible even for the trivial case of a shared memory consisting of a single bit of storage. For any given technology, there is a limit, say b, on the number of signals that one can fan-in during a single cycle. Thus to connect P processors to a common point requires at least $\log_b P$ cycles. An even more elementary argument is that P processors require volume $\Theta(P)$, and thus the distance from the common memory to the processor farthest away grows as the cube root of P.

In our definition, a PRAM has just one input tape, and thus reading in a problem must require time that is linear in the physical size of the problem no matter how big P is. Indeed this "I/O bottleneck" is seen to occur in real machines as well as in their mathematical models. For example, the IBM RP3 project is based on a machine designed to have 512 processors but a far smaller number of disks.[93]

4.2.4   A Message-Passing Model: MP-RAM

In the message-passing model that is discussed below we again have a collection of RAMs, but in contrast with the PRAM model above, the memories are also replicated. Indeed the memory of each RAM is inaccessible by the others, and thus some other means for communication, namely passing messages, is provided. More formally, a *P-processor message-passing RAM,* or an *MP-RAM of size P,* consists of the following:

---

[93] One question is whether 512 disks could be placed together to meet the maximum cable length limitation.

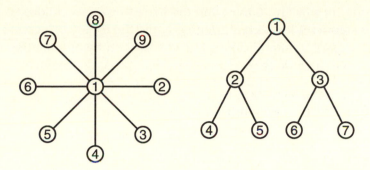

Figure 4.19   *Two simple interconnection graphs.*

1.   *P* unmodifiable programs, each composed of optionally labeled instructions.[94]
2.   *P* memories, one associated with each program.
3.   *P* accumulators, one associated with each program.
4.   A read-only input tape.
5.   A write-only output tape.
6.   An interconnection graph, described below.

We refer to the program-memory-accumulator triples as RAMs even though they are not precisely the same as the RAMs of section 4.2.2, in that these triples do not contain tapes and do support additional (message-passing) instructions not permitted in the original RAM.   The *interconnection graph* has a node corresponding to each RAM in the ensemble.   An edge in the graph indicates that the RAMs on either end can communicate via the send and receive primitives to be introduced.   RAMs so connected are called *neighbors;* the *degree of a node* is the number of edges incident on it, which equals the number of neighbors of the corresponding RAM; and the *degree of an interconnection network* is the maximum of the degrees of its constituent nodes (see Chapter 8 for more details).

Figure 4.19 shows two simple interconnection graphs. In the first graph, often called a *star topology,* all communication involves the central RAM, numbered 1, which has degree 8. In the second graph, often called a *binary*

---

[94] We are defining an MIMD model; an alternative SIMD model would specify just one program that is executed by all *P* of the RAMs, each using its own memory.

tree topology, a RAM can communicate with its parent or either of its children (naturally the root has no parent and the leaves have no children). Interior nodes have degree 3, leaves have degree 1, and the root has degree 2.

Interprocessor communication is accomplished by augmenting the RAM instruction set to include these explicit message-passing primitives:

> Send Neighbor
> Receive Neighbor

Associated with each pair of neighbors (or equivalently with each edge in the interconnection graph) is a bidirectional communication channel. The send instruction copies the value from the accumulator to the channel associated with the neighbor; receive copies the value from the channel to the accumulator.

An important question to ask is what happens if a receive occurs before the corresponding neighbor sends, or if two sends occur without an intervening receive? We shall adopt a synchronous, or blocking, model and say that in either of these cases the instruction in question is delayed until the anomalous condition no longer holds. One can think of (each direction of) the channel as having an associated full/empty flag: A send blocks until the channel is empty and then copies its data and sets the flag to full. Similarly, a receive waits until full and sets to empty.

4.2.5 Emulating Message-Passing with Shared Memory

It is important to realize that a PRAM is a more powerful model than an MP-RAM in that any message-passing algorithm can be executed on a shared-memory architecture with no additional running time. This execution is accomplished by emulating the message-passing architecture as follows. Logically divide most of the shared memory into regions, each to be used as the private memory of one processor. Divide the remaining shared memory into two-word buffers used for message transmission from one processor to another. Two such buffers are needed for each edge in the interconnection graph, one for each direction of information flow. One word of the buffer is used for the value being transmitted; the other is a full/empty flag, which is initialized to empty. Now a send command of the MP-RAM can be emulated on the PRAM by constantly testing the appropriate full/empty bit until it is found to be empty, at which point the value to be sent is placed in the buffer, and then the flag is set to full. Similarly, receive consists of looping until the flag is full, removing the value from the buffer, and then setting the flag to empty.

One can argue that the PRAM is actually *too* strong a model. That is, algorithms will run faster on this model than on real computers since the constant-time access to shared memory is not realizable. The best that one can hope for is that access time is proportional to $\log(N)$. The reader is referred to [407] for a substantially more comprehensive discussion of this topic.

4.2.6   *Parallel Computational Complexity*

In order to formulate a precise definition of parallel computational complexity and related concepts, and thus obtain a suitable yardstick with which to measure the efficiency of parallel algorithms, we extend the treatment given above for serial computational complexity to include the existence of multiple processors. We begin with an informal discussion and then proceed to a more rigorous treatment, always concentrating on the time (as opposed to space) complexity.

Informal Discussion

The key point to observe is that whereas the time complexity of a sequential algorithm is a function of just the size of the problem instance, the time complexity of a parallel algorithm is a function $T(P, N)$ of not only the problem size N, but also of the parallel processor size P, where the latter is defined to be the number of processing elements (PEs) available. It is actually a simplification on our part to assume that the parallel computer size can be specified by a single parameter. In effect, we are considering a family of computers whose members differ only in the number of PEs each contains. For shared-memory computers, this family is simply the PRAM model. For message-passing architectures we are thinking of families, such as binary trees, whose interconnection topologies all have the same structure but differ in size. Commercial computer families are rarely so easily characterized.

As an example of two-parameter computational complexity, consider an algorithm whose running time with P processors on problem instances of size N is given by

$$(1) \qquad T(P, N) = \lceil \frac{N}{P} \rceil \; + \; \log(P)$$

Recall that the *ceiling* function $\lceil x \rceil$ gives the smallest integer not smaller than x. For example, $\lceil 3.5 \rceil = \lceil 4 \rceil = 4$. As we shall see, the new parameter P in equation (1) gives rise to various questions that do not occur in the study of serial complexity. We should remark that formula (1) is representative of a common occurrence in parallel complexity: A serial algorithm has complexity $f(N)$, and the corresponding parallel algorithm is constructed by dividing the N data points into P groups, each of size approximately N/P. The parallel algorithm begins with a local phase in which the serial algorithm is run in each processor using one of the groups as data. This phase requires time $f(N/P)$, which, if f is the identity function, gives rise to the N/P term found in equation (1).[95] Then a second global phase is needed in which the P partial results computed during the local phase are combined. Often this phase is accomplished by first combining pairs of results to obtain $P/2$ values, then combining pairs of these values, and so on. Each step halves the number of partial results and thus when repeated $\log(P)$ times, produces the single final result. If the original partial results and all the intermediate values calculated are of constant size (i.e., size independent of N and P), then it is often possible to perform each combining step in time bounded by a constant independent of N and P, in which case the entire global phase has complexity $\Theta(\log P)$. To obtain formula (1), consider the special case in which each combination requires just one operation; the global phase will then have complexity exactly $\log(P)$. The summing algorithm (see page 205) illustrates the analysis just presented.

One important new question that arises when considering parallel complexity is to determine the *speedup* attained for a given algorithm when multiple processors are employed. That is, how much faster is the problem solved using P PEs than when solved serially? This question normally does not have a simple answer. The speedup S attained when using P processors to solve a problem instance of size N is defined by the formula

$$S(P, N) \;=\; \frac{T(1, N)}{T(P, N)}$$

Often, to emphasize the difference between the two parameters, this last equation is written

$$S_P(N) \;=\; \frac{T_1(N)}{T_P(N)}$$

---

[95]   Unless N is a multiple of P, the groups cannot all be of the same size. Usually, we try to make the sizes as nearly equal as possible (thus minimizing the maximum, and probably rate-limiting, size). The result is that some of the groups have size $\lceil N/P \rceil$, while others have size $\lfloor N/P \rfloor$, where the *floor* function, $\lfloor x \rfloor$, yields the greatest integer not greater than x. Hence, in formula (1) we assign a charge of $\lceil N/P \rceil$ for the local phase.

Thus we see that the speedup is a function of both P and N and can be vastly different as these parameters vary. Once again consider an algorithm whose complexity satisfies (1) above. Then

$$S_P(N) \;=\; \frac{N}{\lceil N/P \rceil + \log(P)}$$

and it is easy to see that if N is much larger than P, the complexity is essentially N/P, and thus the speedup is P. This speedup means that P processors solve the problem P times as fast as 1, implying that the machine is working at maximal efficiency. Such a speedup is the ideal state in parallel processing and is a kind of holy grail for developers of parallel algorithms.   Algorithms that achieve linear (i.e., proportional to P) speedup as processors are added are called *completely parallelizable* and not surprisingly are highly desired. The *efficiency E* of a parallel algorithm is defined to be the speedup divided by P, which has the effect of scaling the speedup to a value between 0 and 1. Symbolically, we write

$$E(P, N) \;=\; E_P(N) \;=\; \frac{S_P(N)}{P} \;=\; \frac{T_1(N)}{P \times T_P(N)}$$

For example, if a 60-PE machine achieves an efficiency of 75% on a given algorithm, the machine is running 45 times faster than for a serial machine and thus is effectively employing 45 processors on the problem itself, the remaining 15 processors being lost to various overheads.

To illustrate the dependence of speedup on P and N, let us now replace the assumption that N dominates P with the assumption that P dominates N. In this case formula (1) becomes essentially

$$T(P, N) \;=\; \log(P)$$

which says that the problem actually takes *longer* to solve as more processors are added.   This anomalous behavior can indeed occur.   Referring to the model solution technique given above, there is some value of P such that executing the local phase, in which one solves subproblems each of size N/P, takes time comparable to executing the second global phase, in which the P partial results are combined. Thus (speaking asymptotically), the time for the entire task is equal to the time for each of the two phases. At this point the amounts of local and global work are in balance.   Further increasing P will lower the time for the first phase and raise the time for the second, which can only increase the total execution time.

As with serial complexity, we are often not able to get exact values for the parallel complexity $T(P, N)$ and thus must settle for asymptotic results. But now it is not so clear what this means. Presumably asymptotic results are obtained by considering arbitrarily large problems, that is, letting N approach infinity; but on what size machine?

Certainly, we must also let the machine size grow as well, since if we bound the number of processors and let the problem size grow arbitrarily large, then just employing an optimal serial algorithm on one processor and letting the others go idle is asymptotically optimal. We need to make two remarks concerning this, perhaps somewhat surprising, assertion. First, recall again that asymptotically optimal does not imply the best one can do. The hyperopic Greeks believe that walking (to California from New York, say) has the same asymptotic time complexity as taking an airplane since both are linear functions of distance. Only the scale factors differ. Second, the assertion itself is actually quite trivial. If the optimal serial complexity is $f(N)$, then an optimal parallel algorithm would have complexity $\Theta(f(N)/P)$. But since P is bounded, this is just $\Theta(f(N))$, which can be attained by solving the problem on one processor. It is thus clear that when considering asymptotic complexity, we must have P grow with N.

But it is not enough just to specify that P and N are permitted to grow arbitrarily large; we need to know in addition how the two are related. Recall our discussion of formula (1). We had an exact formula for $T(P, N)$ and considered two different situations: first N much larger than P, and then P much larger than N. These two possibilities give rise to radically different speedups, even if N and P are arbitrarily large in both situations, thus illustrating the necessity of specifying the relation between P and N in addition to asserting that both are large.

Another question to ask is whether the parallel algorithm in question is applicable for all values of P. In a formal sense the answer to this question is always yes since any algorithm can be trivially extended to operate for all values of P. If there are more processors available than the algorithm specifies, simply let the excess computational power go idle. Of course, this approach has the effect of lowering the efficiency as the number of idle processors increases, and thus one often says that the algorithm is only applicable for $P \leq P_{max}$ instead of the more precise statement that only $P \leq P_{max}$ processors can be profitably employed. If, instead, there are fewer processors than specified, one can multiprogram each of these real processors to create the correct number of virtual processors and implement the algorithm on the latter. This transformation does not affect the asymptotic efficiency attained, since if the P virtual processors are obtained by k-way multiprogramming real PEs, then both the speedup and the number of processors are reduced by a factor of k.[96]

A real complication is that there may be two algorithms for the same problem, one preferred when P is related to N in one way and the second algorithm preferred when the relationship is different. For example, consider the problem of finding the minimum spanning tree (MST) for a connected graph containing N vertices on an MIMD shared-memory parallel processor having P PEs. In this problem one is given a connected graph with a weight assigned to each edge and must choose a subset of the edges such that these edges form a tree containing every vertex, and the sum of the weights is minimal.[97] We note that instances of this problem typically have two size parameters: the number of vertices and edges in the original graph. However, in order to simplify the discussion that follows and stay within the framework specified above, in which the size of an instance is a single integer, we restrict the problem to *dense* graphs, that is, graphs in which the number of edges grows quadratically with the number of vertices. Thus the instance size is just N, the number of vertices, and the number of edges is $\Theta(N^2)$. Optimal serial algorithms for the MST problem are known and have complexity $\Theta(N^2)$. In [93] we find a parallel MST algorithm using

$$\Theta\left(\frac{N^2}{\log^2 N} \right)$$

processors that requires $\Theta(\log^2 N)$ cycles to complete. Since the speedup is

$$\frac{\Theta(N^2)}{\Theta(\log^2 N)} = \Theta\left(\frac{N^2}{\log^2 N} \right)$$

the efficiency is $\Theta(1)$ and the algorithm is completely parallelizable. If, however, the number of processors is increased to N^2, then an algorithm of [41] (using [395]) is faster, since it requires time only $\Theta(\log N)$. Note that this second algorithm, which is not completely parallelizable, does not dominate the first; that is, there are values of P for which the first algorithm is faster. Specifically, if we employ multiprogramming to lower the processor requirement of the second algorithm to

---

[96] We are assuming that the time required to switch a processor's attention from one task to another is bounded by a constant, independent of P and N. Thus, the task-switching overhead goes undetected by our hyperopic Greek friends.

[97] The discussion to follow is applicable to the more general problem of finding the minimal spanning forest for an arbitrary graph.

$$\Theta\left(\frac{N^2}{\log^2 N}\right)$$

then the time required would be $\log^3 N$. For completeness we should mention that in [103] there is yet a third algorithm that outperforms both of the above for a certain range of values for P. Given

$$\Theta\left(\frac{N^2}{\log\ N\ \log\log\ N}\right)$$

processors, the third algorithm finds the minimum spanning forest in time

$$\Theta(\ \log\ N\ \log\log\ N\ \log\log\log\ N)$$

A natural attempt at combining the best features of each algorithm would be to incorporate all three as subalgorithms of a new algorithm that simply examines the values of P and N and then invokes the subroutine having minimal complexity for these parameter values. The time complexity of the resulting algorithm would be quite complicated because it would contain the three complexities given above with an indication of the range of parameter values for which each applies. One must note that this analysis is not necessarily complete, in that there are ranges of values for which faster algorithms might exist. Should such algorithms be found, the overall time complexity for the problem would become yet more complicated.

One way of simplifying the complexity formulas, at the expense of limiting the information presented, is to specify once and for all the relationship between the size of the problem and the size of the parallel computer, instead of attempting to give results that cover the full range of possibilities. Although not the only possibility, the approach we shall adopt is to assume that the problem size is to grow more quickly than the machine size, that is, $N >> P$. The practical justification for this assumption is that, as has occurred with serial machines, the important problems that are to be solved on parallel processors will usually be very large, and making the machines larger will only whet the appetite of users and encourage them to attempt yet larger problems. If we define the loading factor L to be N/P, which measures the amount of data stored in each processor, then our approach is to consider arbitrarily large parallel processors with each processor loaded arbitrarily heavily.

An alternative approach that we shall not pursue is to consider *unbounded parallelism* and define

$$T^*(N)\ =\ \inf_{P}\ T_P(N)$$

that is, let the complexity be the smallest obtained for any number of processors. One could then apply the (one-variable) asymptotic limits to T^*.

Formal Definitions

Our treatment follows that of Gottlieb and Kruskal [201]. The reader is encouraged to see [297] as well.

We continue to assume that the size of a problem instance can be expressed by a single integer parameter, N. The *size of a parallel computer,*
which we consistently denote by P, is the number of processing elements that
it contains.

The *(time) complexity* of a parallel algorithm when executed on a problem
instance of size N by a parallel processor of size P is denoted as either $T_P(N)$ or
$T(P, N)$. In a *dependent-size problem,* N is some specified function f of P; that
is, the size of the problem is determined by the size of the machine. When this
is not the case, we have an *independent-size problem*. An important special
case of a dependent-size problem occurs when f is the identity function, that
is, when $N = P$, in which case we have an *identity-size problem*. If the model
is message-passing, the initial distribution of the data items to the PEs is important; often one assumes a balanced distribution in which each processor
contains either $\lfloor (N/P) \rfloor$ or $\lceil (N/P) \rceil$ items. For example, in a balanced distribution of an identity-size problem, each processor contains one datum.   A
dependent-size algorithm is one used to solve a dependent-size problem, an
independent-size algorithm is one used to solve an independent-size problem,
and an *identity-size algorithm* is one used to solve an identity-size problem.

The *loading factor* of a problem is

$$L = N/P$$

We will see later that the time complexity of the independent-size summing
problem (for a certain computational model) is

$$T_P(N) = \Theta\left(\frac{N}{P} + \log P \right) = \Theta(L + \log P)$$

For N much larger than P (i.e., for L large, the right-hand side is essentially
$\Theta(N/P)$. To make this last assertion precise we introduce another asymptotic
order, which describes the asymptotic behavior of two-variable functions at
an asymmetric limit where one variable is much larger than the other. In light
of its intended application, we refer to this asymptotic order as the *heavily-*

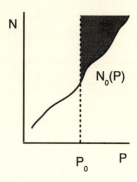

Figure 4.20 *The heavily-loaded limit* of a two-variable function, indicated by the shaded region.

loaded limit or *HL-limit*.[98] The idea is to restrict attention to the region indicated in Figure 4.20 and let P_0 increase. Then f is $o_{HL}(g)$ if f/g approaches 0, f is $O_{HL}(g)$ if f/g is bounded, f is $\Theta_{HL}(g)$ if f/g is bounded and is bounded away from 0, f is $\Omega_{HL}(g)$ if f/g is bounded away from 0, and f is $o_{HL}(g)$ if f/g approaches infinity. More precisely, let f and g be functions of P and N. Then:

$o_{HL}(g)$ is the set of f such that, for all $\epsilon > 0$, there exists a constant P_0 and a function $N_0(P)$ such that, for all $P \geq P_0$ and $N \geq N_0(P)$, $f(P, N) < \epsilon g(P, N)$.

$O_{HL}(g)$ is the set of f such that there exist constants P_0 and C and a function $N_0(P)$ such that, for all $P \geq P_0$ and $N \geq N_0(P)$, $f(P, N) < Cg(P, N)$.

$\Theta_{HL}(g)$ is the set of f such that there exist constants P_0, C_1, and C_2 and a function $N_0(P)$ such that, for all $P \geq P_0$ and $N \geq N_0(P)$, $0 < C_1 g(P, N) < f(P, N) < C_2 g(P, N)$.

$\Omega_{HL}(g)$ is the set of f such that there exist constants P_0 and C and a function $N_0(P)$ such that, for all $P \geq P_0$ and $N \geq N_0(P)$, $0 < Cg(P, N) < f(P, N)$.

$\omega_{HL}(g)$ is the set of f such that for all C there exist a constant P_0 and a function $N_0(P)$ such that, for all $P \geq P_0$ and $N \geq N_0(P)$, $g(P, N) < f(P, N)$.

In analogy with one-variable asymptotic orders discussed previously, when f is contained in $o_{HL}(g)$, we write $f = o_{HL}(g)$ and similarly for O_{HL}, Θ_{HL}, Ω_{HL}, and ω_{HL}.

Recall that the independent-size summing algorithm has time complexity

---

[98] These same concepts were studied by Gottlieb and Kruskal (among others), who called them *supersaturation limits*. We do not adopt their terminology, since the supersaturation limit (in physical chemistry), unlike the mathematical limit we desire, does not correspond to an arbitrarily large loading (of the solvent with the solute).

$$T_P(N) \;=\; \Theta\!\left(\frac{N}{P} + \log\, P\right)$$

Using these definitions of heavily loaded limits, we may formalize the remark that for N large compared to P, N/P dominates log P by writing the complexity as

$$\Theta_{HL}\!\left(\frac{N}{P}\right)$$

We conclude by remarking that using the unbounded parallelism model alluded to previously, summing has complexity logarithmic in N.

4.3   Selected Parallel Algorithms

Armed with the material on computational complexity presented above, we are now ready to discuss algorithms designed for parallel computers. This is a subject for which there is a large and explosively growing literature, so we cannot even begin to present a comprehensive treatment. Instead, we will describe and give a complexity analysis for just a very few algorithms and present in tabular form the complexity of several others, including algorithms designed for both message-passing and shared-memory computational models. We shall see that for many of these algorithms, the speedup increases when, for a fixed-size machine, the problem size is allowed to grow. This situation occurs in the summing algorithm discussed in detail and in many of the tabulated algorithms, because these algorithms each divide into two phases, one in which purely local computation is performed and one in which global computation occurs. As the problem size grows, the local phase becomes dominant. Since, for the algorithms in question, the local phase is performed at maximal efficiency, it follows that the computation becomes increasingly more efficient as the problem size increases. Indeed, our hyperopic Greeks declare such algorithms to be *completely parallelizable* (i.e., maximally efficient) for large problems.

As indicated previously, an important advantage of having a precise mathematical computational model is that it enables one to assign a cost to executing a given algorithm on a specific problem instance. Thus one has a basis on which to choose among algorithms for the same problem. We hope to give the reader a feeling for the importance of choosing a good (i.e., low computational complexity) algorithm for the problem to be solved. We also point out limitations of this approach by explaining why it is that sometimes the best algorithm is *not* the fastest and why the whole is sometimes greater than the sum of its parts, that is, why an implemented solution to an entire problem can require considerably more computing resources than would be predicted by summing the analyzed complexity of its constituent algorithms.

Given a good algorithm for an important problem, it is tempting to design a special-purpose computer containing just the hardware needed to implement the algorithm effectively. A pioneer in this line of work is H.T. Kung, who, working with colleagues at Carnegie Mellon University, has derived "systolic algorithms" for a variety of problems and has shown how these algorithms can be essentially embedded in silicon. The special-purpose vs. general-purpose parallel processor debate has certainly not been resolved and sometimes gets pretty hot and heavy. This issue is discussed in the architecture chapters later in this book, in which we also consider why some algorithms are more amenable to direct VLSI implementation than others.

One aspect of the special-purpose vs. general-purpose question does seem clear. It is risky to develop hardware for problems for which good solutions or at least good solution techniques are not yet established. For example, imagine building a computer for a specific algorithm used for computer vision. By tailoring the machine to this algorithm it might perform a factor of, say, 3 to 10 better than a more general-purpose computer using an equivalent amount of hardware. However, during the hardware development period an improved vision algorithm might be found that performs 50 times faster than the old algorithm. If this new algorithm is run on the general-purpose computer, but the special-purpose computer can only run the old algorithm, the latter will not be competitive. Thus it is not surprising that the first targets of special-purpose machines are in mature areas where it is unlikely that vastly improved algorithms will be discovered soon. Since the FFT algorithm is asymptotically optimal, it has been the subject of several special-purpose designs. Moreover, many AI-tailored architectures can be seen as hardware realizations of efficient searching techniques. Although AI is in an early (prescientific) stage of development and asymptotically optimal algorithms have not yet been discovered for most problems, it does seem very likely that, for the next several years at least, searching will play an important role.

Although it is generally advantageous to choose algorithms having the lowest asymptotic complexity, we now turn our attention to several caveats that must be added to this principle.

4.3.1   *Issues*

Imprecision in Asymptotic Complexity

As indicated previously, a great deal can be "swept under the Θ rug". Two algorithms with equivalent asymptotic complexity can have their running times differ by an arbitrarily large constant factor. Moreover, the asymptotically inferior algorithm may actually be the method of choice for problems of practical sizes: the crossover point may occur for problems so large as to be infeasible for either algorithm on any computer likely to exist in the foreseeable future. Perhaps Larry Snyder put it best: "We don't live in asymptopia."

A well-known example of a superior but slower parallel algorithm is the so-called Hungarian sorting algorithm. Since the serial complexity of sorting N values is $\Theta(N \log N)$,[99] a completely parallelizable, and hence optimal, N-processor algorithm would have complexity $\Theta(\log N)$. Such an algorithm has been discovered [12]. However, the authors acknowledge that the constants hidden by using asymptotic complexity are so large as to render the algorithm impractical.

Worst Case vs. Real-World Behavior

In addition to the issue of large constants, another reason why a complexity calculation may not indicate the best algorithm to use in practice is that our analyses have been for worst-case data and do not consider how likely the worst case is to occur. An illustration of this shortcoming actually appeared in the newspapers several years ago when the Russian L.G. Khachiyan discovered the "ellipsoid" method for solving linear programs [278].[100] The standard solution technique, George Dantzig's "simplex" method [117] was known to require (in the worst case) a number of computation steps that grows exponentially in N, the number of unknowns. The ellipsoid method, with a worst-case computational complexity only polynomial in N, is thus a vastly more effective solution technique.[101] Although Khachiyan's discovery is interesting

---

[99]   As mentioned above, this complexity estimate is only accurate for comparison-based sorting, so we must restrict the computational model to eliminate other techniques, such as radix sorts.

[100]   In a linear program, one wishes to minimize the value of a linear "objective function", such as $7x + 3.5y + 9z - 12w$ subject to a series of "linear constraints" such as $x \geq 0$, $4x + 7y \geq 9$, $y + 2z + w \geq 8$, and $-x - y - w \geq -15$. In commercial applications the objective function often represents the cost of an activity (e.g., shipping oil), and the constraints represent various physical limitations such as storage capacities and maximum flow through pipes.

[101]   The initial newspaper accounts erroneously claimed that a polynomial time solution to the linear programming problem yields a polynomial time solution to the traveling salesman

theoretically, the ellipsoid method has not displaced the simplex method in applications because the worst-case exponential complexity growth is not observed in practice.[102]

Needed Data Movement

Many large-scale problems encountered in practice require a series of diverse algorithms to be applied, and the results of one algorithm are not distributed among the processors in the manner needed by the successor algorithm. Indeed, for current (mostly hypercube) message-passing computers the performance obtained on important problems is often rate-limited by the time required to move data. Thus, one must not forget to include the cost of required interalgorithm data motion when choosing between alternative solutions to a given problem.[103] We return to the topic of data motion later in this chapter when we discuss the complexity of permutation algorithms.

I/O

A related issue is input/output, which may be regarded as data motion into and out of the computer. It is not a significant benefit to improve the algorithms used if the problem is already I/O-bound using current technique. Although the values to be read in and written out are usually specified by the problem and thus are algorithm-independent, the choice of algorithm can determine the required distribution of the input values as well as the final results. Given a 2D $P \times P$ mesh-connected parallel computer with I/O ports located at each of the $4P$ boundary processors, an algorithm that produces its results evenly distributed along the boundary can output these results $4P$ times as fast as an algorithm that produces its results all in one processor. As a result the latter algorithm may require an additional redistribution phase in which the results are spread out along the periphery.

---

problem, which, were it true, would have given an affirmative answer to the P=NP question that remains the leading unsolved problem in theoretical computer science.

[102] A faster polynomial time algorithm has been discovered by Narendra K. Karmarkar [272] that may prove to be competitive with the simplex algorithm in practical applications.

[103] Perhaps the best way to do this is to specify and analyze the data-motion algorithm to be used.

4.3.2   A Simple Message-Passing Algorithm: Summing

To illustrate the analytical formulation given above, we shall study three sample algorithms, two using message-passing and the other shared memory, and calculate their computational complexities. We will then present in tabular form the corresponding results for several other algorithms and cite references in which the reader may find detailed presentations.

We begin by considering the simple example of summing N numbers. The natural sequential algorithm in which we initialize a variable to zero and then increment it by each of the N numbers has complexity $\Theta(N)$, which is easily shown to be optimal. Let us now consider the identity-size problem on a private-memory (i.e., message-passing) machine with P processors, where we have $N = P$ items, one in each processor.

The Dependent-Size Analysis

The idea of the parallel algorithm is to add pairs of numbers and then pairs of pairs, and so on.[104] For this procedure to work in a straightforward manner, it is necessary to assume that the interconnection topology contains a binary tree; that is, a binary tree can be obtained from the interconnection graph (see Figure 4.19 on page 191) by removing edges (but not nodes). The simplest example of such a topology is the binary tree itself, and the presentation that follows is for a binary-tree machine having tree height H. Therefore,

$$N \;=\; P \;=\; 2^{H+1} - 1$$

and thus

$$H \;=\; \Theta(\log P)$$

For the moment let us pretend that we are trying to sum just $N = 2^H$ values evenly distributed across the 2^H leaf nodes of the tree. Subsequently, we will modify the algorithm to include the $2^H - 1$ values stored at the interior nodes.

During the first step of the algorithm, each leaf node sends the stored value up[105] to its parent, where the two values received are added. During the second step, these parents send the sums just calculated up to their parents, each of which sums the two values received, thus producing $N/4$ values, each the sum of four original values. Proceeding iteratively, we see that the Hth step

---

[104] This is an example of a parallel algorithm fitting the model used to justify formula (1) above, but without a local phase.

[105] Perhaps for typographical reasons, trees in computer science, unlike their biological analogues, exhibit positive geotropism; that is, they grow downward.

produces one value (at the root of the tree) that is the sum of all N initial values, as desired. Since each of these H steps consists of two data transmissions and one arithmetic operation, which can clearly be accomplished in time $\Theta(1)$, we see that the entire algorithm has complexity

$$T_P(N) \;=\; T(P,N) \;=\; \Theta(H) \;=\; \Theta(\log P) \;=\; \Theta(\log N)$$

Recall our assumption that the values to be added reside only at the leaves of the tree. To include the values initially located at the interior nodes, we modify the algorithm to have the parents form the sum of three values, two received from their children and one stored at the parent itself. The new algorithm still consists of H steps each requiring a constant number of operations (now two additions and two data transmissions), and thus the overall complexity remains

$$T_P(N) \;=\; \Theta(H) \;=\; \Theta(\log P) \;=\; \Theta(\log N)$$

Since the serial algorithm has complexity $\Theta(N)$, we see that the speedup of this algorithm is

$$S_P(N) \;=\; \frac{T_1(N)}{T_P(N)} \;=\; \frac{\Theta(N)}{\Theta(\log N)} \;=\; \Theta\!\left(\frac{N}{\log N}\right) \;=\; \Theta\!\left(\frac{P}{\log P}\right)$$

The efficiency is thus

$$E_P(N) \;=\; \frac{S_P(N)}{P} \;=\; \Theta\!\left(\frac{1}{\log P}\right)$$

which is very discouraging, since it says that if we scale the problem and machine size up together, the efficiency tends toward zero! This result is not surprising when we consider that the algorithm utilizes only two levels of the tree at a time, leaving the remaining $H-2$ levels idle.

The Independent-Size Analysis

Now let us consider the independent-size problem in which the problem size is not tied to the machine size. In particular, let us put L items in each processor, where we permit L to vary. Recall that parallel algorithms often consist of local and global phases. The summing algorithm just presented contains only a global phase; we now augment it with some local processing.

Begin the new algorithm by having all processors locally sum the L items they contain using the standard sequential algorithm, which requires time $\Theta(L)$. These partial sums can themselves be (globally) combined in time

$\Theta(\log P)$ using the identity-size algorithm just presented. Thus we have summed $N = LP$ values in time

$$\Theta(L) + \Theta(\log P) \;=\; \Theta(L + \log P)$$

The Heavily Loaded Limit

If we consider the heavily loaded limit, in which L becomes arbitrarily large, we see that the time complexity is just

$$T_P(N) \;=\; \Theta(L + \log P) \;=\; \Theta_{HL}(L)$$

$$S_P(N) \;=\; \frac{T_1(N)}{T_P(N)} \;=\; \frac{\Theta(LP)}{\Theta(L + \log P)} \;=\; \Theta_{HL}(P)$$

$$E_P(N) \;=\; \frac{S_P(N)}{P} \;=\; \Theta_{HL}(1) \;.$$

Instead of having the efficiency tend toward zero, as in the $N = P$ case, the problem is seen to be completely parallelizable, that is, to have optimal efficiency, in the heavily loaded limit, where each PE has been given a lot to do during the (fully parallel) local phase.

The explanation for this change is that the local work is clearly being performed at maximal efficiency, and as we increase the loading factor L, the amount of local work grows, whereas the amount of global work remains constant. Thus as L approaches infinity, essentially all the time is spent at maximal efficiency.

The final question we wish to ask is how large must L be for this limiting behavior to occur? This question is not hard to answer. We have a maximally efficient local phase and a less efficient global phase whose complexity does not grow with loading. All we need to do is to "balance the work", that is, increase the loading so that the local and global phases have the same asymptotic complexity. To see that this increase is sufficient, let us break up $T_P(N)$ into its local and global components, $T_P^{loc}(N)$ and $T_P^{glo}(N)$, respectively. Then the speedup may be written

$$S_P(N) \;=\; \frac{T_1(N)}{T_P^{loc}(N) + T_P^{glo}(N)}$$

Figure 4.21   Time complexity of the summing algorithm *as a function of the problem size N and the processor count P. Note that when N is small, the complexity increases with P, but for N large the reverse occurs. For simplicity we have replaced* $\Theta(f)$ *with* f.

If the two terms in the denominator are asymptotically equal (i.e., within a constant factor of each other), then the Greeks would give you two for the price of one,[106] and thus the speedup becomes

$$S_P(N) \;=\; \Theta\!\left(\frac{T_1(N)}{T_P^{loc}(N)}\right)$$

which is just the speedup of the local phase that we have assumed to be optimal.   If the loading is increased further so that the local phase has greater complexity than the global phase, it remains true that the complexity of the two phases is asymptotically equal to the complexity of the local phase. For our specific example $T_P^{loc}(LP) \;=\; \Theta(L)$, and $T_P^{glo}(LP) \;=\; \Theta(\log P)$. Thus for the entire algorithm, the ideal speedup and efficiency found in the HL-limit is actually achieved at a loading factor of $L \;=\; \Theta(\log P)$. We can summarize this discussion by stating that the summing algorithm just described is completely parallelizable for $L \;=\; \Omega(\log P)$.

Our initial formulation of the summing algorithm, where the $N = \lceil P/2 \rceil$ values to be added are located at the leaves, can be readily pipelined. This

---

[106] That is, the asymptotic complexity of a sum is the same as that of the largest term.

property, common to many tree algorithms, means that a second instance of the problem can be started before the first is finished. For the summing problem, as soon as the values have been sent from the leaves to their parents, new values can be read. In this way a tree of height H can be solving H instances of the summing problem simultaneously, with the nodes at height i processing instance i. Thus, although each instance requires time $\Theta(H)$ for solution, the tree is capable of solving summing problems at a rate of one every $\Theta(1)$ time units.

Parallel Prefix

An important generalization of the summing algorithm is to ask not only for the overall sum but for all the partial sums as well. That is, if the $N = PL$ input values are

$$a_1, a_2, ..., a_N$$

then we seek N answers

$$s_1, s_2, ..., s_N$$

where

$$s_i = \sum_{j=1}^{i} a_j$$

Naturally, we can consider other associative operators as well as addition. Finding parallel solutions to these questions is often called the *parallel prefix* problem. The reader is encouraged to extend the summing algorithm in the text to calculate the partial sums as well and hence solve the parallel prefix problem (once again using P processors and $\Theta(L + \log P)$ time units). You should assume that the L values in a given leaf processor have consecutive indices.

4.3.3   *Another Message-Passing Algorithm: Permuting*

The previous section described a positive result: For a binary tree of message-passing processors, the summing algorithm is completely parallelizable for large problems. In this section we present a negative result: For any practical network of message-passing processors, the permutation problem is not completely parallelizable. Indeed, the speedup cannot exceed

$\Theta(P/\log P)$. We also reference results that show that for many networks, there are algorithms that achieve this bound. Much of the material in this section is from Gottlieb and Kruskal [201]; the interested reader is referred to that paper for further details and references to related research.

High-performance data-motion procedures are highly desired since, as indicated above, for many important problems, the solution involves a number of different algorithms, and the results of one algorithm are not distributed among the processors in the manner needed by the successor algorithm. For example, the first algorithm may leave each row of a matrix in a separate processor, while the second algorithm requires that each processor contain a column; in this case a transpose is needed.

The data motion specified by a transpose operation is a *permutation;* that is, each datum is assigned to a unique previously occupied location. In particular, the number of items in a given PE does not change as a result of the operation. The results to be given are all stated in terms of permutations; the lower bounds obtained apply to the more general problem of arbitrary data motion. We adopt the standard assumption that all data items are unique since equal data can be permuted by leaving them alone. For example, if all the data are identical, the null algorithm realizes any permutation.

Permuting Is Not Completely Parallelizable

On a uniprocessor, N items can be moved in time $\Theta(N)$, so a completely parallelizable permutation algorithm on a P-processor parallel computer would have complexity $\Theta(N/P)$. We shall see that this asymptotically ideal performance cannot be achieved on realistic hardware. The last assertion is trivially true for certain data distributions: for any P, if $N/2$ items are located in each of two processors, any permutation moving each item to the other processor will need $\Omega(N)$ data communication cycles to complete. The interesting result is that for *any* initial data distribution (in particular, if the data are distributed evenly among the processors), the assertion still holds. To state this result precisely, we need to recall several definitions.

Two PEs are *neighbors* if they are (directly) connected. The *degree of a PE* is the number of neighbors it has. The *degree K of a parallel processor* is the maximum degree of the PEs it contains. In general, K may depend on P; if it does not, we say that the parallel processor is of *bounded degree*. These latter processors are of practical interest, since if the degree is not bounded, then the interprocessor connections will consume an increasingly large portion of the entire machine as P increases. According to this line of reasoning, for large enough P, a full hypercube (page 386) implementation will not be practical. If the machine presents a hypercube to its users, the hardware will need to simulate the hypercube topology using as a hardware base some bounded-degree interconnection such as the binary tree or shuffle-exchange (K=3), or a 2D grid (K=4). Commercial hypercube-based computers from Intel, NCUBE, and FPS have a few hundred processors (K about 8) and do include the full topology in the hardware. At a somewhat larger scale, the connection machine, with $64,000^{107}$ processors ($K = 16$) does not quite have all the necessary wires.[108]

The *diameter of a parallel computer* is the maximum interprocessor distance.[109] The diameter of a bounded-degree parallel computer must grow at least logarithmically with P since, if the degree is K, then at most K^D PEs can be within distance D.[110] Using graph theory (chiefly Dirac's theorem on the existence of Hamilton cycles), Gottlieb and Kruskal [201] show that one can find a permutation of the processors such that the distance between any processor and its image under the permutation is logarithmic in P. We say that such a permutation moves each processor a logarithmic distance. This statement implies that moving data items from any processor to its image requires a logarithmic number of steps. Thus, if the data were evenly distributed among the processors, then the (data) permutation defined by specifying that each item be moved to a corresponding item in the image processor would require $\Theta(N \log P)$ data-routing operations, which would require time $\Omega(N/P \log P)$, a factor of $\log P$ more than a completely parallelizable algorithm would consume. At the other extreme, if all N items are in one processor, any fixed-point free permutation would require $\Omega(N)$ cycles.

With some additional care, arbitrary data distributions can be analyzed and the following key result obtained. Any permutation algorithm for a degree-K parallel processor requires time $\Omega(N/P \log_K P)$, and thus for a bounded-degree parallel processor, the complexity is $\Omega(N/P \log P)$. It follows that (for any data distribution) the permutation problem is not completely parallelizable on a bounded-degree parallel processor.[111]

---

[107] This is the computer science thousand, which equals 1.024 (mathematical) thousands.

[108] The interchip wiring is a full hypercube, but the on-chip interconnection is only a 2D mesh, in terms of which a hypercube is simulated. We describe the Connection Machine on pages 446–458.

[109] The *distance* between two processors is the length of the shortest sequence of PEs that starts at the first processor, ends at the second, and has the property that successive PEs are neighbors. For example, any PE is at distance zero from itself and at distance 1 from any of its neighbors.

[110] More precisely, a degree-K parallel computer has diameter at least $\log_K(P + 1) - 1$.

[111] More precisely, the problem is not parallelizable on any degree $P^{o(1)}$ parallel processor.

Permuting Evenly Distributed Data

Since any degree-1 parallel processor with more than two PEs is disconnected, it cannot permute data at all. Connected degree-2 machines are either chains or cycles. It is easy to see that for such machines there is a permutation that moves each processor a linear distance (essentially $P/2$), and thus permuting evenly distributed data requires $\Omega(NP)$ data operations and hence $\Omega(N)$ cycles, the same number of cycles (asymptotically) as for a uniprocessor.

For degree 3 or higher the situation is much better. Gottlieb and Kruskal [201] show that the degree-3 *shuffle-exchange machine* can permute evenly distributed data in time $\Theta_{HL}(N/P \ \log \ P)$, which is optimal by the results of the previous section. For $K \geq 2$ the degree-$2K$ *K-way shuffle machine* can permute evenly distributed data in time $\Theta_{HL}(N/P \ \log_K P)$, which is again optimal. Both the shuffle-exchange and the K-way shuffle machines are described in Chapter 8. The HL-limit above is attained at a load factor of

$$ L \ = \ \Omega\left(\frac{P^{4.5}}{\log \ P} \right) $$

If the permutation may be analyzed in advance, then upon presentation of the N (evenly distributed) data items, the necessary data motion can be effected in $\Theta(N/P \ \log \ P)$ cycles on a shuffle-exchange machine and in $\Theta(N/P \ \log_K P)$ cycles on a K-way shuffle machine. That is, this variant, called the *static* permutation problem by Gottlieb and Kruskal, is optimal at all levels. If the permutation is not known in advance (the *dynamic* permutation problem), optimality is only achieved at the heavily loaded limit.

4.3.4 A Shared-Memory Algorithm: Sorting

We now present a shared-memory algorithm for sorting N values in time $\Theta(\log \ N)$, which is very fast but uses $\Theta(N^2/\log N)$ processors, which is lavish indeed.[112] Since the asymptotically fastest serial algorithms for sorting (for example, heapsort) can process N values in time $\Theta(N \log N)$, we see that our shared-memory sorter has speedup

$$ S_{N^2/\log N}(N) \ = \ \frac{\Theta(N \log N)}{\Theta(\log \ N)} \ = \ \Theta(N) $$

giving an efficiency of

---

[112]   The table on page 219 includes more efficient sorting algorithms.

$$E_{N^2/\log N}(N) \;=\; \frac{\Theta(N)}{N^2/\log N} \;=\; \Theta\!\left(\frac{\log N}{N}\right)$$

If we are permitted to use the fetch-and-add instruction found on the NYU Ultracomputer (page 572), then we can sort N values with N^2 processors in constant (i.e., $\Theta(1)$) time!

We assume that N values are already loaded in memory (in locations $V[1], ..., V[N]$), that no duplicates are present, and that N^2 processors are present (we shall later reduce the number of processors to $N^2/\log N$). The goal is to place the sorted values into locations $W[1], ..., W[N]$. The idea is to compare each value against all the values, recording the N^2 results, and then determine the rank of each value by counting how many numbers it is not smaller than. The first step is to divide the processors into N groups each of size N; that is, an ordered pair (i,j) with $1 \le i,j \le N$ is associated with each processor, signifying that it is the jth processor in group i. (There are two ways to do this. One is to note that each processor in a PRAM has its own program and simply "hard code" the appropriate ordered pair within each program. A more pragmatic solution is to extend the PRAM model to permit each processor to obtain its "processor number", from which the ordered pair is easily calculated.) We define an N-by-N matrix A and then have processor (i,j) place a 1 into $A[i,j]$ if $V[i] \le V[j]$ and place a zero into $A[i,j]$ otherwise. We next define an N-element vector T and have the N processors in group i cooperate (in a manner described below) to calculate

$$T[i] \;=\; \sum_{j=1}^{N} A[i,j]$$

in logarithmic (i.e., $\Theta(\log N)$) time. Note that $T[i]$ is the number of values in A (including $A[i]$ itself) that do not exceed $A[i]$. Since we have outlawed duplicate values, $T[i]$ gives the index in W where $A[i]$ should be placed; that is, if $T[i] = x$, then $A[i]$ should be placed into $W[x]$. Hence we simply let processor $(i,1)$ set $W[T[i]]$ equal to $A[i]$.

Note that the summing step requires logarithmic time and that all the other steps are constant time, so the entire algorithm has logarithmic complexity. This completes our description of the algorithm, except for the summing calculation. But the summing algorithm has already been given! Recall that *any* message-passing algorithm can be considered a shared-memory algorithm of equal complexity (see page 192), and we have already given a tree algorithm that sums $\Theta(P \log P)$ values in time $\Theta(\log P)$ using P processors (put $\Theta(\log P)$ values at each leaf of the tree). For our sorting application, we have

N processors to sum N numbers in $\Theta(\log N)$ time, which is overkill. This is why we can reduce the overall processor count in sorting to $\Theta(N^2/\log N)$. We again divide the processors into N groups, but this time each group contains only $N/\log N$ processors. Reducing the group size by a factor of $\log N$ increases the complexity of some of the constant-time steps given above to $\Theta(\log N)$ by letting each processor do the work $\log N$ did before. For the summing step, we have $P = N/\log N$ processors and N values. But

$$\Theta(\log P) = \Theta(\log(N/\log N)) = \Theta(\log N - \log \log N) = \Theta(\log N)$$

and thus

$$\Theta(P \log P) = \Theta(P)\Theta(\log P) = \Theta\left(\frac{N}{\log N}\right)\Theta(\log N) = \Theta(N)$$

Hence, we have P processors to sum $\Theta(P \log P)$ values and thus can accomplish the task in time

$$\Theta(\log P) = \Theta(\log N)$$

In summary, reducing the number of processors did not alter the asymptotic complexity of the summing algorithm. Indeed, we have shown that the overall asymptotic complexity of sorting remains logarithmic as desired.

We now return to the situation with N^2 processors to sum N values, but augment our PRAM with the fetch-and-add (`faa`) primitive:[113]

```
faa           operand
```

This augmentation causes the accumulator of the processor executing the instruction to be added to the memory location specified by the operand.[114] Recall that with N^2 processors, all the steps for sorting were constant-time except for summing N values with N processors. But with faa this is also constant-time, and hence so is sorting.

---

[113] We are not using the full power of this primitive.

[114] We assume that this instruction requires only constant time even if many processors are simultaneously incrementing the same memory location. This assumption is not realistic. However, the Ultracomputer architecture description on page 580 shows that concurrent fetch-and-adds have the same complexity as concurrent loads and stores, which are assumed to be constant-time operations in the PRAM model.

4.3.5 Other Message-Passing Algorithms

The tables on pages 216 through 218 reprinted from [201] present results for other algorithms. The lower bounds given hold for any bounded-degree parallel processor, and the upper bounds can be achieved on a (degree-3) shuffle-exchange machine.

4.3.6 Other Shared-Memory Algorithms

The table on page 219 gives the asymptotic complexity for several shared-memory algorithms. This material was kindly provided by Uzi Vishkin. The results are all for problems of size n. In many cases the results can be sharpened by using a second parameter (e.g., specifying m, the number of edges, in addition to n, the number of vertices) rather than making a worst-case assumption, for example, that the graph is dense, so $m = \Theta(n^2)$). All the algorithms will run on the CRCW PRAM model. However, many do not utilize concurrent writes, and thus the results apply on weaker PRAM models. The interested reader should consult the reference given for each algorithm.

Problem	Sequential		Dependent-size		
	Time	Size	Time bounds		Speedup
	$T_1(N)$	$N = f(P)$	Lower	Upper	$S_P(N)$
Summing	N	P	$\log P$	$\log P$	$\dfrac{P}{\log P}$
Permuting (static)	N	P	$\log P$	$\log P$	$\dfrac{P}{\log P}$
Packing	N	P	$\log P$	$\log P$	$\dfrac{P}{\log P}$
Sorting	$N\log N$	P	$\log P$	$\log^2 P$	$\dfrac{P}{\log P}$
Sorting (1 to N)	N	P	$\log P$	$\log^2 P$	$\dfrac{P}{\log^2 P}$
Merging	N	P	$\log P$	$\log P$	$\dfrac{P}{\log P}$
Permuting (dynamic)	N	P	$\log P$	$\log^2 P$	$\dfrac{P}{\log^2 P}$
Median	N	P	$\log P$	$\log^2 P$	$\dfrac{P}{\log^2 P}$
Median average case	N	P	$\log P$	$\log^2 P$	$\dfrac{P}{\log^2 P}$
Set and map operations	$N\log N$	P	$\log P$	$\log^2 P$	$\dfrac{P}{\log P}$
FFT	$N\log N$	P	$\log P$	$\log P$	P
Matrix mult[a] (naive)	$N^{1.5}$	$P^{2/3}$	$\log P$	$\log P$	$\dfrac{P}{\log P}$
Matrix mult[b] (Strassen)	$N^{0.5 lg 7}$	$P^{2/lg 7}$	$\log P$	$\log P \log\log P$	$\dfrac{P}{\log P \log\log P}$
Gauss elimination[c] (complete pivoting)	$N^{1.5}$	P	$\sqrt{P}$	$\sqrt{P\log P}$	$\dfrac{P}{\log P}$
Odd-even reduction (tridiagonal)	N	P	$\log P$	$\log P$	$\dfrac{P}{\log P}$

[a] N is the number of items in the matrix. The speedup is relative to the naive (cubic in $\sqrt{N}$) algorithm (not the fastest known).

[b] N is the number of items in the matrix. The speedup is relative to Strassen's algorithm (not the fastest known).

[c] N is the number of items in the matrix.

Figure 4.22   *Performance of message-passing algorithms, part 1* – *sequential and dependent-size regimes. The tables in Figure 4.22 to Figure 4.24 are reprinted from Gottlieb and Kruskal [201].*

Problem	Independent-size		Speedup
	Time bounds		
	Lower	Upper	
Summing	$L + \log P$	$L + \log P$	$\dfrac{LP}{L + \log P}$
Permuting (static)	$L \log P$	$L \log P$	$\dfrac{P}{\log P}$
Packing	$L + \log P$	$L \log P$	$\dfrac{P}{\log P}$
Sorting	$L \log(LP)$	$L \log L + L \log^2 P$	$\dfrac{P \log(LP)}{\log L + \log^2 P}$
Sorting (1 to N)	$L + \log P$	$L \log^2 P$	$\dfrac{P}{\log^2 P}$
Merging	$L + \log P$	$L \log P$	$\dfrac{P}{\log P}$
Permuting[a] (dynamic)	$L \log P$	$P^{4.5} + L \log P$	$\dfrac{LP}{P^{4.5} + L \log P}$
Median	$L + \log P$	$(1 + \log L) \log^2 P + L \log P$	$\dfrac{LP}{(1 + \log L) \log^2 P + L \log P}$
Median average case	$L + \log P$	$L \log P + \log^2 P$	$\dfrac{LP}{L \log P + \log^2 P}$
Set and map operations	$L \log(LP)$	$L \log L + L \log^2 P$	$\dfrac{P \log(LP)}{\log L + \log^2 P}$
FFT	$L \log(LP)$	$L \log(LP)$	P
Matrix mult[b] (naive)	$L^{1.5} + \log P$	$L^{1.5} + L \log P$	$\dfrac{P}{1 + L^{-0.5} \log P}$
Matrix mult[c] (Strassen)	$L^{0.5 \log_2 7} + \log P$	$L \log P \log \log P + L^{0.5 \log_2 7}$	$\dfrac{P}{1 + L^{1 - 0.5 \log_2 7} \log P \log \log P}$
Gauss elimination[d] (complete pivoting)	$L^{1.5} \sqrt{P}$	$L^{1.5} \sqrt{P} + L \sqrt{P} \log P$	$\dfrac{P}{1 + L^{-0.5} \log P}$
Odd-even reduction (tridiagonal)	$L + \log P$	$L + \log P$	$\dfrac{LP}{L + \log P}$

[a] A faster algorithm is known for $L = O(P^{4.5} / \log^2 P)$.

[b] N is the number of items in the matrix. The speedup is relative to the naive (cubic in $\sqrt{N}$) algorithm (not the fastest known).

[c] N is the number of items in the matrix. The speedup is relative to Strassen's algorithm (not the fastest known).

[d] N is the number of items in the matrix.

Figure 4.23 Performance of message-passing algorithms, part 2 – independent-size regime.

Problem	Heavily loaded limits		Speedup	Remarks[a]
	Time bounds			
	Lower	Upper		
Summing	L	L	P	Optimal at all levels and CP at $L = \Omega(\log P)$
Permuting (static)	$L\log P$	$L\log P$	$\dfrac{P}{\log P}$	Optimal at all levels and scales up
Packing	L	$L\log P$	$\dfrac{P}{\log P}$	Scales up
Sorting	$L\log L$	$L\log L$	P	CP at $L = P^{\Omega(\log P)}$
Sorting (1 to N)	L	$L\log^2 P$	$\dfrac{P}{\log^2 P}$	Scales up
Merging	L	$L\log P$	$\dfrac{P}{\log P}$	Scales up
Permuting (dynamic)	$L\log P$	$L\log P$	$\dfrac{P}{\log P}$	Optimal at $L = \Omega(P^{4.5}/\log P)$
Median	L	$L\log P$	$\dfrac{P}{\log P}$	Reaches the heavily loaded limit at $L = \Theta(\log P \, \log\log P)$
Median average case	L	$L\log P$	$\dfrac{P}{\log P}$	Reaches the heavily loaded limit at $L = \Theta(\log P)$
Set and map operations	$L\log L$	$L\log L$	P	CP at $L = P^{\Omega(\log P)}$
FFT	$L\log L$	$L\log L$	P	CP at all levels
Matrix mult[b] (naive)	$L^{1.5}$	$L^{1.5}$	P	CP at $L = \Omega(\log^2 P)$
Matrix mult[c] (Strassen)	$L^{0.5\log_2 7}$	$L^{0.5\log_2 7}$	P	CP at $L = \Omega((\log P \log\log P)^{\alpha})$, $\alpha = 1/(0.5\log_2 7 - 1)$
Gauss elimination[d] (complete pivoting)	$L^{1.5}\sqrt{P}$	$L^{1.5}\sqrt{P}$	P	CP at $L = \Omega(\log^2 P)$
Odd-even reduction (tridiagonal)	L	L	P	Optimal at all levels and CP at $L = \Omega(\log P)$

[a] CP = Completely parallelizable.

[b] N is the number of items in the matrix. The speedup is relative to the naive (cubic in $\sqrt{N}$) algorithm (not the fastest known).

[c] N is the number of items in the matrix. The speedup is relative to Strassen's algorithm (not the fastest known).

[d] N is the number of items in the matrix.

Figure 4.24 Performance of message-passing algorithms, part 3 – heavily loaded regime.

Problem	Number of Processors	Asymptotic Complexity	References (See Caption)
Maximum	$\dfrac{n}{\log\log n}$	$\log\log n$	a,b
Merging	$\dfrac{n}{\log n}$	$\log n$	a
Merging	$\dfrac{n}{\log\log n}$	$\log\log n$	c,d
Sorting	$\dfrac{n}{\log n}$	$\log^2 n$	a
Sorting	n	$\log n$	e
Median	n^ε	$n^{1-\varepsilon}$	f
Median	$\dfrac{n}{\log n \log\log n}$	$\log n \log\log n$	g
Connected Components	$\dfrac{n^2}{\log^2 n}$	$\log^2 n$	h,i
Minimum Spanning Tree	$\dfrac{n^2}{\log^2 n}$	$\log^2 n$	h
Minimum Spanning Tree	n^2	$\log n$	j,k
Minimum Spanning Tree	$\dfrac{n^2}{\log n \log\log n}$	$\log n \log\log n \log\log\log n$	l
Biconnected Components	$\dfrac{n^2}{\log^2 n}$	$\log^2 n$	m,n
Biconnected Components	n^2	$\log n$	n
Euler Tour	n^2	$\log n$	o,p
String Match	$\dfrac{n}{\log n}$	$\log n$	q,r
Parsing Arithmetic Exp	$\dfrac{n}{\log n}$	$\log n$	s
Max Flow	n	$n^2 \log n$	t,u

Figure 4.25 *Performance of shared-memory algorithms.* References in the last column correspond to items in our bibliography as follows: a-[394], b-[446], c-[296], d-[70], e-[12], f-[13], g-[451], h-[93], i-[449], j-[41], k-[395], l-[103], m-[443], n-[430], o-[40], p-[38], q-[450], r-[187], s-[51], t-[396], u-[196].

4.4 Exercises

1.   Define the following terms.

Computational model	Complexity of a problem
Von Neumann model	
Binding time	$T_P(N)$
SISD	
SIMD	Dependent-size problem
MISD	Independent-size problem
MIMD	Loading factor
Computational complexity	Completely parallelizable
	Speedup
$o(g)$	Efficiency
	Diameter of a parallel computer
$O(g)$	Static permutation problem
	Dynamic permutation problem
$\Theta(g)$	Asymptotic time complexity
	Asymptotic space complexity
$\Omega(g)$	Unbounded parallelism
$\omega(g)$	

2.   Match each of the terms on the left with its attribute on the right

   a.   Degree of a parallel
        computer
   b.   HL-limit
   c.   Harvard architecture
   d.   Hungarian algorithm
   e.   MP-RAM
   f.   PRAM
   g.   Parallel prefix
   h.   RAM
   i.   Shuffle-exchange ma-
        chine
   j.   Space complexity
   k.   Time complexity

   1)   A degree 3 parallel processor
   2)   An asymmetric asymptotic limit
   3)   Computing all partial sums
   4)   Highly efficient but impractical sorting algo-
        rithm
   5)   Maximum number of neighbors
   6)   Message-passing computational model
   7)   Number of computational steps
   8)   Number of memory words referenced
   9)   Separate data and instruction memories
   10) Serial computational model
   11) Shared-memory computational model

3.   What are the implications of a Harvard architecture?

4.   Reread the box entitled Computational Model Attributes and express the contents
     in your own words.

5.   What does it mean to have a hierarchy of computational models?

6.   Discuss how the technology of the 1940s influenced the von Neumann model of
     computation.

7. (Hard) If von Neumann were still alive, what model of computation might he invent today?

8. Why might someone argue that pipelined vector processors are MISD computers?

9. What are the advantages and disadvantages of MIMD vs. SIMD?

10. Consider the MIMD model in more detail. In your own words, express the contents of the figure giving Treleaven's classification.

11. For each of the following tell whether $f = o(g)$, $f = O(g)$, $f = \Theta(g)$, $f = \Omega(g)$, or $f = \omega(g)$. For this problem assume $\log(x) = \log_e(x)$, the natural logarithm and let $abs(x)$ be the absolute value of x..
    a. $f(x) = 3x^2$ and $g(x) = 9x^2$.
    b. $f(x) = x^2$ and $g(x) = 2^x$.
    c. $f(x) = x^2$ and $g(x) = 2^{\log x}$.
    d. $f(x) = (abs(\sin(x)))^x$ and $g(x) = x$.
    e. $f(x) = x \, abs(\sin(x))$ and $g(x) = .5x$.

12. In what ways is the PRAM model unrealistic? Is a PRAM an MIMD or a SIMD model? Is it a synchronous or asynchronous model?

13. The section "Emulating Message-Passing with Shared Memory" on page 192 discusses simulating message-passing with shared memory. What about the reverse problem: Given an MP-RAM, how would you simulate a PRAM? Is the simulation efficient, i.e., does the running time of a problem increase by more than a constant factor?

14. Would an algorithm designer prefer an algorithm that is completely parallelizable at $L = \Omega(P)$ or one that is completely parallelizable at $L = \Omega(\log P)$? Both algorithms solve the same problem.

15. Read the description of *scaled speedup* in Gustafson's 1988 paper [211] and 1992 conference presentation [213] and the description of isoefficiency in the 1993 paper of Grama et al. [204]. Compare these concepts with our heavily-loaded speedups and with the speedup obtained using unbounded parallelism.

16. How should the disk bandwidth grow with the number of processors if the system is to be used for problems having time and space complexity each linear in the problem size? What if the time complexity is cubic but the space complexity is linear?

17. For each of the following functions what is the heavily-loaded limit? At what loading factor is the limit achieved?
    a. $T(P,N) = \log^2 P + N/P$
    b. $T(P,N) = (N + P)/\log P$
    c. $\dfrac{N}{P^2 + \dfrac{N}{P}\log P}$

18. Solve the parallel prefix problem mentioned in the text. That is, modify the summing algorithm so that all the partial sums are calculated as well. You should assume that the L values stored in a given leaf processor have consecutive indices.

19. Consider two algorithms for a given problem. The first algorithm achieves a speedup of P (i.e., is completely parallelizable) for $P = \Theta(\log N)$. The second achieves a speedup of P for $P = \Theta(\log^2 N)$. Which one would an algorithm designer prefer?

Part II: Parallel Software

Einstein argued that there must be simplified explanations of nature, because God is not capricious or arbitrary. No such faith comforts the software engineer.— Fred Brooks

Overview of the Software Chapters

We have now reached a turning point in our book. The previous chapters have discussed the source and nature of potential parallelism in a number of applications, have touched on the capabilities and limitations of the available technology, and have reviewed possible computational models and algorithms for solving problems in parallel. The rest of this book concentrates on the practical problems of how the software and hardware actually do this.

The next three chapters—on languages, compilers, and operating systems—examine the *software* needs of parallel processing. That is, having decided on a problem from the application domain and on a basic computational model for the parallel hardware, how do we enable a user to create and execute a program that solves the problem as desired? The last chapter described the underlying computational models and software constructs that are available. The applications programmer's environment is the subject of the next chapter, Languages and Programming Environments. Translating the user's program into executable form is the subject of the subsequent chapter, Compilers. Our software trilogy concludes with a chapter entitled Operating Systems.

Real Programmers Don't Write Specs

Real Programmers don't eat quiche. They eat Twinkies and Szechwan food.

Real Programmers don't play tennis, or any other sport that requires you to change clothes. Mountain climbing is OK, and real programmers wear their climbing boots to work in case a mountain should suddenly spring up in the middle of the machine room.

Real Programmers don't write specs—users should consider themselves lucky to get any programs at all and take what they get.

Real Programmers don't comment their code. If it was hard to write, it should be hard to understand.

Real Programmers don't write application programs, they program right down on the bare metal. Application programming is for feebs who can't do systems programming.

Real Programmers don't write in Cobol. Cobol is for wimpy applications programmers.

Real Programmers don't write in Fortran. Fortran is for pipe stress freaks and crystallography weenies.

Real Programmers don't write in PL/I. PL/I is for programmers who can't decide whether to write in Cobol or Fortran.

Real Programmers don't write in BASIC. Actually, no programmers write in BASIC, after the age of 12.

Real Programmers don't program in Lisp. Lisp is for people who flunked math.

Real Programmers don't program in APL. The Wizard of Oz programs in APL.

Real Programmers don't write in PASCAL, or Modula, or ADA, or any of those pinko computer science languages. Strong typing is for people with weak memories.

Figure 5.1 Lighthearted overview of the major programming languages. *(See page 229 for a more orthodox summary.) The "strong typing" comment in the last line refers to the fact that these three languages require users to distinguish between many possible types for each of their variables, as a means of achieving program clarity and readability. (Adapted from Datamation.)*

5

Languages and Programming Environments

The limits of my language mean the limits of my world.—Ludwig Wittgenstein

This chapter looks at parallel programming from the viewpoint of the applications programmer, the end user of the parallel system. How will this person obtain parallel execution of a program? What languages or programming environments are available for this purpose? In other words, what computational model(s) will the *user* be dealing with?

In "Essential Constructs for Parallel Execution" starting on page 146 we discussed the extra operations (beyond those for a serial program) that are needed for the profitable execution of a parallel program —the ability to define, start/stop, and coordinate the parallel subtasks, and perhaps the ability to partition and distribute the data —and we gave examples of constructs used in performing these operations. We did *not* say who was actually responsible for these mechanics. Will the applications programmer have to make explicit use of these parallelism constructs? The answer is maybe. Before we discuss possible scenarios, however, a word on language terminology and on how this chapter is organized.

Figure inner content:

```
Foreach longitude, latitude, altitude
    ustar[i,j,k] = n * pi[i,j] * u[i,j,k]
    vstar[i,j,k] = m[j] * pi[i,j] * v[i,j,k]
    sdot[i,j,k] = pi[i,j] * sigmadot[i,j]
End
```

SOURCE CODE   SERIAL EXECUTION   PARALLEL EXECUTION

(a)   (b)   (c)

Figure 5.2 *Illustrative serial and parallel execution of a loop* from the weather code on page 48 for a hypothetical case in which L = 3 (three layers of atmosphere). The compact notation used for the loop indices is explained on page 47. (a) Illustration of the looping construct in the source code. (b) Serial execution showing single thread of control. (c) Parallel execution showing split thread of control.

Imperative and Declarative Languages

Languages can be classified as imperative or declarative [248], [205], and our chapter is divided the same way. Imperative languages are mainstream. Declarative languages may be where we are going—or not. It depends on whether the "new and improved" features of declarative languages really do pay for themselves in increased parallelism sufficiently well to offset the huge investment in imperative programs and programming skills. Meaningful performance comparisons are just appearing, and so we are at an interesting juncture. Read on.

Imperative programs are sequences of commands, and *imperare* means "to command" in Latin. The commands update variables held in storage, and so an imperative program is said to have a *state* that is altered as the program progresses. There has been a 40-year period of tuning imperative languages (Fortran, Cobol, C, Ada, etc.) and their compilers for the von Neumann computational model, so it is not surprising that these languages are the choice of most professional programmers, whose job, after all, is to write efficient programs for von Neumann computers. It is also argued that many real-life processes that one wants to model on a computer lend themselves naturally to representation as imperative programs [455]. The arrival of parallel computers has brought with it parallel extensions to imperative languages and parallelizing compilers for the automatic extraction of parallelism from serial imperative programs. These approaches have had some success, and after a quick review of the non-parallel imperative languages, we describe these imperative approaches to parallel programming in the first part of this chapter.

But there are those who believe that parallel computers need new, non-imperative languages that free programmers not only from the von Neumann model's "do this, then do that" style, but in fact free programmers from this level of detail entirely, and let them declare *what* they want separately from *how* to get it. Declarative languages, unlike imperative languages, are designed to focus on expressing *what* a program's purpose is rather than *how* the computation is supposed to be carried out. Languages for functional programming and for logic programming are both in the declarative category, and the reader will find them discussed in the second part of this chapter.

What options, then, are there for the programmer facing a parallel computer? We sketch out three scenarios.

Three Scenarios for the Programmer

Most potential customers of parallel computing will already have an investment in existing programs and programming skills, and would naturally like to take advantage of those investments. They are not interested in parallel programming for the sport of it. But as we said in the last chapter, profitable execution of a parallel program requires the ability to define, start and stop, and coordinate the execution of the parallel subtasks, and probably to partition and distribute the program's data as well. Who's going to do this, and how? Three scenarios exist today, which represent a range of trade-offs between programmer work required and performance obtained.

Automatic Parallelization of "Dusty Decks"

In the "dusty deck" or "legacy code" scenario, a parallelizing compiler accepts the original (serial) program (typically a huge old Fortran workhorse) and produces a parallel program. The programmer doesn't have to modify the program or learn a new language. This "automatic parallelization" approach has yielded moderate degrees of speedup on some problems, and is described in our Chapter 6 on compilers. These compilers have to work hand-in-glove with the parallel operating systems of Chapter 7, and the boundary between the two is not yet sharply etched, reflecting healthy disagreement between two camps as to whether operations like scheduling are better performed by the compiler or the operating system. The automatic parallelization scenario demands the least from the user, but the performance improvement is often modest, and such compilers are not always available, especially if the programmer's target is a distributed-memory parallel system.

Parallel Extensions for Imperative Languages

The second scenario requires more work from the user, but still avoids the need to learn a completely new language or completely recode the original serial program. The user draws up a plan to partition the execution and data of the original program, and then carries it out using a set of parallelism constructs appropriate to the target system. In effect, the user learns an extension to a language that he or she already knows. Examples are Express, PVM, and Linda for message-passing environments, and other sets of constructs for shared-memory environments. In addition, explicitly parallel variants of sequential languages (principally Fortran) have been devised. We discuss Fortran 90 and Fortran D later in this chapter. Such "toolkits" of explicit parallelism constructs and explicitly parallel language variants are more widely available than automatic parallelizing compilers, and the degree of parallelism obtained can be higher because the programmer knows what the program is really trying to do. This is probably the most widely used of the three scenarios today. However, there is still a strong influence from the fact that the original program was written for a definitely sequential execution model, and one should also ask about the *portability* of the resulting code.

Non-Imperative Languages

In the third scenario, the user decides to learn a new language with less or no vestiges of the sequential von Neumann computational model, and rewrites the program in the new language. This is an area of major activity in language research, but this scenario is not yet used much in practice. Interestingly, the emphasis is not so much on parallel languages (languages geared toward a specific parallel computational model) as it is on high-level languages that do not assume a specific execution model at all, whether serial or parallel. That is, rather than languages like Occam, which is tailored for the Transputer's message-passing mechanism but is still very much an imperative language, the research emphasis has been mostly on declarative languages, which are designed to express *what* to do rather than *how* to do it. Two kinds of declarative languages are *logic programming* languages like Prolog and *functional programming* languages like the early dataflow languages, and Haskell and Sisal. The implementation of most of these languages is not as efficient as today's imperative languages (Fortran, Cobol, C, etc.) but noteworthy results are beginning to appear. Our chapter on compilers describes how Sisal recently outperformed Fortran on some significant parallel programs. Advocates claim that functional languages' greater expressiveness and freedom from low-level detail lead to more efficient programs on parallel architectures, and hence are worth the learning, recoding, and extra memory capacity that may be needed. These third-scenario trade-offs are discussed in the present chapter on languages, which treats the major imperative and declarative examples.

After a brief review of the major serial languages, the remainder of this chapter is organized as follows:[115] Imperative parallel languages are treated first. Then we discuss declarative languages, starting with functional languages and following with logic programming languages. We will examine the trade-offs and try to put the issues in perspective.

5.1   Review of the Major Serial Languages

It is natural for programmers using a serial language to ask how suitable that language is for parallel computing. Also, many parallel languages and programming environments are outgrowths or extensions of serial languages. Understanding the serial version leads to better understanding of the parallel version. Furthermore, understanding the *differences* among serial languages helps to understand some of the differences among parallel ones. For these reasons, we begin with a brief review of the serial languages.

All the major high-level programming languages in use today came into being in order to write programs for a von Neumann computer, and all show vestiges of this sequential execution model, some more than others. (Our definition of a major language is one that is widely used *and* has a substantial body of programs. Despite the large number of languages invented over the years, only about ten meet this test today, with two more on the way [see Figure 5.3 on page 231].) We will first review each of these languages briefly, and then make some comments on this whole class of languages.[116] Readers

---

[115]   Note that we are classifying languages "as seen from above", that is, as defined in their language manuals and seen by the programmer, whereas our first edition took a "view from below" and classified languages by execution model (control-driven, data-driven, demand-driven, and pattern-driven). Starting with a look from above allows us to distinguish more clearly between language *definition* and *implementation* issues.

[116]   Worrying about how to capitalize the names of programming languages can drive you crazy, because there are no universally accepted rules. We tend to follow the widespread current practice of capitalizing names formed from (only) the initials of an acronym. Thus, APL (A Programming Language) is written with all capital letters, but Fortran (FORmula TRANslator) is not.

interested in more detail should consult references [192], [367], [39], [381], [31], and [455]. The last reference contains a capsule history similar to ours.

5.1.1 A Brief History

Fortran is the grandfather language; its influence is widespread and can be seen even in the way that we structure parallel programs—fork resembles branching and goto statements, tasks resemble subprograms, and so on. As the first high-level programming language, introducing features like symbolic expressions and subprograms with parameters, Fortran had to prove that such languages could generate efficient code. The designers placed considerably more emphasis on efficiency than on syntax, and the language bears a number of features tailored for the (sequential) target computer. Array data types are supported, but in versions earlier than Fortran 90, the language primitives can only deal with array elements, not the whole array. One might say that Fortran is more "compiler-friendly" than "user-friendly". Its efficiency made it the language of choice for the computationally intensive scientific/engineering problems that are one of the driving forces for parallel processing, but this efficiency in matching a serial computer also makes such programs difficult to recast onto a parallel computer. This topic, called *automatic parallelization,* is discussed in our chapter on compilers. A number of parallel extensions to Fortran have been developed (see page 239 or the example in Figure 5.7 on page 245).

Algol was designed with more concern for a well-defined and machine-independent syntax[117] and inspired most of the subsequent theoretical work in programming languages. Algol-60 introduced the concept of *block structure,* whereby variables, procedures, and so on could be declared wherever in the program they were needed, resulting in programs with a more hierarchical structure than Fortran. However, Algol-60's original lack of vital file-handling and data-structuring facilities has limited its commercial use. The later Algol-68 contained additional features, including an equivalent to parbegin.

Cobol is the most widely used language in the world. Its highly structured programs are specifically geared toward business applications, and great emphasis is placed on data motion and presentation. The reason it receives so little attention in discussions of parallel processing is that most Cobol applica-

---

[117] Perhaps Algol reflects the fact that the design team included Europeans, who tend to be more grammar-conscious than the more informal, "get it done" Americans who designed Fortran.

Figure 5.3   A rough genealogy of current major programming languages.

tions today are rate-limited not by computation speed but by I/O speed, which is more difficult to remedy with parallel processing (but see pages 503–504).

Lisp–Whereas Fortran was geared toward scientific and engineering problems whose data were well represented by highly regular *arrays,* Lisp was designed for problems in artificial intelligence and other areas with irregular data structures that are well represented as *lists*. (Lisp stands for LIst Processing Language.) Recursive function calls, which are forbidden in Fortran, play a major role in Lisp. An MIMD-parallel extension called Multilisp is discussed later in this section (page 245), and an SIMD-parallel extension for the Connection Machine is discussed on page 456.

APL is geared toward arrays but is a much higher-level language than Fortran in that it features a large number of powerful "aggregate operators" [31] that act on the whole array, not just one array element at a time. (APL has 66 high-level operators; Fortran has only 6, and they operate at a lower level.) The higher-level semantics allow one to think about and program mathematical operations in a style that is much closer to mathematics than to the looping constructs needed in Fortran and other lower-level languages, and also means that the nature of these parallelizable array operations does not get lost because the language gets so involved with the details of sequential execution. (APL and Lisp are ancestors of the functional programming languages we treat later.) However, some of the features that make APL easy to use also make it hard to compile, and this is one reason that APL has not displaced Fortran for computationally intensive problems in the past. The prospects for automatic parallelization using APL-like languages are discussed on page 323 in our chapter on compilers.

BASIC is a popular language but is not often used for programs large enough to need parallel processing (the B stands for "Beginner's"). The original language was designed to be simple enough so that its translator would be small enough (16 KB or so) to fit on very small computers. The trade-off was that standard BASIC lacked some features (like parameterized subroutines) needed to construct large programs.

PL/1 is a large language that combines many features of Fortran, Algol, and Cobol. The IBM version contains the fork and join[118] parallelization primitives and thus allows the *creation/termination* of parallel tasks, but it has difficulty *coordinating* these tasks in practice.

Pascal was originally designed for teaching disciplined programming and has influenced nearly all recent languages, including Ada. However, its simple I/O mechanism and the strong typing that it imposes on the programmer in its quest for reliable, readable programs can become a problem in writing large programs. Concurrent Pascal (page 246) is a parallel extension that uses shared memory and features *processes* and *monitors* for describing and coordinating concurrency. Parallel Pascal [373] was developed for the MPP (page 460).

C is a language commonly used for systems programming. Both C and Pascal are much smaller than, say, PL/1 or Ada and share other characteristics as well.[119] The emphasis in Pascal is on safety, but in C it is on flexibility and lack of restrictions [166]. C's ability to access the hardware helps make it the clear winner over Pascal in writing operating systems (UNIX is written in C). There is also a preference for C for interactive programming because of its more flexible treatment of input/output. With the popularity of UNIX on multiprocessors (page 367), several parallel variants of C have appeared for use in applications. These variants offer constructs analogous to those shown in Figure 5.7 on page 245.

Modula combines the block and type structure of Pascal with the *module* construct (introduced as the *class* construct in Simula [112]) for defining abstract data types (page 288); Ada *packages* are a similar idea. Like C, Modula

---

[118] Forking is done by using a call to a variable that has been declared to be a task name or by attaching the task attribute to the call statement. priorities and events can be attached to the call. Joining is done by a wait statement specifying the events being waited on.

[119] C subroutines pass the *value* of variables to the calling program, whereas Fortran subroutines pass the variable's *address* ("pass by reference"), thus allowing the calling program to modify its value ("we know where you live"). This is an additional side effect (page 235) that makes parallelization harder.

is a general-purpose language at a relatively low level in that it provides enough visibility of the underlying hardware to be useful for concurrency, especially for operating systems.

Prolog is a very high-level language whose heritage is logic programming and automatic theorem proving. Prolog is not a parallel language, but logic programming in general appears to offer parallelism in the execution of production (expert) systems, among others (see page 280 ff.). The Fifth Generation project in Japan was a major driving force. Prolog is the one language summarized in this section that is not an imperative language, and is discussed later in the section on declarative languages. Concurrent Prolog [388] is one well-known parallel variant.

Ada is a general-purpose language strongly supported by the U.S. Department of Defense and designed for numerical computations, system programming, and applications with real-time and concurrency requirements. It was influenced by both Pascal and CSP and supports both a shared-memory and a message-passing model of computation. Among its features are *packages* and *generics,* designed to aid the construction of large modular programs. Its *rendezvous* mechanism implements the CSP message-passing model. Its tasks can also communicate using global variables; synchronization must then be done explicitly. Schonberg and Schonberg [384] discuss an implementation of Ada on the shared-memory Ultracomputer. Ada is probably the best example available of a state-of-the-art concurrent programming language, but it is not intended for fine-grain parallelism. See the related discussions on pages 165 and 247.

5.1.2   Critique of the von Neumann Languages

All programming languages are a compromise between the way the user thinks about solving a problem and the way the computer actually goes about solving it. In his 1978 Turing Award presentation [46], John Backus expressed frustration at how little this point of compromise has moved in 30 years:

> Conventional languages are basically high-level, complex versions of the von Neumann computer. Our thirty-year-old belief that there is only one kind of computer is the basis for our belief that there is only one kind of programming language, the conventional—von Neumann—language. The differences between Fortran and Algol 68, although considerable, are less significant than the fact that they are both based on the programming style of the von Neumann computer.

Although I refer to conventional languages as "von Neumann languages", to take note of their origin and style, I do not, of course, blame the great mathematician for their complexity. In fact, some might say that I bear some responsibility for that problem.

In that same year, Backus added [45]:

I think conventional languages are for the birds. They're really low-level languages. They're just extensions of the von Neumann computer, and they keep our noses in the dirt of dealing with individual words and computing addresses, and doing all kinds of silly things like that, things that we've picked up from programming for computers; we've built them into programming languages; we've built them into Fortran; we've built them into PL/1; we've built them into almost every language. The only languages that broke free from that are Lisp and APL, and in my opinion they haven't gone far enough.

Backus suggests that it is time to be liberated from this programming style. His proposed solution is discussed in "The FP Functional Programming Language" on page 259.

Being the inventor of Fortran, Backus is well aware of the elegant way in which the simple von Neumann model (Figure 4.2 on page 139) made optimum use of the technology of its day. But he also feels that programmer productivity has not improved as it should have, and that the reason is our failure to develop languages that hide the model's low-level details and allow the programmer to concentrate in a more natural, high-level way on *what* is to be accomplished, rather than *how*. Have we lost our perspective on the relation between technology limitations and computational models?

When our definition of a computational model (page 138) is applied to the domain of high-level programming languages, the result closely resembles Pratt's list [367] of a language's essential characteristics:

1. *Data types* (elementary data items and structures) and *primitive operations* (for manipulating data).
2. *Sequence control* to control the execution sequence of primitive operations.
3. *Data control* to control how data are supplied to the operations for execution.
4. *Storage management* to allocate storage for programs and data.
5. *Operating environment* to communicate with the external environment.

Although Backus emphasizes the similarity of the von Neumann languages, they also have key differences that reappear as live issues in parallel language design. Several of these differences are discussed below.

5.1.3   Shared Variables and Side Effects

A key to understanding a programming language and how it differs from another is the meaning and behavior of a *variable* in that language. In mathematics (algebra, for example) a variable is a symbol used to represent a set of possible values (typically those that satisfy a set of equations and/or inequalities). Although, at the point a variable is introduced, we may not know its values, these values are fixed. If $x^2 = 4$, then x is always 2 or -2. Contrast this situation with the assignment statement

    x = x + 1

as used in an imperative programming language like Fortran, where the value of x is changed as a result of executing the statement. Declarative/functional languages like Haskell retain the mathematical meaning of variables.

Languages for von Neumann computers are broadly divided into *imperative* and *declarative* types (the latter includes functional and logic programming languages). In a functional (or *applicative*) programming style, the notion of a variable is very similar to the mathematical sense. Application of a function to a variable can produce a new variable and a new value but *never* changes the old value. In logic programming, too, once a variable acquires a value, it has the same value throughout the program.

However, the vast majority of programming for von Neumann computers is not done with functional languages, but with a style and language that is called *imperative* because the resulting programs have a strong "Do this, then do that" flavor, in contrast to a program written in a functional language, where the mindset is more like "If you give me that, I'll give you this", or a logic program, whose mindset is more like "If this is true and this is true, then that is true". In an imperative language program, the word *variable* has a distinctly different meaning: it becomes a quantity whose value can be obtained from a specified location in memory. The information in this memory location can be read *and modified* by other parts of the program. This modifiable shared-variable concept, or side-effect mechanism strongly reflects the globally accessible memory that is such a key feature of the von Neumann model, and it provides a powerful mechanism for sharing data structures and communicating among various parts of the program. But it also makes the extraction of parallelism considerably more difficult, a point expanded on in our chapter on compilers.

It is indeed possible to write side-effect-free Fortran programs, but they will use a lot more memory. One must remember that the technology of von Neumann's time limited the largest computers to memories smaller than that of the smallest personal computer today. Hence there was strong motivation to reuse and overwrite the memory as much as possible. In some ways, *side effect* is an unfortunate term for this central feature, because it was certainly not an afterthought. However, given the voodoo-doll-like power that it confers upon the programmer, perhaps the name is appropriate, after all.

The rewritable nature of variables in an imperative language can also lead to other kinds of surprises in the contents of a memory location: for example, *aliasing,* a more explicit class of mechanisms such as the COMMON statement, the EQUIVALENT statement, and the parameter-passing protocols of a language like Fortran (see a compiler book such as the one by Aho et al. [11] for details). These mechanisms allow more efficient execution of imperative programs, but they also make it harder to extract parallelism from such a program, a point that is used to argue in favor of functional languages.

5.1.4 *Evolution of Abstraction in Programming Languages*

Languages also differ in their *level of abstraction,* and the history of programming languages shows a discernible trend toward higher levels of abstraction [455]. Machine instructions and most single statements are examples of low-level language constructs. The procedure concept (in Fortran, for example) allows one to treat a larger block of code as an entity that can be conveniently invoked, has its own local variables, and so on. However, this concept does not yet result in a program whose modules are all first-class citizens. For example, if one procedure invokes another, the second can modify the local variables of the first (assuming that it received them as parameters, say), but not vice versa. The direction in language development has been toward making a program more and more a collection of first-class citizens, with their private lives separated from their public lives. Ghezzi [192], [191] gives a good description of this trend. The motivation has chiefly been increased programmer productivity, but it could also be quite beneficial for parallel processing. The problem is that fork, for example, is such a low-level construct that it can activate *any* statement in the program; it is the parallel equivalent of the goto statement of serial languages in the sense that its undisciplined use can create programs that are very hard to understand, maintain, or modify. This negative aspect is especially detrimental in a large program being written by a team rather than an individual.[120]

One reason for the trend toward higher levels of abstraction in the design of programming languages is that if the program can be broken into well-defined modules that are defined by their interfaces and by what they do but not by *how* they do it (software black boxes), then changes in the programming of a module should not affect any of the rest of the program as long as the design discipline is adhered to.

5.1.5   Binding Times

Another distinguishing feature of a language and its computational model is how early or late in the computing process the *binding* of the program's attributes occurs, or, as we put it earlier, at what time the action of the hardware becomes completely specified.   Programs deal with *entities* (variables, subprograms, processes, statements, etc.) that have properties called *attributes*. For example, a variable has a name, a type (scalar, etc.), a scope (territory), a lifetime, a value, and an area in memory where the value is kept. A process can have a number of instantiations. Binding means specifying the exact nature of an attribute.

Serial languages differ in the number of entities they can deal with, the number of attributes per entity, and the time when the binding occurs. A binding is *static* if it is established before run time, as in a compiler-oriented language like Fortran.   A *dynamic,* or *late,* binding is established during runtime and can be changed according to some language-specified rules. This characteristic increases the power and ease of use of interpretation-oriented languages like APL, Lisp, and Prolog, but it makes compilation and efficient execution harder. Ghezzi [192] discusses trade-offs in the choice of binding time with respect to performance, storage requirements, etc.

Parallel languages involve an analogous set of trade-offs. For example, the number of parallel processes can be static, that is, determined before run time, as is the case with parbegin (page 150). Other systems allow the number of processes to be a dynamic quantity, determined at run time and perhaps

---

120 Capron and Williams [84] use the term spaghetti code (a name they ascribe to Dijkstra) to describe a program with too many gotos (by extension, the name should also apply to a program with too many forks and joins). it's interesting to note that in VLSI chip design [439], a similar term (*spaghetti chip*) is used to describe the result of an unstructured design approach.

Figure 5.4 *Hierarchical program structure with procedures* vs. *modular program structure with information hiding. The trend in language design has been toward programs composed of various first-class citizens that interact but also have private lives. The names abstract data types, information hiding, and object-oriented programming all relate to this idea. Ghezzi [192] treats this topic in detail.*

implemented using fork and join (page 149). Once again, there is a set of trade-offs. A static number of processes makes it easier for the compiler to generate efficient code, but at some sacrifice in program flexibility.

5.1.6 Summary

In summary, the trend in programming language design has been toward higher levels of abstraction and program modularity, which may make it easier to adapt such programs for a parallel processor. However, the imperative style with its side effects continues to dominate, and thus automatic extraction of parallelism is quite laborious, especially from programs written in the lower-level languages. It will be interesting to see how this stream of development interacts with the development of parallel processing. Some initial steps in this direction are discussed next.

5.2   Parallel Imperative Languages and Extensions

In our first edition, which was printed in 1988, we described three developing scenarios for programming parallel computers—automatic parallelization, extensions to current languages, and new languages. People were writing programs for specific parallel machines, but none of the three scenarios offered a programming environment for creating portable programs – none offered a practical way of writing programs that would obtain good speedup on a variety of hardware. Since then, considerable progress has been made in the middle scenario. Several sets of extensions to ordinary Fortran and C are becoming accepted and are providing toolkits of standard parallelism constructs that allow the program to run on a variety of parallel systems. These extensions include Fortran-90, Fortran D, Express, PVM, and Linda. Descriptions of these new systems are included below.

We discussed essential programming constructs on pages 146–170. Parallel language and construct issues are also discussed by Andrews and Schneider [27], Ghezzi [191], Halstead [217], Shaw [390], Woodward [461], Carriero and Gelerntner [86], and Szymanski [152]. A nice little book by Osterhaug [350] explains how to write programs in one parallel environment. Other environments are described by Karp [273], Babb [42], Perrott [183], and Hatcher and Quinn [219].

5.2.1 Data Parallelism, Fortran 90, Fortran D, and HPF

Since the earliest days of computing, an important style of computation, especially for numerical computing, is one in which nearly identical operations are performed on each element of an array. In languages such as Fortran this is expressed by a simple loop with the induction variable, that is, the variable whose range is described in a Fortran DO statement, used as the array index. In array-oriented languages such as APL and Fortran 90, which have vector and array operations, the loop is implicit, and just the array name is mentioned. In those cases where the operations on each element are independent and thus suitable for concurrent evaluation, we get a form of parallel processing now known as *data parallelism*. In the CM-5 Technical Summary [435] *data parallelism* is defined as that type of parallelism "in which more or less the same operation is performed on many data elements by many processors simultaneously" and is contrasted with *control parallelism*. The latter includes pipelining and functional parallelism, in which different functions are performed concurrently. (The word *functional* is used in a different sense here than in *functional language*.)

Although often associated with SIMD computers like the CM-2 (page 457) and the MP-1 (page 458), data parallelism is more general, at least as currently defined by Thinking Machines. A prototypical data parallel snippet would be

```
where (boundary_element)
   do something
elsewhere
   do something else
end where
```

As written, this code fragment is most naturally thought of as SPMD (i.e., all processors execute the same program, but not in lockstep as in SIMD). However, the fragment can easily be executed on a SIMD machine in two phases where first the processors containing interior elements are masked out and then the processors containing the boundary elements are masked out.

Fortran 90

The basic idea behind the data parallelism in Fortran 90[121] is to permit expressions in which an array name stands for all its elements processed concurrently, reminiscent of APL. For example, if X is a 50-element one-dimensional array, both

```
DO I=1,50
   X(I) = 2 * X(I)
END DO
```

and

```
X = 2 * X
```

will double each element of X. We can be fancier and describe sections of arrays as well. For example,

```
X(1:25)
```

refers to the first 25 elements of X and

```
X(1:50:2)
```

refers to the entries with odd indices (as in a DO statement with bounds 1,50,2). With higher-dimensional arrays more interesting possibilities arise. For example given a 100×100 array Y,

```
Y(1:50,1:50)
```

---

[121] Fortran 90 is the culmination of what we referred to in our first edition as the "emerging Fortran 8X standard". It was a long and difficult birth.

gives the upper left quarter, and

```
Y(1:100:2,:)
```

gives the odd-numbered rows (: is short for the entire dimension, in this case 1:100:1).

As in APL, various operators and intrinsic functions can be used, so

```
X = SIN(X)
```

calculates all 100 sines. There are also reduction intrinsics like SUM, which calculates the sum of all the elements in an array, and MAXVAL, which calculates the maximum. Shifts are easy using the array section operations:

```
X(1:40) = X(11:50)
```

specifies a left shift of 10. Rotations (circular shifts) can be effected with the CSHIFT intrinsic function. Shifts and rotates on higher-dimensional arrays are also available. If, as is often the case, different elements of an array are stored local to different processors, then these shifts and rotates are actually communication operators. Many other intrinsics are supplied as well.

Fortran D and HPF

The Fortran D language [181] is an extension of Fortran that enables the user to specify the desired decomposition of his or her data. It provides means for both *problem mapping* using array alignments and *machine mapping* using data distribution. These decomposition enhancements can be applied to either Fortran 77 (serial Fortran), producing Fortran 77D, or to Fortran 90, producing Fortran 90D. A version of this last language is also called HPF (High-Performance Fortran). An account of HPF is given in [326].

Problem mapping, a largely machine-independent activity, is concerned with aligning arrays with respect to one another. For example, given two 30×30 arrays, one may wish to have row I of the first array aligned with (and hence stored together with) column I of the second array. In Fortran D this is a two-step process. First one defines a *decomposition,* which syntactically looks like an array but occupies no storage, and then aligns arrays with the decomposition. The following example should be helpful in understanding the process:

```
REAL X(N), Y(N,N), Z(N,N), W(N,N), A1(N,N), A2(N,N)
DECOMPOSITION D1(N), D2(N,N)
ALIGN A1, A2 with D2
ALIGN Y(I,J) with D2(J,I)
ALIGN Z(I,J), W(J,I) with D1(I)
```

The first align statement assures that corresponding elements of A1 and A2 will be aligned so that, for example, the Fortran 90 array-doubling statement

```
A1 = 2 * A2
```

would require no communication. Note that A1 and A2 do not share storage, that is, ALIGN is not some form of reborn EQUIVALENCE.

The second ALIGN guarantees that if Y is set equal to the transpose of either A1 or A2, say via the Fortran 77 loop nest

```
DO 20 I = 1,N
    DO 10 J = 1,N
        Y(I,J) = A1(I,J)
10      CONTINUE
20 CONTINUE
```

no communication will be required. Again note that since Y and A1 do not share storage, *intra*processor data motion *is* required.

The last ALIGN places all of row I of Z and all of column I of W in the same processor (formally, it aligns row I and column J with the Ith element of the decomposition). Thus the diagonal elements of the matrix product of Z and W can be computed without communication.

There are many other alignments possible, including replication of elements; the interested reader is referred to [181] for details.

The final step is to decide how to distribute the elements of a decomposition across the processors. Once we know where D1(I) goes, all the array elements aligned with it go there as well. For simplicity, we begin with one-dimensional distributions and assume that the number of processors P divides N evenly. Then there are two extreme possibilities: *block* and *cyclic*. In a block distribution, D1, which is of size N, is divided into P contiguous chunks of size N/P, with chunk k assigned to processor k. In a cyclic distribution, D1 is divided into N chunks of size 1, with chunks $k, k + P, k + 2P, \ldots$ all assigned to processor k. That is, cyclic distributions spread the decomposition across the processors in a round-robin manner. Using the terminology of memory mapping, block distributions are stored sequentially, whereas cyclic distributions are interleaved.

The more general intermediate distribution block_cyclic(M) is also supported. This distribution divides the decomposition into N/M contiguous chunks of size M and again assigns chunks $k, k + P, k + 2P, \ldots$ to processor k.

Figure 5.5   *Partitioning 1D arrays in memory* [*181*].

Indeed, cyclic is the same as block_cyclic(1), and block is the same as block_cyclic(*N/P*) (see Figure 5.5).

For multidimensional decompositions, one can choose a distribution for each dimension. In addition, a * can be used for a dimension indicating that the dimension is not distributed (i.e., is stored all in one processor). Various possibilities are illustrated in Figure 5.6 on page 244. In fact Fortran D offers even more control over the distributions; see [181] for details.

In order to permit data mappings to change as program execution proceeds from one phase to another, it is possible to specify reALIGNment and reDISTRIBUTion.

Fortran D supports a FORALL loop with semantics rather different from the DOALL loop used in the Ultracomputer. With DOALL the programmer asserts that the different iterates will not interfere. FORALL semantics instruct the compiler to make sure that the iterates do not interfere. For example, if one iterate writes a variable that the other reads, the value read is guaranteed to be the old value, that is, the value at the time the loop was entered. Another feature of Fortran D is the ability to specify on which processor each iterate will execute. One example is

```
FORALL I = 1,25 on HOME(X(I))
    X(I+25) = F(X(I))
ENDFOR
```

which performs the computation where the input data is stored rather than where the results are to be stored.

Some interesting performance results with a Fortran D compiler are described in a paper by Hirandani et al [235].

Figure 5.6 *Various decompositions for a 2D array* [181].

5.2.2 Fortran and C Extensions for Shared Memory

Suppose you wanted to get a Fortran program to run on a parallel computer without the benefit of a parallelizing translator like PARAFRASE [302] (see "Parafrase Fortran Reconstructing Compiler" on page 314). An alternative is to implement a small set of start/stop primitives and synchronization primitives from the first half of this chapter and let the *programmer* create the parallelism. An example of just such a set for the NYU Ultracomputer is shown in Figure 5.7 on page 245, and a similar set exists for C. Some of the listed primitives, like `doall` and `parbegin`, are implemented as actual language *extensions* recognized by a preprocessor to the compiler. Others are library routines that must be called by the program. None are recognized by the compiler itself in this case.

Constructs similar to those listed in Figure 5.7 are included in the parallel Fortran programming environments supplied by commercial vendors of shared-memory machines such as Cray Research [183] and IBM [253]. In these cases, however, serious work has been put into the compiler to allow it to recognize the new parallel primitives directly and implement them efficiently. The number of primitives is also larger. Allan Karp [273] reviews several other shared-memory programming environments.

START/STOP PRIMITIVES

doall/endall: parbegin/end former loop iterates

parbegin/parallel/parend: begin/end execution of statements separated by **parallel**

spawn: create multiple subprocesses (multiway **fork**)

mwait: wait for multiple processes created by spawn (multiway **join**)

SYNCHRONIZATION PRIMITIVES

faa: fetch-and-add routine

tdr, tir: test-decrement-retest, test-increment-retest (for semaphores, queues, etc.)

pelock: set temporary nonpreemptability and signal masking

bwbarr: busy-waiting barrier synchronization (details on page 160)

bwrr: busy-waiting readers/readers locks

bwrw: busy-waiting readers/writers locks

bwsem: busy-waiting semaphores (counting)

NEW DECLARATION

shared: specifies which variables are shared among processes

Figure 5.7   A window into a simple parallel programming environment: The additional primitives or "bag of tricks" available to a Fortran programmer wishing to use the NYU Ultracomputer [82]. **Spawn** and **mwait** are operating system primitives (involving thousands of instructions). **Doall/endall** and **parbegin/parend** are language features implemented using **spawn/wait**. All the constructs shown are implemented via **fetch-and-add**. Figure 4.8 on page 148 illustrates the use of **parbegin/parend** and **fork/join**. Barrier synchronization is discussed on page 160. An example of the use of **doall** can be seen in Figure 2.6 on page 49, where it is called by its generic (non-Fortran) name **forall**.

5.2.3 Multilisp

Another modification of an existing language (Lisp) is described in Halstead's Multilisp paper [217], which also gives a good discussion on some broader issues of parallel language design. The basic idea behind Multilisp is parallel expression evaluation, and the principal construct used for creating as well as synchronizing such tasks is the _future,_ a sort of I.O.U. that allows (future X) to immediately return a future for the value of the expression X and concurrently begin evaluating X. When the evaluation of X yields a value, that value replaces the future. (Note the similarity to the mathematical idea of a variable.) The language uses a shared-memory model, side effects, and explicit parallelism constructs.   The paper explains these choices and makes comparisons with other languages. In fact, it presents an interesting taxonomy based on these three issues.

Shared memory is felt to be important for the exploitation of medium and fine-grain parallelism because the alternative of *explicit copying of shared data* that would be required on a non-shared-memory machine discourages the writing of programs with frequent interactions. Side effects add to the expressive power of a programming language and are important for array, database, and other operations that are best thought of in terms of objects with mutable state information. On the other hand, the presence of side effects makes coarse-grain parallelism hard to extract unless explicit parallelism constructs are used to indicate task boundaries. In Multilisp this is done with PCALL, a sort of fork/join and procedure-call combination.

The recommended programming approach is to write most code without side effects, that is, in a functional style, and to use data abstractions to encapsulate data on which side effects may be performed. Halstead [217] describes the importance of a language with parallelism integrated into the main structure, rather than tacked on, and with useful constructs (such as garbage-collected heap storage) and support of the needed data abstractions. He gives a good discussion of the different language requirements of numeric processing, with its emphasis on matrix and vector processing and its relatively data-independent flow of control, and of symbolic processing, with its emphasis on tree-structured data manipulation and sequences of operations that are often highly data-dependent, less amenable to compile-time analysis, and more in need of explicit parallelism constructs and MIMD operation. The paper also discusses CSP, program determinacy, and conservative vs. aggressive / eager / speculative scheduling of parallel operations. It is well worth reading.

A more recent paper [293] describes a compiler-based Multilisp implementation for an Encore Multimax multiprocessor (shared memory), presents performance results for up to 12 processors, and makes comparisons with other parallel Lisps.

5.2.4 Concurrent Pascal

Concurrent Pascal [218] is a shared-memory parallel language that extends sequential Pascal with concurrent programming tools called *processes* and *monitors*. It was originally intended for structured programming of computer operating systems, which tilts its emphasis toward a few large parallel activities. A process is defined as a private data structure and a sequential program operating on it, and constitutes a portion of a main program that may be executed simultaneously with other processes. One process cannot operate on the private data of another process, but they can share certain data structures such as input and output buffers. The "access rights" of a process mention the shared data it can operate on. A monitor defines a shared data structure and all the operations that processes can perform on it. A monitor also functions to synchronize concurrent processes, transmit data between them, and control the order in which competing processes use shared, physical resources. In terms of our discussion on page 155, monitors provide both sequence control and access control. However, as we discussed later on page 161, a monitor is a *blocking* synchronization mechanism unsuited to large-scale parallelism. Also, programs suitable for large-scale parallelism tend not to be written in Pascal, for reasons mentioned on page 232.

5.2.5   CSP and Occam

Communicating Sequential Processes (CSP)[237] is not really intended as a complete language, but rather as a proposal for a set of primitives for parallel processing using message-passing rather than shared-memory communication; in other words, processes communicate via input/output statements rather than by updating global variables. Sequential control is by means of *guarded commands* [146], a mechanism whereby an executable statement is preceded by a test that must be satisfied if that statement is to execute. The five primitives consist of the following:

1. A parallel command based on parbegin to specify concurrent execution of processes.
2. A send command, denoted (!), that was eventually implemented as the "entry call" portion of the Ada rendezvous mechanism (see Figure 4.12 on page 167). Execution stops if the receiving process is not ready.[122]
3. A receive command, denoted (?), that was implemented as the "accept entry call" portion of an Ada rendezvous. Execution stops if the message has not yet arrived.
4. An alternative, or "fancy if", command that specifies execution of exactly one of its constituent guarded commands.
5. A repetitive, or "fancy do", command that specifies as many iterations as possible of its constituent alternative command.

---

[122] This can be ameliorated by creating extra processes that function as buffers.

Since parbegin is the only construct used to start and stop parallel execution, the number of processes is static; that is, it does not change at run time.

Halstead [217] argues that the absence of shared memory in CSP causes small-grain parallelism to be lost. Although not everyone agrees, he claims that the association of each protected domain of data with a single sequential thread of execution and the nonuniform style of data access (one for data local to a process and another, namely message transmission, for accesses between processes) discourage the use of a large number of processes, which seems to be consistent with the Ada situation. CSP also has some deficiencies in how well it implements abstract data types (see page 288), that is, in how well it encapsulates and controls the access to objects in programs. On the other hand, CSP's *simplicity* helps in proving the correctness of programs.

The message-passing parallelism ideas of CSP have been incorporated in Occam, a language implemented on the Inmos Transputer. The Transputer (see page 495) is a 32-bit RISC-like microprocessor with extra communication capabilities designed specifically to implement the CSP message-passing model of parallel computing. Its special features include an instruction set closely matched to Occam, four special I/O ports for connection to other Transputers, and 4 KB of on-chip memory [139], [150] in the case of the model T800. With respect to programming style, Occam is an imperative language, with assignment statements, and so on. See references [336], [268], and [256] for more detail on the original version of the language.

All Occam programs are built from three primitive processes — assignment, input, and output — and act upon *variables, channels,* and *timers.* Timers supply the time, variables obtain values from assignments and inputs, and channels communicate values. Unlike CSP, parallel processes in Occam communicate indirectly through channels, which are one-way point-to-point links. These channels do not need a buffer, since data is transferred only when both the reader and writer are ready (synchronous message passing).

The simplicity of Occam makes it easy to write message-passing parallel programs, and the requirement that the number of processes and their storage allocations must be fixed at compile time results in quite an efficient implementation on the Transputer (e.g., a context switch takes a few microseconds). However, the original language lacked many features of other programming languages, such as data typing, recursive procedures, and modules. The name comes from Occam's Razor, a term associated with simplicity, and indeed Occam has been called the "assembly language of the Transputer"[49] . Occam 2 has added features like floating-point representation, functions, and a data-typing system [257]. Although it is popular in academic establishments, Occam is still not widely used by serious users with supercomputer applications. The problem is not so much that of *learning* a new language as it is of *rewriting* a 100,000-line program. Inmos now offers Fortran and C support for the Transputer, but the experience with Victor (page 495) shows that good performance on a Transputer-based parallel machine still requires writing in Occam. Trew and Wilson [442] blame much of the failure of the FPS T series (page 490) on the decision to align with Occam.[123] On the other hand, Alfred Rizzi and colleagues [376] write favorably about their use of transputers to build a real-time system for robot control. They like the ease with which the computational capacity and total data bandwidth of their computer network can be increased by the introduction of extra processors.

5.2.6   *Express, PVM, and Linda*

Next we describe three widely used programming environments, or toolkits, for writing parallel programs to run on distributed-memory MIMD hardware. Express, PVM, and Linda all provide constructs that allow a program to perform the three essential functions that we listed on page 146: to define, start and stop, and coordinate parallel execution. However, these three systems differ considerably in *how* they provide these functions, and they also differ in how many *additional* functions they provide: Express has 160 callable routines, PVM 20, and Linda 6. This is because Express and PVM are both designed to provide message-passing semantics, whereas Linda offers the programmer a simpler, shared-memory programming model. These systems are still evolving and improving, so they are not easy to compare. Because of its heritage, Express has a bit more of a hardware flavor to it, dealing with processors and their interconnection topology, whereas pvm operates at a more hardware-independent level of communicating processes, while Linda uses a yet higher-level programming model resembling a relational database. One would expect higher performance from computational models that map more directly to the underlying hardware. Naturally, performance must be balanced against ease of use.

These three systems have been implemented on many of the same parallel architectures, and are particularly in demand as possible ways to obtain parallel execution on LAN-connected workstations. Speedup has been limited by the communication bandwidth and latency obtained with current implementations, which all use IP (Internet Protocol) and tend to give latencies in the 10 millisecond range. Speedup with practical applications are much more likely

---

123   One unkind wag was heard to say, "They who live by the Razor die by the Razor."

to be 10 rather than 100, and so today these systems are not really providing highly parallel operation or massive parallelism. However, parallel message-passing machines with much lower latencies are appearing, and when system software is available that delivers this low latency directly to the application, programs written in these systems may become scalable to massive parallelism.

Express

The Express [355] software package from ParaSoft Corporation provides a programming environment for distributed-memory MIMD parallel systems, including hypercubes and workstation clusters. Express is a descendant of the CrOS crystalline operating system that we discuss on page 479, and has become widely used. The design philosophy behind Express is stated clearly in the User's Guide [355]:

> The most disheartening thing that can possibly happen to a newcomer to parallel processing is to open the manual and read,
>
>   Boot the new, parallel operating system MAGIC_OS.
>
> There you are, seated at your familiar terminal, with your nicely personalized environment under your fingertips and you are told to throw it all away. The manual probably contains some phrase in it which claims that MAGIC_OS is "just like UNIX" or similar, but you would be wise not to be fooled. At this point you may be faced with learning a whole new set of commands, a new editor, new backup procedures—the list is endless. Furthermore you probably have particular software that ran on your old system that you won't be able to use now without some time-consuming switching of operating systems.[124] You are probably going to end up in an environment with no tools, in which you are expected to generate the world's fastest and most parallel piece of software. ...
>
> Express avoids this situation by making absolutely no statements about operating systems. All that is provided are the basic tools to access the parallel processing system at hand *from the native operating system that you started with*.

The alert reader is already guessing (correctly) that there is a trade-off here between convenience and performance. How much speedup can we get with

---

[124] Similar lamentations come from DOS users first exposed to UNIX, among others.

a parallel program that uses the communication facilities of our existing operating system? One answer is provided by the seismic example we discussed on page 51 in our chapter on applications. Here we shall describe Express in more detail, and then compare it with several other software systems for distributed memory computers.

Express offers the application programmer a library of about 160 routines that can be called from C or Fortran. These routines represent a programming environment (a set of tools and utilities) for creating parallel programs that have the basic functionality they need—the ability to communicate, share data, read files, do graphics, get debugged, and analyze performance—in other words, the three key abilities needed for parallel execution that we listed on page 146, plus data partitioning, plus output useful to the programmer and the user. The routines are summarized below.

Express Library Routines

Communication: 22	**Process Control: 16**	**Synch: 11**	**I/O: 14**	**Debug: 5**
snd/rcv {a/sync}	load node(s)	semaphore		
broadcast/combine	alloc/dealloc			
(vectors, too)	start main/node			
Graphics: 36	**Performance: 24**	**Compile: 7**	**Map: 8**	**Util: 22**
parallel creation	analysis		physical	
of graphic images	monitor		to	
(Plotix)			topology	

A typical program uses a small subset of these routines, and the programmer has many choices. Two styles of parallel program are supported—Host/Node and Cubix. A Host/Node program[125] is like the Manager/Workers seismic program in Figure 2.10 on page 55—two different programs, one to coordinate the work, a multiplicity of the other to *do* the work. A Cubix program has only *one* program that executes on all the processors involved, as in the n-body example[126] on page 487. Host/node programs are an easier way to get started. Cubix programs are more sophisticated, receive much more support with regard to I/O and graphics, and require the maintenance of only one program. The choice depends on the nature of the application and its I/O requirements, the memory capacity of each processor, and other factors [355].

---

125 A general warning to the reader about the word *host*—it can mean *manager* in one place and *worker* in another—sometimes in the same publication!

126 That program is not actually a Cubix program.

PVM

PVM (Parallel Virtual Machine) is a software package for utilizing a heterogeneous network of computers as a single computational resource [59],[421]. PVM consists of two parts: a daemon process, *pvmd,* that any user can install on a machine, and a user library that contains routines for initiating processes on other machines, for communicating between processes, and synchronizing processes.   PVM is designed to provide a message-passing environment for applications with relatively loosely coupled, large-grain parallelism.

Before running a PVM application, the user invokes *pvmd filename* on his or her workstation, which in turn starts up a *pvmd* on each computer listed in *filename*.   This collection of running *pvmds* then defines the present PVM configuration for that user.   The user can now run PVM application programs. The second part of the PVM package is a library of about 20 interface routines,[127] summarized below.

PVM Library Routines

Communication: 9	Process Control: 8	Synchronization: 3
snd/rcv	enroll/leave	barrier
put/get	initiate/terminate	waituntil
probe	status/whoami	ready signal

Application programs[128] link with this library to use PVM.   The manager/worker or host/node parallel program model is well matched to PVM, but other models can also be used, since any PVM process can initiate processes on other machines.   User processes communicate through the *pvmd* daemons: packets are first sent to the local *pvmd,* which determines the machine where the recipient is running and transmits the packets to that machine's *pvmd,* which then delivers it to the remote user process.   There is also provision for converting data to XDR (external data standard) and back, since PVM is designed for heterogeneous environments.   As might be expected, transparency and heterogeneity cost something in communication delays: PVM latencies with representative workstations and LANs are on the order of 10 milliseconds,

---

[127]   As listed in the PVM 2.4 User's Guide [59]; the earlier system description [421] also included shared-memory routines.

[128]   Nine of these routines were used in the PVM version of the parallel seismic program whose description begins on page 51:   enroll, leave, receive, send, put, get, nreceive, begin msg, and msginfo.

about the same as remote procedure calls in the same (IP) environment.[129] However, PVM comes for free and with source code, which enhances its attractiveness and wide usage (PVM documents and code can be obtained by sending an email message, "send index from pvm", to netlib@ornl.gov).

Planned additions to PVM include assistance for algorithm partitioning and scheduling, support for automatic compilation for different architectures, a graphical user interface, and debugging and execution-history trace facilities—many of which, incidentally, are also supplied with Express. These functions are being developed for PVM under a program at Oak Ridge National Laboratory named HeNCE (Heterogeneous Network Computing Environment).

Linda

The Linda [85], [86] model of parallel programming adds a few operations to a base serial language (such as C or Fortran) to support the notion of *tuples* residing in a *tuple space*. Linda can be viewed as a modular approach to parallelism in the sense that the notions introduced are independent of the base language—Linda serves to express just the parallelism, specifically, process creation and coordination.[130] Indeed Carriero and Gelernter [87] argue that having the computation language (e.g., Fortran or C) orthogonal to the coordination language (e.g., Linda) is the appropriate choice for parallel language design. Six operations exist:[131]

The 6 Linda Constructs

`in` and `inp`, which *move* a tuple from tuple space "in" to a process.
`rd` and `rdp`, which *copy* a tuple from tuple space into a process.
`out`, which copies a tuple from a process "out" to tuple space.
`eval`, which places a "live" tuple (to be executed) into tuple space.

---

[129] Relative communication speeds are, of course, implementation-dependent. For communication among processors, PVM and RPCs both use Internet Protocol (IP) at the packet level, but at the message level above the packet level, PVM uses its own protocol rather than TCP, that is, PVM does not use TCP/IP. Some RPCs, like the ones provided by Network Computing System (NCS), do use TCP/IP, and with some implementations of TCP/IP, the rate of data transfer can be several times lower with an RPC than with PVM.

[130] Coordination corresponds to synchronization and data exchange.

[131] Four were used in the Linda version of the parallel seismic program whose description begins on page 51: in, rd, out, and eval.

The "Tuplescope" is a useful program visualization tool that presents a graphical view of what these operations did to the tuple space during execution, as well as other aspects of a Linda program.

Although Linda has been implemented primarily on distributed-memory computers and networks of workstations,[132] the tuple-space model offered by Linda is that of a shared memory in which multiple tuples[133] reside (a tuple is a series of typed fields, for example ("xy", 1, 3.4) is a tuple). Managing tuple space efficiently in the absence of physically shared memory is a key implementation challenge.

The simplest use of tuple space is to support producer-consumer parallelism via the **out** and **in** operations. The command **out("task1", 3, x)** places a three-component tuple into tuple space. The first component is the string "task1", the second is the integer 3, and the third is the value of the variable x. The command **in("task1", ?z, r)** removes a single *matching* tuple from tuple space and assigns its second component to **z**, a formal parameter of the **in** operation, as indicated by the **?** that appears. A tuple matches an **in** operation if it has the same number of components, corresponding components have the same type, and corresponding non-formal components have the same value. For the example above, a tuple would need to have exactly three components: the first equal to the string **"task1"**, the second of the same type as **z**, and the third equal to the value of **r**. If many tuples match, one is chosen non-deterministically; if none match, the **in** operation blocks until a suitable tuple can be removed.

The read operation **rd** is similar to **in** except that the matching tuple remains in tuple space. Non-blocking, so-called predicate, versions of **rd** and **in** are also provided: **rdp** and **inp**. If a matching tuple is found, the predicate version returns true and performs the same actions as the original operation. If a matching tuple is not found, the predicate version returns false immediately (i.e., does not block).

The non-formal components of an **out** operation can be expressions in the base language; in particular function calls entailing considerable computation may be specified. To permit the evaluation of these functions to proceed in parallel with further computation in the task issuing the **out**, Linda provides an **eval** operation that places a "live tuple" (i.e., one that is executing) into tuple space. This operation has the effect of forking a new process to execute the

---

[132] Like PVM, Linda avoids TCP in favor of its own protocol atop the Internet Protocol (IP) in order to obtain a higher rate of data transfer.

[133] Similar to the tuples in a relational database.

Send/Receive, RPC, Express, PVM, and Linda—A Tale

Warning–this is one of those boxes where we allow ourselves to be opinionated. We describe five ways to parallelize the seismic program on page 51, and offer some comments on the practicalities and trade-offs of writing parallel programs. These are not meant as universal truths, but rather as a snapshot at a particular point in time. A manager-workers, or host-nodes, or master-slaves model is used in all cases.

RPC: The first successful version of the parallel seismic program used the NCS RPC package (page 166). The programmer divided the program into separate manager and worker portions, and put the computation to be done by the workers into one or more remote procedures that are called by the manager. Information about the names of these remote procedures and the variables they exchange with the manager must then be put in a file that acts as input to an interface generator that produces the RPC stub files (in C), which are then compiled along with the manager and worker.

This is a convenient way to get correct, reliable parallel code. But speedup can be disappointing; the RPCs are implemented using sockets and TCP/IP, which can be a communications bottleneck. The other disadvantage is that most of the programming must be done over again for the next application— the manager and workers you have created are rather specific to the application, and do not offer a ready template for communication for the next application. So a more systematic programming approach and lower communication delays are both needed.

Naked send and receive: Better performance was obtained with send and receive routines that bypassed TCP/IP (see page 51 ff.). But a week-long bug was finally traced to a variable that the manager was treating as a float but that the workers were (incorrectly) treating as an integer. Unlike the input file to the RPC interface generator above, there is no mechanism with naked send and receive that allows the system to detect such errors.

Express: Express (page 250) features a library of about 160 routines that offer the programmer a great deal of control. But the original program's author (no amateur!) regarded this offer as a two-edged sword: the control is offered, but it must also be exercised. Furthermore, message transmission was via TCP/IP, giving latencies no better than the RPC version. He opted to try PVM and Linda first.

PVM: Lean, portable, popular, body of programs. Good seismic speedup.

Linda: Elegantly simple to use. Seismic speedup comparable to PVM.

live tuple, and hence increasing the execution parallelism.[134] When this new process terminates, the tuple becomes an ordinary tuple described above and can then be matched by a **rd** or **in** operation, or their predicate versions.

Linda tuples thus unify the concepts of process creation, synchronization, and communication. Carriero and Gelernter [85] refer to this as generative communication: when a process wishes to communicate, it *generates* a tuple "and sets it adrift in ... tuple space". Note that, unlike CSP, Occam, and Ada, the communication is anonymous. That is, neither the producer nor consumer task references the other.

Linda is available from Yale, where it was developed, and also from SCA, Inc.

5.3 Declarative Languages

Informally, we can say that a *declarative* language differs from an imperative language in that it is concerned with expressing *what* a program does rather than *how*. A more precise statement is that declarative programming languages are based on an abstract formalism, such as lambda calculus (p. 262), whereas an imperative program can only be understood by reference to its effect on the state of some machine [205]. Paul Hudak's excellent review of functional programming languages [248] describes a declarative language as one that, in contrast to an imperative language, has *no* implicit state that can be modified by assignment statements and other constructs in the language, and so the emphasis is placed entirely on programming with *expressions* (or terms). Two examples are functional languages, whose underlying model of computation is the *function,* and logic programming languages, which are based on *relations*.[135] We shall organize our discussion of non-imperative languages accordingly.

5.3.1 Functional and Dataflow Languages

We will first discuss the landmark functional language FP designed by John Backus many years after (some say "to atone for") leading the development of Fortran, and then we will compare the modern functional language Haskell. After that, we will discuss several dataflow languages, essentially functional

---

134 In other words, creating parallelism in Linda requires the **eval** operation.

135 It is tempting to simply say that declarative languages have no side effects, but Prolog is a declarative language and can have side effects under some circumstances, as we will discuss later.

languages that were designed to support dataflow architectures. Significant Fortran programs have been rewritten in the dataflow language Sisal, with good performance results, as described on page 333.

Functional (or *function-level*) programming grew out of the belief that basic characteristics of the von Neumann model were hindering programmer productivity and the ability to prove program correctness. The solution proposed by Backus [48] was FP, a side effect–free language in which the application of a function to its argument was the main execution mechanism (in contrast to the role of assignment statements in imperative languages). In other words, in a functional language program, the computation is carried out entirely through the evaluation of expressions. This solution is very different from the von Neumann model of computation and the imperative languages tailored for it. The side effects of these languages allowed memory to be conserved and reused in an era when memory was quite expensive. Not surprisingly, removal of these side effects results in a language that needs more memory capacity and bandwidth[136] and thus runs into a memory-access bottleneck in a sequential von Neumann machine; many problems of optimization must be solved before a functional language like FP can run on a von Neumann computer at speeds comparable to that of an imperative language. However, removal of side effects should also make programs easier to parallelize (but other problems have been introduced, e.g., removing unneeded copying). The proposed solution, therefore, is a new computational model at the hardware level, one that avoids this memory bottleneck and takes advantage of the parallelism in functional programs. Below, we describe further the motivation and details of FP.

The "Fat and Flabby" von Neumann Languages

The von Neumann method of computation could be called the storage-oriented or "If you need it, it's in the memory" model. Its heart (Figure 4.2 on page 139) is the memory that stores everything needed for the computation at a globally accessible address and passes it back and forth to the processor, as needed, through a channel that Backus christened the "von Neumann bottleneck". Another channel connects the store to an outside world with which it

---

[136] The extra memory is needed for all the items that are now *copied* rather than rewritten. One reason for extra bandwidth is the memory-to-processor round-trip involved in copying entire data structures rather than updating single elements in them. If the compiler is not able to eliminate superfluous copying, the result would be much lower performance than for imperative languages. Indeed, for many algorithms the computational complexity would increase. It is an important open question to see how good a job the compiler can do on this problem.

exchanges input and output.[137] The job of the processor is to make changes in the state of the store. In the domain of machine language, the store is a set of pairs, each pair being the number of a cell and the contents of a cell. The computation thus involves a succession of addresses and data that the processor pumps back and forth to the store through the bottleneck while executing a program that is basically a mapping of stores into stores plus a storage plan for the addresses of the variables involved.

Programs for this computer were originally written in machine code, then in assembly language, then in Fortran, and then in a great variety of higher-level languages. Although these languages have interesting and significant differences ("Review of the Major Serial Languages" on page 229), Backus sees them as more alike than different (see "Critique of the von Neumann Languages" on page 233) and growing "fat and flabby" because they are at too low a level and force the programmer to spend too much time on *how* the program will run on the von Neumann architecture, when the programmer's time should really be spent on describing *what* is to be accomplished by the program. As a result, programs are hard to write, prove correct, and reuse, so that the accomplishment of the vast army of programmers is not even cumulative. Backus [48] explains the role of the storage plan as follows:

> One way to understand the basic problem of von Neumann programming languages is to observe that their programs always map stores into stores. However, the *purpose* of a program is to map objects into objects—for example to map a matrix into its inverse, or a file of transactions into a file of responses. The purpose of a program is *never* to map stores into stores, yet this is what all von Neumann programs do. Thus, the programmer must translate the purpose of the program—say, to map matrices into their inverses—into a mapping of stores in which the input matrix occupies certain cells and the results others.
>
> This disparity between the purpose of a program, on the one hand, and its actual store-to-store mapping, on the other, is the source of the difficulty in building von Neumann programs from smaller ones. Suppose there are two programs, one to invert matrices, the other to transpose them, but they have not been planned together. Now a program to calculate the inverse of the transpose of the matrix is desired. It would seem a simple matter to form the composition of the two programs ... to get the desired program. But unless both

---

[137] Not all languages address this I/O process specifically; Fortran does.

programs have a common storage plan (and independent programs generally do not), with the output cells of "transpose" coinciding exactly with the input cells of "inverse", the composition of the two programs will not achieve the composition of their purposes: the resulting program will be meaningless.

True, it is possible to write von Neumann subroutines whose storage plans can be altered when they are used, so that they can be reused more easily than ordinary programs. But storage plans can involve much detail, and so such subroutines are still less convenient for building larger programs than are functional programs, which do not depend on storage plans. (On the other hand, these low-level storage plans may offer run-time efficiency compared with the higher-level approach used in functional languages.) Backus's proposal for a functional language is described in the next section.

The FP Functional Programming Language

In addition to a set of primitive functions and a set of data objects, the key components of a functional (or applicative) language are a set of *functional forms* for combining functions into new ones, and the *application operation,* a built-in mechanism for applying a function to an argument and producing a value [192]. The following brief example shows how these concepts look in FP and also illustrates some of the advantages of the functional approach.[138]

The example compares a von Neumann and a functional program for computing a vector inner product.

von Neumann program	Function-level program

c:=0;
for i:=1 step 1 until n **do**
    c:=c+a(i)×b(i)
	Def IP= $(/+)\circ(\alpha\times)\circ$ trans

The FP program on the right defines a new program IP in terms of three old ones:

trans, a program for transposing a pair of vectors (pairing their elements).
×, a program for multiplying.

---

[138] Backus [47] distinguishes between *function-level* functional languages like FP and *object-level* functional languages like lambda calculus and pure Lisp.

+, a program for adding.

The new program is executed from right to left and first pairs the vector elements, then multiplies each pair together, and then sums the resulting vector. The small circle (∘) is a functional form or *program-forming operation* (PFO) called *composition*; *f* smcirc *g* applied to *x* gives the result of applying f to the result of applying g to *x*. Another PFO is *apply-to-all,* denoted α, which may be defined as

$$\alpha f: \ < x_1, x_2,..., x_n > \ = \ < f{:}x_1, f{:}x_2,..., f{:}x_n > \ .$$

A third PFO called *insert* (/) performs the following:

$$/f{:}<x_1, x_2,..., x_n> = f{:}<x_1,/f{:}<x_2,..., x_n>>.$$

(This PFO is identical to the "scan" operator in APL.) In the example above, all the elements of an array are combined by addition.

Backus [48] illustrates the workings of this program and points out the differences between the functional and von Neumann versions:

1. The functional program is built from three generally useful, preexisting programs (+, ×, trans). All the components of the other program (the assignment and "for" statements) must be specially written for it alone.
2. The von Neumann program is repetitive—to understand it, one must mentally execute it, or use special mathematical tools. The FP program is nonrepetitive; if its components are understood, its meaning is clear.
3. The von Neumann program computes one word at a time by repetition. The functional program operates on higher-level conceptual units and does not repeat any steps.
4. The first program mentions the length, *n*, of the vectors; hence it lacks generality. The functional program is completely general.
5. The von Neumann program names its arguments—it will only work for vectors called a and b. The functional program can be applied to any pair of vectors without naming them.

The advantages of FP's mathematical properties for proving correctness of programs are elaborated in an earlier paper [46].

Having a program in the form of a big function yields benefits for parallel processing. Since a functional language shares with lambda calculus the property that the only execution step is the application of a function to an argument, it also shares in the benefits of the Church-Rosser theorem (page 262), which states that any reduction sequence that yields a reduced form may be used in evaluating a function (program) written in such a language.[139] In particular, the inner applications can be applied in parallel, leading to a range of possible parallel execution models. The data-driven or dataflow model (based on "greedy" evaluation) will be discussed in a following section. String reduction and graph reduction (see Figure 4.1 on page 136) form two demand-driven models based on "lazy evaluations" performed only when their results are required. Some architectures specially designed to support these models are discussed later in our book, including a string-reduction machine specifically designed for FP programs (page 630) and a more general-purpose graph-reduction machine (page 498).

Modern Functional Languages–Haskell and Others

FP put functional programming "on the map", but the language proved to be neither amenable to efficient execution nor rich enough in new language features of major research interest, and so FP has largely fallen by the wayside. The 15 years since the advent of FP have seen the birth of many new functional languages, along with new ideas for the design and implementation of such languages [248]. Ease of programming and suitability for parallel computers are still claimed as strengths, but the concern with program re-use that Backus stressed is less discussed today, and *expressive power* has become a hot topic. We will discuss some of the distinguishing features of these modern functional languages. (Note that *modern* in this context has come to mean a set of properties, not just a vintage; we shall elaborate.) As a method for programming serial computers, these languages represent varying trade-offs between expressiveness and efficiency. For parallel computers, this becomes a three-way trade-off that also includes the degree and granularity of parallelism [358].

Haskell (named after the logician Haskell B. Curry) is a modern, general-purpose functional language created by a committee of prominent researchers in response to the "tower of Babel" problem that arose with the proliferation of functional programming languages in the years after FP gave the field a new impetus. Haskell consolidates many features of the other languages, with the intention of providing an agreed-upon stable base for communicating ideas, developing applications, and drawing users to functional programming. A good review by Hudak [248] describes and compares Haskell and other functional languages.

---

[139] That is, the serialization principle comes for free.

A Lambda Calculus Primer

Raiders of the Church-Rosser Theorem

(Parallel Processing, Function-Level Programming, and Lambda Calculus)

What brings a parallel processing enthusiast into the jungles of the lambda calculus, a harsh and hostile territory replete with expressions so ugly that only a mathematician could love them? The answer lies in the *Church-Rosser theorem*:

> If a given lambda expression is reduced by two different reduction techniques, and if both reduction sequences yield a reduced form, then the reduced forms are equivalent up to renaming of bound variables.

Aha! If the sequence doesn't matter, then the reductions can be done in parallel without worrying about the order in which they finish. A potential application area for parallel processing!

But how to transfer the benefits of this gem to the real world? The problems we are trying to solve involve addition, multiplication, integers, and so on, not the highly stylized expressions of the lambda calculus world. Luckily, there is an equivalent lambda expression for all of the practical items we need, and in theory we could use the lambda calculus as our programming language. In practice, other function-level languages provide the bridge between these two worlds. But their theoretical foundation is the lambda calculus, and understanding its elements makes it easier to explain where the parallelism comes from. Herewith, a short survival course in lambda calculus:

The lambda calculus is a mathematical formalism developed by Alonzo Church, a logician interested in exploring the limits of computable functions. However, the first thing a new arrival to lambda calculus has to do is to unlearn much of everyday mathematical notation. The familiar-seeming expression x y, for example, does not mean "x times y"; it means "x applied to y". Almost anything in this particular world can be a function. Furthermore, the forbidding-looking term $\lambda x.(x + 1)$ is really only a (hybrid) lambda expression for the function that we mean when we normally write $f(x) = x + 1$.

(continued on next page)

Higher-order functions and non-strict semantics

Two key properties of a modern functional language are *higher-order functions* and *non-strict semantics*. A first-order function takes data objects as arguments and produces new data objects as results [152]. Higher-order functions have the additional ability to take *functions* as arguments and produce new functions. FP's program-forming operations (PFOs) are examples of higher-order functions, but in FP they are pre-defined. *User-defined*

(continued from previous page)

Lambda signals that a function definition is beginning, x. signifies that x is the bound variable in the function, and .x + 1 is the "body" or form of the function. The only execution step is *application* of a function to an argument, and a single argument at that. The function is on the left, and its argument is the next complete expression to the right. The *Beta reduction rule* says that the argument should be substituted where occurrences of the function's bound variable appear in the function's body. So, for example, λ x.(x + 1) 4 reduces to 5, and λ x.(x + 1) y reduces to y + 1. And that's basically all that governs how lambda calculus works; that's its complete syntax.

"Pure" lambda calculus, for which the Church-Rosser theorem holds, doesn't really have terms like 4 and +, but rather only a very small number of symbols, operations, and rules. However, it can combine them into a complete repertoire of practical operations.

How is this possible? After all, everything done in the lambda calculus has to be expressed using only four kinds of symbol: λ, (,), and the name of a variable. How can anything that simple be useful? The feature that saves the day is that the *argument of a function can be another function*. For example, in the expression λ x.(x + 1) y above, y can be another lambda expression, with an argument that is yet another lambda expression, and so on. Using this feature, it is possible to construct lambda expressions equivalent to the things we deal in, like numbers, addition, and so forth. The number 3, for example, can be defined as λ y.(λ x.y(y(y x))), a lambda expression containing three recursive function applications like the one above. Larger or smaller numbers correspond to larger or smaller numbers of function applications. Lambda calculus does 2 + 3 = 5 by combining a program with two loops and one with three loops into one with five loops (Mr. Ed's number system). The point is not that addition is more convenient using the lambda calculus, but that it is *possible,* and hence addition is covered by the Church-Rosser theorem, as are all the other arithmetic and Boolean operations used in normal computation.

higher order functions are not supported in FP, whereas they are in modern functional languages.[140]

In a language with strict semantics, all the arguments of a function must be evaluated before its body is entered. Thus strictness imposes a partial order on evaluation (arguments before bodies) but not a total order (e.g., the arguments to a function can themselves be evaluated in any order, in contrast to, say, applicative order, in which arguments are always evaluated left to right). In a language with non-strict semantics, a data structure may be used before all its components are written, and a function may compute and return a value without evaluating all (or possibly any) of its arguments. Thus far, non-strict is simply "not strict". However, it is further required that an implementation

---

[140] Backus, FP's developer, warned about the "chaos" that would come from the unrestricted freedom to invent new combining forms in systems based on the lambda calculus [248].

of a non-strict language *may not* evaluate an argument if doing so would prevent the program from continuing to make progress [438].   These consequences of non-strictness give valuable expressive power to the programmer, such as a fuller use of recursion and the ability to define more complicated patterns of data dependence, and this is another way in which modern functional languages differ from FP, which has strict semantics (as is also mostly true for Lisp, APL, the other imperative languages, and many dataflow languages).   However, *implementing* non-strict semantics efficiently poses additional challenges for the compiler writer [438] and can result in considerable run-time overhead and reduced performance.

implementing the Semantics—Some Related Terms

To further explain the differences between modern and older functional languages (like some of the dataflow languages), we need to discuss evaluation strategies for these languages, a subject that has its own terminology.   Unfortunately, as is sometimes the case in a new field, the terminology varies from author to author, and as a result, the literature contains many synonyms, near-synonyms, and closely related terms associated with the notion of strict vs. non-strict languages, but no single reference that pulls them all under one roof. It will help us later if we pause now for a brief treatment of these terms and their relationships.   We will draw on references [248], [358], [152], and [438]. For convenience in the discussion that ensues, we begin by taking a broom and sweeping most of the terms in question into two piles of related terms, with the term *lenient* purposely left between the two piles, for reasons that will become apparent.   The results of our broom-strokes follow:

strict		non-strict
greedy, speculative, eager		lazy
call-by-value	lenient	call-by-need
applicative order		normal order
leftmost innermost		leftmost outermost
data-driven		demand-driven
dataflow		graph reduction

Now, at the risk of some oversimplification, let us discuss how these terms are related.

Strict and *non-strict* describe a particular *semantic* property[141] of a programming language, and, by extension, describe a language implementation which achieves that property [438]. As we said above, under non-strict semantics, arguments to a procedure or data constructor are *not* necessarily evaluated; whereas under strict semantics, they are evaluated before invocation.

Dropping down a level brings us to a set of terms starting with *greedy* that refer to evaluation strategies for the semantics in the layer just above, that is, these terms specify the scheduling policy that determines in what order the program's expressions will be evaluated. We will use a simple example to give a preview of what these terms mean. In some fictional language, consider the function invocation

```
(if (equal X 0)
    7
    (reciprocal X))
```

which returns the value 7 if X is zero and otherwise returns 1/X. Under strict semantics, all three arguments of the `if` function (namely, `equal`, `7`, and `reciprocal`) would have to be evaluated, and it would blow up when X was zero, which is why many otherwise strict languages provide a non-strict conditional construct. A simple though wasteful evaluation strategy called *greedy* and *speculative* (and sometimes *eager*) evaluates all expressions as soon as possible, including evaluating both arms of a conditional even though one is eventually discarded. This strategy is therefore not suitable for our example, or for implementing non-strict semantics in general. One strategy that *is* suitable is *lenient* evaluation, which imposes the requirement that the predicate must be completely evaluated before any arm of a conditional is considered, and therefore makes our example work as desired. But lenient evaluation can still result in wasted work if the results of an evaluation are not needed for the final answer. To eliminate such wasted work, *lazy* evaluation, the technique most frequently used to implement non-strict semantics, stipulates the stronger condition that an evaluation cannot be done *unless* it contributes to the final answer, which, for one thing, prevents execution of the wrong arm in our example. These evaluation strategies and their pros and cons are treated in more detail below.

The terms *dataflow* and *graph reduction* are parallel computational models that correspond to the engines (abstract or physical machines) that execute the functional program. In dataflow, the program is turned into a dataflow

---

141　Readers interested in the distinction between *denotational* and *operational* semantics should consult [358].

graph, and computation proceeds as data tokens flow along the arcs to the operators at the nodes. In graph reduction, the program is turned into an expression graph, which is then transformed into other graphs and reduced (simplified) until the final answer is obtained.

From top to bottom, then, the terms in our piles reach from the level of programming language semantics down through the compiler and run-time system to the architecture level. In a functional language program, the computation is carried out entirely through the evaluation of expressions. Compilation is, therefore, a process of choosing the order in which subexpressions will be evaluated, consistent with the semantics of the language. The remaining terms in our piles are related to this process of turning a program into a computation.

A one-sentence summary of the terms in the pile on the right is that many compilers for *non-strict* languages rely on *lazy evaluation* of expressions, which requires a *demand-driven* scheduling mechanism such as *graph reduction*; lazy evaluation corresponds to *call-by-need* parameter passing, which is a special case of *call-by-name*; call-by-name corresponds to *normal order* or *leftmost outermost* reduction. A more detailed discussion follows.

Lazy Evaluation

As Hudak points out, choosing an optimum evaluation strategy can be tricky [152]. We begin with lazy evaluation because its definition is better agreed upon.

One thing that must be specified in the process of evaluating a functional language program's expressions is the mechanism for passing parameters. As Henderson [225] explains, Algol introduced two distinct mechanisms, call-by-value and call-by-name. In call-by-value, (which corresponds to applicative order or leftmost innermost reduction of lambda expressions in lambda calculus), each argument of a function is evaluated (*exactly* once) before the function body is evaluated. By contrast, a parameter that is called by name in Algol (corresponding to normal order or leftmost outermost reduction in lambda calculus) is not evaluated until a reference to it is encountered in the execution of the procedure body, which may be never. However, once evaluated, its value is "forgotten", and so it is possible that a single parameter will be evaluated more than once, perhaps many times. In the context of Algol these multiple evaluations may each return distinct results due to side effects and aliasing. However, in functional languages, multiple evaluations are guaranteed to return the same result, so all but the first evaluation represent wasted effort. Call-by-need, or *lazy evaluation,* evaluates each argument *at most* once, at the time of first reference. It is a call-by-name mechanism that "remembers" the first evaluation,[142] like call-by-value. Thus, parameters whose values are not needed are not evaluated, while those that *are* needed are evaluated only once. Laziness brings with it certain expressive powers beyond those that come from non-strictness, for instance, the ability to use infinite data structures (if only finite portions are actually evaluated) and freedom from concern about unnecessary evaluation of arguments [248]. Many (in fact, most) compilers for non-strict languages rely on lazy evaluation.[143]

This lazy evaluation of expressions requires the support of a scheduling (control) mechanism that prevents the execution of a thread, or whatever the schedulable unit of execution is, until another thread needs one of the values it computes [438]. Such scheduling is called demand-driven (see also Figure 4.1 on page 136), and is often implemented using graph reduction, and less often using string reduction. As illustrated in Figure 4.1 on page 136, under string reduction, each demand for an expression results in delivery of a complete *copy* of the expression for "do-it-yourself" evaluation, while under graph reduction, the evaluation is performed at the time of the first demand, and each demander receives a *pointer* to the result of the evaluation. Graph reduction entails the extra overhead of the pointer mechanism, but is faster and needs less memory than string reduction, whose copying mechanism is usually considered prohibitively expensive [358]. See page 498 and page 630 for an example of each. Peyton-Jones [358] discusses the implementation of graph reduction in great detail.

Eager Evaluation

Eager evaluation brings us a semantics question of another kind: What does the word mean? There is a range of evaluation strategies that stretches from the "as late as possible" *lazy* approach described above all the way to an "as soon as possible" approach that could, for example, evaluate both arms of a conditional expression in parallel, even though only one will be needed. This latter strategy is generally called *greedy* [400], *speculative* [358], or *eager* [249] evaluation. The problem is not what do you call these extremes, but rather what do you call the stuff in the middle? Is eager a point or a spectrum? We will use the former view, that is, the view that lazy and eager are opposite extremes [248] on a spectrum of, say, anticipatory evaluation policies [156]. Thus "closer to eager" would be correct usage; "more eager" would not. But

---

[142] This is sometimes called *memoization* of the pending evaluations, which are themselves called *thunks*.

[143] As a result, non-strict semantics are sometimes called *lazy semantics*; this is a convenient shorthand, but such usage is confusing and should be avoided.

not everyone agrees. There are authors who hold that eager means "not lazy"[438] , [157], and others [358] who hold that lazy means "not eager", which would make the spectrum itself consist of degrees of eagerness or degrees of laziness, depending on the author. So, in this still-nascent field, the reader occasionally shares the experience of Alice in Wonderland, where a word can mean just what the author chooses it to mean:-)

Eager is also sometimes used to mean "strict", but, as with non-strict vs. lazy above, this usage mixes semantics and implementation issues, something we are trying to avoid.[144] Most imperative languages, including Lisp, have strict functions or procedure calls [438], and some authors have also described them as providing eager evaluation[145] or only eager evaluation [455]. Actually, the sequential semantics of an imperative language tightly control the evaluation order, leaving no degree of freedom for eagerness to play any role, and so the name given to the evaluation order is secondary in this case. But the story is different for *functional* languages (even strict ones), and so it would be less confusing if crossover terms like *eager semantics* and *strict evaluation* were not used.

Dataflow computing, with its data-driven mechanism for activating operations, is probably the best-known example of eager evaluation.[146] Early languages written for such systems, like Val, were functional with strict semantics —not surprising, in light of our earlier statement that eager evaluation of non-strict languages was unsafe. Sisal, a descendant of Val, is still a functional language with strict semantics, but there is a lazy interpreter for it (for research purposes); an implementation to run on a dataflow architecture would amount to something close to eager evaluation; and the implementation with the highest performance so far, whose results on the Cray Y-MP are described on page 333, is actually control-driven, that is, more like the implementation of an imperative language. So the strict semantics of Sisal (and other functional

---

[144] Szymanski [152] writes that strict vs. non-strict is often referred to as eager vs. lazy or call-by-value vs. call-by-need, but that from an abstract semantical perspective, strict vs. non-strict is proper. Traub [438] adds applicative-order vs. normal-order and leftmost-innermost vs. leftmost-outermost to the list, with the comment that they are most correct when applied to lambda calculus. He also adds the usage note that call-by-value vs. call-by-need tend to be used when both mechanisms are available in the same implementation, at the discretion of the programmer.

[145] "In an ordinary imperative language (such as Pascal), arguments to a function are evaluated before the function is called (call by value). ... call by value is often called eager evaluation."[358]

[146] *Practical* dataflow systems are probably better described as implementing *variants* of eager evaluation. In particular, *switch* nodes are used to prevent the evaluation of both arms of a conditional (see Figure 5.8 on page 272).

languages) can be implemented in several ways, only one of which is eager evaluation.

Under non-strict semantics, it is dangerous to evaluate an expression eagerly, that is, without being sure that its value is necessary. This is so because an unnecessary expression may have an evaluation that blows up or goes into an infinite loop, causing its program to fail—a failure that would not occur under lazy evaluation (since the unnecessary expression would not have been evaluated). In summary, eager evaluation is safe for strict functions, but dangerous for non-strict functions.

Eager evaluation has the potential for more parallelism but also for more wasted computation than lazy evaluation. Lazy evaluation eliminates unnecessary computation and increases expressiveness but incurs more run-time overhead and may limit the parallelism obtained. Lazy evaluation may safely be used for both strict and non-strict functions, but the latter combination has more benefit.

Lenient evaluation

Lenient evaluation [438], which is used for the Id language (pages 275 and 276), is an alternative technique to lazy evaluation for compiling non-strict languages, and falls somewhere between lazy and eager evaluation. The ability to schedule each subexpression separately permits lazy evaluation to support non-strict semantics, but such fine-grained scheduling incurs a great deal of run-time overhead. (Traub [438] points out that early lazy compilers based on graph reduction were not much more than interpreters.)

Although sufficient, laziness is not necessary to implement non-strictness. Indeed, all that is needed is a simple rule on conditionals. First completely evaluate the predicate and then evaluate the correct arm (i.e., the `then` clause if the predicate is true and the `else` clause otherwise). An implementation following this rule is called *lenient*. Note that a lazy evaluation is necessarily lenient but not vice versa. Lenient is a compromise. It avoids the obvious inefficiency of evaluating the wrong arm of a conditional but does not require the implementation to guarantee that all computation performed is necessary (such a guarantee has a significant run-time overhead). One price of this compromise is that lenient evaluations are not as expressive as lazy ones. That is, some programs terminate under lazy evaluation but not under lenient. For example the ability to work with (portions of) infinite data structures is weakened.

One way to allow more decisions to be made at compile time and thus decrease the run-time overhead is to allow programmers the option of annotating their programs by using something like the scheduling and mapping constructs in the "para-functional" extension to Haskell that Hudak describes [152]. Another approach is to use some form of *strictness analysis,* a compile-time analysis technique [358] for determining which arguments a function is *sure* to evaluate.[147] As Traub [438] points out, one can view such techniques as methods for maximizing the length of execution threads relative to the overhead of switching among threads. But he claims that these techniques will have limited effectiveness as long as they seek to retain laziness, and proposes lenient evaluation as a strategy that maintains non-strictness but gives up laziness in exchange for greater execution efficiency. Producing lazy, instead of lenient, code is an option provided by Traub's compiler.

Summary

In summary, eager, lenient, and lazy evaluation can be regarded as *compilation techniques* for implementing strict and non-strict functional programming languages. Eager evaluation has the undeniable advantage that faster, more highly parallel implementations are possible when the arguments to functions must be evaluated before the function is applied [358]. However, many of these argument evaluations may be wasted effort, which a lazy strategy seeks to avoid by delaying argument evaluation until its need is certain. Another benefit of a lazy implementation is the additional expressive power given to programmers, such as the ability to use infinite data structures. But the delay mechanism needed for lazy evaluation results in a substantial run-time overhead. Lenient evaluation offers a compromise. It can be used to implement non-strict languages (whereas eager evaluation, as we have defined it, is safe only for strict languages), and so the programmer still gets the expressiveness that comes with non-strictness, such as fuller use of recursion, but not the extra expressiveness that comes from a lazy implementation (e.g., infinite data structures). But since lenient evaluation incurs less run-time overhead than lazy evaluation, lenient evaluation is expected to give better performance. As Hudak [249] said, choosing an optimum evaluation strategy for a modern functional language can be a tricky business.

Much of the activity that falls under the umbrella of functional programming languages comes from two diverse groups,[148] united primarily by their dislike for Von Neumann architectures and imperative languages. The first group consists of language designers who are interested in exploring the ben-

---

147   That is, to determine in which of its arguments, if any, the function is strict. Understandably, strictness analysis is more complex if higher-order functions are allowed, that is, if a function's argument can be another function.

148   But both groups are represented in the Haskell committee.

efits to the programmer of expressive power that comes from modern functional language features like non-strict semantics and higher-order functions. The second group consists of dataflow architecture researchers, who needed a language as part of the process of implementing their ideas. The original *dataflow languages* that resulted are functional languages, but they were designed "from the bottom up" and lacked many of the modern features of a functional language designed to explore what is useful to a programmer. A useful partnership has developed between the functional language and dataflow communities; the ultimate outcome of this partnership is not yet clear. We will explore dataflow languages next, and then make some overall comments on both kinds of functional languages.

Dataflow Languages—VAL, Id, LAU, Sisal

Historically, dataflow languages were developed to yield programs that run efficiently on dataflow architectures (page 512), which are an attempt to improve upon the von Neumann architecture by allowing data to flow directly from instruction to instruction (page 138). Dataflow languages have many (sometimes all) of the properties of a functional language because features such as the absence of side effects result in a larger pool of instructions eligible to be executed in parallel. However, to increase the execution efficiency on a dataflow architecture, dataflow languages sometimes have extra features not found in a purely functional language. But a dataflow machine does not *have* to be programmed in a dataflow language—at least one dataflow machine has been programmed primarily with C. And functional programs can certainly run on von Neumann hardware; the question is one of efficiency as compared to an imperative language program. So, to summarize, functional language programs can be evaluated (executed) using dataflow as well as other models of computation, dataflow languages are mostly functional languages, and dataflow machines are most frequently (but not always) programmed using dataflow languages.

The February 1982 *Computer* special issue on dataflow systems [8] provides a good historical perspective on the data-driven or dataflow model. In this section, we concentrate on its language aspects.

To return to the historical perspective for a moment, the data-driven and demand-driven computational models illustrated in Figure 4.1 on page 136 can both be viewed as reactions to the effects of the von Neumann model, but at different levels. Both try to eliminate the bottleneck caused by the steady stream of data exchanged by the processor and the memory each time an instruction is executed. But whereas the demand-driven (reduction) approach was originally *language-driven*, in that it came from concerns about pro-

$$C(i,j) = \sum_{k=1}^{N} A(i,k) \times B(k,j)$$

Figure 5.8 **Dataflow graph of a matrix multiplication inner loop** [305] *presenting an operational (vs. language-based) description of the tagged-token dynamic approach. The indices i and j are supplied by the outer loops; k is generated by the loop in the dashed box. S is a conditional branch node. D creates a new tag from an old one (it increases a token's iteration number, or "color", by 1 but does not change its data). In a static approach, straight lines would replace the D nodes. The loop leading to "Store C(i,j)" acts as an accumulator for the partial sum, initially set to zero using the "Constant=0" node. Unconditional merge and branch nodes are drawn simply as junctures of lines.* **Get** *and* **Store** *are read operations and write-once operations on the (I-) Structure Store. Unlike structured data in a purely functional language, I-structures may be read and written in parallel (but each element can be written only once; see Figure 10.17 on page 532). Hence one part of the program can read C(i,j) as soon as it is written by another part, rather than having to wait for the entire array C to be written.*

grammer productivity and programming style [46], the data-driven (dataflow) approach was originally *hardware-driven* in that it came from concerns that neither shared-memory nor message-passing architectures would allow efficient operation while exploiting fine-grain parallelism in an application [134]. The point is that dataflow language design starts out with a low-level computational model already in place.

This underlying model, as illustrated in Figure 4.1, is that (1) data flow from instruction to instruction *directly* rather than via a shared variable; and (2) rather than waiting for a signal from a central control mechanism such as a program counter, instructions are executed as soon as all the data they need have arrived. In principle, this should uncover all the parallelism available in a program.

This parallelism may be greatly increased if the program is written in a functional (applicative) language (page 235). This approach eliminates the side effects associated with imperative languages, or, in terms of dependencies among program parts (page 309), it eliminates all but flow dependencies. Dataflow corresponds to greedy evaluation of this graph, while reduction corresponds to lazy evaluation (we discuss this more on page 265). Some dataflow languages like VAL are indeed completely functional, with no concept of a variable that can be assigned and reassigned values as if it were a read/write memory cell available to the program. Others, like Id, are called *single-assignment* languages because they allow each element of certain data structure variables (*I-structures* in Id) to be written (assigned) *once* in their lives, in order to increase the efficiency of computations involving arrays, and so on (see page 276).

A dataflow program can be represented as a graph loosely similar to the one produced after dataflow analysis in an optimizing compiler for, say, Fortran. The nodes of the graph represent the operations to be performed, the arcs show the data dependencies between them, and data motion is represented by tokens on these arcs. An example graph is shown in Figure 5.8 on page 272.

The dataflow graph itself has been considered as a programming medium or "language" [127], but is felt to be too error-prone and difficult for human construction and manipulation [185]. The prevalent approach to programming a dataflow computer has been to generate this graph from a program written in a high-level language (such as VAL, Id, LAU, or Sisal) whose *syntax,* at least, resembles that of established imperative programming languages.

Requirements for Dataflow Languages

Ackerman [2] traces how the design of a dataflow language follows from the data-driven computational model. He lists two criteria that a dataflow language must satisfy:

1.   It must allow deduction of the data dependencies of the program operations, or, in other words, it must allow construction of the dataflow gaph.

2.   The order of execution must be limited only by the data dependencies, so that the instruction-execution rule can be based simply on the availability of the data.

Note that this is a bottom-up approach to language design; that is, the language is constrained to meet requirements of the execution model. Ackerman then discusses how a language can meet these criteria by utilizing *locality of effect* (the assignment of a limited scope to every variable) and *freedom from side effects* (by using call-by-value parameter passing or, in a more far-reaching approach, by using applicative languages).

One can limit side effects to a single procedure by outlawing global variables and using call-by-value parameter passing to procedures. In a call-by-value scheme, a procedure *copies* its arguments, rather than being given their address as in a call-by-reference scheme. Thus, the procedure cannot modify the actual arguments in a calling program. An applicative language is one in which *all* processing is performed by applying operators (functions) to variables that are *values* rather than memory locations; in effect, there *are* no procedures or (read/write) shared variables. The removal of side effects and aliasing makes the dataflow graph considerably easier to generate, since it is then no longer necessary to start with a dependency analysis of the entire program, as is done for a language with side effects like Fortran by a parallelizing translator like Parafrase (page 314).[149]

VAL, Id, LAU, Sisal

Ackerman explores a number of other language issues. One set of answers is represented by VAL (Value-oriented Algorithmic Language), a language for a *static* dataflow scheme, that is, one in which at most one data token may occupy an arc in the dataflow graph at one time (see page 512). The parallelism is implicit; no explicit commands like fork or parbegin exist that allow the programmer to control parallel execution. McGraw [334] gives VAL a detailed critique.

Not all dataflow languages are purely functional, shun side effects, and deny the programmer any role in parallel execution. LAU, for example, has side effects on certain operations related to database management. VAL, Sisal, and LAU have parallel *expressions* like FORALL and EXPAND that allow the programmer to *identify* parallelism. Unlike parallel *commands,* these do not impose a particular form of run-time concurrency, but instead allow the com-

---

[149] Parafrase doesn't really analyze the whole program; it makes conservative assumptions instead.

piler or other translator to make that choice. (VAL is described as having both implicit [334] and explicit [185] parallelism; the confusion arises because it has parallel *expressions* but not parallel *commands*.) Id (for Irvine dataflow) is Arvind's language for his dynamic tagged-token architecture (see page 276), which allows more than one token per arc as long as the tokens have different tags or "colors". To handle arrays and other structured data more efficiently, Id uses *I-structures* (page 531) that allow each array element to be individually assigned "von Neumann–style" *once,* thus leading to the name *single-assignment language*. Unlike a purely functional or *zero-assignment* language, I-structures allow incremental creation and reading of an array (hence the *I*) while still avoiding side effects associated with multiple writes or overwrites. The box on page 276 contains further discussion of I-structures and Id.

Sisal (Streams and Iterations in a Single Assignment Language), a descendant of VAL, was the first functional language to perform as well as Fortran on scientific codes running on an 8-processor Cray Y-MP (see pages 333–335). Sisal is a functional language with no explicit parallel control constructs, but its data types and its constructs for *expressing* operations are specifically chosen to produce efficient code for large-scale scientific computations [165]. The result is a language lacking some of the characteristics of modern functional languages (in particular, Sisal is first-order and largely strict), but the compiler writer has appeared to benefit.

Gajski, Kuck, et al. [185] give a comprehensive critique of the entire dataflow approach and compare it with the extraction of parallelism from programs written in imperative languages like Fortran. The review is somewhat dated now, but still worth reading. They argue that functional semantics and freedom from side effects are nice for the programmer and the compiler writer but that well-known compiler techniques applied to a good imperative language allow equal exploitation of parallelism. They point out the importance of memory management and garbage collection in a system in which memory locations are not reused in the imperative sense. They claim that a language with implicit parallelism is weak in handling recurrences and array-index-related spurious flow dependences, with the result that the required translation techniques will be as complicated as those used to extract parallelism from imperative languages. They feel that dataflow notions are appealing at the scalar level but that array, recurrence, and other high-level operations that are important in computation-intensive problems become difficult to manage.

A good discussion of the relationship between functional languages and dataflow may be found in the book edited by Eisenbach [156].

The Rings of Id

A tension can arise between using a purely functional (applicative) language and supporting efficient execution.   This tension was illustrated in a conversation with Arvind about his Id language.   As indicated in the figure above, Id contains a purely functional core, in which Arvind's students write their first programs.

A purely functional language lacks operators that can incrementally fill in a data structure, and so the next ring brings in I-structures, special kinds of data structures whose components are individually available to be written (assigned) *once*.   These structures allow Id to handle arrays and other structured data in parallel more efficiently (allowing concurrent production and consumption of a data structure) but change Id to a single-assignment language, that is, it is no longer purely functional.   The genie is out of the bottle.

Arvind does not, however, recommend the indiscriminate use of I-structures.   His published examples suggest a style in which the I-structures are used to define new *functional* operators.   As an example consider the operator MakeArray (dim, f) which uses I-structures to return an array (call it A) whose shape is determined by "dim" (the pair (5,5) would indicate a square two-dimensional array of size 5) and whose values are supplied by the function "f" (that is, A[i,j] is defined to be f(i,j)).   If one imagines the language extended to include a collection of functional operators and if no other use of I-structures is permitted, we arrive at the next ring, in which a functional language has reemerged.

But the genie is not quite contained.   With the hope that they would be used wisely, Arvind decided to make I-structures available to application programmers so that they could write their own functional operators.   An example illustrates the need for these structures.   Consider defining an array whose boundary values are constrained to be a constant C and whose interior values are determined by g.   This array can be described by MakeArray (dim, f) if we define f(i,j) as

```
        if (i,j) is a boundary point then
            C
        else
            g(i,j)
        end
```

Arvind rejects this solution because of the test that must be performed for all entries in the array. An imperative solution would avoid this test by using different loops to initialize the boundary and interior.   But a functional operator does not allow such incremental creation of the array—it must be done in one step. *(Continued on next page)*

The Rings of Id (continued)

Arvind's solution is to have the programmer use I-structures to create a new functional operator MakeArrayWithBoundary (dim f g) where f is applied to interior points and g to the boundary. Since the shapes and characteristics of boundaries are highly application-dependent, it is unlikely that a prepackaged library would suffice. This dependency is one reason he makes I-structures visible, a decision not universally applauded in the applicative language community.

The next ring gives us accumulators, which resemble FetchAndOpWithoutTheFetch (page 579) for the n-body problem (Op=floating add)

$$(A\ R) = accumulator\ (dim\ op\ init\ count)$$

which, among other uses, can be used to compute histograms concurrently. (Histograms have been presented as a challenge to dataflow proponents by researchers in other areas of parallel processing, present company included.)

Consider a problem in which N events are to be generated stochastically, and then independently analyzed and classified into one of T types. A (serial) imperative program to produce a histogram of the frequency of the event types can be written as

        Do K times
            generate event stochastically
            classify event as type t $(1 \leq t \leq T)$
            increment count[t] by 1
        end

We wish to parallelize this model program. The concurrent-event-generation problem on the first line has led to interesting work on the parallel production of random numbers. We have specified that the events are independent, so the classification on the second line is easily parallelized. On the third line, "count" can be incremented in a fully parallel mode using fetch-and-add (see page 162), and even without this primitive a largely parallel mode is still possible. A dataflow program, however, cannot increment "count", since updating variables is not permitted. Even with I-structures, variables can only be written once. Arvind's solution to this dilemma is to use

$$(A\ R) = accumulator\ (T + 0\ N)\ ,$$

which produces the (addition-based) accumulator (A R) containing T components each initialized to zero and to which a total of N accumulations are to be performed. A is used to accumulate and R is used to read the values in the accumulator. The statement A[t]=e adds e to the tth component of (A R); it also increments by one a hidden counter C used to determine when the accumulated values may be read. If C exceeds N, a run-time error occurs. The statement x=R[t] defines x to be the final value attained by the tth component; this value is not available until C has reached N. An important point to note is that, since intermediate values of the accumulator are not accessible, the procedure is deterministic; that is, if run multiple times with the same input, the same results will occur. (This assumes that op is associative and commutative, which is true for fixed-point, overflow-free addition. General operators give powerful accumulators, but losing determinism may be too high a price to pay.)

In the last ring Arvind does give up determinism in order to permit the writing of software structures similar to the *monitors* of Hoare (page 247). This work is less complete, and we do not discuss it.

Functional Languages for Parallel Computing: Pros and Cons

The most frequently cited advantages of functional programming languages are their increased expressive power and their freedom from the side effects that are the major stumbling block in the extraction of parallelism from imperative programs. Watt [455] and Peyton-Jones [358] cite some further advantages of functional languages for parallel computers. For example, shared variables need no special protection, since they can never be updated, and explicit synchronization constructs are therefore unnecessary. The most frequently cited drawback is efficiency. Since functional languages do not support overwriting data, and simply copying an entire array to change a single entry is grossly inefficient, it is a challenge to compile functional language programs so that good run-time efficiency is obtained. In addition, Watt gives a good discussion of specific features and the costs they incur, such as first-class functions and the need to allocate data on a heap, lazy evaluation and the need to check a function argument each time it is used in case it is an unevaluated argument, and so forth. Hudak [248] cites three common "myths" about functional languages:

1. That functional programming is the antithesis of convential imperative programming
2. That functional programming languages are "toys"
3. That functional languages can't deal with state[150]

To dispel these myths, he says that (1) functional languages represent a logical evolution from Fortran expressions, and abandonment of side effects in functional programming is analogous to abandonment of the goto in structured programming (i.e., both correspond to a discipline for good programming);[151] (2) compilers and real applications with good performance are beginning to appear, and (3) functional languages deal with state "very nicely", although the state is expressed explicitly rather than implicitly. It is only fair to point out, however, that the most impressive performance results for a functional language were obtained using a no-nonsense version of Sisal that lacks many of the features like higher-order functions and lazy evaluation that are associated

---

[150] A system with state has memory, and hence its response to a stimulus depends on history. Mathematical functions have no state; that is, the value returned is independent of previous invocations. This is different from the notion of a variable that can maintain its value from call to call, as in an imperative language.

[151] Note that reasonably efficient alternatives to gotos exist now, whereas techniques for minimizing the added overhead that comes from abandoning side effects is less well established. Hudak addresses this question of efficiency in point (2).

with modern functional languages. To cite an oft-seen statement in the literature on functional languages, "This is an area of active research."

5.3.2   Logic Programming Languages

From an operational perspective, logic programming languages are declarative languages whose basis is the *relation*,[152] in contrast to the *function* that is the underlying computational model for functional programming languages [248]. More formally, logic programming is derived from predicate logic, whereas functional programming is based on the lambda calculus [205]. It has been argued [455] that logic programming is potentially higher-level than functional programming because logic programming implements a *relation* (a many-to-many relationship) rather than a *mapping* (a many-to-one relationship). There is also an argument as to whether programming with functions or with relations is more "human-friendly". We won't get into this debate, though interested readers are welcome to pursue the references above. Our interest is in the potential of logic programming languages for parallel computing. We will look in more detail at the AND- and OR-parallelism that we introduced in our Applications chapter (page 80), review Prolog, the best-known logic programming language, and then discuss other logic programming languages that are better suited for parallel computation.

A Quick Review of Prolog

As we said on page 80, Prolog [378], [292] is a language based on logic programming; its built-in control scheme is based on a specific method for searching state spaces, and appears to be quite suitable for production systems. Logic programming is an ancient and honorable branch of mathematics whose practical importance is that it represents a formalized method of *reasoning* (inferences and deductions).

Artificial Intelligence applications frequently involve searching the state space of a problem to find a solution (see page 76). The search mechanisms that are used involve moving and performing very simple operations on large quantities of data. The term *symbolic processing* is frequently attached to these

---

152 The clause "father(sam,larry)" is a simple relation (also called an *atomic formula*); father is the *relation name* and sam and larry are the *arguments*. When such a clause is encountered in a logic program, it is referred to as a *relation call*.

Prolog Terminology

The Prolog language is based on a branch of mathematics called logic programming, and its mind-set is that of "proving things", in contrast to a language like Fortran, whose mind-set is to assemble a little "factory" that "builds" the desired answer. A brief refresher follows:

Horn Clauses: Structurally, a pure Prolog program is a sequence of **clauses** of the form
   $A \leftarrow B1,B2,..,Bn.$
Clauses like this, having only a *single* term on the left-hand side, are called *Horn clauses.* The clause above can be thought of as either of the following:

1.   A LOGICAL STATEMENT that if all the Bs are true then A is true.
2.   A PROCEDURE for *producing* a state satisfying condition A.

A is the **head** (or **goal**) of the clause, and the Bs form the **body** (or **subgoals**).

Predicate: The As and Bs in the clause must all be **predicates** in the logic sense, which means that they represent *relations* or that they assert that something (truth, for example) is a quality, attribute, or property of something else.

relation: The clause "father(sam,larry)" is a simple relation (also called an *atomic formula*); father is the *relation name* and sam and larry are the *arguments*. When such a clause is encountered in a logic program, it is referred to as a *relation call.*

Statements: The three basic kinds of Prolog statements are formed from this clause as follows:

| $A \leftarrow B1,...,Bn.$ | **Conditional** statement (defines general rule). |

   $grandfather(X,Z) \leftarrow father(X,Y),father(Y,Z).$

| A. | **Assertion** statement (states fact). |

   father(sam,larry).

| $\leftarrow B.$ | **Query** statement (ask questions, *start computations*). |

   $\leftarrow$ father(X,larry).

(continued on page 281)

AI applications[153] to contrast them with the more traditional *numeric processing,* which is characterized by more complicated (arithmetic) operations performed on smaller quantities of data. This search process as the source of opportunity for parallel processing seems qualitatively different from numeric

---

[153]   The name *symbolic* probably came from the Lisp notion of processing lists of symbols that had no numeric values, unlike symbols in other languages such as Fortran.

Prolog Terminology (continued)

Resolution: Theorem-proving mechanism (used in Prolog) which starts by trying to prove the *negation* of the desired proof and looks for a contradiction.

Unification: The process of finding the most general substitutions of variables that make two expressions identical. For example, if the variable *X* were *bound* to the constant term *sam*, then the goal statement and assertion above would match. Unification is pattern matching complicated by the fact that both patterns to be matched may contain logical variables that have not yet been bound to a specific value. There are now many unification algorithms, but Robinson's was a major breakthrough, being the first use of unification in resolution [343].

Term: Bound variables are bound to *terms*. A term may be a constant, another variable, or a more complex structure involving functions applied to arguments that are themselves terms.

Execution: The subgoals in a clause or query are executed in left-to-right sequence. A subgoal can be solved by finding a matching fact, or by finding a rule whose head matches and whose body can be recursively solved (also left-to-right). The matching process, called *unification,* operates on two arguments (terms) at a time; each argument of a subgoal is compared with the corresponding argument in the same position of the fact or rule head with which the match is being attempted. The two terms unify if they are identical, if either (or both) is a variable, or under certain other conditions (see reference [128] for more detail; note that *aliases* can arise in the two-variable case). In case of success, the clause is exited as in a conventional procedure call, having satisfied the goal by binding specific values to a set of variables. In case of failure, the system *backtracks* to the most recent choice point and tries to follow the path flowing from another choice.   The total path traced out is called the **execution graph** (see Figure 2.19 on page 81 for an example).

---

processing examples such as solving systems of partial differential equations, where the method for solving the problem is to carefully divide it into tasks that can be parceled out to different PEs, after which the solution is "constructed" from the "building blocks" that the PEs produced while they were operating in parallel. The development of new languages specifically for symbolic processing is thus not surprising.

The search mechanism implemented in Prolog (see Figure 2.19 on page 81) is highly sequential in nature. As described in the box on page 279, it performs a depth-first, left-to-right search. When a dead end is found, it *backtracks,* or retraces its steps, and *then* goes down another branch of the tree formed by the execution graph (like the explorer of a maze who ties a rope around his or her waist and the other end at the start of the maze). This sequential behavior is quite inherent in Prolog [437], and means that Prolog itself is not a suitable language for parallel execution of logic programs. (Indeed, the Fifth Generation Computer Project, which aimed to apply parallelism to just such programs, eventually switched from Prolog to FGHC, a newer, parallel logic programming language that we shall have more to say about below.) But there seems to be a great deal of potential parallelism in logic programs, and it comes in two forms:

- AND-parallelism, from trying to solve several goals or subgoals at once.

- OR-parallelism, from trying to solve a goal many ways at once.

The two types of parallelism are discussed in more detail below, followed by some words on their implementation in parallel logic programming languages such as Concurrent Prolog, Parlog, FGHC, and OR-parallel Prolog.

OR-Parallelism

As mentioned, OR-parallelism involves trying to achieve one goal in several ways at once; in Prolog terminology, it involves the simultaneous execution of two or more clauses.[154]. It is called OR-parallelism because success may come from executing the first clause *or* the second clause, and so on. If all solutions to a query are required (e.g., if the query corresponding to Figure 2.19 on page 81 were, "Who are Sam's grandchildren?"), then every clause must be examined, and OR-parallelism is highly advantageous. On the other hand, if the goal can be met by producing just one solution (e.g., if the query in Figure 2.19 were, "Is Sam a grandfather?"), then OR-parallelism may perform considerable unnecessary computation. Although not efficient, searching all paths in parallel will find a solution quickly (providing, of course, that the hardware resources are available). In summary, OR-parallelism is best for applications in which all solutions are desired.

Database systems are a prominent example of such an application, and in fact OR-parallelism is used in the "inference engine" of the original Prolog-based Fifth Generation project [337]. Clearly a query like, "Give me the names of all the people who should buy Almasi and Gottlieb's book" has the potential for a high degree of parallelism. Furthermore, all the various parallel activities are working on different problems, each a potential solution to the original query. Because the problems are different, no cooperation or communication between the different activities is required. The advantages for parallel processing are clear. The greatest challenge is management of a large, distributed data space. The OR-parallel activities may not *need* communication, but pre-

---

[154] The next several paragraphs follow the treatment in [130]

venting *unwanted* communication (overwriting, etc.) can lead to considerable copying overhead in a practical implementation.

AND-Parallelism

Instead of investigating various alternative clauses for a subgoal in parallel, AND-parallelism is concerned with trying to solve two or more subgoals in parallel. For each subgoal, only one clause is investigated at a time, and thus no OR-parallelism is exploited. To solve the original query, a series of sets of subgoals will be produced, and for each set, the first subgoal and the second subgoal and so on must all be solved in order to solve the set—thus the name *AND-parallelism*. If at any time a subgoal in a subgoal set cannot be solved, backtracking to a previous subgoal set must occur. (An important aspect of OR-parallelism is that backtracking is eliminated as a basic operation of the execution model.)

An argument for AND-parallelism is that it may produce a single solution more quickly than either sequential or OR-parallel Prolog, since to produce the single solution, the different parts of the problem are solved in parallel. Further, if a program is largely deterministic (has few matching clauses for any subgoal), it may exhibit large AND-parallelism and little OR-parallelism. Expert Systems are such an application.

In AND-parallelism, all subgoals in a subgoal set are working on the same problem, and each must succeed if the subgoal set is to succeed. Because the subgoals are working on the same problem, they share a common set of data and variables. A change to one variable by one subgoal may affect the computation of another subgoal and may even make it fail. But in addition, when two subgoals share an unbound variable and both wish to assign it a value, care must be taken to ensure that they assign it a common value. If they assign different values to the variable and this discrepancy goes undetected, an invalid computation may result. This situation is called the *binding-conflict* problem, and it can make the extraction of the maximum amount of AND-parallelism costly because identifying the maximum number of blocks of code that are free of binding conflicts and may safely run in parallel requires extra analysis (computation) at both compile time and run time. The latter is a potentially costly overhead that reduces the speedup obtained by parallel processing. If the maximum parallelism in a program exceeds the number of processors available, it may be a wise trade-off to use a less computationally expensive execution model and accept a lower degree of parallelism. A recent paper [129] discusses two such AND-parallel execution models.

The first model does worst-case data-dependency analysis at compile time, examining all calling environments of a clause. The second model analyzes each program clause in isolation, determines several possible execution graphs for each, and embeds run-time tests that choose the best execution graph; however, not all calling environments are examined.

Hence the choice between the models represents a gamble. The second one may win because it executes each clause more efficiently, but it may lose because it finds less parallelism to begin with and because it contributes more run-time overhead. Both should be suitable for machines with hundreds of processing elements [128], and of course AND- and OR-parallelism can be used in combination, but experiments with programs of substantial size are needed to determine the extent of each type of parallelism and the best execution model for parallel logic programs.

Concurrent Prolog, Parlog, FGHC, OR-Parallel Prolog, ...

Ehud Shapiro [388], [389] characterizes today's Prolog as a sequential simulation of a parallel computational model and describes a parallel language called Concurrent Prolog that he is designing. He adds two syntactic constructs to logic programming, namely *read-only* annotation of variables and the *commit* operator. Both are used to control the computation, that is, the construction of a proof by restricting the order in which goals can be reduced and restricting the choice of clauses that can be used to reduce them. The side effects of sequential Prolog are eliminated, and its cut control construct (used to limit the search process) is cleaned up.

A Concurrent Prolog program is a finite set of guarded Horn clauses, that is, clauses of the form

$$A \leftarrow G_1, G_2, ..., G_m | B_1, B_2, ..., B_n$$

where the Gs and Bs are the atomic goals, the Gs are the guard of the clause, | is the commit operator, and the Bs are, as before, the body. Operationally, a guarded clause functions similarly to an alternative in a guarded command [146] of the type also used in CSP (page 247). The resulting synchronization mechanism is similar to that of dataflow languages, in that a process suspended on undetermined read-only variables is analogous to an operator waiting for its arguments to arrive. However, this is more a similarity in spirit than one at the implementation level, since the granularity in most dataflow models is much finer. It is not suggested that Concurrent Prolog is a suitable language for dataflow computers [389]. Shapiro also makes interesting comparisons with functional languages, monitors, and Carl Hewitt's "Actors"[9] , and presents a number of Concurrent Prolog program examples.

In recent years, the number of parallel logic programming languages has grown quite large; good overviews and comparisons can be found in the survey paper by Shapiro [389] and in the books by Gregory [205] and by Tick [437]. AND-parallelism and OR-parallelism are both represented, although some of the early flush of enthusiasm for OR-parallelism has been tempered by experience, namely, the effort required to prevent unwanted communication as the branches of the search tree are being explored independently in parallel, and the realization that many of these branches yield rather small amounts of computation compared to the implementation's overheads. A detailed treatment of the language OR-parallel Prolog is found in the book by Tick [437]. More information on OR-parallelism is contained in the papers by Ciepielewski [101], who reviews the scheduling problems in OR-parallel Prolog, and in the paper by Ali and Karlsson [14], who describe an OR-parallel language named Muse.

AND-parallel approaches can be categorized by whether or not the concurrent evaluations share variables [205]. In *restricted AND-parallelism,* a compile-time analysis and/or a run-time system is used to prevent the possibility of binding conflicts by preventing the parallel execution of two subgoals that share one or more unbound variables. We touched on this approach at the end of the preceding section on AND-parallelism, and DeGroot [128] describes one such system in detail. The advantage is that the implementation process is made easier if it is safe to assume that the arguments being evaluated concurrently are independent. The disadvantage is decreased parallelism.

Stream AND-parallelism is the concurrent evaluation of two calls that do share variables, with the values of the shared variables communicated incrementally between the calls [205]. The languages Concurrent Prolog [389], Parlog [205], and FGHC, or Flat Guarded Horn Clauses [437], all implement stream AND-parallelism, and the references cited provide the details.

The word *flat* refers to the nature of the guards present in the clauses of these languages, and represents a trade-off between expressiveness and efficiency, somewhat reminiscent of our discussion of higher-order functions in functional languages. A *flat* guard may contain no user-defined functions, a restriction that makes the language easier to compile. The language Strand is a flat version of Parlog, and flat versions of Concurrent Prolog and other languages have appeared in response to criticisms about difficulty of implementation. As Shapiro [389] put it, non-flat languages are difficult to implement "for real".

Whereas good performance results for real applications have just recently appeared for functional languages (the Sisal results we mentioned earlier), such results have not yet been achieved for logic programming languages. For example, a recent survey of parallel production systems [310] makes no mention of any logic programming language. However, logic programming is a very active area of research, encouraging results are appearing, and the approach still looks interesting for parallel computing.

5.4 The Programmer's View

To recap, there are three possible scenarios for a programmer's view of a parallel computer, that is, for what a programmer would have to do in order to get a program to run effectively on a parallel processor:

1. In the first view, the programmer is spared from having to learn any new languages or constructs. A parallelizing compiler (for example, Parafrase [302]) automatically extracts parallelism from programs written in existing serial languages (even old "dusty decks"). The programmer may aid this process by specifying data partitioning and helping in code optimization. The mechanisms and limitations underlying this approach are discussed in more detail in our chapter on compilers.

2. In the second scenario, the programmer's favorite serial language is augmented with a few new constructs that allow the programmer to specify and properly coordinate the parallel execution of a number of parallel tasks.[155] This world of explicit parallelism is the one that involves PARBEGINs and DOALLs, FORKs and JOINs, semaphores and rendezvous, SEND and RECEIVE, and other low-level control features typically made available to Fortran and C programmers, as well as higher-level approaches like the "futures" construct that Multilisp offers to Lisp programmers.

3. In the third scenario, the programmer would write in an entirely new language designed to make parallelism easier to detect and extract. One way to do this is to eliminate side effects and other features that make it hard to extract parallelism from programs written in existing serial languages. Although substantial relearning might be involved, the degree of recoverable parallelism should be higher than in the first approach, and the programmer would not be involved with the mechanics of parallelism as in the second approach. This world of implicit parallelism is the one that involves functional programming, dataflow, Prolog, and other new and

---

[155] *Task* is used in an informal sense here.

proposed side effect–free languages, and was treated in the second portion of this chapter.

It is interesting to point out how all three of these approaches are influenced by a single concept, namely the *side effect* mentioned in passing above. A language with side effects supports the concept of a global variable that can be modified by many parts[156] of the program other than the part in which it appears. As mentioned, this is a powerful communication mechanism among portions of a program, but it can limit the amount of parallelism that can be extracted automatically in the first scenario because it makes it hard to guarantee that no interdependencies have been overlooked among tasks to be done in parallel, especially if a low-level language is used. To get around this difficulty, the second scenario gives the programmer specific tools to help the compiler by identifying for it specific instances of parallelism in which side effects are not a concern. Alternatively, side effects can be abolished, as in the third scenario. So in a sense, side effects are the straw that stirs the drink in all three cases.

---

[156] An assignment statement is the most common example.

Glossary of Language Terms

Abstract data type: A language construct that encapsulates a type definition and a set of procedures that provide the only way to manipulate objects of the abstract type [191].

Access control: Synchronization needed in the presence of competition for shared resources. *Mutual exclusion* is one form.

Applicative (functional, expression-oriented) language: A language that more closely resembles mathematics, in that function application is the only control structure (no conditional or assignment statements, explicit sequencing, or looping), leading to programs with an "If you give me that, I'll give you this" style.

Block-structured language: (Sub)programs in block-structured languages are organized as a set of nested blocks having their own local environments.

Busy-waiting: A situation in which a process must keep repeating a test until it succeeds before it can proceed further (see page 158).

Concurrent: Processes are concurrent if their execution overlaps in time, that is, if one process starts before the other process ends.

Coroutines: Programs that can swap control back and forth in symmetric fashion. Only one executes at a time (see page 152).

Declarative language: A non-imperative category that includes functional and logic programming languages.

Expression: Compact, higher-level representation of a sequence of machine-level operations used to calculate a value; may be part of a statement.

Fetch-and-add: A newer synchronization primitive in the form of an instruction Faa(X,e) that says, "In one indivisible step, tell me the value of the shared integer variable X and add e to it." Used for concurrent queue access, and so on (see "Fetch-and-Add" on page 162).

Functional language: See **applicative language**.

Imperative (procedural, statement-oriented) language: A language that closely mimics the von Neumann model, including global variables and side effects, and gives a "do this, do that" -style of program with explicitly specified processing operations.

Glossary of Language Terms (continued)

Procedure: A subprogram that may be activated or **called** (given parameters and made to execute) by another program; library routines, functions, and subroutines are examples.

Process: One execution of a sequential program, subprogram, task, or procedure.

Semantics: The *meaning* of a syntactically correct instance of a language; or, what programs in that language can *do*.

Semaphore: Synchronization primitive used to enforce the mutual exclusion form of access control for a shared resource.

Sequence control: Synchronization needed to enable cooperation. Also called *condition synchronization*.

Shared memory: A shared-memory language is one that never requires explicit copying of data in order to make it accessible to some other part of a parallel program [217].

Side effect: Modification of a data object bound to a global variable, as by an assignment statement. Assignment statements must have side effects, but expressions don't always.

Spin-waiting: Synonym for **busy-waiting** (see above).

Statement: The elemental organizational component of some high-level language programs, analogous to a sentence in a natural language discourse. Executable statements are the active portion of such a program; other statements supply information needed for correct execution.

Syntax: (1) A set of rules specifying which forms of a language are acceptable; a *syntax error* message means, "You can't say it that way in this language". (2) A tax on bad behavior.

Task: Sequential subprogram usable as a high-level building block for concurrent programs.

Test-and-set: An older synchronization primitive in the form of an instruction TS(X) that says, "In one indivisible step, tell me the value of the shared Boolean variable X and make its final value 1." Used for mutual exclusion in critical sections, and so on. (See Figure 4.10 on page 157.)

5.5 Exercises

1. Define the following terms.

   Coroutine   Doall
   Doacross   Imperative language
   Recursion   Reduction language
   Functional Language   Monitor
   OR-parallelism   Rendezvous
   AND-parallelism   Semaphore
   Horn clause   Logic programming language
   Unification algorithm   Mutual exclusion
   Call by value   Serialization
   Call by reference   Side effect
   Dataflow language   Synchronization

2. Match each of the terms on the left with its attribute on the right:

a.	ALGOL	1) ALGOL derivative designed for teaching
b.	APL	2) Commercial language with guarded commands and synchronous message passing
c.	Ada	3) Each process waits until all arrive
d.	Barrier syn-chronization	4) First block-structured language
		5) Hardware synchronization instruction—ideal for queues
e.	CSP	6) Hardware synchronization instruction—ideal for semaphores
f.	FORTRAN	
g.	Fetch-and-add	7) Language reflecting architecture of a traditional uniprocessor
h.	Id	8) Language with "futures" for task creation
i.	LISP	9) Large language with rendezvous for message passing
j.	Modula	10) Logic programming language
k.	Multilisp	11) Modern general purpose language supporting abstract data types
l.	Occam	12) Old language still widely used for numerical computing
m.	Pascal	13) Programming emphasizing array operations
n.	Prolog	14) Purely functional dataflow language
o.	Test-and-set	15) Single-assignment dataflow language featuring I-structures
p.	VAL	16) Tiny language with guarded commands and synchronous message passing
q.	von Neumann language	17) Very early symbolic processing language

3.   Implement the left picture in Figure 4.8 on page 148 using FORK/JOIN and show that the right picture in Figure 4.8 on page 148 cannot be implemented using PARBEGIN/PAREND.

4.   Consider the PARBEGIN program in Figure 4.8 on page 148 and replace each line given as a single letter by a statement printing that letter, i.e. replace A by print ("A"), B by print ("B"), etc. When this program is run one possible output is ABCDEFGH and another is ACBDEFGH. Give two other possible outputs. How many outputs are possible?

5.   Consider the FORK/JOIN problem in Figure 4.8 on page 148 and replace single letter statements by print statements as in problem 4. Give two possible outputs. How many outputs are possible? Why?

6.   In problem 4, we have seen a program whose output cannot be determined even if all its inputs are known (problem 4 is especially simple—there are no inputs). Such programs are called nondeterministic. Why is this form of non-determinism called a race condition, i.e. what is the race?

7.   The program of problem 5 is also non-deterministic due to race conditions. Race conditions make programs harder to understand. Which program is harder to understand, the one in problem 4 or problem 5?

8.   Let S and T be binary semaphores, and consider two concurrent processes, A and B, each executing the following program P(S); P(T); V(T); V(S). Can these two concurrent processes deadlock? If so, give a scenario.

9.   Repeat problem 8 with process A unchanged and process B running P(T); P(S); V(S); V(T).

10. Read the manual for your favorite parallel processor and describe the debugging facilities available to the applications programmer.

11. Consider the standard triply nested loop for matrix multiply. In what order should the loops be nested for efficient execution on an SIMD vector processor? On an MIMD shared-memory multiprocessor?

12. We have scrambled the following humorous item from comp.lang.ada. Can you provide the correct matches?

SHOOTING YOURSELF IN THE FOOT

The proliferation of programming languages can make it difficult to remember which one you're currently using. This guide is offered as a public service.

a. Ada

b. APL

c. BASIC

d. C

e. C++

f. COBOL

g. Concurrent Euclid

h. FORTRAN

i. LISP

j. Modula2

k. Pascal

l. Prolog

m. Unix

1) You shoot yourself in somebody else's foot.

2) You shoot yourself in each toe, iteratively, until you run out of toes.

3) You tell your program you want to be shot in the foot.

4)
```
% ls
% foot.c foot.h foot.o toe.c toe.o
% rm * .o
% rm:.o: No such file or directory
% ls
%
```

5) After correctly packaging your foot, you attempt to concurrently load the gun, pull the trigger, scream, and shoot yourself in the foot, but when you try, you discover that your foot is of the wrong type.

6) You shoot yourself in the foot, then spend all day figuring out how to do it with fewer characters.

7)
```
Using a COLT 45 HANDGUN, AIM gun at LEG.FOOT,
THEN place ARM.HAND.FINGER on
HANDGUN.TRIGGER and SQUEEZE.  THEN return
HANDGUN to HOLSTER.  CHECK whether shoelace
needs to be retied.
```

8) You shoot yourself in the foot.

9) You shoot yourself in the foot with a water pistol.

10) You accidentally create a dozen instances of yourself and shoot them all in the foot.

11) After realizing you can't actually accomplish anything in this language, you shoot yourself in the head.

12) You shoot yourself in the appendage which holds the gun with which you shoot yourself in the appendage which holds the gun with which you shoot yourself in the appendage which holds ...

13) The compiler won't let you shoot yourself in the foot.

TYPES OF GRAPHS			
Type	Node	Arc ("Edge")	Notes
call graph	procedures	procedure calling sequence	skeleton of inter-procedural data-flow analysis
control flow, or just "flow" (p.616)	basic block; compound function	possible flows of control	connects basic block with possible successors (Figure 6.6) within a procedure. ("flowchart" may mix in levels higher, lower than basic blocks.)
control	data transfmt or movement	order of node execution	Gajski et al [186]
process flow	synch. points	process execution, statement	introduces parallel processes (see our Figure 4.8; see p. 51 in Shaw[390] .) may change during execution, unlike control flow graph.
dependency, precedence, data precedence	statements	dependencies	may need local, global, or inter-procedural data dependency analysis
(computation) directed acyclic graph (DAG)	exterior: variables, constants. interior: operations.	path of the resulting values	shows how value computed by each statement in a basic block is used by subsequent statements in the block.
dataflow	operation, instruction	destination (address of instruction receiving the result	connects producer of result with its consumers; nodes do the work, arcs serve as storage (Figure 6.5)

Figure 6.1 Types of Graphs of Programs: *Graphs and graph theory are often used in the art and science of compilers. Herewith, a small scorecard to help keep the various kinds and names straight. Note that, generically, the first four rows are all flows of control.*

6

Compilers

Once a program has been written in one of the languages described in the last chapter, what else must happen before parallel execution can begin? The program must be translated into terms that the hardware eventually understands—the machine language (instruction set) of the architecture to be used. The topic of this chapter is the bridge between two computational models—that of the programming languages described in the last chapter and that of the operating system or hardware architecture to be discussed in subsequent chapters. Compilers, interpreters, and other kinds of language-processing programs are used to perform this translation. The principles used to design compilers for serial computers are treated in books by Aho et al. [11] and Fischer and LeBlanc [168]. We review this topic briefly and then examine the additional requirements of a compiler for a parallel computer [364], [472]. Fortunately, it seems that we need not start from scratch; we can use a number of existing optimizing compiler techniques.

Do parallel processors need new compilers? Not always. The adventurous physicist on a budget may be willing to recode algorithms into the machine language of a parallel processor if this effort results in a substantial performance improvement. Or a few simple parallel constructs like those of Figure 5.7 on page 245, hand-inserted into an existing Fortran program and translated to standard Fortran by a simple preprocessor, may be a good way to obtain some parallel execution, especially in the early stages of a new parallel

Figure 6.2 *Illustration showing a compiler translating a high-level language statement into machine language (for a non-RISC architecture).* *The second, improved version uses fewer instructions.*

machine project. But debugging is usually hard with a preprocessor —compiler error messages now refer to the preprocessor's output, not the programmer's code, for example.

Extracting substantial parallelism from large existing serial programs (the "dusty decks", for example) will almost certainly require a new compiler [15]. Even in the future, should some new concept like, say, dataflow succeed, the user will want to program in a high-level language like Id and not worry about the details of the machine design. Furthermore, there is a school of thought that holds that developing a compiler is essential for developing the architecture because it is the only way to discover where the real problems are before the machine is built [28], [170]. In short, whether the language is new or old and whether the parallelism is explicit or implicit, a compiler will be desirable for the same reasons that it is today.

Our approach is to first review the functions performed by a compiler for serial machines and then consider the additional tasks that must be performed for a parallel computer. We discuss the dependency analyses performed on sequential programs before they are rearranged for improved performance and how these techniques may be adapted in order to partition a program for parallel execution. We compare compilers for vector processors and multiprocessors. Much of the emphasis so far has been on the "automatic extraction of parallelism" from serial imperative language programs with no explicit parallel constructs, and we examine "reconstructing" vs. "reassembling" Fortran compilers and compare these with an APL-based approach. We conclude with compilers for dataflow languages, which represent new languages not burdened with old programs and programming styles. APL has some aspects of a functional language, dataflow languages have more, which makes dependency analysis easier than it is with Fortran and facilitates algorithms whose order of execution is less restricted and perhaps easier to parallelize.

Compilers vs. Interpreters

In contrast to the complete machine-code program generated by a compiler, an interpreter executes one statement at a time and retains only some of the information it gained in doing so. Interpretation is easier but less efficient in using resources. For a recipe calling for three egg yolks near the beginning and three egg whites near the end, a good compiler might use three eggs, but an interpreter would use six and take longer. *Compilers plan ahead.*

Interpreters do have a number of advantages. They are smaller and easier to write, execution starts more quickly, and better diagnostics make debugging easier. However, memory must be allocated for the source program as well as for the interpreter, and, of course, there is a performance penalty. A friend working on an APL compiler explained this performance penalty in the following way:

First, as you already realized, an interpreter carries out work one primitive operation at a time.

Second, in the particular case of APL, the interpreter has the added disadvantage of having to construct the parse tree at run-time.

But the fundamental reason is that the interpreter lacks intelligence. For A←B+C it has to treat B and C as a most general array. This is where the power of type-shape analysis comes in. In our compiler, if we do discover that A and B are simple scalars, they are loaded to registers, and one machine instruction suffices to carry out the primitive operation. Even for arrays, if we know their rank at compile-time, we can save a lot of queries required in interpretation.

The interpreter's advantage over a compiler is its structural simplicity. The reason our APL interpreter is a far more complicated program than a PASCAL compiler is all due to the enormous number of the primitives and general dimensional arrays.

6.1   Serial Compiler Essentials

A compiler program ususally consists of a *front end* that analyzes the user's program and a *back end* that generates a corresponding and complete[157] set of detailed marching orders for the computer. To be more precise, the front end starts with the source program that the user wrote in some high-level language, analyzes it, and translates it into some intermediate representation; the back end translates this intermediate representation into low-level object code understood by the computer being used. Various optimizations may be ap-

---

[157] A compiler is used to generate a complete machine-code version of the user's program, whereas an interpreter proceeds more incrementally; see the box above.

plied to minimize memory requirements and run time of the resulting program. Figure 6.2 on page 296 shows a high-level source program segment and two examples of the corresponding compiled object code in assembly language.[158]

In somewhat more specific terms, Aho et al. [11] list the phases of compilation as follows:

1. Lexical analysis
2. Syntax analysis
3. Intermediate code generation
4. Code optimization
5. Code generation
6. Table management
7. Error handling

The first five occur more or less in sequence, while the last two go on in parallel with them. The optimization in step 4 involves both the front end and the back end and thus represents the boundary between them. The actions performed by each phase are as follows.

First, a *lexical analyzer* (or *scanner* or *tokenizer*) breaks the source program into its atomic objects (or *tokens*) and classifies them as operators, constants, separators, or identifiers. This phase is fairly simple.

In the next phase, a *syntax analyzer,* or *parser,* analyzes the grammatic structure of a program; it checks for errors and arranges the tokens in a *parse tree* as a way of denoting the program's syntactic structure (see Figure 6.3 on page 299). This work proceeds at the level of the program's basic blocks, which are branch-free, or straight-line, pieces of code. A basic block has only one entry point and one exit point and is always executed in the same order (see Figure 6.4).

The flow of control among the basic blocks within a procedure is shown by means of a *flow graph,* and the calling relationships among the procedures that make up the entire program are shown via a *call graph* (see Figure 6.1 on page 294). In addition, *tables* are generated to keep track of the names used by the program, their type (real, integer, etc.), and other essential data. These

---

[158] The job is completed by an *assembler* program that translates assembly language into machine language and by a *linker* program that connects compiled program segments into one loadable and executable program.

Figure 6.3   **Parse trees.**   *On the left, the syntax analysis of an English sentence and the resulting parse tree, showing the hierarchical structure of the sentence, that is, how the parts identified by the lexical analysis should be grouped together (somewhat like diagramming sentences in school). On the right, analogous parse trees for the token stream corresponding to the expression A / B * C , showing how the different syntax of Fortran and APL leads to two different parse trees for essentially identical expressions. In Fortran rules, the ambiguity about whether to multiply or divide first is resolved as (A÷B) × C; in APL, the precedence goes to the rightmost operation, yielding A÷(B × C).*

tables, graphs, and trees amount to the essential results of the overall *semantic analysis* carried out by the front end.[159]

     In some cases, the front end uses this information to translate the original program into a lower-level *intermediate code* for purposes of portability (retargetability) and optimization. Intermediate code differs from assembly language chiefly in that it need not specify the actual registers and memory locations to be used to hold the input and output of each operation. The idea is that the front end can then be re-used with several different back ends to

---

[159] *Semantic analysis* means slightly different things to different authors. In the view of Hennessy and Ganapathi [227], it means walking the parse tree performing semantic checks such as type checking and argument compatibility, and producing an intermediate representation of the program. Semantic analysis appears on their list after syntax analysis, in the place where intermediate code generation appears on the list from Aho et al. [11], who take a broader view of semantic analysis as being the overall action of the front end. Sometimes the term *semantic checking* is used to mean a low-level subset of what the front end does.

generate code with detailed register and memory allocation schemes optimized for a specific computational model and architecture.

An optimizing code generator that produces truly efficient object programs is one of the most difficult parts of compiler design. The *purpose* of optimization is to make the program run faster and/or use less memory, and a main *method* is to *rearrange* the compiled code ("code motion" of a loop-invariant computation from inside to outside a frequently executed loop is a simple example[160]). This rearrangement requires the front end's knowledge of what reorderings are permitted and the back end's knowledge of which ones are profitable.

The front end's contribution is an extensive set of dataflow and dependency analyses performed on each procedure. (For our purposes, the program is assumed to be a collection of procedures.) The name *global* has come to be used for this intraprocedural (inter–basic block) analysis, while *local* is used to mean intra–basic block analysis. When we discuss parallelizing compilers, we shall find the word *interprocedural* used to mean analysis of the entire program.

One example of such a set of analyses consists of applying the following key steps to each procedure:

1. Divide the program into basic blocks [11].
2. Construct a control flow graph (nodes = basic blocks, arcs = possible control paths).
3. Reduce the control flow graph to structured subparts called *intervals* (loops, for example) made up of one or more basic blocks; dependency analysis will then be much easier [16].
4. Within each basic block, divide the occurrences of the variables into three categories:
   a. Variables whose use is confined to the basic block (temporaries, for example, such as Y in the middle line of a basic block consisting of
      ```
      Y = W
      X = Y + 1
      Y = Z - 5
      ```
   b. Those *used* (read) in the basic block but defined elsewhere, like W and Z in the above example.
   c. Those *defined* (written) in the basic block and potentially used elsewhere, like X and like the definition of Y in the last line of the example above.

---

[160] An extreme case is shown on page 19 of the article by Haynes [223].

5. For each variable *used* in this block, find all possible *definitions* in other blocks. This process is called finding the *reach* of each variable, or *u-d (use-definition) chaining,* and forms the backbone of global data dependency analysis (see Figure 6.6 on page 311).

6.2   Parallelizing Compiler Essentials

The task facing a parallelizing compiler[161] can be put as follows: given a program that takes a long time to run on a serial computer, and given a new computer containing multiple processing units that can all operate concurrently, the objective is to shorten the program's running time by breaking it up into pieces that can be processed in a parallel or at least overlapped fashion by the multiple processing units. So the compiler's front end acquires the additional task of looking for parallelism, and the back end must now schedule it (arranging or rearranging both the code and the data storage plan) in such a way that the correct result (the same one as before) *and* improved performance are obtained with the new computational model.

The new parallel computational model raises questions for the compiler about what kind of pieces the program should be divided into and how these pieces may be safely rearranged. Figure 6.5 on page 304 illustrates two different answers for two different hardware architectures, one SIMD, the other MIMD. In general, these questions involve the *granularity, level, and degree of parallelism* that we touched on in Chapter 1, and the *analysis of the dependencies* among these candidates for parallel execution, as we shall discuss in this chapter.

Fortunately, there is a body of work to build on. Optimizing compilers for serial computers perform much of their optimization by modifying the code in such a way as to decrease the running time or memory requirements [11]. These modifications require extensive analysis of the original program and the way it "hangs together", and much of this analysis is applicable to rearranging code for parallel execution as well.

An important example of such serial program optimization is called *code motion* [11], in which a loop-invariant computation is removed from the loop and placed before it. For example, consider an assignment statement A = B + C that is at a position in a loop where all possible definitions of B and/or C are

---

161   A compiler producing code for a parallel computer. The term *parallel compiler* could also mean that it runs in parallel but produces serial code.

Figure 6.4   Compiler terminology: interval, basic block, and BAS illustrated
(terms usually used with the intermediate code or lower-level version of a program). A
basic block is a block of straight-line code, with no jumps out except at the end and no
jumps in except at the beginning. The rules [11] for identifying basic blocks follow:

1. Any statement that is the target of a GOTO is called a leader.
2. Any statement that immediately follows a GOTO is a leader.
3. The program's first statement is a leader.
4. Each leader and all statements up to but not including the next leader or the
   end of the program constitute a basic block.

The term BAS[364] means a block of assignment statements and is a special example
of a basic block. An interval is a section of code that has only one entrance and whose
portion of the flow graph is strongly connected, which means that there is a control flow
path from any one basic block to another within the interval. A DO loop is a simple instance. (In fact, intervals originated as a conceptual generalization of loops [16].) Unlike
basic blocks, intervals can be nested; conceivably, the main program could be an outermost nested interval.

The left part of the figure shows a section of Fortran-like code containing a small DO
loop. The partly compiled version on the right contains just enough of the lower-level
mechanics of the DO loop to show how the conditional jump breaks the loop into (at least)
two basic blocks. The corresponding portion of the flow graph is shown in the middle.
Horizontal arrows show the potential jumps into and out of the code sequence. In a basic
block, execution of the first statement guarantees execution of the last statement (as well
as all the ones in between). We cannot guarantee this execution for the entire interval
of code corresponding to a DO loop, even if the test is made at the end of the loop (consider a loop body that contains an IF statement that chooses one of two statements for
execution based on some condition not known at compile time). Thus, the analysis and
scheduling of loops is more complicated than that of basic blocks and is one of the motivations for the Bulldog approach in contrast to the Parafrase approach, as discussed further in the text.

outside the loop. Then the calculation of B + C will be the same each time it is encountered and might as well be moved outside the loop and done only once in order to save time. Then, it might also be possible to move a statement *using* A (D = A + ...) outside the loop, and so on. The analysis that decides which statements are loop-invariant makes use of the u-d chaining information we mentioned earlier (page 301). This analysis can be regarded as a subset of the more extensive dependency analysis done by vectorizing compilers, which we shall discuss shortly.

A program like the weather code on page 48 can be viewed as consisting of a few large work orders such as its procedures ("Compute the atmospheric parameters within the fifth layer") that are successively translated into smaller and more numerous work orders, eventually becoming a huge number of tiny work orders at the machine-instruction level ("Add the values of the variables A and B and assign this value to the variable C") or an even larger number of tinier work orders at the microinstruction level ("Now turn on that adder circuit").[162] Other intermediate-size work orders are listed in Figure 1.5 on page 19. There will be further discussion of these later. What we are searching for on any of these levels are work orders that can be done in parallel, either because they are totally independent or because their interdependence is such that it still results in a reasonable ratio of computation to communication on the computer to be used. Naturally, this ratio depends on the power of the multiple processing units and on the mechanisms provided for communication and synchronization among them.

Since the program pieces as well as the multiple processing units come in a range of sizes, a fair number of combinations are possible, requiring different overall compiling approaches. However, these combinations also have many needs in common, and fortunately a reasonable amount of the needed compiler technology already exists as a result of the work on vectorization as well as on optimized code generation for serial programs, where a correct but nonoptimum intermediate-code version of the original program is rearranged into a new (serial) order that produces the originally computed result more quickly. The compiler performs dependency analysis (page 309) to find those statements that are independent of each other and may be rearranged with respect to each other. These techniques can be extended to find independent pieces of the program that can be executed concurrently. This approach has been applied most successfully at the instruction level, and so we begin our treatment of specific parallelizing compilers with a discussion of vectorizers.

---

[162] These different-size work orders correspond to the multilevel computational model we discussed on page 140.

$$c_0 = 0$$
FOR i FROM 1 to 8 DO
$$a_i = d_i/e_i$$
$$b_i = a_i{}^*f_i$$
$$c_i = b_i + c_{(i-1)}$$

ENDFOR

Figure 6.5 Two ways to parallelize: *SIMDizing (vectorizing) vs. MIMDizing (parallelizing). The small program's dataflow graph can be divided into different schedulable units of computation for the two different models of computation. For example, the DO loop can be "distributed" (divided) into three separate independent loops (labeled "vector", "vector", and "recurrence"). The first two each perform a number of simple, identical, and independent arithmetic operations. Hence each loop can be replaced by a vector instruction that has the effect of performing these simple operations in parallel or in pipelined fashion, depending on the SIMD machine. Good speedup calls for long vectors. The computations of the last loop involve a recurrence (are not independent of each other) and do not easily lend themselves to such vectorization (but good vectorizers don't give up; see Figure 10.16 on page 526).*

The code can also be divided into tasks for an MIMD multiprocessor, with each processor assigned several iterations of the loop, as shown for four processors ("task1 ... task4"). The key here is the ratio between the actual computation time and the overheads incurred, including starting/stopping parallel execution and interprocessor communication time. The overheads are large enough in most practical cases that an economical task work load would have to be much larger than the ones shown here. See the text for more details. (From an example in [186].)

Figure 10.16 on page 526 compares the parallel execution schedule and efficiency of this program on several dataflow architectures vs. a more conventional SIMD processor and optimizing compiler combination.

6.2.1　*Vectorizers*

The most thoroughly explored of these levels of work orders or program granularity is that of machine instructions. Surely at most moments of a program's execution there is a huge backlog of instructions that could be done in parallel, even though the von Neumann model does them one at a time. The dataflow model is sort of an extreme effort to capitalize on this backlog, with an instruction only needing to have received its input data in order to qualify for execution (see "Dataflow Languages—VAL, Id, LAU, Sisal" on page 271). Vectorizing, a more modest approach to exploiting parallelism at the instruction level, has had more commercial success to date and is the basis of the most widely used supercomputers. Since vectorizing represents real experience, we begin our discussion here. We first examine how a vectorizing compiler goes beyond a scalar compiler and then compare it with other kinds of parallelizing compilers.

As discussed in "Vector Processors" on page 415, a vector processor has some extra computing units and fast memory designed for efficient execution of long sequences of identical operations. For example, the addition of two N-element vectors on an ordinary scalar computer is expressed in Fortran as an N-cycle loop of the form

```
      DO 10 I = 1,N
         A(I) = B(I) + C(I)
   10  CONTINUE
```

As you can see, the add instruction must be fetched and decoded N times. The effect of these fetches and decodes on the time needed for the whole vector addition can be ameliorated by the kind of instruction prefetching and pipelining shown in Figure 9.1 on page 412, which ideally reduces the total time to slightly more than N times that needed to execute a single addition. However, this time can still be substantial, especially for floating-point operations, which characterize scientific and engineering computations. Most machine architectures can execute a fixed-point addition in a single cycle, but floating-point operations take multiple cycles (6 cycles for a floating-point addition on the Cray-1, for example) because of the extra manipulations needed when two numbers have different exponents (see Figure 9.4 on page 419). Given this situation, the extra overhead of vector processing can be an attractive trade-off if it reduces the average number of cycles per floating-point operation, as we discuss next (also see Figure 9.4 on page 419).

On a vector processor, the loop above is replaced by a single instruction like

$$A(1:N) = B(1:N) + C(1:N)$$

The idea is that, after some set-up time, the vector elements can be added in parallel. (In practice, this conceptual model is most frequently implemented by a pipelined design, which performs the operations in overlapped rather than completely parallel fashion in order to save hardware, and eventually emits the result of an operation on every cycle; see page 413 ff.) A vectorizing compiler, or *vectorizer*, takes the sequential statements equivalent to the vector statement above and performs a translation into vector machine instructions. For the above addition of two vectors, assuming each has N elements stored contiguously in memory, the assembly code for the IBM 3090 Vector Facility (page 427), for example, is shown below (instructions starting with the letter V belong to the vector facility; all others are regular System/370 instructions; VLD, VAD, and VSTD each advance the vector address in its general register by 128):

```
        L     G0,N      ┐load the vector length N into general register 0
        LA    G1,C      │   and the starting addresses of the three
        LA    G2,B      │   vectors into general registers 1 to 3.
        LA    G3,A      ┘
LOOP    VLVCU G0        —set up loop that does 128 vector elements at a time.
        VLD   V0,G1     ┐load 128 elements of C from memory into vector register 0,
        VAD   V0,V0,G2  │   add to it 128 elements of B from memory & put result in V0;
        VSTD  V0,G3     ┘   store result into a section of A; +128 to G1,G2,G3 contents.
        BC    2,LOOP    —branch back to "LOOP" if more elements are left.
```

The condition that allows vectorization is that the elements of the source operands must be independent of the result operands. For example,

```
    DO 20 I = 1,N
        X(I) = B(I) - A(I)*X(I-1)
20  CONTINUE
```

is not generally considered vectorizable because of the implied recursive use of the X_i values (X_{i-1} <u>must</u> be calculated before X_i). For the same reasons, the code following the first `foreach` in the weather code example on page 48 is easily vectorizable; that following the second `foreach` is not. This loop-carried dependence between X_i and X_{i-1} inhibits vectorization and is the sort of thing that the compiler must check for as it searches a program for parallel portions suitable for vector processing. Such dependency analysis is discussed in more detail below, starting on page 309.

So far, we have shown a loop that is trivial to vectorize and one that is impossible. Most cases of interest fall somewhere in between. For example, the matrix multiplication

$$c_{ij} = \sum_{k=1}^{N} a_{ik} b_{kj}$$

is often coded[163] as

```
       DO 100 J=1,N
          DO 100 I=1,N
             DO 100 K=1,N
                C(I,J) = C(I,J) + A(I,K)*B(K,J)
   100 CONTINUE
```

assuming that the Cs have been initialized to 0. Note that the innermost (K) loop is like

```
       DO 100 K=1,N
             scalar=scalar + A(K)*constant,
   100 CONTINUE
```

which is an example of a loop-carried dependence: the value of C calculated on iteration k is passed on to iteration $k+1$, or, in other words, there is *communication* between iterations k and $k+1$. (This loop is sometimes called "unfriendly"). Because the loop iterations are not independent, this code as written cannot take advantage of the small operations that a vector processor can perform in parallel, that is, it is not vectorizable. (It *is* well suited to a highly parallel MIMD design with processors powerful enough to carry out substantial computations on their own, as we shall discuss later.)

However, this code can be made vectorizable by a simple *loop interchange* on the K and I loops. (Vector people like the unfriendly loop to be on the outside.) After this rearrangement, the code is

```
       DO 100 J=1,N
          DO 100 K=1,N
             DO 100 I=1,N
                C(I,J) = C(I,J) + A(I,K)*B(K,J)
   100 CONTINUE
```

Note that now the inner loop is like

---

[163] Fortran stores arrays in column-major order; hence, one wants the first index (i) to vary fastest.

```
DO 100 I=1,N
    C(I) = C(I) + A(I)
100 CONTINUE
```

in which each element of C has the *corresponding* (like-indexed) element of another vector added to it (denoted as $C \leftarrow C + A$ in APL). The key point is that now there is no communication between iterations of the inner loop, i.e., a "friendly" loop is now in a spot favorable for vectorization. If this code were translated into Fortran 90 by a vectorizing source-to-source translator, the result would be

```
DO 100 J=1,N
    DO 100 K=1,N
        C(1:N,J) = C(1:N,J) + A(1:N,K)*B(K,J)
100 CONTINUE
```

Since the situation is completely symmetrical in I and J, it should not be surprising that the J loop can also be moved inside the K loop, and, in fact, it can—see the paper by Randy Allen and Ken Kennedy[18]. The result is a set of fewer, longer vectors.

The foregoing is a simple example of a rearrangement of (originally) serial code into a form more amenable for parallel (vector) processing. The fact that this rearrangement is permissible (always gives the same answer as before) is so intuitively obvious in this example that formal analytical techniques are not really needed. But most of the time they are. Much work has gone into analysis techniques that allow vectorizers to untangle sections of code that either started out as vector operations or can be cast as such. The example above, as we mentioned, involves "loop-carried" dependence between iterations, which in general brings about a need for a variety of subscript analysis techniques. One example is the following "iteration space" [353] view of the matrix multiplication code:

Dependence graph

Execution picture before
loop interchange

Execution picture after
loop interchange

The dependency graph on the left (valid for both cases) shows how the iterations affect each other (each small circle is a multiply-add operation). The center figure shows the original (serial) execution sequence of the two innermost loops; the sequence after loop interchange appears on the right.

This dependency graph shows pictorially what we have already said in words: the iterations in I are independent, but the ones in K are not. Hence for a vector processor, one would like to fix K, calculate all the I values vectorially, advance K, calculate all the I values vectorially again, and so on, as in the rightmost execution picture. For an MIMD, shared-memory parallel computer, the leftmost execution picture is more favorable: one can assign each iteration of I to a different processing element, which can then compute a full set of K iterations on its own without needing to communicate with another processing element. Put another way, in the MIMD case the execution picture is sliced into parallel tasks horizontally for this example, whereas for a vector processor the slicing is vertical. More on this later.

For this example, one speaks of a (=,<) *direction vector* in the dependency graph, meaning that the "sink" depends on a "source", one of whose indices is *equal* and one *less than* the sink. This level of formalism represents a bit of overkill for this simple example, but it is needed for code with more complex dependencies. In order to extract as much parallelism as possible, a compiler needs precise information on dependencies. It needs economical tests to narrow down the possibilities, and it needs to know what sort of code restructuring is allowed under different dependency situations. These tests and their consequences are discussed in the literature [353] [79], and we shall not treat them in more detail here. Rather, the purpose of this example with its loop-carried dependence was to provide some insight into why dependency analysis and the code restructuring that it makes possible are important for parallel processing and thus to motivate the more general discussion of dependency analysis that follows in the next section.

6.2.2   Dependency Graphs and Analysis

A program in a language like Fortran can be regarded as a collection of statements, the ordering and scheduling of which are subject to dependence constraints [111]. *Data dependence* exists when statements compute data that are used by other statements. *Control dependencies* arise from the ordered flow of control in a program. On machines that support concurrent operations, dependencies can limit the full utilization of the machine by insisting that certain operations complete before others commence. A graph can be constructed for a program such that directed edges (arcs) connect dependent operations (see Figure 6.6). These arcs impose a partial ordering among operations that prohibits a fully concurrent execution of a program. The task of a compiler for a parallel computer is to identify spurious or nonessential dependencies and to make sure that the critical ones are obeyed.[164]

The use-definition chaining mentioned above, although a form of dependency analysis, leads to overly conservative estimates of data dependence; Kuck [302] describes a set of fast tests that allow construction of a more accurate, less conservative dependency graph. Four types of dependence may exist between statements S_i and S_j, assuming that S_j follows somewhere after S_i on a common control path (see Figure 6.6 for examples):

$S_i \delta S_j$: S_j is *flow-dependent* on S_i if a value of a variable used by S_j was computed by S_i (S_i must store its output before S_j fetches its input).

$S_i \bar{\delta} S_j$: S_j is *antidependent* on S_i if a value of a variable used by S_i is re-computed by S_j (S_i fetches data from an area later overwritten by S_j).

$S_i \delta^o S_j$: S_j is *output-dependent* on S_i if both compute the same variable and the value from S_j is to be stored after that from S_i (the two statements share a common storage location in their output lists).

$S_i \delta^c S_j$: S_j is *control-dependent* on a conditional statement S_i if its execution depends on the execution of S_i and the path chosen after that (S_i must complete before a decision can be made about executing S_j). (This example is not shown in Figure 6.6.)

The basic idea behind dependency graphs is simple. In preparing a serial program for optimization or parallelization, the compiler must look for several kinds of dependence among statements to prevent their execution in the wrong order, that is, in an order that changes the program's meaning (see Figure 6.6). Flow (or ordinary) dependence happens when a variable is assigned in one statement and used in a subsequent one. An example is the variable A in statements 1 and 3 in the illustrative program segment of Figure 6.6. Antidependence is the mirror image of flow dependence; it occurs when a variable is used in an earlier statement and then (re)assigned in a later one. An example is the variable A in statements 3 and 6 of Figure 6.6. Output dependence occurs when a variable is assigned more than once, either in different statements (A in statements 1 and 6 of Figure 6.6) or in multiple traversals of one statement (T in statement 5 of Figure 6.6). The latter case can be hard to spot. Note

---

164   In pipeline scheduling, dependencies are called *hazards* [288].

Dependency types:

	δ (flow)
A= =A	
=A A=	δ̄ (anti)
A= A=	δ (output)

1: A=B+C

2: DO 5 I=1,N

3:   D(I)=A*E(I)

4:   S=E(I)*5

5:   T=T+S

6: A=D(N) - 7

Dependencies:
A: 3δ1   6δ̄3   6δ 1
D: 6δ3
S: 5δ̄4   4δ 4   4δ̄5
T: 5δ5   5δ 5   5δ5

Figure 6.6   Dependency graph of a program segment [312]. *This figure shows six statements with a number of dependencies among them that must be reckoned with in any proposed rearrangement of the order of execution, parallel or otherwise. Control dependencies (page 310) are not shown. The control flow graph is shown to the left of the statements, and the dependency graph to the right. (The dataflow graph is left as an exercise.) For example, because of the several appearances of the variable A, statement 3 is flow-dependent on statement 1, 6 is antidependent on 3, and 6 is also output dependent on 1. Unlike this imperative language example, single-assignment (dataflow) language programs have only one kind of data dependence, namely flow dependence.*

that programs written in a functional ("applicative") language have only flow dependencies.

Vectorized and parallelized versions of the code in Figure 6.6 are shown in Figure 6.7 on page 312, and discussed in more detail in the section on the Parafrase compiler that begins on page 314.

6.2.3   Parallelism Beyond the Vector Level

For understandable historical reasons, most of the work on parallelizing compilers so far has been done for Fortran programs, as the reader may already have discerned. The *degree* of parallelism that can be automatically extracted from these programs is often not very high, but the sheer number of Fortran programs and their economic value lead to this choice. However, one should

Figure 6.7 *Vectorized (left) and parallelized (right) versions* of the code segment of Figure 6.6. The dependency graph of the vectorized version is also shown [312]. Note how the loop-associated dependencies have been removed. These examples are from the Parafrase project (page 314).

keep in mind that the resulting view of parallel compilers is strongly influenced by some of Fortran's characteristics and peculiarities discussed in Chapter 5. For example, the most frequently exploited form of parallelism in Fortran programs is that associated with *loops.* These frequently spring from the fact that Fortran operates only on array and vector *elements,* not whole arrays and vectors. Hence, any kind of vector or array operation (an addition, say) must be coded as a loop specifying what is to happen to the individual elements of each array or vector. These loops would not be present in a higher-level language like APL, for example, whose elementary operations can take whole arrays as arguments. Thus a Fortran compiler, but not an APL compiler, must go to considerable trouble to reconstruct the fact that a loop was originally a vector operation and hence can be scheduled on a vector processor. However, APL also has characteristics that make it harder to compile than Fortran. These will be touched on later.

The point we wish to make is that though a substantial body of knowledge exists about compiling serial programs for parallel processors, the resulting picture of parallelism (its origin, granularity, and extent) is strongly colored by the nature of the Fortran language and could have quite a different composition for programs written in other languages (such as APL, PROLOG, or a dataflow language). However, the set of compiling tools and techniques that have been developed seem to have broad applicability not limited to Fortran.

In terms of prominent levels of parallelism, a Fortran program may be viewed as consisting of the following "high-level objects" [448], in rough order of decreasing grain size (see Figure 1.5 on page 19):

- Procedures and functions
- I/O
- Loops
- Conditional statements
- Basic blocks

The finest granularity comes from distributing or *spreading* a basic block among a number of parallel processors, that is, from the parallelism within a basic block. Parallelism *among* basic blocks of a sort is obtained by *loop distribution* of the iterations of an eligible inner loop by an optimizing vectorizer (see pages 307 and 316). In this case one wants as long a vector as possible. For an MIMD multiprocessor like the Ultracomputer and many others (page 572), the emphasis is a large chunk of computation with minimum communication requirements. One way to obtain this favorable ratio is to interchange inner and outer loops, as discussed on page 307. Now the chunks of parallel computation consist of many basic blocks each. For all the chunk sizes or granularities that come from these different levels of parallelism, the compiler must perform an analysis to determine the dependencies among the candidates for parallel execution.

How extensive must this analysis be? The degree of anlaysis required depends on the grain size and degree of parallelism being pursued, which in turn are related to the purview of the compiler [15]: if it analyzes interrelationships only within a basic block of code but not *among* basic blocks, that is, if it performs only local dataflow analysis, then the parallelism will be of the rather fine-grained sort. *Global* dataflow analysis, in which the relationships *among* the basic blocks and other components of a procedure are examined, can lead to levels of parallelism with a larger (medium-sized) granularity. A prominent subset of this is loop-level parallelism, that is, parallelism between different iterations of the same loop. Within loops, statements that do not participate in a cycle of dependence can be vectorized. In particular, a loop having independent iterations and containing only one assignment statement translates directly into a vector instruction. The most extensive and difficult type of analysis is that of the whole program, called *interprocedural* data flow analysis (the assumption is that the program is a collection of procedures). This analysis yields potentially the largest granularity of parallelism. The Sisal compiler discussed on page 333 employs such an analysis.

The *extent* of parallelism will depend on how extensive the analysis is; for example [15], on whether dependencies among individual array *elements* are examined, or only those among arrays as a whole. That is, are subscripts included in the analysis, or is a worst-case assumption made that if one element of array A depends on one element of array B, then *all* the elements of A depend on some element of B. Naturally, this assumption can make a big difference in the extent of parallelism that is extracted.

6.3   Parallelizing Compiler Examples

We next present three different approaches to the creation of parallel code from existing serial programs, or *automatic extraction* of parallelism, as this transformation is sometimes called. We call Parafrase, which is described first, a *reconstructing* compiler because it tries to reconstruct the high-level meaning of the code it sees. It accepts standard Fortran and attempts to recognize vector operations and compound functions and schedule their execution on vector and parallel hardware. The next section describes Bulldog, which we call a *reassembling* compiler because it doesn't really care about the higher-level meaning of the Fortran code as long as its operations can be reassembled into sufficiently large chunks of parallel execution for VLIW (Very Long Instruction Word) hardware. The third example is somewhat different in that it describes a compiler for programs written in APL, in which large chunks of parallel execution occur naturally and with less legerdemain than in the two Fortran-based approaches, although first the difficulty of obtaining a good serial APL compiler had to be overcome. Our final example is a brief discussion on compiling dataflow languages.

6.3.1   *Parafrase Fortran Reconstructing Compiler*

Parafrase (reference [302] and Figure 6.8 on page 315) is an optimizing compiler preprocessor that takes scientific Fortran code, constructs a program dependency graph like the example in Figure 6.6 on page 311, and performs a series of optimization steps (primarily code motion and renaming of variables) that each create a revised version of the original program[165] and gradually optimize it for a particular high-speed architecture. Figure 6.8 on page 315

---

[165] Written at the assembly-language level in legal Fortran.

Figure 6.8   The Parafrase source-to-source optimizing precompiler.

shows the optimization being done for an SEA (equivalent, in this case, to SIMD), pipelined, register-to-register architecture. The first passes bring the program toward one optimized for parallel architectures. The second set of passes optimize the program for SEA parallel architectures. The final set of passes targets the code for register-to-register pipelined vector processors like the Cray or IBM designs described in Figure 9.7 on page 424 or Figure 9.9 on page 428. The revised code usually takes more memory space than the original version, but that is not a bad price to pay for improved performance given how inexpensive memory is today.

Automatic parallelization is a very difficult problem, which is reflected in the scale of effort expended on Parafrase over a number of years. The system software consists of some 50 modules that can be used to transform an internal program representation. After each module it is possible to regenerate a source program. The modules can be connected into different optimization sequences. These can be tailored for a given architecture, and also to establish the value of a potential design feature in a new architecture.

An example of an optimization from the front-end set of passes is shown in the left half of Figure 6.7 on page 312. It is called *scalar expansion* and involves the scalar variable S that is assigned and subsequently used inside a loop in Figure 6.6 on page 311. In the original version, each iteration of the loop must be performed sequentially, so that the scalar can be read before being reassigned in the next iteration. Figure 6.6 shows these *loop-carried de-pendencies* created in connection with statement 5. This situation can be avoided, and the dependency broken, by replacing the scalar with a compiler generated array *S* with one element for each iteration of the loop that we wish to execute in parallel, as shown in Figure 6.7. The cost is extra memory for the new array. This may have been unaffordable in the past, but with memory as cheap and plentiful as it is today, this is probably a good trade-off for added performance. An optimization in the back-end sequence has the option of shrinking this array if the scalar expansion does not pay off.

Another example of a Parafrase back-end optimization is *loop distribu-tion*. This optimization is the process of breaking down a DO loop with mul-tiple statements (Figure 6.6) into several smaller loops. This process has two effects. First, if a loop can be distributed around (shrunk down to) a single assignment statement, and if the statement can be executed in parallel, then a vector operation has been formed (statement 3 in Figure 6.6 is an example). Second, loop distribution can be used to increase the *locality of a program's memory references* by accessing (referencing) all the elements of the arrays in one distributed loop before executing the next distributed loop. In certain memory organizations, there is a performance bonus for increasing locality.[166]

The referenced papers describe many other optimizations, and also point out that these can be reordered for other target architectures. For example, the right side of Figure 6.7 shows the code of Figure 6.6 optimized instead for an MIMD parallel processor. In this case, each loop iteration has been assigned to a different processing element (PE), which then performs all steps of a single iteration. Note the interprocessor communication necessitated by the state-ment $T = T + S$. Each PE computes its element of *D*, the value of its own local variable *S*, reads *T*, adds its *S* to it, and attempts to write the new *T*. The Nth PE then assigns its value of *S* to *S* and completes the computation. The statement $T = T + S$ needs careful synchronization, since the other PEs may try to perform their actions at the same time.[167] Even if these loop iterations and their com-putation were completely independent, however, the *locality of memory ref-erence* that we praised a moment ago could be a bad thing if the processing elements of this shared-memory multiprocessor had private caches. Here's how this problem can come about.

------

[166] This is true for a memory consisting of modules that are accessed in an interleaved fashion; for example distributing an array's elements among the modules allows multiple elements to be delivered during each cycle of a vector processor.

[167] This topic is discussed in more detail on page 353.

Locality of references means that the addresses of the data needed by the program are all close to each other. This proximity tends to improve the performance of systems that use paging (page 124) and/or caching (page 546), since it increases the chance that the needed data can be brought aboard in just one page and/or cache line. Contiguous data storage of an array, in which the array elements are stored at consecutive memory addresses (also called a stride-1 vector) is one way to improve locality. If an interleaved memory (page 124) is used, these consecutive addresses are usually strung out across the interleaved modules to maximize the data rate. If multiple processing elements with individual caches are cooperating on a problem, however, a high degree of data locality may mean that a cache line transferred to processor 1 drags along data being used by processor 2. The processors may be doing completely independent computations (different independent iterations of a loop, say), but since they both touched on the same cache line, care must be taken to keep the memory consistent. For example, it may become necessary for each PE to confer with its colleague when it is ready to return this cache line to memory. This delay is avoided if there is less locality of reference and the data used by each processor are far enough apart in memory that they do not get into the same cache line. So a different sequence of compiler optimizations is called for in this case. Such cache-related issues are discussed in more detail on page 546.

Yet another situation arises if a processing element in the target architecture has much quicker access to one memory module than to the rest; then the compiler should try to ensure that the needed data are all in that module, rather than distributed as before. These are but a few examples of how a compiler is called on for different optimizations and trade-offs for different parallel architectures.

Being as versatile as it is, Parafrase's performance can't really be characterized by a single number. As a vectorizer, the speedups it obtains are in the low to middle single numbers. However, one must remember that whereas the vector processor's conceptual model is parallel, the actual implementation on which these speedup results were obtained is a pipelined design, on which the maximum theoretical speedup is the number of pipeline stages, which tends to be below 10.

Parafrase-2, a successor system described in the book by Polychronopoulos [364], can handle programs written in Pascal and C in addition to Fortran, and is designed to perform communication and synchronization overhead analysis, memory management, and scheduling assistance in addition to program restructuring.

Related Systems: PFC, PTRAN, MIMDizer

Other work on restructuring compilers includes the PFC (parallel Fortran converter) project of Kennedy and co-workers[168] at Rice University [17], [472] and the work at IBM by Allen and co-workers on PTRAN, an approach that utilizes a large database of information about the program that persists throughout the compilation and enables optimizations not otherwise possible [15]. Additional detail on PTRAN may be found in reference [382]. Reference [234] describes work by the Rice group on a compiler for Fortran D, an extension to Fortran that enables users to specify the decomposition of their data for a distributed-memory computer (page 241). The Fortran D compiler then automatically generates node programs with explicit communication (send, receive, collective communication, etc.) for a given data decomposition. Some interesting performance results with a Fortran D compiler are described in a paper by Hirandani et al [235]. An interactive system named SUPERB for generating distributed-memory programs is described by Zima [472]. The resulting programs are similar in form to the manager-workers program described in Figure 2.10 on page 55.

The MIMDizer from Applied Parallel Research started at Pacific-Sierra as an interactive Fortran vectorizer called FORGE, which currently accepts Fortran 77 and produces Fortran 90. FORGE was enhanced in 1987 to perform global program analysis to expose large-grain parallelism for shared-memory computers. The MIMDizer is a later extension that also supports distributed memory systems. As of this writing (1992), versions of MIMDizer were being tested for distributed-memory Intel and nCUBE parallel computers and for workstation clusters. Most previous parallelizers have targeted vector and shared-memory parallel computers.

The program to be parallelized is parsed, and its symbolic and control information is recorded in a database. This information becomes the basis for dependency analysis. During the subsequent transformation to parallel code, the user participates by specifying array decompositions and helping to resolve ambiguities that may result. This is unlike systems such as PTRAN that are fully automatic. The package also includes tools for viewing the database, a parallel debugger, performance prediction and monitoring, and other items. For best results, APR advocates that programmers write in a restricted form of Fortran 77, for which they supply guidelines.

---

[168] We cited one of their papers in connection with loop interchange on page 307.

6.3.2 *Bulldog Fortran Reassembling Compiler*

We remarked earlier that at most moments of a program's execution there is a huge backlog of instructions that could be done in parallel, even though the von Neumann model does them one at a time. On page 305 we characterized vectorization and dataflow as conservative vs. radical efforts to capitalize on this backlog of parallelism. The Bulldog compiler [170] (see Figure 6.9) is another approach to automatic parallelization at the instruction level. Like Parafrase, it is aimed primarily at scientific programs written in Fortran, but it operates in a different way, designed to catch parallelism not amenable to vectorization. The main ideas are the VLIW (Very Long Instruction Word) target architecture (page 622) and the trace scheduling compilation technique (Figure 6.10). We will discuss both of these below, but first we wish to provide a little more perspective on the difference between Bulldog and a vectorizer.

We said that a parallelizing compiler must find parallelism and then schedule it. Vectorizers deal mainly with loops, looking for ones with simple independent iterations that can be scheduled as vector instructions. However, *proving* that loop iterations are independent and suitable for vectorization is a difficult and involved process, as is the subsequent scheduling. Much of the work done by Parafrase and the other restructuring translators discussed in the last section—the dependency analysis, all the business about iteration space, direction vectors, and so on—is devoted to handling loop-carried dependencies.

Life is easier if one stays inside a basic block (Figure 6.4 on page 302) and does not worry about loops. The absence of jumps in its interior code makes a basic block much easier to analyze and schedule. If there is sufficient parallelism within the basic block, then parallelization of a program can proceed by applying the dependency analysis on page 309 to one basic block at a time and scheduling the eligible statements in as parallel a way as possible. This process has previously been done in horizontal microcode compaction [169].[169] The problem is that the basic blocks in Fortran tend to be very small,[170] and the parallelism available within them tends to be very low: it is

---

[169] *Vertical* microcode has been encoded and takes less microstorage but is slower than *horizontal* microcode, in which each bit directly controls something, with no decoding involved.   GF11 (page 436) may have the world's most horizontal microcode—every decision point has a bit.

[170] One out of every four to eight operations is a jump, according to Fisher.

Figure 6.9 *The Bulldog compiler's overall structure* [158]. *The source language is parsed into a traditional intermediate code and optimized. Then the memory-bank disambiguator tries to determine the bank (module address) of every vector reference. The resulting program is then handed to both the trace scheduler and the antialiasing disambiguator. The trace scheduler repeatedly picks traces (highly probable execution sequences of basic blocks) from the program's flow graph, gives them to the code generator, and replaces the trace by the machine code generated, which is then relinked to the rest of the program (see Figure 6.10). While generating code, the code generator asks the (antialiasing) disambiguator whether pairs of vector references v(i), v(j) in the trace could possibly refer to the same memory location. A fair amount of user interaction may be involved.*

rare to attain a speedup exceeding 3 from this kind of parallelism.[171] Fortran programs are typically full of loops, and each loop is broken into at least two basic blocks by the conditional jump statement that makes the loop work (see Figure 6.4). These loops are one reason why Fortran basic blocks are small.

---

[171] Fisher [170] says that the Floating Point Systems FPS-164 can offer speedup by a factor of 5 or 6 in a few special-purpose applications for which code has been handwritten at enormous cost. But this code does not generalize, and most users get only the standard 2 or 3—and then only after great labor and on small programs. Kuck [301] cites the same factor.

Larger basic blocks would presumably yield more parallelism, but how to get them? APL programs are one source, as described in the next section ("An APL-Based Approach" on page 323). But let us stay with Fortran for now. The basic premise behind the Bulldog compiler is that there are many scientific and engineering Fortran programs in which the conditional jumps we just mentioned can be predicted quite well [158]. (The time-critical control structures of scientific code tend to be quite simple, consisting mainly of nested loops with a few conditionals that usually branch one way most of the time.)[172] The program's basic blocks can then be spliced together into much larger "pseudo basic blocks" with a high *probability* of being executed from beginning to end without interruption. These larger pseudo basic blocks are called *traces*. By restricting its attention to traces, Bulldog can avoid having to deal with loop-carried dependencies and the complicated analysis that goes with it in Parafrase in favor of simpler, well-established techniques for dependency analysis within a basic block. Also, the harvestable parallelism is not restricted to the highly regular loop-type structures needed for vectorization. The price paid for this consists of the trace scheduling techniques and work needed to handle the cases when the compiler guesses wrong about the outcome of the conditional jumps. The VLIW architecture that can benefit from the increased parallelism found within such traces is described briefly below and in more detail on page 623.

VLIW Architectures

As described in more detail on pages 622 and 623, a VLIW architecture can be loosely regarded as either a form of liberated SIMD or specially orchestrated MIMD. The net effect is of a central controller that is issuing very long instructions (hundreds of bits). The VLIW idea is related to the generation of horizontal microcode, but has previously been applied only to much smaller collections of much less versatile processing or functional units. The reason is that traditional compilers operate on one basic block at a time; the average Fortran basic block is rather small and hence contains a rather low degree of parallelism, and it wasn't *worth* it to have a highly parallel machine as a target. (The average speedup from parallelism within a Fortran basic block is about 3 or so.) The analysis and compilation were traditionally done one basic block at a time because it wasn't known at compile time which new basic block would be the target of the (conditional) jump at the end of any given basic block. It seemed obvious that operations from different basic blocks couldn't be put into the same instruction. Yet that is precisely what trace scheduling is

---

172　This premise is less likely to be true for other domains, such as systems programs.

designed to accomplish. Basically, this capability amounts to guessing which way the jumps will go and then removing the results of harmful guesses.

Trace Scheduling

The underlying premises of trace scheduling are that the most likely execution paths through a program can be predicted at compile time, and that most of the execution time is spent in these paths [158]. The proponents of this approach feel that this is a valid assumption for most scientific programs, as mentioned above. The outline of the method is sketched in Figure 6.10 on page 324. The two most prominent jump-prediction strategies are programmer-specified guesses and execution of sequential code on sample data. These strategies are used to find highly probable execution sequences of the basic blocks of a program. These sequences are called *traces*; one is shown in Figure 6.10.

For various reasons [171], a trace never extends past a loop boundary. That is, a trace can include blocks from the same loop, but no blocks from contained or containing loops. To further increase the parallelism of traces, the compiler unrolls the bodies of inner loops (32 times, say) immediately after parsing the source program into intermediate code. (This process is equivalent to guessing that the loop will be executed at least 32 times, which would be nice for a 32-processor VLIW.)

After a trace is identified but before any rearrangements are made within it, the same kind of dependency analysis that we discussed earlier on page 309 is applied within the trace to prevent the scheduler from making absolutely illegal code motions between basic blocks, ones that would "clobber" (incorrectly overwrite) the values of "live" variables (ones still to be used) outside the trace. The data precedence graph built for the trace is augmented with new edges drawn between (1) the test operations that conditionally jump to where the variable is live and (2) the operations that might clobber this variable. After this, the scheduler is permitted to treat the entire trace like one large basic block. Guided by estimates of execution frequency, the compiler picks the most probable trace, generates code for it, picks the next most likely trace, generates code for it, and so on until the entire flow graph has been translated to machine code.

After scheduling is complete, the scheduler will have made many code motions (rearrangements) that speed the execution of the trace but do not correctly preserve jumps from the stream to the outside code (or rejoins back). A postprocessor inserts new code at the stream exits and entrances to correct this problem. Some simple examples are shown in Figure 6.10.

The middle sequence in that figure illustrates code rearrangement in the trace in the presence of a conditional jump off the trace. Suppose that the trace consists of operations 1, 2, and 3, and suppose the code generator decides that operation 1 is not time-critical and should be moved below the conditional jump 2. But then operation 4, which reads the variable *a* written by 1 (i.e., is flow-dependent on 1) will get the wrong ("old") value of *a*. So the compiler has to make a copy of 1 (labeled 1' and also *S*) on the off-trace edge of the jump, as shown. An example of an illegal code motion that cannot be compensated in this way would be to move 3 before the jump. Because 3 writes the variable *d* and 5 reads the *previous* value of *d*, this move would cause 5 to get the wrong ("new") value of *d*. If the value of *d* were not used on the off-trace edge of the jump, then moving 3 above the jump would be permissible.

The bottom sequence in Figure 6.10 shows the analogous situation for conditional jumps *onto* the trace. There, moving 3 above the jump means that 4 can no longer send 3 the correct value of *a* as it is supposed to. The solution is to make a copy of 3 (labeled 3' and also *R*) on the incoming edge right below 4. In this way, no matter which path is executed, *d* will still get the same value.

Once again,[173] we see here a potential way to trade more memory for improved performance, which, as we mentioned earlier, often makes good sense in today's memory marketplace, assuming that the number of copied operations is acceptable. Experiments indicate that good performance can be obtained [171].

In a sense, trace scheduling, like cache memory, is a gamble. The former bets that jump probabilities are predictable; the latter assumes the same about memory reference patterns. Of course, the circumstances under which each works well are much better established for caching. The original Bulldog compiler goal was 10 times more speedup than the factor of 3 or so obtained just within basic blocks. More recently attention has been given to extending this analysis beyond compile time [172]. That is, the program is first run one or more times with statistics gathered giving the probability that each conditional branch is taken. This data is then used to augment the program to indicate whether to predict that each branch will be taken or not taken. The question is whether the past will be a good predictor of the future, that is, if the probability that a given branch is taken changes much from run to run. Fisher and Freudenberger [172] write:

> Although it is possible to pick previous runs that are not effective, it appears that a variety of runs with their branch direction counts added together make a good predictor. ... This result is not unexpected in FORTRAN/Floating-point codes, but holds for systems codes as well.

----

[173] As when Parafrase makes extra copies of variables to eliminate aliasing, etc.

Figure 6.10   Trace scheduling [*170*], [*171*]. *The upper left shows a trace picked from a flow graph (the small squares are basic blocks). In the upper middle, the trace has been rearranged and scheduled for parallel execution, but has not yet been re-linked to the rest of the code. This is done by adding blocks of code marked S (split) and R (rejoin) as shown on the upper right. Examples of such extra relinking code are shown in the lower half of the figure. The middle sequence shows a trace in which the first two operations are swapped. Operation 4 outside the trace reads the variable a written by 1 and would now get the wrong value of a if the compiler did not place a copy of 1 (labeled S) on the off-trace edge of the jump. An analogous solution is shown on the bottom for jumps onto the trace.*

6.3.3   An APL-Based Approach

Much of the discussion to this point has been about a compiler that takes existing serial programs in a procedural language with side effects (like Fortran). What about the case when these two conditions are relaxed? What about programs written in a more parallel-thinking environment, like APL? What about function-oriented or function-level programs written in single-assignment (i.e., side-effect-free) dataflow languages like Val or Id? The E-compiler project [94] provides some answers to the first question. Figure 6.11 on page 326 shows the structure of the E-compiler, which is discussed further on page 329. Dataflow architectures and languages have their own sections in this book.

One of APL's advantages for parallel processing is easy to explain: it speaks the language of vectors and arrays—not just array elements, like Fortran, but whole arrays.[174] The operation $+/A$ adds all the elements of a vector, and $A + B$ adds two vectors without resorting to loops and other specifics of how the elements are to be shuffled around. Much of the Sherlock Holmes-like reconstruction that Parafrase must do with Fortran code ("I wonder if this is a loop? I wonder if it corresponds to a vector operation? I wonder what it does?") is not needed with APL code, because such information is not lost during the coding process and is available to the compiler. So it is not particularly daring to say that APL offers strong advantages for vectorization. In modern terminology, APL supports data parallel programming (see page 239).

But APL has a second advantage for parallel execution: As a consequence of the power and number of its primitive operators and functions,[175] as well as its ability to speak the language of arrays, the basic blocks in scientific and engineering code written in APL are much larger (measured in execution time) than when these problems are encoded in Fortran.[176] Thus, for the same kind

---

[174]   The language of vectors and arrays is also spoken to some extent by the new parallel Fortran 90 (page 240), which contains part of APL's functions.

[175]   APL has 66 primitive functions plus five operations that generate additional derived functions, such as inner product.

[176]   For example, the summation of the elements of a vector A is written in APL as $+/A$. This is one basic block at the APL level. In Fortran one would define some variable and then write a loop that adds the vector elements to that variable one by one. This code is split into two basic blocks by the test required to see whether the last iteration has been reached. APL basic blocks contain two to three times more operations (interior nodes in the parse tree) than Fortran's on average, according to one estimate [94]. In addition, an APL operation generates considerably more work on average than a Fortran operation and may, in fact, correspond to several Fortran basic blocks.

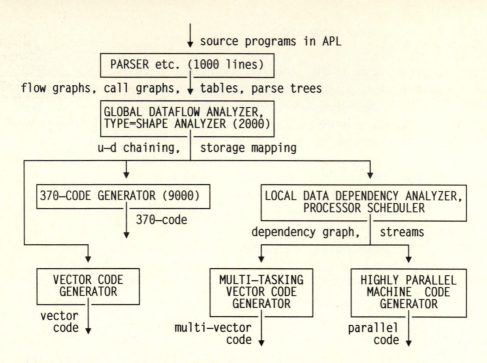

Figure 6.11   E-compiler structure. *See [94] for details. (Note that vectors are generated without either the local or global analysis needed by Parafrase.)*

of intra–basic block analysis as Bulldog's,[177] a substantial amount of the same kind of parallelism (instruction-level, not limited to vector operations) should be available, but this time in *real* basic blocks, meaning that the complex trace-scheduling mechanism for handling wrong guesses is not needed. Larger basic blocks also mean that for the price of Parafrase's inter–basic block analysis (loop analysis), one potentially obtains substantial chunks of processing (the basic blocks) suitable for MIMD computers with powerful processing elements but expensive communications.

As we said, the power and number of APL's primitive functions and operators, in addition to making vectorization easier, are also what make the basic blocks larger. An example may be the best way to explain this situation. We quote from a paper by Ching [95] and use Figure 6.12 on page 327 to explain his example.

---

[177] The analysis is more expensive, however, due to the larger basic blocks.

This example finds all the primes up to N. A prime number can't be divided evenly by any other whole number (except 1), so it certainly won't be found in a multiplication table. One method, then, is to construct a multiplication table whose largest entry exceeds N and then list the missing numbers. That is precisely what this little APL program does:

```
∇Z←PRIME N;V
Z←(~V∈V∘.×V)/V←1↓ιN      ∇
```

The right part $/V←1↓ιN$ creates a local vector variable $V = 2\ 3\ 4 .. N$. The left part $(~V∈V∘.×V)$ creates a V-length boolean vector with 1's that correspond to the elements of V missing from an $N×N$ multiplication table. The compression operator / selects the missing elements of V for assignment to Z.

The detailed operation (from right to left) is as follows:

N	is the input parameter
$ιN$	uses the iota operator $ι$ to create a vector 1 2 3 ...N.
$1↓ιN$	uses the drop operator $↓$ to create a vector 2 3 ...N.
$V←1↓ιN$	assigns 2 3 4 ...N to a local vector variable V.
$/V←1↓ιN$	readies V via the compression operator / to be acted on by a boolean vector for a selecting action like this: 1 0 1 / 1 2 3 returns 1 3.

The rest of the function creates the proper boolean vector:

$V∘.×V$	constructs an $N×N$ multiplication table using the outer product operator " . " to create all possible products of the elements of V.
$V∈V∘.×V$	uses the membership function $ε$ to create a V-length boolean vector with 1's for every element of V that *is* in the multiplication table and 0's elsewhere.
$~V∈V∘.×V$	uses the negation function $~$ to create a boolean vector with 1's for each element of V *missing* from the table.

This latter vector is then applied to V via the compression operator discussed above, creating a vector whose elements are the values of the missing elements of V (the prime numbers up to N).

This function works perfectly well, but can be made more efficient in several ways. First, only odd numbers need be checked. Second, an N/3 $× \sqrt{N}$ multiplication table is large enough to check whether a number in 3 ... N is prime. But then we must remember to put 2 itself back in the list of primes. The improved code is as follows:

```
∇Z←PRIME N;V
Z←2,(~V∈(2↓ι⌊N*.5)∘.×2↓ι⌈N÷3)/V←1+2×ι⌊(N-1)÷2    ∇
```

The additional symbols are:

- the ceiling and floor operations $⌈$ and $⌊$ which round a number up or down to the nearest integer.
- the exponentiation operation, as in $N*.5$
- The catenation operator $,$.

The basic action is the same as before, but needs much less time and memory.

Figure 6.12   *Annotated APL program with large basic blocks* suitable for par-allel processing.

We shall briefly illustrate the scheduling and intra-block multi-functional parallelism based on compile-time dependency calculation by the following example: Find all the prime numbers from 2 to *N*. Unlike in Fortran or Pascal where loops are most likely to be used, we have

```
∇Z←PRIME N;V
Z←2,(~V∈(2↓ι⌊N*.5)∘.×2↓ι⌈N÷3)/V←1+2×ι⌊(N-1)÷2
∇
```

and its parse tree is shown in [Figure 6.13 on page 330]. Basically, it sets up a multiplication table and checks the vector of odd numbers up to *N* against that table. The ones not in the table are prime numbers. The instruction stream corresponding to the right corner subtree that calculates *V* is independent of the instruction stream corresponding to the subtree (2↓..)∘.×2↓..3, rooted at the outer product node that set up the multiplication table. In short, the two subtrees delineated by the two dotted semi-circles in [Figure 6.13] are data independent. They are the main parts of the computation and can be executed in separate hardware components if such components are available.

Note a very important point about this example: The action is performed *entirely* by high-level operations. There are no loops, no conditional branches that fracture a Fortran program into many tiny basic blocks. Each APL operation not only does a lot, but it also fits up against its fellow high-level operators seamlessly, uninterrupted by low-level operations and jumps that break a basic block.[178]

The parse tree of this one-basic-block function is shown in Figure 6.13 on page 330. The dashed lines in that figure mark two large subtrees that have no data dependency between them and correspond to two basic blocks that can safely be scheduled for concurrent execution and that can keep two processing elements profitably occupied even if they are quite powerful. Just the single outer-product node that produces the multiplication table creates a tremendous amount of computation. The Fortran version would require a double DO loop and a substantial amount of global dataflow analysis to establish that this operation can proceed in parallel with others, whereas local analysis suffices here because the basic blocks are so much bigger with APL. So the

---

[178] A somewhat analogous situation is a hardware system built solely from a few well-designed VLSI chips that need no small "glue" chips or discrete circuits to interconnect them. One might say that APL basic blocks are to Fortran basic blocks as VLSI is to LSI.

same features of APL that can give rise to infamous one-liners also encourage a programming style that is beneficial for parallel processing. In terms of the program parse tree, nested vector loops in Fortran degenerate into simple 2- or 3-node subtrees in APL, and many function calls in Fortran can be replaced by primitive function nodes, resulting in "bushy" trees with large independent branches.

To be fair, APL also has features that make it quite difficult to compile. For example, a Fortran programmer must declare, at compile time, whether a variable is a scalar or array, what its rank and size are in the latter case, and so on. APL has the ability to figure out that if you multiply a 2×3 matrix by a 3×6 matrix and assign it to a variable M, then M's rank is 2 and its size is 2×6. Not only does APL lack declared typing, it also has dynamic typing, that is, the type of a variable (character, integer) can change in the middle of a program. Dynamic typing makes APL easier to use (some Fortran programmers argue that programming in APL isn't really programming), but it makes compilation much more involved.

These differences are reflected in the nature of the experimental E-compiler (Figure 6.11 on page 326), which handles a subset containing a majority of APL's operators and primitive functions. The front end is freed from worrying about many of the special cases of low-level dependency, as a Fortran translator like Parafrase must do. On the other hand, the E-compiler must perform extensive analysis to infer the type and shape of the program's variables based only on (compile-time) information about the program's input parameters; a Fortran compiler has the advantage of having this information at the start.

A second consequence of a large arsenal of powerful and versatile primitive functions and operators is that the back end becomes huge because most of these primitives can accept several types of arguments, and almost each combination requires its own implementing code.

There are also some APL functions that are simply impossible to compile. However, these are mostly related to the interactive use of APL, whereas the E-compiler is intended to be used for computation-intensive batch jobs. It recently demonstrated its mettle by producing code that outperformed code from the very good Fortran compiler for the IBM 3090 Vector Facility on problems like prime number computation and Poisson equation solving [97]. A comparison of results for the Prime function discussed here are as follows:

Figure 6.13   The parse tree of the PRIME program in the text. *The detailed version created by the compiler is at the bottom, and a simpler, stylized version is at the top. The whole tree is one basic block. The two subtrees below the dotted semicircles (top) are data-independent and constitute large tasks that may be scheduled readily for parallel execution. (Details of the bottom version: The node numbers are in the left-to-right order seen by the compiler. Shape 1=scalar, 2=one-element vector, 3=vector of unknown length. Type 0=Boolean, 1=integer, 2=floating-point, 3=character.)*

	Fortran Prime	Fortran Prime3	APL Prime
Non-vector	3ms	54ms	4ms
Vector	2.8ms	52ms	2ms

Note:

1. All times are on an IBM 3090; output time excluded.
2. Fortran Prime uses the traditional sequential algorithm of finding one prime at a time.
3. Fortran Prime3 is a hand-translated version of APL Prime, which uses the sieve method.
4. The vectorizing VS2 Fortran compiler was used for the vector case.
5. The APL compiler implements the membership function ϵ with a hash table; this implementation is more efficient than an interpreter's linear search.

APL is not everyone's cup of tea, partly because the lack of a compiler has kept APL out of the running for the really computationally intensive jobs. But APL does offer a large variety of real programs to guide the design of a parallelizing compiler, and it offers the chance to deal much more directly with the inherent difficulties of parallelization as opposed to those introduced by a language historically designed for a specific hardware model of either sequential or parallel execution.

Reference [96] describes a compiler that translates APL to C, and describes results obtained using a run-time environment that supports the parallel execution of these C programs on the RP4 64-way parallel prototype.

6.3.4 Dataflow/Functional Language Translators

From the standpoint of a compiler or other language translator, the most significant thing about a functional or dataflow[179] language is the single-assignment feature discussed in the last chapter (page 271). Variables are

---

179 According to Hudak [248] the name *dataflow language* is normally used to describe early functional languages like Val and Id that were in some sense tailored to the dataflow machines then being designed. These languages were generally fairly simple, lacking such modern functional language features as higher-order functions and nonstrict semantics. Recent descendants of Val and Id are Sisal and Id Nouveau, respectively, both of which have sophisticated compilers. We discuss the performance of the Sisal compiler OSC later

assigned a value only once, and maintain this value throughout the course of a program, a condition called *referential transparency,* under which there are no side effects. In terms used earlier in this chapter, this feature means that output and antidependencies are eliminated, which greatly simplifies the front end's task of analyzing the program prior to translation. Parallelism can now be detected without global analysis of the program [34]. Also, since the execution order is largely unspecified, algorithms are likely to be less sequential. However, one can argue that the back end's job becomes more difficult, because the construction of the data flow graph (the machine code of a dataflow computer) is more complicated than ordinary code generation, mostly because of array variables, and Gajski et al. [185] suggest that this complication may completely offset the advantages gained for the front end by the dataflow approach.

This disagreement cannot be resolved until more experience is obtained with real dataflow programs and compilers. In the meantime, we provide a summary of the arguments on both sides, based on discussions with two of our colleagues, Wai-Mee Ching, whose work we described on page 323, and Kattamuri Ekanadham, author of several papers on dataflow (e.g., [157]).

Ching makes the point that code generation in a dataflow compiler back end has to be harder than, say, Parafrase's vectorizing back end because dataflow operations are at a lower level than vector operations, and one must specify the details of how things will be done. True, one must specify details for a sequential von Neumann machine, too, but that process is simpler because there is only one stream of control; that is, only one thing is happening at a time, whereas in dataflow all kinds of things are (potentially) going on in parallel. So the comment by Fisher [171] on the impossibility of hand-coding a VLIW computer would seem to apply in spades here.

Ekanadham maintains that, except for arrays, the front end of a dataflow compiler should be easier, and the back end should be no harder than for Parafrase. Nothing comes for free, we objected. True, he says, the price is the extra work that the *programmer* had to do (!).[180] How about what Gajski et al. said, we asked. Well, said Ekanadham, if you care about handling arrays efficiently (I-structures), then (in the back end) you have to get into the same kind of analysis that Parafrase does about collisions of array indices, and so on, and needing this analysis is probably why Gajski et al. say the overall work is about

---

in this section. Id Nouveau, unlike Sisal, has the features typifying a modern functional language. Traub [438] discusses the compilation of such languages.

[180] Compare Veen's [447] comment about programmers needing to take care to avoid creating serial sections of code.

Figure 6.14   Sisal language processing [165]

the same; that is, "You can pay me now, or you can pay me later." Ek says that Arvind argues that even so, dataflow is less work.

A favorable performance comparison was reported recently [83] between Fortran and Sisal, a descendant of the VAL dataflow language (page 274) specifically designed to produce efficient code for large-scale scientific computations [165]. Sisal is a functional language with no explicit parallel control constructs, but its data types and its constructs for *expressing* operations are chosen with the above objective in mind. The result is a language lacking some of the characteristics of modern functional languages (in particular, Sisal is first order and largely strict), but the compiler writer has appeared to benefit.

A suite of eight benchmark programs coded in both Fortran and Sisal was compared on an 8-processor Cray Y-MP. The benchmarks included the Livermore Loops (24 scientific kernels), the SIMPLE hydrodynamics program, and a weather-prediction program (somewhat smaller than the example we describe on page 39). Each Sisal program was a transliteration of its Fortran equivalent; the algorithms were not changed to improve performance.

The Optimizing Sisal Compiler (OSC) that was used generates C and Fortran and thus relies on local compilers to finish compilation. The optimization with the most dramatic effect is *copy elimination*. If one needs to change a single value in an array using a language with functional semantics, the programmer needs to produce a copy of the original array with this value changed. However, if the old value is no longer needed, it is *much* more efficient to simply update the element in place (i.e., not to produce the second array at all). Since Sisal is functional, the programmer writes code including both arrays, but the compiler detects that the original array is no longer needed and avoids the copy. In some experiments OSC prevents over 99% of the copies that a naive implementation would have made.

Compared to Fortran, the Sisal run time was 5% worse for the Livermore Loops, four times better for SIMPLE, and almost six times better for the weather code. One reason for the improved performance on the weather code is the lack of interprocedural analysis in the Fortran compiler (as we shall see below, the Sisal optimizer always sees the entire program). Perhaps the most interesting explanation is the one for the SIMPLE results: the Fortran compiler was unable to unravel the true behavior of the equation of state package. This is an example of what functional language advocates mean by an imperative language masking what a program is really trying to do.

The structure of OSC is shown in Figure 6.14 on page 333, which is adapted from [165]. The parser is fairly conventional and produces a language called IF1 (intermediate form 1), which consists of dataflow graphs and has functional semantics. The IF1 linker IF1LD is placed *before* the backend; the result is that the entire program, including any library routines referenced, is optimized as a whole. This technique permits interprocedural optimization but can increase compile time. The first optimization phase IF1OPT is fairly conventional, but the next phase IF2MEM is more interesting. In Sisal an array is defined one element at a time, so a naive implementation would first create an array of size one, then copy it and append the second element, then copy the two-element array and append the third element, and so on. The total number of elements copied would be quadratic in the array size! Instead, IF2MEM determines when the array can be built in place. The output of this phase is IF2, an extension of IF1 that no longer has functional semantics. The next phase IF2UP attempts to avoid other copies (such as those mentioned two paragraphs previously), replacing them with updates-in-place. The analyses needed for these copy optimizations are based on research reported in [250]. The resulting optimized IF2 is then partitioned into parallel subtasks by IF2PART. This is similar to loop-level parallelism (in Sisal parlance, only `for` expressions and stream producers and consumers are parallelized [165]). Finally, CGEN generates C code from IF2.

6.4 Summary and Perspective

The creation of a parallel program involves pinpointing and then scheduling sections of code that may be executed in parallel. In the *explicit* parallelism approach, these activities are done by the programmer, using specific parallelism constructs provided by or added to a language for the control of parallel execution. However, this approach often results in hardware- or architecture-dependent programs, requires programmers to be familiar with the hardware, and has had its major successes only with certain easily recognized forms of parallelism, either a few very large blocks of code or else loop-level parallelism with a high degree of regularity. The alternative, *implicit* parallelism, is to use a language that hides the details of parallel execution and have a compiler or other translator identify and schedule a range of types of parallelism efficiently.

One important class of implicit parallelism occurs when using conventional sequential languages. Existing sequential-language programs, which often represent a substantial investment (the so-called dusty decks), must all be modified if the explicit parallelization approach is chosen. Instead of leaving this task to the programmer, one can construct a translator that converts the sequential program to parallel form. This solution is called *automatic parallelization*.

The leading example of automatic parallelization applied to an existing sequential language is the Parafrase project at the University of Illinois, with related projects at Rice University and IBM. Parafrase accepts standard Fortran and attempts to vectorize, recognize compound functions, and schedule their execution on vector and parallel machines. It tries to *reconstruct* the high-level meaning of the code it sees. A somewhat different approach to extracting parallelism from Fortran programs is followed in the Bulldog approach, which doesn't really care about the higher-level meaning of the code as long as its operations can be *reassembled* into sufficiently large chunks of parallel execution. The choice of Fortran is understandable, since the bulk of computationally intensive programs are written in this language. However, the von Neumann model and its sequential nature reflect themselves strongly in Fortran, and this nature makes the extraction of parallelism difficult. Potentially concurrent operations become serialized code because that is the only mode of operation recognized by Fortran, and the parallelism is hard to recover because it must first be proved that the variables involved are not dependent on other parts of the program via the side-effect and aliasing mechanisms that Fortran allows.

Another approach to implicit parallelism is to define new languages that make detecting parallelism easier, for example by eliminating side effects and aliasing. An important class of such languages are those based on function evaluations rather than assignment statements. This *functional-language* approach removes many of the restrictions on the order in which instructions can be executed and presents several new possibilities for scheduling their parallel execution. One extreme is greedy evaluation, in which instructions are executed as soon as their data are available. This approach is the data-driven, or dataflow, model. But this greediness has a high cost in work and overhead, especially for small chunks of computation. Another approach is lazy evaluation, in which an instruction is executed only when another instruction needs its result. This model is the demand-driven, or reduction, model. Dataflow has received considerably more work than reduction as a method for evaluating functional-language programs. The projects at MIT and the University of Manchester include work on dataflow hardware, languages, and language processors. Recent success with Sisal has spurred new interest in the area. However, the body of real programs in functional languages is small as yet.

Both Fortran 77 and the dataflow languages perform array operations at a low level; that is, their primitives can operate on single array elements only, not on the entire array. Even a simple vector addition must be coded as a set of operations on the vector elements. These low-level operations are the source of much potential parallelism, but the side effects of Fortran make the delivery of this parallelism difficult.

APL and Fortran 90 have side effects, too, but operate at a fundamentally higher level. Arrays are the dominant data structure, and the primitives operate on whole arrays. The fact that something is an array operation does not become obscured by the coding process, and so scheduling such fine-grain parallelism on vector and array processors becomes much more straightforward.

As a second advantage, APL's support of a large number of high-level primitives leads to larger basic blocks of branchless code (some six times larger than those of Fortran 77, on the average). Assuming that the program in question is rich in array or vector operations, APL's large basic blocks can contain enough substantial vector operations to keep several vector processors or a large number of scalar processors busy, assuming the vector operations are independent. Independence can be determined from local dataflow analysis, that is, done only within the basic block. A Fortran program would require global dataflow analysis to achieve such large parallel chunks of work. The E-compiler project aims to exploit these factors to achieve the programming of multi-(vector) processors and massively parallel machines without the need for much of Parafrase's extensive analysis and VLIW's sophisticated trace scheduling. Naturally, APL compilation has its own problems.

New languages do not solve the dusty-deck problem. Moreover, the only production compilers available for most commercial parallel processors are those for sequential languages: specifically Fortran, C, and occasionally Lisp.

6.5   Exercises

1. Define the following terms.

Basic block	Horizontal microcode
Interval	Vertical microcode
BAS	Microcode compaction
Dataflow analysis	Trace scheduling
Vectorization	Lexical Analyzer
Parallelization	Parser
Dependency analysis	Control flow graph
Reconstructing compilers	Loop carried dependency
Reassembling compilers	Loop distribution

2. Match each of the terms on the left with its attribute on the right

    a. Anti dependency

    b. Bulldog compiler

    c. Flow dependency

    d. Output dependency

    e. Paraphrase compiler

    1) Reassembling compiler for VLIW featuring trace scheduling
    2) Reconstructing FORTRAN compiler
    3) Two statements assign to the same variable
    4) Variable assigned in one statement used in a preceeding statement
    5) Variable assigned in one statement used in a succeeding statement

3. Consider the following FORTRAN program fragment.

```
        DO 20 I = 1, N
            DO 10 J = I, M
                C(I) = C(I) + A(I,J)*B(I,J)
10          CONTINUE
20      CONTINUE
```

   Draw the dependency graph.

4. Take the program from problem 3 and interchange the I and J loops. Draw the dependency graph of the resulting program.

5. If the goal is vectorization, which of the two preceeding programs would you prefer. What if the goal is parallelization for a shared-memory MIMD computer? Explain your answer.

6. Identify the basic blocks in the following C program:

```
void f(int x) {
        int a,b,c;
        a = x + 3;
        b = a + x;
        if (b > a) {
            c = x + b;
            b += c;
        } else {
            c = x - b;
            b *=c;
        }
        while (x > b) {
            x -= a*a + 1;
        }
        printf ("x is %d\n", x);
}
```

7. Why is an APL compiler (producing good machine code) much harder to construct than a Fortran compiler.

8. (For APL experts) Propose an APL-like language for use with SIMD machines as described in chapter 9. Why would your language be good for SIMD, and have you eased the difficulties you mentioned in answering the previous problem?

9. Consider the following real-life occurence. A competent group produces a parallel program P that attains high speedup on a parallel computer. Another competent group rewrites P in a straightforward way as a serial program S to include in a standard benchmark. S is then given to a good parallelizing compiler, but very little parallelism is found. How could this happen?

10. Consider the following program that processes N data items using nproc processors (assume N is a multiple of nproc)

```
chunksize = N / nproc
forall pe = 0 to nproc-1    {create nproc tasks one per pe}
    for j = pe * chunksize to (pe+1) * chunksize - 1
        compute (j)
    endfor
endforall
```

Assume compute (j) requires 1 millisecond for any j and that creating k tasks requires k milliseconds. Ignore the (trivial amount of) time required for loop overhead and the computation of chunksize. How long (in terms of N and nproc) does the complete computation require? For a given N, how many processors should be assigned (i.e. what value should be assigned to nproc) if the goal is minimum execution time? What if the goal is maximum efficiency?

11. For the Serial Access Paradigm (SAP) introduced on page 179, derive an expression for the speedup as a function of the number of processors (look in the index for the definition of speedup, if necessary). How does your result compare with the speedup expression given for the seismic example in the applications chapter? What do you conclude about the relationship between the seismic program and the SAP model of communication among parallel processes?

12. As in the above exercise, derive an expression for the speedup of the Concurrent Access Paradigm (CAP). Explain similarities and differences between the SAP, CAP, and seismic expressions. How do the assumptions made in the three cases compare?

Last night I dreamed that the Real World had adopted the Unix Philosophy.

I went to a fast-food place for lunch. When I arrived, I found that the menu had been taken down, and all the employees were standing in a line behind the counter waiting for my orders. Each of them was smaller than I remembered, there were more of them than I'd ever seen before, and they had very strange names on their nametags.

I tried to give my order to the first employee, but he just said something about a syntax error. I tried another employee with no more luck. He just said Eh? no matter what I told him. I had similar experiences with several other employees. (One employee named ed didn't even say Eh?, he just looked at me quizzically.) Disgusted, I sought out the manager (at least it said man on his nametag) and asked him for help. He told me that he didn't know anything about help, and to try somebody else with a strange name for more information.

The fellow with the strange name didn't know anything about help either, but when I told him I just wanted to order he directed me to a girl named oe, who handled order entry. (He also told me about several other employees I couldn't care less about, but at least I got the information I needed.)

I went to oe and when I got to the front of the queue she just smiled at me. I smiled back. She just smiled some more. Eventually I realized that I shouldn't expect a prompt. I asked for a hamburger. She didn't respond, but since she didn't say Eh? I knew I'd done something right. We smiled at each other for a little while longer, then I told her I was finished with my order. She directed me to the cashier, where I paid and received my order.

The hamburger was fine, but it was completely bare... not even a bun. I went back to oe to complain, but she just said Eh? a lot. I went to the manager and asked him about oe. The manager explained to me that oe had thousands of options, but if I wanted any of them I'd have to know in advance what they were and exactly how to ask for them.

He also told me about vi, who would write down my order and let me correct it before I was done, and how to hand the written order to oe. vi had a nasty habit of writing down my corrections unless I told her that I was about to make a correction, but it was still easier than dealing directly with oe.

By this time I was really hungry, but I didn't have enough money to order again, so I figured out how to redirect somebody else's order to my plate. Security was pretty lax at that place.

As I was walking out the door, I was snagged in a giant Net. I screamed and woke up.

Figure 7.1   Humorous look at Unix *from an electronic bulletin board at Stanford University. A partial explanation for the popularity of Unix is on page 367.*

7

Operating Systems

In any computer system it is the combination of hardware and software that determines the obtainable performance. In this chapter we discuss operating systems (OSs) for parallel computers. Compilers, the other major system software component, are the subject of Chapter 6.

When discussing operating systems for parallel computers, two aspects of parallel processing must be carefully distinguished. On the one hand, the operating system, as the dispenser of hardware resources to users, must be able to support parallel user programs, that is, single programs that wish to make use of multiple processors. On the other hand, the operating system runs on the parallel processor and thus is itself a parallel program. It is possible for a system to do one of these tasks well and the other poorly. For example, consider a master-slave OS in which the operating system will execute on only a single (master) processor but in which user processes may execute on either the master or any of the other (slave) processors. Such a system can give full support for parallel user programs and can efficiently allocate processors to the individual processes that constitute the user's job, but the requirement that the OS run only on the master processor means that the OS itself is essentially a serial program.

It is interesting to note that modern operating systems are *all* parallel programs controlling parallel hardware, even when the hardware is labeled a uniprocessor. Parallelism is present because many of the peripherals, or more specifically their controllers, which are often computers in their own right, can issue asynchronous interrupts that may cause the operating system running on the central processor to switch execution from its current code sequence to the sequence specified for the particular interrupt.[181] If not controlled, this unpredictable context switching could result in arbitrary interleaving of the main-line operating system code and all the various interrupt handlers, which is essentially a concurrent execution of these multiple code sequences. We shall see (page 353) that such interleaving can lead to erroneous computation. Indeed much of the traditional "charm" of operating system development and maintenance involves the inappropriate (and not easily repeatable) consequences of an unanticipated interleaving. A fear often whispered at technical meetings is that the coming generation of true parallel hardware will bring this same charming behavior to the world of applications programming. Advocates of functional programming (page 259) see this behavior as a strong argument in favor of dropping our traditional computational models and adopting instead an applicative style that guarantees repeatable results. Although one might wish to carry this argument further and advocate functional programming for operating systems in order to make their outcome repeatable, a significant additional difficulty is that these systems must respond to *external* stimuli that are by their very nature nonrepeatable. For example, barring artificially controlled environments, the time between initiation and completion of an I/O event is not repeatable, and thus one cannot predict which instruction the operating system will be executing (if any) when the interrupt signaling completion of the I/O event occurs.

The remainder of the chapter is organized as follows: We begin with a review of selected topics in conventional uniprocessor operating systems and expand on our claim that all such systems have aspects of parallel programs. We then discuss concurrency control methods, noting the tension between the need for control to insure correctness, as in *the critical section problem* (page 359), and the desire to relax control to increase parallelism, as in *the second critical section problem* (page 359). Next we classify operating systems for parallel computers into separate supervisors, master-slave, and symmetric according to the method used internally to cope with the existence of multiple processors, and we give a short historical account of several early systems, including an example in each class. We then consider operating systems for more modern parallel processors,[182] restricting our attention to tightly coupled systems in which a primary objective is to utilize all the processors in a coordinated solution to a single problem. The more loosely coupled distrib-

---

[181] It is for this reason that, in the previous paragraph, we referred to a master-slave operating system as *essentially* a serial program.

[182] The authors acknowledge the help of Jan Edler and James Wilson as well as the survey by Enslow [159] in preparing the historical accounts of both the early and modern systems.

uted systems in which the processors are controlled by largely autonomous operating systems are not discussed. The reader interested in these distributed systems is referred to the proceedings of the yearly ACM Symposia on Operating Systems Principles. Specific systems reported there and elsewhere include VAXclusters [294], V [92], Accent [369], Sprite [351], DUNIX [324], the Alto operating system [433], Roscoe [408], Tandem [52], Eden [22], Amoeba [338], DEMOS/MP [366], and Locus [452]. Finally, we study two recent university efforts: Mach, from CMU, which runs on a variety of uniprocessors and MIMD machines, and Symunix, from New York University, which runs on the NYU Ultracomputer and IBM RP3 simulator. Discussing Mach leads us to the quest for lightweight processes, and discussing Symunix leads us to the quest for bottleneck freedom.

7.1   Operating Systems for Serial Machines

In this section we review various aspects of OS design and illustrate the presence of concurrency issues even when the hardware is a uniprocessor. In his *Vade Mecum* [167], Raphael Finkel gives two views of an operating system:

> **The resource principle:** An operating system is a set of algorithms that allocate resources to processes.

> **The beautification principle:** An operating system is a set of algorithms that hide the details of the hardware and provide a more pleasant environment.

These views are clearly related, since by allocating resources the OS relieves the user of the details required to do the allocation. Moreover the resources allocated may not correspond directly to hardware resources but instead may represent a more easily used abstraction. For example, the memory granted to a process may exceed the primary memory of the machine, and the OS assumes the task of automatically moving the data to and from secondary storage. Also the I/O resource presented to the user is typically a device to which one can simply issue read and write requests. Real disks are considerably more complex. The most important resources managed by the OS are the processor, the central memory, and the I/O devices and file systems.

7.1.1 *Process Creation, Destruction, and Scheduling*

In most modern operating systems, processes are created dynamically, and hence the number of active processes,[183] called the *multiprogramming level,* varies with time. Each process is in one of three states (see Figure 7.2 on page 345): It is called *running* if executing on the CPU (for parallel machines there may be more than one running process). It is called *blocked* if waiting for resources such as addition memory or an I/O device. It is called *ready* if it has the resources it needs currently but some other process is executing on the CPU.

A simple model of process creation is fork [104] (see page 149), where a running process creates a replica[184] of itself. Similarly, it is easy to understand an operating system primitive that causes the executing process to terminate. It is important to understand that these operations, although conceptually simple, can be quite expensive to implement. For example, a UNIX fork is about 55 ms on a Sequent Balance (a multiprocessor using National Semiconductor NS32032 microprocessors) running Sequent's Dynix operating system [350], which represents a few tens of thousands of instructions. An implementation of fork in the Mach operating system of CMU takes 3069 Vax instructions [432].[185] Mach also offers *lightweight processes,* called *threads,* that do not carry the full state of a UNIX process. A thread create costs 375 Vax instructions. Similar costs occur for process termination. We discuss lightweight processes below (page 370).

Processor management, normally referred to as *scheduling*, can be broadly classified as preemptive or nonpreemptive. With nonpreemptive scheduling, a task that begins execution continues to execute until it voluntarily relinquishes the processor.[186] On the other hand, an OS that employs preemptive scheduling initiates context switches even when the currently executing task has not yielded the processor and is ready to run. These switches

---

[183] A process can also be suspended, indicating that it is not to run in the immediate future. We do not consider such inactive processes; an interested reader is referred to [167] and [428].

[184] Typically the child process is not an exact copy of the parent; perhaps the process ID, program counter, or some other bit of state is different.

[185] The Mach fork employs *copy-on-write;* as the child runs and modifies private memory, additional costs attributable to the fork will occur.

[186] Note that voluntarily does not imply explicitly. For example, a task that issues an I/O request must often wait for the I/O to complete. A context switch at this point to another task, one that is ready to run, is considered to be a voluntary yielding of the processor resource, even though the original task did not explicitly ask to relinquish the processor.

Figure 7.2   *Process states and transitions.*

can occur, for example, when a task of higher priority becomes ready or when the current task has executed continuously for a certain period of time.

Perhaps the simplest policy is *first come, first served* (FCFS) scheduling. In its strictest interpretation, this nonpreemptive discipline runs a process from start to finish, choosing processes in the order of their creation.   It is implemented by establishing a queue of jobs awaiting execution, called the *ready queue.* When a process is created, it is placed at the tail of this queue; when a process completes, the head entry of the queue is removed and executed. The queue discipline used by FCFS leads to its alternate name of *first in, first out* (FIFO) scheduling.

A common variation is to permit a process to yield the processor. As described above, the usual cause for a voluntary yield is that the process needs to wait for either a resource that is in use or an event to occur (e.g., for an I/O to complete). The OS places the process on a waiting list for the needed resource or event and then completes the *context switch,* that is, the switching of execution from one process to another, by removing the head entry of the ready queue and executing it.   The processes on waiting lists are called *blocked,* those on the ready queue are called *ready,* and the process executing on the CPU is called *running* (for parallel machines there may be many running processes). When the event occurs for which a blocked process has been waiting, the process becomes ready (i.e., is placed at the tail of the ready queue). Another variation is to assign a priority to each process and establish one ready queue for each priority. Processes are placed on the ready queue corresponding to their priority, and when a context switch occurs, the operating system chooses for execution the head entry of the highest priority nonempty queue.

The preemptive analogue of FCFS is round robin (RR) scheduling, in which the operating system, in addition to permitting a process to yield the CPU, actually forces it to do so if the process has executed continuously for a long time.   Specifically, a time interval, or *quantum,* is established, and whenever a process is run for this period without interruption, it is *preempted* and placed at the tail of the ready queue; the head entry is then run.   A small quantum makes the system more responsive to short jobs but performs more context switches, each of which is expensive.   The value chosen is typically around 0.1 second.   As the quantum is made larger, RR approaches FCFS.   As the quantum is made smaller, RR approaches processor sharing (PS), an idealized policy in which there are no ready processes.   Instead, all nonblocked processes are running, but at a speed inversely proportional to their number. Although this policy cannot be realized on traditional computers since it requires instantaneous context switching, a parallel system with the same number of processors as nonblocked processes realizes it automatically.   The HEP parallel processor (see page 566) has special hardware that does context switches with extremely low overhead and can thus be said to give a good approximation of PS for any number of nonblocked tasks (within certain limits).

Note how the operating system treats user tasks as objects to manipulate. Finkel refers to this as the level principle:

> **The level principle:**   Active entities are data structures when viewed from a lower level.

This principle can be used to explain the view of some OS designers that the computer actually belongs to the operating system, the latter scheduling user jobs at its convenience.   This view reminds us of Senator (then "Dollar") Bill Bradley's remark that when he was a member of the world champion New York Knicks basketball team, "The ball belonged to Clyde" (all-pro Walt Frazier, who orchestrated the offense and to a large degree determined when his teammates handled the basketball).

7.1.2 *Memory Management*

In modern multiprocessing operating systems, there are normally many ready tasks competing for use of the processor and its memory.   As a result the amount of real memory provided to a given task varies with time and system load. Were the competition visible to the tasks, they would need to determine how much storage is available for their use and at what address this storage is located.   One goal of the memory manager is to hide the presence of other tasks in memory and thus to give each task a view of memory that does not vary with time or load.   In addition, many operating systems permit each task to access a memory space that is larger than the primary memory of the machine. A third objective of the memory manager is to permit processes to share storage regions in a flexible way (e.g., some memory can be declared private, some fully shared, and others shared but read only). These issues of *protection* and *sharing* also arise for files (page 353). Presenting the user with a more easily managed model of memory than really exists is an example of the beautification principle.

The key technique used by the memory manager to achieve all these goals is memory mapping, or virtual-to-physical address translation, in which the address specified by the program, the *virtual* address, is first transformed[187] into another address, the *physical* address, which is then used to reference memory. Virtual addresses are also called *logical* addresses, and physical addresses are also called *real* addresses. To describe memory mapping, let us first consider the program and its data as existing in some additional idealized storage that is outside the computer. By the beautification principle, we give this (virtual)[188] memory some attributes that make it convenient for the programmer (and compiler-writer). One such convenience, called *segmentation,* is to treat memory as composed of *segments,* that is, contiguous regions each having differing properties. For example, the program text (i.e., the machine instructions) would be placed in an execute-only segment, the data would be in several segments, some read-only, others read-write. For a parallel program, some of the data segments would be shared, and others would be accessible by only a single task. There are other attributes as well. We may choose to assume that each segment starts at location zero and is 100 MB in size (even though the target computer has only one location zero and just 8 MB of central memory). Memory mapping is then the function that assigns addresses in this virtual memory to addresses in the real memory of the computer.

The simplest mapping imaginable is the identity function (i.e., the virtual address *is* the real address), but this function fails to satisfy the beautification principle: there is only one segment, its size is limited to the size of the computer's memory, and addresses used in the program depend on where the program is loaded.

UNIX traditionally defines three segments: text, stack, and data. The text segment contains the program instructions. It is write-protected, and if several processes are executing the same program concurrently, they all share one

---

[187] We describe one such transformation below when we discuss having both segmentation and paging.

[188] Often the term *virtual memory* is used to mean what we will define below as demand paging.

copy. The other two segments are both used for data. The stack segment automatically grows in size as accesses are made just beyond its current extent. It is most often used for data accessed in a stacklike manner, such as activation records for a block-structured language. The data segment, which grows only on explicit request, is typically used for "heap" storage and for variables whose lifetime exceeds that of the procedure in which they are defined.

In order to dispense more memory than exists in primary storage, it is necessary to utilize secondary storage (normally disks) for some of this memory. Since disk accesses are five orders of magnitude slower than memory accesses, for the machine to run efficiently, it is important that the overwhelming majority of references be satisfied by central memory. Since to achieve fast access the data must be in central memory *before* the access occurs, an interesting question, discussed in all OS texts, is how the memory manager should decide which data will be accessed in the future. The heuristics employed all make use of the principle of locality:

> **The locality principle:** Memory references in the recent past can be used to predict references in the near future.

Thus, locations just referenced are copied into central memory, and locations that, according to some metric, "haven't been accessed much lately" are moved out to disk. The hope (which has been borne out by many well-behaved programs) is that for significant periods of time, a small subset of the program's virtual memory accounts for a large fraction of the actual references. Then the policy just mentioned will result in having this subset mapped to central memory and much of the rest of the program mapped to disk. This adheres to Finkel's cache principle:

> **The cache principle:** The more frequently data are accessed, the faster access should be.

Unfortunately, the scheme as described above implies that data are copied from disk to memory and vice versa in very small units, essentially one machine word. As noted in Chapter 3, transferring such small units is extremely inefficient, so we must find larger chunks to transfer. One choice might be the segments we just talked about. Such a scheme, which should be called *demand segmentation,* would bring an entire segment into central memory (unless it was already there) whenever any part of it was referenced. But this scheme has problems. In UNIX, for example, where there are only three segments, all of which are frequently accessed, we would need to keep the entire program in central memory to prevent excessive I/O. Naturally, smaller and more numerous segments would help, but the fact that the segments are of varying size means that some would be too small and some too large for convenient demand loading. In addition, the varying segment size means that the free space in real memory, which consists of space formerly occupied by segments, consists of regions that vary in size, often called *holes*. Deciding which hole should be used for a new segment (assuming that there is a hole big enough) is called the *placement problem*. A danger of course is that there could be many holes, each too small to hold the new segment even though in total there is ample free space. This possibility is called *external fragmentation*. Various heuristics are used for the placement problem. Examples include *best fit, first fit* (which is normally better than best fit), and the *buddy system;* all these examples are discussed in [428].

We come now to the other important memory management policy, *paging*.[189] One divides the virtual memory of the program into fixed-size pieces called *pages* and divides the real memory of the computer into fixed-size pieces called *page frames,* which are the same size as the pages. With all pages and frames the same size, the placement problem disappears: a page is simply put into any available frame. In addition, there is no external fragmentation. However, when a program is divided into pages, it is likely that the last page will not be fully utilized: Such partial utilization is referred to as *internal fragmentation,* and, unless the pagesize is unusually large, it is not nearly as severe a problem as the external fragmentation described above. Finally, the trouble with demand segmentation, in which some segments are too small and others too large, is also absent with paging. The resulting policy, *demand paging,* which is the analogue of demand segmentation but in which the regions swapped in and out of central memory are pages, not segments, is very popular today. Indeed, one of the major determining factors in selecting the page size for a modern computer system is to facilitate demand paging.

We have seen that segmentation, in which the program is broken up into visible variable-size segments, is good for specifying flexible protection and sharing, and that paging, in which the program is broken into fixed-size pieces (the breakup is essentially invisible to the program), is good for memory allocation and especially for on-demand allocation. A natural suggestion is to put these two techniques together and support segmentation and paging. The program is visibly broken into segments, with varying attributes, and each segment is invisibly broken into fixed-size pages that are automatically moved on demand into central memory with no placement problem and only minor

---

[189] Often the term *paging* is used to mean what we will define below as demand paging.

(internal) fragmentation. This composite technique, pioneered by Multics [347], is now popular (e.g., IBM 370).

We end this section by describing a possible implementation of the memory mapping that occurs for a system employing segmentation plus demand paging.[190] The first point to observe is that a memory address is no longer a single number. Instead, it is a segment number plus an offset into the segment. This offset is then treated as a page number plus an offset into the page. The actual implementations all statically divide a memory address into three fields: a segment number, *s#;* a page number, *p#;* and a page offset, *poff.* For example, on the IBM RP3 (see page 603) the 32-bit addresses are divided into 10-bit segment numbers (allowing one program to have up to $2^{10} = 1024$ segments), 8-bit page numbers (allowing each segment to have up to 256 pages), and 14-bit offsets (forcing each page to contain 16 KB, which is somewhat larger than usual):

When such a memory address is issued by the processor, the following actions occur (see Figure 7.3 on page 351). The address of the segment table for the currently running process is known (obtaining this address is part of context switching). First *s#* is used to index the segment table. The entry found is examined to determine whether the memory reference is valid (for example, writing to a read-only segment is invalid) and to find the pointer to the page table for this segment. Assuming the reference was valid, *p#* is used to index the page table, and the entry found is examined to determine whether the page is resident (i.e., is loaded in central memory) and if so, its starting address. If the page is not resident, a free frame is chosen (to obtain a free frame may involve evicting a currently resident page and modifying its page-table entry accordingly), the requested page is read in, and its page-table entry is updated. Once the page is resident, the original memory reference is satisfied by accessing location *poff* in the frame.

---

[190] Other implementations and various optimizations, for example, translation-lookaside buffers, may be found in [167] and [428].

7.1.3   *Input/Output and File Systems*

A major problem with I/O is that we can never seem to get enough.   This problem, however, is primarily a hardware limitation, as discussed in Chapter 3. It is interesting to note that a techinque suggested for masking unacceptably long I/O latency is an OS change: increasing the multiprogramming level.   In this section we give a brief indication of the operating system issues involved in supporting I/O and (tree-structured) file systems.

The first point to note is that I/O is a slow operation when compared to typical computer instructions, about 5 orders of magnitude slower than a 32-bit integer add on a modern machine. Hence, when the operating system issues the I/O request, it is not viable simply to wait until it has completed.   One possibility is to start the I/O and periodically check whether it has completed. Instead of the *polling* technique we just described, most systems use a procedure in which the I/O device *interrupts* the processor when the request has completed.   On receipt of the interrupt, the processor automatically switches control to a predefined *interrupt handler* that *services the interrupt*. As with procedure calls, interrupt processing saves and restores the state of the previous context (e.g., the machine registers and the address of the next instruc-

Figure 7.3   *Memory-address translation using segmentation and paging.*

tion). The novelty of interrupts is that they are not explicitly invoked. Instead they occur as a response to an essentially unpredictable external event (e.g., the completion of a disk read), and hence the interrupted instruction cannot be determined by inspection of the program text. One may think of an interrupt as an "asynchronous procedure call", which introduces nondeterminacy into operating systems, as alluded to above.

In addition to the nondeterminacy just described, I/O offers another problem. The devices themselves are often complicated and present a variety of software interfaces to the OS. For this reason the care and feeding of each device type is relegated to a separate module of the operating system called a *device driver;* the drivers present a uniform I/O interface to the main line OS, which in turn, following the beautification principle, presents a uniform interface to users.

This interface includes read and write *system calls* (also called *supervisor calls)*. We have already seen that the operating system begins to execute when an interrupt occurs. A more direct method of transfering control to the operating system is for the currently executing task to issue a system call, that is, to specifically request one of a predefined list of system services provided. Through some machine-dependent mechanism, the state of the user processes is saved, control is transferred to the provider of the specified service, and (normally) the computer is switched into *supervisor mode* (also called *privileged mode, system mode,* or *kernel mode)*. When executing in supervisor mode, the system is able to execute certain otherwise forbidden instructions, such as those that manipulate I/O devices. Equally important, the memory mapping is changed when entering supervisor mode. This is used to protect portions of the operating system programs and data from direct user access. Hence erroneous (or malicious) programs cannot (in theory) damage the operating system itself, which is important if the system is to remain running despite faulty user programs. When the OS module has completed its requested function, another machine-dependent mechanism is invoked, and control returns back to the user task with the computer once again executing in *user mode*. The read and write system calls are decidedly nontrivial. A reader wishing details is encouraged to see Bach's book [43], which describes the UNIX implementation, a comparatively simple I/O system.

The next point we wish to discuss concerning I/O is file naming. It is clear that for any system with large numbers of unrelated users, it is not feasible to assume that all distinct files will be given distinct names whenever referenced. Names like *test, temp, chapt3,* and *data* will probably be employed by several users. A simple scheme is to give each user a separate namespace, probably with some provision for accessing selected files owned by other users or by the system itself. Compilers would be a common example of the latter. Normally more flexibility is offered to users so that they can have, for example, many data files, each associated with a different project on which they are working. Most modern systems[191] present a *tree-structured file system* in which the files are thought of as the leaves of a tree whose interior nodes are called *directories* (see the box on page 356 for an example).

Once we can name files, the issues of *protection* and *sharing* arise, just as they did for memory segments (page 347).   To provide the most flexible method of protection and sharing, one first specifies the kinds of accesses possible (e.g., read, write, execute, delete, append, etc.) and then defines an *access matrix*. This matrix has a row for every user and a column for every file; entry (r,c) contains the *access rights* granted to user r for file c. For example if (r,c)=<read,execute>, user r can read or execute, but cannot write, file c. Row r is often called the *capability list* for user r, and column c is often called the *access list* for file c. Normally *user* and *file* are replaced by the more abstract terms *subject* and *object* respectively, permitting, for example, concurrent jobs submitted by the same user to have different capability lists.

7.1.4   Even a Serial OS Is Concurrent

Recall our earlier comment that OS theory is related to parallel computing, even ignoring the goal of developing operating systems for parallel machines. For example, consider incrementing x by 1 on a serial computer. An applications programmer would immediately code the obvious assignment statement

$$x = x + 1$$

knowing that no trouble could ever arise. However, as we shall soon see, a systems programmer must be more careful.[192]

Unless the machine in question has an explicit "increment memory" instruction, the assignment statement given above will be compiled into a sequence of instructions.   For example, many compilers would generate three instructions: a load, an increment, and a store. Specifically, we might find the following sequence:

---

191   There *are* important exceptions.
192   The problem to be described is characteristic of the shared-memory programming model. It is an advantage of the (synchronous) message-passing model that no processor interferes with another processor's memory (and no processor receives asynchronous requests to update its own memory).

```
load reg1,X
incr reg1,1
store reg1,X
```

The essence of the problem is that the sequence may not be executed *atomically* (i.e., without interruption), and an interrupt occurring between the first two statements can produce erroneous results, as we shall see.

Let us consider a variable `NumBlocks.` used by the OS to record the number of blocks currently enqueued waiting to be written to a specific disk. Then, a "write-block" system call would enqueue a block and increase `NumBlocks.` by 1; the handler for the disk completion interrupt would dequeue a block, send it to the disk, and decrement `NumBlocks..` However, a straightforward solution using simple assignment statements to update `NumBlocks.` can fail, as the following possible scenario illustrates:

1. Assume that the current value of `NumBlocks.` (stored in memory) is 10 and that task A is executing and issues the write-block system call.
2. Control passes to the operating system and eventually reaches the three-instruction sequence used to increment `NumBlocks..`
3. The first (load) instruction of this sequence is executed.
4. The disk in question finishes writing a previously enqueued block and issues an interrupt, causing the processor to save the values of the registers and then switch control to the corresponding interrupt handler. Note that the saved value of register 1 is 10.
5. Assume that the queue is nonempty. The handler then removes another block and decrements `NumBlocks.` by 1, using a three-instruction sequence analogous to the one displayed above for an increment. Since `NumBlocks` is currently 10, it will become 9.
6. The handler terminates, and task A resumes with register 1 restored to the value it contained at the time of the interrupt, namely 10.
7. The remaining two instructions

```
incr reg1,1
store reg1,NumBlocks
```

store an 11 into `NumBlocks.`

But `NumBlocks,` initially 10, was both incremented and decremented by 1, and thus should again be 10. The root cause of this anomaly is again that the increment and decrement were not atomic.

Thus, in the presence of asynchronous interrupts, even the most innocent-looking program can produce mysterious results. Similar examples can be found in database systems, in which there is a large literature on concurrency control [61]. Before reviewing solutions to these problems, it is appropriate to ask why they have been tolerated. That is, since concurrency can cause subtle bugs and needs to be controlled, why is it used at all? The answer is that concurrency, like true parallelism, enables increased performance.[193] Asynchronous disk interrupts could be eliminated by having the processor explicitly wait for each I/O operation to complete, but overall system performance would suffer.

Although the example given involved just the CPU currently executing in both normal and interrupt modes, similar situations occur involving the parallel execution of the CPU and a data channel. It is not surprising, therefore, that, just as with multiple-CPU parallel computers, proper coordination is required for the "multiprocessor" consisting of CPU and data channel.

To repeat, the essence of the problems just discussed is that the operations (in these cases increments and decrements) were not atomic; that is, multiple increments and decrements performed concurrently may give a result different from serial execution. The requirement that concurrent execution of multiple operations have the same effect as some serial execution is often called the *serialization principle*, and an execution satisfying this principle is called *serializable*. In the examples discussed above the operations were trivial, and some computers have single instructions that indivisibly add to memory. Sometimes, however, the operations that need to be atomic are decidedly nontrivial. As an example, the box on page 356 describes a well-known pitfall in the UNIX operating system, in which a file can become disconnected from the file system tree.

7.2 Controlling Concurrency

Researchers have developed a variety of techniques to control concurrency. Andrews and Schneider [27] survey many of the techniques for operating systems, and [61] discusses related database issues. In this text we describe just a few of the more widely used techniques. The strongest of these techniques,

---

[193] Common practice is to context-switch whenever a process needs to perform I/O. As compared with waiting, context switching increases the *throughput* of the system as a whole, but does not decrease the *turnaround time* for running a single job.

The Importance of Being Atomic

The figure above shows a small portion of the tree-structured file system found in UNIX. The names in circles represent directories, other names represent ordinary files, and the top slash is the root of the entire tree. Each directory contains one entry for each of its immediate children. In the diagram these entries are represented by lines that are implicitly directed downward; that is, directories know their children but children do not know their parent directory. (Actually, subdirectories do know their parents, but ordinary files do not, and it is the latter that are used in the example.) For example, directory b contains entries for gottlieb and almasi, and gottlieb contains entries for mbox, bin, ideas, and book. By UNIX convention, bin (short for binary) directories hold executable programs, and we have followed the common convention of using each user's surname (but in lowercase) for both his/her user id and for the name of his/her "home directory". To facilitate their joint work, Gottlieb has set his (group) permissions so that Almasi can add, delete, read, execute, or write files in the gottlieb subtree.

One day, Gottlieb decided to remove his ideas directory, since it had been empty for years, and (while in his home directory) typed

rmdir ideas

to accomplish this task. The rmdir utility first invokes the operating system to read the ideas directory in order to ensure that the directory is indeed empty (the danger in removing a nonempty directory will be made clear later). Assuming the test is passed, rmdir then removes (*unlinks* in UNIX parlance) the ideas entry from its parent directory, which in this case is gottlieb. The unlink operation also returns to the free list the disk blocks used for the ideas directory. (For UNIX experts we remark that in our example we are assuming that no aliases exist, that is, that all link counts are minimal.)

Meanwhile, Almasi, having a surplus of ideas, typed

mv ideas/cube /b/gottlieb/ideas/cube

to give his cube idea to Gottlieb. The mv utility first links cube into the ideas subdirectory of gottlieb and then unlinks it from the ideas subdirectory of almasi.

The Importance of Being Atomic (continued)

Although the scenario described will work most of the time, it can fail, and for the same reason as the concurrent increments to `NumBlocks` failed earlier; namely, the necessary actions are not atomic. Specifically, the following sequence of events can occur:

1. rmdir reads ideas and finds it empty.
2. mv links cube to /b/gottlieb/ideas .
3. rmdir unlinks ideas returning its blocks to the free list.
4. mv unlinks cube from /b/almasi/ideas .

But now cube is an orphan: it does not occur as an entry of any directory and thus cannot be referenced. However, its disk blocks remain in use and thus are unavailable. Since the ideas directory cannot even be named, it cannot be deleted, and the blocks appear lost forever. Fortunately, however, UNIX has a file-system checker /etc/fsck that is run periodically. This program will detect that there is an unreferenced file owned by almasi. Although the file name cannot be determined (this is stored in the parent directory, not in the file itself), a unique identifier is available, the so-called inode number. The fsck program then attaches this file to the directory /lost+found using the inode number as the file name.

The cause of the problem is that rmdir is not atomic, and hence its reading and unlinking subactions can be separated by other operations, in this case the linking of cube by mv. These race conditions, where actions can occur in an unpredictable order and the outcome depends on the order, often lead to unpleasant bugs that are hard to reproduce and hence can be quite difficult to fix. We remark that some new versions of UNIX (e.g., 4.3BSD) have an atomic rmdir operation, which is invoked by the rmdir utility, thus avoiding the pitfall given. Other race conditions are possible based on the nonatomicity of mv (i.e., the separate link and unlink operations), and new versions of UNIX supply an atomic rename operation as well. Nonetheless, plenty of races remain.

Many of these same considerations apply to real-time software. Indeed, the following excerpt from [319] concerning the fatal radiation accidents of the Therac-25 medical electron accelerator illustrates well how serious races can become.

> It is clear from the AECL documentation on the modifications that the software allows concurrent access to shared memory, that there is no real synchronization aside from data stored in shared variables, and that the "test" and "set" for such variables are not indivisible operations. Race conditions resulting from this implementation of multitasking played an important part in the accidents.

in which one uses *semaphores* and the *P* and *V* operations to enforce *mutual exclusion* and guarantee *atomicity,* has already been discussed on page 159. Semaphores, especially the busy-waiting (as opposed to task-switching) variety, are also often called *locks.* As we note in more detail below, introducing critical sections to control concurrency can easily lead to poor utilization of highly parallel architecture. On page 247 we also describe *monitors,* a mechanism for mutual exclusion that provides a higher-level user interface than the semaphores provided by P and V.

An ever-present danger accompanying the use of mutual exclusion is *deadlock,* in which processes are waiting for events that cannot occur. For example, assume two tasks have already executed P (but not yet V) on separate semaphores, and now each task tries to execute P on the semaphore it has not yet referenced. Neither of these P operations can ever succeed, since each task is waiting for the other task to execute a V. Deadlock has occurred.

Techniques have been devised to avoid deadlocks and to recover from them. For example, deadlock cannot occur if all tasks obtain locks in the same order. To describe a technique used when it is necessary to obtain an out-of-order lock, we first modify the *P* operation so that, if the semaphore is not positive, the operation *fails,* and the semaphore value is unchanged. We call this new operation *conditional-P.* To obtain an out-of-order lock, a task uses conditional-P (instead of P). If this operation fails, the task stops trying to obtain the lock[194] and may need to relinquish previously obtained locks and undo other actions taken in anticipation of obtaining the last lock. A more centralized approach would be to let the deadlock occur and then have an arbitrator detect the problem and break the deadlock, perhaps by aborting some task. Examples of systems that always get locks in a fixed order and of systems that use conditional-P are presented later in this chapter where we give a history of operating systems for parallel computers.

An important consideration for any system that employs locking is the *granularity* of the locks. At one extreme, the entire operating system can be protected by a single lock. This very coarse granularity leads to the floating master design described on page 361, in which the OS itself exhibits no parallelism and may become a serial bottleneck. A system with extremely fine-grain locking might associate a distinct lock with each shared variable. Such a design can potentially support very high concurrency, since tasks exclude each other only if they both access the same variable. A task that accesses many shared variables must, therefore, obtain many locks, and the lock-management overhead (including avoiding or recovering from deadlocks) can be significant.

Sometimes, correct execution can be assured by employing a concurrency control mechanism less severe than mutual exclusion. One such mechanism, which also arises naturally in database applications, is *readers-writers coordi-*

---

[194] If instead the task repeatedly executes conditional-P until the operation succeeds, the effect would be the same as executing a (busy-waiting) P, and hence deadlock can occur.

nation, introduced in [106]. This mechanism is used when one has two classes of tasks to coordinate, readers and writers. Multiple readers may execute concurrently, but writers demand exclusive access. That is, when a writer is active, no other writer and *no reader* may be executing. A typical usage is that some tasks need to update a data structure or database atomically (these are the writers) while other tasks (the readers) need simply to query the data. To ensure that a reader obtains a consistent view of the data, updates are blocked while the reader is active. If reader activity predominates, reader-writers coordination offers considerably more concurrency than does mutual exclusion. The Symunix operating system (page 371) employs readers-writer coordination internally.

7.2.1   The (Second) Critical Section Problem

As we have seen, unconstrained concurrent access to shared data structures can lead to erroneous results (page 354). One common approach to avoiding errors is to serialize the accesses by making each a critical section. Finding correct, effective implementations of critical sections has been called the *critical section problem*. Note that in this setting, the errors caused by unconstrained access are the problem, and the critical sections are the solution. But in the world of highly parallel computing, there is a second critical section problem, one in which the critical sections are the problem and not the solution. Specifically, a simple application of Amdahl's Law (page 24) shows that the inherently serial execution implied by critical sections limits the overall speedup obtainable by parallelism. Moreover, the limit becomes increasingly more important as the degree of hardware parallelism increases. It is fair to say that when striving for maximum parallelism, critical sections are an important enemy. Whereas the original critical section problem arose from a desire to control concurrency to obtain correctness, the second critical section problem arose from a desire to loosen this control to obtain more parallelism.

Although critical sections can be found in all programs, they are especially prevalent in operating systems. Their presence is not surprising, since semaphores, critical sections, access control, and so on were all introduced for use in operating systems. More importantly, a fundamental goal of any operating system is to allocate the hardware resources to user processes in a controlled manner, and therefore large parts of the operating system code deal directly with the data structures used to represent the resources and processes. When the operating system is itself a parallel program with many concurrent threads of control, accesses to these data structures must be managed, and critical sections are a natural, albeit serial, approach.[195]

7.3   Classifying Parallel Operating Systems

In this section we shall be concerned with the way in which an operating system deals with the presence of multiple processors. As we shall see in the next section, when we present a brief history of operating systems for parallel computers, three approaches have been adopted.

7.3.1   Separate Supervisors

The simplest approach to implement for dealing with multiple processors is to use *separate supervisors* in which each processor has its own (copy of the) operating system and has its own files and I/O devices. This approach effectively treats each processor in a multiprocessor as an independent system. Indeed, the operating system, or more precisely each copy, can be said to be running on and controlling a uniprocessor. Hence very little new structure is needed to support the multiprocessor aspects of the hardware. Not surprisingly, the separate supervisor approach has several shortcomings. For one, since the processors are controlled independently, there is no support for multiprocessing within a single job. In addition, since process migration is generally not supported, load balancing can become a problem. In short, these are not truly parallel systems.

7.3.2   Master-Slave

The simplest system to implement that does support multiprocessing within a single job is a *master-slave* organization in which a predefined processor is declared the *master* and is permitted to execute the operating system. The other processors, denoted *slaves,* may execute only user programs. In practice a master-slave system does permit the slaves to perform some easily

---

195   This argument has been given under the assumption of (or at least using the terminology of) a shared-memory design. The distributed-memory alternative is discussed briefly in the box on page 362.

parallelized operating-system functions. For example, a clock is often associ-ated with each processor, and most interrupts generated by the clocks can be fielded locally.[196] Slaves are also allowed to service supervisor calls that simply query the state of the system (e.g., the time of day, the priority of the current process, or the identity of the user who submitted it).

Unlike separate supervisors, a master-slave system permits true parallel-ism within a single job, but only for user processes. The OS itself is essentially serial, with all but the most trivial functions executed on the unique master processor. For a modest number of processors and a computationally heavy work load, parallelizing the user's jobs may be adequate and the master-slave system does have the advantage of simplicity over the more ambitious sym-metric systems described below. Naturally, the single master can become rate-limiting: If a job requires 5% of its execution in the operating system, then the speedup is limited to 20, independent of the number of CPUs. The master is also a single point of failure. That is, should it fail, the entire system stops running. Hence fault-tolerant systems like Tandem (page 503) adopt a sym-metric organization.

7.3.3 *Symmetric*

In a symmetric organization the hardware resources (e.g., I/O devices and any central memory) are pooled so as to be available to all processors. The oper-ating system is also symmetric in that it may be executed by any processor, which in principle allows operating-system functions to be parallelized in the same manner as application programs. However, the ideal of achieving speedup equal to the number of processors is not achieved and often not even approached. As pointed out before, unconstrained parallel execution, in par-ticular unconstrained updating of shared data, can lead to erroneous results. The need to organize the system to ensure atomicity of important operations can have the effect of shifting the serial bottleneck from being the single master processor to being the shared data structures themselves, that is, from the hardware to the software.

For example, in the simplest symmetric configuration, the so-called *float-ing master,* the entire OS is viewed as one big critical section; that is, it may be

---

196 Normally the time quantum used in round robin scheduling (page 345) is a multiple of the clock period. If, while processing a clock interrupt, a slave detects that a quantum has ex-pired and hence a context switch may be required, we no longer have a simple clock in-terrupt, and the master must complete the servicing of this interrupt.

Comments on Distributed-Memory Operating Systems

The text emphasizes parallel operating systems with a shared-memory orientation. To implement an operating system on a distributed-memory machine, message passing must be used instead of the shared data structures that are found in shared-memory designs. As in any distributed-memory program, such an operating system can be efficient only if the overwhelming majority of its memory references are for values stored locally. However, operating systems have a great deal of state information that is frequently referenced and modified. Since the state must be distributed across the processors, and nonlocal memory references are expensive, it is important to minimize the number of accesses by processor A to data that are stored in processor B. (The distributed state consists primarily of data describing the user tasks and the resources furnished by the hardware.)

A possibility is to partition the resources and tasks statically among the processors and have each processor manage the resources and tasks assigned to it. It is natural that primary storage, a very important resource, would be managed locally; that is, a task could request memory from only the node on which it was running. However, one cannot be too rigid about this partitioning or else poor load balancing will result. Consider, for example, another crucial resource, the processors themselves. If they were managed in a strictly local manner, each task would execute on the same processor as its creator, and thus the entire tree of tasks descendant from any given task would all execute on one processor. The result would be very poor performance for some applications that exhibit highly dynamic parallelism.

Certain distributed operating systems for loosely coupled machines (e.g., Locus [452]) do permit tasks to migrate from one processor to another. However, the computing environments in which these systems run are characterized by a low interprocessor communication rate and a relative independence of the operating systems running on each processor, at least when compared to the parallel computing systems that form the subject of this text.

The challenge for the designer of an operating system for a distributed-memory parallel computer is to achieve adequate load balancing without using excessive interprocessor communication. This task is not easy. To date, no complete operating system (with, e.g., file-system support) has been implemented for this class of machine. To be sure, programmers using these computers do have complete operating systems to use, but this software runs on a support processor; the parallel computer itself hosts only what might be called a run-time monitor.

---

executed by only one processor at a time. This organization may be thought of as a master-slave system in which the master is not predesignated but "floats" from processor to processor as required. As in a pure master-slave system, there is no speedup for OS execution, but neither is there an associated single point of failure.

Less extreme measures can be employed in the quest for atomicity. The OS can be divided into a number of components having little interaction. Although each component is executable only serially, parallel execution among the components is supported. We shall see several examples of this approach, each differing in the number and size of the components, that is, in the granularity of the parallelism. We shall also see that it is sometimes possible, perhaps with hardware assistance, to devise data structures that can be updated concurrently and yet remain consistent.

7.4   History of Parallel Operating Systems

7.4.1   First Steps

As we indicated previously, we are primarily interested in operating systems for highly parallel systems that are capable of supporting parallel applications in which multiple processors cooperate closely on a single problem. We shall, however, begin by mentioning operating systems for very early parallel computers, even though these machines had low levels of parallelism.

Perhaps surprisingly, a commercial multiprocessor, the Burroughs D825, [159] was available in 1960. It was a shared-memory design with up to four (identical) processors and an up-to-date operating system called the Automatic Operating and Scheduling Program (AOSP). Although it was possible to run parallel applications on the multiprocessors introduced during the 1960s, this mode of execution was not done routinely. Instead, those multiprocessors were intended as a cost-effective alternative to multiple uniprocessors. Like central memory, I/O devices were pooled on the D825; AOSP permitted processors to request and release devices as necessary. Today we would categorize AOSP as employing a floating master organization (page 361), in which any processor can execute the operating system, but only one processor at a time.

Other multiprocessors introduced during this decade included the Burroughs B5000/B6000 series (two processors in 1963) [348], the GE-645 (four processors in 1965), the UNIVAC 1108 (three processors in 1965), and the IBM System/360 model 67 (two processors in 1966). In addition to the true multiprocessors just mentioned, several early systems employed special processors for dedicated functions. IBM data channels are used for I/O, and the CDC 6600 employed "peripheral processors" to run the operating system. The BCC-500 contained five roughly comparable processors, two dedicated to user programs, one to memory management, one to terminal I/O, and one to scheduling.

In the early 1970s DEC introduced the PDP-10 model KL-10 [144], a two-processor shared-memory computer that could be configured as either a master-slave or symmetric system. The operating system TOPS-10 supported both configurations. In the master-slave version, all the peripherals were attached to the master processor, and it alone serviced most OS requests. However, the slave was permitted to schedule itself; in particular it could access the ready list. Shared access to this data structure was serialized, the mutual exclusion being enforced via a semaphore. In the symmetric mode both processors could execute TOPS-10 concurrently, provided that they did not reference the same data structure. Again mutual exclusion was enforced via semaphores, a separate one for each data structure. Since there were many structures, we see that the parallelism was at a comparatively fine level.[197]

The IBM System/370 models 158 MP and 168 MP [32] [327] were, like the PDP-10s, two-processor shared-memory computers with two configurations. Unlike the DEC design, one of these configurations essentially separated the processors. This configuration, called *uniprocessor mode* for obvious reasons, gave each PE its own main memory, I/O devices, and copy of the operating system OS/VS2 (Operating System Virtual System 2, which has evolved into MVS). The uniprocessor mode of OS/VS2 was an example of the separate-supervisors (page 360) approach. The multiprocessor mode is more interesting for us and can be viewed as somewhere between the floating master AOSP and the symmetric TOPS-10. Like the latter, VS2 was divided into components that were each serially executed. However the granularity was coarser; there were only 13 components, and each contained several related data structures. Obtaining the single semaphore lock associated with a component was less expensive than acquiring all the data structure locks separately. The disadvantage is that less parallelism was possible. To prevent deadlock, where each processor requests a lock held by the other, a convention was established requiring that locks be obtained in a fixed order. Also introduced with these machines were two new coordination instructions, compare-and-swap, which atomically tests and possibly modifies a memory location, and signal-processor, one use of which was to recover from the failure of one processor.

---

[197] In contrast, if there were a single lock for the entire OS, we would have a floating master system (page 361) with no effective parallelism.

7.4.2   Higher Levels of Parallelism

The primary reason for the low level of parallelism in these early systems is that individual processors were expensive.   In the 1970s, the development of minicomputers, especially DEC's PDP-11, considerably lowered this barrier, and assembling larger numbers of processors became feasible.   Two larger PDP-11 projects developed during the 1970s were C.mmp [463] [465] (page 561) and Cm* [422] [266] (page 563), both done at Carnegie-Mellon University. During the same period, the PLURIBUS special-purpose multiprocessor [274] was constructed at Bolt, Beranek, and Newman (BBN) using Lockheed Sue processors.   The CMU designs were the hosts for significant experiments in parallel operating systems, namely Hydra, Medusa, and StarOS, which are described in the next two sections.

The microprocessor explosion of the 1980s has further lowered the hardware cost associated with assembling a multiplicity of processors.   Indeed, a million-dollar budget can buy hundreds of (diskless) workstations, each containing more powerful processing elements than any of the uniprocessors discussed above.   Although it is true that much recent research on operating systems has emphasized support for multiple processors, the majority of this work has been targeted at distributed operating systems, in which the processor ensembles form loosely coupled networks of largely independent computers rather than the tightly coupled parallel systems emphasized in this book.   In particular, direct OS support for highly parallel application programs is, in general, not provided by these network operating systems.   This is not to say that tightly coupled systems have been ignored.

Hydra

C.mmp (page 561) was a shared-memory MIMD computer with 16 processors connected via a crossbar to 16 memory modules.   Its operating system was called Hydra [464] [465], after the mythological multiheaded beast.   Like TOPS-10, Hydra permitted multiple processors to perform OS functions simultaneously, providing they did not access the same data structure.   The mutual exclusion needed was provided by several means, the most interesting being a *kernel lock* that did not consume memory bandwidth.   If the resource was not available, the processor executing the kernel lock essentially went idle waiting for an interrupt indicating that the data structure could be accessed exclusively.

Results on the use of lock primitives were encouraging.   A study showed that although a process may spend over 60% of its time executing kernel code, less than 1% of the time is spent waiting for locks.   Two reasons for this low waiting time were that 90% of the lock requests were granted immediately and the average time spent in a critical section was only about 300 microseconds.

Unlike the earlier systems mentioned, Hydra was (in part) a capability-based object-oriented system [264] [138]: An *object* is an individual, named resource such as a file or a procedure, and a *capability* consists of an unforgeable identifier of an object together with a set of access rights indicating the actions that the holder of the capability can perform on the object. Possible actions include calling (a procedure) and reading (a file).

Hydra was written as a kernel containing a collection of basic mechanisms that allow most of the facilities generally provided by an operating system to be written as user programs, thus allowing many user-level definitions of a facility to coexist.

Medusa and StarOS

Cm* (page 563) contained 50 processor-plus-memory modules grouped into five clusters of ten modules each. A significant consequence of this hierarchy is that memory-access times were nonuniform; the ratios for local:intra-cluster:intercluster were 1:3:9. Two operating systems were developed: Medusa [352] and StarOS [267] [265]. Like Hydra, both were object-oriented and supported capabilities, but they departed from Hydra by introducing *task forces,* that is, collections of tasks cooperating closely to solve a single problem. Both systems attempted to *coschedule* [352] the members of a task force, meaning that the entire force would run concurrently (on separate processors, naturally). Medusa and StarOS were themselves implemented as task forces; interprocess communication was via message passing. StarOS differed from Medusa by hiding more of the details of the underlying hardware.

Embos

The Embos [346] operating system for the Elxsi System 6400, a bus-based 10-processor system with shared memory, is itself organized in a strict message-passing manner: each resource is managed by an operating-system task, and these tasks share no data. Embos does, however, support both message passing and shared memory for user processes. The latter was added late in the development cycle; several of the designers originally believed that users would not want it, but they were urged to change their minds by their first customer.

7.4.3 *UNIX-Based Parallel Systems*

The UNIX operating system has become popular with many researchers since it is reasonably powerful but not nearly so large as many other complete operating systems. Moreover, the source code of UNIX is readily available, especially for universities, and (again in comparison with other systems) it is easy to port to different architectures. Many developers of operating systems for parallel machines are using UNIX as a base for these reasons and because it is emerging as a quasi standard. A little background from an article by Peter H. Lewis [321]: "UNIX was developed by AT&T Bell Laboratories in the early 1970s and quickly gained favor with research and academic institutions because it was written in a high-level computer language called C, which made it capable of being easily customized to run on different machines. It quickly gained a cult following among computer scientists, who found it to be a powerful and elegant system. Other users have complained that it was difficult to learn" (see page 340).

Lewis notes that UNIX is popular on personal computers and workstations but then goes on to say that "Cray Research Inc. of Minneapolis last week announced that all of its models of supercomputers—arguably the meanest machines in the world ...—will be able to use the UNICOS operating system, which is based on UNIX System V. Each model previously had its own operating system ... . Once an elegant piece of software has been written, it would be nice to know it will not have to be substantially rewritten with every new hardware advance. This holds true for the biggest computers as well as the smallest." UNIX is available on most computers sold today.

MUNIX and Purdue UNIX

Possibly the earliest multiprocessor adaptation of UNIX was the MUNIX system developed at the U.S. Naval Postgraduate School [220] together with the host hardware, a dual PDP-11 configuration. MUNIX was a symmetric system (except for I/O) of fairly simple design: Although not a floating master organization, MUNIX had very few different locks, and each serialized a large part of the system.

Purdue University assembled a dual DEC VAX system on which a master-slave version of UNIX [194] was implemented. This OS was ported to DEC's first multiprocessor VAX, the 782.

Tunis

Toronto University reimplemented UNIX in Concurrent Euclid [240] and extended the resulting system to run on a multimicroprocessor system based on the National Semiconductor 32000 series. The operating system Tunis was a strictly hierarchical program, with each of the five layers implemented as a Concurrent Euclid *module* and no procedure calls permitted from a lower layer to a higher one. We classify the Tunis design as symmetric, but the implementation, in order to minimize (expensive) nonlocal memory accesses, did not permit tasks to migrate freely among processors and performed memory management on a per-processor basis. In addition to its implementation language, Tunis was unique among the surveyed systems in using monitors (page 247) for internal synchronization.

Dynix and 3B20A UNIX

The Sequent Balance was a commercial shared-memory MIMD computer containing up to 30 processing elements based on the National Semiconductor 32032 microprocessor. A later-generation system, the Symmetry, employs Intel 80486 microprocessors. The processors, memory modules, and peripherals are interconnected via a high-speed system bus. Snooping caches (page 542) are used to reduce bus traffic.

The Sequent operating system Dynix is a fully symmetric version of UNIX that comes with a collection of software tools for the support of parallel application programs [54] [350], including compilers and a debugger. However, the primary market target for Balance was a time-sharing system running multiple serial jobs concurrently, and Symmetry is used primarily to support database activity.

Like several other systems already mentioned, internally Dynix uses locks to obtain exclusive access to central data structures. However, a different technique is used to avoid deadlocks. Although a fixed order for obtaining multiple locks was established, it could not always be followed. When an out-of-order lock was needed, a conditional-P (page 358) was executed, and if it failed, the potential deadlock was avoided by relinquishing previously obtained locks and restarting. Since this procedure is likely to involve backing out previous actions and requires obtaining the same lock more than once, an efficient implementation can occur only if conditional-Ps succeed with high probability. Dynix has succeeded in this respect in part because locking is done at a fine granularity, that is, with many locks each protecting a small data structure, and in part because only very few structures are locked at any one time.

The AT&T 3B20A is an asymmetric, dual-processor, shared-memory minicomputer. However, the operating system 3B20A/UNIX[44] was organized in a symmetric manner and was applicable to configurations with symmetric hardware and more processors. The internal organization was similar to that of Dynix, having fine-granularity locking and using conditional-P to avoid deadlocks when obtaining out-of-order locks.

Mach and Lightweight Processes

Perhaps the most portable (and ported) multiprocessor operating system is CMU's Mach [1] and [471], which already runs on the Sequent Balance, Encore Multimax, BBN Butterfly, multiprocessor DEC VAXen, and the IBM RP3 simulator. Mach also provides good support for distributed systems, due in part to its Accent heritage, and runs well on DEC Microvax, IBM RT, and Sun 3 workstations. Although Mach can run serial UNIX applications, and hence is often called a UNIX extension, there is an important distinction between it and the other systems in this section. These others are based on UNIX (possibly with significant extensions, for example to support parallel programs); Mach, on the other hand, is a new operating system containing a unique interface and set of system calls (which in addition can emulate UNIX). Like Hydra, the Mach design specifies that only the kernel of primitive operations should be included in the operating system; the remaining functions are supplied by user-mode modules.   In particular, the design specifies that much of the UNIX emulation will be performed in user mode.

Internally, the current version of Mach is a mixture of symmetric and master-slave organizations. The Mach system itself is fully symmetric, with fine-granularity locking as in Dynix and 3B20A UNIX. Much of the UNIX emulation is, however, a master-slave implementation. When the emulation is moved outside the operating system proper, a symmetric organization may be chosen.

Once again like Hydra, Mach is in part a capability-based object-oriented system but supports a different set of abstractions, namely *messages, ports* (which are kernel-protected communication channels for messages), *tasks, threads* (of control), and *memory objects.* the designers' past experience with Accent had shown them that a message- and capability-based network operating system can be successful. Mach goes beyond Accent in providing, via tasks and threads, direct operating-system support for shared-memory multiprocessors and applications programs. A Mach task is an environment in which one or more threads may execute; it is a protection domain to which resources may be allocated, and includes a paged virtual address space. Threads, which are roughly independent program counters operating within a task, are the execution units scheduled by the OS. A task plus a single thread gives a traditional process, and in the remainder of this section the term *process* is used to mean a task plus a thread. The interesting case occurs when multiple threads are associated with a single task. All these threads share access to the allocated resources; in particular, they share the task's memory objects and have identical memory mappings. Although not always ideal (for example, when private memory is desired), execution units with shared address spaces have proved to be quite useful for parallel applications.

The Quest for Lightweight Processes

As mentioned on page 344, creating a thread (given the task) is an order of magnitude less expensive than creating a new process. In addition, context switching between two threads executing the same task is faster than switching between unrelated threads. The reason for both of these improvements is that there is much less state associated with a thread than with a process. For this reason threads are sometimes called *lightweight processes,* a term used to denote processes in any operating system that can respond more quickly than their heavyweight (i.e., more state-laden) counterparts. There is no doubt that reducing creation and switching costs is an important asset.

There is a question whether the Mach approach, with *operating-system-visible* threads, can lead to an implementation sufficiently efficient to support fine-grained parallel applications in which the parallelism available changes rapidly. Another approach is to have the kernel supply only traditional (heavyweight) processes and to have the language run-time system create and manage lightweight processes without invoking the operating system. Since any interaction with the OS is far from free, this approach leads to even lower costs than achieved for threads. However, it assumes that the need to change the number of traditional processes will occur at a much lower frequency than the need to change the number of (OS-invisible) lightweight processes. A third approach is to combine the first two, using threads for lightweight processes and OS invisible processes for even lighter weight processes; this approach can be implemented under Mach. More experience is needed before any conclusions can be drawn. The interested reader is referred to [25] and [332] for recent results in this area.

The weight of a process

Process implementations containing less state permit more rapid context switching and creation at the cost of less protection and flexibility. The table below shows four different process types: The heaviest is a Unix-like process (UP), next comes a Mach-like thread (MT), then a user-mode thread (UT), and finally a special case of the latter in which a thread once started is run to completion (RC). RC threads might be created to represent the iterates of a doall requesting no I/O or other system service. The first row gives the chores needed to create an RC thread and to switch between two RC threads created together. Since RC threads are always run to completion, such switching only occurs when one thread completes and one of its (already created) siblings is to be started. The second row gives the *additional* chores needed to create a general UT and to switch between two of them. The third row repeats this for MTs, and the fourth for UPs. There is actually considerable variability in implementations, and the table should be viewed as only a rough approximation.

Process Type	(Extra) Overhead to Create	(Extra) Overhead to Switch
RC	Create task control block (TCB) and link into task list. Only one TCB for all RCs created together.	Like getting the next iterate of a loop (bump index, test, jump).
UT vs. RC	Allocate stack for task (number of active tasks not known until run time). Create additional TCBs.	Save/restore as for subroutine call. Link/unlink TCB.
MT vs. UT	Enter and leave kernel (cross protection domain, marshall arguments, etc.).	Enter and leave kernel.
UP vs. MT	Copy (on write) address space. Switch address spaces (refill TLB). Set up files, signals, etc.	Switch address spaces.

Symunix and Bottleneck Freedom

The NYU Ultracomputer (page 572) is an MIMD shared-memory design that includes a novel interprocess coordination primitive fetch-and-add and a memory system that combines simultaneous references to the same location (including fetch-and-adds). Using this hardware, NYU has written a variety of coordination routines that introduce no critical sections. (The important example of queues is discussed on page 588.) The system design is tailored for hundreds or thousands of processors, but to date only 8-processor (bus-based) prototypes have run real applications and a 16-processor (network-based) prototype is nearing completion.

The operating system Symunix [153] [154] is, as the name suggests, a symmetric organization, once again with fine-granularity locking. Symunix emphasizes the traditional UNIX self-service paradigm, in which a process switches to OS state to perform supervisor calls rather than invoking a separate "server" process. A second version of Symunix, currently under development, will support coscheduling of cooperating processes, as in Medusa and StarOS.

Software tools for developing parallel application programs, including compilers and a debugger, are also provided. The Fortran system supports parbegin and doall, (page 151), which may be nested to arbitrary levels. The run time system supports OS-invisible processes.

Consider a parallel application program that is written with a number of doalls, and assume that a constant number of processors are assigned to this job for its entire duration. Then the overhead of each doall executed (which is essentially the cost of creating and destroying the OS-invisible processes) is approximately $150 + 10T$ instructions, where T is the number of iterates (i.e., processes). For large T, this is an order of magnitude better than for OS-visible tasks. Naturally, for some applications, having a constant number of processors assigned is very inefficient.

The Quest for Bottleneck Freedom

The most noteworthy aspect of Symunix is the considerable attention paid to removing critical sections. As we discussed on page 359 when describing the second critical section problem, these inherently serial program sections can lead to bottlenecks that limit overall speedup. Some of the changes to serial UNIX involved a high-level reorganization; for brevity we limit our discussion to lower-level data structure changes.

Variants of the concurrently accessible queues mentioned above are now central data structures for both the process- and memory-management components of the operating system. One example is the scheduler ready queue (page 345). This structure has the additional properties that a delete removes the oldest process of *highest priority,* and one can insert (in constant time) an item with *multiplicity K* representing K identical processes, for example, the (OS-visible) iterates of a doall loop.[198] Another example is the queue of processes waiting for an event. When the event occurs, all the processes can begin execution in constant time if enough processors are available.[199] Our final example is the set of queues[200] used to hold free memory blocks in the buddy system [285] [286].

---

[198]   NYU and IBM have added this ready queue structure to the RP3 version of Mach. Multiplicities are not used, however, since there is currently no system call to create multiple Mach threads.

[199]   The current implementation uses a logarithmic time algorithm instead of the more recent constant time algorithm in [459].

[200]   For this application, the FIFO property is irrelevant.

Sometimes, critical sections can be removed simply by observing that even when fully concurrent behavior is not possible, mutual exclusion is not required. For example, consider readers-writers coordination [106], in which there are two classes of procedures, readers and writers, accessing a shared structure and only the writers require exclusive access. If the reader activity dominates, significant parallelism is obtained. Readers-writers coordination occurs naturally in database applications; Symunix uses it to query and update various data structures, for example the descriptors of recently accessed files (UNIX incore inodes). Readers-writers algorithms are well known. The Symunix version is unique in not having any critical sections in the reader algorithm.[201] Two possible reasons why many operating systems do not use readers-writers coordination are that (1) the latter are more expensive than simple P and V, so if only a modest level of hardware parallelism is available, a semaphore may be more efficient; and (2) without combining and fetch-and-add, a critical section is required in the reader algorithm. Symunix also uses a variation dubbed *readers-readers coordination,* in which each class of procedures permits concurrency, but members from both classes are not permitted to run simultaneously.

---

[201] The reader algorithm given in [372], using eventcounts and sequencers, does not have a critical section but solves a somewhat different problem: readers must be prepared to fail and undo their actions.

7.5 Exercises

1. Define the following terms.

    access list
    beautifications principle
    capability
    cache principle
    context switch
    coschedule
    critical section
    deadlock
    demand paging
    interrupt handler

    level principle
    lightweight process
    locality principle
    multiprogramming level
    mutual exclusion
    readers-writers coordination
    resource principle
    semaphore
    serialization principle

2. Match each of the terms on the left with its attribute on the right:

    a. AOSP
    b. Dynix
    c. Floating-master
    d. Hydra
    e. Mach
    f. Master-slave
    g. Separate supervisors
    h. Symmetric OS
    i. Symunix

    1) All processors execute the OS
    2) Capability based OS for c.mmp
    3) Highly portable OS featuring OS visible threads
    4) Most OS functions done on one processor
    5) OS executed on one processor at a time
    6) OS with OS invisible threads stressing bottleneck freedom
    7) One OS per processor
    8) Symmetric OS for Sequent multiprocessors
    9) Very early floating-master OS for Burroughs multiprocessor

3. What would be the effect of removing the arc labeled create in Figure 7.2 on page 345? What if instead you remove the arc labeled terminate? Both arcs? Just the arc labeled preempt?

4. Describe one of the distributed operating systems mentioned in the introduction.

5. What are the advantages and disadvantages of preemptive scheduling?

6. The procedure for converting a virtual address to a physical address illustrated in Figure 7.3 on page 351 requires two additional memory accesses: one to read the segment table entry and one to read the page table entry. This would be unacceptable overhead so the cache principle is applied and a *Translation Lookaside Buffer (TLB)* is constructed to speed up the process. Read the TLB section in the book by Hennessy and Patterson [228] and describe the mechanism in your own words.

7. Consider a shared memory machine using demand paging and having a TLB (see the previous problem) at each processor. How can theses TLBs become inconsistent? (Hint consider a page fault.) Why would this be disastrous? What can one do to prevent these inconsistencies from arising?

8. Read Bach's book and describe the purpose and operation of the UNIX buffer cache.

9. Consider a private memory machine with a disk and a buffer cache (see the previous problem) at each processor. Describe how these caches can become inconsistent? How might UNIX semantics then be violated? Suggest a remedy.

10. The text describes two examples (incrementing NumBlocks and moving the cube idea) where a lack of atomicity (i.e. a race condition) could cause faulty OS behavior. Describe another one.

11. Consider a shared memory multiprocessor. The operating system could keep one central ready list (list of tasks ready to run) or could keep many ready lists one for each processor. What are the advantages of each scheme?

12. What are the advantages of using fine granularity locking? Of using coarse granularity locking?

13. Discuss OS-visible and OS-invisible lightweight processes. What are the advantages of each.

14. Can you implement P in terms of conditional-P? If so, give an implementation. If not, explain why? Can you implement conditional-P in terms of P? If so, give an implementation. If not, explain why.

Part III: Parallel Architectures

Overview of the Architecture Chapters

In the following four chapters, "the rubber meets the road", that is, the ideas and influences of the preceding chapters take shape in the form of specific parallel computer designs. We have organized these designs into three major architectural groupings: SIMD, MIMD, and hybrid combinations of the two. We begin with the networks used to connect the processing elements in these architectures. Our aim is not a catalogue of all designs but coverage of the key concepts. We present detailed case studies of a few selected designs, and then use these to discuss the key issues and make comparisons with other designs.

The chapters include discussions of pipelined processors (especially pipelined vector processors) and bus-connected multimicroprocessor systems. Although neither class can be expected to exhibit *highly* parallel processing, they are included for two reasons. First, they serve as introductions to architectures that do achieve large-scale parallelism. Second, the pipelined and bus-based machines add a strong measure of reality to the discussion. They offer a performance yardstick against which the upstart highly parallel designs must be measured. For example, referring to the table on page 379, we see that the NEC SX-3/44 achieves 20 GFLOPS on the Linpack TPP benchmark. (The table gives other Linpack performance results as well but the reader is cautioned not to extrapolate from results on a few benchmarks to grandiose pronouncements on overall system desirability.)

The pipelined vector processors lead naturally (but not historically) to other SIMD architectures such as the original ILLIAC IV, the CM-1, the GF11, and the MP-2. On problems sufficiently dominated by vector operations, the ILLIAC IV obtained speedups approaching its processor count of 64. Modern SIMD machines perform similarly. GF11 achieved 10 GFLOPS on QCD and 9.6 GFLOPS on TPP. The latest SIMD machines in the CM and MP series achieve 9.0 and 1.6 GFLOPS respectively on TPP.

The bandwidth limitations of modest bus-based systems underscore the need for a higher communication bandwidth in large MIMD designs, thus leading to the more powerful (and expensive) networks found in the commercially available Paragon, CM-5, T3D, SP1, NCUBE-2, and KSR-1. The first five have demonstrated 72.9, 59.7, 9.4, 3.9, and 1.9 GFLOPS on TPP.

The SIMD group has the longest history. By and large, this group represents a rather fine grain of parallelism, consisting of a single stream of instructions that are each executed in parallel on multiple sets of data. Historically, this model was first used on data in the form of *vectors* or *arrays* of *floating-point* numbers, characteristic of many scientific and engineering problems, and so there is a strong association between the terms *SIMD computer*, *vector processor*, and *array processor*. The ILLIAC IV, in particular, was both an array *of* processors and a computer good for processing arrays of data. More recently, however, the SIMD model has been applied to other kinds of problems as well, and there have evolved computers that are intended to process vectors and arrays but that are not themselves arrays of processors, so that the terms *vector processor* and especially *array processor* now mean different things to different people. Hence, these terms will be used cautiously and sparingly.

In a MIMD computer, the processors have sufficient memory to store their own individual programs and perform their executions in response to the instructions in these stored programs rather than in response to a single stream of instructions broadcast time from an external source, as in the SIMD case. One would expect to find a coarser granularity of parallelism (larger chunks of work) associated with this model, and one would be right most of the time, but not always (dataflow, for example). MIMD is currently the most active area of parallel architecture design. Both shared-memory and message-passing designs abound, usually consisting of processing elements at least as powerful as commercial microprocessors and geared for chunks of work of at least several hundred instructions. Recent experimental designs are beginning to unify the shared-memory and message-passing models by discovering and implementing *mechanisms* needed by both. Also popular, due to their ease of construction and resulting short time to market, are clusters of workstations cooperating on a single problem. MIMD computers are not as restricted to problems with a high degree of regularity as are SIMD designs, but of course there is a price to pay in extra hardware.

Architectures also exist that combine features of SIMD and MIMD, and these hybrids appear in the last chapter. Included there is the VLIW approach already discussed in Chapter 6, as well as several Multiple-SIMD (MSIMD) designs.

Performance Benchmarks for Some Supercomputers

Computer (#PE, MHz)	Measured (N=Nmax)			Theor	Measured (N=1000)			
	Max GF	Nmax size	N 1/2 size	Peak GF	all-PE GF	one-PE GF	Spdup	Eff
Intel Paragon XPS (1872, 50)	72.9	55000	17500	94	--	--	--	--
TMC CM-5 (1024, 33)	59.7	52224	24064	131	--	--	--	--
NEC SX-3/44 (4, 345)	20.0	6144	832	22.0	13.4	4.5	3.0	.75
Intel Delta (512, 40)	13.9	25000	7500	20	0.45	.030	14.7	.03
Cray Y-MP C90 (16,238)	13.7	10000	650	15.2	9.69	.872	11.1	.69
Cray T3D (128, 150)	9.4	11968	2688	19	--	--	--	--
TMC CM-200 (2048, 10)	9.0	28672	11264	20	--	--	--	--
Alliant Campus (192, 40)	4.8	17024	5768	7.7	--	--	--	--
IBM SP1 (64, 62.5)	3.9	26500	8000	8	--	--	--	--
IBM ES/9000-982VF (8, 141)	--	--	--	4.51	2.28	.422	5.40	.68
Cray 2S/8-128 (8, 244)	--	--	--	3.9	2.17	.379	5.73	.72
Intel iPSC860 (128, 40)	2.6	12000	4500	5.0	.238	.030	7.7	.06
nCube 2 (1024, 20)	1.9	21376	3193	2.4	.258	.002	128	.12
MasPar 2216 (16384, 12.5)	1.6	11264	1920	2.4	--	--	--	--
IBM PVS (32, 40)	.925	6000	1560	1.3	.307	.0327	9.35	.29
Convex C3880 (8, 60)	--	--	--	.96	.793	.113	7.02	.88
IBM RS/6000 (8, 62.5)*	.694	10000	1500	1.0	--	.104	--	--
KSR (32, 20)	--	--	--	1.28	.513	.031	16.5	.52
IBM GF11 (500, 19.2)**	5.6	2500	1060	9.6	--	--	--	--

*IBM RS/6000 cluster results from Oak Ridge National Lab

**IBM GF11 results are single-precision, and GF11 is an experimental machine

Note: Selected performance benchmarks [148] using standard linear equation software (Linpack). The first three columns are for the TPP benchmark, where any matrix size may be chosen. The best performance and corresponding matrix size are given in the first two columns. The third column gives the matrix size for which the optimum performance is cut in half. The theoretical peak performance in the fourth column is just the peak performance of one processor times the number of processors. The last four columns are again measured quantities, now for a fixed matrix size of 1000.

380

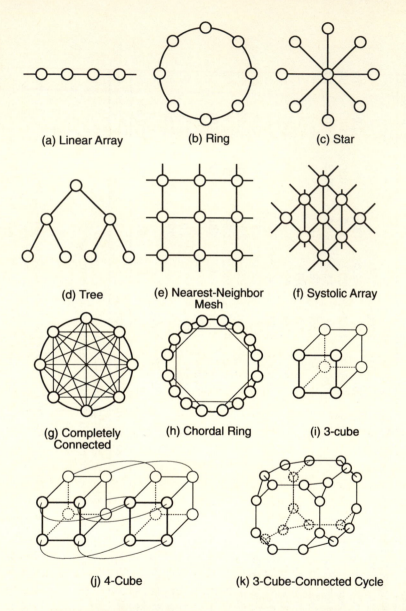

(a) Linear Array   (b) Ring   (c) Star

(d) Tree   (e) Nearest-Neighbor Mesh   (f) Systolic Array

(g) Completely Connected   (h) Chordal Ring   (i) 3-cube

(j) 4-Cube   (k) 3-Cube-Connected Cycle

Figure 8.1 **Static interconnection topologies** in order of increasing capacity and cost (from Feng [164]).

8

Interconnection Networks

In order for our processing elements to cooperate on solving a single problem, we must supply some interconnection scheme so that they can communicate with each other. The reasons for communicating (synchronization, exchange of partial results) and the extent (amount, degree) of communication needed will depend on the application, algorithm, computational model, and language used—in short, on most of the topics discussed so far. Conceptually, the interconnection network starts out to perform a very simple and mundane function for our parallel processor, but as we get into the details, the reader may agree with the comment that the design of such networks is hard because they actually do most of the computation [232]; by the time we are finished, the network becomes an interesting window into the operation of the machine as a whole (Or a window into the soul of the machine?).

In general terms, the measure of an interconnecting network, whether we are discussing parallel computers or a highway system, is *how quickly it can deliver how much of what's needed to the right place reliably and at good cost and value*. Translated to our case, the performance criteria for a network connecting a set of computing elements are the following:

1. *Latency* (transit time for a single message)
2. *Bandwidth* (how much message traffic the network can handle)

3.   *Connectivity* (how many immediate neighbors each node has, also known as the node's *degree*, and how often each neighbor can be reached)
4.   *Hardware cost* (what fraction of the total hardware cost the network represents)
5.   *Reliability* (redundant paths, etc.)
6.   *Functionality* (additional functions performed by the network, such as combining of messages and fault tolerance)

The main choices available to the designer of such a network are these:

1.   Topology (static or dynamic, with subclasses in each category)
2.   Operation mode (synchronous or asynchronous)
3.   Switching strategy (circuit, store-and-forward, or cut-through)
4.   Control strategy (centralized or distributed)

As Feng points out in his review article [164], the cross product of these four design decisions represents a space of interconnection networks. This chapter is primarily a discussion of how these two lists interact, that is, of the trade-offs in performance criteria represented by different points in this design space.

The first three performance criteria above would be optimized by an all-to-all connection topology, but this topology becomes prohibitively expensive for more than a few processors. Otherwise, there would be little need to write this chapter.[202] The networks discussed here can be viewed as a series of lower-cost engineering approximations to this ideal but unaffordable topology. As a first step toward explaining the available design choices, we show that static topologies are appropriate for problems whose communication patterns can be predicted reasonably well, whereas dynamic topologies (switching networks), though more expensive, are suitable for a wider class of problems. After discussing the various cubelike, mesh, tree, and other static topology networks, we turn to switching networks. An important design decision is the choice of a switching strategy. We review circuit switching, store-and-forward switching, and cut-through switching and its wormhole variant. We then comment on the closest approximation to the all-to-all topology, namely the crossbar network, and the least expensive switching network, namely a bus. We next turn to the family of shuffle-exchange networks, beginning with the omega network as a simple example that illustrates the basic functions performed, and then show the additional features and ca-

---

[202] Some of the multistage networks that we treat later, although inferior in performance criteria 1–3, may have advantages in criterion 6 by providing facilities for combining messages and other special functions.

Figure 8.2 *Conceptual progression from static to dynamic networks.*

pabilities of some of the larger, more complex members of this class of networks. The last dynamic topologies we present are the switching mesh and the switching (fat) tree, currently popular choices. We conclude the chapter with discussions of message combining and fault tolerance.

Static vs. Dynamic (i.e., Switching) Networks

The basic distinction we wish to make between static and dynamic networks is that in the former, processors are connected to each other directly by wires, whereas in the latter there are switches in between. To make this point clearer, and as a by-product see how blurry the distinction really is, let us look at the series of diagrams in Figure 8.2.

In the first diagram, which is typical of a static network, we have four nodes, each a processor plus memory, connected by wires. The communication primitives supported by the *hardware* are determined by the connectivity itself. Viewing the diagram as a two-dimensional mesh (it can also be viewed as a two-dimensional hypercube, which would give different terminology), the communication primitives might be called *send up, send down, send left, send right, receive down, receive up, receive right, receive left*. A message sent via a send up would be received via a receive down, and so on. This hardware is similar to the original Caltech Cosmic Cube (page 475) in which case a (hardware-supported) message is a 64-bit quantity. There is no hardware support for sending a message from the lower left processor to the upper right. Instead, the message must first be sent to either the upper left processor (via a send up) or to the lower right processor (via a send right), received at this intermediate processor and then re-sent to the upper right processor, where it is finally received. (As we shall discuss later, pipelining of message transmissions is possible.)

In the second diagram, we have added a switch to each processor. Now the hardware provides a general send primitive that is given two arguments: the message and the destination processor. Thus, there is hardware support for sending a message from the lower left processor to the upper right. This support consists of having the switches perform the intermediate routing and transmissions previously done by the main processor. The last two diagrams are just redrawings of this second one and result in a generic figure that is often used to depict dynamic networks.

Of course, even with the switchless hardware in the first diagram, arbitrary communication can be supported. One simply writes software, most likely in the form of a communications library, to do the necessary retransmissions. On the Cosmic Cube itself, the *distributed process* environment, advocated by Seitz, contained such a library; whereas the *crystalline* environment, advocated by Fox, did not. Users of crystalline wrote their own communications libraries.[203] Thus the distinction between static and dynamic networks is partly a discussion of what is done in hardware vs. software (somewhat analogous to the RISC/CISC debate).

8.1   Static Connection Topologies

Figure 8.1 on page 380 shows some of the many designs that have been studied. A wide range of connectivity is represented. At one extreme is the simple *ring*, in which each processing element (PE) is wired to only two other PEs; messages to other PEs must get there by hopping from PE to PE, like a hot dog being passed along the stands in a baseball park. However, the network is cheap; its cost grows no faster than the number of PEs.[204] At the other extreme in connectivity is the all-to-all network, in which each PE has its own private "hot line" to every other PE. Connecting a thousand nodes this way would take some multiple of a million wires, which is why neither your telephone system nor highly parallel computers are wired this way. The network cost grows as the square of the number of PEs and can rapidly dominate the cost of the computer. In between these two extremes there are a number of other configurations with intermediate numbers of nearest neighbors.

---

203   There are other differences between the crystalline and distributed process environments, for example in process creation (see our Cosmic Cube discussion beginning on page 475).

204   One example is ZMOB [375], a ring of up to 256 Z80 microprocessors.

A parallel computer with such a fixed communication topology can be expected to do well on problems that can be divided into parts having light and predictable communication patterns consisting mostly of exchanges among neighboring processing elements. One application domain that fits this category is the analysis of events in space, ranging from vision to weather modeling to VLSI design. Indeed, there have been successful matchups between such applications and parallel computers with static (and frugal) interconnection networks, including the ILLIAC IV for hydrodynamic problems, the MPP for image processing, and the WRM for chip wiring, all of which use rectangular mesh connections. The disadvantages of such machines are seen with problems that do *not* have such predictable locality, because the delay between non-neighboring processors may be considerable. This need to closely match the problem's communication topology means that computers using static interconnection networks (except all-to-all networks, of course) tend to be more special-purpose than those using the switching networks we will discuss shortly.

The range of computational models used with static topologies includes both SIMD and MIMD, but not shared-memory designs, presumably because of the importance of uniform memory access time in the latter.

8.1.1 Descriptions

In this section we briefly describe some of the topologies given in Figure 8.5 on page 393. The next section gives routing algorithms to be used for each topology. We use the term *nodes* to refer to the items being connected. For the static topologies being considered in this section, a node consists of a processor plus memory. Later, when we discuss dynamic topologies, the nodes may be heterogeneous, with some consisting only of processors and others only of memory.

Meshes and Rings

The simplest connection topology is the one-dimensional mesh, or linear array, in which the nodes are arranged in a line and adjacent nodes are connected. Interior nodes thus have two connections, and boundary nodes have one. If we connect the two boundaries, we get a ring with all nodes of degree 2 (i.e., each has two neighbors). A higher-dimensional mesh is constructed analogously; with k dimensions, interior nodes have degree $2k$. Very common is the two-dimensional (2-D) mesh, exemplified by the ILLIAC IV, MPP, DAP, and WRM. There is not a consensus on what to do at the boundary nodes. The

WRM is a pure mesh: boundary nodes have degree 3, and corners have degree 2. On the ILLIAC all nodes have degree 4, bottom nodes are connected to the top node in the same column, and rightmost nodes are connected to the leftmost nodes in the next row (thus embedding a 1-D mesh); the MPP has several options for the boundary.

Stars

In a star the single central node is connected to all the others. Since the central node has degree $N - 1$ for an N-node star, large configurations are impractical.

Binary Trees

In the basic binary tree, interior nodes have degree 3, with two children and one parent; leaves have degree 2; and the root has degree 1. This pattern has been augmented in various ways; for example, the Berkeley X-tree has horizontal interconnections between nodes of the same level of the tree. Binary trees are well matched to VLSI and other planar layouts (see Figure 8.3 on page 387).

Fully Connected Nodes

In this most-powerful interconnection pattern, each node is directly connected to all the others. With all nodes of degree $N - 1$ and $N(N - 1)/2$ connections, the fully connected topology can only be implemented for modest values of N. It does, however, serve as a performance yardstick against which other, more practical designs can be compared.

Hypercubes

Hypercubes[205] have been much studied; several companies, including Intel, NCUBE, and FPS, have marketed machines having this topology. In a k-dimensional hypercube we have $N = 2^k$ nodes, each of degree k. Figure 8.4 on page 388 illustrates a 3-D hypercube in which each node is labeled with its Cartesian coordinates.

By treating each label as a binary value, we number the nodes from 0 to $N - 1$. The edges in the cube are all parallel to the axes and thus connect nodes differing in only one coordinate (e.g., $(a,0,b)$ is connected to $(a,1,b)$ for any a and b). This observation is equivalent to saying that, using the numbering given above, neighbors differ by a power of 2 (e.g., $(a,1,b) - (a,0,b) = 2^1$).

---

[205] Actually we are discussing only binary hypercubes, but we follow current practice and refer to them simply as *hypercubes*.

Figure 8.3   Planar tree layouts for VLSI chips and circuit boards.   (a) *Binary tree with its single Tree (T) external connection.* **(b)** *The equivalant "H"-layout.   Area required for N nodes grows linearly with N, instead of NlogN as in (a).* **(c)** *Leiserson [314] approach for building a tree recursively is based on this building block: a tree, a "free" (unconnected) node, and four external connections.* **(d)** *New block formed recursively from two of the blocks in (c); result contains a tree with one more level, a free node, and the equivalent four external connections.* **(e)** *The same procedure applied to four blocks using the H layout of (b). Note that the two blocks on the right are rotated 180 degrees. Since the new and old blocks have the same aspect ratio, it is easy to see how to apply the procedure recursively.* **(f)** *Possibly more familiar view of (e). An advantage of trees is that they can grow without requiring more I/O pins. See pages 505, 630, and 634.*

Figure 8.4 Three-dimensional hypercube and cube-connected cycles. *A three-dimensional hypercube (left) with the nodes labeled in binary, and the cube-connected cycles graph (right) obtained by replacing each node of the hypercube with a 3-cycle of nodes.*

For higher dimensions the diagrams become more difficult, but the idea is the same.   Number $N = 2^k$ nodes from 0 to $N - 1$, and connect two nodes whose numbers differ by a power of 2. If the difference is 2^i, we are in effect drawing a line parallel to the *i*th coordinate. Since i ranges from 0 to $k - 1$, we see that each node is of degree k. [206]

Cube-Connected Cycles (CCC)

Preparata and Vuillemin [368] observed that many of the connectivity and routing advantages of a hypercube can be maintained while preventing the node degree from growing with the dimension of the cube. First, they replace each node of the original k -dimensional cube by a ring (or cycle) of k nodes, giving us $k \times 2^k$ nodes in all. Number the rings from 0 to $2^k - 1$ as before, and number the nodes on a ring from 0 to $k - 1$.   Now if two rings have numbers differing by 2^i, connect node i on these rings. Thus the k connections to each node on the original hypercube have been distributed to the k nodes on the ring replacing this node.   Thus each node has degree 3, independent of k. This procedure is illustrated in Figure 8.4 for the special case $k = 3$. Preparata and Vuillemin consider a more general construction in which the ring size need not equal k.

Shuffle Exchange

Like the hypercube topology discussed above, interconnections based on the *perfect shuffle* mapping are gaining increased attention since a commercial product, the BBN Butterfly, has appeared. This mapping, under the name *faro shuffle*, was used for many years by magicians when performing card tricks.

---

[206] Hypercubes are actually meshes. This fact is used in the section on routing that follows.

Imagine shuffling a deck of $N = 2^d$ cards numbered from 0 to $N - 1$ with the numbers written in binary. This action interleaves cards in the top half of the deck (i.e., cards whose numbers begin with 0) with cards in the bottom half (i.e., whose numbers begin with 1). Hence the shuffle can be accomplished by rotating the card numbers one bit to the left and reordering the cards based on their new numbers. More formally, the *shuffle map* is the function *sigma* mapping the integers from 0 to $N - 1$ onto themselves defined by

$$\sigma(x_{d-1}x_{d-2}...x_0) = x_{d-2}...x_0 x_{d-1}$$

where $x_{d-1}...x_0$ is the binary representation of x. We also define the *exchange map epsilon* by

$$\epsilon(x_{d-1}...x_1 x_0) = x_{d-1}...x_1 \overline{x_0}$$

where the bar indicates binary complement. Finally, we define a *shuffle-exchange network* to contain N nodes $v_0,..., v_{N-1}$, with v_x connected to v_y if $y = \sigma(x)$, $x = \sigma(y)$, or $y = \epsilon(x)$.

We also define the related *K-way shuffle network* to contain $N = k^d$ nodes each connected to $2k$ others as follows: Number the nodes from 0 to $N - 1$ using base k, and connect $x_{d-1}x_{d-2}...x_0$ to nodes $x_{d-2}...x_0\alpha$ for $\alpha = 0, 1, ..., k - 1$. Note that two nodes x and y in the two-way shuffle network are connected if and only if one is the shuffle or shuffle-exchange of the other; that is, $x = \sigma(y)$, $y = \sigma(x)$, $x = \tau(y)$, or $y = \tau(x)$, where $\tau = \epsilon\sigma$.

8.1.2 Routing

In this section we show how to route data from one node to another for each of the topologies given above. For some topologies, such as stars and fully connected configurations, routing is trivial; for others, it is more interesting. The routing algorithms for meshes, hypercubes, cube-connected cycles, and shuffle exchanges are related, and routing on an omega network, the most heavily studied dynamic topology, will be seen as a step-by-step application of the hypercube algorithm. Indeed the omega network can be drawn in such a way as to make this correspondence clear, and the resulting graph is often called the *indirect binary cube.*

For each topology, we shall give an algorithm that, when presented with an ordered pair of nodes (A,B), produces a path from A to B along which data can be routed. The interested reader can easily check that, except for the cube-connected cycles, the paths obtained are of minimal length. We ignore issues of redundant paths (perhaps of nonminimal length) that can be used to introduce fault tolerance or to split the load between nodes that communicate heavily. Also ignored is the possibility of node contention. For example, the reader should not conclude that stars route better than hypercubes from the fact that paths on stars have length at most 2, while on cubes the lengths can reach log N.

Fully Connected Nodes

Since all nodes are connected, the minimal-length path from A to B is simply the edge connecting them.

Stars

If either A or B is the central node, then A and B are connected, and the path is just the edge connecting them. If not, the path consists of two edges, the first connecting A to the central node and the second connecting the central node to B.

Trees

The idea is simple. Travel up the tree from A until you reach an ancestor of B and then travel down to B. To implement this algorithm, we need to detect the lowest ancestor of B while ascending and then determine whether to go right or left while descending. One way to do this is to first number the root node 1 and number the left and right children of x as $2x$ and $2x + 1$, respectively. We write these numbers in binary and note that the nodes at level i (call the root level 1) are i bits long and the left and right children of a node have a 0 or 1 appended to their parent's number, respectively. Now the lowest common ancestor of A and B is the node numbered P, the longest common prefix of the numbers of A and B, and thus it is easy to see how many levels up the tree we must proceed from A. The descent to B is determined by reading from left to right the suffix of B's number that remains when P is removed, and going left on 0 and right on 1.

Meshes and Rings

Since there is no consensus on how boundary nodes in rings are connected, we restrict our attention to meshes and note that routing is simply performed one dimension at a time. For example, on a three-dimensional mesh a minimal path from the node numbered (a,b,c) to the node numbered (x,y,z) is constructed by moving along the first dimension to (x,b,c), then along the second dimension to (x,y,c), and finally along the third dimension to (x,y,z). This technique is often called *dimension-order routing*.

Hypercubes

Since a k-dimensional hypercube is simply a k-dimensional mesh in which each dimension contains only two nodes, we have already given the routing algorithm. However, it is useful to recast it slightly for this important special case. Given two nodes A and B, the exclusive or, X, of their node numbers contains a 1 in precisely the dimensions in which the numbers differ and thus tells along which dimensions the data must move. Thus the routing algorithm contains k steps: During step i the data are sent to the adjacent node in dimension i if the ith bit of X is 1; otherwise, the data remain where they are. Since $N = 2^k$, we see that routing takes at most log N steps. (The use of this algorithm in the Connection Machine is described on page 451.)

Cube-Connected Cycles (CCC)

We refer the reader to Preparata and Vuillemin [368] for a detailed analysis, and simply show that routing can be accomplished within 2.5 log N steps. First recall that a k-dimensional CCC is a k-dimensional hypercube in which each vertex contains k nodes, and thus the ensemble contains $N = k2^k$ nodes. It is easy to get from any cycle to any other cycle within $2k$ steps by alternating movement along the cycles with movement across the hypercube if necessary. Once we are at the desired cycle, a path to the destination node can be found with length not exceeding $0.5k$, and thus the entire path from source to destination has length no more than $2.5k < 2.5$ log N.

Shuffle Exchange

Routing from a node x to a node y in a shuffle-exchange network is quite easy and requires 2 log N steps. Recall that the shuffle rotates a node's number one bit to the left. Hence applying log N shuffles to x yields x again. To reach y (instead of returning to x), precede the jth shuffle by an exchange if the jth low-order bit of x differs from the corresponding bit of y. This procedure also gives the routing algorithm for an omega network (page 398), in which the shuffles are performed by the wires, and the exchanges by the boxes.

8.1.3   *Cost-Performance Tradeoffs*

Figure 8.5 on page 393 shows performance trade-offs among some of the static topologies of Figure 8.1 on page 380. The rectangular mesh has the longest history (ILLIAC IV, MPP, WRM), and experience bears out the need for the close match between problem regularity and network topology. The mesh is cheap, but the network *diameter*, or latency, that is, the maximum delay of a message from one of N processors to another, is $\sqrt{N}$, which is bad because there is a large range of delays and also because of the way the maximum delay increases with N.

The hypercube designs add more connections and reduce the network latency by connecting each of the N PEs to $\log N$ neighbors. The number of wires increases (by $1/2 \log_2 N$), but the latency (the network diameter) is reduced by $\log_2 N / \sqrt{N}$.

The tree network might appear to be quite a bargain since its latency is the same as that of a cube, but its wire cost is that of a mesh since the degree of a node (the number of its nearest neighbors) is independent of N. Tree networks also lay out nicely in two dimensions, which makes them especially attractive for designs that use multiple processors per VLSI chip. As technology progresses and linewidths decrease, more processors can be put on a chip by simply adding more levels to the tree. As illustrated in Figure 8.3 on page 387, the chip I/Os need not be changed, and the processor design need only be photographically reduced, not redesigned.

It is true that a single message can go from a leaf node to the root and thence to any other leaf node in $2 \log N$ steps. However, networks must also be compared on their fully loaded behavior, that is, when *all* the inputs are trying to reach an output. When no two inputs seek the same output, this behavior can be looked at as a *permutation* between the inputs and the outputs, and the network is judged on how well it can perform an arbitrary permutation. Trees do well on permutations that correspond to leaf nodes talking to immediate neighbors, but trying to talk to leaf nodes farther away rapidly causes increasing congestion as one nears the root, and the performance rapidly becomes worse than that of the corresponding hypercube network.

Perhaps at least as important as the parameters in Figure 8.5 on page 393 is the *fit to available technology*, such as the maximum number of I/O pins on a chip or circuit board. One disadvantage of a hypercube network (but not a tree network) is that the degree per node grows as N. As described above, a fixed-degree version of the hypercube network called *cube-connected cycles* replaces each vertex in the hypercube with a ring of trivalent nodes (see Figure 8.4) but the routing algorithm for messages is trickier because of the two types of structures (cubes and rings) involved. The routing algorithm for hypercubes is particularly simple and is discussed in the sections on the Connection Machine and the Cosmic Cube in the chapters on architectures. More discussion on static topologies may be found in the review article by Feng [164] and the books by Hillis [232] and by Johnson and Durham [150].

NETWORK SCALING FACTORS

(diameter)

Network	Latency with no con-tention	Maximum Bandwidth per PE	Connectivity (neighbors)	Wire Cost	Switch Cost	Users
Crossbar	const.	const.	any to any non-busy	N	N^2	YSE, C.MMP, Alliant FX/8
bus	const.	$1/N$	any to any if bus free	N	N	bus based systems
multistage fat tree	$\log N$	const.	any to any non-busy if not blocked in network	$N \log N$	$N \log N$	Ultra, RP3, Rediflow, GF-11, TRAC, Cedar, Butterfly CM-5
all-to-all	const.	const.	any to any	N^2	----	
hypercube	$\log N$	const.	$\log N$ nearest neighbors	$N \log N$	----	Cosmic Cube, CHOPP, Connection Machine
Cube connected cycles	$\log N$	const.	3 nearest neighbors	N	---	
Binary tree	$\log N$	const.	3 nearest neighbors	N	----	NonVon, DADO, Cellular
2-D mesh	$\sqrt{N}$	const.	4–8 nearest neighbors	N	----	ILLIAC IV, DAP, MPP, WRM, Systolic, CHiP

Figure 8.5 Interconnection network tradeoffs *showing how performance characteristics scale with number of processors N being interconnected. Dynamic topologies are in the upper portion, static in the lower. Within each of these two groups, higher performance is at the top, lower cost is at the bottom.*

8.2 Dynamic Connection Topologies (Switching Networks)

Static topologies have been used in designs ranging from small systolic arrays to large supercomputers such as the ILLIAC IV and the Goodyear MPP. Computers designed this way can have very good performance on specific problems to which their network topologies are well matched, but it is hard to achieve a multipurpose highly parallel processor using only a fixed interconnection topology, short of an all-to-all network. This difficulty has given rise to much work on dynamic interconnection networks as well communication libraries for static network machines that support in software the

send *message* to *destination*

operation typifying dynamic networks. As with static networks, there is a range of performance and a price tag for each dynamic network. They are, in order of increasing performance and cost, as follows:

- Bus networks.
- Multistage switch networks.
- Crossbar networks.

A bus network is very much like a party-line telephone: it works as long as only a small number (say, 10) PEs are on it, and on the average the service they get is equally good (or bad). The bandwidth available to each is inversely proportional to the total number of PEs. A crossbar network, on the other hand, is like a private exchange that allows any PE to contact any other nonbusy PE at any time and with a constant delay, which is basically the switching time of one switch element. A multistage switching network falls in between these two extremes. Examples of these dynamic topologies are shown in the drawing at the beginning of this section, and the trade-offs among them are shown in Figure 8.5 on page 393. The progression starts from the top with the (static) all-to-all network, with its uniformly fast access to any other node any time, and proceeds through a progression of more restricted but more affordable switching-network approximations to this almost ideal topology.

8.2.1   Switching Strategy

(Much of the material in this section is adapted from Susan Dickey's NYU dissertation, supervised by the second author [141].) Network bandwidth and latency are strongly affected by the speed of the switches, the capacity of the channels, and the number of hops a message must take. Also important is the switching strategy used. In *circuit switching*, a circuit is first established from the source all the way to the destination, after which a contention-free, low-latency transmission takes place, and the circuit is released. With *store-and-forward switching*, the message travels one link at a time. It is sent first to a neighbor of the source, where it is buffered in its entirety and then retransmitted. Since circuit switching does not use buffering and holds links while circuits are being set up, system bandwidth is reduced. For example, an unbuffered omega network with N inputs can have bandwidth at most $N/\log N$ rather than N in this case. However, the minimum latency for circuit switching is the sum of the message length and the number of hops (i.e., the message is pipelined), whereas for store-and-forward the minimum latency is the product. *Cut-through* strategies, including *wormhole routing*, combine some of the advantages of circuit and store-and-forward switching.

Circuit switching is most appropriate when the setup time is small compared to the transmission time, that is, when the circuit will be used for a prolonged period. Once setup is complete, the message is pipelined across the circuit and all the links involved are active simultaneously. The standard example is telephone switching.

Store-and-forward switching, commonly used in long-haul computer communications, gains the bandwidth advantages of buffering and holding links only when in use, but gives up the latency advantage of pipelining. Why not add pipelining? Before answering that question, we discuss a matter of (unfortunately confusing and inconsistent) terminology involving message and packet switching.

Several researchers, the authors included, have used the term *packet switching* to mean simply that circuits were not set up in advance of transmission; pipelining might or might not be implemented. However, packet switching (and the related term *message switching*) have also been used to imply store-and-forward, for example by Kleinrock [283]. The distinction between packet and message switching is that in the former there is a higher-level protocol that breaks up messages into packets at the source and reassembles them at the destination.

Returning to our main discussion, one can indeed add pipelining to a buffered network that holds links only when in use. Kermani and Kleinrock [277] have coined the term *cut-through* switching for a strategy in which a message is broken into parcels that, in the absence of contention, are then pipelined through the network (a header is only added to the first parcel, so we do not use the term *packet*). In their terminology, when (the head of) a message arrives at a switch and the desired link is free, the message can "cut through" and begin transmission immediately. Only if the message is blocked during transmission is it buffered at an intermediate switch. As in circuit switching, all the links on the path from the source to the destination can be active simultaneously, but in contrast to circuit switching, there is no setup time, buffering is possible, and links are released as soon as the last parcel passes through.

What happens if the desired link is busy when the message begins to arrive but becomes free before all the message is present? One possibility is to buffer the entire message; another is to start sending as soon as possible. Kermani and Kleinrock refer to the latter as a *partial cut*, which has given rise to the terminology *partial cut-through* for systems permitting partial cuts and *full cut-through* for systems that do not. The reader should be careful, since partial cut-through requires greater hardware capability and offers better performance. Although it is at first surprising that "part" is superior to "full", it is somewhat akin to a memory system that supports partial word writes.

Dally and Seitz [116] use the term *wormhole routing* to describe a variant of cut-through with only minimal buffering. Instead of providing enough buffer space for an entire message, the switch-to-switch flow control permits stopping reception in the middle of a message. This leads to interesting deadlock issues, which are addressed successfully both in their paper and their "torus routing chip". We now turn our attention to some specific switching networks.

8.2.2 Crossbars and Buses

The first switching network shown in the diagram on page 394 is the crossbar, in which each node is equipped not with N but with two connections, leading to a central switch that has a constant delay corresponding to one logic gate independent of the number of nodes. (A crossbar is a grid of logic gates; adding more PEs increases the capacitive loading, but the switch delay is increased only slightly as long as packaging boundaries aren't exceeded, e.g., an intraboard connection becomes an interboard connection.) The delay grows a little with N and access is provided to any other *nonbusy* node rather than to *any* node as before, but otherwise life is the same as with an all-to-all network. The third drawing down on page 394 shows the inside of the switch in a schematic way. The intersections each represent a logic gate.

So far we have been talking as if all the nodes in the network were processing elements. Often, half of them are memory modules, and we want each processor to have equal access to each memory module, as in a shared-memory computational model. The fourth drawing down on page 394 shows a modified crossbar connection for this situation.

The problem with crossbar networks is that, although the wire cost now scales as N, the switch cost still adds an N^2 cost component. This problem is alleviated in the multistage switching network (second from the bottom), but at the cost of added latency, and is further alleviated in the bus network drawn at the bottom of page 394, but now at the additional cost of a bandwidth per processor that is inversely proportional to the number of processors on the bus. Multistage networks are discussed in the next section. We now offer a few words on buses.

Buses are simple in concept, well understood, and readily assembled from existing technology [150]; but the very simplicity of the bus concept also limits its scope for future development. The bandwidth of a bus is simply the product of its clocking frequency and the width of the data path, and this product must be matched to the total processing power of the attached processors. The Concurrent Computer Corporation, for example, marketed a design consisting of six processors, each with roughly 6 MIPS of processing power and connected with a 64 MB/sec bus, which left some margin of capacity. Sequent Computer Systems, by contrast, markets a design consisting of thirty processors, each with roughly 20 MIPS of processing power and still connected with a 64 MB/sec bus. Large caches are used to keep the processors' bus utilization low. Bus widths over 128 bits are rare, and the only other way to raise bandwidth is by increasing the clocking frequency. But the same technological advances that make higher bus clock rates possible will also make faster processors possible, so the ratio between processor power and bus bandwidth is likely to remain roughly the same, and the number of processors that can be supported on a single bus will remain limited.

8.2.3 Multistage Switching Networks

The omega network (Figure 8.7 on page 399) provides a convenient starting point for discussing a class of switching networks with characteristics in between those of a crossbar and a bus interconnection scheme. The omega network is a member of a large group of networks based on the shuffle and exchange permutations. This group includes the banyan, baseline, Benes butterfly, delta, and many others [195], [60], [356], [164], [91]. Many of these networks have been shown to be topologically equivalent [462] and we shall here lump them all under the name *multistage shuffle-exchange networks*, for want of a universally accepted name.

All these networks are slightly different, but they are all collections of 2×2 or slightly larger crossbar switch elements arranged in an array whose dimensions are close to N by $\log_2 N$. They are all attempts to approximate the connectivity and throughput of a crossbar while reducing its cost-scaling factor from N^2 to $N \log_2 N$, at the price of an increase in the network latency on the order of $\log_2 N$. That is, the processors are still equidistant from each other in communication terms (unlike the static topologies of Figure 8.1), but that distance is roughly $\log_2 N$ times greater than in a crossbar net. Their designs differ primarily in the exact connection topology, operation mode, control strategy, and nature of the switch boxes.

All of these networks are capable of connecting any *single* input terminal to any output terminal. However, they differ in how many different *all-to-all* connection patterns (how many permutations) they can achieve, and also in the extra functions, such as message combining, that they may be designed to provide. Our treatment of this class of networks starts with the elegantly simple omega network. We discuss its advantages and its limitations, and then we show how adding hardware to improve its performance leads to some of the other multistage networks.

Omega Networks

The omega network is sort of a basic, no-frills, economy model. It provides exactly one unique connection path from every input to every output. This property has its advantages and disadvantages, as we shall see.

Figure 8.6   The four switch functions for an omega-net switch box: *straight-through, criss-cross, upper broadcast, lower broadcast.*

Figure 8.7   Omega network topology. *The switch boxes perform the functions shown in Figure 8.6. The distributed control scheme uses a simple, fast routing algorithm (Figure 8.8 on page 400) that makes this switch economical to use with short messages in a packet-switching network.*

The original omega network [311] embodied a set of design choices that we will now discuss. It consisted of 2×2 crossbar switches that could perform the four functions illustrated in Figure 8.6. The interconnection topology is shown in Figure 8.7 and consists of $\log_2 N$ columns each containing $N/2$ switch boxes interconnected in *perfect shuffle* wiring patterns, so called because of their analogy to the process whereby the top half of a deck of cards is perfectly interleaved with the bottom half.

The switching method chosen is packet switching. This method resembles the postal system, in that messages are sent through the network in the form of data plus an address that is read at each node; the packet is then forwarded to the next node according to some control scheme until it arrives at its destination. A circuit-switched network, on the other hand, is more like the telephone system, in that a direct connection is set up between origin and destination and maintained for the duration of message transferral. As might

Figure 8.8 *Message routing and blocking in an omega network.* *The routing algorithm used by the distributed control scheme is that each switch box peels off the leading bit of the address of the incoming message; if the bit is zero, the message is sent out the upper port of the switch; if the bit is 1, the message leaves via the lower port. The bold line traces the path of a message leaving processor #2 (binary 010) bound for memory module #6 (binary 110). The text explains how the message finds its way back. The algorithm can be this simple and fast because there is only one path from each input to each output. Note, however, that this property can also give rise to blocking of one message by another when both try to use the same wire, as shown by the bold and the dashed paths in this example.*

be expected, packet switching is more economical if the communication consists mostly of many short messages.

The omega network uses a *distributed* control scheme that takes advantage of a simple message-routing algorithm suitable for both SIMD (synchronous) operation, in which many different permutations have to be performed in a short time, and MIMD (asynchronous) operation, in which connection requests are issued dynamically. This routing algorithm (illustrated in Figure 8.8) allows the packet to steer its own way through the network.[207] The alternative is *centralized* control from a remote source. Such a control scheme may be designed to control individual switches, it may operate on a column-by-column basis, or it may reset the full network each time, depending on the scheme's complexity.[208]

---

[207] A clever way of getting back is described on page 580.
[208] This is like asking, Do all the traffic lights in the city turn green at the same time?

The omega network's sparseness and simplicity make the simple routing algorithm possible and keep the network small, cheap, and fast, but the price paid is a high probability of *blocking* among potential message paths. Put another way, there are many input-to-output permutations that the omega network cannot perform in one pass.[209] There are several ways to solve this problem. The Ultracomputer (page 572) and the RP3 (page 603), for example, both use omega networks, but the switch boxes not only perform the four simple functions illustrated in Figure 8.6 but also combine messages bound for the same address as one way to reduce blocking and improve network bandwidth. Naturally, this capability requires more hardware. The GF11 (page 436) uses a nonblocking Benes again at the cost of additional hardware. We shall discuss both of these approaches in this chapter.

Benes Networks

The omega network is called a *blocking* network because there are certain combinations of input-output connections that it cannot achieve because one path blocks another. An example of this was shown in Figure 8.8 on page 400. A crossbar is a *nonblocking* network because it can achieve any input-output connection pattern (permutation). However, it is much more expensive than an omega network. The Benes described in this section belongs to an intermediate category called *rearrangeable* nonblocking networks. Unlike the omega, these have multiple ways to "get from here to there" and can achieve all the permutations of a true nonblocking network like the crossbar, but only if *all* the desired connections are specified before the routing computation begins. That is, with a crossbar, one can make the connections in any arbitrary time sequence, but if one tries this with a rearrangeable network, one is most likely to reach a point at which the network in effect says, "Oh, if I had known you wanted *that* connection, I would have routed some of the previous connections differently!" It can make the desired connection but may have to *rearrange* some of the previous ones to do it.

As can be seen by comparing Figure 8.9 on page 403 with Figure 8.7 on page 399, the Benes network can be thought of as an omega net that has had extra hardware added to it and now has many possible paths from each input to each output, instead of just one. As can be seen, the Benes net has no trouble making the pair of connections that was not possible with the omega net, and readers should be able to find many other noninterfering paths besides the two shown in Figure 8.9.

---

[209]   Three passes through an omega network have been proved sufficient for any permutation. The two-pass case remains unproved.

There is, however, a price for this reduced blocking and increased bandwidth. The additional stages increase the size, cost, and latency of the network. In addition, the permutation pattern takes a while to calculate. For this reason, Benes networks are appropriate for circuit-switched, SIMD designs. The GF11 (page 436) uses a Benes network of 24×24 crossbars to interconnect 576 processing elements.

Banyan Networks

The number of inputs and outputs of the switch boxes need not always be equal. Figure 8.9 on page 403 shows an SW-banyan network used to connect four processors to nine memory modules. What's in a name? Banyans are trees, and in a sense, multistage networks (including banyans) give each input node its own tree connection (sideways now) to all the output nodes, although the trees are interlinked and not independent. The *SW* sounds sporty, although ostensibly it is there to distinguish these SWitching banyans from the more obscure *CC* (crosshatched cylinder) banyans.

In the topological sense, an omega network is actually a special case of a banyan network (see the exercises at the end of this chapter). The existence of a single unique path from each input to each output is true for banyans, too. The TRAC project (page 635) uses a circuit-switched banyan network like the one in Figure 8.9 to *partition* the resources of the overall parallel machine into several concurrently running subsystems, each with resources matched to its task.

8.2.4   *Single-Stage (Recirculating) Switching Networks*

The omega network shown in Figure 8.7 is a multistage network ($\log_2 N$ stages). Its function could also be performed by $\log_2 N$ passes through a single-stage shuffle network [417] equivalent to just one of the omega network's multiple stages. Such a network would be $\log_2 N$ times cheaper and would still have the same delay, or latency. However, the bandwidth is $\log_2 N$ times less for the single-stage network because it cannot be pipelined—all $\log_2 N$ passes must be completed for one wave of messages before the next wave can be accepted. A multistage network can accept a new wave each time the preceding wave moves on to the next stage.

Figure 8.9   *Benes network (left) and banyan network (right).* The banyan network shown here was used in the TRAC prototype (page 635). A Benes network much larger than the one shown here is used in GF11 (page 436).

8.2.5 Dynamic Meshes

Several new designs have employed a low-dimensional mesh with switching. The Intel Paragon, the Stanford Dash, and the MIT Alewife are 2-D meshes, and the J-Machine and Tera are 3-D meshes. All these designs consist of switches interconnected in a mesh topology with each switch having five inputs and five outputs for 2-D meshes, or seven inputs and seven outputs for 3-D meshes. That is, the switch connects the associated processor with its (four or six) nearest neighbors. On the J-machine a switch and its associated processor are integrated onto one chip! On the Tera, some links are missing so any node has only four nearest neighbors, and the mesh is "depopulated", as described in the next section.

Both the T-800 and T-9000 Transputer series include four I/O ports and the processor on one commercial chip. Not surprisingly, this has led to a number of 2-D mesh designs. Since these chips do not themselves route, a design consisting of just RAM, Transputers, and wires would exemplify a static network. However, router chips do exist for the T-9000 series, and their addition results in a dynamic network.

Depopulated Meshes

If one assumes that messages generated from a given node are equally likely to go to any other node (i.e., no locality), then meshes do not have enough wires and buffers, at least asympotically, to support a constant message rate as the mesh size grows: with no locality, messages must on average traverse (about) $\sqrt{N}$ links in a 2-D mesh with N nodes (we are, in the best spirit of asymptotic analysis, ignoring constants). Even without contention, this means that a given message is present for $\sqrt{N}$ cycles. If each processor issues messages at a constant rate independent of the size of the machine, there will be (again ignoring constants) $N\sqrt{N}$ messages in the network at any one time. But there are only N wires and buffers, so something has to give. Below are two solutions designed for machines of widely different size. (The analysis for 3-D meshes is similar.)

Burton Smith depopulates the (3-D) mesh in his Tera design (see page 571). That is, he builds a 3-D mesh of switches but connects processors (or memory modules) to only a subset of the switches, and the ratio of processors to switches is decreased with machine size, so big machines are more sparsely populated with processors than small ones.

The XILINX 4000 family of field-programmable gate arrays (FPGAs) is not often considered a line of parallel processors; but it could be. A 4000 contains, inside the chip, a 2-D array of CLBs (computational logic blocks, small general-purpose logic elements composed of a few dozen gates). The chip contains routing resources as well, and for the same reasons given above, XILINX includes more routing resources per CLB in larger members of the family. Once again, the processors become sparser as the system becomes larger.

8.2.6 Dynamic (Fat) Trees

As with meshes, one can add switches to each node of a static tree topology and get a dynamic tree. A well-known deficiency of trees is that nodes near the root get a disproportionate share of the network traffic. On the other hand, there are not so many nodes near the root so perhaps if we throw a little extra hardware their way, the entire network will improve. This idea, due to Charles Leiserson, has led to his development of fat trees, that is, trees that, like their biological namesakes, are thicker (i.e., have higher bandwidth) near the root. One way to do this would be to have wider datapaths higher in the tree; another way would be to clock them faster. On the CM-5, well known for its fat-tree data network (see page 509), the greater bandwidth is accomplished by replicating switches. Specifically, (non-root, non-leaf) switches in the CM-5 fat tree have four children and two or four parents. The cost and performance of the network can be adjusted by choosing whether to use two or four parents at each level of the tree. A simpler fat tree, one where intermediate switches

*Figure 8.10   A binary fat tree where all non-root switches have two parents.
If you view the ovals as nodes and view the edges between a pair of nodes as a
single edge, a tree appears. If, instead, you ignore the ovals and view the squares
as nodes, an omega network appears.*

all have two children and two parents, is shown in figure Figure 8.10 on page
405.

Fat trees have interesting theoretical properties. As made precise in
[315], a fat tree of a given size is nearly the best network possible of that size.

8.2.7   Added Features: Combining and Fault Tolerance

Combining of Requests in the Network

As we mentioned, an omega network has the advantage of a simple, fast
scheme for routing messages but the disadvantage of being a blocking network, which can lower the effective network bandwidth. The Benes network
removes the blocking, but at the cost of increased size and latency as well as a
more complex routing algorithm. An alternate way to increase the omega
network's bandwidth and still keep its simple routing algorithm is to keep its
topology but to increase the switch boxes' duties to include the combining of
messages bound for the same address. Combining can be especially significant if the network has non-uniform traffic in the form of "hot spots" [362]
corresponding, for example, to an address accessed significantly more frequently than the others, as might be the case with a the shared variable used in
a synchronization scheme like semaphores (page 155) or fetch-and-add (page
162), for instance. Simulations have shown [362] that relatively small amounts

Figure 8.11   *An omega network switch node able to combine messages.* *This is the Ultracomputer switch, further discussed on page 580. The simulations reported in Figure 8.12 used a slight variant of this design.*

of this effect can seriously degrade the latency of *all* paths through the network, not only the ones leading to the hot spot, unless provision is made to combine these competing messages in the network before they reach the hot spot.

Naturally, there is a hardware cost for combining, too. Figure 8.11 is a schematic drawing of an omega network switch node enhanced to support combining. Message combining works by detecting the occurrence of memory-request messages directed at identical memory locations as they pass through each switch node. Such messages are combined at the switch node into a single message. The fact that combining took place is recorded in a *wait buffer* in each switch node.

When the *reply* to a combined message reaches a node where it was combined, multiple replies are generated to satisfy the multiple requests. Since combined messages can themselves be combined, the generation of multiple replies has the effect of a dynamically generated broadcast of data to

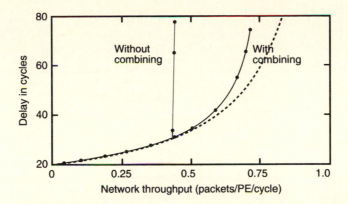

Figure 8.12 *Average memory latency with and without combining in a 64-input, 64-output buffered omega network with 2×2 switches for the case when 2% of the memory references are to a single memory location. The dashed curve is the prediction of a simple model for uniformly distributed network traffic. Message length is 4 packets, queue length is 4 messages, and wait buffer size is 6 messages. See [362] and page 600 for further details.*

multiple processors.[210] Combining can make dramatic improvements in the throughput (bandwidth) of a network with hot spots (see Figure 8.12 on page 407), but the hardware cost to implement should not be ignored and with some technologies and design methodologies can be significant. One early estimate [362] was that message combining would have increased the size and/or cost of the ECL switches in the RP3 by a factor of at least 6. More recently, the Ultracomputer project has implemented combining switches with a more modest cost: they increase the pin count by 50% and double the number of gates [63].

Another consequence affects technology choices. By now, the switch node has become complex enough that it starts to resemble a microprocessor itself. Thus, for a 1024-processor machine using a multistage interconnection network with 2×2 switches, the minimum (round-trip) memory-access delay is increased by 20 switch-cycle times. If both the switch and the PEs use the same technology, their cycle times may be comparable, so that the memory-access time is increased by nearly 20 times the PE cycle time. This increase is bad even if the average PE instruction takes a relatively large number of cycles,

---

[210] Note that this is somewhat analogous to car-pooling as a way of reducing vehicular traffic congestion.

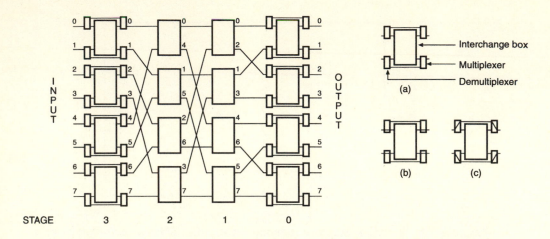

Figure 8.13 **The extra-stage cube network for fault tolerance.** *This network is formed from the indirect binary cube by adding an extra stage (left) along with a number of multiplexers and demultiplexers. Their details are shown at the right of the figure: (a) Detail of switch box with multiplexer and demultiplexer for enabling and disabling. (b) Switch box enabled. (c) Switch box disabled. PASM (page 636) uses such a switch.*

but it is especially bad if the PEs use a RISC-like architecture where the average instruction takes only a little more than a PE cycle. Then the memory-access time looms large compared to the time needed to execute an instruction. One way to partially alleviate this problem is to use a significantly faster technology for the network than for the processors. The RP3 (page 603), for example, uses bipolar technology for the switch to interconnect RISC-like microprocessors made with FET technology. It is possible that this is fairly fundamental and that a multistage interconnection network may always have to use a faster technology than the processing elements. However, even if very fast technology is used, it seems likely that non-local memory accesses will incur a latency equivalent to a significant number of processor cycles.

Fault Tolerance via Redundancy

Another consequence of the fact that there is only one path from each input to each output in the omega network is that the network is not fault tolerant at all. One broken wire, and it's in big trouble. The extra-stage cube network [3] shown in Figure 8.13 allows a second path to be taken for each connection when necessary. This is one of several similar ways to provide fault tolerance in such a network.

8.3   Exercises

1.   Define the following terms.

Mesh	Crossbar
Ring	Bus
Star	Omega network
Tree	Benes network
Hypercube	Banyan network
Cube-connected cycles	Recirculating network
Shuffle-exchange	

2.   Match each of the terms on the left with its attribute on the right:

a.	Bandwidth	1)	All sets of connections possible
b.	Blocking networks	2)	Centralized or distributed
c.	Control strategy	3)	Latency is packets plus stages
d.	Degree	4)	Latency is packets times stages
e.	Latency	5)	Maximum number of messages per second
f.	Non-blocking networks	6)	Message delay
g.	Operation modes	7)	New connection possible if change old connections
h.	Rearrangable networks	8)	Number of immediate neighbors
i.	Store & forward	9)	Packet or circuit
j.	Switching methods	10)	Some sets of connections not possible
k.	Topologies	11)	Static or dynamic
l.	Wormhole (cut-through)	12)	Synchronous or asynchronous

3.   What are the advantages and disadvantages of static vs. dynamic networks?

4.   Compare the requirements for a good highway system with those for a good interconnection network.

5.   With regard to part c of Figure 8.3 on page 387, consider the alternative of omitting the free node and instead supplying an external connection to each leaf. Why is Leiserson's method much better?

6.   Consider the shuffle-exchange static network with N nodes. Show that one can get from any node to any other by applying at most $2 \log(N)$ mappings, each of which is a shuffle σ or an exchange ϵ.

7. Would you think that the nationwide telephone network is blocking, non-blocking or rearrangable? Give evidence to support your claim.

8. Complete the table of network scaling factors on page 393 to include 3D-mesh, kD-mesh (for $k \geq 2$), shuffle-exchange, star, ring, k-ary tree (for $k \geq 2$).

9. What are the advantages and disadvantages of a crossbar vs. a multistage network? When is each appropriate?

10. Why was much of the early good work on networks done at Bell Laboratories?

11. a. In how many ways can N objects be permuted?
    b. How many permutations of its $N = 2^n$ inputs can be achieved with one pass through an omega network composed of 2x2 switches?
    c. For $n = 3$, what percentage of the possible permutations can be achieved?
    d. Repeat part c for $n = 4$ and for $n = 10$. What is the trend?

12. Show that, by using the broadcast function of its constituent switch boxes, an omega network can perform any multicast, i.e. a single input can be broadcast to any subset of outputs.

13. Read the 1962 paper by Benes and compare the costs and performance of Benes and omega networks.

14. How does combining messages in a network help to solve the hot-spot problem? Suggest alternative software-based solutions.

15. What additional issues arise if combining of messages is used in a network that has more than one path between a given input and output?

16. Describe circuit and packet switching. What are the pros and cons of each?

17. A network can be either circuit or packet switched and it can have either central or distributed control. Describe the four possible combinations.

18. Show that banyans and omega networks are topographically equivalent by replacing all the switches of Figure 8.9 on page 403 with 2-input, 2-output switches. Remove any wires and switches that have become superfluous and then consider moving some of the boxes and wires around.

412

SERIAL EXECUTION:

8 cycles per simple instruction,

9 average including complex instructions

OVERLAPPED INSTRUCTION FETCH:

4 cycles per simple instruction,

5 average including complex instructions

IDEAL OVERLAP (PIPELINING):

1 cycle per simple instruction ideally   etc.

2 cycles (approx.) with complex instructions ideally

3 actual (due to branching etc.)

Figure 9.1 *Cycles per instruction*:   Key for serial execution:

A1	1	Get address of next instruction
Fetch I1	2,3	Fetch that instruction from cache memory
D/A	4	Decode instruction, generate operand address
Fetch oprnd	5,6	Fetch operand from cache memory
E	7	Execute instruction on operand
PA	8	put result into register

8 cycles per simple instruction,
9 cycles average including complex instructions.

9

SIMD Parallel Architectures

As we explained previously, an SIMD computational model corresponds to a single stream of instructions, each of which is applied to multiple data items. We are mainly interested in fully parallel implementations, that is, in SIMD computers in which each instruction processes multiple data items *simultaneously* on separate hardware. These computers are the primary focus of this chapter. We study ILLIAC IV, GF11, and the Connection Machine in some detail and round out this discussion with briefer treatments of other processor arrays, including systolic ones. SIMD/MIMD trade-offs are discussed on page 442. We precede the treatment of parallel SIMD with two related topics, for reasons explained below.

The SIMD computational model has also been implemented using pipelining, an engineering technique that trades off performance for lower cost by executing the data items for each instruction in *overlapped* fashion on shared hardware, rather than in fully parallel fashion on fully replicated hardware. Although pipelining of vector instructions yields less speedup than a fully parallel approach, it forms the basis of the current generation of supercomputers, and so we study them in a fair amount of detail as a perspective on the later discussion of parallel SIMD.

We begin this chapter with a very brief description of several ways in which the von Neumann computer, although still serial, has grown considerably more sophisticated than the simple model that we introduced on page 138.

9.1 Evolution from von Neumann Machines

Figure 9.1 on page 412 shows how the number of clock cycles required to perform an instruction on the simple von Neumann computer described on page 138 has improved over the years [365]. If the cache access time is assumed equal to two processor cycles,[211] a typical early embodiment requires eight cycles, as shown in the top part of the figure. By fetching the next instruction while the present one is still executing, and by improving the execution cycle, the cycles per instruction can be reduced to four to five, as shown in the middle part of Figure 9.1.

Further improvement is obtained by pipelining the instruction unit,[212] that is, allowing it to work on several instructions in different stages of completion at once, as illustrated in the bottom part of Figure 9.1. The well-studied IBM 3033, for example, typically achieves three cycles per instruction when all the needed information is in the cache. This number of cycles is still three times larger than the ideal one cycle/instruction that one might expect for simple instructions with this pipelining approach. The principal reasons for the difference are the following:

1. Complex instructions (floating-point operations, for example; see Figure 9.4 on page 419), which add roughly one cycle to the average execution time.
2. Branches in programs, which cause delays in fetching instructions. These and other delays keep the pipeline from being full all the time and add roughly another cycle.

---

[211] Loosely defined, a CPU cycle is the minimum time needed for a register-to-register operation. See page 110 for a more precise definition.

[212] Pipelining the *execution* unit is what is done for vector processors (see the next section).

Figure 9.2   *Basic vector processor block diagram.*   *The two leftmost boxes correspond to the von Neumann model of Figure 4.2 on page 139.*

9.2   Vector Processors

SIMD, vector, and *array processor* are often regarded as synonymous terms. However, they have also grown to have more restrictive and distinct meanings to many people. A historical perspective may help explain.

Broadly speaking, vectors are one-dimensional arrays (or arrays are multidimensional vectors), and so vector and array processors are the same. A broad definition of a vector processor is that it contains special hardware (Figure 9.2) that allows a sequence of identical operations on data arranged in a regular array to be performed faster than a sequence of nonidentical operations. An SIMD architecture means that a *S*ingle *I*nstruction causes the execution of identical operations on *M*ultiple pairs of *D*ata (presumably in less time than that needed for an equal number of non-identical operations). So *SIMD, vector,* and *array processor* are synonymous when looked at in   way. However, these terms are often used with narrower meanings. For example, people also take *vector processor* to mean specifically a pipelined machine designed to do well on floating-point operations. A brief history helps to clarify this situation.

Detailed books and papers on vector processing [239], [288], and [78] are available to the interested reader, and so the following treatment will concentrate on the essentials. The idea originated with the observation that scientific and engineering programs like the weather code discussed on page 48 frequently contain long sequences of floating-point operations. A simple example is the multiplication of two 100-element vectors. The code to accomplish this multiplication in serial Fortran would be something like

```
      DO 10 I=1,100
10       A(I)=B(I)*C(I)
```

that is, a loop equivalent to a string of 100 consecutive statements each causing a multiply operation. In Fortran 90, the code would look something like

$$A(1:100)=B(1:100)*C(1:100)$$

more nearly with the power of an APL statement.

What happens at the machine-language level of an ordinary sequential computer is that, in addition to fetching 100 pairs of operands, the multiply *instruction* is also fetched and decoded 100 times. Instruction prefetching and pipelining can remove this overhead and reduce the total execution time to the sum of the individual execution times, but unlike the simple instructions shown in Figure 9.1, floating-point operations take multiple machine cycles to execute (like six for addition), and so a procedure in which each pair of vector elements must be completely processed before execution of the next pair begins still takes a long time.

In a vector processor, this repeated fetching and decoding of the instruction for each pair of vector elements is replaced by a single *vector instruction* decreeing that the same arithmetic (or logic) operation be performed on all the corresponding pairs of elements of two vectors. Thus, one vector instruction causes a large number of floating-point operations (100 in this case).[213] However, this process in itself does not give higher speed than the highly pipelined scalar machine of Figure 9.1. The speedup comes from the concurrency that the vector processor allows, that is, the extent to which it allows an operation on a pair of vector elements to start before the operation on the previous pair is finished. For the simple example shown above, the 100 multiplications are completely independent and can be done in any order—pipelined, parallel, backwards, mixed—as long as the results are eventually put in the proper order at their final destination, for example in a register being used for the output.[214]

Conceptually, these 100 multiplications could be sent off to 100 complete replicas of the original scalar execution unit, and in the ILLIAC IV discussed, on page 430, this is close to what happens. However, this implementation is expensive in hardware, especially for the times when vector processors were first developed, and inefficient in hardware usage because the different stages

---

[213] This result is why vector processor performance is measured in MFLOPS (Millions of FLoating-point Operations per Second) rather than MIPS (the instruction rate).

[214] Most loops found in real programs, like the weather code on page 48, do have some dependencies among their component computations (also called *hazards* in pipeline scheduling). Thus, either the user or the compiler must do the kind of dependency analysis described on page 309 in order to establish the allowed scheduling.

of a floating-point operation tend to use different circuits, and hence at any one time only a small fraction of the circuits would be active. Pipelining was a cost-saving engineering compromise (Figure 9.3 on page 418). Extra circuits were added to the execution unit to allow the different stages of a floating-point operation to function independently, and arrangements were made so that the floating-point operations could be fed in and processed in a staggered or overlapped fashion, as shown in Figure 9.4 on page 419. After the initial overhead of setting up the pipe and filling it, the floating-point operations are completed at a rate of one per cycle. The total execution time is longer than that of a completely parallel processor, but the hardware cost is less. For very long vectors, the speedup over a scalar process approaches a factor equal to the number of pipeline stages (the degree of overlap) (see Figure 9.5 on page 420).

9.2.1 Vector Processor Performance

Some of the key aspects of vector processor performance can be understood from a simple analytical model. The treatment here is based on work by Hockney and Jesshope [239].

In the "ideal overlap" scalar case depicted in Figure 9.1 on page 412, in which instruction prefetching and pipelining have made it possible to execute one instruction per cycle, the time needed to perform a vector operation may be written

$$T_{serial} = (s + nl)\tau$$

where s is the (loop) setup time, l is the number of suboperations performed on each pair of vector elements, τ is the CPU clock or cycle time, and n is the vector length. After the loop is set up, it takes a time $t = l\tau$ to execute an operation on each pair of vector elements. The value of l depends on the operation being performed. If the code is not written in assembly language but in a higher-level language such as Fortran, then the startup time depends on the compiler. It is usually still quite small in the serial case, however, and the average execution time per element $\bar{t}_{serial}$, defined as $\dfrac{T_{serial}}{n}$, is approximately $l\tau$ even for rather short vectors, that is,

$$\bar{t}_{serial} = \frac{T_{serial}}{n} \rightarrow l\tau \qquad (9.1)$$

(a) True SIMD or vector computer

(b) Pipelined SIMD

AU - Arithmetic/ logic unit
CPU - Central processing unit
M - Memory module

Arithmetic/ logic
pipeline

1 2 3 4 5 6

1. Vector register readout
2. Compare exponents
3. Shift
4. Add
5. Normalize
6. Vector register write

Figure 9.3 *Comparison of pipelined and parallel vector processors.* Two different implementations are shown of the extra vector memory and arithmetic units of Figure 9.2 on page 415. (Adapted from [291]).

as is shown in Figure 9.5. (Note that we use $\bar{t}$ where Hockney and Jesshope use t.)

The time required for pipelined execution of a vector is

$$T_{pipe} = (s + l)\tau + (n - 1)\tau$$

where the first term is the time to start and fill the pipe and produce the first result, and the second term is the time to produce the remaining $(n - 1)$ results. For long vectors $(n \to \infty)$, the average execution time per pair of vector elements approaches τ; that is,

$$\bar{t}_{pipe} = \frac{T_{pipe}}{n} \to \tau \text{ as } n \to \infty \tag{9.2}$$

The speedup over the scalar case, namely $\bar{t}_{scalar} / \bar{t}_{pipe}$, therefore approaches l, the number of pipeline stages (see Figure 9.5).

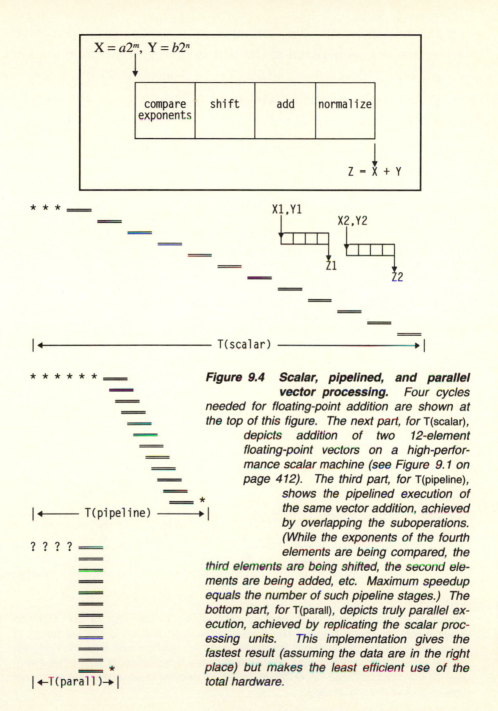

Figure 9.4　Scalar, pipelined, and parallel vector processing.　*Four cycles needed for floating-point addition are shown at the top of this figure. The next part, for T(scalar), depicts addition of two 12-element floating-point vectors on a high-performance scalar machine (see Figure 9.1 on page 412). The third part, for T(pipeline), shows the pipelined execution of the same vector addition, achieved by overlapping the suboperations. (While the exponents of the fourth elements are being compared, the third elements are being shifted, the second elements are being added, etc. Maximum speedup equals the number of such pipeline stages.) The bottom part, for T(parall), depicts truly parallel execution, achieved by replicating the scalar processing units. This implementation gives the fastest result (assuming the data are in the right place) but makes the least efficient use of the total hardware.*

If a parallel rather than pipelined approach is being used to perform the vector operations, as depicted at the bottom of Figure 9.4, then the same amount of time is needed for 1 and for n vector elements, as long as n does not exceed P, the number of processing elements. Thus, the vector execution time in the parallel case is

$$T_{parallel} = \lceil \frac{n}{P} \rceil (s + l)\tau$$

where $\lceil \rceil$ is the ceiling function defined on page 193, so that $\lceil 1 \rceil = 1$, $\lceil 1.01 \rceil = 2$, and so on. Once again, the average execution time per vector element is T/n, and for $n < P$, the expression becomes

$$\bar{t}_{parallel} = \frac{1}{n}(s + l)\tau \tag{9.3}$$

Figure 9.5 *Serial, pipelined, and parallel vector processing times (left) and rates (right) vs. vector length. The pipelined result on the left is representative of register-to-register operations in assembly code for vectors with less than 64 elements on a CRAY-1 [239]. The parallel results are a hypothetical illustrative example. In the pipelined case, $n_{1/2}$ is the vector length needed to get half of the maximum speedup over the scalar case.*

The processing rate r (in megaflops, say) is just the inverse of $\bar{t}$ in each case and is shown vs. vector length in the right half of Figure 9.5, which illustrates the vector and parallel speedups $\bar{t}_{serial} / \bar{t}_{vector}$ and $\bar{t}_{serial} / \bar{t}_{parallel}$.

For more general examples, T_{pipe} may be more complex than equation (9.2), but its measured value still often has the same form as above; that is, it can be written as

$$T_{pipe} = T_0 + n\tau$$

which can be rewritten as

$$T_{pipe} = r_\infty^{-1}(n_{1/2} + n)$$

but T_0 and r_∞ should in general be considered as empirical, measured quantities. T_0 is the time to start and fill the pipe, while r_∞ is the asymptotic processing rate (MFLOPS) for very long vectors. The quantity $n_{1/2}$ is derived from these two measured quantities by $n_{1/2} = T_0 r_\infty$ or $n_{1/2} = T_0 / \bar{t}$; its usefulness is that it characterizes what *long vector* means to the processor at hand, and it can be thought of as the vector length needed to obtain half the ultimate speedup over scalar processing. Alternatively, $n_{1/2}$ can be thought of as the number of vector elements that could have been processed during the startup time. For the simple example above (register-register operations, assembly code, short vectors), these quantities are

$$T_0 = (s + l - 1)\tau, \qquad r_\infty = \tau^{-1}, \qquad n_{1/2} = (s + l - 1)$$

These numbers depend only on the machines involved; for example, $n_{1/2}$ is in the low teens for the CRAY-1, in the high 20s for the IBM 3090 Vector Facility, about 50 for the Cray X-MP, and about 100 for the CDC Cyber 205. The respective values of r_∞ are 80, 54, and 50 single-pipe MFLOPS. We must immediately note, however, that these are not the peak MFLOPS for the entire machine. Both the Cray and IBM machines can link pipes to perform two floating-point operations per cycle (multiply and add, for example), and the CDC machine can have up to four pipes running concurrently, so the respective entire-machine peak rates are 160, 108, and 200 MFLOPS, respectively.

We are immediately led to a second caution: peak MFLOPS are related to the time needed for an entire job in the same way that the rate at which a master carpenter can drive nails is related to the time needed to build a house. One can imagine the frenetic scheduling and flow of material needed to keep the hammering going uninterrupted. In much the same way, the peak MFLOPS rating is, as one knowledgeable wag put it, "a rate that the manufacturer guarantees will not be exceeded during your job". The differences between job, loop, and peak MFLOPS are discussed in the paper by Clark and Wilson [78].

Figure 9.6 shows what happens when several real-world effects are introduced into the ideal example treated in Figure 9.5 on page 420: vector lengths greater than the register length or number of processing elements, Fortran rather than assembly code, and memory-to-memory rather than register-to-register operations. The startup time T_0 now has a dependence on the quality of the compiler, while r_∞ is less than τ^{-1} because of the time taken to refill the registers from main memory after every 64 elements. For the simple dyadic vector multiplication shown, values of T_0 near 1 microsecond and $r_\infty = 22$ MFLOPS were measured on the CRAY-1, yielding $n_{1/2} = 18$ floating-point operations (FLOPS). The value of r_∞ is degraded to 28% of its peak value of 80 MFLOPS by the finite register length, but even more by the fact that the CRAY-1 allows only one memory read or write per cycle; the second read can be chained with the multiply operation, but slightly more than three cycles are required per pair of elements [239], and credit for only one floating-point operation is obtained.

The Cray X-MP has two more memory ports than the CRAY-1, which allows chaining the two reads, the multiply, and the write, so that r_∞ is 70 MFLOPS or 74% of the peak MFLOPS. But since the startup time T_0 has not

Figure 9.6 *Influence of real-world effects on vector processing rate. The pipeline curve corresponds to measurements [238] on one CPU of a Cray X-MP (9.5 nsec clock cycle, 64-element registers) of memory-to-memory operations coded in FORTRAN. The parallel curve is for a hypothetical machine with 64 processing elements, for comparison purposes.*

changed significantly between the two machines, $n_{1/2}$ increases to 53 FLOPS, or, to put it another way, 500-element vectors are now needed to obtain 90% of r_∞.

For the reader interested in more performance numbers and comparisons among a range of commercial vector supercomputers, minisupercomputers, superminicomputers, and workstations, the paper by Dongarra, Martin, and Worlton [149] contains a nice compendium of such data.

9.3 Pipelined SIMD Vector Processors

9.3.1 CRAY Series

Overall, the CRAY-1 architecture (Figure 9.7 on page 424) comprises a main memory feeding data to and from a set of scalar and vector registers [239]. The instruction processor performs all instruction decoding and system control and holds all scalar registers. The arithmetic and logic are performed by 12 independent functional units working to and from the registers. All functional units are pipelined and may operate concurrently. Six are used strictly by the instruction processor for address calculation, scalar integer addition, logical and shifting operations, and so on. [288]. Three are used strictly for vector operations on integer or logical data. The other three perform floating-point operations for both vector and scalar instructions. Their pipeline stage lengths vary from 2 to 14. Clock time for all stages is 12.5 nanoseconds. Startup time for a register-register vector operation is three clock times. Thus, $n_{1/2}$ for register-register multiplication is a very short nine clock times.

The CRAY-1 memory-register data path may be visualized as an 11-stage pipeline, 64 bits wide, transferring data in one direction at a time. This relatively low memory bandwidth becomes a bottleneck in such operations as a memory-to-memory multiply, which requires two memory reads and a memory write to support each floating-point vector multiplication. This machine is designed on the basis that many of the arithmetic operations will be performed on data resident in the registers. Careful assembly language coding can usually achieve this result, but performance from (compiled) FORTRAN code is often less than hoped for due to this relatively low main memory bandwidth. The newer Cray Y-MP C90 features four memory ports that each deliver 128 bits per processor cycle, which itself decreased to 4 nanoseconds.

Figure 9.7 CRAY-1 processor architecture showing the 12 independent functional units and the number of pipeline stages in each. (Memory in the CRAY-2 can have up to 256 million 64-bit words.)

The 120 instructions (7-bit opcode) provide the logical, shift, branch, and arithmetic scalar and vector operations that one would expect from the nature of the 12 functional units. Most are three-address instructions. Since 3 bits suffice to address the eight registers, the opcode, plus the three addresses, just fits in a 16-bit "parcel" for most instructions; the rest need two parcels, or 32 bits.

The CRAY-1 has no specific instructions for the reduction operations (such as summing all the elements of a vector) that are important in many scientific programs. However, the design permits almost any vector instruction to be converted into a reduction operation by specifying that one of the input vector registers be the same as the one that receives the result [288].

"Chaining" of vector instructions is another useful feature, achieved by allowing the same register to serve as the output for one vector operation and the input for another. If the two vector operations use two separate functional units, then the second operation can start as soon as the first result from the first operation leaves *its* functional unit, rather than waiting for *all* results of the first operation before beginning the second. This optimization is equivalent to gluing two pipelines into one longer pipeline. Arithmetic as well as memory-register transfer operations can be chained. In practice, chaining four vector instructions is considered a noteworthy achievement.

Because of chaining, the peak processing rate of the CRAY-1 is listed as 160 MFLOPS (80 million additions and 80 million multiplications per second, done strictly among registers). However, this rate drops to 27 MFLOPS (80/3) or less for memory-to-memory vector multiplication[215][239] . The first reason for this drop is that only one floating-point operation is being performed, which cuts the potential top rate to 80 MFLOPS. The second reason (shown pictorially by Hockney and Jesshope [239]) is as follows. Two memory reads and one memory write are needed to support each vector operation. Because of the memory bandwidth limitation discussed above, however, only one memory-register transfer is allowed per cycle, and only one of the three memory operations can be chained with the multiplication, which means that three clock cycles are needed for each additional floating-point operation once the pipeline is set up and running. This would result in a peak rate of 27 MFLOPS (80/3) for long vectors, were it not for the fact that the vector registers need to be reloaded after every 64 vector elements, thus introducing an additional delay. The measured value of r_∞ is 22 MFLOPS.

An examination of the code generated by the compiler in this case shows that, while the code within the loop cannot be improved on, the loop setup (counters, etc.) can be reduced from about 46 to 15 clock periods by coding in assembly language instead of Fortran. This coding reduces $n_{1/2}$ from 18 to 10 for a memory-to-memory floating-point vector multiply.

On the Cray X-MP, two extra ports are added to the main memory, which allows three concurrent memory-register transfers and allows all three memory operations to be chained with the multiply. With a cycle time of 9.5 nanoseconds, r_∞ for memory-to-memory vector floating-point multiplication increases to 70 MFLOPS using Fortran [238]. Because the startup time remains approximately unchanged, however, $n_{1/2}$ increases to 53 FLOPS, meaning that vector lengths over 500 are needed to come within 90% of this 70 MFLOPS rate. In this regard, the CRAY X-MP becomes more like the Cyber 205 in the programmer's eyes.

The above results are all for one CPU of the Cray X-MP, which can be configured with up to four CPUs. The nature of the much larger-grained parallelism *among* these CPUs is taken up later in our discussion of multiprocessors. Performance results for the 16-processor Cray Y-MP C90 are listed on page 379.

---

[215] Clark and Wilson [78] would call this "LOOP_MFLOPS".

Figure 9.8 *Vector processor of the CDC Cyber 205* with up to four identical *general-purpose floating-point arithmetic pipelines. (Adapted from Levine [320].)*

9.3.2 CDC Cyber 205

The vector processor of the CDC Cyber 205 (Figure 9.8) has up to four identical general-purpose floating-point arithmetic pipelines. Each can add, multiply, divide, and take square roots, but at any given time all of them are performing the same operation on different pairs of elements in one vector operation. The clock period is 20 nanoseconds, yielding a peak of 200 MFLOPS for four pipes. The vector-stream unit manages the traffic between the four pipes and the central memory. Since central memory serves as both the source of vector operands and the destination of the results (i.e., there are no registers), the total vector pipeline is long, and startup overhead is large. Typical values of $n_{1/2}$ are in the 100 range. But since the transfer rate to central memory is much higher than the CRAY-1's (800 million words per second vs. 80), CYBER 205 outpaces CRAY-1 when vector length exceeds a certain value [320].

The ETA-10, a multiprocessor successor to the Cyber 205, was for a time the fastest computer on the 100×100 Linpack benchmark. Up to eight 205-like processors could share up to 8 GBytes of memory. This was the culmination of the line of memory-to-memory vector supercomputers that began with the CDC STAR-100.

9.3.3   IBM 3090 and ES/9000 Vector Facility

Vector processors are available in two forms. One is a separately programmed special-purpose unit that attaches to standard commercial computers as a peripheral device (Floating Point Systems FPS 164, IBM 3838). The other is integrated into a supercomputer design, as in the Cray Research or CDC Cyber series. The IBM Vector Facility [78], [193] combines aspects of both types. It is integrated, in that the 171 new vector instructions[216] can appear directly in the S/370 or S/390 instruction stream. It is separate, in that it is implemented using a set of vector registers and a pipelined arithmetic unit (Figure 9.9 on page 428) on a separate board. We describe the 3090 Vector Facility first.

The 16 vector registers, each with 128 elements of 32 bits each, can be coupled to form 8 registers instead, each with 128 64-bit elements, for double-precision floating-point computations. The interleaving and organization of the vector registers allows two elements to be read out and one element to be written in on every cycle.

The multiplier is a particularly simple example of the trade-off that pipelining costs in extra hardware. It consists of three scalar multipliers, each capable of producing a product three cycles after receiving the input, ganged together in interleaved fashion. The multiplier can be combined with the pipelined ALU to form one long pipeline that allows both a multiply and an add (the basic operations of matrix multiplication, for example) to proceed at a one-cycle rate. (This combining of functional units is similar to the chaining allowed among the functional units of the CRAY-1.)

The delivery rate of operands from the memory system is a key factor in the performance of any vector processor. The IBM Vector Facility is integrated into the 3090 or ES/9000 machine design and is thus a *cache-based* structure. This memory policy leads to some special design considerations and optimizations aimed at providing a stream of double words (64 bits) to the Vector Facility at a rate close to one per cycle. On a cache miss, for instance, the Vector Facility must ordinarily wait for an entire cache line (1024 bits, say) to be transferred from memory to cache. However, for stride-one vectors (with elements stored contiguously in memory), the double words are passed on to the Vector Facility at the same time they are being put into cache. Naturally, this influences the storage plan of the compiler. More details may be found in

---

216 The instruction set consists of eight basic arithmetic and Boolean operators, three array-arithmetic compound operations, and four that operate on vectors to produce scalar results. The total swells to 171 as each operation is replicated several times for different operand types and instruction formats.

Figure 9.9 Data flow in the IBM 3090 Vector Facility.

the cited references. The TCM technology that is used is shown in Figure 3.11 on page 111.

In the ES/9000 Vector Facility, the 16 registers are organized into two even/odd sets that are each associated with an ALU and a multiplier, so that a peak of four floating-point operations per cycle is possible. One measure of performance is shown in the table on page 379: an eight-processor ES/9000-982VF with a clock cycle of 7 nanoseconds achieved a performance of 2.28 GFLOPS and a speedup of 5.4 on the Linpack benchmark for a matrix size of 1000.

9.3.4 The NEC SX System

The SX system [454] [340] is a heterogeneous multiprocessor with a single control processor (based on NEC's ACOS mainframe computer) and multiple high-speed vector arithmetic processors. In early models, all operating system functions were executed on the control processor but later models shifted much of this software to the arithmetic processors so that now the former is used mostly for I/O. During execution, the control processor services I/O requests while computation proceeds on the arithmetic processors. In addition, user programs executing on the control and arithmetic processors can call each other. The operating system is a Unix derivative.

The most powerful model in the SX series, the SX-3/44 achieves 20 GFLOPS on Dongarra's TFP benchmark. An SX-3/xy consists of x arithmetic processors each with y pipeline sets. A pipeline set contains 4 vector pipelines so the largest system, an SX-3/44, contains 64 pipelines and, with a clock rate of 2.9ns, has a peak performance of 64/2.9=22 GFLOPS.

Each processor in an SX-3 contains up to 144 KB of vector registers, a 4-KB instruction buffer with branch history, and a 64-KB cache. The SX system contains up to 2 GB of central memory interleaved across 1024 memory banks and 16 GB of extended memory used as a RAM disk. The scalar architecture is a RISC design that also operates on a 2.9-nanosecond clock.

The arithmetic processor is designed to execute Fortran programs compiled by the SX's vectorizing Fortran compiler. By using vector mask registers, certain Fortran DO loops containing IF statements can be executed in vector mode.[217] Gather/scatter operations are provided to permit vectorization of expressions like A(IDX(I)). In addition special instructions permit recurrences like

$$A(I) = B(I) + A(I-1) * C(I)$$

to be executed faster than for strictly scalar operations.

9.3.5   Comparison of Pipelined Vector Processors

The table below entitled "Early Vector Processors" compares several of the earliest pipelined vector processors.

9.4   Parallel SIMD Designs

Our treatment of parallel SIMD computers begins with three fairly detailed case studies that we then draw upon to discuss other such designs. The three case studies are the ILLIAC IV, the GF11, and the Connection Machine. If we were proceeding chronologically, we would swap the last two; this would also correspond to the increasing degree of connectivity—ILLIAC IV was mesh-connected, the Connection Machine is cube- (and mesh-) connected, and GF11 is fully connected (by a Benes network). However, ILLIAC IV and GF11

---

[217] As an example, the hypothetical vector instruction "VR1 = VR2 + VR3 using MR" , where the VRs are vector registers and MR is a (Boolean) mask register, updates VR1(i) only if MR(i) is TRUE.

Early Vector Processors				
Name	Memory Hierarchy	Memory Bandwidth (64-bit words per cycle)	CPU Clock Cycle (nanosec)	Minimum Pipeline Delay (cycles)
Cray-1, X-MP	memory: 4 cycle, 8MB registers: 1 cycle, 4KB	1 (Cray-1) 3 (Cray X-MP)	12.5 (Cray-1) 9.5 (Cray X-MP) 4 (GaAs)	11
CDC Cyber 205	memory: 4 cycle, 8-32MB	8	20	about 50
IBM 3090 Vector Facility	memory: 11 cycle, 16+MB cache: 2 cycle, 64KB registers: 1 cycle, 8KB	3	18.5	27
Floating Point Systems FPS-164	main memory: 2-3 cycle, 8MB table memory: 1 cycle, 0.5MB registers: 1 cycle, 0.5KB program memory: 0.3 cycle, 32KB		167	2-3
NEC SX	memory: 12 cycle 256MB cache: 2 cycle 64KB instruc. buffer: 1 cycle 2KB registers: 1 cycle, 80KB	8	6	9-13

are closer in that both are "number crunchers" designed to do well on floating-point computations, whereas the Connection Machine is a "symbol cruncher" designed primarily for data manipulation, and by treating GF11 while ILLIAC IV is still fresh in the reader's mind, we can profitably compare these two designs, including the difference made by 20 years of progress in technology. This latter order also places these machines in order of increasing number of processing elements—from 64 to 566 to 65,536. As different as these machines are, they also have interesting similarities reflecting their SIMD nature. We shall point these out.

9.4.1 UI ILLIAC IV

It is instructive that the original paper on ILLIAC IV hardware [50] had six coauthors, whereas the paper on software [299] had only one author. ILLIAC IV has been described as a hardware-first approach to parallel computing. It is also interesting that the one author whose name appeared on both papers, David Kuck, is now spearheading the CEDAR project (page 611), a software-first approach to parallel architecture that we shall describe later on, in Chapter 10.

ILLIAC IV was a pioneering project, and it offers many lessons that are still important 20 years later. The very readable personal memoir of Daniel Slotnick [402], the project's leader, is especially recommended. The two papers mentioned above are also worth reading, although some of the machine's final details were different, such as the memory technology. Another paper by Slotnick [401] contains good pictures of the machine, and Hord's book [244] gives an updated description of the entire project. More concise descriptions may be found in several sources, such as the book by Hayes [221].

ILLIAC IV was intended for applications involving matrices and partial differential equations like those found in the weather code discussed on page 39, in which the solution involves a function defined as a grid of points, and the value of the function at each point depends on the values of its neighbors.[218] This intention is reflected in the hardware structure, which is sketched in Figure 9.10 on page 432. Sixty-four processing units (PUs), each consisting of a processing element (PE) and a processor memory (PM), are driven by instructions from a common control unit. The supervisory system consists of an ordinary computer that handles most of the system software, such as compiling a user's program into instructions that are passed on to the control unit, which decodes the instructions and generates the corresponding control signals for all the PUs in the array. The control unit has random access to the information in all 64 PMs, but a PE has access only to its own PM. Thus, all 64 PEs execute a common instruction simultaneously, but each uses data from its

---

[218] Slotnick [401] gives a simple example for the parallel solution of the temperature distribution of a rectangular slab. The temperature distribution is discretized onto a set of 64 gridpoints, each assigned to a different PU. There follows a series of relaxations during each of which all the processors simply compute in parallel the average of their four neighbors' temperatures, after which each processor stores the number it obtained. This stored number is used in the next relaxation, and so on, until the steady-state temperatures at each gridpoint are reached. Since the temperature at the boundaries is fixed, the speedup is roughly the number of PUs assigned to interior gridpoints, namely 36. (Unfortunately, grids with other than 64 points do not work out quite so neatly.)

Figure 9.10   The structure of ILLIAC IV. *The left part of the figure shows the common data and control buses that link the 64 processing units (PUs) to the central control unit. The right part of the figure shows the additional direct data paths that connect each PU to four neighboring PUs, forming a two-dimensional array of processing units. This diagram does not convey the machine's huge size—the 64 PUs employed over a million logic gates (six million discrete components) and occupied a 32-foot long row of 16 racks in a room almost as large as a basketball court.*

own memory—a classical example of SIMD operation, that is, a single instruction stream controlling multiple data streams.[219] Superimposed on the control and data buses that link the PUs to the control unit is a second interconnection pattern that provides each PU with a direct data link to four neighbors, forming a rectangular array, as shown in Figure 9.10.

Each PE was originally designed to perform a 64-bit floating-point multiplication in 400 nanoseconds and addition in 240 nanoseconds at a CPU clock cycle of 40 nanoseconds. This clock cycle time had to be almost doubled by the time the hardware was delivered. The PE instruction set was similar to that of conventional machines, with two exceptions: a set of routing instructions allowed communication of data to four neighbors, and another allowed each PE to set its own (8-bit) mode register to enable or disable itself. This latter

---

[219] One visitor likened this to a Marine drill sergeant who yells "ADD!" instead of "Present arms!"

feature gave the PEs a modicum of local control beyond a purely SIMD model. For example, the program could cause the control unit to broadcast the instruction, "Set your mode register to the contents of your memory location X (which was previously loaded with 0 for those PEs that were to be turned off at this point)." The control unit could now issue a sequence of instructions to be performed only by those PEs whose mode value was still 1. Physically, each PE used 210 printed circuit boards (*cards* to some people) holding 20 DIP (dual in-line pin) chip packages (7 ECL logic gates/chip), plus resistors, and so on.

Each PM had a 240-nanosecond cycle time and stored 2048 64-bit words (four boards each holding 128 256-bit, 16-pin DIP chip packages), for a total primary memory of 8×10^6 bits. As we mentioned earlier (page 32), by today's standards this memory is very small for a computer with a peak processing power of 10^3 MFLOPS (10^{-3} MB/MFLOPS). The Cray-1 that eventually replaced ILLIAC-IV, for example, had only one-sixth of its theoretical peak processing rate but had at least eight times more memory.

However, the small size of ILLIAC IV's primary memory was at least partly compensated for by an impressive secondary storage system (mass memory). It consisted of a 10^9-bit head-per-track disk system in which 128 heads were accessed in parallel, giving a transfer rate (on a 1024-line bus) of 5×10^8 bits per second. Thus, the entire set of PMs could be loaded in 16 milliseconds after an average access time of 20 milliseconds. Since this access time is about 100,000 times longer than the access time of the primary memory, however, skillful programming and scheduling of both the disk and the PUs are required to obtain good sustained performance.

The designs of both the PEs and the PMs were quite aggressive with respect to the state of the art of their respective technologies, at the cost of considerable grief to the project in both cases. Each PE required about 10^4 high-speed (ECL) transistor circuits. The original machine layout assumed these circuits would come in 64-pin packages (20 gates/chip), but the final version had to be built using less aggressive and less space-efficient 16-pin packages (7 gates/chip). The physical layout had to be substantially redesigned, at the loss of considerable time; and furthermore, there was now not enough room for the original PMs. The magnetic thin film memories successfully built for this purpose had to be discarded and were eventually replaced by units using the just-developing semiconductor memory technology (256 bipolar memory cells/chip). Although much valuable technological ground was broken, these events were disastrous for ILLIAC IV's schedule and cost and were largely responsible for the fact that, although the architecture and hardware were designed for four control units and 256 PUs, only one-quarter of this configuration (as shown in Figure 9.10) was actually delivered. Slotnick [402] wrote afterwards, "My hindsight is clear—I should have used more comfortable technology.... By sacrificing a factor of roughly three in circuit speed,[220] it's possible that we could have built a more reliable multi-quadrant system in less time, for no more money, and with a comparable overall performance level." And, one might add, four times more memory, an important consideration in a machine that we already pointed out as having a very low ratio of memory to processing power by today's standards (see page 32).

Software was not ILLIAC IV's strongest point. The operating system was rudimentary [244], performing monitoring of I/O and loading of data into the PMs, but leaving management of the disk memory and other functions to the user. Three high-level languages designed to hide at least some features of the machine architecture were at least partly implemented:

1. GLYPNIR,[221] a block-oriented, ALGOL-like language augmented with 64-word superwords, or *swords*, and control statements like FOR ALL. It presented ILLIAC IV as a set of PEs operating simultaneously. Slotnick [402] writes that for ten years GLYPNIR was the only working ILLIAC IV higher-level language.

2. CFD (Computational Fluid Dynamics), a Fortran-like language written after ILLIAC IV was delivered to the NASA Ames Research Center. It required more knowledge of machine details than GLYPNIR. For example, the user had to know about the single control unit and the linear ordering of the PEs.

3. IVTRAN can be regarded as a Fortran compiler that attempts to isolate DO loops that can be done in parallel and generates code for ILLIAC IV (a forerunner to Parafrase, in other words; see page 314) or as a Fortran-based language with some parallel facilities. Unfortunately, the compiler was never completely debugged and was replaced by CFD after delivery to NASA.

All three of these languages are criticized for failing to abstract and hide enough of the machine's details. (A variation of APL, with its very high-level

---

[220] That is, by using slower but better established technologies for both the PEs (TTL transistor circuits) and PMs (magnetic core memories).

[221] In Norse mythology, GLYPNIR is a magic chain made of the noise of a cat's footfall, the beard of a woman, the roots of stones, the breath of fish, the sensibilities of bears, and the spittle of birds. The gods used it to bind the Fenris wolf that would otherwise devour the world.

capabilities for vector and array processing, was worked on but eventually abandoned because of the difficulties of implementing such a general and dynamic language efficiently on ILLIAC IV. These difficulties and a more recent solution were discussed on page 323.

What about performance? We warned you that this was a tricky question when we mentioned during our discussion of pipelined vector processors that care must be taken to distinguish peak vs. sustained processing rates, simple operations vs. substantial programs, high- vs. low-level languages, and so on. Hord [244] presents some benchmarks using simple, 64-bit, floating-point vector arithmetic operations that generally peak at about 40 MFLOPS for long vectors, well below the theoretical peak rate (500 MFLOPS with the eventual cycle time). Two hundred MIPS is also mentioned as having been achieved. However, these benchmarks are somewhat beside the point. ILLIAC IV was designed to be a marathoner, not a sprinter. Its very high disk-memory bandwidth gave it superior performance on problems too large to fit into the central memories of other computers. To quote Levine's 1982 summary [320], "The Cray-1, because of its short cycle time, is the fastest computer for problems dominated by scalar and short vector operations. The CYBER 205, because of its large central-processor-to-memory bandwidth, is the fastest for problems that can be programmed to include long vectors. ILLIAC IV, because of its large-bandwidth link to secondary storage, was faster than any model of the Cray or CYBER yet delivered for problems with the largest database". (See page 39 ff. for an example of such a problem.)

ILLIAC IV wound up with 64 processors, only one-fourth of the original design, at a cost of $31 million, four times the original estimate. Nevertheless, it made major contributions in a number of fields. Its main application was in solving aerodynamic flow equations; beyond that, it was used for weather prediction and climate modeling, signal processing (and Fast Fourier Transforms), beam forming, seismic research, radiation transport, and linear programming with large numbers of constraints. Its positive contributions included the acceleration of both semiconductor logic and memory technology and increased knowledge in the fields of parallel algorithms, programming, software, and hardware design (particularly with regard to reliability and fault tolerance). To quote Slotnick, "ILLIAC IV remained the world's fastest computer until August 1981 when it was shut down to make way for a physically smaller, more readily programmable, and less erratic [CRAY-I] successor."

Near the end of Hord's book [244] is a list of ILLIAC IV's contributions to hardware technology, machine architecture, system architecture, and applications. One interpretation of this list is that a large part of what was learned was how to design hardware and how not to interconnect processors. The hardware achievements included the following:

- First large-scale use of ECL integrated circuits.
- First successful use of (circuit-card) design automation outside IBM.
- Barrel-switch logic circuit for full-word shifts during one clock cycle (for floating-point normalization, etc.).
- First significant large-scale use of semiconductor memory.
- First successful use of large (16" × 20") multilayer (up to 12 layers) circuit boards.
- First use of dense belted-cable interconnection technology.

Significant contributions were also made in other areas, but the most interesting comment for the present audience is the negative one about the difficult programmability and lack of self-repair capability of the hard-wired processor interconnection scheme. To quote a prophetic sentence from Hord's book, "Future systems will have modular configurations for improved problem matching and will be able to switch ailing PEs out and good PEs into the configuration all under software control."

9.4.2 IBM GF11

As shown in Figure 9.11 on page 437, GF11 is a modified[222] SIMD parallel computer with 566 processing elements interconnected via a nonblocking Benes network (see page 401). Each processor is capable of 20 (32-bit) MFLOPS (single precision) and has space for 2 MBytes of memory, giving the total machine a peak of 11.4 GFLOPS and 1.14 GBytes of memory. The network can realize any of 1024 preselected data-path permutations among the processors at each 200-nanosecond machine cycle (i.e., every time a data word arrives). The switch settings and most of the control decisions are made at compile time.

The main intended application was a set of calculations needed to verify quantum chromodynamics (QCD), a basic theory of matter; more specifically, it is a theory of the elementary particles that make up the nucleus of an atom. The needed computations were estimated to take a year on GF11. The designers also felt that the GF11 architecture was flexible enough to sustain 5 to 10 GFLOPS on a wide range of problems in science and engineering [58],

---

[222] See the discussion of relocate and mode registers in the "Processors" section that follows.

Figure 9.11   *The GF11 architecture. As shown, 566 processing units and 10 disk units are connected to a nonblocking Benes switch with three stages of 24 x 24 crossbars. The figure gives a misleading impression of the physical size distribution: the processors occupy 20 racks, the switch 5.*

which has turned out to be true [304]. The following description draws generously on two GF11 publications [57], [58].

Processors

Each processor can perform 20 million floating- or fixed-point operations per second. The floating-point portion is built around four commercial floating-point chips, each capable of 5 MFLOPS in pipelined mode. The fixed-point unit, implemented in TTL, includes a general-purpose ALU and a barrel shifter. Each processor also contains 64 KB of static RAM memory (50-nanosecond cycle) for frequently accessed data and up to 2 MB of slower dynamic RAM (one access every 200 nanoseconds) to store long-term data. In order to get data where they are needed quickly enough to keep ALUs occupied and pipelines filled, each processor has a huge (by previous standards) register file—256 words (32 bits each), 12.5-nanosecond cycle time, implemented in ECL. In one 50-nanosecond processor cycle, two operands can be sent to the fixed- or the floating-point unit, a result can be obtained therefrom, and a word can be received from the switch or transferred to or from the static RAM. With this provision, over 90% utilization of the processors is expected for typical QCD computations.[223]

Each processor also contains 256 base registers to relocate static RAM addresses. Thus, for a given instruction, each processor can have a different base value, so that each can be processing a different variable or array. (ILLIAC IV accomplished the same thing via index registers in each PE. Otherwise, in response to an ADD instruction, each processor could only add numbers located at the *same* two local memory addresses within each processor. Adding two 64-element vectors would then require that the elements of each vector reside at the same pair of local addresses within each processor. A_1 could not readily be added to B_2 without some sort of provision like the ones above.) A processor can skip or slightly modify a given instruction depending on eight locally stored *condition code bits*, thus exerting some local control beyond that allowed by a strict SIMD model, in a similar manner as that described for ILLIAC IV on page 432.

The GF11 processors are implemented as 566 identical 22" × 16" boards, each with 642 chips and a 300-pin connector. The chips implement the logic and memory functions described above and also some features useful for the Monte Carlo integration techniques used for the calculations. The majority of the I/O pins are for a 180-bit-wide channel that brings address and control signals every 50 nanoseconds. A pair of 32-bit ports handle data traffic between the static RAM and the switching network, at one (9-bit) byte every 50 nanoseconds, and allow a processor's register file to be loaded with a word from some other processor's static RAM after the switch's pipeline delay (600 nanoseconds). Another pair of 32-bit ports exchange data with the central controller at 32 bits/50 nanoseconds.

Disks

The disk system consists of 10 450-MB disk units, each interacting with the rest of GF11 through the switch in the same way as a processor. Each disk unit transfers data at 8 Mbyte/second. An IBM PC/AT acts as a file server controlling the 10 disk units; it also transfers data to and from an IBM 3090 host for archiving purposes. The disk system's total bandwidth of 80 MB/second allows unloading the entire GF11 memory in under 15 seconds, which makes hourly checkpointing practical.

---

[223]   The static RAM may appear 3 times too slow and the dynamic RAM 12 times too slow to keep the functional units satisfied, but in scientific calculations (especially QCD) the results and inputs of one operation are often quickly reused as inputs to a new operation.

Network

The other major hardware innovation in GF11 is the interconnection of the processors. This interconnection is achieved with a high-speed Benes network, a nonblocking switch capable of realizing any permutation of the processor interconnections and able to reconfigure among 1024 preselected permutations in one processor cycle. It takes considerably longer to set the switch for an arbitrary permutation *not* included in the preloaded set of 1024, but this number of switch settings is more than adequate for many useful topologies. A hypercube of dimension d, for example, requires $2d$ switch settings—one to pass data from each processor to its nearest neighbor in the positive-1 direction, one to the neighbor in the negative-1 direction, one to the neighbor in the positive-2 direction, and so on. A QCD computation in which GF11 is configured as an 8x8x8 array uses only 6 of the available 1024 switch settings. A photo of part of the network (left) suggests some of what is involved in implementing the innocent-looking diagram of Figure 9.11. The Benes network has 576 (9-bit-wide) inputs and consists of three stages of 24 nodes each. Each node is a 24x24 crossbar 9 bits wide and occupies a single board. The node's key elements are 18 CMOS gate array chips, each of which is a 24-to-12 crossbar 1 bit wide. The board also has enough memory to store 1024 switch settings. The controller chooses one of these every 200 nanoseconds by transmitting only the 10-bit address of the configuration's location in memory. At one word/200 nanoseconds/port, the peak network traffic capacity is 2.88×10^9

words/second (11.5 GB/second), and the time for a word to pass through the switch is 600 nanoseconds, even in heavy traffic, thanks to the nonblocking nature of the Benes network (page 401).

The switch can also be used to replace failed processors with spares. GF11's full state is saved on disk periodically. When a failed processor is found, the switch-setting data are modified so that program data originally sent to and from the failed processor is now sent to and from its replacement. GF11 is then reloaded with the most recent checkpoint file from disk and started again.

Controller

The action of a GF11 processor board during each 50-nanosecond microcycle is specified by a 59-field, 180-bit microcode word, and so the main requirement of the central controller is that it dispatch one of these microcode words to the processors every 50 nanoseconds. In principle, a special-purpose unit could be built to generate control words on the fly from a higher-level instruction stream. However, designing such hardware is hard (sorry) and also requires a choice of *instruction set* that might limit the machine's flexibility and sustained performance. The strategy adopted instead for GF11 is to precompute large, optimized blocks of microcode (to be used as subroutines), store them in a fast (50-nanosecond) 512K-word × 200-bit memory, and then dispatch them to the processors as required. Although this is a huge microcode store by most standards, GF11 uses microcode so rapidly that this store represents only 25 milliseconds of execution, and sustained operation is possible only by reusing at least some microcode sequences a large number of times. Fortunately, this is possible in QCD, in which the time-consuming portions of the algorithms consist of a large number of iterations of an inner loop that uses the same instruction sequence on each pass.

In addition to this microcode memory, the controller consists of an address relocation unit, an IBM PC/RT acting as the control CPU, and an interface through which the PC/RT acts on the rest of the controller and on the file server CPU and its data channel to the processors. The control CPU is also linked to the IBM 3090 host. The intelligence of the GF11 lies in the control CPU; it decides which sequence of microcode is to be executed next, sets up the necessary relocation and remap values, and starts the next sequence when the previous one finishes.

The operation of the controller makes certain assumptions about the size (granularity) of the parallel computations. The control processor runs at about 2 MIPS, at which rate it takes a minimum of about 30 microseconds to prepare a typical block of microcode. This work can be fully overlapped with GF11 execution if the preceding block of microcode takes more than 600 operations on each GF11 processor (20 MFLOPS). Transmitting the microcode preparation commands to the control interface (during which GF11 cannot execute) typically takes 2 microseconds. In order for this to be no more than a 4% loss, the block of microcode must take 1000 operations (50 microseconds) on each processor. Typical QCD inner-loop blocks take between 4000 and 100,000 GF11 50-nanosecond clock cycles, and thus satisfy both conditions above.

Programming

A GF11 program is divided into two parts—a set of subroutines in GF11 microcode, and a master program that runs on the control CPU (the IBM PC/RT) and calls these subroutines, which have been preloaded into the control RAM by a process we shall describe in a moment. Microcode subroutines are executed on all GF11 processors simultaneously, at a peak rate of 11 GFLOPS, but they have no decision or looping capability—they execute for a fixed number of cycles and then stop. The master program is responsible for their efficient scheduling.

GF11 is much too complicated to program entirely at the microcode level, and so the user clearly needs a higher-level programming language. However, until more experience had been obtained, the designers did not want to create a new language and compiler or select an instruction set and thus restrict the available combinations of microcode. As a compromise, GF11 programs are written in standard Pascal or C that is then processed by a standard compiler followed by two special GF11 software packages. The user writes the program, identifies the computation-intensive parts such as inner loops, and rewrites them (still in Pascal or C) as procedures called by the original program. The main program, procedure calls and all, is then translated into the master program by a standard compiler for the PC/RT.

The special computation-intensive procedures are sent along a different path. The user writes each of them as one or more calls to a predefined subroutine, such as MULT for matrix multiplication. Each of these predefined subroutines is a small Pascal or C program, compiled for either the host or the PC/RT; when it is executed, it generates a program graph for GF11 microcode. When the compiled version of MULT is executed, for instance, it examines its input parameters (matrix size, for instance) and generates a program graph for a sequence of GF11 microinstruction words that will perform matrix multiplication on GF11. This library of predefined, microcode-generating subroutines is one of the two special sets of GF11 software that we mentioned above. It constitutes a de facto instruction set for GF11 that can be easily changed because it is implemented in software.

The Case for SIMD

The following is a condensation of the advantages of SIMD architectures as given by Beetem et al [58] in their GF11 paper:

SIMD architectures are less general-purpose than MIMD but do offer important advantages. We first restrict attention to SIMD algorithms and compare the GF11 to a hypothetical MIMD machine that uses the same floating-point computation engine. SIMD machines are inherently synchronous; our MIMD competitor is not, so that even when executing the same instructions (as is the case for SIMD algorithms), its multiple processors will get out of step with each other. (Contention for shared memory can cause large degrees of asynchrony, but even private-memory MIMD machines usually do not have both a single clock and the ability to start all processors at the same clock cycle.) The GF11 will then surpass its MIMD analogue in performance, design simplicity, memory efficiency, and processor cost. When we permit the MIMD machine to execute MIMD algorithms, then serious questions of programmability and debugging arise. We consider these points in turn.

Performance. At the very least all processors must wait for the slowest to finish. More likely, there will be many synchronization points during program execution. In addition to requiring fast processors to wait for slow ones, there is the delay associated with the explicit synchronization requests. This SIMD perfomance advantage will be larger if the MIMD machine has shared memory and thus significant processor asynchrony.

Design. An SIMD design is simpler since there is never an asynchronous contention problem where multiple processors compete for the same critical resource, such as a specific memory location in a global memory—in an SIMD machine, either no processor wants a resource or every processor wants it, in which case the control processor broadcasts it to every worker. Similarly, hardware deadlocks can occur with MIMD but not with SIMD since a resource is either strictly private (such as local RAM) or else always shared by all (like the common instruction stream).

(Continued on next page)

To create the microcode for the entire computation-intensive procedure, its constituent, predefined, microcode-generating subroutines are linked together and executed, creating a composite program graph. This is then processed by the second and most important piece of special GF11 software, an optimizing compiler that does dependency analysis (see page 309) on the program graph, rearranges it for more efficient traffic flow and parallel usage of the processors, allocates the registers to be used within them, and so on. The resulting microcode sequence, with the same name as the original computation-intensive procedure, is then stored in the GF11 control RAM, so

The Case for SIMD

(continued from previous page)

Memory Efficiency. In an SIMD design there is one common instruction memory for the whole machine. For private-memory MIMD machines, the entire program text must be replicated on each processor or else as yet unsolved problems in demand paging for such machines must be resolved. Indeed, current machines in this class cannot run programs of more than a few hundred kilobytes. If the cost of memory continues to decrease faster than the cost of processors, this problem may become less severe. For a shared-memory MIMD design, it is not necessary to replicate the program text. However, every large-scale design proposed to date does include private caches at each processor so that at least the "active" part of the program is replicated.

Processor Cost. A general-purpose processor that can support a 20-MFLOP nonvector floating-point unit is still very costly. No microprocessors (and few mainframes) are fast enough. GF11 needs only one such processor (the central controller); an MIMD equivalent would need 566.

Programming and Debugging. In an SIMD program all processors are doing the same thing at the same time. In an MIMD computation, the processors are free to execute separate instructions, and they may proceed at their own rates. This inherent asynchrony means that the composite effect of the individual instruction streams is guaranteed only to be equivalent to *some* interleaving of the instructions; it is not possible to predict which one. Designers of MIMD algorithms must consider all possible total orderings of the operations (consistent with the partial orders prescribed by the program running on each processor) and include sufficient coordination commands to ensure that only proper interleavings can occur. Operating systems programmers can well attest to the difficulties involved and the insidious, nonrepeatable "race conditions" and deadlocks that can arise. Debugging such situations is difficult unless expensive trace aids are included in the design.

---

that it can be called by the master program. The process is repeated for the remaining computation-intensive portions of the user's program.

For best results, the microcode for all the computation-intensive procedures identified earlier should be resident in the control RAM.[224] The compiled

---

[224] Note that the microcode acts as an instruction set specifically tailored to the program being executed. Tailoring the instruction set is possible because the control RAM can be both written and read. Such a structure is called a *writable control store* (WCS) and is much less common than the read-only memory (ROM) microcode store used for most non-RISC processors.

microcode subroutines should be several thousand operations long.[225] Shorter sequences finish too quickly—the control CPU is unable to start the next one in time, and cycles are wasted. Longer sequences should be avoided, since the control RAM is of limited size; loading it with new microcode is very slow, so it is preferable to have all microcode subroutines resident, and hence at least some of the microcode sequences are reused a large number of times. As mentioned already, QCD meets this requirement.

QCD

Quantum chromodynamics (QCD) is a theory about the particles that make up atomic nuclei. These particles are collectively called *hadrons* and include the familiar proton and neutron as well as the more exotic delta baryon, pion, and others. According to QCD, these particles are composed of still more elementary objects called quarks and antiquarks, bound together by something called the chromoelectric field [58], in analogy with the electromagnetic field that binds the electrons and nucleus of an atom together.[226] The proton and neutron, for example, are each modeled as a bound system of three quarks.

The motion of a quark through the chromoelectric field is partly random, as is the behavior of this field itself. QCD provides a formula for the probability that any specified configuration of quarks and field at one instant will arrive at another specified configuration at some later instant. Given such a transition probability, relatively simple formulas can be used to extract a variety of testable predictions.[227] The mass of the proton, for example, can be obtained from transition probabilities for systems of three quarks. This calculation is one of the first planned for GF11. It may well take 10^{17} steps and consume a good part of a year. To understand why, we give a brief sketch below of the method used to solve this many-body problem.

The space-time continuum is approximated by an $N \times N \times N \times N$ four-dimensional rectangular lattice, and the problem is reduced to the evaluation of an integral over $56 \times N^4$ variables. The quark field ϕ at each lattice site is represented by a 12-element complex vector and thus contributes 24 variables to each lattice site. The chromoelectric field U at each pairwise link in the lattice is represented by a 3×3 complex matrix, and four links per lattice site

---

[225] Note the parallel with the discussion of large basic blocks on pages 319 and 325 in Chapter 6.

[226] Whereas packets of electromagnetic field are called *photons*, packets of chromoelectric field are called *gluons* [98].

[227] Transition probabilities in time-space can be related to time constants characterizing a particle's observable behavior, time constants are related to energy, and energy, as Einstein told us, is related to mass.

must be considered, but only eight of the matrix elements are independent, so 32 more variables are contributed to each lattice site, for a total of 56. The probability of transitions from one configuration of the quarks to another is expressed as an integral depending on these two fields as well as the transition in question, and it is evaluated over all the variables mentioned above.

There is some evidence that a lattice as small as $8 \times 8 \times 8 \times 8$ produces a useful approximation to the theory's infinite volume continuum limit. Even with such a small lattice, deterministic methods of numerical integration such as the trapezoidal rule would require astronomical amounts of time even on GF11 (the time for such methods increases as the *product* of the number of variables). Therefore, integration methods based on Monte Carlo statistical sampling are used. Following the procedure outlined in [58], a random sequence of lattice configurations of the U and ϕ variables is generated, the function of U and ϕ inside the integral is evaluated for each random configuration, and this set of values is averaged to give an approximation to the transition probability. For a $24 \times 24 \times 24 \times 24$ lattice, 10^5 random configurations is felt to be reasonable. Generation of each new random configuration involves a matrix equation that can be solved with about 10^3 passes of an iterative method like the conjugate gradient or Gauss-Seidel algorithm. Each iteration takes about 2400 operations on GF11 for the formulations of U and ϕ described above. Therefore, for a $24 \times 24 \times 24 \times 24$ lattice, the number of operations needed to calculate one transition probability is $24^4 \times 2400 \times 10^3 \times 10^5$, or about 10^{17}. At 10 GFLOPS, these operations require 10^7 seconds, or about 100 days. Note that by this reckoning, an $8 \times 8 \times 8 \times 8$ lattice takes only 4 days.

As it turned out, the larger computation was needed. The results, described in reference [81], were that the theoretically computed hadron masses deviated from the experimentally measured values by at most 6%, which was taken as a validation of the theory and a contribution toward establishing the legitimacy of computer experiments, as compared with actual physics experiments like those done with particle accelerators.

Other GF11 Appplications

The QCD results mentioned above bore out the hope that such a physics problem, with laws that are local and homogeneous in space-time, would do well on a machine like GF11. As Weingarten [457] phrased it, "Seen as a computer, the universe has an independent arithmetic unit at each point of space-time each executing the same program and communicating only with its nearest neighbors." What has been a pleasant surprise is that a number of other applications have performed well, ranging from 10 GFLOPS for petroleum reservoir modeling to 5 GFLOPS for PAMCRASH, an irregular-grid program used to simulate automobile crashes. A large share of the credit is given to the versatility of the GF11 network.

Other QCD Machines

Another QCD machine project described in the literature [98] is at Columbia University and has produced three special-purpose parallel computers. The most recent, with 256 nodes arranged in a square mesh with nearest-neighbor communication and periodic boundary conditions, has a theoretical peak performance of 16 GFLOPS. This simplicity as compared to GF11 has some advantages and drawbacks, which are discussed in a paper by Weingarten [457] that also describes several other QCD machines.

9.4.3 CM-1 Connection Machine (MIT/TMC)

The CM-1 Connection Machine [232] was a collection of 65,536 1-bit processors designed primarily for massively parallel solutions to artificial intelligence problems, although its manufacturer, Thinking Machines Corp., also demonstrated its use on other applications, such as database search. Like ILLIAC IV and GF11, it was an SIMD computer, driven by a conventional computer that acts as host and runs the main program that contains all the intelligence in the system. But unlike those "number crunchers", the CM-1 was a "symbol cruncher" designed to answer questions more like "Is Clyde an elephant?" than "What proton mass does QCD predict?". It was designed for problems that can benefit from parallel pattern-matching search algorithms rather than algorithms that are heavy in floating-point computations. Floating-point computations are handled much better by the subsequent CM-2 and CM-5 offerings, which are discussed on page 457 and page 509, respectively.

Unlike the ILLIAC IV or GF11, the CM-1 uses a large number of small processors. Indeed, the CM-1 and CM-2 are the current champions in that department, with four times as many processors as the runner-up MPP (page 460). The processors in CM-1 are connected in a 256×256 grid; in addition, clumps of 16 processors are also interconnected by a packet-switched, 12-dimensional hypercube network for routing messages, and the 16 processors within a clump are linked in daisy chain fashion. Each processor performs a single-bit add in 750 nanoseconds; addition of 32-bit integers has a peak rate close to 2000 (32-bit) MOPS (millions of operations per second).

Figure 9.12   The CM1 Connection Machine. *The upper part of this figure shows the CM1's external host and microcontroller, and one of the 4096 nodes that are connected into a 12-dimensional hypercube. Each node has four memory chips, a processor chip holding 16 processors, and a router connected to the hypercube network. The lower part of the figure shows one of the simple bit-serial processors as it performs the ADD operation.*

There are several ways to view the Connection Machine. One is that it tries to solve the von Neumann bottleneck (page 271) by replacing one big processor over there talking to one big memory over here with instead many little processors distributed throughout the memory (in fact, it was originally called the Connection *Memory* [231]). A second view is that it is an experiment in pushing the degree of parallelism to the limits allowed by technology. A third view has to do with a model of the brain as a highly parallel collection of relatively slow processes, with information stored as *connections* rather than "bits on a shelf" (see "Computing with Connections" on page 87). Thus one would *expect* drastic differences from ILLIAC IV and GF11, but there are some surprising similarities as well; we shall point these out as we go along.

Processing Elements

The processing elements are so small that 16 of them fit on a single 1-cm^2, 68-pin CMOS chip, along with a message router that is connected to the hypercube network and a nanoinstruction decoder that controls the processors and the router (see the top part of Figure 9.12 on page 447). This chip is surrounded by four 16-Kbit static RAM chips whose read/write ports are 4 bits wide, so that each processor can have its own private 4 Kbit memory. The processors are almost deceptively simple—as shown in the bottom part of Figure 9.12, each has a three-input, two-output, bit-serial arithmetic-logic unit (ALU), a little decoding logic, and 16 1-bit flag registers that are used for intermediate results, for personalizing the chip, and for communicating with other chips. In CM-1 terminology [232], a microcontroller positioned between the host and the Connection Machine executes a set of *microinstructions* that tell how to translate *macroinstructions* sent by the host into *nanoinstructions* to be executed by each processor on the chip. Unlike microcode in the GF11, these nanoinstructions can be generated on the fly because the processors are so much simpler.

To give the reader an idea of the simplicity of the ALU, if it were implemented in logic gates instead of the scheme used in CM-1, it would have about twice as many gates as the 1-bit full adder shown in Figure 3.8 on page 108, plus some decode logic. The basic operation performed by the processor is to read 2 bits from locations A and B in memory and 1 bit from flag register F, perform a specified ALU operation on them, and write one of the output bits back to A and the other to the destination flag register Fdest. (The flag output also goes to the flags of neighboring processors via the daisy and grid connections.) The addresses of A, B, F, and Fdest are specified by the nanoinstruction. Examples of ALU operations are

```
                  Memory Output:           Flag Output:
ADD               A←XOR(A,B,F)             Fdest←MAJORITY(A,B,F)
AND               A←AND(A,B,F)             Fdest←AND(A,B,F)
OR                A←OR(A,B,F)              Fdest←OR(A,B,F)
MOVE              A←B                      Fdest←AND(XOR(A,B),F)
SWAP (CROSS)      A←F                      Fdest←B
```

and variations of these. The inputs can be inverted, and SUBTRACT, for example, is obtained by changing B to $\overline{B}$ in ADD. Each processor operation takes three clock cycles, one for each memory access, for a total instruction cycle of 750 nanoseconds. (When the daisy flag is the read flag, the design permits a signal to pass through all 16 processors on a chip in one instruction cycle.)

In the implementation of the CM-1 prototype, the ALUs do not really compute their outputs by performing logic operations; rather, they look up the proper outputs in a 16-bit register that contains the two output columns of the truth table corresponding to the ALU operation being performed (since there are three ALU inputs, the truth table has $2^3 = 8$ rows). Each ALU consists of a decoder and some special gates that give it concurrent access to this latch. In CM-1, the 16 truth table bits are part of the nanoinstruction broadcast to the processors. By reprogramming the microcontroller, the instruction set can be easily changed, as in GF11, and for similar reasons—the desire to gain more experience before freezing the instruction set. Theoretically, the 16 bits allow 2^{16} "instructions", although most of these would be useless logical combinations of the ALU inputs. After an instruction set is chosen, the nanoinstructions can be shortened by generating the truth table bits on-chip from a shorter opcode, perhaps by using a PLA (programmed logic array). For example, a 5-bit opcode can specify 32 different ALU operations.

In addition to the 16 truth table bits specifying ALU operation, the microcontroller sends the following parameters to the processors during each ALU cycle:

- *A-* and *B- address* (12 bits each) specifying the external memory address from which the ALU's two memory-input bits are read. The memory-output bit is also written into A.
- *Read Flag* (4 bits) specifying which one of the 16 flag registers is to supply the ALU's flag input bit.
- *Write Flag* (4 bits) specifying the flag register that is to receive the ALU's flag output.
- *Condition Flag* (4 bits) specifying which flag to consult for permission to proceed with the operation (like "Mother, may I?" in the children's game).

- *Condition Sense* (1 bit) specifying whether a 1 or a 0 shall mean "proceed" in the Condition Flag.
- *NEWS Direction* (2 bits) specifying whether data are to move to the north, east, west, or south neighbor during this instruction.

This nanoinstruction is relatively wide and does contribute to a longer processor cycle. As Figure 9.12 shows, there are many more chip I/Os than pins, even neglecting the pins needed for control signals and power and ground connection, and so substantial time-sharing of the pins used for data must be done.

Much of the processor's capability comes from clever use of the 16 1-bit flag registers. Some of these are general-purpose, with no predefined hardware function, and are used for such things as carry bits in ADD operations. The remainder have special hardware-related roles. Several are used for communication via the grid, daisy chain, or router:

- The read-only *NEWS Flag* receives the flag output of the ALU to the north, east, west, or south, depending on the NEWS parameter sent by the instruction.
- The read-write *Router-Data Flag* is used to receive data from and send data to the message router via a special on-chip bus.
- The *Router-Acknowledge Flag* is set by the router when it accepts a message from a processor.
- The *Daisy Chain Flag* reads the flag output of the preceding processor on the daisy chain connection, and is used to resolve contention among the chip's processors during message routing.
- The logical NOR of the *Global Flag* of all the processors on a chip is available on one of the chip's pins for communication with the host.

Together, these 16 bits hold the state of the processor, and since any of them can serve as the condition flag, they can be used to give a processor some independence beyond a strict SIMD model, in rather the same way as the 8 local condition-code bits of the GF11 and ILLIAC-IV processors are used.

Parts of the memory are also set aside for special information, such as the processor's absolute address. The processors can be sent a pattern to match against anything in their memories and told to set their flags in a certain way if they succeed, after which the selected processors can behave differently from the others even though all receive the same macroinstruction. For example, this technique is used to deliver a message from the router to the desired processor on the chip. Other special areas of memory are a status word that includes a bit indicating when a message is ready to be sent to the router, and another area set aside to receive messages from the router. The router also uses part of the memory to buffer messages going elsewhere.

Routing Element and Network

In addition to quick access to its immediate neighbors, a processor also has slower access to any other processor via a 12-dimensional hypercube network formed by the connections between the routers. How much slower depends on which of two routing mechanisms is used, *cut-through* or *store-and-forward*. As we discuss on page 478, store-and-forward routing in a hypercube network means that the entire message has to arrive at one node before any of the message is forwarded to the next node. The time to transmit a message is, therefore, the *product* of the message length and the number of cube stages. Cut-through (or *wormhole*) routing means that a message element (bit, byte, or word) is forwarded to the next node right away, that is, without waiting for any trailing pieces of the message (the network is *pipelined*). The message transmission time is therefore the *sum* of the message length and the number of cube stages; thus it is much faster than store-and-forward.

The trade-off in the case of the Connection Machine is that the cut-through routing requires bypassing, or "short-circuiting", the router elements and making the user's program totally responsible for steering each message to its destination and avoiding collisions with other messages. By contrast, although the router uses store-and-forward and is therefore slower, it handles the routing automatically. We will describe how below.

A router's function is to accept messages from its 16 local processors for transmission to one of the 12 other routers to which it is directly connected; it also receives messages from those other routers and either delivers them to its local processors or else forwards them to other routers. A typical CM-1 message consists of 32 data bits, plus the address information needed to reach the destination, plus a return address, for a total of slightly more than 60 bits.

The routing algorithm used is the one described on page 391. It consists of 12 steps, or *dimension cycles*; during step i the message is sent to the adjacent node in dimension i if the ith bit of its router address is 1. This router address is the address of the destination node *relative to the originating node* and is obtained from the exclusive OR of the two absolute addresses (see page 391). This relative address is used to guide the message to its destination; each

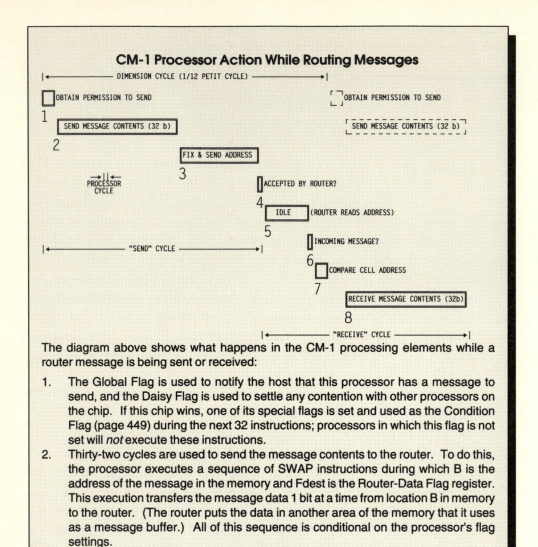

The diagram above shows what happens in the CM-1 processing elements while a router message is being sent or received:

1. The Global Flag is used to notify the host that this processor has a message to send, and the Daisy Flag is used to settle any contention with other processors on the chip. If this chip wins, one of its special flags is set and used as the Condition Flag (page 449) during the next 32 instructions; processors in which this flag is not set will *not* execute these instructions.

2. Thirty-two cycles are used to send the message contents to the router. To do this, the processor executes a sequence of SWAP instructions during which B is the address of the message in the memory and Fdest is the Router-Data Flag register. This execution transfers the message data 1 bit at a time from location B in memory to the router. (The router puts the data in another area of the memory that it uses as a message buffer.) All of this sequence is conditional on the processor's flag settings.

(continued on next page)

time it is sent along some dimension, the corresponding 1 in the address is set to 0. When the address is all 0s, the message has arrived.[228]

The complete process of sending and receiving a message via the hypercube network involves a SEND cycle, during which a processor injects a

---

[228] Another way to look at this situation is that every processor thinks that it is at the origin. The reader is encouraged to experiment with the simple 3-cube shown on page 451.

(Continued from previous page)

3. Next, the message address (in absolute coordinates) is read out and "fixed", including making it relative to the router in question. This process is accomplished by XORing the router's own address and the message's absolute address, using a series of MOVE instructions.

4. The router sends back an acknowledge bit if it accepted and stored the message. This step completes the SEND cycle. The RECEIVE cycle begins next.

5. The processor sits idle for some cycles while the router prepares to deliver a message. It reads the address of the message in its highest-priority buffer. This message could be one that has been previously delayed by traffic and thus takes precedence over a more recent arrival. If the address is different from the router's, the message is switched onto one of the 12 outgoing router wires and sent out. If the address matches the node's, the router prepares to deliver it locally.

6. The router broadcasts a bit to its local processors that there is an incoming message.

7. The local processors compare their own local address with that of the message.

8. Another 32 cycles of SWAP instructions are used to put the message's contents into the receiving processor's local memory. This step ends the RECEIVE cycle. Since the SWAP instruction can read and write the memory at the same time, the RECEIVE cycle can be overlapped with the next SEND cycle as shown, at the cost of a small gap between steps 7 and 8. The delay between message initiations matches the length of a dimension cycle.

If the message address does not match that of the local node, the router may start transferring the message to another router (start filling the buffer of another router) at step 8 above.

message into its router; one or more petit cycles to reach the target router; and then a RECEIVE cycle, in which the router ejects the message into a local processor. The processor SEND and RECEIVE cycles are synchronized with the router dimension cycle as shown on page 452. *At the beginning and end of a dimension cycle, a message (address + data) is completely in either a router buffer or in a processor's private memory* During a dimension cycle, a message may move from one router to another (along one of the 12 edges, or dimensions, of CM1's hypercube), or a message may move from a processor's memory to a router's buffer or vice versa.

Each message bit takes one processor instruction cycle (750 nS) to transmit, and so a dimension cycle is a little over 60 instruction cycles long. The set of 12 dimension cycles is called a *petit cycle*, which is thus about 800 instruction cycles long. This time is the minimum spent by a message going all the way across the router network, assuming it is not delayed by traffic.[229] A message moving only from one adjacent router to the next and not running into conflicts with other messages could take as little as 3 dimension cycles or as many as 14, depending on the phase of the petit cycle during which it leaves the processor. Since the algorithm accesses the dimensions in a cyclical fashion, a message that runs into a conflict with another message during a dimension cycle must wait at least one full petit cycle before it gets a second chance to move along that dimension. The average network delay can easily be several petit cycles or several thousand instruction cycles, amounting to several *milliseconds* in CM1.[230] Thus, this mechanism should *not* be used for casual one-on-one communication, but rather for parallel set-up of and communication within / among the *active data structures* discussed on page 456.

The diagram in the box on page 452 shows what a processor does to send or receive a message via the router. Note that all processors perform these instructions, even though the inputs and outputs of some are inhibited by their flag settings, and so no other processing can be done until all messages are delivered. One could say, therefore, that communication dominates computation in the Connection Machine. Its builders might reply, however, that communication *is* computation for the problems of interest.

The mechanics of the router itself[231] are as follows. All messages reaching a router go into buffers unless these are full. The router is continually cycling messages into and out of its buffers. During a dimension cycle, it can accept a message from either a local processor or another router and put it in a buffer, and it can take a message from a buffer and deliver it to a local processor or another router. On dimension cycle i, the router tries to send any stored message with a 1 in bit position i. Messages leaving these buffers encounter a cross-point-like switch that sends one message onto output wire i and the rest (if there are any) back to the buffers. The time of one of these round trips is equal to a dimension cycle. A first in, first out (FIFO) discipline is imposed, so that the most recently arrived message is put in the lowest-priority buffer, and the oldest message goes out first.

---

[229] A grand cycle is the time for *all* messages generated by some operation to arrive through heavy traffic.

[230] By contrast, the nonblocking Benes network keeps the GF11 network pipeline delay constant.

[231] By way of analogy, the router can be thought of as a train station's waiting room, with passengers moving in accord with a dictatorial set of rules. (The whole Connection Machine may owe more inspiration to the MIT Model Railroad Club than is generally recognized.)

If the buffers are full and multiple messages arrive, one is put in the lowest-priority buffer, and the old contents of this buffer plus the other messages are sent out to other routers even if this process moves them a step further from their destinations.   By way of consolation, these involuntarily rerouted messages get an increase of priority.   This *desperation routing* is expected to occur only rarely.   However, its effects are not yet fully known.

Programming Environment

CM-1 compilers have been written for C, Fortran, and Lisp.   Extensions are added to these languages to allow parallel data structures.   Programs are described in terms of *virtual processors* to make them independent of the number of hardware processors, which are multiplexed to the extent necessary to support this abstraction.   Hillis's book [232] describes one such extension called CmLisp.   With respect to parallelism, its computational model is similar to that of APL.   All concurrent operations involve a generalized, vectorlike data structure called a *xector*, each of whose elements is stored in a separate processor.   Xector operations are specified by using "alpha notation" to denote the kind of "apply-to-all" parallelism inherent in APL operations.   For example, the addition of two vectors 1 2 and 2 3 to produce a vector 3 5 is expressed in CmLisp as

$$(\alpha +\ '\{a \rightarrow 1\ \ b \rightarrow 2\}\ '\{a \rightarrow 2\ \ b \rightarrow 3\})$$

and in APL as

$$1\ 2 + 2\ 3$$

(In the xector enclosed in { } brackets, the arrow $\rightarrow$ connects the index and value of each element of the xector.   This mapping performed by a xector can involve symbols as well as numbers.)   "Beta notation" is used to reduce the elements of a xector into a single value, much like the APL reduction operator.   For example, the addition of all elements of a vector 1 2 3 to produce the sum 6 is represented in CmLisp as

$$(\beta +\ '\{A \rightarrow 1\ B \rightarrow 2\ C \rightarrow 3\})$$

and in APL as

$$+/1\ 2\ 3$$

Hillis [232] describes the use of these constructs in more detail. To quote his summary, "A Connection Machine is the direct hardware embodiment of the α and β operators. Processors [perform] α, routers [permit] β. The contents of the memory cells are xectors." It is interesting to compare the SIMD parallelism of CmLisp and these constructs with the MIMD parallelism of Multilisp and its "future" construct (page 245).

CM-1 Applications

One of the primary motivations for the design of the CM-1 Connection Machine [232] was the retrieval of common-sense knowledge from a semantic network, a data structure frequently used in artificial intelligence to model the human brain's ability to manipulate relatively unstructured data and quickly extract (i.e., infer) facts that were not explicitly put into the database. A parallel method for doing this modeling using an earlier, simpler system called NETL was described on page 85. This approach is one touched on by Fahlman [162] when he discusses message-passing systems with "three flavors of parallelism"; in order of increasing complexity, the three are *marker passing* (such as NETL's 1-bit markers), *value passing* (a kind of multiple-bit marker passing), and true *message passing* (as supplied by the Connection Machine). Markers and values are passed among nodes and perhaps combined at a node to form a sum, minimum, or maximum, but they are not kept separate, as true messages are. The processors in the Connection Machine are considerably more powerful than NETL's in that they transmit and maintain individual messages of (more or less) arbitrary length and perform arbitrary logical and arithmetic operations on them. The router can "soft-wire" two arbitrary processors together, since it can deliver a message between any two processors and since the received message includes the sending processor's return address. Hillis [232] describes how "active data structures" such as semantic networks are built up out of trees of processors and how Lisp's CONS operation is related to the building up of such networks.

However, the early demonstrations of the Connection Machine have not been on semantic network problems, but on such applications as document retrieval and fluid flow. These demonstrations have indeed used a processor per data item, but most have not used the router network, relying instead on only the grid connections. One performance example cited [411] is the retrieval of a news story matching some key words from among 50,000 news stories and the subsequent retrieval of all related stories in a time as low as a few milliseconds. Considerable work has been done by the Connection Machine people on "thinking in parallel" and using parallel algorithms, but the computational model used so far has not used the most unique feature of the

Connection Machine, namely the routers, and so many of the results are applicable to other massively parallel machines made up of large arrays of small processors, such as the DAP and the MPP (see page 460). It is not yet clear what the Connection Machine's most important application will be.

Comparisons

Other examples of massive parallelism via many small processors in SIMD mode have been configured as meshes or trees. The mesh-connected MPP and DAP are treated on page 460ff. Tree machines are discussed on page 629. Trees are nice data structures, but as hardware structures they pose a problem: you want to be able to put the root at any PE, which you can't do with tree machines; you can with shuffle and cube networks.

Another example of a cube-connected, message-passing architecture is provided by the Cosmic Cube (page 475), but the processors there are much more substantial and fewer in number, and the operation is MIMD.

CM-2

When introducing the CM-2 successor, Thinking Machines shifted their emphasis from symbolic to numeric processing; a trend that has continued with their subsequent offerings, including the CM-5 MIMD machine mentioned on page 509. The major architectural change from the CM-1, is the addition of a Weitek-based floating-point coprocessor with every 32 of the of 1-bit integer processors. This ensemble of 2048 floating-point units is able to achieve several GFLOPS (billions of floating-point operations per second) on favorable problems well suited for SIMD operation. Not surprisingly, such high floating-point performance has attracted considerable attention in the numerical computing community, and the Connection Machine is now considered more a number cruncher than a symbolic processor. The model 200, introduced in 1991, operates the 1-bit processors and also the Weitek chips at 10 MHZ, thus obtaining 10 MFLOPS (64-bit) from each Weitek chip and a peak of 20 GFLOPS from a full-scale CM-2.

Early versions of the software stored a floating-point variable in the memory associated with a single bit-serial processor, and hence 32 data transfers were needed to send a single-precision (32-bit) value to the Weitek.[232] Newer

---

232   During these 32 cycles, each of the 32 processors associated with a Weitek can transfer a value. There is a buffer present to hold these 32 values as they are (simultaneously) arriving and then deliver them sequentially to the Weitek. Hence 32 cycles after they arrive in the buffer, they have all been sent to the processor.

slice-wise software spreads each single-precision value across the 32 processors so that it can be transmitted all at once.

When using the slice-wise model, the CM-2 is often viewed as a parallel computer containing 2048 32-bit processors. That is, the machine has become a collection of Weiteks with an integer support unit (that happens to contain 32 1-bit processors) rather than as a collection of 1-bit processors with Weiteks added to boost floating-point performance. It is interesting to note that a software change was the last step needed for the architecture to change appearance. One should also recognize that the slice-wise CM-2 has proven to be quite an effective performer on numerical problems. The 1989 Gordon Bell award for highest performance was won by a team using a CM-2, as was the 1990 Gordon Bell award for highest compiler-generated speedup (an impressive 1900 out of a maximum possible 2048).

Other improvements include a vast increase in memory from 32 MB in the CM-1 to 8 GB (8 billion bytes) in the CM-2, support for parallel I/O to a Data Vault disk system, and an integrated color frame buffer for visualization. More details can be found in [444] and in [434].

9.4.4 Other Arrays of Processors

The MasPar MP-1 and MP-2

Given the success of the CM1 and CM2, it is not surprising to see another manufacturer produce a machine in the same architectural class (SIMD, tiny processor). What perhaps *is* surprising is that Thinking Machines, with the new CM-5, has moved to an MIMD design (see page 509). The MasPar Computer Corporation's MP-1 system, introduced in 1990, features an SIMD array of up to 16K 4-bit processors organized as a two-dimensional array with each processor connected to its eight nearest neighbors (i.e., the NEWS of CM1 plus the four diagonals). MasPar refers to this interconnection topology as the X-Net. The MP-1 also contains an array control unit that fetches and decodes instructions, computes addresses and other scalars, and sends control signals to the processor array.

An MP-1 system of maximum size has a peak speed of 26 GIPS (32-bit integer operations) or 550 MFLOPS (double precision) and dissipates about a kilowatt (not including I/O). The maximum memory size is 1GB, and the maximum bandwidth to memory is 12 GB/sec. When the X-Net is used, the maximum aggregate inter-PE communication bandwidth is 23GB/sec. In addition, a three-stage global routing network is provided, utilizing custom routing chips and achieving up to 1.3 GB/sec aggregate bandwidth. This same network is also connected to a 256 MB I/O RAM buffer that is in turn connected to a frame buffer and various I/O devices.

Although the processor is internally a 4-bit device (e.g., the datapaths are 4 bits wide), it contains 40 programmer-visible, 32-bit registers and supports integer operands of 1, 8, 16, 32, or 64 bits. In addition, the same hardware performs 32- and 64-bit floating-point operations. This last characteristic is reminiscent of the CM1 design, but not the CM2 with its separate Weiteks. Indeed a 16K MP-1 does perform 16K floating-point adds as fast as it performs one; whereas a 64K CM2 performs only 2K floating-point adds concurrently (one per Weitek). The trade-off is naturally in single processor, floating-point speed. The larger, and hence less numerous, Weiteks produce several MFLOPS each; the MP-1 processors achieve only a few dozen KFLOPS (which surpasses the CM1 processors).

MasPar is able to package 32 of these 4-bit processors on a single chip, illustrating the improved technology now available (two-level metal, 1.6 micron CMOS with 450,000 transistors) compared to the circa 1985 technology used in CM1, which contained only 16 1-bit processors per chip. Each 14" by 19" processor board contains 1024 processors, clocked at 80 nsec, and 16 MB of ECC memory, the latter organized as 16KB per processor and implemented using page-mode 1Mb DRAMs.

A DECstation 5000 is used as a host and manages program execution, user interface, and network communications for an MP-1 system. The languages supported include data parallel versions of Fortran and C as well as the MasPar Parallel Application Language (MPL), which permits direct program control of the hardware. Ultrix, DEC's version of UNIX, runs on the host and provides a standard user interface. DEC markets the MP-1 as the DECmpp 12000.

Further information on the MP-1 can be found in [99], [341], [67], and [333]. An unconventional assessment of virtual processors, as used for example in CM2, appears in [100].

The MP-2

The second generation MasPar maintains the same system architecture as the MP-1 but with the processors upgraded to 32-bit engines. MasPar is still able to fit 32 processors on one chip, and the heat load remains a relatively modest kilowatt. The VLSI technology used is now two-level metal, 1 micron CMOS (the MP-1 used 1.6 micron technology), and the clock is 80 nsec. Performance has improved as well. Peak speed is now 68 GIPS (32-bit integer operations) or 2.4 GFLOPS (double precision), and memory capacity has increased to 4 GBytes. The router and I/O performance have remained the same.

Goodyear MPP

The Goodyear MPP (Massively Parallel Processor) predates the Connection Machine (page 446) and has a number of similar features, as well as some differences. Batcher's paper [53] gives a good, concise description of the MPP and compares it briefly with its predecessor, the STARAN.

MPP is a 128×128 grid of bit-serial processors designed primarily to process satellite image data[233] for NASA. There is also a daisy chain connection that threads through all the processors as in CM1, but there is no hypercube routing network. The processing elements operate bit-serially with a clock rate of 10 MHz (vs. 4 MHz for CM1). There are eight PEs on a CMOS chip that is made using the somewhat exotic silicon-on-sapphire (SOS) process, which is partly responsible for the shorter clock cycle. They each have a full adder, six 1-bit registers, and some combinatorial logic; they have only 1 mask bit (vs. CM1's 16 flag bits) to represent the local state, but they do have a shift register for improved performance on floating-point computations. The memory chips are 4×1Kbit static RAMs with 45-nanosecond access time, and they provide each PE with 1024 bits. Sufficient address bits are allocated to allow expansion to 64 Kbits/PE using higher-density chips.

Addition of 8-bit integers proceeds at 6553 MIPS, as compared to 4600 MIPS on CM1 for the same operation, which is interesting given that CM1 has four times as many processors. Thus, CM1 is the parallelism champ but MPP is the performance champ, at least for this operation.

Parallel Pascal [373] was the first operational high-level language on the MPP.

The ICL DAP

The ICL DAP (Distributed Array Processor) is described succinctly by Bowler and Pawley [72] and in more detail by Hockney and Jesshope [239]. It predates the MPP and consists of a 64×64 array of bit-serial processors, each with 4 Kbits of memory[234] and a clock cycle of 200 nanoseconds. Each processor contains a 1-bit full adder and three registers, one of which (the *activity* or A-register) acts like MPP's mask bit or one of CM1's flag bits in determining how each PE complies with the instruction broadcast by the master control unit. DAP Fortran allows operations and assignments to be made conditional on a logical mask defined over the array of PEs, which in effect sets the A-register. The operation is thus SIMD with this small amount of local autonomy. The DAP is constructed by associating a processor with each memory chip of a

---

[233] That is, it's an array *of* processors as well as an array processor.
[234] Eventually increased to 16 Kbits.

standard 2-MB storage module of an ICL 2900 series mainframe that is acting as the host computer. Thus there is no overhead associated with loading the DAP, as there is with array or vector processors that are attached to a mainframe as back-end processors.

Some of the raw performance numbers on 32-bit data listed by Hockney and Jesshope are 186 MOPS for integer addition and 15 MFLOPS for matrix inversion (with full pivot). Applications requiring shorter word lengths do better, while those requiring extreme accuracy do "rather poorly". Bowler and Pawley describe a number of physics problems that have been done on the DAP, including an $8 \times 8 \times 8 \times 8$ lattice Monte Carlo simulation of the QCD calculations described in the section on GF11 (see page 444).

9.4.5　Systolic Arrays

Systolic array research was pioneered by Kung and Leiserson [309] and focuses on the advantages obtainable by designing algorithms and architectures that lay out well in two dimensions and that therefore adapt well to the restrictions of VLSI technology. This technology favors compute-bound vs. I/O-bound computations (matrix multiplication vs. addition, for example, and also favors simple, regular, and modular layouts, both for their shorter design time and for their more efficient use of the space on a VLSI chip. The name *systolic* derives from the analogy between pumping data through one of these computing arrays and pumping blood through a heart. Systolic array processors are already used in signal processing and also appear well suited for other special applications characterized by simple control and data flow.

A classic example of a systolic array is the two-dimensional structure for matrix multiplication shown in Figure 9.13 on page 462. The problem is to compute $c_{ij} = a_{i1}b_{1j} + a_{i2}b_{2j} + \ldots$. The figure shows the computation being done with a hexagonal mesh of three-input, three-output computing cells that perform the depicted multiply-add operation on every clock cycle. The size of the hexagonal array is determined by the fact that A and B are *banded* matrices whose nonzero elements are all contained in a four-element wide band along the diagonal, which makes Cs band seven elements wide. Thus, 16 cells are needed, no matter how large the matrices are. In a VLSI implementation, each cell consists of a few registers and control circuits and a simple ALU. The a's, b's, and c's form three (carefully phased) data streams that flow into the array,

Figure 9.13 **Two-dimensional systolic array** for multiplication of banded matrices A and B. The operation is explained on page 461.

intersect, are processed in SIMD[235] fashion, and flow out again. Note how this process corresponds to making transparent copies of the three matrices, flipping *A* and *B* over, and sliding the three transparencies toward the systolic array by the corners indicated.

Figure 9.13 illustrates a key feature of systolic algorithms: they schedule computations in such a way that a data item is used when it enters the array and is *reused* as it moves through the pipelines of the array. As Fortes and Wah [176] wrote:

> This results in balancing the processor and input/output bandwidths, especially in compute-bound problems ... . Conventional [von Neumann] processor designs are often limited ... because data items are read/written every time they are referenced.

In this last sense, systolic arrays bear more resemblance to dataflow, although they are control driven rather than data driven, since the operations are executed according to a schedule determined by the systolic array design and not by the arrival of data. Note that this two-dimensional array exhibits both parallel and pipelined processing.

Another two-dimensional example is the VLSI chip used in the Ultracomputer switch to speed the process of finding and combining memory requests with matching addresses. This design is shown in Figure 9.14 on page 464.

This systolic queue is an enhancement of earlier work by Guibas and Liang [206] and operates as follows. Items added to the queue enter the middle column, check the adjacent slot in the right column, and move into this slot if it is empty. If the slot is full, the item moves up one position in the middle column, and the process is repeated. (Should the item reach the top of the middle column and still be unable to shift right, the queue is full.) Meanwhile, items in the right column shift down, exiting the queue at the bottom.[236]

The queue is enhanced by adding comparison logic between adjacent slots in the right two columns, permitting a new entry moving up the middle column to be matched successively against all the previous entries as they

---

235 "This would be a Johnny one-note" SIMD in the case of the simplest VLSI implementation, since all processors perform the same instruction in synchrony, and furthermore the instruction is the same each time.

236 Four observations: The entries proceed in a FIFO order; as long as the queue is not empty and the switch in the next stage can receive an item, one item exits the queue at each cycle; as long as the queue is not full, a new item can be entered at each cycle (the number of cycles between successive insertions must, however, be zero or even); and items are not delayed if the queue is empty and the next switch can receive them.

Figure 9.14 *Systolic matching queue used in the Ultracomputer switch* for *combining memory requests bound for the same address. The outputs of two of these VLSI chips are multiplexed together to form the "Combining Queue" shown in Figure 10.26 on page 581. The operation is explained in the text.*

move down the right column.[237] In other words, half of the queue entries are compared pairwise to the other half during each systolic cycle. If a match is found, the matched entry moves (from the middle column) to the left column, called the *match column*. Entries in the match column shift down at the same rate as entries on the right column of the queue. A pair of requests to be combined will therefore exit their respective columns at the same time and will thus enter the combining unit simultaneously. For more details, see [199] and the references cited therein.

We give examples of two different ways to make systolic arrays less special-purpose: extra hardware to make them reconfigurable (CHiP, page 502) or reprogrammable (Warp).

---

[237] Actually, an item is matched against half of the entries moving down the right column. Since messages are packetized, one can arrange for each item to be matched against its corresponding item in each request moving down the right column (this is particularly easy if each message consists of an even number of packets). If, however, an entire request is contained in one packet, then one needs either twice as many comparators or two cycles for each motion.

Figure 9.15   *The Warp programmable, one-dimensional systolic array* [*28*]. *Each cell is a 32-bit processor. The two data streams (X and Y) can flow in the same or in opposing directions. Local memory addresses and systolic control signals travel the "Address" path. The lower part of the figure shows an algorithm from* [*308*] *that corresponds to the latter case.*

CMU/GE Warp

Not all systolic arrays are two-dimensional, and not all are VLSI designs. The Warp computer[238] shown in Figure 9.15, for example, is a linear systolic array of 10 or more identical cells, each of which is a programmable processor [28]. In the version built by General Electric, each cell occupies a 15" by 17" circuit board and has a peak capability of 10 (32-bit) MFLOPS. Each cell is implemented as a programmable horizontal microengine (112-bit-wide microinstructions) with its own sequencer and a control store of 8 K instructions. The 32-bit-wide data path consists of two (Weitek) 32-bit floating-point processing elements, a 4 K-word memory for resident and temporary data, a 128-word queue for each communication channel, and a 32-word register file to buffer data for each floating-point unit. Each cell can transfer up to 80 MBytes per second to and from its neighboring cells. A skewed SIMD model[239] of com-

---

[238]   The name connotes speed, as in "Star Trek".

[239]   The same instruction is still broadcast to each PE, but the executions can be staggered rather than simultaneous.

putation is used. The authors feel that their machine is well matched to applications that include few conditional branches and consist primarily of tight, data-independent loops.

The machine's first application is in vision research. A 10-cell Warp can process 1024-point complex fast Fourier transforms at a rate of one FFT every 600 microseconds and can also perform many other computations, such as two-dimensional convolutions and matrix multiplication (each Warp cell can be time multiplexed to perform the function of a column of cells).[240] An enhanced, VLSI version of Warp, called iWarp is produced by Intel.

9.5 Exercises

1. Define the following terms.

   SIMD   Systolic array
   Vector processor   Pipelined machine
   Array processor   Peak megaflop rating
   Array of processors   MFLOPS

2. Match each of the terms on the left with its attribute on the right:

a.	r_∞	1)	Megaflops for long vectors
b.	$n_{1/2}$	2)	Vector size for half speed
c.	Chaining	3)	Linking two vector operations
d.	CRAY-1	4)	Register based vector processor
e.	Cyber 205	5)	Memory based vector processor
f.	IBM Vector Facility	6)	Cachee based vector processor
g.	ILLIAC IV	7)	Early parallel SIMD computer
h.	Desperation routing	8)	Send the data SOMEWHERE

3. Explain the difference between MFLOPS and MFLOPs.

4. We give the values of r_∞ and $n_{1/2}$ for specific CRAY, CYBER, and IBM vector processors. What megaflop rate would be obtained by each when processing vectors of length 10? Length 50? Length 250? Length 1000? Assume only one pipeline is used on each machine.

5. Why were two extra memory ports added when the CRAY-1 was replaced by the CRAY X-MP

---

[240] The definition of systolic gets a little fuzzy when it's not VLSI: is the n-body algorithm used by the cosmic cube (page 487) systolic?

6. What is currently the highest performance obtained on Dongarra's TPP benchmark? (You can obtain a list of performance benchmarks by sending a mail msg to netlib@ornl.gov with subject **send performance from benchmark** and no body.)

7. For what application classes was ILLIAC IV intended? How is this reflected in the machine design?

8. Compare and contrast the machine designs of the ILLIAC IV, the GF-11, the MP-1, and the CM-2.

9. Compare and contrast the programming environment for the ILLIAC IV, the GF-11, and the CM-2.

10. Why do QCD programs obtain high performance on the GF-11? Would you expect these programs to also work well on the CM-2 and MP-1? Why or why not?

11. Is the GF-11 network packet or circuit switched? Does it use central or distributed control?

12. Critique "The Case for SIMD" on page 442.

13. What was the intended primary application for the CM-1? For the CM-2? How do the hardware designs reflect this difference?

14. Describe, with respect to CM-1, macroinstructions, microinstructions, and nanoinstructions.

15. Why did CM originally stand for Connection Memory? Relate your answer to the von Neumann bottleneck.

16. Compare the CM-1, MPP, MP-1, and DAP.

17. "SIMD parallelism" is often mistakenly taken to mean only vector parallelism. Explain how document matching on the CM-1 Connection Machine is an example of *non-vector* SIMD.

18. How many cycles are needed to multiply two 100x100 matrices on a 100x100 systolic array? What if the systolic array is bigger, say 1000x1000?

19. The systolic matching queue illustrated in Figure 9.14 on page 464 can only combine pairs of requests. If three requests are for the same location, at best two will combine and the third will not. Design a structure that can combine up to three requests.

20. What are the advantages and disadvantages of a *programmable* systolic array such as Warp?

Figure 10.1 A 1024-processor CM-5 Connection Machine. *See page 509 for details. (Photo courtesy of Thinking Machines Incorporated.)*

10

MIMD Parallel Architectures

Suppose we change the rules of the game and let each processor march to its own drummer rather than the single drum of an SIMD architecture by expanding each processor's memory so that it can now hold a substantial number of instructions as well as data. Suppose, too, that the problem to be computed is broken into substantial programlets (processes or tasks) that can be distributed to the processors for execution. The existence of these programlets suddenly creates some new concerns that we didn't have to worry about before. First of all, they must somehow be *spawned*. Their execution time is usually unpredictable, so they must be *scheduled* on the processors in some intelligent and flexible way that allows balancing the load on the processors for efficient operation. Once on the processors, the programlets will need access to various system resources as well as to each other, and thus *synchronization/coordination* must be provided in order to obtain the desired result and avoid any one of a number of possible disasters. There will also be a need for more *flexible communication* than that needed for SIMD operation. We already introduced the need for these functions in our chapters on languages and on operating systems (Chapters 5 and 7). We will now discuss their implementation by various architectures.

10.1 Stepping Up to MIMD

In the course of this discussion we will revisit a number of choices treated in our chapter on computational models (Chapter 4). Chief among these is the question of the mechanism for sharing data among the programlets. Two approaches are being pursued, namely *message-passing*[241] and *shared memory*, and we have divided MIMD architectures into these two groups.[242]

10.1.1 Private Memory (Message Passing) vs. Shared Memory

Eugene Brooks [73], who designed much of the early crystalline system software for the Cosmic Cube (page 475), explains how the choice between these two models is seen differently by a programmer and a hardware designer (also see page 29 for a complementary view). From the user's viewpoint, the most attractive parallel system is one that provides a globally shared physical address space. A shared address space leaves the choice of programming model up to the programmer. A message-passing model can be set up using buffers in the shared memory, or else the shared-memory model can be used directly; in the latter case, undesired data sharing can be prevented by using the standard data-hiding methods of modern programming languages (page 238), and processes can communicate in a simple and unconstrained fashion by sharing data using commonly known addresses. Because of this ability to support a variety of programming models efficiently, a shared-memory multiprocessor will always be the first choice of the user.

The hardware designer has a different perspective (page 29). Providing simultaneous access to a shared memory by many processors is expensive. The hardware cost of the switching network that is implementing the shared memory can be reduced at the expense of increased memory latency. This latency can be masked by vector operations, but typical programs have a significant amount of scalar variable access. These references are often to data that are private to a task, and thus the hardware designer is led to propose adding local storage to the programming model. This reduces the number of accesses to shared memory, but it also reduces task mobility; tasks that use local storage must now be bound to the processor that has access to the local

---

[241] Message passing is also called *distributed memory* or *fractured memory* depending on whether or not one likes this approach.

[242] The terms *multiprocessor* and *multicomputer*, respectively, are also used to distinguish these two designs.

Figure 10.2 The blurring of shared and distributed memory systems. *The left-most figure is a prototypical shared-memory diagram and the rightmost is a prototypical distributed-memory diagram. The key transformation is the second memory port added in the second figure from the left.*

memory. Thus, tasks cannot migrate to underutilized processors unless the memory is copied. Such copying may be profitable if done occasionally but is too costly to do frequently. Another way to reduce traffic to a shared memory is the use of local cache memories; the problem then becomes one of cache coherency, a subject discussed on page 546.

In summary, shared memory has traditionally placed more of the burden of parallel processing on the hardware designer, whereas message passing placed it more on the programmer. However, recent developments are making this distinction more blurry, as illustrated in Figure 10.2.

10.1.2   The Effect of Grain Size

In this section, we consider mostly architectures for which the grain of parallelism is large; that is, designs in which the individual activities executed concurrently are substantial, ranging from entire processes down to a few iterations of a loop. This approach should be contrasted with the designs discussed in Chapter 9 on SIMD architectures, in which the corresponding parallel activities are often single arithmetic operations.

Macro Dataflow

To illustrate the effect of grain size, let us consider increasing the granularity of two architectures discussed elsewhere in this chapter, static dataflow and pipelined vector processors. A large-grain dataflow architecture would have the overall computation driven by the flow of data, but a typical scheduled operation, which for static dataflow would be an arithmetic operation on two numbers, would be instead a complex computation on a data structure. For example, consider the following dataflow graph for computing $A^{-1} \times B \times (A^T)^{-1}$ given two nonsingular matrices A and B.

If we ignore for the moment the labels inside the boxes, this diagram could have been drawn when describing the static dataflow architecture (page 271), and thus, from the topology of the diagram, we see the potential for concurrent execution of certain boxes.[243] Since the dataflow principles are being applied to the computation in the large, but not necessarily to evaluation of individual boxes, such a scheme is called *macro dataflow*. The University of Illinois CEDAR architecture (page 611) is an example of a macro dataflow design.

Macro Pipelining

We now turn our attention to increasing the grain of a pipelined vector processor. Instead of pipelining the various micro-operations into which a single floating-point operation is decomposed, we pipeline more substantial computations. As an example, consider the following pipelined implementation of pcc, the UNIX portable C compiler.[244]

In this pipeline cpp, the C preprocessor, expands simple macros and inserts text (normally common declarations) from other files; ccom compiles the expanded text into assembly language, which is then processed by the as as-

---

[243] Note that each box is free of side effects.

[244] Readers familiar with the UNIX make utility may recognize how a typical make innovation involving multiple compiles could be parallelized in the macro dataflow style described above. It is interesting to note that just as the macro dataflow make generalizes the pipelined pcc, a pipelined vector processor can be considered a (very) special case of a static dataflow design.

sembler, producing an object module; finally, the linkage editor `ld` converts this module into executable form. This pipelined C compiler has been implemented on an early prototype of the New York University Ultracomputer, which is described on page 572. In a typical execution of the compiler, each pipeline stage runs in a separate processor.

As illustrated by the previous examples, a large-grained design requires that the individual processing elements be capable of executing large program segments that are to run independently of the other elements. Thus, at least at the macroscopic level of the diagrams just discussed, the architectures will be MIMD. Since these units must fetch their own instructions and decode them, a substantial size is required, and we cannot expect the near future to bring the millionfold parallelism at this level that is anticipated for several of the designs discussed in the last chapter. Moreover, at this macroscopic level very general communication patterns will develop between processing elements. This communication requirement will also limit the number of processing elements. We note that the (static and dynamic) dataflow designs presented later in this chapter are also MIMD with general communication and that millionfold parallelism is not expected for them either.[245]

Of course, there can be additional parallelism at lower levels that raises the machinewide parallelism to very high values. For the macro dataflow and macropipeline designs, the processing element that is assigned to an individual box could itself be a parallel processor. Indeed, the CEDAR macro dataflow design follows this approach: each box is assigned to a tightly coupled (MIMD) cluster containing a modest number of processors. Finally, within each processor, circuit-level parallelism can be used, enabling, for example, multibit arithmetic to be performed in a single step.

As indicated above, in this chapter we will discuss designs specifying from dozens to thousands (but not millions) of processors. At one extreme, exemplified by the CRAY-3 and NEC SX-3, one interconnects a small number of very powerful processors to form a configuration of modest (MIMD) parallelism. In many cases, including the CRAY and NEC, the processors are themselves (SIMD) vector processors. Designs at the other end of the spectrum are often assemblages of hundreds or thousands of the most powerful microprocessors available. In the remainder of the chapter, we discuss both large-processor- and microprocesser-based architectures, as well as certain chameleonlike designs that can undergo a partial reconfiguration during program execution. We conclude with a consideration of some special-purpose computers, each optimized for solving a limited class of problem.

---

[245] These are called *highflux* by Ullman.

10.2   Private-Memory (Message-Passing) Designs

10.2.1   *What to Look for in Private-Memory Designs*

Even though we divide MIMD private- and shared-memory designs cleanly into two separate sections here, there is actually a nearly continuous spectrum running from your and my digital watches at one extreme to, say, a multi-processor 3090 at the other, with most designs falling at different points in between. We define a shared-memory parallel computer as one in which all processors have equally direct access to one large memory address space. There is not much doubt that the Cosmic Cube (page 475) is a private-memory design belonging in this section and that the Ultracomputer (page 572) is a shared-memory design belonging in the next. Rediflow (page 498) and the Butterfly (page 594) are also on opposite sides of this dividing line, but they are much closer. Rediflow proposes a pressurelike mechanism that allows tasks to move to less busy processors (dynamic load balancing), whereas in the Cosmic Cube a process is assigned to a unique processor. Rediflow also proposes a globally addressable address space. However, the access mechanism is the same as in the Cosmic Cube, namely, messages routed to the processor whose private memory it really is. Cosmic Cube could implement this global address space by combining the processor address with the memory address, but each processor would not have equally direct access to all the memory, and hence the Cosmic Cube fails to meet our definition of a shared memory. Butterfly, on the other hand, has an omega network that provides each processor equal access to all the memory modules, and so it is in the shared-memory section, even though it lacks some of the other features of the Ultracomputer that are designed to improve the flow of memory traffic. Dataflow, although basically private memory, acquires a bit of the flavor of shared memory if I-structures are used and is hence the last item discussed in this section on private memory.

The reader may notice that the private-memory designs are arranged according to their interconnection networks, whereas shared-memory designs are not. This arrangement may seem like a dichotomy, but actually there is a reason for it, namely that the shared-memory programming model hides the interconnection.

10.2.2   *Clusters of Workstations (Farms)*

Curiously, the first large-scale, commercially significant use of parallel processing may well be clusters of workstations working together on a local area network, an arrangement sometimes called a processing *farm*. Not surprisingly, communication is much slower in a LAN-connected cluster than in most of the other architectures we describe, and so the applications that have been tried tend to be those that have only modest communication requirements among the parallel computations. Some parallelism researchers regard such applications as bordering on being "embarrassingly parallel", but many computer users see "low-hanging fruit" instead. Fermilabs has a cluster of over 100 off-the-shelf IBM RISC/6000 processors working on particle-event analysis, computations that require no communication after startup. But there are many examples of smaller clusters running problems that do involve communication. Lawrence Livermore National Laboratory, for example, transferred a number of applications from a Cray X-MP to a parallel cluster of 16 RISC/6000 workstations. And as the table on page 379 shows, performance can be impressive. For example, a cluster of eight IBM RISC/6000 workstations running at 62.5 MHz achieved 694 MFLOPS on the TPP benchmark.

We do not really discuss the architecture of such clusters, because there isn't much to discuss—they are collections of off-the-shelf workstations connected by an off-the-shelf LAN, which has much to do with their appeal. But in our chapter on languages, we describe Express, PVM, and Linda, three of the most popular software systems used to write programs for such clusters (page 249). Our applications chapter uses a parallel seismic migration program as a case study to derive theoretical speedup predictions that are compared with actual performance on a cluster of workstations (page 51). And the IBM SP1, which we describe on page 512 later in this chapter, can be viewed as a better packaged cluster (in both the hardware and software sense) equipped with a faster communication system.

10.2.3   *Hypercubes*

The largest body of parallel scientific computation has almost surely been performed using hypercube-connected distributed-memory MIMD machines, which are the subject of this section. We begin with the university project that started it all, go through a programming case study, and then describe several commercial designs.

The Caltech Cosmic Cube

Hardware and Architecture of a Message-Passing MIMD Machine

The Cosmic Cube shown in Figure 10.3 on page 477 grew from a G. Fox–C.Seitz collaboration [387] [178] and is a prototype MIMD message-passing computer with 64 computing nodes, designed primarily for physics problems having a high degree of regularity. Each node has a direct, point-to-point connection[246] to six others like it, forming a binary six-cube network that is in some ways a smaller version of the 12-dimensional hypercube network of the Connection Machine (page 446). But although the Cosmic Cube's processing nodes are fewer in number, they are considerably more powerful. Each is built around an Intel 8086/87 16-bit microprocessor and floating-point coprocessor running at 4-5 Mhz; each node also has enough memory (128 KBytes) to store programlets as well as data,[247] which allows each node to run in an asynchronous (MIMD) mode, unlike the CM-1 and other SIMD designs.

It is also interesting to contrast the Cosmic Cube with the GF11 (page 436), since they were both originally designed for the same kind of (highly regular physics) problem. GF11 is an SIMD design with tight central control, and tries to exploit mostly inner-loop parallelism. It is designed for all-out performance, with 20 MFLOPS available from each of its 566 nodes, which are connected by a separate, high-performance, dynamic interconnection network that allows a node to access any other node equally quickly. The Cosmic Cube is more of an experiment in capitalizing on VLSI to build an economical "mini-supercomputer" for the adventurous physicist on a budget as simply as possible. It is a MIMD architecture, designed to capitalize on outer-loop parallelism. The 64 nodes together have a peak floating-point rate of about 3 MFLOPS. Instead of using a more expensive dynamic network containing multiple switches, the nodes communicate in "do-it-yourself" fashion using a static interconnection pattern formed by each node's connections to its six nearest neighbors. The other nodes can also be reached, but this communication takes longer because intermediate nodes must forward the message; the most successful algorithms tend to be those with the least extensive communication patterns. Fox [180] lists 20 scientific problems that have run on cubes varying in size from 32 to 128 nodes; the average efficiency (speedup divided by number of processors) is 85%. QCD in particular is cited as achieving 97% efficiency on the 64-node Cosmic Cube [178].

---

[246] Seitz calls these *channels*; we use *connection* since *channel* can also mean an I/O controller.

[247] Typically, about 4 MB, or half of the overall memory, is available to hold data.

Figure 10.3 The Cosmic Cube. *The photo shows the 64-processor prototype. The eight black objects in front are fans, each cooling a group of eight processor node cards. The node interconnections run underneath the circuit cards in a pattern similar to that drawn at left for a smaller eight-processor design. Note the hardware simplicity obtained in this message-passing design due to the use of a static topology and elimination of the switching network needed to implement a shared memory, compared schematically in the drawing above right. (The large flat cable connects processor node 0 to the intermediate host (IH) on the shelf above it.)*

Unlike the shared-memory MIMD multiprocessors and parallel processors discussed elsewhere in this chapter, the Cosmic Cube and its relatives have no shared global address space; that is, the memory in each node can be directly addressed only by the processor in that node. (In the sense discussed on page 470, this is a hardware designer's approach to parallel processing.) Other processors seeking access to a node's memory must send a message to the node's processor. This is done via 4-bit-wide, 2-4 Mbit/second data paths between neighboring nodes.

Messages are made up of 64-bit packets, corresponding to double-precision floating-point numbers (a representative message in the n-body example used later is about 10 packets). In a six-cube, a message may have to be relayed up to five times by intervening processes. This routing time can be quite long since there is no special hardware support for routing, which must therefore be done by software. In the *distributed process* environment described in the next section, routing is handled by the operating system kernel at each node. Also, a store-and-forward protocol is used, meaning that the node must receive the entire message before it forwards any part of it to the next node. This protocol makes the message-routing time proportional to the *product* of the message length and the number of cube stages (this observation is also true for the Connection Machine described on page 446).

Dally and Seitz [115] describe a special VLSI chip that should speed the routing considerably because it handles the routing by hardware rather than software and because it uses a cut-through method, in which the network is pipelined. Each byte of a packet is forwarded to the next node as soon as it arrives, making the routing latency proportional to the *sum* of the message length and number of forwardings. (This routing is also called *wormhole routing* because the path can be arbitrary, but once it is started, all parts of a message follow the head. This process can be regarded as a cross between packet and circuit switching in some ways.) The paper also explains how the routing is made deadlock-free by dividing each physical channel, or connection, into two separate virtual channels with their own queues. (Note that although the routing network itself is deadlock-free, it is still the programmers' responsibility to prevent other kinds of deadlocks in their programs.) The chip increases the internode bandwidth to 64 Mbits/second (8-bit-wide path with 150-nanosecond routing latency per routing step) and makes message locality considerations considerably less important in concurrent programs for machines like the Cosmic Cube.

Programming Environments—Distributed Process vs. Crystalline

The Cosmic Cube has been used primarily in two related but different programming environments. In both, programs are written in an ordinary language like C, with no new parallel processing constructs; instead, calls to special subroutines transfer data among processes. However, these two environments reflect opposing views on whether to *mask* or *exploit* the hypercube topology.

Seitz [387], the computer architect, writes, "The hardware structure of the Cosmic Cube, when viewed at the level of nodes and channels [connections], is a difficult target for programming any but the most highly regular computing problems." He views the distributed process environment as a more flexible and machine-independent abstraction of the hardware. Programs are written in terms of *processes* connected by *virtual communication channels* rather than *nodes* and *physical interconnections*. A small operating system kernel,[248] resident at each node, routes messages between processes and hence between any arbitrary pair of nodes. The kernel can spawn and kill processes, schedule their executions, spy on them, manage storage, and deal with error conditions. Processes instantiated in one node are not relocated to another.[249] A host computer running UNIX has overall control.

Fox [179], the physicist, on the other hand, argues that the computation of a typical physics problem is demanding not because its algorithm is conceptually complex, but because a relatively simple procedure (e.g., partial derivatives in computing ∇^2) must be applied to a basic unit (a field at a grid point, for example) in a world that consists of a huge number of such units. He produces a long list [178] of applications with algorithms that map efficiently onto specific topologies and writes that "the important feature of the hypercube architecture is that it includes all topologies that seem necessary in the class of problems studied so far."[250] In the "crystalline" applications environment developed by physics users like Fox, the user decomposes the problem so that each node has only one part (process). There is no dynamic (data-dependent) creation of processes and no routing of messages; they are sent by direct I/O operations to a specified neighbor. This hands-on, low-level programming of the machine has produced very efficient programs for problems with highly regular computations.

---

[248] It is not a full operating system, because it does not do file management, among other reasons; see chapter 7 on page 341.

[249] In other words, this scheduling is static, with no automatic load balancing, as in Rediflow, for example.

[250] A similar claim is made for GF11.

An example is the class of problems of a local nature, such as those characterized by short-range forces, so that field variables, for example, evolve as a function of only the other variables that are nearby in physical space. Such problems benefit from an interconnection topology that matches the physical space. A subvolume of the space is assigned to each node, and the algorithm within each node is almost the same as in the sequential case, except that variables in the subvolume develop under slightly more complex boundary conditions that include values communicated by neighboring nodes. In this kind of problem, the computation per subvolume is proportional to its volume, and the communication scales as its surface; the subspace per node that is chosen should be large enough to keep the communication-to-computation ratio at a reasonably low value.

A nonlocal problem with long-range forces must be treated differently. As an example, Figure 10.4 on page 486 shows the message-passing process code used in the *distributed process* environment to solve the "n-body Newtonian gravity problem" by means of a parallel program consisting of processes that *do* have substantial interaction and hence require careful synchronization. Message passing imposes a certain ordering on a parallel program, since a process needing something not in its local memory must have that item sent to it by another process. On page 163 we called this a *self-synchronizing* feature. This feature can be undesirable, but Seitz shows how to put it to good use in providing the synchronization that this parallel formulation of the n-body problem needs anyway. We shall use this example as a case study to show some of the differences between message-passing and shared-memory programming environments.

Case Study—Message-Passing vs. Shared-Memory n-Body Program

The problem treated in this section is the time evolution of a system of n bodies that each interact with all the other bodies by gravitational attraction or some other symmetrical force. Our solar system is an example. We shall contrast parallel message-passing and shared-memory programs.

In mathematical terms, the following happens: At time t, an $N \times N$ matrix is created by computing the force between each pair of bodies from

$$\vec{f}_{ij} = \frac{G \, m_i \, m_j \, (\vec{x}_i - \vec{x}_j)}{\left| \vec{x}_i - \vec{x}_j \right|^3}$$

which is an expression for the force exerted by body j (with mass m_j and location $\vec{x}_j$) on body i. The quantities $\vec{f}$ and $\vec{x}$ are three-dimensional vectors, m is a scalar, and G is a scalar constant. The total force on body i is then obtained from

$$\vec{\mathbf{F}}_i = \sum_{j=1}^{N} \vec{\mathbf{f}}_{ij}$$

Time is advanced to $t + \Delta t$, and each body's velocity and position are recalculated from

$$\vec{\mathbf{F}}_i = m_i \frac{d^2 \vec{\mathbf{x}}_i}{d\, t^2}$$

The new values of $\vec{\mathbf{x}}$ are used to update $\vec{\mathbf{f}}_{ij}$, and the cycle repeats endlessly. Periodically, after some number of time steps Δt, the information on each body is sent to a printer or something that records how the system develops.

A straightforward (but suboptimum) sequential program for this might look as follows:

```
Do Time = 1 to Number_of_Time_Steps
      Do i = 1 to n
            F(i) = 0
            Do j = 1 to n
                  F(i) = F(i) + COMPUTE_FORCE (i,j)
            End
      End

      Do i = 1 to n
            UPDATE (i)
      End
End
```

The Do j loop uses a routine COMPUTE_FORCE to calculate the force f_{ij} between body i and each other body j, and sums these forces to obtain the net force F_i acting on body i. After these are all done,[251] the next Do i loop uses a routine UPDATE to update body i's position $\mathbf{x}_i$ based on the new value of $\mathbf{F}_i$.

This program is easy to parallelize, because the iterations of the outer (i) loop are independent, and hence the Do i ... End pair can simply be re-

---

[251] The two separate Do i loops ensure that all the interactions are computed using the "old" positions.

placed by `Doall i ... Endall`, leading to *n* (identical[252]) parallel processes.[253] However, this program doesn't take advantage of the fact that **f** is a symmetrical force (i.e., $\mathbf{f}_{ij} = -\mathbf{f}_{ji}$) and hence invokes `COMPUTE_FORCE` twice as often as necessary.   This problem can be fixed easily enough in the serial case by using `Do j = 1 to i-1` to halve the number of inner loop iterations and by changing `COMPUTE_FORCE` a little so that it updates both `F(j)` and `F(i)`. The inner loop would now be

```
Do j = 1 to i-1
        COMPUTE_FORCE (i,j,FORCE)
        F(i) = F(i) + FORCE
        F(j) = F(j) + FORCE
End
```

Unfortunately, both these changes cause a problem in the parallel case. First, each outer loop iteration now contains a different number of inner loop iterations, resulting in different-sized processes and work-load balancing problems.[254] Second, the outer loop iterations are now no longer independent, since each component of `F` now receives contributions from more than one iteration of the outer loop, which means that in the parallel case we can no longer just replace `Do i` with `Doall i`. We now have to have the proper synchronization between processes in order to avoid race conditions and erroneous results that depend on which process wins the race.

A more clever algorithm helps to solve both these problems. The basic idea is contained in the drawing on page 484. We describe the message-passing implementation used on the Cosmic Cube and then give a corresponding shared-memory version.

---

[252] The fact that the processes are identical corresponds to an SPMD (single program, multiple data) programming model, a popular subset of MIMD (see page 609).

[253] The inner loop cannot be so easily parallelized, because it contains a loop-carried dependence identical to the one discussed on page 307 and shown on line 5 of Figure 6.6 on page 311. For a given `i`, all iterations of the inner (`j`) loop update the same variable `F(i)`, and to attempt this in parallel leads to *race conditions* and erroneous results that depend on which process wins the race, for reasons we previously discussed on page 353 and in Figure 4.10 on page 157, namely, that the addition `F(i)` + `COMPUTE_FORCE(i,j)` is not *atomic*. Each of the *j* parallel processes reads `F(i)`, adds the result of its `COMPUTE_FORCE`, and *writes* (not *adds*) the result back into `F(i)`. In between the time that one process reads `F(i)` and then writes it again, a second process could write *its* updated value back into `F(i)`, which then gets overwritten and disappears when the first process does its write. The contribution of the second process will be missing from the final value of `F(i)`.

[254] See previous footnote regarding static scheduling on page 479.

In the message-passing version shown by Seitz [387], the algorithm that is used is as follows. A process is assigned to "host" each body and to compute the forces between it and half of the other bodies. The host body is "cloned", and one of the resulting twins stays home while the other visits half the neighbors. In a seven-body example, the traveling version of body 1 visits process 2 to obtain the mutual force with body 2 and then repeats this procedure for body 3 and body 4. It then goes home to process 1, leaving the trail shown in the drawing on the left. In the meantime, all the other bodies have traced out corresponding paths, and so the stay-at-home twin of body 1 has received visits from the traveling twins of bodies 7, 6, and 5 and has recorded the mutual force with those three bodies. The forces accumulated by the traveling twin and the stay-at-home twin are then added together for the net force acting on that body. This force is used to calculate a new position and velocity for the body, and the visiting cycle starts again. Superimposing the individual paths yields the interconnection pattern needed between the processes, which is the chordal ring shown in the drawing on the right. The code that implements one of these processes on the Cosmic Cube is shown in Figure 10.4 on page 486.

For comparison, Figure 10.5 on page 489 shows a parallel shared-memory program that uses the same idea. The similarities as well as the differences between these two programs are interesting. Both use a routine COMPUTE_FORCE to calculate the force between two bodies according to the formula given above for $\mathbf{f}_{ij}$ and then they add this force to the value in two different storage locations. In both cases there are seven identical processes that each perform three such computations of $\mathbf{f}_{ij}$ per time step (yielding the needed $n(n-1)/2 = 21$ computations), after which a routine named UPDATE uses the new value of $\mathbf{F}_i$ to calculate the new position $\mathbf{x}_i$ for each body. After a certain number of time steps, the message-passing program sends the data to the intermediate host, which can then perform analysis and recording of the development of the n-body system, such as the positions of the bodies. This forwarding of data is accomplished by the statement send_wait(&my_body_out) in Figure 10.4. The shared-memory machine can perform this analysis and housekeeping itself, via the line PEEK_AT_BODIES in Figure 10.5.

The need to have a `barrier_sync()` in our Figure 10.5 can be explained with the drawing at the left, which shows a fragment of the process flow graph for the parallel algorithm being used and applies to both the message-passing and shared-memory implementations. Given the asynchronous MIMD situation we are dealing with here, there is no assurance that each process will proceed at the same rate. Note that processes 1, 2, and 3 each eventually update G_7. The following sort of mischief must be prevented. Process 1 reads G_7, but before it rewrites it with the updated value $G_7 - f_{17}$, process 2 comes along and reads the *same* old value of G_7 that process 1 is using. Process 1 then stores its updated value, but process 2 then overwrites it, and the net update will be $-f_{27}$ instead of $-f_{17} - f_{27}$. This sort of thing can happen because the updates are not atomic, indivisible operations (see page 353 and Figure 4.10 on page 157). In the shared-memory case, these race conditions are prevented by using a barrier synchronization construct that prevents any process from passing until all have arrived. Neatly message passing solves this problem neatly, because a message can't be in two places at the same time.[255] However, the barrier mechanism's shared-memory implementation often makes it much faster than message passing. This efficiency is discussed further below.

In the shared-memory case, a process encountering a barrier must either busy-wait or else perform a task switch (see page 158). We can implement a barrier as a global variable that one can envision as being initialized to the number of processes and then decremented by each process arriving at the barrier. In a busy-waiting implementation, this variable is also constantly being checked by the waiting processes to find out whether it has reached zero yet. This checking can generate a large volume of traffic all aimed at one memory location and thus create a "hot spot" [362] with cascading delays that are very detrimental to performance.

---

[255] The message-passing and barrier synchronization mechanisms do have some differences, but they both achieve the goal of providing enough synchronization among the parallel processes to prevent wrong answers.

One way to reduce such hot spots is to have the processes that arrive at the barrier do a task switch, that is, have them temporarily dump their tasks at the side of the road and go on to other tasks, rather than going into busy-wait mode. However, the cost of a task switch in most operating systems is high (on the order of several hundred to 1000 instructions or more) and hence is sensible only with large tasks and long expected delays at the barrier. These delays, unfortunately, are hard to predict. Special hardware such as that in the HEP multiprocessor (page 566) or the Alewife (page 556) can make the overhead of task switching much, much smaller.

The other solution to the potential hot spot problem associated with the barrier is special hardware added to the interconnection network to allow *combining* of requests (or at least reads) aimed at one memory location (see page 405). This is the approach taken in the Ultracomputer project, among others; it is discussed further on page 572.

The remaining code in Figure 10.4 is the overhead of message passing. Although the COMPUTE_FORCE routine performs the same calculation in both cases, the shared-memory version has "longer arms" in that it can "see" and access all n positions, masses, forces, and so on, equally well; the message-passing version is more "nearsighted" and can only access whatever is in the host and guest buffer regions of the local memory. The rest of the code in Figure 10.4 is needed to make sure that the right data are in these two buffers at the right time. (In some ways this data motion is the software analogue of all the GF11 hardware described on page 436, whose purpose it is to get data where they are needed quickly enough to keep the ALUs occupied.) Note a vital difference from the CSP send-receive (and Ada rendezvous) protocol: enough buffering is provided so that send_wait does *not* suspend processing until a receive occurs. Were this not so, the processes in Figure 10.4 on page 486 would deadlock, since each does a send before it does a receive.

The message-passing COMPUTE_FORCE is simpler since its arguments are simpler; it can also get things from its own memory more quickly, since the global access feature in the shared-memory case comes at the expense of extra hardware and increased access time. However, the means for getting things into those faster local memories and also for providing the synchronization is a message-passing mechanism that takes considerably longer than the shared-memory access time, even counting memory-access conflicts. Each process in Figure 10.4 sends four messages, each of which involves a memory read, a message transmission time, and a memory write. These messages must be added to the three pairs of local accesses made by COMPUTE_FORCE and compared to the three pairs of global memory accesses made per time step in the shared-memory case. The global access time is usually on the order of

```
/* process for an n-body computation, n odd, with symmetrical forces*/
#include "cubedef.h"       /* cube definitions*/
#include "force.h"         /* procedures for computing forces and positions */

struct body    {     double pos[3];        /* body position x,y,z        */
                     double vel[3];        /* velocity vector x,y,z      */
                     double force[3];      /* to accumulate forces       */
                     double mass;          /* body mass                  */
                     int    home_id;       /* id of body's home process  */
               } host, guest;

struct startup {     int n;                /* number of bodies           */
                     int next_id;          /* ID of next process on ring */
                     int steps;            /* number of integration steps */
               } s;

struct desc my_body_in, my_body_out, startup_in  /* IH channels          */
struct desc body_in, body_out, body_bak;          /* inter-process channels */

cycle() /* read initial state, compute, and send back final state */
{
    int i; double FORCE[3];

    /* initialize channel descriptors */
    /* init (*desc, id, type, buffer_len, buffer_address); */
    init(&my_body_in ,0,0,sizeof(struct body)/2,&host); recv_wait(&my_body_in);
    init(&startup_in ,0,1,sizeof(struct startup)/2,&s); recv_wait(&startup_in);
    init(&my_body_out,     IH_ID, 2, sizeof(struct body)/2, &host);
    init(&body_in    ,       0, 3, sizeof(struct body)/2, &guest);
    init(&body_out   , s.next_id, 3, sizeof(struct body)/2, &guest);
    init(&body_bak   ,       0, 4, sizeof(struct body)/2, &guest);

    while(s.steps--) /* repeat s.steps computation cycles */
    {
        body_out.buf = &host;              /* first time send out host body */

        for(i = (s.n-1)/2; 1--;)                   /* repeat (s.n-1)/2 times    */
        {
            send_wait(&body_out);              /* send out the host|guest   */
            recv_wait(&body_in);               /* receive the next guest    */
            COMPUTE_FORCE(&host,&guest,FORCE); /* calculate force           */
            ADD_FORCE_TO_HOST(&host,FORCE);    /* may the force be with you */
            ADD_FORCE_TO_GUEST(&guest,FORCE);  /* and with the guest, also  */
            body_out.buf = &guest;             /* prepare to pass the guest */
        }
        body_bak.id = guest.home_id;                   /* send guest back    */
        send_wait(&body_bak); recv_wait(&body_bak);    /* the envoy returns  */
        ADD_GUEST_FORCE_TO_HOST(&host,&guest);
        UPDATE(&host);                                 /* integrate position */
    }
    send_wait(&my_body_out);   /* send body back to host, complete one cycle  */
}

main() { while(1) cycle(); }  /* main execute cycle repeatedly */
```

Figure 10.4 A message-passing program for the n-body problem (from [387]).
See the explanation in the box on the next page. More program details are found in
reference [418].

microseconds, whereas the time to pass a message in the Cosmic Cube is on
the order of 100 microseconds.

Further message-passing vs. shared-memory program comparisons and
examples are found in the paper by Karp [273]. His discussion is generally

---

Commentary on the Message-Passing Program

In the message-passing program of Figure 10.4 on page 486, the innermost loop computes the gravitational force between the host body and $(n-1)/2$ visiting guest bodies. The macro COMPUTE_FORCE computes the force, which is then added to both the host and guest bodies; the other code in the inner loop shuttles the guest bodies in and out. The next outer loop sends the host body's "clone" out to visit other processes, waits for $(n-1)/2$ inner-loop iterations, brings the half-updated traveling clone back home, combines its baggage with that of the half-updated clone that stayed at home, and then uses a macro named UPDATE to recalculate the host body's position, using the new force and Newton's second law of motion. The outermost loop (starting at cycle()) initializes the channels (communication paths), cycles the middle loop *s* times, and then sends the host body's data back to the intermediate host (IH) *computer* (to plot the bodies' courses, for example). Note that this takes a while; that is, the Cosmic Cube *isn't* the machine for jobs with lots of I/O. The two lines above cycle() define the channels connecting a process to the IH and also to other processes. struct body defines a body's baggage to be 10 double-precision floating-point numbers and an integer, resulting in messages with about 700 bits of data. The symbol & means "address of" and changes C's normally pass-by-value semantics to pass-by-reference.

---

consistent with ours, and he makes several interesting additional comments. He points out that shared-memory systems inherently need more language extensions because they need to distinguish private from shared data, because they need to prevent out-of-sequence access to shared data, and because they enable a larger number of programming styles. Algorithm design is easier for shared-memory programs, but debugging is harder because an error often involves picking up wrong data from a global variable; the program continues however, and produces wrong final results. Designing efficient message-passing algorithms is hard because the data must be distributed in a way that minimizes communication traffic, but debugging is easier because errors normally cause the system to stop. On balance, then, it is not so easy to say which of these two systems results in faster development of correct programs.

To summarize this section: The program of Figure 10.4 makes clever use of the synchronization that comes with message passing to prevent the race conditions we discussed above. The shared-memory version (Figure 10.5) is almost surely faster and is easier to write and understand (though probably harder to debug). However, as pointed out previously (pages 29 and 470), implementing a fast, globally accessible shared memory takes a major hardware effort, whereas message-passing machines take less time, effort, and expense to build. The products on the market reflect these differences. For a fixed amount of money, one gets more processing elements and hence more

---

Commentary on the Shared-Memory Program

In the shared-memory program of Figure 10.5 on page 489 the $h = n$ processes that are activated by the `forall` each perform three specific iterations of the inner (`g`) loop, as shown in the execution picture below. The dependence graph shows the barriers that are used to ensure that only independent iterations are executed concurrently. (See the text.) (The execution picture and dependence graph of the simpler but less efficient program at the start of this section are basically identical to the two leftmost drawings on page 309. Note that that program was written in Fortran, whereas this one is in C to facilitate comparison with Seitz's program in Figure 10.4 on page 486.) The barrier synchronization algorithm `barrier_sync` is described in more detail in the section on the Ultracomputer (page 572).

Execution picture   Dependence graph

---

raw performance from a message-passing machine. The challenge is in the programming.

Intel iPSC and iPSC/860

The first commercial hypercube to be delivered was the iPSC (Intel Personal Supercomputer), which is based on the Cosmic Cube and is available with between 32 and 128 nodes [29]. The 32-node system is about as big as a four-drawer file cabinet. Each node occupies a 9" by 11" circuit board (card) and consists of an 80286/87 (16-bit) processor/coprocessor, 512 KBytes of memory, and a 10-Mbit/second communication link. The peak performance of a 32-node model is about 2 MFLOPS. Ethernet chips were used for internode communication because of their availability. However, these are really designed for distributed rather than parallel systems and result in very slow

```
struct body      {    double pos[3];
                      double vel[3];
                      double force[3];
                      double mass;
                 } host [n], guest [n];


main ()
{
    int h, g;   double FORCE;


    forall (h=0; h<n; h++)
    {
        while (1)
        {
            while (s.steps--)
            {
                /* repeat (n-1)/2 times */
                for (g=h-(n-1)/2; g<h; g++)
                {
                    /* Recall % is modulo operator */
                    COMPUTE_FORCE (FORCE, h, g%n);
                    ADD_FORCE_TO_HOST (h, FORCE);
                    ADD_FORCE_TO_GUEST (g, FORCE);
                    barrier_sync();
                }
                ADD_GUEST_FORCE_TO_HOST (h, g);
                UPDATE (h);
            }
            PEEK_AT_BODIES;
        }
    }
}
```

Figure 10.5 Shared-memory program for the n-body gravitational problem *us-*
ing the same algorithm as the message-passing example of Figure 10.4 on page
486. See the explanation in the box on the previous page. Also see page 579 for
another shared-memory solution.

internode communication—about 10 milliseconds for an 8-Byte message, or
about 50 times longer than the Cosmic Cube [289]. Compilers for Fortran and
C are available.

The more recent iPSC/860 has considerably better performance. The
system consists of 8 to 128 compute nodes with an internode communication
bandwidth of 5.6 MBytes/sec. The processing node is based on an Intel i860

chip, a 40 MHz, million-transistor, 64-bit RISC processor whose on-chip features include a floating-point multiplier and adder, an 8-KByte instruction cache, and a 16-KByte data cache. As shown in the table on page 379, an iPSC/860 with 128 nodes achieved a TPP Linpack performance of 2.6 GFLOPS, about half of its theoretical peak rating. The successor to the iPSC/860 is the Intel Paragon, a mesh-connected arrangement of i860 processors that we describe on page 491.

Floating Point Systems FPS/T

The nodes in the Floating Point Systems T-series n-cube designs [212] are 64-bit floating-point computers built around the Inmos Transputer, a special 32-bit CMOS microprocessor whose instruction set is closely matched to the Occam language (page 248). Each one-board node also includes several commercial floating-point chips and has a peak performance of 16 MFLOPS (one add and one multiply every 125 nanoseconds). Internode communication proceeds at 0.5 MByte/second, using DMA (direct memory access) transfers with a startup of 5 microseconds. A 64-node configuration has a peak performance of 1 GFLOPS and 64 MBytes of memory, is air-cooled, and needs no special installation facilities. Each node has 14 links; reserving two for external I/O and mass storage leaves enough for a maximum 4096-node system. This system would have 65 GFLOPS and 4 GBytes.

 The commercial success of the FPS/T was hampered by the original strategy of relying on Occam (page 247) as the only language in which the machine could be programmed [442].

The NCUBE/ten and NCUBE 2

The NCUBE/ten [222] consists of up to 1024 32-bit, single-chip custom processors. A node consists of this chip plus six 256-Kbit memory chips (128-KByte local memory). *Sixty four* of these nodes plus their interconnections fit on a *single* 16" by 22" board (the same size as one of GF11's 20 MFLOPS processors). The maximum system consists of 16 of these boards plus eight I/O boards, in an enclosure less than 3 feet on a side and consuming 8 KW. The processors run at a 10-MHz clock rate and achieve 2 MIPS on register-register nonarithmetic operations, a peak of 0.5 MFLOPS on single-precision arithmetic operations, and a peak of 0.3 MFLOPS on double-precision arithmetic. Internode communication is via asynchronous DMA transfers at about 1 MByte/second. The I/O boards can transfer data at video rates (30-1 MByte frames/second). The maximum system has a peak performance of 0.5 GFLOPS, or 2 BIPS, and a memory of 128 MBytes. The host computer uses an 80286 to run AXIS, a UNIX-based operating system that manages to make the whole machine look like one distributed file system. VERTEX is a small (< 4-KB) kernel or nucleus in each node; its primary function is internode communication (message routing and store-and-forward buffering). Fortran and C are supported.

The processing nodes of the more recent NCUBE 2 are based on a custom single-chip processor, which combines a 64-bit CPU, 64-bit floating-point unit, and a message-routing unit onto a single 500,000-transistor chip. The processor architecture is VAX-like. With a 20-MHz clock, the processing node's performance is 7.5 MIPS and 2.4 MFLOPS (3.5 MFLOPS single-precision). Node memory is between 1 and 16 MBytes. The maximum configuration is 8192 nodes. As shown in the table on page 379, an NCUBE 2 with 1024 nodes achieved a TPP Linpack performance of 1.9 GFLOPS vs. a theoretical peak rating of 2.4 GFLOPS. Programming in C and Fortran is supported under the Express parallel programming environment (page 250).

10.2.4 Meshes

The designs in this section differ in many ways but share the fact that their processors are connected in a mesh pattern.

Intel Paragon and Touchstone Delta

The Intel Paragon XP/S Supercomputer [258] is powered by a collection of up to 4096 Intel i860 XP processors and can be configured to provide peak performance ranging from 5 to 300 GFLOPS (64-bit). Although in some ways the Paragon is a successor to the Cosmic Cube and the Intel iPSC series, its processing nodes are connected in a rectangular mesh pattern, unlike the hypercube connection pattern used in those earlier machines. Some of the reasons for changing to a mesh are discussed by Dally [113].

The i860 XP node processor chip (2.5 million transistors) has a peak performance of 75 MFLOPS (64-bit) and 42 MIPS when operating at 50 MHz. The chip contains 16-KByte data and instruction caches, and can issue a multiply and add instruction in one cycle [139]. The maximum bandwidth from cache to floating-point unit is 800 MBytes/s. Communication bandwidth between any two nodes is 200 MByte/sec full duplex. Each node also has 16-128 MBytes of memory and a second i860 XP processor devoted to communication.[256]

---

[256] iPSC/860: 8 to 128 compute nodes (0.48 to 7.6 GFLOPS peak), 5.6 MBytes/sec internode bandwidth. i860: 40 MHz, 32-bit RISC processor (64-bit floating-point unit), FP multiplier,

The prototype for the Paragon, the Touchstone Delta, was installed at the Jet Propulsion Laboratory (JPL)[257] in 1991 and immediately began to compete with the CM2 Connection Machine for the title of "world's fastest supercomputer". The lead changed hands several times.[258]

The Delta system consists of 576 nodes arranged in a mesh that has 16 rows and 36 columns. Thirty-three of the columns form a computational array of 528 numeric nodes (computing nodes) that each contain an Intel i860 microprocessor and 16 MBytes of memory. This computational array is flanked on each side by a column of I/O nodes that each contain a 1.4 GByte disk (the number of disks is to be doubled later). The last column contains two HIPPI interfaces (100 Mbyte/sec each) and an assortment of tape, ethernet, and service nodes. Routing chips are used to provide internode communication with an internode speed of 25 MByte/sec and a latency of 80 microseconds for short messages. The peak performance of the i860 processor is 60 MFLOPS (64-bit), which translates to a peak performance for the Delta of over 30 GFLOPS (64-bit). JPL advertises achievable speed in the range of 1–15 GFLOPS. Total memory is 8.4 GBytes, on-line disk capacity is 45 GBytes, to be increased to 90 GBytes.

The operating system consists of OSF/1 (which is based on Mach; see page 369), with extensions for massively parallel systems. The extensions include a decomposition of OSF/1 into a pure Mach kernel, and a modular server framework that can be used to provide distributed file, network, and process management service.

The system software for interprocess communication is compatible with that of the iPSC/860. The Express environment is also available. Language support includes Fortran and C. The intention at JPL is to allocate 80% of the Delta's time for "Grand Challenge" problems.

FP adder, 8KByte i-cache, 16 KByte d-cache, peak 60 MFLOPS double, 80 MFLOPS single. "Million-transistor" chip.

[257] The machine is owned by the Concurrent Supercomputing Consortium, an alliance of universities, laboratories, federal agencies, and industry.

[258] One point of reference is the 16 GFLOPS reported at the Supercomputing '91 conference for seismic modeling on the CM2 [339].

HSCP PAX

The PAX-128 is a rectangular array of 128 processing units (PUs)[259] developed by the Japanese High-Speed Computing Project.[260] Each PU occupies a circuit board and includes an 8-bit microprocessor (MC68B00), an attached 32-bit arithmetic processor (AM9511), and 32 KB of memory. Of this memory, 8 KB is used for four 2-KB *communication memories* (CMs) that are shared with the four neighboring processors.[261] The edges of the array have end-around connections, forming a torus. A TI990/20 minicomputer acts as host [246].

The authors define a "quasi-MIMD" mode [245] of parallel processing that excludes fully asynchronous fork/join-type MIMD parallelism but suffices for many scientific applications (see Figure 10.6 on page 494). Users write main programs in Fortran for the host and in SPML[262] for the PU nodes. As in the Cosmic Cube (page 475), the node programs describe how data are taken from the CMs, how they are processed, and how they are replaced in the CMs, but no explicit language extension for the control of parallelism is used. In fact, PAX is very much like a Cosmic Cube with a less extensive interconnection pattern ("Cosmic Grid?").

An average floating-point operation in one of the PUs takes about 65 microseconds, leading to a peak of 4 MFLOPS for the 128-processor array. It may be convenient to view PAX as a message-passing MIMD version of ILLIAC-IV, but note that 4 MFLOPS is equivalent to just two of ILLIAC-IV's 64 nodes. On the other hand, the cost of a FLOPS is about 10 times lower in PAX (about $20K/peak MFLOPS, based on the companion PAX64J workstation), which is consistent with how much the market in general has improved in 10 years [149].

The references describe performance on a number of scientific problems similar to those used on the Cosmic Cube. Continuum models (characterized by short-range forces; see page 480) are processed in parallel with high effi-

---

259 PAX stands for Processor Array eXperiment.
260 Not the Fifth-Generation Project.
261 Since the memory is read in half a processor cycle, contention is avoided by sending clock signals 180 degrees out of phase to every other processor.
262 A conventional structured programming language that facilitates the distribution of variables across the memories. It does not contain explicit parallelism constructs.

Figure 10.6 SIMD, "quasi-MIMD", and MIMD parallel processing. *Horizontal lines bespeak synchronization, thick vertical lines are tasks, PU means processing unit, and A_1, A_2, and so on, are parallel processes. PAX uses the quasi-MIMD mode shown above, in which several synchronization points appear during the course of a computation, and different processes appear only between successive synchronization points. This description fits DOALL, PARBEGIN, and BARRIER but not the fully asynchronous MIMD possible with FORK/JOIN and hand-tailored synchronization routines (see Figure 4.8 on page 148).*

ciency (as in the Cosmic Cube). Particle models and linear equation models can also be parallelized successfully. Direct mapping of physical space to the PU array is easy to achieve and generally satisfactory, although degradation due to uneven work loads can occur, since (as in the Cosmic Cube) there is no software support for moving processes from one processor to another. However, since the memory devices are distributed and not globally accessible from all processors, it is expected that it will be "difficult to develop automatic software for PAX that can be used to partition a job into parallel sub-tasks, map the partitioned tasks to PUs, and generate an object program for them"[245] —in other words, an automatically parallelizing compiler.

QCDPAX [260] is a more recent machine intended primarily for quantum chromodynamics computations (see page 444). Each node has an MC68020 processor and an LSI Logic 32-bit, floating-point coprocessor that can perform two operations every 60 nanoseconds. The communication memories for nearest-neighbor communication were increased to 8 KB each; synchronization takes 2.5 microseconds, broadcasting 1 KB takes 0.56 milliseconds. The nodes are connected in an 18-by-24 2D-torus; peak performance is 12 GFLOPS (single precision), with about half that value being reached for QCD computations. The physical configuration looks like a hexagon from the top rather than a square as in the PAX-128.

A machine with perhaps a thousand processors and performance in the 300 GFLOPS range (double precision) is being worked on for 1997. The target for link bandwidth is 400 MB/s (8B/20nsec), and the latency target is 1-2 microseconds.

IBM Victor: A Transputer-based Design

Victor [393] is a 16×16 mesh of Inmos T800 transputers [139] that was built at IBM Research as a learning vehicle for the development of parallel software and programming environments for distributed-memory MIMD architectures.[263] At 1.5 MFLOPS per transputer, the 256 nodes represented a peak performance of 384 MFLOPS. About 70% of this performance was achieved by several applications, including ocean modeling and circuit simulation.

The Inmos T800 Transputer is a 32-bit RISC-like microprocessor with extra communication capabilities designed specifically to implement the CSP message-passing model of parallel computing. Context switching is fast,[264] and messaging and instruction processing can be overlapped. The T800 chip has a 64-bit floating-point unit and 4 KB of memory. Its special features include an instruction set closely matched to the Occam language (page 247), and four special I/O ports for connection to other Transputers. The total memory per Victor node is 4 MB, for a system total of 1 GB. Four transputer nodes are packaged per circuit card. Serial links between the cards operate at 2 MB/sec (4 microsec per 64-bit floating point number).

Graphics nodes are connected to the left and right sides of the processor mesh. The top edge of the mesh is connected to 16 I/O nodes, each connected by a 1.6 MB/s link to a 600-MB medium performance disk. The I/O nodes are also connected to the lower edge of the mesh, thus forming a cylinder, which can be divided (spatially) among four users.[265] Non-intrusive monitoring is provided by a dedicated IBM PS/2, which collects performance information such as memory usage and link activity and displays it graphically (see

---

263 There were also several smaller Victor machines with 16 to 64 processors
264 Switching from a blocked process to a new active process takes 17 clock cycles on the T414 [442], and presumably somewhat longer on the T800, which has a floating-point unit not found on the T414 and thus has more context to save.
265 Spatial sharing avoids the performance penalties associated with protecting users from each other in a time-shared system.

Figure 10.7 The Victor monitor, which provides information about partitioning, link activity, and processor state.

Figure 10.7 on page 496) or else files it for future analysis. Several programming environments were implemented, including Occam with Pascal subprograms, Trollius, and Express. Although hardware latency was in the microseconds, the latency with the then-implemented version of Express was more in the millisecond range. Figure 10.8 on page 497 shows the speedup obtained on Victor for a 2-D FFT program. The peaking and subsequent decrease of speedup that is observed for small values of N is a manifestation of the smaller ratio of computation that is obtained when the array is smaller.

The 150-200 MFLOPS performance that was mentioned earlier was obtained with programs written in Occam and doing single-precision floating-point operations. For double precision and programs written in Fortran or C,

Figure 10.8 Victor speedup experiment with 1-D FFT

performance was more like 50 MFLOPS. This has to do with the long-held insistence by Inmos that Occam be the only programming language for the Transputer. Support was eventually added for Fortran[266] and C, but not enough to bring these languages up to the level of Occam as first-class citizens.

Transputers have been used to build many other systems. Most of these are smaller than Victor. One large commercial system being developed by Parsytec is to have between 64 and 16,384 T9000 Transputers, and a peak performance of as much as several hundred GFLOPS. We also mentioned the T-series by Floating Point Systems on page 490. In their book, Trew and Wilson [442] link the demise of the latter machine to the reluctance of most programmers to learn the new language Occam, which these authors feel has been the impediment to more widespread use of Transputers for supercomputing. Also, transputers are a cheap, easy, and hence popular way to knit yourself a parallel computer, but the transputer's computing power is less than that of several more conventional RISC chips.

IBM WRM

The WRM (Wire Routing Machine) was an experimental 64-PE computer [242] built at IBM to develop efficient parallel algorithms for automatic wiring of VLSI gate-array ("master-slice") chips and other carriers of regularly placed

---

266   For example, Occam's concept of channels was eventually exposed to Fortran programmers.

circuits. The processing elements were in a square mesh with end-around connections in both directions. Each PE contained an 8-bit microprocessor (Z80-A, 4 MHz), 15 KB of memory, and hardware for communication with the control processor via an X,Y selection mechanism and with its neighbors via a memory-map mechanism with a mailbox flag protocol (a more ambitious design would have individual output ports and banks of neighbor input buffers). The PEs were slaves of the control processor, which was connected to the disk units and host computer. The mode of operation was the SPMD subset of MIMD (each PE was loaded with the same program).[267]

Using a parallel version of the well-known Lee-Moore algorithm, the memory size of 15 KB per PE is adequate to perform wire routing for a chip of 24 × 24 cells. A folding technique was used to accommodate cell arrays larger than the processor array. This folding allows use of a smaller processing array at the expense of increased processing time, but the total memory requirement of the system stays constant; that is, the memory per PE must increase. The authors felt that a processing array size between 16 × 16 and 32 × 32 was a cost-effective trade-off for foreseeable VLSI chips.

Global wiring of a 19 × 23 cell chip, folded nine times, took about 1 minute of CPU time on the WRM. An almost identical algorithm programmed in PL/1 and run on an IBM 3033 ran in about 45 seconds.[268] Thus, the WRM demonstrated that an inexpensive array of microprocessors could successfully exploit parallelism in this application. However, this particular implementation lacked both the speed advantage and the user interface (it was programmed in Z80 assembly language) needed to displace the established tools of the day.

U. Utah Rediflow

Rediflow [276] is a collection of ideas for a private-memory multiprocessor architecture designed to execute functional-language programs using lazy evaluation, that is, a demand-driven or reduction model of computation (see pages 144 and 256). Primarily because it is free of the side effects found in a von Neumann program, a functional-language program can yield (more and smaller) parallel processes whose important feature is that they can more easily migrate from processor to processor. We will discuss why this is so and

---

[267] These programs were sufficiently complex that depending on its data, status, and position, each PE often processed different program sequences.

[268] This is an interesting if rough measure of the communication overhead in the WRM. The cycle time of the 3033 is about 60 nanoseconds, and it uses 32-bit words, for a factor of 17 over the Z80. But even though the WRM is programmed in Z80 assembly language and the 3033 in the higher level (and presumably less efficient) PL/1, the 3033 still beats 64 Z80s.

how it influences the Rediflow hardware design as compared to other private-memory MIMD architectures such as the Cosmic Cube.

Concept: As we mentioned previously, a key concept in a von Neumann program is the existence of a store consisting of a set of pairs, each pair being the number of a cell and its contents, which can be made accessible to any part of the program for repeated reading and writing. The reuse of these cells effects a considerable saving in the amount of memory needed to run a program, but it also allows *side effects* (page 288) or interactions among parts of the program that constrain the scheduling of these parts for parallel execution.[269] We discussed this in some detail for the n-body example in the Cosmic Cube section (see page 484).

By contrast, a functional-language program has no concept of a reusable von Neumann-style store; it has no side effects, and it carries its own data. Another way to say this is that in the reduction model, both the program and data are treated as an integrated but distributed data structure. Data values are never modified in place; they are only created and destroyed (by storage reclamation, i.e., "garbage collection").[270] A less formal way to describe this attribute is that the von Neumann model is "If you need it, it's in the memory", and the reduction model is "Everything you need is in your pockets."

As might be expected, reduction uses more memory, but since side effects are absent, "subprocesses" can now be executed in parallel.[271] If the data that a process needs are reasonably close by (i.e., if there is high *locality* in the program), then it is not critical which processor performs which process, and processes can (at least conceptually) easily be moved from a very busy processor to one that is less busy. The authors conjecture that applications of medium grain and larger usually do possess sufficient locality to minimize nonlocal memory references and make the boudoir approach attractive.[272]

The Rediflow design reflects these points. It uses a graph reduction model that is augmented, for reasons of efficiency, with a second, more memory-efficient (but less easily parallelized) model to execute sections of code for

---

[269] The ease of erroneous scheduling has led to the suggestion that the motto for a shared-memory multiprocessor should be, "But I *know* I put a 5 over there!"

[270] A standard garbage collection method is used—divide the memory in half and periodically copy from one half to the other half all objects that still have pointers pointing to them, and then erase the old half.

[271] Since there are no side effects, the serialization principle (page 572) is automatically obeyed.

[272] Presumably the fact that reduction programs carry their own data benefits locality.

which further concurrency would add little overall speedup.[273] Such sections of code are encapsulated as special "von Neumann processes", thus forming a second category in addition to the processes that come from using the reduction model. The goal is to combine the load-spreading potential of reduction with other methods that are less storage-intensive. Internally, these special "von Neumann processes" are ordinary sequential programs, but they are allowed to influence their exterior environment only by sending messages (no external side effects),[274] which they do using send and wait operations similar to those defined by Kahn [270].[275] Externally, these processes appear as a type of (macro) dataflow function, which explains the second part of Rediflow's name.

In a comparison of reduction vs. dataflow, reduction is at a *disadvantage* in processing strict operations such as those found in arithmetic expressions $(+,\times,...)$, where every operand normally contributes to the final result. Reduction is *superior* for nonstrict operations such as "if-then-else" that do not require all their arguments. This fits with Rediflow's orientation toward applications in artificial intelligence and database management.

Hardware Design: In general, the Rediflow hardware is envisioned as an interconnected set of processors, each having a private memory, an arrangement that the authors dub a *boudoir* configuration to distinguish it from the *dance hall* configuration of some shared-memory designs in which all the memory modules are on one side of the network and all the processors on the other (like boys and girls at a school dance). A global address space is provided to support the pointer mechanism needed by the graph reduction model (see Figure 4.1 on page 136).[276]

---

[273] In a similar vein, it has been said that the problem in Prolog programs is not that of *finding* sufficient parallelism but of *controlling* its degree.

[274] Echoes of information hiding, Ada packages, and, to a lesser extent, objects in object-oriented programming, in that private life is ignored as long as public behavior is acceptable.

[275] Kahn defined a simple message-passing language for parallel processing that predates and differs from CSP (page 247) in that, as in the Cosmic Cube, a process performing a send is *not* forced to wait for an acknowledgment of receipt. CSP is *so* synchronous that deadlock arises easily.

[276] This allows the sharing of subexpressions (definitions). In graph reduction, unique expressions are evaluated only once. In string reduction, by contrast, the expression is copied every time it is needed. Thus, graph reduction requires more addressing overhead, but string reduction needs more memory. These trade-offs are discussed further on page 630 ff.

The specific implementation discussed [276] is based on a Transputer-like node containing a processor, a memory, and a moderately intelligent switch that connects the node to four neighbors in a rectangular mesh. (The memories have a combined global address space, but a processor in one node accesses a memory in another node via a request packet that is routed by intermediate nodes. Hence, this is a message-passing rather than a shared-memory design, since access to the globally addressable memory is not equally direct for all processors.)

The distinguishing feature is the distributed task-scheduling[277] and load-balancing mechanism, which works as follows. Each node has a queue used for the backlog of tasks[278] to be done in that node. The node maintains a count of the local backlog and periodically compares this number with that of its neighbors. In case of a big difference, some tasks are moved to a less busy processor. The authors draw an analogy between local task backlog and pressure in a fluid, with the switch having the capability to guide tasks along "pressure gradients" to less busy nodes.[279]

The spawning of tasks within a node is controlled with a "throttling" mechanism that can (reversibly) change the way the task queue works from its normal first in, first out (FIFO) to a last in, first out (LIFO) mode of operation (i.e., the task queue becomes a stack). This throttling action effectively switches the system from breadth-first to depth-first traversal of the tree of successive function evaluations generated by the reduction model.

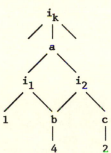

An example may help to see why this reduces the number of enqueued tasks. Consider the simple computation in part (d) of Figure 4.1 on page 136. Task i_k calls for the evaluation of a; this evaluation is enqueued as a task that eventually calls for two evaluations, i_1 and i_2. In FIFO mode, these are evaluated successively, and the evaluations demanded by *both* are placed in the queue, until eventually all the leaves of the tree are enqueued. In LIFO mode, i_2 is evaluated first, then the last of

---

[277] The reader is encouraged to compare this scheduling approach to the parallel central task queue in the Ultracomputer design (page 572).

[278] Called *chares*, an Old English word for a small task or chore.

[279] The Rediflow approach assumes that the Ultracomputer approach won't work; that is, that the network used for the shared memory will be a bottleneck, the introduction of caches will create cache-coherency problems, and both will limit the number of processors and hence the degree of parallelism. It is better, Rediflow advocates argue, to have a large number of processors and memories that are pairwise tightly coupled.

the evaluations it demands, and so on; only some time after the bottom of the tree is reached is i_1 evaluated. No more than one evaluation per tree level is ever enqueued, so the maximum number of enqueued tasks is the tree height, which is generally less than its breadth at the leaf level;[280] that is, the number of tasks in the queue is smaller in the LIFO (depth-first) case.

Results: Simulation experiments involving on the order of 50 processors were carried out on toy programs (divide-and-conquer algorithms) as well as real examples from database and signal-processing programs. Typically, between 5% and 20% of data references generated by a node were nonlocal.[281] The embodiment envisioned for this approach is a machine with medium-grain parallelism, having somewhere between 100 and 10,000 processors.

Purdue/UW CHiP

The CHiP (Configurable, Highly Parallel) computer [406] is a lattice of identical processing elements (PEs) set into a lattice of identical switches and can assume the configuration of many different systolic arrays and other "algorithmically specialized processors". Figure 10.9 shows an example of a CHiP array configured as the systolic array of Figure 9.13. The number of ports per switch is usually four or eight (Figure 9.13 corresponds to the latter case), while the number of PE ports is usually eight or fewer (six in the present example). The perimeter switches are connected to external storage devices. Each switch in the lattice has local memory capable of storing the switch setting for several different configurations, like a decentralized version of the

Figure 10.9 A CHiP lattice of intermixed switch and processing elements [406] configured into the systolic array of Figure 9.13 on page 462. The circles are switches, and the squares are processing elements. The lattice can be reconfigured for other algorithms by resetting the switches.

---

280 Remember that computer science trees are upside down.
281 This proportion is also about what was assumed for the RP3 design. Note that, as a rule of thumb, about two-thirds of memory references are instructions; note also that data can be prefetched.

GF11 operation (page 436), and, as in that case, circuit switching rather than packet switching is provided. The switch memory is loaded before processing, at the same time that the PE memory is loaded. Processing begins with the controller broadcasting a command to all switches to invoke a particular configuration setting. The advantages of this reconfigurability in regard to flexibility, fault tolerance, and wafer-scale integration are discussed by L. Snyder [406].

"Pringle" prototypes[282] with 64 PEs were used to investigate design trade-offs at Purdue University and the University of Washington. The PEs were 8-bit Intel 8031 microprocessors, and a polling bus was used to simulate a network of switches.

10.2.5 Bus-Connected Designs

Tandem

The Tandem NonStop™ System [275] shown in Figure 10.10 is a bus-connected MIMD message-passing design available with 2–32 PEs (3 MIPS each). The operating system is symmetric (i.e., not master-slave). At least two

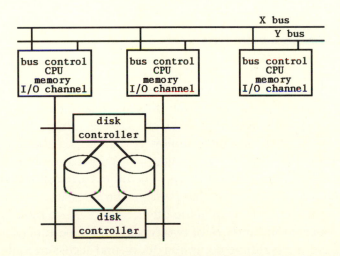

Figure 10.10 Tandem system diagram.

---

[282] Pringle is a brand of homogeneous potato chips.

paths connect any two components in the system, as part of a hardware redundancy scheme that can tolerate single-module failures without stopping
the system (graceful degradation).

Tandem systems are being used to obtain high performance in distributed
on-line transaction processing systems. As we said on page 66, a multiuser
database system affords two main sources of parallelism: *among* many (simple) independent transactions and *within* a single complex transaction. Here
we are talking about the first category. The interesting thing is that the parallel
hardware in Tandem was not originally designed to exploit parallelism in database applications, but rather to provide high reliability and availability.
However, these features made possible the design of a database management
system without the encumbrance of some of the software safety features
needed by less reliable hardware, which in turn created opportunities for more
highly parallel transaction processing [71]. Transaction rates up to 208 per
second were reported for NonStop SQL running on a 32-PE system [426].
Higher performance[283] is offered by the more recent Integrity 300 system,
which is based on RISC processors from MIPS Computer Systems Incorporated.

10.2.6 Trees

The Teradata Database Machine

Teradata's DBC/1012 Data Base Computer [431] is a
tree-connected collection of up to 1024 PEs, operating in MIMD, message-passing mode. The desig-
nation "1012" (for 10 to the 12th power) refers to the
product's ability to handle databases of up to a
terabyte. Unlike NonVon (page 634), only the leaf
nodes are PEs. The others are formed into a treelike
"Y-net" that performs broadcast in one direction and
sorting in the other. The PEs are based on the Intel
8086 and its successors, and are of two types: interface-function processors
(IFPs) that parse, analyze, and compile a query, and access-module processors
(AMPs) that control disks and execute database operations. The DBC/1012
attaches to a mainframe computer and handles the mainframe's database
management activities. A relational database model is used; that is, data are

---

[283] Rates of 1000 simple transactions/sec were reported in 1992.

represented as tables (see page 67). This is not a small machine; a 512-PE system would require a minimum floor space of 56 feet by 61 feet (about 19 by 20 meters).

To repeat what we have said, a multiuser database system affords two main sources of parallelism: *among* many (simple) independent transactions and *within* a single complex transaction. Here we are dealing with the second category. Complex queries as large as 10-table (i.e., 10-relation) joins on 4-GB to 10-GB tables have been reported for a 208-PE configuration.

The hardware of this machine has been described as harnessing the cost-efficient power of multiple microprocessors operating in parallel, but at least equal credit must go to the software (over a million lines of code), which achieves such things as *partitioning* the database "right", that is, on independent disks when needed, and so on. This, together with the improving economics of microprocessors and the availability of cheap memory for buffers, is the major element responsible for the success of this parallel database machine.

The Columbia DADO Production-System Machine

The DADO project[284] at Columbia University has developed a tree-structured MIMD parallel processor [415] designed for the kind of rule-driven "production-system" applications we described on page 74 (see Figure 10.12 on page 507). As we said before, the tree interconnection scheme offers simplicity and is well matched to the layout of VLSI chips and circuit boards (see Figure 8.3 on page 387), but it can suffer from traffic jams at the root if there is much communication among the processing elements (PEs) located at the tree's leaves. DADO's builders feel that these traffic jams are not a problem with production-system applications, because of the local nature of the communication involved [416].

The DADO2 prototype built at Columbia University consisted of 1023 PEs based on the Intel 8751, a 1-chip 8-bit microcomputer (processor + memory) incorporating 4K of EPROM and 256 bytes of RAM. The PE also included a 16-KB RAM and a gate-array I/O chip (1600 gates) that improved global communication among the PEs. This prototype was used for a number of programming and performance experiments [415]. A commercial version with between 3 and 8191 PEs built on the (32-bit) Motorola 68020 has been announced by Fifth Generation Computer Corp. [410]. There are two versions, one for rule-based and sorting and matching problems and one for signal in-

---

284 The dictionary defines *dado* as that part of a pedestal included between the base and the surbase. A similar three-tier structure is visible in Figure 10.11.

Figure 10.11 *Functional division of the DADO tree* corresponding to the original *DADO algorithm for production-system execution (from reference [415]).*

terpretation. Languages include Parallel C, Parallel Lisp, Parallel Fortran, and OPS5.[285]

Before we discuss production systems on DADO, we pause for a brief review. As summarized in Figure 10.12 on page 507 and described in more detail on page 74, a production system program applies a set of "if ... , then do ..." rules (*productions*) to a set of facts about the world. A production memory (PM) holds the rules, and a working memory (WM) holds the facts. Program execution is controlled by the inferencing system, which can be an interpreter, as in the case of OPS5, a compiler, as in the case of OPS83, or special inference-engine hardware, as in the case of the PIM-D dataflow machine (page 537).

In the serial case, the inferencing system cycles in sequence through the MATCH-SELECT-ACT steps of Figure 10.12. As Gupta *et al.* [208] put it, during the MATCH phase, the program's knowledge (represented by the production rules) is tested for relevance against the existing problem state (represented by the working memory). During the CONFLICT RESOLUTION phase the most promising piece of knowledge that is relevant is selected. During the ACT phase, the action recommended by the selected rule is applied

---

[285] Note that Prolog is absent from this list.

Figure 10.12 Essential components of a (rules-driven) production system.
*LHS and RHS refer to the left- and right-hand sides of a rule in the production
memory.*

to the existing problem state, resulting in a new problem state. The process is
repeated until no unsatisfied rule remains.[286]

Algorithms for performing the MATCH operation fall into two classes:
non-state-saving algorithms match the complete working memory against all
the productions on each cycle; that is, they start from (almost) scratch every
time. This policy can be inefficient if only a small and stable number of rules
is matched on each cycle, as, for example, in the R1 production system. The
only new rules added to the conflict set during a new cycle, or, in other words,
the only rules that match this time that didn't also match last time, are the rules
that are associated with *changes* in the working memory. *State-saving algorithms* take advantage of this slow rate of change; they store the results of executing MATCH from previous cycles, so that only the changes made to the
working memory by the most recent production firing need be processed ev-

---

[286] This description omits many subtleties, and for more details the reader should consult the
references cited in this section.

ery cycle. An example is the *Rete algorithm*[287] that forms the basis of the OPS5 production-system language [208], [175]. Whether it is advantageous to store state depends on the fraction of working memory that changes on each cycle and the amount of state stored. In the parallel case, state-saving also imposes some additional sequentiality. These trade-offs are discussed in reference [208].

As with databases, the key to speedup from parallel execution of a production system is the method used for partitioning and distributing the data, which this time are the rules in the PM and the facts in the WM. Stolfo discusses several DADO algorithms for partitioning and distributing this data, one of which is illustrated in Figure 10.11 on page 506.

Each PE can execute in either of two modes under control of run-time software. In SPMD mode (page 609), the PE executes instructions broadcast by some ancestor PE in the tree. When a PE enters MIMD mode, it no longer receives instructions from an ancestor, but it can still broadcast them to an SPMD subtree of descendants. These instructions are not machine-level instructions and are not executed in lockstep, as in SIMD operation. Rather, addresses of prestored code are broadcast to PEs for local execution, which may take different amounts of time on each PE (due to different branching conditions, etc.).

Stolfo [416] discusses several ways to partition a production system for parallel processing on DADO. One way is to give each PE some rules and some facts. By contrast, the "original DADO algorithm" makes use of the ability to operate in the two modes described above and logically divides the machine into the three conceptually distinct components illustrated in Figure 10.11 on page 506. An appropriately chosen level of the tree called the *PRODUCTION MEMORY level* consists of MIMD-mode PEs executing the MATCH phase. A number of distinct rules are stored in each of these PM-level PEs. Working memory elements relevant to each PM-level PE's rules are stored in that PE's subtree. During MATCH, this WM-level subtree functions as a collection of SPMD-mode PEs implementing a content-addressable memory. The upper tree consists of SPMD-mode PEs that perform CONFLICT RESOLUTION and synchronization. Stolfo and Miranker [416] describe other DADO algorithms, including a parallel Rete, and discuss the trade-offs. This work overlaps a little with the paper by Gupta, Forgy, Newell, and Wedig

---

[287] *Rete* is a word meaning "network". The Rete algorithm uses a dataflowlike discrimination network (compiled from the left-hand sides of the productions) to perform MATCH. Forgy's title [175] gives the objective nicely: "A fast algorithm for the many pattern/many object pattern match problem".

[208], who also compare DADO with other architectures for production system execution.

The MATCH phase is the most obvious source of parallelism in the execution of a production system. However, the resulting speedup is still a matter of some controversy. One reason is that the execution of a production system often involves only a small subset of the rules, and thus most of the MATCH operations will fail. In such cases, a sequential implementation of an algorithm that can predict and avoid useless MATCH operations[288] will do respectably well against a parallel algorithm that performs MATCH on all the rules during each cycle, especially when there are large variations in the processing requirements of the relevant rules, since many PEs in the parallel case must then wait for the slowest to catch up and synchronize for the resolve operation. The OPS5 team [208] claims that in practice the true speedup from parallelism is less than tenfold and feels that a shared-memory multiprocessor with 32–64 powerful PEs running a parallel Rete algorithm is the way to go. Defending DADO against this "depressing view", Stolfo [415] acknowledges the problems, but he points out that the observations are based on the serial execution of programs in one particular language and may not be universal. He is also optimistic about reducing the rule-match variance time and increasing the average affected set size via multitasking and source-to-source transformational techniques.

The TMC Connection Machine CM-5

In the previous chapter on SIMD architectures, we discussed the CM-1 and CM-2 designs from Thinking Machines Corporation. Somewhat surprisingly their next offering, CM-5, has moved into the MIMD world (although, as we shall see, there is still hardware support for a synchronous style of programming). Readers seeking additional information should consult [435].

Architecture

At the very coarsest level of detail, the CM-5 is simply a private-memory MIMD machine, another descendant of the cosmic cube. But such a description leaves out a great deal. The interconnection topology is a fat tree, there is support for SIMD, a combining control network is provided, vector units are available, and the machine is powerful. We discuss each of these in turn.

As discussed in the interconnection networks chapter on page 404, a fat tree is a tree in which links higher in the tree have greater bandwidth (e.g., one can keep the clock constant and use wider busses near the root). Unlike the

---

288 As can the Rete algorithm, for example.

nodes in hypercube machines such as CM-1 and CM-2, a node in the CM-5 has a constant number of nearest neighbors (four) independent of the size of the machine.[289] In addition, the bandwidth available per processor for random communication patterns remains constant as the machine size increases, whereas this bandwidth decreases for meshes (or non–fat trees). Local communication is favored by the CM-5 but by only a factor of 4 over random communication (20MB/sec vs. 5MB/sec), which is much less than in other machines such as CM-2. Also attached to this fat tree are I/O interfaces. The device side of these interfaces can support 20MB/sec; higher-speed devices are accommodated by ganging together multiple interfaces. (If the destination node for the I/O is far from the interface, the sustainable bandwidth is also limited by the fat tree to 5MB/sec.)

The fat tree just discussed is actually one of three networks on the CM-5. In addition to this data network, there is a diagnostic network used for fault detection and a control network that we turn to next. One function of the control network is to provide rapid synchronization of the processors, which is accomplished by a global OR operation that completes shortly after the last participating processor sets its value. This "cheap barrier" permits the main advantage of SIMD (permanent synchrony implying no race conditions) without requiring that the processors always execute the same instruction.

A second function of the control network is provide a form of hardware combining, specifically to support reduction and parallel prefix calculations. As discussed in Chapter 4, parallel prefix computation for a given binary operator ϕ (say addition) begins with each processor specifying a value and ends with each processor obtaining the sum of the values provided by itself and all lower-numbered processors. These parallel prefix computations may be viewed as the synchronous, and hence deterministic, analogue of the fetch-and-phi operation described on page 578. The CM-5 supports addition, maximum, and logical OR and XOR. Two variants are also supplied: a parallel suffix and a segmented parallel prefix (and suffix). With a segmented operation (think of worms, not virtual memory, and see [386]), each processor can set a flag indicating that it begins a segment, and the prefix computation is done separately for each segment. Reduction operations are similar: each processor supplies a value, and all processors obtain the sum of all values (again MAX, OR, and XOR are supported as well).

Each node of a CM-5 contains a SPARC microprocessor for scalar operations (users are advised against coding in assembler, a hint that the engine may change), a 64-KB cache, and up to 32 MB of local memory (which will

---

[289] Only the leaf nodes of the tree are processing elements.

increase as DRAM technology improves). Memory is accessed 64 bits at a time (plus 8 bits for ECC). An option available with the CM-5 is the incorporation of four vector units in between each processor and its associated memory. When the vector units are installed, memory is organized as four 8-MB banks, one connected to each unit. Each vector unit can perform both floating-point and integer operations, either one at a peak rate of 32 million 64-bit operations per second.

As we said above, the CM-5 is quite a powerful computer. With the vector units present, each node has a peak performance of 128 64-bit MFLOPS or 128 64-bit integer MOPS. The machine is architected for a maximum of 256K nodes but the current implementation is "limited" to 16K due to restrictions on cable lengths. Since the peak computational rate for a 16K node system exceeds 2 Teraflops one might assert that the age of (peak) "teraflop computing" has arrived. However, as we write this in 1993, the largest announced delivery of a CM-5 is a 1K-node configuration (a photo is shown in Figure 10.1 on page 468). A full 16K system would cost about one-half billion dollars.

Software and Environment

In addition to the possibly thousands of computation nodes just described, a CM-5 contains a few control processors that act as hosts to which users can log in. The reason for multiple control processors is that the system administrator can divide the CM-5 into partitions, each with an individual control processor as host. The host provides a conventional UNIX-like operating system; in particular, users can timeshare a single partition. Each computation node runs an operating system microkernel supporting a subset of the full functionality available on the control processor acting as its host (a master-slave approach; see page 360).

Parallel versions of Fortran, C, and Lisp are provided. CM Fortran is a mild extension of Fortran 90 (see page 240). Additional features include a `forall` statement (see page 151) and vector-valued subscripts. For an example of the latter, assume that `A` and `P` are vectors of size 20 with all `P(I)` between 1 and 20; then `A=A(P)` does the parallel assignments `A(I)=A(P(I))`.

An important contribution is the CM Scientific Software Library, a growing set of numerical routines, hand-tailored to exploit the CM-5 hardware. Although primarily intended for the CM Fortran user, the library is also usable from TMC's versions of C and Lisp, C* and *Lisp. To date, the library developers have concentrated on linear algebra, FFTs, random-number generators, and statistical analyses.

In addition to supporting the data parallel model of computing typified by Fortran 90, the CM-5 also supports synchronous (i.e., blocking) message passing in which the sender does not proceed until its message is received. (This is the rendezvous model used in Ada and CSP.) Limited support for asynchronous message passing is provided, and further support is expected.

10.2.7   Multistage Networks

IBM 9076 SP1

The 9076 SP1 is the first member of the IBM Scalable POWERparallel series [255], a distributed-memory architecture based on RISC/6000 processing elements that communicate via messages through a multistage interconnection network. The SP1 has 8–64 processors, providing 1–8 peak Gigaflops. The architecture is scalable to Teraflops. The software supports interactive, batch, serial, and parallel jobs. Performance results are shown on page 379 and in Figure 2.11 on page 58.

The computing nodes are 62.5 MHz RISC/6000 processors (125 MFLOPS peak) with 64–256 MB of memory. The interconnection network, or "switch fabric", consists of 8×8 crossbar switches arranged in an extra-stage omega network that provides 40 MB/s peak bandwidth per (bidirectional) connection. The hardware delay across the network is below a microsecond. Applications typically see 8.2 MB/s bandwidth and 29 microsecond latency. The network provides buffered wormhole routing for the self-steering packets of a message. The switch boards of each 16-processor rack implement the first two stages of a multistage network, which has been "folded" in such a way that a packet between two nodes in the same rack traverses three switch stages if the two nodes are not connected to the same switch element, or one switch stage if they are (see Figure 10.13 on page 513). When source and destination are in separate racks, the packet traverses four switch elements. Because of the redundancy provided by the extra network stage, there are four routes possible between any two nodes in SP1, so that four different links would have to fail before a node was cut off from communication.

10.2.8   Dataflow Machines—Manchester and (Many) Others

The message-passing parallel computers we have discussed so far have all used rather conventional processing elements. Even Rediflow's hybrid

Figure 10.13 Illustration showing how redrawing a switch element with four unidirectional inputs and four such outputs as a 2x2 switch element that has bidirectional inputs and outputs makes drawing a folded multistage network easier. The two networks at the bottom of the figure are identical; both allow four processors to talk to each other or to the rest of the world via four different paths. The SP1 switch elements are larger than those shown here. They have eight unidirectional inputs and a like number of outputs, and are drawn as 4x4 bidirectional switches.

reduction/dataflow computational model (page 498) is implemented using von Neumann processing elements that have been beefed up with a few extra instructions to implement the CSP message-passing protocol. In this section, however, we describe parallel message-passing machines in which the processing elements themselves are dataflow computers. In other words, "Warning—Hardware 'Paradigm Shift' Ahead!"

The basic idea of the dataflow model, as we illustrated in Figure 4.1 on page 136, is that (1) data flow from instruction to instruction *directly* rather than via a shared variable, and (2) rather than a program counter or other central control mechanism, instructions may execute (fire) any time after arrival

Figure 10.14 Illustrative dataflow processing element. *Division into Enabling Unit, Memory, and Processing Unit holds for most designs. Details here resemble those of the Manchester Dataflow Machine prototype, but we show a two-level design with concurrency among function units and among processing elements; the Manchester prototype had one PE and hence only pipeline concurrency. (I-structure memory from MIT tagged-token design is an alternate way to package Structure Store.) Small box at right: dataflow graph snippet with a token going from node 15 to 16. Token's details are above the box; graph's representation in Instruction Memory is below. Token pool and matching unit of this dynamic design are absent in a static dataflow machine.*

of the data they need[290] (this simple enabling, or firing, rule may be expanded to include additional restrictions in practice, as we discuss later). A dataflow program is compiled into a graph whose nodes represent instructions and whose arcs represent the program's structure (data dependencies). Data-carrying tokens flow along these arcs during program execution (see page 271). Implicitly, each arc contains buffers to hold tokens. Tokens on a node's input arcs are held until each input arc for that node has a token. Then the node is said to fire. It consumes the first token from each input arc, performs the designated operation, produces a result token, and sends a copy of this token on each output arc. Although the original program can be written in an imperative language like Fortran, the full benefit of this model is obtained with dataflow languages (page 271) that eliminate side effects and hence make more instructions eligible for concurrent execution. We briefly discussed re-lated compiler issues on page 331. Here we treat dataflow hardware.

The job of a dataflow processing element is to receive a data token, wait for its mate(s), use this collected information to compute and form new result tokens,[291] and send them on to their next destinations in the dataflow graph. Figure 10.14 on page 514 shows a representative processing element, divided into an Enabling Unit that collects the tokens needed to enable an instruction, Memory that holds the program and provides temporary storage for tokens, and a Processing Unit that executes enabled instructions.

To be more specific, the Enabling Unit coordinates concurrent activities at a node by managing the storage of tokens and administering the enabling rule for those nodes (instructions) that require more than one input. It se-quentially accepts a token and stores it in memory. If this process enables the node to which the token is addressed (i.e., if this results in a token on each in-put port of the node), then the input tokens are extracted from memory and combined into an *executable packet* consisting of the input tokens' values (data), the opcode, and a list of destinations. This packet is sent to the Proc-

---

290   For a *strict* function or instruction, this firing rule means a token on each input arc to the node. An example of a nonstrict function is a *merge* node—multiple inputs, one output, but it can fire with just one input token.

291   The plural is important, since multiple output tokens give the parallelism. For the sake of clarity, our examples may show only a single token moving through the dataflow graph, but in reality one should think of this graph as simply *crawling* with tokens, the more the better from the viewpoint of the dataflow people, as long as the resource constraints of the machine are not exceeded (otherwise, deadlock can occur). For tagged-token architec-tures, these resources are token storage, structure storage, program memory, and the number of tasks (i.e., the number of contexts or names). Resource management policies are an active area of dataflow research.

essing Unit, which computes the output values, combines them with the destination addresses into new tokens, and sends these back to the Enabling Unit (of this or another processing element), where they may enable other nodes [447]. Since the enabling and functional stages work concurrently, the processing element (PE) is sometimes referred to as a *circular pipeline*, or *processing ring* (not to be confused with the interconnection topology of the PEs). At this level of generality, this model holds for most dataflow designs. It is the inner workings of these three units that distinguish one design from another. An example follows in the next section.

"It is no exaggeration to say that *all* dataflow projects started in the seventies were directly based on seminal work[292] by Dennis"[137] , writes his MIT colleague Arvind [33], himself a prominent researcher in this field. A general-level introduction [318] as well as detailed surveys [33], [447], [409] and critiques [185] are found in the recent literature, and so we confine our discussion of dataflow architectures to the central issues influencing the opportunities for massive parallelism. These issues include static vs. dynamic dataflow, modified enabling rules, and provisions for structured data. We illustrate our discussion with examples from the Manchester Dataflow Machine [209], [210], a design of the dynamic type, since this machine represents a superset of some of the other designs and also represents experience with real hardware.

Special thanks go to K. Ekanadham for patience in clarifying many aspects of dataflow.

The Manchester Dataflow Machine Prototype

The Manchester Dataflow Machine (MDM) is an example of a dynamic, tagged-token architecture. The essence of a dynamic machine is that the criterion to fire an instruction is simply the availability of all its operands. Potentially, this enables all the parallelism in the program, but provisions must be made for this parallelism. For example, the different iterations of a loop may be eligible for parallel execution, but the nodes corresponding to the loop body are now fired many times during the program and may well find more than one token on an input arc. To exploit such parallelism, a tagged-token design provides tokens that carry tags identifying their roles in the computation (iteration number, for instance) and represent a mechanism for allocating storage to the arcs dynamically (needed because the number of iterations is not

---

[292] An outgrowth of a method for designing and verifying multiprogrammed systems like MULTICS, whose development provided the first experience with the complexities of large scale asynchronous parallelism [447]. Note our discussion of concurrency in uniprocessor operating systems on page 353.

Figure 10.15 Token flow in the Manchester Dataflow Machine prototype. *This is a dynamic, tagged-token architecture. In this embodiment, three simple 2×2 switch elements connect a processing element to the host and to two special memory modules used to store array data in the form of I-structures for better efficiency. Pipelined (overlapped) parallelism is obtained from the concurrent Function Units (ALUs), whose number is adjusted to the speed of the Matching Unit. The text provides more details.*

known at compile time). We want to examine a concrete example of hardware that allocates storage in this manner. After that, we will discuss alternative design choices and trade-offs.

The MDM prototype [209] and [210], shown in Figure 10.15 on page 517, consists of a switching network connecting some number of processing elements (processing rings) and structure stores (storage rings) to a host computer (VAX 11/780). The MDM is a *two-level* design, intended to permit (pipeline) concurrency among the multiple function units *within* a processing element as well as (truly parallel) concurrency *among* processing elements when more than one is present. In the implementation described in the cited references, there are two structure stores and one processing element. The speed of the link to the host is 168-KB/second (14K tokens/second), with a substantial upgrade planned.

Structure Store, Network: Two structure store modules can hold a total of 1 million data values with access rates of 0.75 million reads per second and half as many writes per second. Arrays and other data structures are stored in this special memory as *I-structures* (page 531) that improve the parallelism and efficiency of computations involving data structures by allowing these structures to be created incrementally, that is, by allowing the production and consumption of a data structure to proceed concurrently (something not allowed with the purely functional array operators used in some other designs). A further advantage is that data values in the structure store are stored without their tags. However, space is needed for tokens that try to read a data element before it is written, since the entire read token is then stored in the structure store (and a pointer is returned) until the write takes place.[293] Each location in the structure store has a present bit like the HEP full/empty bit (page 568) to indicate whether the element has yet been written (and hence is available to be read).[294] The structure store provides reference counts to support garbage collection of I-structures no longer needed by the program.

The switching network is organized as a sequence of three 2×2 (bus-) switching elements that have an internal clock period of 50 nanoseconds and a capability of transferring 5 million tokens per second. A multistage version (page 398) of this linear switch is planned for the future.

Processing Element: One processing element was constructed. It consists of four independent modules connected in an asynchronous pipeline. Data values, encapsulated in packets known as tokens, enter the Queue, are paired in the Matching Unit, fetch the corresponding instruction from the Instruction Store, and are executed with that instruction by the Processing Unit to produce new tokens that may reenter the Queue and each enable a subsequent instruction. The name *processing ring* that is also used for this processing element (PE) comes from this circulation of tokens during program execution and does not refer to PE interconnection topology. The 96-bit tokens entering and leaving the PE are formatted as follows:

37 bits for data (5 of these are for the data type).
36 bits for tag (fields for activation name, iteration number, and array index).
22 bits for destination (instruction node address and input port number).
1 bit for marker (number of tokens needed to enable destination instruction).

---

[293] Therefore, all writes must spend time checking for deferred reads.
[294] This protocol resembles readers/writers coordination but is asymmetric (only one write) and hence more constrained.

The designers would have preferred a 64-bit data field (rather than one of 32 bits) but felt they could not afford it.

The Token Queue (used to smooth out uneven rates of generation and consumption of tokens) consists of three pipeline buffer registers surrounding a first-in, first-out (FIFO) circular store with a capacity of 32K tokens and an access time of 120 nanoseconds. The store and registers are 96 bits wide. The clock period is 37.5 nanoseconds, giving this queue a maximum throughput of 2.67 million tokens/second.

The most visible sign that this machine is a tagged-token design is the Matching Unit that pairs tokens destined for the same instruction if their tags match (tokens destined for one-input instructions bypass this unit). A hardware hashing mechanism is used to approximate the action of an associative memory that can hold up to 1.25 million unmatched tokens awaiting their partners. (This memory plus the various buffers in the PE define the size of the common pool of tokens that is the mechanism for dynamic allocation of token-storage capacity to the arcs of the dataflow graph.) In addition to eight buffers, the building blocks of this unit are 20 64K-token memory boards that also contain a comparator. An incoming token's 54-bit matching key (18 bits for the destination and 36 bits for the tag) is hashed to a 16-bit address corresponding to the same cell on each board. Each board compares the key of the token stored at that address against the incoming token's key. If there is a match, the two tokens are combined into a 133-bit packet (token plus extra data field) and sent to the Instruction Store. If there is no match, the incoming token must be written at that address on one of the 20 boards. In other words, a full system can simultaneously accommodate 20 tokens that hash to the same address. The twenty-first and subsequent such tokens are sent to continue their search in an Overflow Unit (simulated by the host and to be replaced by a hardware version with an initial capacity of 32K tokens). The overflow unit is an essential safety mechanism, but for good performance its population of tokens should be kept reasonably low. The Matching Unit has a clock period of 155 nanoseconds and a memory cycle time of 150 nanoseconds, giving rates of 1.29 million matches/second for dyadic operators and 6.45 million bypasses/second for monadic operators. The Overflow Unit is slightly slower.

The Instruction Store is a buffered random-access memory with a capacity of 64K instructions; these come in three formats, with lengths up to 70 bits. The clock period is 40 nanoseconds, and the memory access time is 150 nanoseconds, resulting in a maximum processing rate of 2 million instruction fetches/second. The 166-bit output packet is longer than the incoming token-pair packet by a 10-bit opcode and an optional 23-bit destination address and marker bit.

The Processing Unit[295] contains a preprocessor that executes a small number of instructions, but the majority are passed to a homogeneous bank of 20 microcoded Function Units (ALUs) with 51 internal registers and 4K words of writable microcode memory. The internal word length is 24 bits, with facilities for microcoding 32-bit floating-point arithmetic. Microinstructions are 48 bits wide. The clock period is 67 nanoseconds, and the Function Unit microcycle period is 267 nanoseconds.

Performance: Microcoding is valuable for fast design iterations in an experimental situation but extracts a performance penalty. The instruction execution time ranges from 16 to 480 microcycles, giving a maximum 0.23 MIPS per Function Unit and making the optimum number of Function Units strongly dependent on the instruction mix. Twenty Function Units have achieved processing rates over 1 MIPS on real programs [209], [210]. About 50-fold software parallelism is then needed to keep all the hardware modules in the processing element busy. The matching unit's million-token capacity is found to be barely adequate.

Design and Efficiency Considerations

The processing of dataflow tokens, like the processing of floating-point numbers, requires operand manipulation that takes several steps and is amenable to pipelined processing. However, processing a dataflow token is more complex, and the pipelines are longer. A typical floating-point adder has six pipeline stages (see Figure 9.4 on page 419 and Figure 9.7 on page 424), a dynamic dataflow processing element can have 30–40 stages [447]. For example, the following breakdown of the pipeline latency in the MIT tagged-token dataflow multiprocessor is largely true for the MDM as well (the steps correspond to the token flow in the processing element of Figure 10.14 on page 514):

---

[295] Veen [447] changed the terms *Processing Unit* and *Function Units* used in the MDM papers [209], [210] to *Functional Unit* and *Functional Elements*, respectively. We use the original MDM terms.

Operation	Clock Cycles
input	1
token match	4
instruction fetch	8
decode & execute	4
fetch destination list	4
build token	1
route	1
transmission network	4–8
PIPELINE LATENCY	27–31

If the instruction being executed involves structured data (such as an array) and hence access to the I-structure[296] memory, the pipeline latency increases by about 15–20 clock cycles. Thus, a substantial performance improvement is possible for programs that contain a sufficiently high degree of parallelism. By the same token, however, a high degree of parallelism is *needed* for efficient operation of such a dataflow machine.

Understandably, the question has been asked whether the amount of hardware needed for a dataflow machine would not be better used by another architecture. Gajski et al. [185], for example, argue that the effective utilization of a dataflow machine's hardware will be unacceptably low because most programs do not have sufficiently high degrees of parallelism except when large arrays are processed, in which case the overhead of handling large data structures in a dataflow machine will result in excessive storage or processing requirements.

Veen [447] highlights the considerations that influence the design and efficiency of a dataflow machine like the Manchester prototype as follows: The network hardware in this prototype, as for that of others in this chapter, is a relatively small fraction of the total,[297] with the remaining cost fairly evenly split between memory and processors. Thus, the question becomes how well the processors are kept busy, what fraction of their work is useful, and how much memory they need to do it.

The processors may be idle for three reasons: (1) improper hardware balance within a processing element (PE), (2) improper load distribution among PEs, and (3) insufficient parallelism in the program. The hardware within a PE must have the proper balance between the number of Functional Units and the

---

[296] I-structures are defined on page 531.

[297] However, a multistage network for *n* processors grows as *n* log *n* and eventually dominates the cost for large *n*.

speed of the Matching Unit. Experiments and simulations showed that the number of Functional Units should be about 20. Including the other pipelines in the PE, this estimate calls for program parallelism of at least 30 per PE, with 50 preferred for smooth buffered operation. Thus, even a moderate dataflow multiprocessor (64 PEs, say) needs parallelism on the order of several thousand in the program. Furthermore, this work load must be properly allocated to the PEs.

In summary, the concern is the utilization of time and resources by a dataflow machine. The effective speed of such a machine is a complex problem, and we have touched on only a few key aspects. The utilization of resources is also complex. The allocation and deallocation of tags, processors, I-structure store memory blocks, and token space in wait-match memory are difficult problems, and optimal solutions are not easy to find. Each decision is complex, often cannot be made at compile time, and can take considerable time at run time. The redeeming feature of dataflow (dynamic especially) is that other instructions can be executing while these decisions are being made. However, to maintain the high throughputs needed to mask these overheads, the problem must have enormous parallelism.

Static and Dynamic Dataflow and Reentrancy

Static and Dynamic Dataflow: The data of a dataflow program are contained in tokens,[298] and these tokens require storage. In dataflow, token storage replaces the von Neumann addressable memory, and the *method* of token storage is the key feature that distinguishes the various dataflow architectures at the hardware design level. The abstract dataflow model assumes unbounded FIFO (first in, first out) queues on the arcs and FIFO behavior at the nodes, but it is difficult to implement this model exactly, and practical approximations are needed [33]. In a *static dataflow* design an arc may contain at most one token, and hence the token storage may be allocated statically; in contrast the arcs in a *dynamic dataflow* design like the MDM may contain multiple tokens, and hence token storage is allocated dynamically from a common pool [33].

Handling Reentrant Code: Multiple tokens occur because dataflow programs permit multiple concurrent use of the same piece of code, that is, they are *reentrant*.[299] To cite but one reason why this feature is important, the weather code that we discussed on page 39 contains a potentially enormous amount

---

[298] Except for structured data, as we discuss later.

[299] Note that a reentrant execution can occur on serial hardware via interleaving of two instruction streams (see the discussion of *coroutines* on page 152).

of parallelism between individual loop iterations (assuming the dependencies can be handled) because the number of mesh points involved is so large. Theoretically, the potential speedup is proportional to the product of the nested loop limits. To support reentrancy on a von Neumann architecture, private read-write data must be stored separately for each invocation, so that the executions do not interfere. The analogue for dataflow architectures is that provisions are needed to enforce the logical FIFO order of tokens. An example may be helpful.

Recall Figure 5.8 on page 272, a dataflow program to calculate $C(i,j) = \sum_{k=1}^{N} A(i,k) \times B(k,j)$. The subgraph that generates k's accepts one token and then produces *in order* all N values. Suppose that the Get A node is faster than the Get B node (for example, store each matrix in row major order). The multiply node will receive many A's before it receives a B. These A's must be stored and the correct one paired with each B.[300]

The approach in static dataflow is to *prevent* the problem by forbidding multiple tokens to accumulate at a node; in dynamic dataflow the approach is to *solve* the problem by guaranteeing that the tokens are correctly paired at the nodes. That is, dynamic dataflow is an attempt to *exploit* the fully parallel execution of such reused code (at the cost of extra hardware), whereas the philosophy of static dataflow is to *prevent* it, keep the hardware simpler, and work with the remaining forms of concurrency. (Note that the previous comments apply to *fully* parallel execution; static dataflow still has the option of applying *pipeline* concurrency to the execution of such loop iterations [135].) Four approaches have been used to handle reentrancy in dataflow: the *lock* method and the *acknowledge* method in static dataflow, *tagged tokens* and *code copying* in dynamic dataflow [447].

Reentrancy in Dynamic Dataflow: In a tagged-token architecture, the tag is the mechanism for handling such reuse of code, as explained by Arvind [33]:

> Each token in a static dataflow machine must carry the address of the instruction for which it is destined. This is already a *tag*. Suppose, in addition to specifying the destination node, the tag also specifies a particular firing order of the node. Then, two tokens participate in the same firing of a node if and only if their tags are the same. [Thus,] another way of looking at tags is simply as a means of maintaining the logical FIFO order of each arc, regardless of the physical arrival order

---

[300] In this example the arrival is FIFO, so a simple queue would suffice; however, in general a more sophisticated pairing is necessary [33].

of tokens. The token that is supposed to be the ith value to flow along a given arc carries i in its tag.

Instead of tags, an alternative (but potentially more space-consuming) method for dynamic dataflow is *code copying,* proposed for the Form IV family of designs by Dennis and colleagues at MIT. We are referring to run-time code copying, in which copies are created during execution. In any dataflow design (indeed, in any design without a shared instruction memory) a processor can only execute instructions that it contains. So if a loop, for example, is to be executed in parallel, its code must be replicated, but the replication can be done when the program is loaded.

Reentrancy in Static Dataflow: In static dataflow, reentrancy is handled by the *lock* method or the *acknowledge* method. We previously defined static dataflow as providing storage for no more than one token per arc. Static dataflow may also be defined as adding a restriction to the enabling rule, so that an instruction node can be fired only if all its operands are available *and* all its output arcs are free of tokens. (Readers are encouraged to convince themselves that these two definitions are equivalent.) The acknowledge method and the lock method are two different ways to enforce this restricted firing rule.

The acknowledge method requires that a signal be sent back to the node whenever a token leaves one of its output arcs (i.e., is consumed by the next node on that arc) and that the node wait for these signals before producing more tokens. This protocol can be implemented by adding extra acknowledge arcs between consuming and producing nodes. Acknowledgment is implemented at the architecture level in the Form I static dataflow design of Dennis at MIT by including two fields in each instruction that state how many acknowledge signals are needed to enable the instruction and how many have been received [135].

The lock method enforces the "single-token-per-arc" constraint in a more economical way, but one that permits less pipeline parallelism. It operates at a higher level than the acknowledge method and reenables nodes in a reentrant subgraph only after all tokens of a previous activation have left the subgraph, in effect, collecting acknowledgments not from individual arcs but from larger units of code that have been carefully chosen so as not to require internal acknowledgments.[301] For example, if each iterate of a loop is an acyclic graph and hence cannot cause reentrant execution, then one need only ensure

---

[301] One can view the lock method as applying acknowledgments to large units, or view the acknowledge method as locking single nodes.

that no iterate begins before its predecessor completes, which Veen [447] shows can be accomplished by inserting a compound branch node, for example. This approach needs extra instructions or hardware to test the completion of an iteration and allows no parallelism among the iterations [185], unless the compiler creates copies of reentrant subgraphs [447], which usually requires programmer directives. The LAU (Langage a Assignation Unique) project in Toulouse, France (mentioned on page 274), uses extra hardware to test the completion of an iteration.

Comparisons: Although the lock method is more efficient than the acknowledge method, it supports less parallelism because it allows loop iterations to be performed only serially. The acknowledge method allows more concurrency (although less than the dynamic tag or code-copying methods) because it allows overlap of consecutive iterations in pipeline fashion. However, the acknowledge signals approximately double the number of arcs *and* tokens and also increase the traffic flow. The dynamic methods provide the most parallelism—they allow fully parallel execution of loop iterates but at the cost of extra hardware. Gajski et al. [185] compare the performance implications of these different methods against each other and also against a good optimizing compiler for a von Neumann language. Their results are summarized in Figure 10.16 on page 526. With respect to this figure, note that each iterate must be executed serially due to data dependencies. The lock method executes iterates one at a time and thus forces totally serial execution. The acknowledge method, which forbids concurrent execution of a single program operation, permits pipelined execution. Dynamic dataflow is free of either restriction.

Summary: To recap, then, static dataflow gives up some of the parallelism that a dynamic approach can exploit, but since the hardware is simpler in the static case, it also has a lower break-even point with regard to the amount of parallelism needed to justify the investment and to obtain efficient operation. Since an arc may hold at most one token, there is no need to "color", or tag, tokens; resource management is simpler, and tokens can be smaller. There is no need for a complex associative matching of tags nor for a waiting-matching memory to hold the pool of unmatched tokens (space for the token is provided in the instruction node itself). Thus the processing unit's pipeline latency is shortened. Finally, the efficient distribution of code onto multiple processors is simpler since more of the information needed for the distribution is available before run time. However, the enforcement of the single-token-per-arc rule

```
input d,e,f
      c₀ = 0
for i from 1 to 8 do
    begin
        aᵢ: = dᵢ + eᵢ
        bᵢ: = aᵢ + fᵢ
        cᵢ: = bᵢ + cᵢ₋₁
    end
output a,b,c
```

Static dataflow, lock method (48 clock cycles):

Static dataflow, acknowledge method (27 clock cycles):

Dynamic dataflow, tag method (14 cycles):

More traditional parallel compiler (14 cycles):

where
$s_1 = b_2 + b_1, f_1 = b_3 + s_1, c_1 = b_1 + c_0, c_5 = b_5 + c_4$
$s_2 = b_4 + b_3, f_2 = s_2 + s_1, c_2 = s_1 + c_0, c_6 = s_3 + c_4$
$s_3 = b_6 + b_5, f_3 = b_4 + s_3, c_3 = f_1 + c_0, c_7 = f_3 + c_4$
$s_4 = b_8 + b_7, f_4 = s_4 + s_3, c_4 = f_2 + c_0, c_8 = f_4 + c_4$

Figure 10.16 Performance comparison of several dataflow methods (from Gajski et al. [185]). The execution of the programlet of Figure 6.5 on page 304 (repeated above), on several dataflow architectures is compared with the execution on a conventional (control-driven) parallel processor (see page 525). The machines are idealized by neglecting network and memory delays; thus, we obtain upper bounds on performance. It is assumed that there are four processing elements and that division takes three time units, multiplication two, and addition one. The theoretical minimum number of steps is 13, set by the critical path, which is $a_1b_1c_1...c_8$.

represents an overhead and a limitation not present with dynamic dataflow. The acknowledge method requires every arc to be able to send an "all clear" signal back to the preceding node, which approximately doubles the number of arcs as well as the dataflow traffic and also means that even if the iterations of a loop are independent, they can only be executed in pipelined, rather than fully parallel, fashion. The lock method has less overhead but limits such iterations to completely sequential execution. In summary, static dataflow machines have simpler hardware, less software overhead, and are better matched to problems with lower degrees of parallelism and applications dominated by pipeline parallelism, such as signal processing.

Data Structures in a Dataflow Machine

To the discerning reader, the mere juxtaposition of the words *structure* and *flow* may hint at a problem, since these words connote two distinctly different states of matter, namely solids and fluids. The reader would be right—data structures[302] are indeed a special problem in dataflow machines. To be fair, however, three factors are really involved—functional languages, data-driven computation, and parallel execution. We look at the array problem from this perspective before we discuss how dataflow machines propose to solve it.

Data Structures and Their Importance: Structured data are essential to the efficient formulation and computation of many problems. Examples are the use of arrays in the weather model on page 48 and the many-body problem on page 481. The correct yet efficient manipulation of such data structures is a challenge in any parallel environment but is a special problem in a purely functional (assignmentless) dataflow language because of the total lack of updateable storage, which is abolished in order to banish side effects and ease parallelization (page 271).

Data structures are characterized by the operators used to *construct* them from their component data objects and to *select* one of those components. For example, the *first* element and the *rest* of a list are selected by *CAR* and *CDR* in Lisp, while *CONS* constructs new lists by "gluing" CARs and CDRs together. The construction of an array involves placing its elements on an imaginary grid by, for example, a prearranged plan for storing its elements in some contiguous fashion in memory; these elements can be accessed with integer selectors

---

[302] Arrays, lists, records, sets, trees, stacks, and queues are common data structures. Arrays are most frequently mentioned in these discussions because of their importance in scientific/engineering computation, but much of what follows applies to other data structures as well.

called *indexes*. The indexes can be expressions that include variables and function references, which makes possible the iterative loops widely used to save memory space and programmer time in carrying out array operations.[303] Imperative, array-based languages like Fortran and APL (page 229) combine these indexes with assignment statements that mimic the von Neumann model's storage mechanism; thus, the reading and writing of individual array elements can be accomplished as desired.

Data Structures in a Functional Language: *Any* parallel method of executing such a program involving incremental updates of an array demands proper precautions to prevent incorrect sequences of read and write operations. A program written in Fortran needs careful analysis (page 314) and judicious use of coordination primitives (as in the weather and many-body examples cited above) to guard against undesirable side effects from assignment statements.[304] Writing in a functional language makes parallelization easier because assignment and hence side effects are outlawed. Such a language may, however, reduce the efficiency of handling arrays because it also eliminates the ability to update arrays incrementally. The only way to change a single element is to create an entire new array that is an exact copy of the old array except in one spot. It is no longer possible to *rewrite* (parts of) arrays,[305] and thus we have the "array problem". It comes from the nature of the operators in a functional language (see page 259) and is not limited to the dataflow model. Not surprisingly, dataflow researchers have put considerable effort into solving this problem or at least reducing its deleterious effect. One result of these efforts is the notion of accumulators (see page 277).

Data Structures in Dataflow: Arvind and coworkers [37] showed at some length how the problem of data structures in functional languages impacts dataflow machines and discussed a number of solutions that have been explored. When it comes to efficient handling of structured data, the dataflow model is brought to grief by its method of storing data, namely in mobile tokens. The only satisfactory solutions have been various kinds of limited reintroductions of the von Neumann model's method of storing data. Almost all practical dataflow machines have such a structure store, which holds the values of the data structure's elements while tokens carry their addresses (rather than their values). What varies from one machine to the next is the nature of the oper-

---

[303] Just think of translating a program that manipulates a large matrix whose size is unknown at compile time into a language with only scalar variables.

[304] Much of this discussion also holds for scalar variables.

[305] As our friend Manuj Kumar put it, it is like having the eraser taken off one's pencil.

ations allowed on this structure store.   We expand on this structured data problem and its solutions below.

In a von Neumann computer, data structures live in a central memory, and if a user wants to read an array element, say, the user goes there with his or her indexes and receives the value of the corresponding array element.   In dataflow, there's no "there" *there* (as someone once said about Los Angeles), since the data storage mechanism consists of mobile tokens.   Theoretically, the entire array could be represented as one token, but such large tokens are not practical.   One could also put each element's value plus its index into a separate token, but then each token must be directed separately, losing much of the array's advantage over multiple scalars.[306] Therefore, a *complete copy* of the array has to be sent in response to every request, even if it is only to read a single element.   Direct implementation of this concept is called *structure copying* [447].   A retrieve (read) operation, for instance, consumes an entire array and an index and produces a copy of the retrieved element.

Structure Stores: For some applications, sending the entire array is precisely what the problem needs.   An example is the weather code (page 39), according to the analysis by Dennis et al. [135].   However, copying and sending an entire array when only a single element is requested is clearly an unacceptable burden for all but the smallest data structures. Many dataflow machines therefore have a special facility that stores structures and hands out an individual element value rather than the whole array in response to the arrival of a retrieve (read) request.   In other words, the values of the array elements are stored by index as in the von Neumann case, and a token carries the index of one of these elements rather than its value.   (Early versions of the Manchester Dataflow Machine tried to avoid the need for such a store by instead using "sticky" tokens that could be temporarily pinned down in the Matching Unit, but this procedure proved unsatisfactory [210].)

A structure store eliminates excess copying associated with read operations, but the extent to which it alleviates the problems of creating and updating (i.e., *writing*) data structures depends on the nature of these array-definition operators.   Three cases discussed by Arvind et al. [37] are illustrated below.   Starting from the left, they are (1) a fine-grain functional `update` operation, (2) a bulk functional `make-array` operation, and (3) the

---

[306]   In other words, "the third dancer from the left" is no longer a meaningful identification after the dancers leave the stage.

incremental array creation associated with the I-structures [37] for which Arvind's research group has become well known.[307]

DEFINING AN ARRAY		
Basic Dataflow	**Basic Dataflow + Bulk Definition**	**Basic Dataflow + Incremental Definition**

`A1 = array(1,10)`
`A2 = update(A1,1,V1)`
`A3 = update(A2,2,V2)`
.
.
`A = update(A10,10,V10)`
	`A = make-array(1,10,f)`	`A = array(1,10)`
		`A[1] = V1`
		`A[2] = V2`
		.
		.
		`A[10] = V10`

In the example above, an array is allocated initially using the expression `array(1,u)` which returns an array whose index bounds are `(1,u)` and all of whose locations contain some standard initial value (nil). The expression `update(A,i,V)` returns an array identical to A except at index `i`, where it contains the value `V`. Though it sounds imperative, this is a *functional* operation—it returns a *new* array and does not disturb A. The two big problems with this approach are demonstrated by a simple example [37], namely to build an array of size N with `A[i] = i`. If only the `array` and `update` operators described above are available, it will be necessary to create (and store!) $N + 1$ arrays, of which only the final one is of interest. (Building an $M \times N$ array would waste MN arrays!) Furthermore, their order of creation is overspecified. Although the computations for the elements are all independent, *these intermediate arrays cannot be produced in parallel*—it is necessary to *chain* all the updates involved because of the nature of the `update` primitive. (One might say that "producer-producer" parallelism is not possible.) So, although a structure store solves the copying problem associated with *reading* an array element, the use of these strictly functional write operators still leads to gross inefficiencies in performance and memory usage during structured data operations. Arvind et al. discuss the use of *reference counts* to reduce storage requirements and *subscript analysis* to increase parallelism but show that these are not general solutions to the problem.

The middle column of the table above shows the "bulk" functional data-structure operator `make-array (1,u,f)`,[308] which returns an array whose index bounds are `(1,u)` and whose *i*th component contains `f(i)` as specified by the "filling function" `f`. This procedure eliminates the need for intermediate copies in the previous example and poses no serious problem for an efficient

---

[307] Recall that *I* is for "incremental".
[308] Called `make-structure` in the MDM's language.

parallel implementation in which, say, the rows of a matrix are filled in concurrently by multiple processors. Note one very important point, however: to create a new array under this system, the entire array must be filled in at once, that is, in one operation. In other words, if you have writing of an array in mind, you are given access to it only once, and you'd better get it *all* right the first time.[309] There is no chance to create an array incrementally.[310] Furthermore, all reading of a shared array must wait until the array is completely written, and concurrent read and write operations are not permitted.

These restrictions rule out the possibility of "producer-consumer" parallelism, a scenario in which the producer and consumer are two concurrently running subprograms, or perhaps two different iterations of a loop. The loss of the latter form of parallelism would be especially galling in a dynamic dataflow machine (like the MDM), with its heavy investment in mechanisms that allow tokens from different iterations onto the same arc. What is needed is a more efficient way to make *incremental* definitions. Appropriately we now discuss I-structures and the derivation of their name.

I-structures: Arvind's I-structure memory and the MDM's structure store differ in packaging details but are identical at the architectural level. An I-structure is a data structure whose elements can be individually written *once*. An I-structure array, for example, has the same allocate and read operators as the functional case shown at the left in the table on page 530, but writing is not done with an update operator but rather with the element definition A[1] = V1 that may be applied to each element once.[311] The "big deal" about I-structures, however, is the change in the nature of the retrieve (read) operator A[i]. Although it looks the same as before, it can now get a response token from the array any time after the element that is requested has been defined, even if the rest of the array has not been filled in yet. To provide the proper synchronization between writes and reads, each location in Arvind's I-structure memory contains a "presence bit" similar to the "full/empty" bits in

---

[309] This situation is like a fresco painting, which must be completed before the plaster dries and cannot be changed afterwards, in contrast to, say, an oil painting, which can be built up and reworked in many steps. The limitations on parallel processing also carry over—Leonardo da Vinci presumably did nothing else once he started creating the *Last Supper*.

[310] You can take multiple steps to create an array with the values you want, but this process is very wasteful of time *and* space, as we discussed above.

[311] Writing an element more than once causes a run-time error.

the HEP (see page 568)[312] to indicate whether that element has been written. An operation trying to read a yet unwritten location is deferred; the read request token is stored in a special place in the I-structure. When the token to write that location arrives, it checks for and activates all the pending reads of that location (see Figure 10.17 on page 532). Thus, the production and parallel consumption of the array can proceed at the same time. Nothing is free, however. Special hardware can allow deferred reads to be processed almost as quickly as conventional reads, but the write operation takes longer when it must process deferred reads. Hence the overhead and performance penalty of this scheme are low only if most read requests follow the corresponding write [33], which is an additional constraint that the dataflow programmer must try to observe.

It is interesting to contrast the occurrences of `array(1,10)` in the first and last columns of the table above. The first one produces an array, all of whose values are nil. This array will *never* contain a non-nil value. The other one produces an array whose values are not *yet* defined but presumably will be in the future. Attempts to reference elements of the array in the third column will be delayed until the elements have become defined. The difference between the two behaviors of `array(1,10)` may be illustrated by the following erroneous program:

```
A = array(1,10)
B = A[4]+3
```

With the first version of `array`, the second statement will produce a runtime error, since we are trying to add 3 to nil. With the second version, the addition will never occur; it will be indefinitely postponed awaiting the completion of Get(A,4).

Dataflow languages are often classified as *single-assignment*, since there is no notion of updating a variable.[313] It is arguably better, however, to refer to basic dataflow languages as *zero-assignment*, viewing the "assignment statements" that occur as (permanent) definitions. The term *single-assignment* would be reserved for the incremental definitions that occur in

---

[312] The difference from HEP is that deferred reads are not recirculated (not busy waiting) and hence have less impact on processor cycles and do not limit the number of parallel activities as much. But 10 deferred reads take much longer than 10 nondeferred reads.

[313] Recall that the `update` operator used above produces a new array and does not update its argument.

Figure 10.17 How I-structures work. *The top figure shows the two dataflow nodes used to get and store array elements. The bottom figure shows a finer level of detail: the Get node is split with an I-structure reference in between. Even if A[I] has not yet been defined (by a store) when Get-1 fires, the ISS accepts the token shown in the diagram. This token represents a deferred read. When the store of A[I] finally does occur, the value is sent from the ISS to Get-2. This is the value produced by the Get node in the top figure. From now on whenever a Get-1 token requests this same element, the value is immediately sent to Get-2. This action implements a conventional read. An application was shown in Figure 5.8 on page 272.*

column three, since in these languages a structure is first defined, and later its values are assigned.

Static dataflow machines have by and large used only functional operators on their structure stores. Could static dataflow benefit from I-structures? Yes, but not as much as dynamic dataflow, because of static dataflow's limit of one token per arc at a time. The example in the box on page 532 discusses this question further.

Other Hardware

To exploit the parallelism available from all those concurrently executable instructions in a dataflow program, many different dataflow machines have been designed and at least partly implemented over the years, offering interesting similarities as well as contrasts with regard to the hardware we have discussed so far. Almost all are "boudoir"-type, private-memory multiprocessors that are outwardly much like the others we have described in this chapter—collections

	Static Dataflow	**Dynamic Dataflow**
Static Connection Topology	DDM1	DDPA
Dynamic Connection Topology (Packet Communication)	Form I DDP LAU μDP7281 HDFM	Form IV* MIT Tagged Token MDM DFM-1 EM-3 DDDP PIM-D SIGMA-1

*Form IV uses code copying to protect reentrant graphs and the designs below it use
tagged tokens; MIT's Tagged Token design uses both.

Figure 10.18 _A categorization of the most important dataflow machines_ _according to the nature of storage allocation for dataflow tokens (static or dynamic) and communication among processing elements (direct or packet). This figure is a composite of two tables in Veen's survey_ [447]_, which contains references to all these projects. We discuss some of these designs in our text._

of processor/memory elements (PMEs) that pass messages to each other via one of the static or dynamic interconnection networks described on page 381 ff. As we mentioned before, it is the inner workings of the processing elements that distinguish dataflow machines from other architectures. Not surprisingly (given the nature of the dataflow model) there is usually no central memory, although each PME has plenty of memory used in other ways, as we have already shown.

Figure 10.18 on page 535 tabulates these projects by two parameters, one characterizing the processing elements and the other characterizing their communication, and the figure provides a sort of histogram of how the design activity has been distributed. Although substantial work has been done in both static and dynamic dataflow, the latter has generated a larger number of projects. (We have already discussed the trade-offs among these two choices.) For communication, most designs use packet-switched dynamic networks. The dynamic network allows better load distribution, and packet communication is appropriate since the messages are small (typically one token). The main drawback of direct communication machines is that for many graphs it is difficult to find a good mapping (allocation) onto the network. The two static-topology machines are discussed first.

I-Structures for Static Dataflow ?

Could static dataflow benefit from I-structures? Yes, but not as much as dynamic dataflow. A simple example illustrates the difference. Consider the program

```
A(2)=13
Do I=1,2
   A(f(I)) = A(I) + 2
End
```

where the array A is an I-structure. The parts of the dataflow graph that we need for this discussion are shown in Figure 10.17 on page 532.   First consider the simple case $f(I) = I - 1$. If the token for $I = 1$ reaches the Get node first and fires it, this sends a read request to the I-structure store (ISS) asking for A(1); however, A(1) is computed by iteration $I = 2$ and hence is not in the ISS yet. In a dynamic dataflow architecture, there is no problem. The read is deferred by storing the read-request token in the ISS as shown in Figure 10.17 on page 532. The second iteration can proceed to use the same Get node, compute A(1), and store it in the ISS. Now the read-request token from the first iteration can be consumed and used to return the value of A(1), which enables the first iteration to finish by computing A(0). So the two iterations can proceed in parallel even though there is a producer-consumer relationship between them.

In static dataflow, however, the results under this scenario are less happy. Because A(1) does not get into the ISS until the second iteration, the read-request token from the first iteration asking for A(1) is not consumed by the ISS. But in static dataflow, with no more than one token at a time allowed on an arc, the GET node cannot be fired again while there is an unconsumed token on its output arc, and so the second iteration is blocked from storing A(1) into the ISS, and deadlock occurs. In the simple case $f(I) = I - 1$ used here, this problem can be avoided by running the loop backwards, that is, doing $I = 2$ before $I = 1$, but this procedure will not work if $f(I)$ is unknown at compile time. In fact, a statement like A(f(I))=A(I)+2 is not allowed in the VAL language used for Dennis's static dataflow machines for just such reasons.

So the use of I-structures can enable a type of parallelism in a dynamic architecture that is not available in a static architecture. Note, however, that I-structures also make life more complicated. For example, suppose that $f(1) = f(2) = 3$ is true but not known at compile time. A run-time error is generated when the program tries to store twice in A(3).

Static-Topology Machines: DDM1 (Data-Driven Machine #1) was completed at Burroughs in 1976, making it the oldest working dataflow machine. It uses the static dataflow approach and has its processing elements arranged as a tree. Program allocation is simple but far from optimum with respect to load balancing, and the root of the tree forms a communications bottleneck [447]. The published description of the hardware is rather vague.

The DDPA (Data-Driven Processor Array) from Nippon Telephone and Telegraph is some six years newer and is a dynamic tagged-token design intended for large scientific calculations. The processing elements (PEs) are arranged on a two-dimensional grid and are connected to eight other PEs (nearest and next-nearest neighbors). A hardware simulator consisting of 4×4 PEs was built and used to test small applications [425].

Dynamic Topology, Static Dataflow Machines: Static dataflow machines using (dynamic) packet communication constitute the next largest group. The prototype for this category (and indeed for *all* dataflow machines, as we said) is the "Form 1" family of designs started in 1971 by Jack Dennis at MIT. His 1984 paper [135] is a good description of the architectural design choices that have been made. There is no structure store of the type we described. The paper contains a nice analysis of the parallelism available from the same weather model we described on page 39 ff., and it is shown that sending an entire array is often exactly what the program requires, which helps one to understand why the structure store is absent. It was shown that it was feasible to use the technology of the day to design a dataflow machine that would compute a time step representing 20 minutes of weather in 5 seconds, a speedup of about 20 over the nonvector supercomputers of the day. A prototype has been built consisting of eight PEs (emulated by microprogrammable microprocessors) and an equidistant packet routing network using 2×2 routing elements; it is used primarily as an engineering model [136].

The Texas Instruments DDP (Distributed Data Processor) is a one-level (multiple-PE) design that became operational in 1978. Reentrant graphs were protected by a lock method. The compiler could create additional copies of a procedure to increase parallelism, but the creation had to be done before run time (statically). A prototype was built consisting of four PEs connected by a simple ring to a TI990/10 minicomputer host. This prototype is the machine that actually ran dataflow graphs derived from Fortran programs and found average parallelism ranging from 5 to 20. The authors feel that parallelism of 1000 or more is possible [263].

The Toulouse LAU project [423] has been studying dataflow since 1973 and has constructed a prototype containing 32 "elementary processors", some based on the Intel 8085 engine and others on the AMD 2900. Each processor requires one circuit board. There are eight 32-KB memory banks configured to hold a total of 32K 64-bit instructions. A novel feature is the $32K \times 3$-bit instruction control unit (ICU) that associates 3 tag bits with each instruction. An instruction is fireable (in particular its operands are available) if, and only if, its tag is 111 and there is special hardware in the ICU that searches for these tags and sends the corresponding instructions to the ready instruction file, from where they are dispatched.

The NEC Electronics μDP7281 and the Hughes Aircraft HDFM are both small processing elements designed to be used in a dataflow machine for signal processing applications. The NEC chip has a seven-stage circular pipeline, memory for 64 instructions and 560 tokens, and a reported peak performance of 5 million tokens per second [447]. The parallelism is dynamically regulated: when the chip is underutilized, the pipeline gives preference to tokens addressed to instructions that increase parallelism. It is interesting to compare this throttling mechanism to the one used by Rediflow (page 498).

Dynamic Topology, Dynamic Dataflow Machines: The last and largest category consists of dynamic dataflow machines that use (dynamic) packet communication. Most of the machines listed above use tagged tokens to protect reentrant graphs from the multiple tokens per arc of dynamic dataflow. The notable exception is the Form IV family of designs (from Jack Dennis's group at MIT), which uses on-demand copying of subgraphs (*code copying*) instead. Another distinguishing feature is a special unit that stores data structures in the form of a tree and has hardware support for counting the number of outstanding pointers to the array. The reference counts are used to determine when it is safe to update the array in place without risk of a read-write race. The tree representation means that only the nodes along the path to the appended element need be regenerated (the rest of the tree can be shared). Thus, the amount of allocation and copying is reduced, but the time for selection is increased [33].

The Tagged Token architecture from Arvind's group at MIT [36] and the MDM (page 516) from the University of Manchester are quite similar, even though they were developed independently, and we have already given their essential features (Figure 10.14 on page 514) as well as a detailed description of the Manchester prototype (page 516). At MIT, Arvind's group has put together an emulation facility consisting of 32 Texas Instruments Lisp machines connected by a packet-switched network. Each Lisp machine emulates a dataflow PE. A rather small tag space is used, and when the tag supply is exhausted, new copies of a subgraph are allocated (code copying). A software simulator also exists and is being used to study hydrodynamics code and other large benchmarks [33].

The remaining five dynamic dataflow projects listed in Figure 10.18 are all located in Japan. Two of them are Lisp machines intended primarily for list processing—the EM3 (ETL data driven machine-3) from the Electrotechnical Laboratory, and the DFM (Data Flow Machine) from Nippon Telephone &

Telegraph [467] and [24]. Both designs use a "lenient CONS" operation that can generate a pointer token before its arguments are available, similar to the "lenient update" array operation described in our discussion of I-structures (page 531). The EM3 has an eight-PE hardware emulator, while the DFM prototype consisted of two PEs and two structure stores.

The PIM-D (Parallel Inference Machine Based on the Dataflow Model) is a joint venture of ICOT (Institute for New Generation Computer Technology) and OKI Electric Industry Co. [259]. The languages to be supported include AND-parallel and OR-parallel Prolog (discussed on page 282). One of the special features is a primitive that supports nondeterminate merging of streams and enables PIM-D to be used for the efficient implementation of unification (see pages 281). A prototype with four PEs and three structure stores has been built.

The remaining two designs are oriented toward arithmetic operations and array data types. The DDDP (Distributed Data Driven Processor) from OKI Electric has a centralized tag manager and performs token matching using a hardware hashing mechanism similar to that of the MDM (page 519). A prototype consisting of four PEs and one structure store connected by a ring bus has achieved 0.7 MIPS on small benchmarks [280]. The SIGMA-1 is based on the MIT tagged-token architecture and is being developed by the Electrotechnical Laboratory under the auspices of the Japanese National Supercomputer Project [33]. The aim is a 100-MFLOPS, 32-bit prototype. A 1-board PE and a one-board structure memory are being developed for a machine with up to 304 boards, divided roughly half and half between PEs and structure memories. As in the MDM, a chained hash table is used for the waiting-matching store, and "sticky tokens" are employed for loop constants, although (as in the MDM) the practicality of the sticky tokens is being questioned. A six-board version of the PE has been operational since 1984.

Veen [447] and Arvind [33] make further comparisons among these designs, and additional details can be found in the individual references.

Programming and Software

We have already touched on issues related to dataflow programming in this section as well as in previous parts of this book, notably our chapter on languages and, to a lesser extent, our chapter on compilers (Chapter 6). When it comes to programming a dataflow machine, the most prominent impact of the *architecture* (as opposed to factors like the vagaries of programming in a functional language) is the long pipeline latency of a dataflow processing element, a point we discussed on page 520. This latency is especially long for dynamic dataflow and means that programs for such machines must contain parallelism on a grand scale in order to amortize the startup delays and extra hardware expenses of this approach to parallel processing.[314] Commenting on the point made earlier that an average rate of parallelism close to 1000 is needed to utilize even a moderate (64-PE) dataflow multiprocessor, Veen [447] writes, "experience so far suggests that realistic programs can indeed achieve such rates of parallelism, if the programmer carefully *avoids sequential constructs*" and has a sufficiently *sophisticated compiler* available (our italics). It remains to be seen how well these requirements can be achieved in practice.

Conclusions

Dataflow is the most genuinely different new architecture we have discussed, and its theoretical potential to extract the maximum amount of parallelism from a program is undeniable. The chief concern is that the overhead involved in handling data structures, load balancing, and control of parallelism may lead to excessive consumption of time and resources when applied to the fine instruction-level granularity that has been explored so far. Chief among these resources are the structure store and the matching unit. The rejoinder is that careful programming and sophisticated compilers can provide enough parallelism to pay for this overhead, but proving this assertion requires the execution of large programs, which are difficult to simulate and analyze and hence are awaiting more powerful prototypes. One alternative is to stay with fine-grained parallelism but to try to exploit it with much more control-driven SIMD techniques, such as in the Connection Machine (page 446). Another approach is to adapt the principles of dataflow to coarser-grain levels of parallelism, such as procedure bodies. We describe such an example of macro-dataflow in the Cedar architecture on page 611.

As Veen puts it in his recent summary [447], at this point "there is [still] no consensus as to whether data-driven execution, besides being intuitively appealing, is also a viable means to make these visions become reality". We have of necessity omitted many of the finer details of this subject, and interested readers are encouraged to continue their reading in the cited references.

---

[314] It is important to note that coping with latency is not unique to dataflow designs. Indeed, the significant memory latency inherent in shared-memory MIMD von Neumann architectures offers the key challenge to the designers and users of such machines. Dataflow, especially dynamic dataflow, is able to extract more of the available parallelism in a problem than is a von Neumann design. However, dataflow, again especially dynamic dataflow with its various associative memories, needs more parallelism for high utilization.

10.3   Shared-Memory MIMD Designs

10.3.1   Comparing Shared-Memory Designs–What to Look For

The essence of the shared-memory model of parallel computation is that all processors have equally direct access to one large memory address space.[315] Such access results in a less constrained programming environment than a private-memory (message-passing) design at the cost of more elaborate hardware: *enabling* the global access costs something, and *preventing* undesirable accesses to shared variables adds more cost.   Our case study of the n-body problem (page 487) explored these two programming environments. We now turn to the architectural consequences of the shared-memory model—how the extra features that are needed influence the design of a computer that supports this environment.

As pointed out by Arvind and Ianucci [35], two very basic issues must be addressed by any shared-memory multiprocessor:

1.   How to tolerate long latencies for memory requests
2.   How to achieve unconstrained, yet synchronized, access to shared data

(The dataflow approach, which is preferred by Arvind and Ianucci and which we have just discussed, can be viewed as an extreme solution to the memory-latency problem: Use instructions that are expected to have received their data *before* they bother the processor.) Both questions arise from the nature of the shared-memory model. The first one reflects the fact that the designer is basically asked to provide an n-port memory in a world in which a two-port memory is still (somewhat of) a big deal. Even under ideal circumstances, increasing the number of ports to a memory will lengthen the access time.[316] With presently affordable interconnection networks and technologies, the memory latency becomes significant compared to the processors' instruction execution time, and the architecture/machine design must make specific provisions to avoid having processors idle while awaiting responses to their memory requests. The way those provisions are accomplished is one of the

---

[315]   Still unanswered however, is the question of whether the processors may also have access to other memory on a less equal basis, as in HEP.

[316]   For a fixed fanin/fanout technology, one needs on the order of $\log n$ stages of fanin/fanout to have n processors access even a single bit of shared memory.   Moreover, these processors occupy a volume proportional to n, so the average distance to memory grows at least as the cube root of n.

interesting differences among the architectures that we will be looking at. The HEP solution, for instance, is a heavily pipelined processing element with special hardware that allows very fast task switching to avoid inefficiency ("bubbles") in the pipeline. The Ultracomputer and several other designs use processing elements with local caches. Dataflow is a third approach: "Somewhere there must be an instruction that's ready to go."

The second issue listed above is one that we treated already in our chapter on languages (Chapter 5) when we discussed communication and coordination among parallel processes (see page 155). There, we pointed out the need for two kinds of coordination: *sequence control,* to allow cooperating processes to do things in the right order, and *access control* (mutual exclusion, for example), to handle processes competing for a shared resource. In both cases, one must avoid unnecessary serialization and maintain as much parallelism as possible. The HEP meets both requirements by using extra bits associated with each data storage location. The Ultracomputer uses a combining network and the special fetch-and-add primitive. Dataflow avoids much of the problem by restricting itself to languages without side effects.

In summary, two key questions to ask about any parallel processor design is how it handles memory latency and how it achieves parallel synchronization. The reader is encouraged to look for answers to these questions in the machine descriptions that follow as well as in those that appear elsewhere. We will return to these points after we introduce the architectures.

10.3.2   Caches and Modest Bus-Based MIMD Systems

In order to obtain high performance from modest processors, it is clearly necessary to use many effectively. Thus, unlike architectures that consist of a few powerful vector processors, the supercomputer designs described later in this chapter specify hundreds or thousands of processors. Of course, architectures composed of multiple microprocessors are not limited to the supercomputer end of the performance spectrum. Currently an area of significant commercial activity is the use of bus-based designs comprising a few or possibly a few dozen microprocessors to produce cost-effective machines in the midrange class. Early examples were produced by Sequent (Balance, then Symmetry), Encore (Multimax), and Elxsi (System 6400). We shall describe certain aspects of these designs below, especially their *cache-snooping* techniques. As will become clear later, these snooping techniques cannot be extended to more highly parallel designs containing hundreds or thousands of processors. Ironically, it is the fundamental limitation of these modest systems, the single bus, that *enables* snooping caches. By having every cache controller monitor the bus continually (i.e., snoop), we get a kind of Turkish bath situation in which everyone knows what everyone else has got, and it is not too hard to keep all the caches consistent. We discuss how this is done below. For larger systems without a single bus, more sophisticated consistency-preserving techniques are needed. These directory-based algorithms are explained later in the chapter.

Another area of commercial interest, which we shall discuss only briefly, is the use of parallelism as hardware redundancy to produce fault-tolerant systems. This avenue was first explored by Tandem and subsequently by Synapse and others.

Bus-Based Systems

Using current technology and an effective (uniprocessor) caching scheme, a microprocessor does not saturate the potential bandwidth of the bus that connects it to primary memory. This excess bandwidth naturally leads to the possibility of having several processors share the bus with a single shared memory, giving the following configuration:

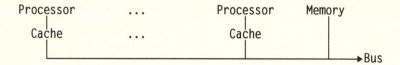

Since the bandwidth supplied by the single bus provides a clear limitation on total system performance, it is important to use this resource only when necessary.[317] Total bandwidth is conserved by effective caching, thus reducing the number of central memory requests, and by reducing the bandwidth used by each of the remaining memory requests. One consequence of this latter observation is that systems in this class adopt a *split-phase* bus protocol. That is, when a processor is granted the bus to access central memory, the request is transmitted to the memory module, and the bus is released for use by another processor. When the memory is ready to respond (about 150

---

[317] One can of course use multiple buses. To employ snooping caches it would be necessary for every cache controller to monitor every bus. It is unlikely that controllers could manage to do this. We have just shifted the limitation from the single bus to each controller. There still is a fixed total bandwidth that can be supported. It is definitely possible to have a sparse interconnection; that is, employ P processors, M memories, and B buses but with each bus connected to only k devices, $k << M + B$. Cache-snooping techniques are not possible since we have lost the Turkish bath advantage of a single bus.

nanoseconds later), the bus is re-acquired, and the response is sent to the originating processor. The alternative *tenured* protocol, in which a processor maintains control of the bus while the memory is processing the request, would keep the bus idle during the 150-nanosecond memory-latency period, thus wasting bandwidth. The split-phase protocol does increase hardware complexity, however, since the memory is no longer a passive slave and requires logic capable of actively seizing the bus. For this reason, single microprocessor systems (e.g., workstations) often use the tenured protocol.

As the reader is likely to have noticed, freeing the bus while the memory is busy does not seem especially useful. Yes, another processor can get the bus, but with the memory busy what is the bus good for? Moreover, the memory bandwidth appears to be just as limiting as the bus bandwidth. There are two answers to the question of how to use the bus while the memory is busy. First, the memory could be pipelined. That is, while the memory is busy, the bus could be used fruitfully by another processor[318] to transmit a request to memory, where it would be buffered while waiting for the memory to finish the previous request.

The second, and more significant, answer is to have multiported memory. In this scheme, the (logically) single central memory is (physically) divided into multiple banks, or memory modules (MMs), that may be accessed independently. The resulting system configuration may be depicted as follows:

With multiple memory modules, the extra bus bandwidth made available by adopting a split-phase protocol can be used effectively even with non-pipelined memory, since, when one module is busy, another can be accessed. Moreover, the total memory bandwidth is no longer limited to the one request per 150 nanoseconds that a single bank can supply. That is, the cycle time of the memory chips that are used is no longer an absolute limit on system performance. This scheme is clearly useless if all the memory requests are to the same module. It is most effective if the consecutive requests are spread uniformly across the modules. Due to spatial locality, consecutive requests are

---

[318] It could even be used by the same processor if this processor supports multiple outstanding memory requests. Thus, even for uniprocessors with one central memory, the split-phase protocol is advantageous.

likely to be to nearby locations and thus it is advantageous to interleave memory across the banks.

Multiple memory modules have other advantages as well. Indeed, they are often used in uniprocessor designs. One reason is that packaging requirements often dictate multiple MMs. For example, the desired memory capacity may not fit on one circuit board, or the amount of data to be transmitted in a single memory request (typically a cache line of a few hundred bits) may exceed the I/O capacity of the board. Another reason for specifying a split-phase bus protocol and multiple MMs in uniprocessor design is that sophisticated processors can issue a second memory request before the first one has been satisfied.

Caches

We now turn our attention to the caches used in the system. As is the case with uniprocessors, caches significantly reduce the average memory latency. However, for bus-based multiprocessors, caches have yet another advantage: they reduce the bus bandwidth consumed by an individual processor and thus permit more processors to be used. The result is a higher-performance system. For example, consider a highly simplified situation in which a processor always issues a memory request exactly A seconds after its previous request has been satisfied, all these requests are loads, and a tenured bus protocol is adopted. To show that a cache is more helpful for multiprocessors than for serial machines, let us make the unreasonably pessimistic assumption that a cache hit takes as long as a miss (providing that the bus and MM are available when the miss occurs); call this time B seconds. Thus, for a uniprocessor machine the cache would have no effect regardless of the cache hit ratio. But, this is not the case for our multiprocessor system. Without caches each processor uses the bus for B seconds out of each $A + B$ seconds. Thus, one processor consumes $B/(A + B)$ of the bus, and the system cannot exceed the performance of $(A + B)/B$ processors. If, however, a cache is used that achieves a 90% hit ratio, then each processor uses the bus for 1 out of 10 instructions and thus consumes $B/(10A + 10B)$ of the bus, thereby permitting a maximum performance of $10(A + B)/B$ processors.

We conclude from the above discussion that caches are critically important for bus-based multiprocessors and thus that considerable effort can be justifiably spent on the goal of increasing the cache hit ratio.

Cache Consistency (Cache Coherence)

With multiple caches present in the system, we must deal with the problem of maintaining *cache consistency*, often called *cache coherence*. In order for the system state to be consistent, it must be the case that if one processor updates a location of shared memory and another processor subsequently[319] queries this location (with no other update intervening), then the value obtained by the second processor must be the updated value placed in this location by the first processor.

With caches in the system, there are two ways that this property can be violated. First, the update may be done only to the cache in the first processor and, thus, when the second processor reads central memory, the (incorrect) old value is found. Second, even if the update is written to central memory, the query may be satisfied by the cache in the second processor, which was not updated. We now consider these two possible failures in turn.

Cache Consistency via Noncacheable Variables

The simplest method of avoiding both failures is not to cache read-write shared variables. The linker, with guidance from the compiler and/or user, places all such variables into segments that are marked noncacheable, and the cache ignores all memory references to uncacheable segments. This approach places no restriction on the topology of the processor and memory modules. Indeed, as reported in Yen et al. [469], it was first employed in C.mmp, a crossbar design. Although this solution can maintain cache coherence, a significant cost can be incurred: marking variables noncacheable may well lower the cache hit ratio substantially, thereby increasing bus traffic and lowering performances. In addition, there is the danger that a shared read-write variable may be missed by the (manual or automated) analysis and be marked cacheable. Nasty bugs can result.

In the C.mmp design, cacheability is a *static* property—a memory location is either cacheable or not—the decision being effective for the duration of the program's execution. A more *dynamic* approach has been studied in which the cacheability of a memory segment may be varied under program control. Simulation studies by McAuliffe of several scientific application programs have shown that a significantly increased cache hit ratio is obtained when cacheability is treated dynamically.[320] An example of dynamic cacheability occurs in those iterative solution techniques for partial differential equations where an old and a new matrix are employed. During one phase the old matrix is queried and the new one updated. Then, after the processors synchro-

---

[319] The exact definition of *subsequently* is somewhat subtle, as is the appropriate notion for a consistent memory system.

[320] Although dynamic cacheability does increase performance, it does not ameliorate the potential problem of nasty bugs that would occur if memory locations were erroneously marked cacheable.

Uniprocessor Cache Update Policies

An excellent introduction to uniprocessor caching policies and their effect on system performance can be found in Smith [403]. Here, we are content to describe briefly just one policy choice, write-through vs. write-back updates. In a write-through system (also called *store-through*), all updates are sent to central memory. If the location to be modified is cache-resident, the cached value is updated as well. If the update generates a cache miss, some write-through policies leave the cache as is, while other write-through policies allocate a line for the new value, likely at the cost of evicting another line. The interested reader is referred to Smith for the trade-offs involved in this write-allocate vs. write-no-allocate decision. We note that either write-through policy guarantees the following (advantageouns) properties: *central memory is always up-to-date* and a cache line can be invalidated without writing it to central memory. The second property simplifies the logic needed for processing a read that misses the cache. When the new line is brought to the cache, an old line can simply be overwritten (and the directory updated). Naturally, this argument applies equally well to uniprocessors. Perhaps surprising is the observation that keeping central memory up to date is also important for many uniprocessors; the point is that, from the standpoint of central memory, a single CPU with one or more direct memory access (DMA) I/O devices acts like a multiprocessor.

In the alternative write-back (also called *copy-back* or *write-in*) policy, an update that hits the cache modifies only the cache; the central memory retains its previous value. We again refer the reader to Smith for consideration of an update that misses the cache. When a dirty (i.e., updated) line is subsequently evicted from the cache, its contents must be written back to central memory.

Since write-back caches permit central memory to become out of date and require more sophisticated control hardware (to effect the write-back on cache eviction), one may question why a designer would ever choose this policy over write-through. The reason is that write-back potentially generates fewer central memory requests, since a location updated many times by a single processor is only updated once in central memory (at eviction time). One must add, however, that a write-back policy is likely to cause bursts in memory traffic since a context switch (or a phase transition in a user program) will cause a flood of memory writes. Some hardware designs, especially those using multistage interconnection networks, are adversely affected by bursts in traffic.

---

nize, the old matrix is declared new, the new one is declared old, and the process is repeated. Between synchronization points, the old matrix is cacheable, and the new one is not. Hardware support for dynamic cacheability has been included in several designs; for example, the IBM RP3 (page 603) allowed one to mark selected cache entries and then invalidate all marked entries at once.

Cache Consistency via Write-through and Snooping

The first failure (stale central memory) may be prevented by employing a write-through cache update policy. As noted in the box on page 546, which compares write-through and write-back policies, a disadvantage of adopting write-through is increased bus traffic.

To prevent the second failure (stale caches), one could adopt what we might call a *write-all-the-way-through* policy. That is, a store from one processor updates not only its cache and central memory but also any other cache that contains this entry.[321] More precisely, the originating processor updates its cache and sends the store request to central memory. The cache controllers on the other processors snoop on the bus and respond to the store request by updating their caches if necessary. Although we are unaware of any system that actually stores all the way through, an approximation, called *cross-invalidation,* is widely used. In this technique a store updates the local cache and invalidates (i.e., deletes) the entry in other caches (once again it is really the remote cache controllers that snoop and perform the invalidation). Cross-invalidation has been used in commercial multiprocessors for some time. It was introduced in the multiprocessor version of the IBM 370/168 (see [469]). Also uniprocessors with DMA I/O devices often cross-invalidate. In many of these uniprocessor systems, the I/O devices do not have caches, so there is only a cache for the CPU, and cross-invalidation degenerates into the requirement that DMA I/O invalidate the (CPU) cache. Deleting entries when they become stale is called a *write-invalidate* coherence technique by Stenstrom et al. [413].

Cache Consistency via Write-back and Snooping

The final method we shall discuss for lowering bus traffic is to use more aggressive cache hardware that permits one to adopt a write-back cache update policy. The additional problem that must be solved is to prevent other processors from using the stale value in central memory. In particular, a read miss (i.e. a load request not satisfied in the cache associated with the processor making the request) cannot be satisfied by central memory. Instead, some remote cache that does contain the correct value must satisfy the load request. This is achieved by having all cache controllers snoop the bus and, if its cache contains the needed value, the controller satisfies the request (normally the protocols adopted guarantee that when central memory is out-of-date, exactly one cache has the entry).

---

[321] This policy is called *broadcast update* by Yen et al. [469] and similar policies are referred to as *write-update* by Stenstrom et al. [413].

Goodman [197] has proposed a related technique that combines write-through and write-back. In this *write-once* technique a cache first employs a write-through update to seize ownership of a line. Subsequent updates can employ write-back if no other cache has taken the ownership away. Several other related techniques have also been proposed; the interested reader is referred to the proceedings of the several *International Symposia on Computer Architecture* that occurred during the mid-1980s and to the performance evaluations given in [30].

Directory Based Cache Consistency

Snooping techniques work well when the number of processors is small but the single bus does not scale to highly parallel systems. When snooping is not available, other techniques must be used. To date these have been directory-based. A key point noted in [7] is that for these schemes the location of caches containing copies of shared items is known, and hence broadcasts are not required to find all such copies.

The first technique, proposed by Tang [429], was to augment each cache entry with a dirty bit and keep a central directory containing the status of all cache lines. This directory can be thought of as a copy of all the local cache directories (i.e., the cache tags and dirty bits). Furthermore, caches acquire read or write locks on requested lines. Like most coherence schemes, clean blocks (obtained with a read lock) may be present concurrently in many caches, whereas a dirty block (obtained with a write lock) can only be in one cache at a time. Reminiscent of database techniques and readers-writers algorithms, Tang's proposal also includes lock conversion from a (shared) read lock to an (exclusive) write lock, which occurs when a previously read-only shared value needs to be updated.

Censier and Feautrier [89] proposed a similar technique but with the directory organized by memory block not by cache block. The difference is that when a cache miss is forwarded to memory, only the single directory entry for the requested memory location need be searched to determined if the value is cached elsewhere. In Tang's scheme the central copy of each cache directory must be searched.

Stenstrom [412] suggested a directory-based protocol organized by cache line (as was Tang's) but with the information distributed to each cache (rather than having Tang's central repository). All three of these schemes share two characteristics: the directory entries describe which of the n caches in the system contain the data, and (as a result) broadcast is not required. The point is that if a cache wishes to obtain exclusive access, it must invalidate (or update, but we will consider only invalidations here) all the other copies. To do this it must either know where all the other copies are, or it must broadcast the invalidation to all caches. The three schemes above all do the former and are thus classified as Dir_nNB by Agarwal et al. [7]; that is, the subscript indicates how many pointers are stored, and NB signifes No Broadcast. These are often called *full-map schemes*, since the directory map is complete. The Stanford DASH (page 553) employs a full-map directory.

The full-map schemes require n bits of storage for each directory entry (a bit map is used). An alternative is to keep a limited number of pointers (each of length $\log n$). For example, in a Dir_4B scheme, up to four pointers are kept and, if more than four caches hold a copy of the block, the broadcast bit is set so that when an invalidation is needed it is broadcast to all the caches. In a Dir_4NB scheme, when a fifth cache wishes to share a block, one of the other caches is sent an invalidation request maintaining the limit of four sharing caches. Note that Dir_0NB is not a viable alternative. The idea behind these limited schemes is that large-scale sharing is not common and does not justify the storage expense of a full-map protocol (see [7] for an evaluation).

The MIT Alewife project [90] suggests implementing a limited-map scheme without hardware support for the overflow case. Instead, overflows trap to software, which can then emulate a full-map protocol (or others). Chaiken et al. [90] refer to this technique as LimitLESS.

Finally, the Scalable Coherent Interface (SCI) [262], an IEEE standard, specifies that sharing caches be linked together (in software). An invalidation then consists of traversing the list.

Although all these hardware-consistency techniques appear conceptually simple, there are a number of technical details that must be worked out for an actual implementation, a feat that is far from trivial. We now discuss two completed implementations: the Stanford Dash and the Kendall Square Research KSR1, and more briefly describe the MIT Alewife and the SICS Data Defusion Machine.

10.3.3 Kendall Square Research KSR1

The KSR1 is a shared-memory MIMD computer with private, consistent caches; that is, each processor has its own cache, and the system hardware guarantees that the multiple caches are kept in agreement. In this regard the design is similar to the MIT Alewife (page 556) and the Stanford Dash (page 553). There are, however, three significant differences between the KSR1 and the two university designs. First, the Kendall Square machine is a large-scale, commercial effort: the current design supports 1088 processors and can be extended to

Figure 10.19 The "ring of rings" used in the KSR1

tens of thousands. Second, the KSR1 features an ALLCACHE memory, which we explain below. Finally, the KSR1, like the Illinois Cedar, is a hierarchical design: a small machine is a ring, or Selection Engine, of up to 32 processors (called an SE:0); to achieve 1088 processors, an SE:1 ring of 34 SE:0 rings is assembled. Larger machines would use yet higher-level rings. Much of the material below was obtained from [377].

Hardware

A 32-processor configuration (i.e., a full SE:0 ring) with 1 gigabyte of memory and 10 gigabytes of disk requires 6 kilowatts of power and 2 square meters of floor space. This configuration has a peak computational performance of 1.28 GFLOPS and a peak I/O bandwidth of 420 megabytes/sec. In a March 1992 posting to the comp.parallel electronic newsgroup, Tom Dunigan reported that a 32-processor KSR1 at the Oak Ridge National Laboratory attained 513 MFLOPS on the 1000×1000 LINPACK benchmark. A full SE:1 ring with 1088 processors equipped with 34.8 gigabytes of memory and 1 terabyte of disk storage would require 150 kilowatts and 74 square meters. Its peak performance would be 43.5 GFLOPS and 15.3 gigabytes/sec of i/o bandwidth.

Each KSR1 processor is a superscalar 64-bit unit able to issue up to two instructions every 50 nsec, giving a peak performance of 40 MIPS (KSR refers to this as 20 MIPS since only one of the two instructions issued can be computational). Since a single floating-point instruction can perform a multiply and an add, the peak floating-point performance is 40 MFLOPS. A KSR1 system contains from 8 to 1088 processors (giving a system-wide peak of 43,520 MIPS and 43,520 MFLOPS), all sharing a common virtual address space of one million megabytes. The processor is a four-chip set, a control unit and three coprocessors, implemented in 1.2 micron CMOS. Up to two instructions are issued on each clock cycle. The floating-point coprocessor supports IEEE single and double precision and includes linked triads similar to the multiply and add instructions found in the Intel Paragon (page 491). The integer/logical coprocessor contains its own set of 32 64-bit registers and performs the usual arithmetic and logical operations. The final coprocessor provides a 32-MB/sec I/O channel at each processor. Each processor board also contains a 256KB data cache and a 256KB instruction cache. These caches are conventional in organization though large in size, and should not be confused with the ALLCACHE (main) memory discussed below.

ALLCACHE Memory and the Ring of Rings

Normally, caches are viewed as small temporary storage vehicles for data, whose permanent copy resides in central memory. The KSR1 is more complicated in this respect. It does have, at each processor, standard instruction and data caches, as mentioned above. However, these are just the first-level caches. *Instead* of having main memory to back up these first-level caches, the KSR1 has second-level caches, which are then backed up by *disks*. That is, there is no central memory; all machine-resident data and instructions are contained in one or more caches, which is why KSR uses the term ALLCACHE memory. The data (as opposed to control) portions of the second-level caches are implemented using the same DRAM technology normally found in central memory. Thus, although they function as caches, these structures have the capacity and performance of main memory.

When a (local, second-level) cache miss occurs on processor A, the address is sent around the SE:0 ring. If the requested address resides in B, another one of the processor/local-cache pairs on the same SE:0 ring, B forwards the cache line (a 128-byte unit, called a *subpage* by KSR) to A again, using the (unidirectional) SE:0 ring. Depending on the access performed, B may keep a copy of the subpage (thus sharing it with A) or may cause all existing copies to be invalidated (thus giving A exclusive access to the subpage). When the response arrives at A, it is stored in the local cache, possibly evicting previously stored data. (If this is the only copy of the old data, special actions are taken not to evict it.) Measurements at Oak Ridge indicate a 6.7 microsecond latency for their (32-processor) SE:0 ring.

If the requested address resides in processor/local-cache C, which is located on *another* SE:0 ring, the situation is more interesting. Each SE:0 includes an ARD (ALLCACHE routing and directory cell), containing a large directory with an entry for every subpage stored on the entire SE:0.[322] If the ARD determines that the subpage is not contained in the current ring, the request is sent "up" the hierarchy to the (unidirectional) SE:1 ring (see Figure 10.19 on page 550), which is composed solely of ARDs, each essentially a copy of the ARD "below" it. When the request reaches the SE:1 ARD above the SE:0 ring containing C, the request is sent down and traverses the ring to C, where it is satisfied. The response from C continues on the SE:0 ring to the ARD, goes back up, then around the SE:1 ring, down to the SE:0 ring containing A, and finally around this ring to A.

Another difference between the KSR1 caches and the more conventional variety is size. These are *big* caches, 32MB per processor. Recall that they replace the conventional main memory and hence are implemented using dense DRAM technology.

The SE:0 bandwidth is 1 GB/sec, and the SE:1 bandwidth can be configured to be 1, 2, or 4 GB/sec, with larger values more appropriate for systems with many SE:0s (cf. the fat trees used in the CM5; see page 509). The idea of having only cache memory was introduced into the literature by the team at Swedish Institute of Computer Science working on the *Data Diffusion Machine* ([214] and [215]). They refer to the organization as COMA (cache only memory architecture). A performance comparison of COMA and NUMA (specifically CC-NUMA—cache coherent, nonuniform memory access) designs is given in [414]. To complete the alphabet soup of memory organizations, we note bus-based systems like the Sequent Symmetry are termed UMA (uniform memory access) designs and private memory architectures are termed NORMA (no remote memory access) designs.

Software

The KSR operating system, an extension of the OSF/1 version of Unix, is symmetric and thus runs on all the processors concurrently. Processor allocation is dynamic; that is, the number of processors assigned to a specific job varies with time.

A fairly rich software environment is supplied, including the X window system with the Motif user interface; Fortran, C, and Cobol; the Oracle relational database management system; and ATC Tuxedo for transaction processing.

A Fortran programmer may request automatic parallelization of his/her program or may specify the parallelism explicitly; a C programmer has only the latter option.

---

[322] Actually, there is an entry for every page giving the state of every subpage.

Figure 10.20 The Stanford DASH architecture. *(Drawing from [317])*

10.3.4   The Stanford University DASH

The Stanford DASH (Directory Architecture for SHared Memory) project is exploring the feasibility of large-scale shared-memory computers with hardware cache coherence. DASH is quite a comprehensive project that has studied cache coherence, applications programming, simulation techniques, and weak models for memory consistency. Here we concentrate on the DASH prototype constructed in 1992 [317].

Architecture

The DASH architecture has a two-level structure, illustrated in Figure 10.20, which is taken from [317]. It consists of a two-dimensional mesh of clusters, each of which is itself a bus-based multiprocessor. All the caches in the system are kept consistent by the hardware. Within a single cluster (i.e., within each bus-based multiprocessor), consistency is maintained using a snooping cache protocol, as one might expect. On the other hand, intercluster consistency is maintained via a distributed, directory-based protocol of the full-map variety.

For the moment let us restrict attention to a single-cluster machine and consider a load instruction issued by processor P. The best case, referred to as the *processor level* of the memory hierarchy, occurs when the referenced location is found in P's own cache. If the request misses in P's cache, the request is put on the cluster bus, and the snooping protocol is invoked. Either main memory or a cache on another processor will respond to the request. This interaction is called the *cluster level* of the memory hierarchy.

When we expand our example to a full (i.e., multi-cluster) DASH, the situation is more complicated, since the memory location may reside in another cluster, and both the processor and cluster-level lookups may miss (since the address determines the cluster, the cluster-level lookup is restricted to just the caches; main memory in P's cluster is not searched). When such a cluster-level miss occurs, the request is sent to the cluster containing the referenced memory location. Normally, this second cluster, called the *home cluster*, can satisfy the request. This part of the memory hierarchy is referred to as the *directory home level*. However, if some processor Q in a third cluster has cached the location and modified the cached value, then the lookup in the home cluster will reveal that the home value is stale, and the request is forwarded to Q's cluster, where the request is finally satisfied. This fourth and final level of the memory hierarchy is called the *remote cluster level*.

Prototype Hardware

The current prototype consists of 16 clusters arranged in a 4×4 mesh, with each cluster a four-processor, single-bus computer. The clusters are interconnected using two "wormhole-routed" (page 396) networks, one for request messages and the other for replies. Each network is composed of mesh routing chips developed at Caltech and modified to have 16-bit datapaths.

Cluster Hardware

A DASH cluster is based on a commercial multiprocessor, the Silicon Graphics POWER Station 4D/340, a bus-based system containing four MIPS R3000 processors and R3010 floating-point coprocessors clocked at 33 MHz. Each processor contains two levels of caches. The second level caches are connected via the POWER Station system bus to main memory. Together the second-level caches and the memory implement the snooping needed for cluster-wide cache coherence. The specific coherence protocol chosen is often called the Illinois protocol [354]. The system bus can achieve a maximum bandwidth of 64MB/sec.

The primary modification to the POWER Station is the inclusion of two new circuit boards to support the directory memory and the intercluster interface. The boards are each named after one of their main functions. The first board, called the *directory controller*, or DC, contains the directory for main memory (a full map directory (page 549) used for intercluster cache consistency) as well as logic for initiating all network requests and replies. In addition, DC includes a performance monitor for a variety of intra- and intercluster events, the outbound network logic, and the *X* dimension of the network itself (the routing chips always route first in one dimension, usually called the *X* dimension).

The other board, the reply controller, or RC, monitors requests made by this cluster that are outstanding in the network and receives all replies. In addition, RC receives remote requests directed at this cluster and presents them on the system bus, acting as a surrogate for the remote processor (responses to these requests are sent out of the cluster by DC). Finally, RC contains the network inbound logic and the Y dimension of the network.

Performance of the Prototype

DASH performance has been intensively studied. Real programs have been run and timed; the hardware performance monitor has yielded detailed non-invasive measurement of internal events; and extensive simulation studies have been performed. See [317] and the studies referenced therein for details. Here we comment briefly on the performance of the memory system and application performance of the entire system.

As one would expect, the four-level memory hierarchy offers four levels of performance (actually there are five levels of performance, since the processor level of the hierarchy really includes two levels of caches). A load request that hits in the (first level) processor cache is satisfied in one 33-nsec processor clock or *pclock* for short. At the other extreme, a load that must be satisfied by a remote (non-home) cluster takes typically 132 pclocks.

A number of applications have been run on DASH. Lenoski et al. [317], in summarizing their results, make several points, including the following: (1) "While the coherence protocol and hardware are not trivial, such systems can be built." (2) "It is possible to get near linear speedup on DASH for a number of real applications." (3) "Even with caches, ... locality is still important. If locality is very low ..., then speedup will be poor."

10.3.5   The MIT Alewife

The goal of the Alewife project is well stated in the following passage from [5], which is itself a good source of additional information on Alewife.

> The Alewife project explores methods for automatic enhancement of [communication or memory reference] locality in a scalable parallel machine. The Alewife multiprocessor uses a distributed shared-memory architecture with a low-dimensional direct network. Such networks are cost-effective, modular, and encourage the exploitation of locality … . Unfortunately, non-uniform communication latencies usually make such machines hard to program because the onus of managing locality invariably falls on the programmer. The goal of the Alewife project is to discover and to evaluate techniques for automatic locality management in scalable multiprocessors.

The DASH diagram, Figure 10.20 on page 553, can be used to describe Alewife as well. Like DASH, Alewife is a 2-D mesh, with each node containing a processor, some hardware-coherent cache, a portion of the shared memory, and a switch. But the differences are important as well. For example, DASH processors are MIPS R3000s straight from commercial SGI offerings, whereas Alewife uses a modified SPARC (called Sparcle [6]); and DASH uses a full-map cache-directory scheme, whereas Alewife introduced LimitLESS directories [90].

The Sparcle processors are especially interesting, in part due to their use of a latency-hiding technique called *block multithreading*. Whenever a memory reference misses in the local cache and must be satisfied by a remote memory, there is an unavoidable delay before the information is available. To hide this latency, a variety of techniques are used. The HEP system (page 566) introduced multithreading. Specifically, whenever HEP issued *any* instruction, the processor did a context switch to another runable thread. Providing there were sufficient threads, all latency is hidden. In an effort to reduce the number of threads needed for full performance and to improve the speed of a single thread, designers are turning to block multithreading, in which a block of statements is issued from the same thread before a context switch occurs. (This technique is also referred to as *coarse multithreading*, and the HEP style is referred to as *fine multithreading*. The Sparcle processor, like a conventional SPARC, normally issues instructions from one thread. A cache miss requiring a remote transaction is detected off-chip and causes a trap to occur. The Sparcle modifications permit fast trap processing. At a cost of just 14 cycles, Sparcle can switch to a new thread. The main change is that the SPARC register windows are used instead as independent (non-overlapping) register sets. This prevents the saving and restoring of registers during context switches. The program counter and status register are not replicated, but the trap handler is quite short (only five instructions). Another modification permits the floating-point instructions to be modified on the fly, in a context-dependent fashion, as they are loaded into the off-chip FPU. Since the total number of floating-point registers remains the same, each context has fewer than with a conventional SPARC.

In addition to hiding memory latency, rapid context switching permits certain synchronization delays to be masked as well. When a synchronization fault occurs, Sparcle is able to rapidly switch to another thread. For another approach to block multithreading, see the description of the Tera design on page 571.

The LimitLESS cache-coherence technique emulates a full-map scheme (page 549) by just keeping a limited number of pointers in the cache controller (the current hardware can hold up to five pointers), and trapping to sofware when an overflow occurs. This again takes advantage of the fast trap handling in Sparcle. An interesting observation made in [5] is that even with *zero* hardware pointers, that is with all coherence requests trapping to software, the performance for some applications is only a factor of 2 worse than with an infinite number of pointers, that is, a full-map scheme.

Although we have only discussed the architectural aspects of the Alewife approach, the group has also studied software techniques for locality management. They are developing compiler technology to enhance the static communication locality of applications by performing intelligent mapping of the task graph onto the machine. When the compiler cannot glean sufficient information to make good placement decisions, placement is deferred to the run-time system. For further information see [5].

10.3.6 The MIT J-Machine

The J-machine is somewhat hard to classify as either private-memory or shared-memory. The basic hardware primitive for communication is message-passing but it is provided in a manner that makes implementing a shared address space both simple *and* efficient. The key component, indeed almost the sole component, of the J-machine is the Message-Driven Processor (MDP), a single-chip, million transistor VLSI microcomputer whose designers wished to meet the following two goals (as stated in [114]):

... to implement a general-purpose multicomputer processing node provides the communication, synchronization, and naming mechanisms required to efficiently support several different parallel programming models.

... to create an inexpensive, VLSI component for cost-efficient parallel computers.

The designers believe that an ideal multicomputer node should be a commodity VLSI part, as inexpensive as jellybeans, that one can network together to form a *Jellybean* or *J-Machine* multicomputer.

The largest J-Machine built to date contains 1024 nodes arranged as an $16 \times 8 \times 8$ (bidirectional) 3-D mesh. Each node consists a single MDP chip and three 1M×4 DRAM chips, dissipates 1.5 Watts, and measures just 2" by 3". A board containing an 8 by 8 plane of nodes with elastomeric connections to vertically adjacent boards is 20.5" by 26". A vertical stack of eight boards forms a 512-node machine. Two parallel stacks, connected by short ribbon cables, are used for the 1024-node machine, currently in use at MIT. The unused connections on the boundary of the mesh are available for I/O ports.

Although the J-machine suggests a number of interesting areas for discussion, we will concentrate on one: the extremely efficient messaging system that begins to blur the distinction between shared- and private-memory and causes one to reconsider various "obviously inefficient" communication strategies. The interested reader is encouraged to consult [114] or [345] for more information.

The MDP chip has an 80 nS cycle time and contains, in addition to an (integer) computational unit the switching logic and buffers for the mesh routing. With three dimensions and bidirectional channels, each MDP has 6 inputs and 6 outputs to the network. The system supports *dimension-order routing* in which a message first travels in the X direction, then Y, and then Z. Hence, an arriving X message might continue out the other X side or might exit via any of the four Y or Z outputs (naturally, if the destination is the current node the message is consumed locally). This gives 5 routing possibilities for each X direction. Similarly, each Y input can be routed to any of 3 outputs and each Z input has a unique output, giving a total of 18 paths, each of which contains buffers, comparators, and output arbitration. Since the router is independent of the computation unit, the later is unaffected by messages (destined for other processors) passing through its node.

The J-machine achieves extremely low end-to-end message latency. A user-level task can send a message anywhere in a 4096-node machine in 2 us. assuming no network congestion. After another 1 us. the receiving node has created and dispatched a task to handle this message. This one to two order-of-magnitude latency improvement over common practice is why the J-machine, which is basically a message passing design, can nonetheless provide a shared-memory model with reasonable efficiency.

Many modern machines have fast networks. The J-machine's advantage comes in needing very little software to send and receive messages. There is a hardware SEND instruction that reads two words from registers or memory and queues them for transmission. Back-to-back SENDS are used for longer messages. An initial SEND is needed to specify the destination; the final SEND, which contains data, is flagged to indicate the end-of-message. Thus an N word message requires $1 + \lceil N/2 \rceil$ instructions. A typical three-instruction four-word send requires four processor clocks. All formatting for the network is done by the hardware.

Message reception benefits from the inclusion of three register sets, which as in Alewife (page 556) and HEP (page 566) enable rapid context switching. In the J-machine, each register set is associated with an execution priority. The MDP executes in the lowest, or background, priority when there are no messages pending. Message arrival creates a task at priority PO or P1, depending on the priority of the message, which is specified by the SEND operation. Task creation takes only three cycles after which the message handler, whose address was specified in the first SEND instruction, begins execution. Hardware managed queues are provided for messages that arrive when the processor is already executing at the specified priority or higher.

A number of benchmark programs have been run [345] and the consequences of such low latency communication have been noted. In the author's own words:

> The data presented here demonstrates that the J-machine's communication, synchronization, and naming mechanisms are effective in supporting programs with small task size (150 instructions). These programs also demonstrate that a fast communication facility makes it possible to operate with only a small amount of memory per node (1MB) by fetching instructions and data from remote nodes when needed.

10.3.7   Cray T3D

The processing elements (PEs) in the CRAY T3D system are based on a DECchip 21064 (Alpha) 64-bit microprocessor and have a peak performance rating of 150 MFLOPS. Each Alpha contains an 8-KB instruction cache and an 8-KB data cache. In addition each PE contains 16 or 64 Mbytes of local (DRAM) memory. Although this memory is local to an indvidual PE, it can be accessed by all processors directly (i.e., PE A can access memory local to PE B without message passing and without involving the microprocessor in PE A). Such an arrangement is referred to as physically distributed, logically shared memory. Of course, although access is provided to all of memory, access to the local memory is more rapid. Access times to remote memory are dependent on load and access pattern but should typically be in the microsecond range, a significant improvement over message-passing latencies in most private memory architectures.

Two of these processing elements share a high-speed network interface that connects the PEs into a 3-D torus system and supports a peak interprocessor communication rate of 300 Mbytes per second. Dimension-order routing is used as discussed on page 390. Since the topology is a torus (i.e., the highest numbered node in a dimension is connected to the lowest) and the links are bidirectional, there are two paths possible for each dimension and the hardware uses this redundancy to achieve fault-tolerance.

Cray-designed logic circuits provide synchronization and communication functions, including fetch-and-increment (i.e., fetch-and-add with an addend of 1), swap (i.e., an atomic exchange of a value in the microprocessor and in memory), barrier synchronization, and a messaging facility. These features make it possible to support SIMD, message-passing MIMD, and also shared-memory MIMD programming models.

The CRAFT (Cray Research Adaptive Fortran) programming model is an extension to Fortran 77 that also supports Fortran 90 array syntax and intrinsics. The functions of the UNICOS MAX distributed operating system are divided between the host (a CRAY Y-MP or CRAY C90) and the processing nodes. The intent is to minimize the amount of operating system software running on a processing node and release most of its local memory for application data storage and processing. The OS can be classified as a master-slave approach (360). System calls and exceptions generated by an application are first passed to a UNIX handler running on the same PE. This slave OS can respond to some system calls but passes the others on to the master OS running on the host.

System configurations range from 32 to 2048 processors in both air-cooled and liquid-cooled packaging, with peak performance ranging from 4.2 to over 300 GFLOPS. Some actual performance numbers are contained in the table on page 379. More information on the T3D can be found in [107].

Figure 10.21 The C.mmp (Carnegie-Mellon multi-mini-processor). Sixteen DEC PDP-11s were connected by a crossbar network to the 16 modules of a shared global memory [463]. The address translators were needed since the physical address space of the shared memory (32 MB) greatly exceeds the logical address space of the PDP-11 (64 KB). The cache was designed and prototyped but never used due to cache coherence problems [35].

10.3.8 CMU C.mmp

Hardware

The C.mmp (Computer with multiple mini-processors) was a research project started in 1971 at Carnegie-Mellon University (see Figure 10.21). It consisted of 16 minicomputers (DEC PDP-11s)[323] connected through a circuit-switched crossbar network to 16 memory modules, forming a shared-memory MIMD design.[324] In addition to the 32-MByte physical address space formed by these 16 memory modules, each PDP-11 processing element (PE) had access to an 8-KByte private memory, used primarily for operating system functions (handling PDP-11 traps and interrupts). The crossbar speed was comparable to the

---

[323] Some of the PDP-11s were Model 40s, and some were Model 20s.
[324] Or *multiprocessor* in the language of the day. Flynn [174] coined *MIMD* in 1972.

speed of a local memory reference.[325] Sixteen memory references can be in progress at once, provided that each reference is to a different memory port. There is a scalability question, however, since the cost of building a larger switch that maintains the same performance level grows approximately quadratically.[326] I/O and other peripheral devices are assigned to the Unibus of specific PEs and *cannot be shared* (a processor cannot initiate an I/O operation on a peripheral that is not on its own Unibus). The Hydra operating system described in Chapter 7 allowed many of these details to be hidden from the user.

Results

Experience showed that the failure rates of the processors, memory modules, and interprocessor bus outweighed that of the crossbar switch, which was quite reliable and usually available. Fault detection, diagnosis, and recovery were handled by Hydra as follows: A "watchdog" mechanism was implemented to detect processors that halt or become trapped in endless loops. Each PE must set a special bit every 4 seconds or it becomes a "suspect". For recovery, the system is quiesced, and a PE is chosen at random to test the suspect by stepping it through a simple diagnostic. If the suspect PE fails, it is removed from the configuration immediately; otherwise, the error is logged, and more extensive tests are conducted to determine its cause.

Unfortunately, this procedure was ineffective against transient errors. The addition of a processor-error counter helped somewhat, but a flaw was that the PE detecting the error was charged with causing it, even though the cause could be another PE, bad memory, or software. System restart took less than 2 minutes typically, so system availability was relatively high, but the loss of user jobs was an extreme inconvenience.

A number of design experiments were conducted involving such parameters as processor and memory speeds, memory-contention effects, semaphore wait-time constants, and so on [463]. Studies of several applications show that there are several classes that achieve a speedup that is linear with the number of PEs being used [223].

Wulf et al. [466], [465] offer an interesting discussion of the shortcomings and lessons of Hydra and C.mmp. The most significant hardware difficulty

---

[325] The average time to execute an instruction on a PDP-11/40 is about 2.5 microseconds. The model 20 is 50% to 60% slower. The time needed for address translation, switch overhead (without contention), and round-trip cable delay was 1 microsecond [251].

[326] The C.mmp crossbar is $(16 \times 16) \times (16 \times 16)$. The YSE crossbar on page 627 is $(256 \times 3) \times (256 \times 3)$, or nine times bigger by this one measure.

noted was the *small address space provided by the PDP-11;* the designers felt they could have provided a much more comfortable user environment had they not faced this addressing limitation. *Debugging* and *checkpointing* a collection of processes emerged as major unresolved issues. The failure to construct adequate *tools* was considered a serious failing.[327] The Hydra kernel itself was felt to be reasonably successful, but the paper concludes by saying that the test of success for the *user-specified* features that could be built using the kernel lay in the future, when many more people would be using the system. Unfortunately, this expectation was not realized, for reasons encountered before (see page 31): the design of C.mmp was ahead of its technology, and the system did not offer the combination of performance and user-friendliness needed to motivate users to reprogram their applications for a new computer like C.mmp.

10.3.9   CMU Cm*

Hardware

Cm* was a modular, multimicroprocessor design [422], [230] from Carnegie-Mellon University (Figure 10.22 on page 564).[328] It differed from its predecessor, the C.mmp (page 561) in several ways. Cm*'s basic building block was a processor-memory pair called a *computer module,* or *Cm.*[329] The processor was a DEC LSI-11. The memory local to a processor was also the shared memory in this MIMD system. The interconnection network was a three-level hierarchy of buses:

1. A local switch connects the LSI-11 to either its own local bus (for access to its local memory or I/O) device) or to a shared Map bus.

2. Up to 14 Cm's can share this Map bus and a (K.map) controller, forming a cluster.

3. Finally, clusters are connected via intercluster buses (450 nS per word).[330]

---

[327] Ironically, the Stanford/Livermore S-1 project set out to reimplement the C.mmp architecture with more powerful processors, but is remembered mostly for its tools (SCALD, etc.).

[328] *Cm* stands for "Computer module", a processor-memory pair. The star is metamathematician S.C. Kleene's formal-language closure operation (for example, $(a + b) \times .aaa$ is the set of all strings of *a*'s and *b*'s ending in three consecutive *a*'s). The names of hardware components use Bell and Newell's PMS notation, with the leading capitalized letter indicating the unit's function, e.g., Computer, Processor, Kontroller (as in K.map), Switch, Link [422].

[329] Thus Cm* was a boudoir, whereas C.mmp was a dance hall (see Figure 1.2 on page 7).

[330] Compare this bus hierarchy with the clusters and hierarchical design of Cedar (p. 611).

Inter-cluster buses

Cm
(Computer module):
P=processor (DEC LSI-11, up to 14 per cluster)
M=memory (up to 0.25 MByte)
S=local switch
(Computer module):
P=process

Figure 10.22 The Cm* multiprocessor. *Five clusters with 10 PEs each were built.*

The processors saw this hierarchy as a set of three different memory-access times (in a 1:3:9 ratio). The system was "reconfigurable" at "milliday bus re-plugging speeds" [230]—in other words, it took minutes to move the cables manually. A 50-module/5-cluster system was built and operated.

The system's memory formed a single 2^{28}-byte segmented virtual address space; any processor could directly access memory anywhere in the system. Message-passing provided a second type of communication, giving the user the option of using tightly or loosely coupled processes, that is, of viewing Cm* as either a multiprocessor or a computer network.

Cm* was designed to have fewer memory-contention problems than C.mmp. The hardware showed this intention in its three-level memory hierarchy, which was designed to take advantage of the spatial locality (of reference) found in most programs (and also places a premium on it). Another difference was that Cm* used buffered packet switching (rather than circuit switching as in the C.mmp) to eliminate the possibility of processor deadlock over memory-bus allocation. (Since multiple buses are needed for remote references, it is possible that two requests in a circuit-switched design each have seized one bus and now need the bus held by the other request. With a buffered design the request is copied at each stage, and the bus used to reach that stage is released, eliminating the deadlock possibility. Actually, as Swan [422] points out, this technique just transfers the deadlock from bus allocation to buffer allocation; but with available technology it was much easier to supply an excess of buffers than an excess of buses.)

Since the cost of the K.map controller was distributed across many cluster processors, it could be endowed with considerably more flexibility and power. Its heart was a horizontally microcoded processor with a 150 nanosecond cycle time. Because of its commanding position in the cluster, the K.map controller could ensure mutual exclusion on access to shared data structures with very little overhead.

A normal PDP-11 instruction mix has about 70% code references and 30% data references. Because of the 1:3:9 ratio of local:cluster:out-of-cluster memory-access times, a simple programming strategy was to execute code locally (and data remotely if necessary).[331] Under worst-case conditions, with the LSI-11s remotely executing code sequences maliciously contrived to generate high traffic, a K.map could handle up to six processors before saturating. With a reasonable balance of local to remote references, the K.map had no trouble handling the address-mapping traffic generated by a cluster [230].

Software

Algol 68 was extended to include *eventual values*, which allow a programmer to specify lazy evaluation (page 265), and *parallel clauses*, which furnish fork-and-join primitives (page 149). The compiler and run-time system for this language were first implemented on C.mmp.

Parallel subtasks (known as *activities*) are mapped onto available processors by a distributed high-level scheduler contained in the run-time system and remain on that processor until either blocking on a user semaphore or terminating. Associated with each activity is a master processor in charge of its execution. To exploit low-level parallelism, Cm*, unlike C.mmp, places operations such as floating-point arithmetic on a queue of pending work that can be picked up by other processors acting as slaves. The reader should compare this technique to a lookahead processor (the master) with multiple functional units (the slaves) and to the dataflow approach used by the LAU project (page 274). Data dependencies are reduced by compiler techniques and by structuring the run-time system to have the flavor of one for a single assignment language. The additional speedup from mining this low-level parallelism was only a factor of 2 or 3, limited by the overheads of queue manipulation and also by the relatively large proportion of operations performed

---

331   Note that this strategy implies replicating code that is to be executed by multiple processors. With the PDP-11's limited 64-KB address space, this replication can be particularly troublesome.

by the master. Reducing the overheads by microcoding the queue operations was expected to increase the parallelism to about 5 [230].

Experiments with various applications yielded the desired linear speedup for some (integer programming, partial differential equations) and gave Minsky's dreaded logarithmic speedup in other cases (quicksort). Overall, all the software components were operational; however, the user interface "left much to be desired" [230]. To quote Swan, "It will not be possible to declare the overall system a success until it is regularly and reliably supporting a community of satisfied users." Although much was learned from Cm*, this latter happy state was not reached, for the same reasons we discussed for C.mmp—insufficient computing power and user-friendliness to lure users.

10.3.10 Denelcor HEP

The Denelcor HEP [404], [291] is a shared-memory, pipelined multiprocessor that was the first commercial product to give programmers a chance to experiment with MIMD parallelism involving as many as 256 concurrent (potentially parallel) processes. From the hardware standpoint, it is a collection of up to 16 Process Execution Modules (PEMs). Each PEM is a register-to-register, pipelined, MIMD processor. In place of the normal (von Neumann) program counter, the instruction-issuing mechanism in this PEM contains special hardware in the form of a set of multiple task queues, each of which can be the source of the next instruction (a rather dataflow-like approach, actually). This hardware makes possible a fast, instruction-level, task-switching mechanism that is used to mask memory as well as pipeline latency. Synchronization among processes is a message-passing protocol that uses extra bits associated with each data storage site, as described below. A packet-switching network can connect these PEMs to a maximum of 128 data-memory modules (the largest configuration actually built had 4 PEMs and 4 data-memory modules). A PEM can address a portion of data memory directly and access the entire data memory through the switch. The network bandwidth is 10 million words per second per link, and each I/O cache (maximum of four) sustains I/O at 32 MB/second.

A key feature of the HEP architecture is extensive pipelining of both memory and ALUs in order to hide their inherent latencies. To handle dependencies, or "hazards", (page 416) among instructions that might be in the pipeline at the same time, other heavily pipelined designs have required either extensive resource scheduling using hardware interlocks (such as deTomaso's algorithm for the IBM 360/91) or software scheduling of instructions to avoid

Figure 10.23 A HEP processor (left). *The system delivered to the Aberdeen Proving Grounds consists of four of these processors (P) connected to four data memories (M) via a network of 3-input, 3-output switches (right). The hardware in the upper left corner of the diagram implements very low-overhead task switching.*

the need for interlocks (as in the MIPS design). The novelty of HEP is that it uses *instruction*-level multiprogramming and multitasking[332] to ensure that all the active instructions (i.e., those currently under execution) come from different processes and thus have a high probability of being independent. The pipelining problems caused by branch instructions are eliminated by allowing only one instruction from a given process to be in the pipeline at a time. Naturally, with process switching occurring after each instruction, the switching must be accomplished in hardware with extremely low overhead. Rapid process switching is the role of the task queues mentioned above.

The HEP Architecture

In addition to queues and floating-point logic units, the PEM includes up to a million 64-bit words of instruction memory, 2048 general-purpose registers, and 4096 words used to hold program constants. When a task is initiated, it is assigned a contiguous range of instruction, register, and constant storage, each

---

[332] Multiprogramming usually means time-sharing of equipment by programs that are solving unrelated problems; multitasking refers to a situation in which pieces of a program (tasks) are cooperating to solve the *same* problem.

specified by a pair of base and limit registers. A task consists of from 1 to 64 cooperating threads of control, called *processes* in HEP, all having the same protection domain; that is, the same base and limit register values.[333] A PEM can support up to 16 user tasks; however, the total number of user processes on a PEM is limited to 64. These tasks are executed in a time-multiplexed manner.

An active process in a PEM is represented by a Process Tag (PT), which contains a modest amount of the process's state, including, for example, the program counter but *not* the register contents. The PTs awaiting execution are located in the task and snapshot queues shown at the upper left in Figure 10.23. The hardware injects PTs from different processes successively into the execution pipeline.[334] This entire process can be viewed as extremely fine-grained (instruction-level) multitasking achieved by the hardware with much, much less overhead than that of a normal operating system task switch. Arithmetic instructions, which reference only registers and constants, are executed in the eight-stage pipeline shown in the upper right. References to local memory are also completed synchronously in eight clocks.[335] A separate set of queues is provided for the Storage Function Unit (SFU) instructions that access the shared data memory through the network (this access takes 20 to 30 pipeline steps in a small, moderately loaded system).

Coordination (communication and synchronization) among processes in HEP is accomplished via the famous full/empty bit, which is used to implement a one-word message-passing mechanism (see Figure 10.24 on page 570). Every location in the shared data-memory word and every general-purpose register has an extra bit used to indicate its access state (either full or empty). To allow a process to send a message via the data memory, there is a special store instruction that waits until the addressed location is "empty" and then indivisibly (i.e., without allowing an intervening reference to the location) writes into that location and sets it to "full". Reception of a message uses a special load instruction that waits until the address is "full" and then indivisibly reads it and sets it to "empty".[336] Registers have an additional "reserved" bit used to guarantee that these operations will be *atomic*, that is, un-

---

[333]   Here we have yet another use of the words *task* and *process.*

[334]   If no other process was ready to execute, then, under certain additional conditions, the next instruction was issued from the process just serviced. This second instruction might cause pipeline bubbles.

[335]   But these synchronous memory references may not use the full/empty bits described below.

[336]   The hardware is actually more general, but these are the most important functions supplied.

interruptible by other operations. If a location is not in the required state, the instruction is recycled through the task queues.[337] Thus, any writable storage location can be used as a safe one-word message buffer—one that will accept a message, keep it safe, deliver it (potentially as soon as the next access cycle), and ensure that the correct sequence is observed. Smith [291] points out that this low-overhead message passing allows processes to cooperate on tasks as small as the evaluation of a single scalar arithmetic expression—fine-grained parallelism, indeed. The message passing can be used for synchronization directly, as in Figure 10.4 on page 486, or it can be used to implement other synchronization mechanisms such as semaphores or barriers. Barriers are especially favorable in HEP because processes arriving at the barrier can use the low-cost process switch instead of busy-waiting, which lowers the potential for memory-access "hot spots" (see page 484). Since most synchronization methods can simulate each other, the choice should be based on performance and usefulness.

As we said, registers have an extra "reserved" bit that, when set, prevents use of that register by *any* instruction. This reserved bit is needed to make sending and receiving messages via the registers atomic. The explanation is interesting. Message passing can be used to coordinate both cooperating and competing processes; that is, it can provide both access and sequence control (page 155), provided that both send and receive are atomic operations, uninterruptible by other operations. In the Cosmic Cube (page 475) atomicity is achieved relatively easily, since there are no shared variables (a processor cannot directly access another's memory), and very little access control is required. However, HEP has shared memory, and also *shared registers*, because it is possible for the execution pipeline to contain instructions from several processes that all correspond to the same task and hence (by definition) share the same registers. To prevent erroneous results, an instruction entering the execution pipeline must have uninterrupted access to its registers until it leaves. But the pipeline takes eight processor cycles, during any of which another instruction could try to read or write a register used by the first instruction. Empty/full bits alone cannot prevent such an attempt. A "full" register is fair game to be read by another instruction, and an "empty" register is fair game to be written into. The solution is to equip registers with a third state, "reserved", which is set for the result register of an instruction entering the execution pipeline and prevents use of that register by another instruction until the first instruction leaves.

---

[337] The recycling causes a one-cycle "bubble" in the pipeline; the fast task-switching mechanism can supply an instruction from another process on the next cycle.

```
        ⋮
        PURGE $IP, $NP
        $NP = NPROCS
        DO 10 I = 2, NPROCS
            $IP = I - 1
            CREATE S($IP,$NP)
    10  CONTINUE
        $IP = NPROCS
        CALL S($IP,$NP)
C       WAIT FOR ALL PROCESSES TO FINISH
        N = $NP
    20  $NP = N
        IF (N .NE. 0) GO TO 20
        ⋮
        SUBROUTINE S($IP,$NP)
        MYNUM = $IP
        ⋮
        $NP = $NP-1
        RETURN
        END
        ⋮
```

In the code at the left, the new CREATE statement is used to effect a DOALL loop that performs NPROCS iterations of subroutine S in parallel. A $ in front of a variable indicates that it is an "asynchronous variable" used for synchronization and communication among processes. It is "protected" by an extra bit that determines its access state ("full/empty"). The semantics are

$VAR = means "wait for empty, write, set full"

= $VAR means "wait for full, read, set empty".

These are atomic (uninterruptible) operations. PURGE sets such a variable to "empty". $IP is used to give each process a unique ID number; $NP is used to implement the DOALL loop.

Figure 10.24 A snippet of HEP Fortran code [404] *illustrating the parallel extensions for process creation and synchronization.*

This architecture differs from the SIMD pipeline we discussed earlier (see page 423), which is designed to perform the *same* instruction on a number of input data pairs; that is, only the data flow through the pipeline. By contrast, the HEP PEM can be thought of as 16 independent SISD (serial) processors that were implemented by someone who didn't want to pay the cost of fully replicating the ALUs 16 times, and instead arranged for the processors to share one pipelined ALU. As in the pipelined SIMD case, however, the maximum speedup on a single PEM is the number of pipeline stages, namely eight. Experiments show that this maximum occurs when about 15 processes are concurrently placing instructions into the pipeline [236]. Since this pipeline can complete one instruction every 100 nanoseconds, a single PEM has a maximum performance of 10 MIPS, and thus the delivered four-PEM configuration can attain 40 MIPS, which for floating-point intensive programs translates into about 10 MFLOPS [291].

Programming the HEP

Two extensions were added to HEP Fortran to allow the programmer to create processes, the more important one being `CREATE`. This primitive creates a child process identical to the invoking parent and then immediately returns control, after which both processes may execute simultaneously. It is identical to Conway's fork (see page 149). Execution of `RETURN` terminates the child process. A third extension, *asynchronous variables*, which are specified by beginning the variable name with a dollar sign, essentially make available to the programmer the full/empty hardware bits discussed earlier. These variables are used for synchronization and communication among processes and are each "protected" by a full/empty bit that determines its access state. The semantics of an assignment to an asynchronous variable are "wait until empty, update the value, and set the state to full", all atomically. The semantics of evaluating an asynchronous variable are "wait until full, read the value, and set the state to empty", all atomically. A `PURGE` primitive is also supplied that simply sets the state of an asynchronous variable to *empty*.

The Tera Architecture

The idea of using rapid context switching to mask memory access and other machine latencies is not unique to the HEP design. Indeed, the dataflow architectures discussed in Chapter 9 represent another attempt to utilize this idea, as does the Sparcle processor used in the MIT Alewife project (page 556). Not surprisingly, Burton Smith, the HEP architect has continued to champion the idea in his subsequent designs, Horizon [303] and Tera [23].

Tera was designed to achieve three goals:

1. High speed—a fast clock and many processors
2. Wide applicability—suitable to a broad spectrum of problems
3. Good compilability—easy target for compilers

Many factors, at both the architectural and detailed-design level, contribute to meeting these goals, and we will just touch on a few.

As we described in Chapter 8, Tera is topologically a (depopulated) 3-D mesh. That is, Tera consists of a three-dimensional grid of switches with processors, memories, and I/O caches connected to *some* of the switches. A 256-processor system would contain 4096 switches arranged in a $16 \times 16 \times 16$ mesh that wraps around in all three dimensions. Connected to these switches would be 256 computational processors, 256 I/O processors, 512 data memories, and 256 I/O memories.

As with HEP, a Tera single processor can execute multiple instruction streams interleaved on a cycle-by-cycle basis. For HEP an individual stream could rarely have more than one instruction executing simultaneously. This meant that to get full performance out of a HEP processor, at least 11 active streams were normally needed. With the technology improvements in processor speeds outstripping memory-access times, the corresponding number for Tera would be about 70. While there are undoubtedly applications that can furnish 70 active streams, this would limit applicability. Moreover, even the most important stream could execute little faster than one instruction per 70 clocks and previous multistream processors have been criticized for poor single-stream performance. Tera uses two techniques to lessen this problem. First, it is a superscalar design: each instruction typically specifies three operations. The second technique is novel: each instruction contains a count specifying the number of subsequent instructions that are guaranteed *not* to depend on the current instruction. Since independent instructions can be active simultaneously, the processor can continue to issue instructions from a single stream at full speed until a dependency is encountered. The traditional approach to utilizing this observation is to employ register scoreboarding; the novelty in Tera is that the dependencies are made explicit in the architecture and are the responsibility of the software. Since the dependency count is a 3-bit field, up to 8 instructions (24 operations) from a given stream can be executing concurrently and thus only 9 streams would be needed to extract the full performance of the processor and each stream would execute at a rate of one operation per 3 clocks. It will be interesting to see how close in practice Tera will come to this best case.

Tera expands upon the HEP concept of tagged memory. In addition to full/empty bits, Tera memory has tags to support application-specific lightweight traps and indirect memory references (the latter without the processor complications that RISC advocates have rightfully criticized). The memory also supports the Ultracomputer fetch-and-add operation (but the network does not combine multiple references; see page 577).

10.3.11 *The NYU Ultracomputer*

"Basic Techniques for the Efficient Coordination of Very Large Numbers of Cooperating Sequential Processes" is the title of a key paper [202] on the NYU Ultracomputer. This title is also a good description of this project's motivation. Like HEP, the Ultracomputer is a shared-memory design with processors on one side of a network connecting to memory modules on the other side (Figure 10.25, left), and as with HEP, the schedulable units of computation are *processes*. However, the scale of parallelism here is significantly higher: A

Figure 10.25 Two views of the Ultracomputer. *The hardware view (left) features the realization of a shared multiport memory, and the software view (right) features process management with a parallel access queue (self-service paradigm).*

4096-processor machine is a representative design point, whereas most experiments with the HEP were limited to several dozen parallel processes.[338] Such a large jump in the scale of parallelism renders many previous coordination techniques unsuitable. The aim of this project has been to develop a new set of techniques suitable for such a highly parallel MIMD computer. The emphasis has been on the design and implementation of a set of truly parallel coordination mechanisms and data structures that can be used for both writing parallel application programs that contain a minimum of serial bottlenecks and creating an efficient operating system that is itself parallel.

The Ultracomputer approach to shared memory MIMD has two key underpinnings: the fetch-and-add synchronization primitive (page 162) and an enhanced interconnection network that can combine two or more requests bound for the same memory address (page 405). Fetch-and-add, in conjunction with such a combining network, makes it possible to construct a family of data structures that can be accessed by N processors in the same time required by one, thus satisfying one basic multiprocessor requirement mentioned on page 540, namely, "unconstrained, yet synchronized, access to shared data". An example is the parallel access queue that, among other applications, is used by the operating system for scheduling processes. A simplified version of such a queue is sketched at the right in Figure 10.25 and discussed further on page 588. The other basic multiprocessor issue, namely memory latency, is approached by equipping the processors with local cache memories and by interleaving memory addresses across the memory modules to distribute references and decrease congestion as much as possible. The combining feature of the network reduces network traffic, especially for hot spots that can otherwise increase memory latency for *all* processors.

---

[338] In the terms of a friend who divided parallel processing projects into the "tensies, thousandsies, and millionsies," the Ultracomputer is a "thousandsie".

The following is a list of the most important hardware features of the Ultracomputer that are intended to provide high performance for shared memory programs:

1. The processing elements are allowed to have multiple requests to memory outstanding (as in most high-performance serial computers).
2. The hardware interleaves consecutive memory addresses across the memory modules to reduce the chances of avoidable conflicts in accessing different data (the elements of a matrix, for example) in the same memory module.
3. Cache memories are placed in the processing nodes to keep the effective latency down by reducing the percentage of data that must be fetched from across the network.
4. The switch nodes are equipped with queues to handle messages that collide at the switch.
5. The switch is also equipped to combine messages that are bound for the same memory address.
6. The memory module is equipped with an adder to perform an at-memory fetch-and-add synchronization primitive.

These points are discussed in more detail below. An alternate and even more detailed description of the Ultracomputer is given in reference [199].

Hardware for Coordinating N Processes in Log N Time

The Ultracomputer approximates the paracomputer, or CRCW PRAM, model of computation (page 189), whose key features include one-cycle access by any processor to any memory module and enforcement of the serialization principle, which insists that, although a set of concurrent actions might be done much more quickly than if they were performed serially, the net result of the concurrent actions must nevertheless be the same as if these actions took place in some (unspecified) serial order.[339] The Ultracomputer's memory system (including an enhanced omega network) preserves the model's serialization principle. However, a memory access (load or store) is physically unrealizable in one cycle (due to fanout limitations, etc.) and is instead approximated as an access by N processors to N memory modules in a time that grows as $\log N$. By contrast, this penalty grows as N for the other shared mem-

---

[339] In other words, after the parallel actions are finished, the state of the world must correspond to that obtained after *some* sequence in which each action was performed from start to finish. There can be no results that could *only* arise if the actions were performed in some kind of piecemeal or interleaved fashion.

ory multiprocessors we have discussed so far. In addition, the Ultracomputer extends the CRCW PRAM model by including as a primitive the fetch-and-add operation, which shares with loads and stores the properties of satisfying the serialization principle and executing in log N time.

As we shall see, these features of the Ultracomputer hardware often permit processes to be coordinated in a bottleneck-free manner. In other designs, this interprocess contact usually involves *critical regions* of code that can only be executed by one process at a time (Figure 4.10 on page 157, for instance). During this time, the parallel processor may limp along at the speed of only one of its processing elements. For small, infrequent critical sections and few processors, these serial code segments may still represent an acceptably small portion of the running time, but they can be totally dominant when one is discussing thousands of processes (Amdahl's argument revisited; see page 24). Even the HEP "full/empty-bit" synchronization mechanism that we just described (page 568) involves serial sections[340] that, while small compared to those found in most multitasking operating systems (using semaphores, say), nevertheless introduce a time penalty that is linearly dependent on the number of processes (i.e., the HEP technique changes only the constant multiplier of the time penalty). The effect is still that of a structure accessible by one processor at a time.

useful parallel work   serial portion

A simple example is the barrier synchronization used in the n-body program of Figure 10.5 on page 489. The dilemma is that, although one cannot *count* on each process taking exactly the same time, one must be *prepared* for the processes to do so. Suppose a barrier for 4000 processes were implemented as a shared variable that was initially set at 4000 and had to be decremented by 1 and checked for 0 by each process arriving at the barrier. The problem, as we mentioned on page 161, is that each of these tests is itself a small critical section. If 4000 processes arrive at the barrier all at once, these tests must ordinarily be performed *one at a time, which is expensive.* Furthermore, the 3999 processes that flunk the test ("no, it isn't zero") have to do *something*, and the options are busy-waiting or task switching. Busy-waiting involves further testing of the variable controlling the barrier. The HEP

---

[340] The HEP allows creating many small, fast buffers (queues of length 1), but they still have serial access: a word location set at "full" is not allowed to be written, and an "empty" one is not allowed to be read, until their access states are changed.

can at least reduce this retesting traffic, because it can use its fast task-switching mechanism instead of having the processes busy-wait at the barrier. However, the initial tests are still not eliminated, and when the process that was switched out comes back, the test may fail again.

In the Ultracomputer implementation of barrier synchronization (pages 484 and 587), the variable controlling the barrier is tested using the fetch-and-add instruction. The result is a substantial speedup for the case in which all processes reach the barrier together (although not if they arrive separately). Since fetch-and-add is implemented at the memory (see page 577), it takes no longer than an ordinary memory read and write,[341] and because the interconnection network is able to combine simultaneous fetch-and-adds accessing the same memory location, all 4000 processes can arrive at the barrier at the same time and receive an answer (3999 nos and one yes) in the same time required by just one process. This is one simple example of the Ultracomputer approach to avoiding serial bottlenecks both in application programs and in operating systems by providing coordination primitives and data structures that can be used by multiple processes in parallel.

Software: Application Programming Environment and Operating System

In Figure 5.7 on page 245 we already listed a set of fetch-and-add–based parallel constructs for the application programmer, and several of these will be discussed in more detail later. The Ultracomputer operating system supports a UNIX environment. This OS, called Symunix, is a derivative of UNIX, with several key internal changes:

1. Process scheduling extends the UNIX self-service paradigm to a distributed implementation using a parallel access queue, a simplified version of which is described on page 588.
2. Memory management is also performed in parallel. The current implementation, running on the Motorola 68451 memory management unit, uses a parallel buddy system.
3. I/O management uses readers/writers code that is bottleneck-free when no writer is active.

All three of these enhancements are built on fetch-and-add; their highly parallel nature is due to the message-combining hardware mentioned above and described on page 580. Symunix is discussed in more detail on page 371.

---

[341] That is, two memory cycles.

Recap

In summary, the Ultracomputer approach to avoiding serial bottlenecks is to create coordination primitives and data structures that can be used by multiple processes in parallel. At the hardware level, this approach is accomplished by the memory system (the network and memory modules) and hence involves a delay that scales as log N, but during this delay *all* processors can, say, place an item on a queue or receive an item from it. The key idea is to add one rather special instruction called fetch-and-add to the otherwise ordinary repertoire of the processing elements, at the cost of an adder at each memory module, and to combine requests from different processors to the same memory location before they get there, that is, within the omega network,[342] at the cost of extra memory and logic (comparators and adders) in the network switch elements. We discuss the power and cost of fetch-and-add next, then that of combining, and then some of the parallel functions such as semaphores, barriers, and queues that can be achieved when fetch-and-add and combining are used together.

The Power and Cost of Fetch-and-Add

The reader of the earlier Ultracomputer papers [203] will remember that they are written in terms of a replace-add primitive, which is almost but not quite identical to fetch-and-add. The relationship is

V = integer variable, stored in shared memory
e = integer number or expression
F&A = fetch-and-add instruction
RA = replace-add instruction

Fetch-and-Add	**Replace-Add**
Y ← F&A(V,e) means that the following two things happen as one indivisible instruction: Y ← V V ← V + e	Y ← RA(V,e) means that the following two things happen as one indivisible instruction: Y ← V + e V ← V + e

---

[342] Like car pooling and a set of park-and-ride lots.

Note that *Y* gets the "*old* value of *V*" with F&A and the "*new* value of *V*" with RA. The primitives F&A and RA are equally powerful, since

RA(V,e) is equivalent to F&A(V,e)+e

and

F&A(V,e) is equivalent to RA(V,e)-e

The significant difference between these primitives becomes apparent when one considers generalizations to operations other than addition. The first equivalence remains valid for any other binary operation; the latter equivalence only holds for invertible operations (note the minus sign).[343]

In our earlier discussion of language synchronization constructs (page 162), we pointed out that unlike test-and-set, for example, the fetch-and-add primitive is geared toward quickly handing out a group of unique identification numbers and keeping track of how many are in circulation. Exactly what "quickly" means depends on the implementation. The two key results of the Ultracomputer implementation are that the fetch-and-add is performed at the memory module in two memory cycles and that concurrent fetch-and-adds aimed at the same memory location can be combined in transit in the processor-memory interconnection network and handled in no more time than a single fetch-and-add. The full benefit is obtained from the joint action of both of these features. We shall discuss the benefit and cost of each one individually and then show examples of the power of the full implementation.

Making Fetch-and-Add an Atomic Operation: Performing a fetch-and-add at the memory costs an adder circuit at each memory module. The present Ultracomputer design uses a 32-bit fixed-point adder, corresponding to the use of fetch-and-add as a coordination for an integral number of events.[344] The benefit of performing the addition at the memory can be explained by considering the alternative. Fetch-and-add is by definition atomic, that is, the fetch, add, and store must be performed as one indivisible operation. If the add is to be

---

343 For example, after executing replace-max(V,e) it is not possible to determine the old value of *V* unless it was greater than *e*. More interesting is to consider the Boolean operation Or and note that fetch-and-or(V,true) is identical to test-and-set(V). In contrast, replace-or(V,true) is simply V ← true since the value returned is always true and hence of no use. In general, the hardware used to combine fetch-and-add can be extended to support fetch-and-phi for any associative binary operator phi, whereas the replace-add hardware performs a subtraction and hence is limited to an invertible operator.

344 An interesting application for a floating-point fetch-and-add is discussed not far below.

done by the processor, then other processors must be prevented from access-ing the variable between the fetch and the store, perhaps by semaphores or HEP-style full/empty bits. The variable is thus locked unavailable for at least two memory cycles, one processor cycle, and one round-trip delay through the network, which could add up to 10 or 20 memory cycles. By performing the fetch-and-add at the memory, this period of unavailability is reduced to 2 memory cycles. In this regard, fetch-and-add done at the memory (but with no combining in the network) achieves the same thing as the HEP full/empty-bit synchronization mechanism—the cost of synchronization is reduced to one memory cycle per processor, but is still a serial bottleneck that grows linearly with the number of processors attempting simultaneous access. The combin-ing of fetch-and-adds in the network avoids this bottleneck.

However, if the memory accesses are distributed uniformly, without sig-nificant hot spots caused by competing accesses, fetch-and-add can be of sig-nificant benefit even without combining. The example below is fanciful in that the present Ultracomputer memory modules contain only fixed-point adders. With floating-point adders, the following alternate and much simpler version of the n-body program on page 489 would be possible:

```
Doall h = 0 to N-1
    Doall g = 0 to h-1
        COMPUTE_FORCE (FORCE, h, g)
        FloatingFetchAndAddButDoNotNeedTheFetch (FORCE, F(h))
        FloatingFetchAndAddButDoNotNeedTheFetch (FORCE, F(g))
    Endall
Endall

Doall h = 0 to N-1
    UPDATE (h)
Endall
```

The barrier in the solution on page 489 was needed because the updates to the net force on a body were not atomic. They are atomic, however, if imple-mented with floating-fetch-and-add, and so $N(N - 1)/2$ independent processes can be generated, and the barrier is no longer needed. Each of the N memory locations holding the net force on a body would be accessed $(N - 1)/2$ times during the course of the new program, giving an overall algorithmic complex-ity of $\Theta(N)$.[345] When compared with the $\Theta(N^2)$ serial algorithm, the speedup is

---

[345] Θ is defined on page 182 ff.

$\Theta(N^2)/\Theta(N)$, which is $\Theta(N)$. If we combine these fetch-and-adds, the time required reduces to $\Theta(\log N)$, and the speedup increases to $\Theta(N^2/\log N)$.

Making Fetch-and-Add a Parallel Operation: Although we have argued that just making fetch-and-add atomic can lead to improved parallelism in situations in which memory references are relatively uniformly distributed, the thinking in the Ultracomputer project was that the worst-case scenario of a large number of simultaneous references to the same memory location could not be neglected and demanded a truly parallel solution, namely, an interconnection network that could combine such simultaneous references into one reference before arriving at the memory. This solution requires extra memory and logic in the network switch elements but allows multiple fetch-and-adds accessing the same memory location simultaneously to be handled in the same time as a single fetch-and-add. In the next section we discuss the operation and costs of this combining in more detail.

Enhanced Omega Network with Combining

Here we shall describe how the omega network is augmented to perform message combining and what the augmentation costs. The reader may wish to review quickly Figure 8.7 on page 399 for its description of how message routing works in an omega network, and then we shall throw in a clever addition to the algorithm used there. After each switch reads its bit of the address, it still sends the message out the upper or lower port, depending on whether that bit was 0 or 1, but it also replaces the bit it just read with a 0 or a 1, depending on whether the message came *in* on the switch's upper or lower port. This way, the message steers its own way to the correct destination, and when it arrives, its address field contains the address whence it *originated*, and it is ready to steer its way back.[346] (The reader is encouraged to work out the modified address field for the example in the figure.)

This procedure is fine as long as only one message at a time arrives at a switch, but additional hardware is required to handle conflicts between messages arriving simultaneously when the traffic is realistic. Figure 10.26 on page 581 shows some of the extra hardware that a network switch must then contain. We first explain the needs and then the operation of this switch.

An omega network connecting a group of processors to a group of memory modules provides a unique path between each PE-MM pair. The uniqueness simplifies the routing algorithm above, which can be used for the messages generated by the processors as part of such memory-access oper-

---

[346] Like Hansel in the fairy tale.

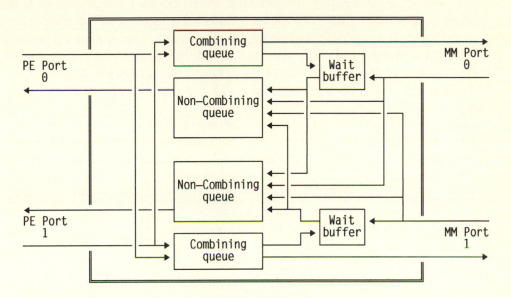

Figure 10.26 The insides of an omega network switch *(page 398) in the Ultra-computer, equipped for queueing and combining conflicting messages. This design corresponds to the VLSI chip described in reference [142]. Its operation is explained in the text (see Figure 10.27 on page 584).*

ations as load (memory read), store (memory write), and fetch-and-add. Unfortunately, two such concurrent requests can conflict; that is, the paths corresponding to these two requests can enter the two input ports of a switch but require the same output port (we called this conflict *blocking* on page 161). One solution is to "kill" one of the two conflicting requests and have it resubmitted by the PE, as in an earlier proposal by Burroughs [80], but this limits the network bandwidth to $O(N/\log N)$[298] . The solution adopted instead for the Ultracomputer is to add queues to each switch node, so that the two conflicting requests can be forwarded one after the other.[347] Such a "buffered" network can emit a wave of messages during each switch cycle rather than at intervals equal to log N switch cycles (the latency of the entire network). Then the network bandwidth is $\Theta(N)$, assuming infinite queues and a processor that can tolerate the latency. In practice, queue lengths of 8–16 messages[348] are usually found to be adequate.

---

347 Such "buffered" omega nets are also used elsewhere.
348 A representative message on the Ultracomputer is 2–4 packets of 37 bits each.

Another enhancement added to the switch nodes besides queues is the combining feature. The motivation for this enhancement is the observation [202] that there is such a thing as a *favorable* conflict: when concurrent loads and stores are directed at the same memory location and meet at the switch, they can be combined (and thereby satisfied), and network traffic can be reduced without introducing any delay, provided the right circuitry is added to the switch node.

Such combining is valuable when there is a hot spot [362] in the memory, that is, when references are not uniformly distributed among the memory modules but instead there is an above-average rate of accesses to one address, for example, to a memory location used by a counting semaphore used in the parallel queue algorithm shown below or to a central variable of some other coordination construct. In our networks chapter (Chapter 8) we cited experiments (Figure 8.12 on page 407) showing that concentrating even a very small percentage of the total accesses on one memory location can cause significant access-time degradation, not only for those processors involved in the hot spot, but for *all* processors trying to use the network in the meanwhile. Queued-up requests bound for the hot spot back up into the network and create a traffic jam for all requests. The mechanism is discussed in more detail under the title "The Great Hot Spot Controversy" on page 598, where we explain the significance of buffered networks and processors supporting multiple outstanding memory references. The point to remember here is that combining in such a situation benefits not only those processes trying to access the hot spot but also all the other "innocent victim" processes as well.

The following actions are consistent with the serialization principle and are appropriate for favorable conflicts involving loads and stores:

Load-Load (two memory reads): Transmit one, return to each the value obtained from memory.

Store-Store (two memory writes): Transmit either one, ignore the other, and acknowledge both (this gives the same effect that occurs if the stores are executed serially).

Load-Store (memory read, memory write): Transmit the store and return its value to satisfy the load.[349]

---

[349] This decision to act as if the store preceded the load is the subject of some recurring controversy that involves the serialization principle and is beyond the scope of the present discussion.

The circuits required are basically address comparators (to determine combinability) and additional memory (short-term parking for one of the requests); fetch-and-add also requires an adder (for the response to the parked request). See Figure 10.26 on page 581 and its discussion.

Since combined requests can themselves be combined, any number of concurrent memory references to the same memory location can be satisfied in one memory cycle (assuming the absence of conflicts with requests destined for other memory locations, which would introduce delay). It is this property that, when extended to include fetch-and-add operations, permits the bottleneck-free implementation of many coordination protocols. Figure 10.27 on page 584 illustrates how the combining of fetch-and-adds works.

The action in Figure 10.27 on page 584 corresponds to the serial order "`F&A(X,3)` immediately followed by `F&A(X,1)`" (the upper input is arbitrarily treated as occurring first). Barring unequal delays, however, the processors issuing these two `F&A`s receive their replies simultaneously, in the time one reply would have taken. If the reverse order were assumed, then `F&A(X,1)` would receive Y, and `F&A(X,3)` would receive $Y+1$, but the contents of memory location X would still become $Y+3+1$ as before.

Fetch-and-adds can also be combined with loads and stores. `Load(X)` is simply treated as `F&A(X,0)`. Combining a fetch-and-add with a store is done in a manner analogous to that described above for combining a load with a store: the store is arbitrarily treated as having occurred first. In other words, when a `F&A(X,e)` meets a `Store(X,f)`, the rule is to transmit `Store(X,e+f)` and, upon receiving the acknowledgment, satisfy the `F&A` by returning f.

How the Switch Works: Here's how the switch in Figure 10.26 on page 581 performs the sequence of steps shown in Figure 10.27 on page 584. As seen in Figure 10.26, a queue is associated with each output port of the switch: two "combining queues" for requests going toward the memory and two "non-combining queues" for responses returning from memory and bound for a processor. Optimum queue and message sizes are still the subject of some research, but a representative queue size is eight messages, each consisting of four packets of 37 bits each. A memory request sent by the processor and transmitted by the switch consists of *function indicator* (Load, Store, or Fetch-and-Add), *address*, and *data*. The address is an amalgam of part of the source processor's number and part of the target memory module's number (per the routing algorithm described on page 580) and the internal address

Figure 10.27 Combining of two concurrent fetch-and-add instructions *accessing the same variable, shown in a four-step time sequence.*

Time t1: *Two fetch-and-adds,* `F&A(X,e)` *and* `F&A(X,f)`, *referencing the same shared variable X meet at a switch.*

Time t2: *The switch forms the sum* $e + f$, *stores* e *(in the Wait Buffer of Figure 10.26), and transmits* `F&A(X,e+f)`.

Time t3: *The value Y (formerly stored in X) is returned to the switch in response to* `F&A(X,e+f)`.

Time t4: *The switch transmits Y to satisfy* `F&A(X,e)` *and transmits* $Y + e$ *to satisfy* `F&A(X,f)`.

(The Ultracomputer switch presently implemented associates a queue with each input-output pair and only combines messages in the same queue, which means that combinable messages on separate inputs don't get combined until the next switch stage. The next design is intended to work as shown here.)

within the memory module. For simplicity, only the combining of requests with like function fields will be described here.[350]

The Combining Queue compares the MM number and address of each entering request with the requests already in the queue.[351] If there is no match, then no combining is possible, and the new request takes its place at the tail of the queue. Otherwise, the addresses of the two matching requests are put in the Wait Buffer, and the new request is deleted from the queue. If the requests being combined are stores, the datum of the old request (in the queue) is replaced by the new request's datum. If the requests are fetch-and-adds, then the old datum is sent to the Wait Buffer and replaced by the sum of the two data.

After returning from memory, a request is both routed to the appropriate Noncombining Queue and used for an associative search of the relevant Wait Buffer. If a match occurs, the matching entry is removed from the buffer and sent, equipped with the following data field, to the Noncombining Queue leading to the appropriate PE.

1. The data field of the returning entry in the case of a load (memory read).
2. The sum of its own data field and that of the returning entry in the case of a fetch-and-add.

This procedure effects the serialization discussed earlier; that is, the end effect is as if the old request had been received at the memory before the new request.

Reflection and Refraction

Although shared memory offers straightforward support for message-passing (as discussed on page 470), a special *reflect* message-passing operation is also proposed to increase efficiency in some cases. Associated with each process is a *reflector* in shared memory containing the PE number of the process, or a "disabled" indication if the process is not running. When a reflect request[352] arrives, it is acknowledged and forwarded to the indicated PE, where it generates an interrupt; a disabled reflector generates instead a negative acknowledgment.

---

[350] This restriction also occurs in the initial switch design [142], which does not combine "heterogeneous" requests, e.g., loads with stores.

[351] The queue is implemented as a VLSI systolic array (see page 463) that permits half of the queue entries to be compared pairwise to the other half during each systolic cycle [200], [199].

[352] These requests may not be combined by the network.

To move a process, its reflector is first disabled,[353] and when the new PE has obtained the process, it stores its number in the reflector. If the memory is dual-ported and on its other side are located, for example, specialized I/O processors, reflection is replaced by *refraction*. Reflections and refractions can be broadcast to multiple destinations by having network switches replicate the requests.

Case Study: Semaphores Using Fetch-and-Add

The box at the left shows an implementation of *counting semaphores* (page 160) using fetch-and-add: A subtle point about P: note that each processor trying to enter the critical section through P must test S <u>twice.</u> This double testing may appear redundant. However, if the first test (while S < 1) is removed, the remaining code can fail due to unacceptable race conditions [202]. Suppose, for example, that three processors execute P(S) at the same time with S having an initial value of 1. The values 1, 0, and -1 are returned to the three processors, and S is set to -2. The processor receiving the 1 enters the critical section; the other two each go into a cycle of resetting and then retesting S. Now, suppose the first processor leaves the critical section at a time when each of the other processes has executed the first F&A but not the second, that is, when $S = -2$. The first process then executes V, thus incrementing S to -1.

The box:

(Correct) Semaphore

(Initially S=1)

P :

```
α: While S < 1: DoNothing
   If F&A (S,-1) < 1
      F&A (S,1)
      GOTO α
```

(Critical Section)

V :

```
F&A (S,1)
```

The section is now free to be entered by either of the waiting processors as soon as S is incremented to +1. However, this event may never occur, because more than one processor is performing cycles of test-reset on S. Incrementing S to +1 requires two resets in a row, but instead, the following endless scenario is possible. Call the two waiting processors B and C. Processor B increments S to 0 and then decrements S back to -1 *before* processor C executes its next instruction. B thus fails to enter the critical section. Then, while B is between instructions, C increments and immediately decrements S. This

---

[353] When this operation is acknowledged, reflections can no longer be headed for the processor.

process can continue indefinitely, with S varying between 0 and −1 and neither processor ever entering the section. This race condition becomes steadily more probable as the number of processors grows, since the probability is increased that some processor has executed the first F&A but not the second.

This failure mode is prevented by P's first test. If $S=1$, a number of simultaneous processes are still allowed to go charging by to see whether they can get into the critical section. However, when the losers (all those getting less than 1 from the second test) come back to α, they are told for their own safety to test S by *reading* it rather than by performing the fetch-and-adds that got them into trouble before.

Case Study: Barriers Using Fetch-and-Add

When a number of processors in the Ultracomputer simultaneously execute fetch-and-add instructions that access the same shared variable, the network is able to combine these into one fetch-and-add before they reach the memory.[354] Hence, the N processes can read and update a shared variable in the same time needed by one process, and the N numbers that they receive are the same as if they had read and updated the shared variable individually in some (unspecified) serial order. This capability can be invaluable in eliminating the serialization that would otherwise occur when a number of processes arrive at a barrier synchronization point and check whether the requisite number of processes has arrived yet (consider the n-body example in Figure 10.5 on page 489 for large n). The code used to implement a barrier using fetch-and-add is quite short, but explaining it requires that we say a bit more about barriers first.

When a program contains barrier synchronization points, no process executing that program may continue past a barrier until some preset number of processes (N, say) have reached that barrier. If this were the *only* condition, the code for a barrier like **barrier_sync** in Figure 10.5 on page 489 could be as simple as

```
F&A(X,1)
WAIT FOR X=N
```

where X is initially zero. But barriers must be reusable (and hence resettable). One might think about using a different variable for each barrier, but in general the number of barrier synchronizations needed by a program can be very large and unknown at compile time or even at the start of run time, and a separate

---

354 Remember that fetch-and-add is made an indivisible instruction by performing it at the memory.

variable per barrier becomes impractical. Instead, a resettable barrier using a single variable is used. The following might at first appear suitable:

```
If F&A(X,1) = N-1 then
     X←0
Else
     wait for X = 0
```

However, this code fails because it can only be used once,[355] even though it does reset X after N processes have passed. Look again at Figure 10.5 on page 489 and its commentary. The processes don't all rush past the barrier as soon as the N th one arrives, as if in response to a starter's pistol; each process must first test the barrier variable again before it knows that it may proceed. The problem is that, since the barrier is reused, it is possible for a process to pass the first barrier, reach the second barrier, and increment X to a nonzero value *before* all the other processes have passed the first barrier. This possibility creates a deadlock: X can never reach $N - 1$ again, and all processes are stuck forever at barriers. One solution is to alternate barriers with two different shared variables $X1$ and $X2$, but it becomes awkward to decide which to use when.

The following simple and correct barrier algorithm [147] uses one shared variable X (initially 0), one constant N, and one private Boolean variable `wasless` to automatically give the *effect* of an alternating series of barriers. Premature closing is prevented by allowing $N - 1$ processes to arrive at a previously opened barrier before it is reset (reclosed):

> **Procedure barrier_sync**
> ```
> boolean wasless ← (X<N)
> If F&A(X,1) = 2N-1 then
>      X←0
> wait for (X<N) ≠ wasless
> ```

Lill Tschudi's linocut, *Tour de Suisse.*

In other words, "test to see whether X is less than N and assign the test result (true or false) to the local variable `wasless`; do a F&A on X; if you get $2N - 1$, set X to 0. Test again to see whether $X < N$ and compare the test result with `wasless`. Wait until these two Boolean values disagree, and then proceed." The effect is that of a barrier that opens when N processes reach it, allows N processes to pass, and then closes. The processes at one barrier wait for $X \geq N$, at the other barrier for $X < N$; the variable X cycles between 0 and $2N - 1$.

---

[355] Like Daffy Duck's great finale in which he blows himself up with dynamite.

Case Study: Highly Parallel Queue Management Using Fetch-and-Add

Queues are used in most multiprocessor organizations to hold the backlog of work. As mentioned earlier, when a processor in the Ultracomputer finishes an assigned task, it will interrogate a global queue of tasks awaiting attention, claim a task, and go on to perform this task.[356] A queue that can be shared among many processors without using any code that could create serial bottlenecks is thus essential for the scheduler of the Ultracomputer operating system (and is also used in many applications programs). Here we show how fetch-and-add can be used to achieve a simplified version of such a queue.[357] More details may be found in the literature [200].

In the algorithm below, a queue of length `SIZE` is represented by a public circular array `Q[0:SIZE-1]`, depicted in Figure 10.28 on page 590. Public variables I and D point to the locations for inserting and deleting the next item (the rear and front of the queue, respectively). Initially the queue is empty, and $I = D = 0$. As concurrent inserts and deletes occur, the body of the queue (the part between I and D) fluctuates in size and rotates clockwise. I and D are changed only via F&As.

If one didn't have to worry about queue overflow and underflow, the procedures for inserting and deleting could be done with a simple fetch-and-add on I and D. In reality, however, it is essential to prevent attempts to insert into a full queue and delete from an empty one. One might think next that the empty condition would simply correspond to $I - D = 0$ and the full condition to $I - D = SIZE$, but this is not so. Of necessity, the insert procedure below in-

---

[356] In the assumed environment of large numbers of simultaneous insertions into the queue and deletions from it, the first in, first out property of a queue is defined as follows: If insertion of data item p is completed before insertion of data item q starts, then it must not be possible for a deletion yielding q to complete before a deletion yielding p starts. In other words, if q goes in after p, it can't come out before p (no Hungarians allowed). But if they arrive simultaneously, all bets are off!

[357] One way in which the queue actually used for scheduling tasks differs from the simpler example shown here is a feature called *multiqueues* (or queues with multiplicity). The SPMD model (multiple copies of the *same* program executed by many processors) becomes increasingly important as the number of processors grows into the thousands, since it is unlikely that there will be thousands of *different* pieces of code in execution at the same time. A more likely scenario is that 1000 iterations of an outer loop will be enqueued as 1000 separate tasks by a process containing a `DOALL i=1 to 1000`, say. The model in Figure 10.28 on page 590 would lead one to believe that the enqueuing must be done in 1000 consecutive steps by the processor containing the code for this outer loop, and thus the parallel effect of the queue is lost. Instead, the problem is solved by using a fancier data structure, which allows *one* item with a *count field* for the multiplicity. Only when this count reaches zero does the item get dequeued. This is an optimization for an important special case—an SPMD DOALL.

Figure 10.28 Illustration for Fetch-and-Add–based parallel queue. *(This illustration is a simplified version of the queue used by the scheduler of the Ultracomputer operating system.) The total number of slots in the queue is* SIZE. *Items are inserted at the rear of the queue at* I *and removed from the front of the queue at* D. *The expression* SIZE-#QU *gives the number of definitely empty slots (the variable* #QU *is used to maintain an Upper bound on the number of elements in the queue), and* #QL, *the corresponding Lower bound, gives the number of definitely full slots. At any one time,* SIZE-#QU *inserting processes and* #QL *deleting processes may access the queue simultaneously. (Note that the full slots are not always contiguous as in this snapshot. For example, the middle one of the three inserting PEs might fill its slot first.)*

crements I *before* it actually transfers data into the queue, and the delete procedure decrements D before it transfers data out; thus, at any moment there can be a number of queue slots that are being filled but are not ready to be emptied, and vice versa. Therefore, two additional counters are maintained:

1. #QU is the total number of queue slots that are occupied or being moved into or out of (i.e., an Upper bound on the number of items in the queue) and when *this* number reaches SIZE, the "no vacancy" sign goes up.[358] (More formally, a *QueueOverflow* notification is returned to a process that attempts an insert while *#QU ≥ SIZE*. Depending on the application, the

---

[358] Most real-life innkeepers are not this conservative!

appropriate action for the QueueOverflow and QueueUnderflow conditions might be either to retry the operation or to switch to another activity.)

2. #QL, on the other hand, is the total number of occupied queue slots that are *not* being moved into or out of (i.e., a Lower bound on the number of items in the queue), and when this number hits zero, the "empty" light goes on (more formally, a *QueueUnderflow* notification is sent to a process that attempts a delete while *#QL* ≤ 0).

Thus, *#QU* − *#QL* is the number of processors currently doing either inserts or deletes.

The critical-section-free insert and delete programs are as follows:

Insert	**Delete**
`If #QU≥SIZE: Full`	`If #QL.≤SIZE: Empty`
`If F&A(#QU,1)≥SIZE:`	`If F&A(#QL,-1)≤0`
` F&A(#QU,-1)`	` F&A(#QL,1)`
` Full`	` Empty`
`MyI←Mod(F&A(I,1),SIZE)`	`MyD←Mod(F&A(D,1),SIZE)`
P`(InsertSem[MyI])`	**P**`(InsertSem[MyD])`
`Q[MyI]←Data`	`Ans←Q[MyD]`
V`(DeleteSem[MyI])`	**V**`(InsertSem[MyD])`
`F&A(#QL,1)`	`F&A(#QU,-1)`

The insert procedure is really trying to accomplish only `Q[Mod(F&A(I,1),SIZE)]←Data`, which is embodied in the two lines `MyI←Mod(F&A(I,1),SIZE)` and `Q[MyI]←Data`. The rest of the code detects queue overflow and performs coordination with other processes. The first four lines are a test to see whether the queue is full (the reason for the double test is the same as that discussed for the correct vs. "naive" implementation of semaphores earlier). `Full` means set the *QueueOverflow* flag. `InsertSem` and `DeleteSem` are each Boolean vectors of dimension `SIZE`, while **P** and **V** implement the semaphores we described on page 586. The reason that the two procedures look so symmetrical is that a delete operation is equivalent to the insertion of empty space.[359]

---

[359] We thank Boris Lubachevsky for this insight.

The reason that the semaphores are needed is a bit tricky. A simple scenario starts with two insert processes arriving at an empty queue. The inserts are assigned to slots 1 and 2. Suppose the second insert finishes first. Now a delete arrives at the queue. Without the semaphore, it would access slot 1. But this access is premature, since the first insert has not yet filled slot 1. The delete is susceptible to getting old, wrong, or meaningless data instead of whatever the first insert was supposed to leave for it.

A more complex scenario that is possible without the semaphores is that two processes desiring to perform an insert are assigned the *same* slot. This could happen even though the tests in the first four lines of the insert procedure allow through only a number of processors that does not exceed the number of (really) empty queue slots. The semaphores ensure that only one process at a time can perform the insert (*or* delete) procedure on a given slot.

Furthermore, using *two* semaphore variables and cross-coupling the **P**s and **V**s of the two procedures as shown sets up precisely the alternation needed to resolve such conflicts. For example, if two inserts were given the same MyI, a delete with MyD=MyI following one of the inserts is just what is needed to empty that slot and allow the other insert to proceed. Note that the **V** performed by the completing insert sets the **P** of precisely the right delete to "go ahead".[360] The HEP full/empty bits (page 568), incidentally, enforce this kind of alternation automatically;[361] the semaphores could be discarded, and the lines they were protecting could be written

$$\$Q[MyI] \leftarrow Data \qquad and \qquad Ans \leftarrow \$Q[MyD]$$

Prototype Hardware

In the 1980s, the NYU group built several reliable bus-based Ultra II systems, the two largest each containing eight PEs and 8 MB of central memory. The processors were 10-MHz Motorola MC68010s augmented with Weitek 1164/65 floating-point units, 32-KB 2-way set associative caches, and hardware support for fetch-and-add. The central memory was packaged as four 2-MB memory modules, each containing an adder used to support fetch-and-add. A second port on the shared memory was connected to an I/O-laden PDP-11 that, in addition to serving as an all-purpose I/O controller, connects the prototype to the NYU network and hence to the internet as well. These prototypes were in

---

360 Put another way, the only way to relieve multiple inserts into the same queue location is to alternate them with deletes to the same location.

361 Note the following fine distinction between the full/empty bits and fetch-and-add. The former enforce alternation of reading and writing, whereas the latter does the read and write together and does not change the state of the variable.

routine use for software development, algorithm and application studies, and scientific production, both within and outside NYU, and the university has offered courses on programming MIMD shared memory computers for which students were required to develop, run, and analyze programs on Ultra II systems.

In 1992 a 4-processor Ultra III prototype began operation with full hardware support for combining memory references. A 16-processor system is being constructed in 1993.

Ultra III uses AMD 29050 processors, each with a 32-KB data cache and a 128-KB instruction cache. Both caches are direct-mapped; the I-cache has a 16-byte linesize, and the D-cache has a 4-byte linesize. Each Ultra III processor has a 4-byte wide, bidirectional port to the processor-to-memory interconnection module. For flexibility and, more importantly, to permit detailed performance measurements, the control logic on the processor board is controlled by two XILINX FPGAs (model 4010).

The primary novelty is in the omega network, which is composed of NYU-designed, MOSIS-fabricated, full-custom switch chips that buffer conflicting requests and combine simultaneous references to the same memory location. In addition to fetch-and-add, operations that may be combined are *fetch-and-or, fetch-and-andnot, fetch-and-store* (also known as *swap*), *fetch-and-store-if-0*, and *fetch-and-store-if-not-neg*, all of which operate on a 32-bit word, and *load double*, and *store double*, which operate on a pair of 32-bit words. Only like operations can be combined. Non-combinable operations supported are partial word store, reflect, and broadcast; the latter two are used for interprocessor interrupts. The current switches are implemented in 2-micron CMOS, packaged in 132-pin PGAs, and require 8 chips per 2×2 bidirectional crossbar. These switches are pin-limited. NCR has agreed to fabricate switches using a 1.5-micron process and package them in 208-pin PGAs. This packaging halves the number of chips needed.

The shared memory consists of sixteen 16-MB memory modules each with an ALU to support fetch-and-phi and a network interface.

The system has run successfully at its target clock speed of 15 MHz. The 32-bit datapaths, 1 clock-per-stage network, 3-clock processor-board latency, and 2-clock memory latency, give a minimum round-trip memory latency of 14 cycles, or just under a microsecond for the 16-PE Ultra III prototype. The latency grows by 2 clocks every time the number of processors is doubled. Peak network bandwidth is 60 MB/sec per port in each direction.

Many of the Ultracomputer ideas are also incorporated in the RP3, which is described on page 603.

10.3.12 *The BBN Butterfly*

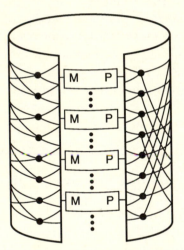

At first glance, the wraparound nature of its omega network makes the BBN Butterfly parallel processor [108] look quite different from the design of the Ultracomputer (page 572). Then, after realizing that the Ultracomputer topology is the same as that of the Butterfly with the processor-memory pairs mentally ripped apart along the dotted line, we see that the two designs appear quite similar. In actuality, these two designs have interesting similarities as well as differences.

Both use a shared-memory architecture at the hardware level (all processors have equally direct access to all parts of shared memory), but they differ in how they support shared-memory programs. The Ultracomputer design incorporates a number of extra hardware features (page 574) whose purpose is to mask the effects of memory latency and to provide unconstrained yet synchronized access to shared data. The Butterfly approach uses simpler hardware (the only item shared with the Ultracomputer list above is fetch-and-add at the memory) and relies more on software for these purposes. Both are designed to use an omega network to connect Motorola 68000-series processors to the memory modules, but 128-processor Butterfly systems with omega networks have already been delivered,[362] whereas Ultracomputer hardware is at the much earlier stage of 8-processor, bus-connected

---

362 We believe the Butterfly is the first working computer system using an omega network. The largest system demonstrated as of this writing was a 256-processor configuration formed from two 128-processor systems that were eventually delivered to separate customers.

prototypes.[363] We will make more comparisons after we describe the Butterfly in more detail.

Architecture and Hardware

The Butterfly architecture [109] and [374] permits up to 256 processing nodes. In the first generation, each 0.5-MIPS node is a 12" by 18" board that includes an MC68000 processor, a microcoded Processor Node Controller (PNC), and 1 MB of memory, expandable to 4 MB by a daughter-board arrangement. These nodes can be upgraded to an MC68020 processor supplemented with an MC68881 arithmetic coprocessor. This upgrade doubles the node performance to 1 MIPS. (Floating-point results have not been published as of this writing, but a peak of 0.2 to 0.4 MFLOPS per node is a reasonable guess.)

All memory is local to some processor node, but each processor can access any of the memory in the machine. The PNC uses the memory management unit to translate the virtual address used by the MC68000 into physical memory addresses in such a way that the memory of all processor nodes, taken together, appears as a single global memory to application software. The omega network makes all the remote memory-access times uniform in the absence of contention (about 6 microseconds for a 256-input network vs. 2 microseconds for a local access). However, the memory addressing is sequential in each node, not interleaved across the nodes, and the network is not buffered; that is, there are no queues in the switches. If two conflicting messages collide at a switch node, one is "killed" and resubmitted later.

The packet-switched omega network interconnecting these nodes has up to four stages of 4×4 crossbar switches. Each path through the switch can transfer 32 Mbit/second. Each 4×4 switch element is a custom VLSI chip. Eight such chips on a board make a two-stage 16-input, 16-output switch; combine it with 16 processor boards and you have an entry-level Butterfly, able to accept increments of capacity in every subsystem that contributes to the overall throughput. A 256-processor configuration achieved a maximum of 115 MIPS (on matrix multiplication), representing a speedup of about 230 (91% efficiency) over a single (0.5 MIPS) node. A 128-processor Butterfly system occupies four standard racks and dissipates up to 20 KW. The initial selling price was about $8000/node.

---

[363] On the other hand, the body of literature describing the theory, principles, and details of the Ultracomputer is much more extensive, and so we discuss it first because that allows fuller initial coverage of the issues involved.

Software and Programming

A UNIX-like environment is provided by the Chrysalis operating system kernel, which resides in each processor node and provides processor and memory management,[364] in the form of subroutines that may be called from the user's programs. Two programming environments that are supported are Cooperating Sequential Processes (message passing) and the Uniform System (shared memory). The former was developed for Butterfly's original communications and networking applications and is still the most widely used mode. The latter includes two special kinds of subroutines, *generators* that identify the next task for execution and *workers* that carry out the task. The Uniform System provides a library of commonly used generators. The programmer is required to structure the application into a collection of generators and workers.

A copy of the code needed for all the tasks is distributed to each processor (SPMD model; see page 609). In other words, code is stored in local memory, not fetched across the network; constants and stack variables are also stored in local memory. The application data are spread uniformly across the memory of the machine using *software interleaving* supplied by the Uniform System. This form of interleaving involves a performance penalty but frees the programmer from worrying about data placement and allows all processors to be treated as identical workers able to do any task.

Fetch-and-add is implemented in hardware at the memory, thereby making this an atomic operation, but since there is no message-combining hardware, simultaneous fetch-and-adds are serialized, and the type of parallel access queue discussed in the Ultracomputer section (page 572) is not possible here. Consistent with this situation, the task-scheduling algorithm is a distributed computation. Each processor runs just enough of the scheduling algorithm to decide what its next task should be (similar to the Ultracomputer, but not in parallel).

Software combining can be done by spreading the load on one variable over many intermediate variables stored in different memory modules and then using pairwise combining of results. Experiments show that for over 100 processors, fetch-and-add with software message combining gives better performance than at-memory fetch-and-add with no combining.[365]

C was the original language available on the Butterfly; Lisp and Fortran are later additions. The references cited previously provide additional details.

---

[364] It does not provide file management, as in a full operating system (page 343), and hence the word *kernel*.

[365] In other words, for more than 100 processors, we really want combining with fetch-and-add.

Figure 10.29 Hardware and program computational models. *The point is that both shared-memory and message-passing programs can be supported by either shared-memory or private-memory hardware. The question is how efficient an implementation can be obtained in each case, and what will be the performance? Linda is a shared-memory program model. In [88] Linda was implemented via message passing on S/Net.)*

Comparisons and Controversies

The Butterfly was originally designed for a satellite message-processing application called the Voice Funnel, with very little communication between parallel processes, and the original purpose of the shared-memory hardware was to implement a message-passing model of computation suitable for infrequent sending and receiving of large messages (chunks of compressed telephone conversations). In this mode it differed from the Cosmic Cube chiefly in having faster and uniform transmission time between any pair of processors.

There is some controversy about whether the Butterfly is really a shared-memory multiprocessor. We shall show that two different levels of the computational model are involved: at the hardware level, one can have shared memory or private memory. There is no question that the Butterfly is a shared-memory design at this level. A separate but related question is whether (or, actually, how well) the hardware supports shared memory or message-passing *programs* (see Figure 10.29). As Pfister put it while making a general comment, "The use of underlying shared-memory hardware must be distinguished from the use of higher-level paradigms for programming"[361].

Two points of controversy about the Butterfly have to do with hot spots and shared-memory operation. Actually the two are related. The Butterfly's designers describe it as a tightly coupled, shared-memory multiprocessor that does not exhibit network tree saturation in the presence of hot spot non-uniform memory-access patterns. An opposing camp holds that tree saturation is absent because the Butterfly is designed much more for efficient execution of message-passing programs than (in general) shared-memory programs and that the experiments corresponded to the first type of program. The hot spot aspects are discussed in the following section, "The Great Hot

Spots Controversy". It does seem that the normalized network loading was very light during the Butterfly hot spot experiments. The shared-memory aspects boil down to two different design philosophies with regard to supporting shared-memory programs and underscore that this is still an area of active research. The approach followed by the Ultracomputer project and the RP3 project, for example, is to assume that a high degree of contending accesses to shared memory will be occurring and to provide a number of extra hardware features geared toward these. A partial list of these features appears on page 574. The Butterfly approach is to keep the hardware much simpler and to use a combination of some software equivalents to the list mentioned above combined with programs that place fewer demands on the network than envisioned by the other group. Time will evaluate these two approaches.

10.3.13 *The Great Hot Spots Controversy*

Do hot spots [362] affect innocent bystanders, or not [436]? As shown in Figure 10.30 on page 599, a hot spot in a multiprocessor interconnection network is a weak link, typically a memory module, that becomes overloaded by a non-uniformity in the memory traffic and creates a backup that can affect all messages entering the network. This phenomenon occurs in buffered networks[366] and can be cured by providing message combining at the switch nodes, as done in the RP3, Ultracomputer, and original CHoPP designs (pages 603, 572, and 625). However, an alternate view is that buffering causes the problem in the first place, and the solution is an unbuffered network such as that used in the Butterfly (page 594). Examining both sides of this controversy reveals differing assumptions about the network traffic (and hence about the applications).

Consider an N-input, N-output buffered network composed of $K \times K$ switches with message queues of infinite capacity. Let each processor send memory requests to the network at a rate that averages out to r packets per switch cycle per network input port ($0 > r > 1$), and suppose that these requests are *uniformly* distributed among the memory modules on the other side of the network. Then the one-way network latency T as a function of network utilization r is [199]

---

[366] In such networks the switch node handles contention for an output port by enqueueing rather than erasing messages.

Figure 10.30 Network tree saturation developing from a memory hot spot. *The hot spot here is an overloaded memory module, one receiving requests at a rate that approaches or exceeds its service rate. The scenario is one in which the average rate of memory requests is low enough to cause no problems if the requests are uniformly distributed among the memory modules, but one module receives an above-average rate of requests, as might happen with a shared variable used for interprocess coordination (synchronization). In a network intended for high through-put and therefore equipped to buffer messages at the switch nodes (i.e., enqueue rather than erase one of two messages competing for the same switch output port), the traffic headed for the hot spot can back up into the network and disrupt all traffic. Message combining in the switches can prevent this effect [362].*

Without such combining, the output queue leading to the hot spot fills rapidly [306]. Messages bound for that queue can enter either input port of the switch, and so both inputs are "turned off" by rescinding the "clear to send" signal to the two connecting switches in the previous stage. An output queue in each of those switches then fills up, and the process repeats until a tree pattern of saturated switches rooted at the hot spot stretches all the way to the other side of the network, and all messages entering the network are delayed. This sequence is illustrated in the figure [370]. (A more elaborate design with two "clear to send" signals per input port allows messages to keep flowing to the nonfull output queue; this improvement lessens but does not eliminate the hot spot effect.)

Another way to avoid hot spots is to eliminate the message queues in the switches and use the Ethernet protocol — resubmit a request if it runs into a conflict [436]. This simplifies the network's design but reduces its throughput capability. There is controversy about the need for a buffered network with combining as used in the Ultracomputer and RP3 designs vs. the unbuffered network of the Butterfly. The answer depends on the application and its communication needs. The results published for the Butterfly so far correspond to relatively light use of the network.

$$T = \frac{\log_2 N}{\log_2 K} \left[1 + \frac{Mr(1 - 1/K)}{2(1 - r)} \right] + M - 1$$

where M is the number of packets per message, and T is in units of switch cycles. The second term in the brackets is from queueing theory, the multiplier is the number of switch stages, and $M - 1$ accounts for the time to get the message into the network. $T(r)$ is the basis for the dashed curve in Figure 8.12 on page 407.[367]

However, averages can be deceiving, and one can drown in water averaging 2 feet deep. In real life, the distribution of memory requests can be non-uniform enough so that, while the average request rate may not be a problem, the local request rate approaches or exceeds the local service rate at, say, a memory module.[368] Since real-life switch queues have finite capacity, the output queue leading to the overloaded hot spot backs up and overflows into the previous stage of the network, as shown in Figure 10.30 on page 599, until hot spot traffic backs up all the way to the other side of the network and slows *all* messages, not just those going to the hot spot. A tree of saturated switches grows from the hot spot and cripples the network. This condition is called *tree saturation*. A small imbalance in network traffic [362] can create tree saturation, and create it quite rapidly [306].

If each of the N network input ports contributes an average of hr requests per switch cycle to the hot spot memory module (over and above the uniform distribution), one would expect trouble when Nhr approached the service rate of the memory module. Assuming equal memory and switch cycle times, $T(r)$ should go into a steep climb when r approaches $1/Nh$, which is indeed the behavior of the simulation results in reference [362] and Figure 8.12. For a buffered 1000-input network without combining, a hot spot rate of $h = 1\%$ reduces by 10 the maximum available network throughput and computational speedup. The same thing happens for $h = 16\%$ with the 64-input network of Figure 8.12 on page 407. The simulations in reference [362] show that combining significantly reduces hot spot effects in the 64-input network; the throughput for $h = 16\%$ is increased tenfold, for example. Other simulations [313] for larger networks show that *pairwise* combining becomes inadequate as $N = 1000$ is approached but that three-way combining is sufficient. The true test will come from real hardware and real programs.

---

[367] To be exact, $M - 1$ is replaced by M, the round-trip time is approximated by $2T$, and 1 cycle is added for the memory, yielding $9 + 12/(1 - r)$ for the equation of the dashed curve in Figure 8.12.

[368] Other "weak links" can also cause hot spots.

This approach of buffered networks with message-combining was challenged by some hot spot experiments on the Butterfly that showed that, although the access time of the hot spot increased as expected, the effect on processors not using the hot spot was small. This result was ascribed to the nonbuffered nature of the network.[369] However, there are significant differences in the normalized network loading used by the two camps (reflecting differences in intended applications), as we explain below.

The Butterfly hot spot experiments [436] were done using a 256-input network capable of 32 Mbits/second/input, for a maximum network carrying capacity of 8 Gbits/second. However, no more than 101 processors were sending messages to the network, and they were sending them roughly every 10 microseconds (because a processor must wait for one memory access to complete before starting the next one), and so the total input to the network was less than 320 Mbits/second, corresponding to a network utilization of $r = 0.04$, a rather low value. Put another way, there were never more than 101 messages in the 256-input multistage network. This light loading would account for the low contention seen at the switches.

The second set of experiments, multiplication of two 400×400 matrices, made similarly light use of the network. Software floating-point operations were used first to verify the correctness of the algorithms and then were replaced by operations that simulated a hardware floating-point unit's timing and memory references. The inner loop then accomplished two floating-point operations (multiply and add) in 10 microseconds. The reconstruction of network usage is as follows. Each processor computed a 6×6 subset of the output matrix (one element at a time created too much contention; see page 17), and row-wise and column-wise storage of the input matrices were both used to capitalize on the Butterfly's block transfer mechanism. Hence, each processor did something like this:

6×400 get row elements
6×400 get column elements
Do 36 entries
    Do 400 elements
        Multiply
        Add
6×6 store answers

---

369 The authors use the word *nonblocking* for the network, but this term is inconsistent with our usage (page 401) and that of most others.

The 400 multiply-adds take 4 milliseconds, the 36 entries therefore take 144 milliseconds, and the get and store operations (chiefly the gets) take about 5 milliseconds, since they use the 10^6 elements/second block transfer mode. So the network is used for about 5 out of 150 milliseconds, for a network utilization a little over r=0.03.

As compared to the MC68000 processor in the Butterfly used for the hot spot experiments, the RP3's ROMP processor differs in two important ways:

1. It is RISC-like, performing instructions in 1 or 2 cycles[370] rather than 10 to 20

2. It can have multiple (up to 16) outstanding memory requests vs. just one.

Given that four processors are multiplexed into one network input, the RP3 network is facing up to 64 outstanding memory requests per input port, vs. a value of 0.04 in the Butterfly experiments. The reasons that the RP3 network can cope are that the clock cycle time of its switch is almost 10 times faster than that of the processor and that the processor cache satisfies many of the memory requests before they get to the network. But the network utilization is still expected to be much greater than 0.04, which predicts that contention will *not* be tolerable at the switch nodes unless they have message buffers, as in the model used for the original hot spot simulations [362]. This analysis helps to explain why switch contention and tree saturation were much more prevalent when the combining feature was turned off in these original experiments. Note, moreover, that references to a synchronization variable cannot by definition be cached,[371] and so the caches do nothing to ameliorate this source of hot spots, which reinforces the argument for message-combining in the switch nodes. We have already described how message-combining keeps hot spots from "blowing up" the average network latency. Once again, note that this benefit accrues to all memory accesses, *including* those to the hot spot.

These differences in network loading reflect differences in intended applications. The Butterfly was originally designed for the Voice Funnel, an application in which numerous telephone conversations were compressed and decompressed for a satellite communications link. This application involves much processing, occasional receiving and sending of a large block of data, but little communication among processors. The RP3 is designed to allow ex-

---

370   The cycles are about twice as long.
371   Remember that these caches cannot communicate; that is, they are not like the "snoopy" caches discussed on page 542.

periments with a wide range of computational models and applications.[372] Nevertheless, a fair question at this point is what are the trade-offs involved? Is it cheaper to use extra paths to reduce the effects of switch contention, as in the Butterfly experiments, or to beef up the switch nodes, as in the Ultracomputer and RP3 designs? This remains an active research area.

10.3.14   *The IBM RP3*

The IBM Research Parallel Processor (RP3) is a testbed for the hardware and software of highly parallel MIMD supercomputer designs. It aims to provide sufficient flexibility to examine a variety of computational models and sufficient computing power to justify the effort of converting a variety of real applications to parallel form. Basic questions to be addressed include whether there *is* a multipurpose parallel architecture, whether this can be programmed with normal skills, whether there is enough parallelism in applications to make the machine interesting, and whether it can be implemented cost-effectively.

In order to accommodate a wide range of applications, the RP3 is an MIMD design, and in order to explore how to combine the best features of both shared and private memory, the RP3 hardware provides a variable global/local partition capability that makes it possible to have as much of both as needed. The initial application can thus be done in a global memory context. This context is easier since fewer algorithmic changes are needed, although the network traffic and memory latency are higher. Then, through a gradual tuning process, the data for the computation-intensive parts can be migrated to local memory for higher efficiency.

As we mentioned on page 540, Arvind and Ianucci [35] listed two basic issues that must be addressed by any shared-memory multiprocessor: (1) how to tolerate long latencies for memory requests, and (2) how to achieve unconstrained, yet synchronized, access to shared data. In their solution, dataflow, instructions are expected to have gotten their data *before* they bother the processor; the cost includes that of circulating a relatively large number of instructions through a long pipeline, as we discussed on page 512 ff. The RP3 solutions are more traditional—a cache at each processor node to reduce latency, and parallel accessing algorithms based on the fetch-and-add synchronization primitive with hardware support, as we will describe.

---

[372] The RP3 has hardware to support memory addressing that is completely interleaved across the memory modules (as in the Ultracomputer), completely sequential (as in the Butterfly), or mixtures of both.

(a) System connection diagram

128-port network, 13 GB/s (20 nS clock cycle)

8 X 50 MB/s per port

Processor-memory element

ROMP processor (200 nS)
32 KB cache
custom MMU
4 MB memory

PME 0

PME 7

ISP 0

192 MB/s total

Disk system (shared with host S/370)

ISP 63

PME 511

(b) 64-PME subsection (top view)

(b)

32 PMEs

Network

I=ISP
P=PME

(c) 512-PME machine (top view)

Figure 10.31 512-processor configuration of the RP3 (Research Parallel Processor Prototype).
(a) *Overall system connection diagram. The design incorporated two networks: a faster one, built from water-cooled bipolar technology, would perform reads and writes but not message combining, while a slower but denser CMOS combining network (sketched as mostly hidden behind the bipolar network) would be used for synchronization, e.g., fetch-and-add. Each PME (processor-memory element) is connected to both networks. Total memory was 2 GB, performance target was in the range of 1000 MIPS.* **(b)** *Top view of the physical layout of the 64-processor subsection that was built and operated for several years. The power supply cabinet is shown by dashed lines. Each end of the H-shaped cabinet holds 32 PMEs and 4 ISPs (I/O and support processors). The bipolar network is in the middle (the combining network was not completed). Note that this network takes less than one-third of the total volume of the machine.* **(c)** *Top view of the overall physical layout. The diameter of the outer circle is 10 meters.*

Architecture and Hardware

RP3 was initiated in cooperation with the NYU Ultracomputer effort and is in many ways a superset of that architecture.[373] However, its purpose is not to make a highly detailed architectural statement, but rather to allow a broad range of such statements to be tested.[374] RP3 is designed to accommodate 512 processing nodes interconnected by a high-speed omega network. As shown in Figure 10.31, each node contains a 32-bit ROMP microprocessor, a 32-KB cache, a floating-point unit, and a portion (up to 8 MB) of the main memory of the system. The initial hardware consists of a module comprising an octant of this system.

To allow experiments with various architectures, RP3 features a special memory organization that allows its entire 2–4 GB of storage to act as one global shared memory or as a collection of purely local memories with message passing or various intermediate mixtures of local and global memories. Other RP3 design properties include

- Peak performance of 1300 MIPS, 800 MFLOPS
- Interconnection network throughput of 13 GB/second, latency equal to 1–2 processor cycles
- High-function ("request-combining") memory communication
- I/O rates of 192 MB/second
- Software cache control
- Built-in performance measurement hardware

Exploration of a diverse range of application areas is planned, including scientific/engineering problems, artificial intelligence and expert systems, design automation, computer graphics, and mathematical optimization.

The RP3 is designed to be flexible enough to assume the hardware characteristics of designs as diverse as those of the NYU Ultracomputer (page 572) and the BBN Butterfly (page 594), that is, interleaved memory for efficient support of shared-memory programs, sequential memory for efficient support of message-passing programs, as well as mixtures of the two chosen at run time,[375] and to do so with sufficiently high performance to justify the effort of converting real applications to the corresponding parallel forms.[376] RP3 in-

---

[373] Strictly speaking, RP3 is a superset of a certain vintage of the Ultracomputer; the present Ultracomputer design has evolved some features not in RP3, such as the reflection/refraction message-passing mechanism (page 585).

[374] As one project member joked, "This is a machine to tell us what machine we *should* have built."

[375] That is, both flavors of memory are supported *and* the percentage can be changed dynamically, as we will describe below.

[376] We spoke previously of the importance of raw processing power for attracting real users (see page 31).

cludes all the shared-memory-related hardware features listed for the Ultra-computer on page 574, but it can alter most of these and assume the hardware characteristics of the Butterfly (no message-combining, no memory interleaving). The Cedar [301] is an intermediate design with a fixed partitioning of private and shared memory. In the RP3, this partition can be changed under software control, thus permitting a wide range of experiments.

Processing Nodes

Each processor-memory element (PME) includes a 32-bit ROMP [229] micro-processor (the same one used in the IBM RT-PC), a custom memory management unit (MMU), a 32-KB cache, a floating-point unit, an I/O interface, 4 MB of memory, a performance monitor, and a network interface (Figure 10.32).

The PME is designed to allow the ROMP microprocessor, floating-point unit, and I/O interface device all to operate asynchronously (with multiple outstanding memory requests). The 32-KB, 2-way set associative cache (1024 lines per set, 16 Bytes/line) is designed to support these multiple requests without locking up (waiting for line fetches), thus masking the network latency. Store-through is used to avoid the bursts of network traffic that would arise from a store-in cache. A store-allocate-non-fetch (SANF) policy is used to reduce startup costs. Software-initiated invalidation is supported for a line, a page, or the entire cache. In addition to private and shared data, RP3 supports a third category called "temporarily cacheable data", the use of which can significantly improve program speed.

Software control of cache consistency sounds frightening at first, but *any* optimizing compiler for MIMD shared memory must be aware of shared read/write data. The syntax and semantics for this control are already in the latest ANSI standard for the C language. At present, the cacheability of data is decided by the user, but the algorithms for automatic detection of cacheability are already being installed in the PTRAN compiler.

Perhaps the most unique feature of the RP3 architecture (as distinguished from its hardware implementation) is the memory mapping. An interleaved memory mapping is one that spreads each processor's memory addresses over all the memory modules, as is done in the Ultracomputer for better support of shared-memory programs. A sequential mapping keeps each processor's memory addresses within its local memory, as is done in the Butterfly for better support of private-memory, message-passing programs. In order to make this happen, the MMU is equipped to translate *virtual* addresses generated by the processor into *real* addresses recognized by the memory hardware. As an option in RP3, this address to be used by the memory hardware can first be transformed into an interleaved *absolute* address (Figure 10.33). Each page

Figure 10.32 The RP3 processor-memory element.

carries an attribute specifying the degree of interleaving to be used when it is stored.

Network

RP3 uses two networks. One of them does not combine messages but obtains a fast 20-nSec clock cycle[377] by using ECL bipolar circuits in a TCM package [68]. The other uses slower CMOS technology but does perform message-combining. A single network was preferred, but logic fast enough to provide the desired latency did not have sufficiently high integration levels at the time of design.

The 128-port noncombining network consists of four stages of 4×4 switches and provides dual paths between every input and output port, each of which is multiplexed among four PMEs. (Two such dual path networks are actually used, one for requests to the memories and one for replies.) Topologically, this is quite similar to the Butterfly network, but the RP3's has one-sixth the latency due to its faster technology, which allows an 8-byte

---

[377] A packet takes 2 clock cycles to move from one switch to the next (latch-to-latch design), so the latency is 20 nSec × (2 × #stages + pipeline fill) = 160 nSec + 20 nSec × packets/message.

Figure 10.33 Memory address translation on the RP3.

message to traverse the network in 320 nanoseconds (assuming no contention). The ratio of bandwidths is even greater, since RP3's switches buffer messages and the Butterfly's do not.

The combining network proposed was a 64-port, six-stage omega network with 2 × 2 switches; an extra stage of multiplexing at the network ports accommodates the 512 PMEs. Each stage can combine queued references to identical memory locations. The combining network may match the peak bandwidth of its noncombining partner by using a wider data path, but its latency is apt to be longer.

I/O Subsystem

The I/O subsystem consists of 64 data channels (one per ISP), for a peak bandwidth of 192 MB/second. The designers preferred more bandwidth, but made a practical compromise. The I/O requirements of a computer with several GB of main memory[378] are unknown, and this system moves data and programs in and out of RP3 at reasonable speeds. In stream mode, one of the eight PMEs serviced by an ISP can receive 3 MB/second. At the hardware

---

[378] Not just extended memory or RAM disk.

level, any disk is equally accessible by 64 PMEs. Otherwise, the operating system routes requests automatically.

Software and Programming

The RP3 software provides support for initial applications and an infrastructure for experimentation. A UNIX-like environment is provided by the CMU MACH operating system, modified by IBM and NYU to eliminate internal serial sections and support highly parallel operation, using the "combining fetch-and-op" synchronization primitives developed at NYU [198] and supported on RP3. Extensions for efficient shared-memory operation and low-overhead message passing are also being added. Other features include user cacheability control, support for non-uniform memory architecture, and jobwide scheduling of families of tasks. Normal-weight tasks (parbegins, for example) and lightweight tasks (doalls, for example) will both be supported. Jobwide scheduling permits identification and scheduling of a family of tasks to be all active at the same time, which can benefit lightweight tasks in particular.

Programming language support for RP3 at this point consists of minimal extensions of C and Fortran. Users annotate their programs to indicate parallel and serial sections, shared and private data, and so on, and a preprocessor converts these annotations to macros in the standard languages, which are then compiled by existing ROMP compilers. Work is in progress to automate this entire process as part of the PTRAN project [15]. Ada and Common Lisp support may be added, as well as support for functional languages.

While the hardware was being built, a number of potentially parallel applications were examined using a system called EPEX, or Environment for Parallel Execution [121], [189]. The IBM VM operating system supports multiple virtual machines in time-shared mode. By using a standard but lightly used feature of VM called *writeable shared segments*, VM/EPEX allows these virtual machines to work on a single problem, thus simulating parallel execution on a uniprocessor and actually achieving it on a multiprocessor.

Most of the investigation was done using the SPMD (Single Program, Multiple Data) model, a special case of MIMD, in which all processors execute the same program, although at any one time the instruction (and of course the data) can be different in each processor due to data-dependent branches, varying memory-access times, and so on [122]. In SPMD, the number of processes or tasks[379] is decided before run time and remains constant throughout the run, thus avoiding the operating system overhead associated

---

[379] Again we are using *task* and *process* as synonyms.

Figure 10.34 Speedup curve vs. number of processors *for three problem sizes of a molecular dynamics application. The degree of parallelism for each problem is 27, 64, and 127, respectively. Note that a speedup of almost 40 can still be obtained for 40 processors.*

with fork-and-join–style spawning of processes during run time. SPMD can be used in both shared-memory and private-memory (message-passing) modes. It should be understood that although both EPEX and RP3 provide efficient support for SPMD, neither is limited to the SPMD subset of MIMD.

The RP3 software environment also included a set of useful "postmortem" analysis tools: SPAN (SPeedup ANalyzer) to analyze potential speedup in the serial program, TDNS (Trace-Driven Network Simulator) to predict the amount of network traffic, and PSIMUL (Parallel SIMULator) to analyze traces, cache activity, and so on, in the parallel program. Over 20 scientific, engineering, and graphics applications have been parallelized in this environment, using real programs. Some of the results have been analyzed in detail [123], [120], [119], [118]; an example is shown in Figure 10.34. By and large, there was pleasant surprise that it was possible to parallelize existing programs better than expected.

One of the most interesting lessons learned from the RP3 is the effect of NUMA (Non-Uniform Memory Access) on parallel programming style: even though there was less than a 2:1 ratio between the time it took a processor to access remote vs. local memory,[380] performance-conscious programmers would still spend considerable effort to distribute their data in a way that min-

---

[380] If there was no significant contention in the network, RP3 had a 1:12:20 ratio of times needed to access cache, local memory, and remote memory [77].

imized accesses to remote memory — in other words, they were writing distributed-memory programs on shared-memory hardware. Localizing the data in this fashion could improve performance as a result of improved memory-access time and cache utilization.[381] Such experience can be used as an argument favoring MIMD hardware designs that are based on distributed memory and fast message passing rather than on NUMA shared memory[382].

Some nice work was also done on parallel program visualization [279]. Program visualization (as distinguished from data visualization) is the use of computer graphics techniques to show what a parallel program is doing while it is executing. This has become an excellent tool for experienced programmers as well as new learners. RP3 also influenced the design of the IBM PVS (Power Visualization System), a 32-processor shared-memory design aimed at visualization applications and described below.

10.3.15   IBM PVS

The IBM Power Visualization System [254] consists of up to 32 i860 processors running at 40 MHz and provided with up to 2 GBytes of shared memory by a multistage switching network. The bandwidth to each processor is 8 MB/s. The shared memory can also be used for fast message passing: latencies as small as 3 microseconds from application to application have been achieved for short messages.[383] The theoretical peak performance is 1.3 GFLOPS in double precision and 2.5 GFLOPS in single precision. As with RP3, cache consistency is provided via non-cacheable variables, that is, by the software. PVS is primarily intended for use as a visualization engine with the Data Explorer software that was developed for it, and this combination is making inroads in the entertainment industry. As a scientific computer running under UNIX, PVS has achieved 925 MFLOPS on the TPP benchmark (see page 379).

---

381 *Local* did not necessarily imply *cacheable* because of the way memory interleaving worked. If someone, however, took the effort to move data into the memory module that was associated with the processor (thus treating it as local memory in the more traditional sense) it was probably private data, and therefore cacheable.

382 MIT J credo?

383 Bill Dally of MIT is reputed to have said that if you have fast communication means, it is a shame to limit its use to load/store programming, so he would presumably approve this expansion to send/receive programming.

10.3.16 UI Cedar

Cedar[384] is a parallel supercomputer being designed and built by a group at the University of Illinois [301] primarily to run Fortran programs restructured by the Parafrase compiler that this group has developed over the years (see page 314). The architecture is thus a compiler-driven design that shows the influence of keeping one eye on the nature of Fortran programs and the other on the hardware requirements of supercomputers, particularly their memory requirements, all areas in which this group has considerable experience (several members are veterans of ILLIAC-IV). Prominent characteristics include *clusters* of processing elements, a multilevel *memory hierarchy*, and a *macro-dataflow* method of controlling the parallel execution of the *compound functions* (page 616) into which the compiler has divided the program. We discuss these key ideas in more detail.

Hardware

The current embodiment of Cedar is shown in Figure 10.35 on page 613. Like several of the other shared-memory MIMD designs that we have treated on the preceding pages, this one includes a number of memory modules connected to a multistage interconnection network, but the resulting global memory is not directly connected to individual processing elements (PEs) but rather to *clusters*, each of which is itself a parallel computer with its own disk storage (I/O) system, memory, and cache shared among multiple PEs.

Cluster: Each cluster shown in Figure 10.35 on page 613 is a slightly modified Alliant FX/8 "mini-supercomputer". Like the machines discussed in "Caches and Modest Bus-Based MIMD Systems" on page 541, the Alliant's eight PEs represent what we call *modest* parallelism, but rather than a bus connection and private caches, the Alliant's PEs are connected by a crossbar, and they *share* a cache, thus guaranteeing cache consistency, but at the cost of possible contention. These choices reflect the small number of PEs for which an FX/8 is designed. The modification for Cedar consists of four boards that constitute an interface to the global memory network. These boards take half of the physical space available for memory within the cluster, limiting the cluster memory to 32 MB. The following description of the cluster is based on the papers by Kuck et al. [301] and by Yew [470].

Each (custom-built) PE implements the Motorola 68020 instruction set enhanced with three-operand vector instructions executed by Weitek and

---

[384] The name carries no hidden meaning.

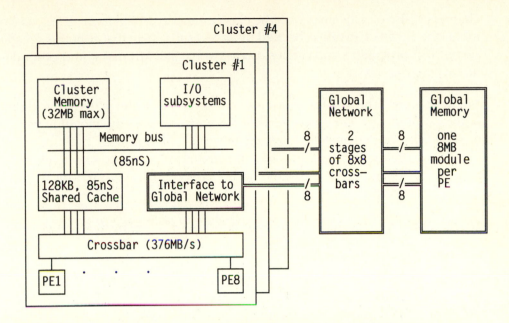

*Figure 10.35 **Block diagram of the Cedar prototype.** Each cluster is a modified Alliant FX/8. Bold lines denote hardware designed specifically for Cedar. Each PE contains fixed- and floating-point ALUs, scalar and vector registers, and an instruction cache. The shared cluster cache's ports are twice as fast as a PE's.*

(Alliant-designed) Fujitsu[385] floating-point chip sets. The resulting clock period is 170 nanoseconds. Each PE also has a set of vector registers and an instruction cache and shares a concurrency control bus for fast synchronization. With some special instructions, this bus allows processors to do self-scheduling of parallel loops by dynamically assigning loop iterations to available processors at run time. It also provides a fast mechanism to enforce data dependencies between loop iterations, so loop structures such as *doacross*[386] can be executed like parallel loops.

The crossbar allows the eight PEs in a cluster to share a 128-KByte, 4-way interleaved, write-back cache (see page 546) whose ports are twice as fast as a PE's. (The cache size was quadrupled in later models). This cache ex-

---

385 Gate array, 8-K gates.
386 Cedar's doacross, unlike doall, does not require loop iterations to be completely independent and allows iterations with dependencies between them to be executed in overlapped "parallel" (pipelined) fashion rather than completely sequentially.   Sequent's doacross, however, is a doall.

changes 32-Byte cache lines with the cluster memory (maximum 32 MB, as we mentioned), which in turn is backed by an I/O subsystem that contains several sets of I/O processors and caches, up to twelve 395-MB disks, and other devices.

Global Network: The same crossbar also connects the cluster's PEs to the global network interface. This provides each PE with access to the global network, a two-stage, packet-switched omega network composed of buffered 8×8 crossbar switches leading to the global memory. These latter switches have an 85-nanosecond clock cycle and an 80-bit-wide data path (64-bit word, 8 error correction bits, 8 control bits).

Global Memory: The global memory consists of as many 8-MB, two-way-interleaved memory modules as there are PEs. Access time at the system level is 1.5 microseconds, followed by a sustainable stream rate of one word every 170 nanoseconds to each PE (assuming no network conflicts). Physical address space is divided as 2 GB for the Global Memory and 2 GB for the cluster memories. Each process sees a virtual memory of 4 GB.

Each global memory module also contains a special on-board processor that implements synchronization operations using a 32-bit "key" field that may be associated with each 64-bit data word stored in that module. This allows the global memory to be used for intercluster shared data and synchronization without the need to lock the memory port for the duration of several round trips through the network each time such an operation occurs. As described by Kuck et al. [301], this key-bit mechanism for coordinating parallel processes is a superset of some other approaches we have described:

> Probably the simplest form of synchronization is the full-empty bit [page 568] used in the HEP computer, whereby a word cannot be written if its full-empty bit indicates full and cannot be read if it is empty.[387] Only slightly more complex is the common test-and-set form of instruction [page 162], which tests for a particular value, and if the test is true, writes a new value into the key. Still more complex is the fetch-and-add instruction [page 162] used in the Ultracomputer and the IBM RP3, which allows an arithmetical or logical operation instead of just a write. Cedar uses a general and flexible synchronization mechanism wherein each 64-bit data word may have an associated 32-bit integer key stored in the same global memory module. Each global memory module has a simple dedicated processor that

---

[387] A similar mechanism is used in Arvind's I-structure memory described on page 531.

performs an indivisible sequence of synchronization operations in response to a single-packet request transmitted from a processor. If the test is successful, an arithmetic or logical operation may be performed on the stored key, and transmitted data may be stored. A return packet to the processor contains the test result and (if the test is successful) key or data values (or both) as requested.[388]

I/O System: The I/O (disk) system is the remaining portion of Cedar's memory hierarchy. Since disk speeds (page 129) have not kept up with processor speeds, the system uses solid-state memory *disk caches*, as well as *disk striping*, in which data structures are interleaved across disks that are accessed in parallel to provide the needed data rates. Note that the disk system does not directly connect to the global memory but, in fact, resides in the clusters (on the "other" side of the switch).[389]

The Memory Hierarchy: The global memory, cluster memory, cluster cache, and instruction cache[390] and registers in each PE amount to a four-level memory hierarchy. Whenever distinct copies of shared data are allowed to exist in such a system, a *coherence* problem exists. The logical consistency of these copies must be maintained, as we discussed on page 546. The main problem is the read-write data that are used by more than one PE. In Cedar, the compiler (or user) will identify such variables that could cause incoherence, and these will remain in the global memory. Read-only data (including program code), private data used by only one PE, and "partially shared" data used only by PEs within a single cluster can be stored in the corresponding (and faster) cluster memory, thereby lowering the access time and reducing the load on the global network. If, as observed in the Cedar experiments, most accesses are in this second category, then the few remaining (global) accesses should not cause much performance degradation, especially with the synchronization hardware mentioned above [301]. On the other hand, sophisticated system software is needed to manage this memory hierarchy in such a way that it achieves the

---

[388] The synchronization instruction format is *if (key condition) then (key operation) and (data operation)*. Key conditions include $>$, $<$, $\geq$, $\leq$, $=$, $\neq$. Key operations include fetch, store, inc, dec, add, and, or, exor. Data operations include fetch and store.

[389] The Ultracomputer project calls this *front-end* I/O; it is also used in Butterfly. The alternative *back-end* I/O with a second (customized) network connecting memory to the disk system would be more expensive.

[390] The i-cache is read-only and hence easier to manage, but the vector registers probably qualify for a legitimate level.

traditional aim: an effective access time near that of the fastest memories and a cost per bit near that of the cheapest.

Software and Programming

Alliant's operating system is called Concentrix, and Cedar's is called Xylem.[391] Both are extensions of UNIX with support for parallel tasks. However, the Cedar approach also depends heavily on a sophisticated compiler to restructure a program to exploit this complex memory hierarchy effectively. The belief that this restructuring can be accomplished is based on the Parafrase project that we discussed on page 314.

Three levels of *program* parallelism that one could attempt to exploit on a parallel computer are as follows:

1. The first are the compound functions into which the main program is divided. These should be large chunks of work, each of which can be allocated to one or more clusters in such a way that the time needed for their computation within a cluster far exceeds the time used for intercluster communication. The implication, therefore, is that compound functions are much larger than the individual arithmetic operations that are typical of the granularity in most dataflow proposals. Gajski et al. [184] list six categories of compound functions. Four operate on array data and two on scalar data. Examples are matrix additions, forall loops, and basic blocks of assignment statements. Exploiting only the large-grain parallelism *among* these compound functions is expected to yield only a small speedup in most programs.

2. The potential for medium-grain parallelism *within* a compound function, however, is enormous (although its discovery can be intricate). For nested loops, for instance, the potential speedup is proportional to the product of nested loop limits.

3. The lowest granularity of parallelism includes arithmetic expressions and blocks of control and assignment statements (see Figure 6.4 on page 302). Speedups at this level are small (two to three, based on many real Fortran programs) because of the limited complexity of individual statements or even blocks of statements.[392]

The Cedar *hardware* offers the algorithm designer three levels of parallelism to work with:

---

391 The dictionary defines xylem as a complex tissue providing life support to plants (including cedar trees).

392 But see "Trace Scheduling" on page 319.

	Sparse Linear System Solvers	Linear Least Squares Algorithms	Nonlinear Algebraic System Solvers	Sparse Eigenvalue Problem Solvers	Fast Fourier Transforms	Rapid Elliptic Problem Solvers	Multigrid Schemes	Stiff O. D. E. Solvers	Monte Carlo Schemes	Integral Transforms
Lattice-Gauge (QCD)	X	.	.	X	.	.	.	.	X	.
Quantum Chemistry	.	.	.	X	.	.	.	X	X	X
Weather Simulation	.	.	.	.	X	X	.	.	.	.
Computational Fluid Dynamics	X	.	X	.	X	X	X	.	.	.
Adjustment of Geodetic Networks	X	X	.	.	.	.	.	.	.	.
Inverse Problems	.	X	.	.	X	.	.	.	.	.
Structured Mechanics & Dynamics	X	.	X	X	.	.	.	.	.	.
Electronic Device Simulation	X	.	X	.	.	X	X	.	X	.
Circuit Simulation	X	.	X	.	.	.	.	X	.	.

Figure 10.36 Application areas used to evaluate Cedar's performance and corresponding basic algorithms [301].

1. Among clusters. This parallelism is exploited using a macro-dataflow concept in which the operating system manages a list of compound functions (CFs) with precedence constraints, and schedules clusters to perform CFs when their predecessors have completed.

2. Within clusters. The fast communication among the PEs in a cluster is especially valuable for the (overlapped parallel) execution of *doacross* loops (loops whose iterations do have certain kinds of interdependencies). These doacross loops are "self-scheduled" in the sense that the iterations are gotten in turn by the processors.

3. The *vector* processing capabilities of each PE.

One example is a triply nested loop. In this case, what one would like to do, using *loop interchanging* (page 307) if necessary, is to have each iteration of the outer loop running on a separate PE that runs the middle loop serially and runs the inner loop on its vector hardware.

At the risk of oversimplification for the purpose of providing some perspective on approaches to parallelism, we note that the Cedar project,[393] with its strong emphasis on smart compilers, represents an intermediate point on the spectrum of when to schedule parallel execution, namely at compile time.[394] The message-passing MIMD designs such as the cubes (page 475) can be said to represent earlier scheduling by "smart programmers", while a project like the Ultracomputer (page 572) represents an emphasis on later (run-time) scheduling, via a highly parallel operating system.

Performance

When the benchmarks discussed here were run, an Alliant FX/8 (with eight PEs) had a theoretical peak performance of 94.4 MFLOPS on (64-bit) triadic vector operations [149], or about two-fifths the theoretical peak performance of one CPU of a Cray X-MP. For dense matrix multiplication, one cluster of Cedar has achieved over 40 MFLOPS. On complete application codes, the designers expect one Cedar cluster to achieve from 20% to 100% of the performance of one Cray X/MP CPU [301]. Figure 10.36 on page 617 shows the application areas in physical science research, physical simulation, and engineering design that will be used to evaluate and compare Cedar's performance.

---

[393] As distinguished from the Cedar *design!*
[394] Note that Cedar and Multiflow (page 623) are *both* heavily compiler-dependent.

10.4 Exercises

1.   Match each of the terms on the left with its attribute on the right

a.	Alliant FX/8	1)	Bus connected fault-tolerant database machine
b.	C.mmp	2)	Early 16-processor crossbar connected computer
c.	Cedar	3)	Early 50-processor hierarchical machine
d.	Cm*	4)	Early MIMD machine used to calculate VLSI wiring
e.	Cross invalidate	5)	Fine grain synchronization–ideal for producer/consumer
f.	DADO	6)	First commercial hypercube
g.	Fetch-and-add	7)	Graph reduction demand-driven computer
h.	Full/empty bit	8)	Hardware synchronization instruction—ideal for queues
i.	HEP	9)	Hardware synchronization instruction—ideal for semaphores
j.	NCUBE/ten	10)	High performance tagged-token dataflow machine
k.	PAX	11)	Hypercube with 64 nodes per board
l.	Rediflow	12)	Machine with fetch-and-add that combines memory references
m.	SIGMA I	13)	Machine with full-empty bits and instruction-level multiprogramming
n.	SPMD	14)	Maintains coherence by monitoring broadcasts
o.	Snooping cache	15)	Multiprocessor with a shared cache
p.	Tandem	16)	Multiprocessor with local, cluster, and global memory
q.	Teradata	17)	Rectangular array of 128 processors
r.	Test-and-set	18)	Restricted form of MIMD
s.	Ultracomputer	19)	Tree connected database machine with upto 1024 processors
t.	WRM	20)	Tree-based computer for production systems
u.	iPSC	21)	Update entry in local cache and remove from others

2.   Define the following terms.

Producer/consumer parallelism	Hot spots in memory systems
Cache coherence	Load balancing
Memory latency	
Static dataflow	Macro dataflow
Dynamic dataflow	Macro pipelining

3.   Compare the Teradata and Tandem database machines. What type of database parallelism does each exploit? How is this emphasis reflected in the architecture?

4. What are the advantages and disadvantages of a *reconfigurable* systolic array such as CHiP.

5. Describe busy-waiting and context-switching synchronizations. What are the advantages of each?

6. What is the cache coherence problem? Describe techniques used to achieve cache coherence in parallel systems.

7. Read the Archibald and Baer paper mentioned in the bibliography and compare two of the coherence protocols discussed.

8. Read the Stenstrom paper mentioned in the bibliography and discuss directory based cache coherence techniques.

9. Why is latency an inherent problem in shared-memory computers? Discuss techniques used to hide latency.

10. Compare write-through and write-back caches. What are the pros and cons of each?

11. (Requires VLSI knowledge.) A VLSI implementation of the combining switch illustrated in Figure 10.26 on page 581 presents a packaging challenge. The switch has eight (unidirectional) ports. If 32 bits of data or address are in a single packet, the number of pins per port approaches 40 (including control). If this switch is implemented on one VLSI chip, the pin count is excessive. Why is bitslicing difficult? (Hint: see Figure 9.14 on page 464.) If the chip is partitioned into forward path (processor to memory) and return path components, how many ports are needed for each chip (the answer is not 4)? How would you partition the design into more chips, each having fewer ports?

12. Distinguish between zero- and single-assignment languages. How do I-structures help in implementing the latter?

13. We have discussed parallel processors at great length. Also important, but typically discussed much less, is parallel I/O. We discuss the subject briefly in the Cedar section, where we mention the possibility of disk striping. What degree of parallelism would you expect to occur with this technique and what sets this limit. (Hint: a disk transfers data in multiples of sectors, not bytes.) Does striping improve latency, bandwidth, or both?

14. Load balancing can be achieved with centralized or distributed data structures. Ultracomputer applications often keep all work items in a single pile with processes concurrently accessing the pile in a self-service manner. Message-passing machines normally distribute the work items and redistribute them when the load is out of balance. For example, in the Rediflow approach, work items migrate in response to a pressure-like quantity. What architectural features would favor the central or the distributed solution?

15. Discuss the relative advantages of programming environments that mask vs. those that exploit the hypercube communication topology.

16. In what sense are the Paragon and Delta logical continuations of the Cosmic Cube? In what sense are they vastly different architectures from the Cosmic Cube requiring significantly different application programs?

17. How would one solve the n-body problem on a dataflow computer? On a SIMD machine like the CM-2? How do these solutions compare to the ones given in the text for private and shared memory?

18. Why is a tree (with its inherent bottleneck at the root) nonetheless appropriate for the DADO parallel processor?

19. Discuss the relative advantages of static vs. dynamic dataflow architectures.

20. Compare the approaches used to hide memory latency in the HEP, Alewife, Tera, and dataflow architectures.

21. Discuss the relationship between HEP's use of full/empty bits and the TEST-AND-SET primitive discussed in the chapter of languages (Chapter 5). Include comments about the time required by the operation, and whether a separate variable that can quickly be tested by other processes is used.

22. First discuss the worth and cost of an atomic fetch-and-add operation. Then discuss the additional costs and benefits of making (an atomic) fetch-and-add into a parallel operation?

23. Several new synchronization algorithms have the property that each processor busy waits on a unique variable that is rarely set by any other processor. Discuss the suitability of the Ultracomputer and Butterfly approaches to the location of shared memory for these algorithms.

24. How can the RP3 hardware emulate both Ultracomputer- and Butterfly-like memory management? Why are both useful?

25. What are the three levels of parallelism provided by the Cedar hardware?

26. As noted in the text, Dir_0NB is not a viable alternative for hardware cache consistency. Why?

SIMD vector machines, VLIWs, and MIMD multiprocessors all share the above structure. However, the architectures differ in their control flow, in the connecting of processors, in the accessing of memory, and in the programming requirements of each architecture. The table below compares these points (adapted from [173]). A, B, and C are instructions.

	SIMD	**VLIW**	**MIMD**
Flow of Control (Architect's view)	One instruction at a time von Neumann style, all processors doing the same operation. Mask bits may disable a subset of processors.	All processors fetch instructions from the same next address, but instructions differ from processor to processor. Von Neumann-style control flow with very long instructions.	Each processor has its own control flow. Processors must be synchronized by the program. See, for example, "Fetch-and-Add" on page 162.
Programming Requirements (Programmer's view)	Code must be expressed as regular operations on aggregates and must match inherent regularity of hardware.	Not likely to be hand-coded. Compiler must figure out that ACB is useful, do greedy scheduling (*trace scheduling*) & elaborate run-time analysis to choreograph data movements etc.	Code must be broken into relatively independent tasks that minimize communications and synchronization.
Interprocessor Communications	Subvectors must be moved in patterns fitting the regularity of the interconnections and algorithm.	Individual data movements completely specified at compile time; hence data need not carry destination addresses or be buffered in network. Runtime resource scheduling not needed.	Hardware scheduling of datapath resources, data packets with destination addresses, and buffering of data in network; lots of hardware for this run-time partitioning.
Memory Bandwidth	Vectorized reference allows full access to all memory banks; unvectorized references like a uniprocessor.	Memory banks must be predictable at compile time to get maximal bandwidth for scalars and aggregates, which may be mixed in a single instruction. When the aggregate bank is unpredictable, uniprocessor action results.	When possible, local memory is used. Global memory references involve interconnection network delay.

11

Hybrid Parallel Architectures

As implied by its title, this chapter deals with architectures that do not fit neatly into either the SIMD or the MIMD computational model. Two main categories are treated. The first one is that of Very Long Instruction Word (VLIW) machines, the target for reassembling compilers such as the Bulldog, which we discussed on page 319. The second category is that of multiple SIMD (MSIMD) machines and includes several tree-connected and circuit-switched reconfigurable designs that can be partitioned into multiple subconfigurations, each operating in SIMD mode.

11.1 VLIW Architectures

11.1.1 Multiflow TRACE

As we described in detail on page 622, a VLIW (Very Long Instruction Word) architecture is one step up from an SIMD/vector/array processor in the following sense: An SIMD processor can be viewed as a collection of processing elements marching in lockstep under orders from a central controller and each performing the *same, identical* operation on different data elements. Vector addition is a prime example. In a VLIW architecture, the processing elements are still in lockstep and under centralized control, but the individual processing elements can each be performing a *different* (though carefully preplanned) operation on different data elements. One could thus regard this architecture as a somewhat liberated SIMD. One could also regard it as specially orchestrated MIMD, but an essential difference is that there is only one thread of control. The net effect is that of a central controller issuing very long instructions. For example, the ELI-512 machine [170] is a cluster of sixteen 32-bit RISC[395] processors and has an overall instruction word length of 512 bits.

The VLIW idea is related to the generation of horizontal microcode but has previously been applied only to much smaller collections of much less versatile processing or functional units. The reason is that since traditional compilers operate on one basic block at a time, and the average Fortran basic block is rather small and hence contains a rather low degree of parallelism, it wasn't *worth* having a highly parallel machine as a target. (The average speedup from parallelism within a Fortran basic block is about 3.) The analysis and compilation were traditionally done one basic block at a time because it wasn't known at compile time which new basic block would be the target of the (conditional) jump at the end of any given basic block. It seemed obvious that operations from different basic blocks couldn't be put into the same instruction. Yet that placement is precisely what trace scheduling, the compiler optimization technique that is at the heart of VLIW, is designed to accomplish. Basically, achieving this placement amounts to guessing which way the jumps will go and then removing the results of harmful guesses. The sophisticated compiling techniques needed to do this are discussed on page 319 ff.

Multiflow Computer Inc. offered a line of long-instruction-word machines built on the ELI-512 research.[396] The Trace 7/200 has a 256-bit instruction word and can perform up to seven operations at a time [453]. Peak performance is cited at 30 MFLOPS, with 6 MFLOPS obtained on Linpack. The instruction length and number of simultaneous operations double in the model 14/200 and double again in the model 28/200.

Several other computers, such as CHoPP and Cydra 5, also use extremely wide instruction words. We discuss CHoPP in the section that follows. The

---

[395] Reduced Instruction Set Computers, each with a repertory of 10–30 simple instructions in this case.

[396] Historical footnote: the company ran into financial difficulties in 1990 and no longer exists. Trew and Wilson [442] present an interesting post-mortem. Although the compiler technology was regarded as very sound, there was perhaps not enough emphasis on hardware technology early on, which made it harder to compete with other high-end minisupercomputers that had faster hardware. Meanwhile, increasingly powerful workstations provided fierce competition from below.

Cydra 5 architecture [371], [55] and compilation technique [131] are described in the literature. The last two references appear in a special issue of the *Journal of Supercomputing* on instruction-level parallelism, which contains a number of interesting VLIW articles

11.1.2 CHoPP

The name CHoPP comes from Columbia Homogeneous Parallel Processor. In the late 1970s, when the powerful SIMD ILLIAC IV still held the center of the parallel processing stage, the CHoPP project was at the forefront of research into shared-memory MIMD computers with a plan for a multistage network connecting up to a million processing elements, with program organization achieved not by a host computer but by "negotiation between running processes"[419] and [420]. The CHoPP 1, announced a decade later [330], is still a shared-memory MIMD design but with a much smaller number of more powerful processors than in the original concept and with several key features also found in other designs that we have already described. High sequential performance is expected from issuing multiple instructions on each clock, from zero-delay branch-instructions, and from fast execution of individual instructions. High performance with both large-grain and small-grain parallelism is expected from a "conflict-free memory" shared by multiple processors and from fast context-switching hardware.

Up to 16 processing elements (computing nodes) are connected by a proprietary "conflict-free network" to a set of memory modules. Figure 11.1 on page 626 shows one of these processing elements. Each PE contains nine functional units that can concurrently execute nine operations under control of a 256-bit-wide "superinstruction", very much like the 256-bit long instruction word of the Multiflow Trace 7/200 (see page 623). (By comparison, the Cray-1, shown on page 423, has 12 independent functional units.)[397]

Each PE can support one active task and up to 63 waiting tasks (a task is defined as a *single instruction stream* controlled by a *single program counter* with its *own register set*). The task manager contains hardware that allows any one of the waiting tasks to be "swopped" (internally swapped) with the active task in just three clock cycles. This rapid switching allows efficient execution of code that has very few instructions between task-swopping events, that is, of small-granularity tasks (although not as small as in HEP, which could per-

---

[397] The FUs are parallel in both cases.

*Figure 11.1 **A processing element (processing node) from CHoPP 1.*** *The machine accommodates up to 16 of these PEs [330]. The Branch Unit executes branch instructions. The four Address Functional Units share a set of registers and perform integer and logical address arithmetic. The four Computational Functional Units perform floating-point operations and share a second set of registers. Under control of a 256-bit "superinstruction", each functional unit can do one operation per clock cycle, expected to be 60 nanoseconds [102].*

form a task switch on every clock, corresponding to instruction-level parallelism).

Empty	Wait	64-bit Data
Full	NoWait	

Creation of one or more tasks is done using an instruction similar to the two-way or multiway fork described on page 245. Synchronization of these tasks is done as follows: Each location in the memory has space for a 64-bit datum plus 2 extra bits used for synchronization, an empty/full bit that indicates whether the datum has yet been stored, and a wait/nowait bit that indicates whether a recipient task has arrived prior to the storing of the datum and is waiting. (Note the similarity to the HEP full/empty bit on page 568 and the dataflow I-structure memory "presence bit" on page 531.) These two control bits are used to implement (message-passing) task-synchronization primitives. One of these transfers a 64-bit word between *two* tasks, and another distributes copies of a word to *many* tasks. As in CSP (page

247), these are synchronous transfers, in that a task attempting to use such data is held in the wait state until the data are created and sent by a task.

Two instructions are also provided to permit rapid indivisible operations on memory locations. The first is a match-and-replace operation (similar to a compare-and-swap) used for efficient implementation of "blackboard" algorithms. The second is fetch-and-add, for which CHoPP provides hardware support that allows combining simultaneous fetch-and-adds to the same memory location (a capability also available in the Ultracomputer and RP3 designs found on pages 572 and 603).

Performance estimates based on the 24 Livermore Loop kernels indicate that a four-PE CHoPP is slightly faster than a one-PE CRAY X-MP for about half of the loops (those that vectorized well on the Cray X-MP) and substantially faster (by a factor of 2 or more) for most of the remaining loops that did *not* vectorize well in the Cray case. This comparison is felt to be particularly interesting because both machines are one-fourth of the maximum configuration, and both contain about the same number of components [102].

11.1.3   IBM YSE/EVE

The YSE (Yorktown Simulation Engine) is a special-purpose parallel processor [133], [295] built at IBM to speed the development of large computers by providing rapid simulation of the large network of logic gates that such machines represent. A full YSE configuration simulates networks of up to 2 million logic gates at a rate exceeding 3 billion gate computations per second. This is far beyond the capabilities of existing register-level software simulators.

As shown in Figure 11.2 on page 628, the YSE design accommodates 256 processing elements (PEs) interconnected by a full crossbar switch. A Control Processor provides the interface to a host computer to enable YSE program loading, and so on. The design has two kinds of PEs: *logic simulators* for the logic-circuit portion of the machine being simulated and *memory simulators* for the RAMs and ROMs.

Unit-delay simulation is provided, meaning that it is assumed that every gate has the same delay, called one *unit-delay*, and that external inputs change only on integral unit-delay time boundaries (There is also a second *mixed* mode that we do not discuss here). In other words, the YSE tests the correctness of the detailed logical design but does not simulate the technology details beneath it (see Figure 3.16 on page 118). A compiler translates the RTL (register-transfer level) description of the machine to be simulated into a *nodes file* of rather powerful hypothetical logic gates (they have infinite fanout, a

Figure 11.2 The YSE (Yorktown Simulation Engine).

4-input XOR counts as one gate, etc.), partitions a large network into pieces small enough to fit into a PE, and distributes these pieces to the PEs.

Each logic simulator PE contains an *instruction memory* that stores the interconnection and function-type information for a logic network, a *data memory*[398] that holds logic values for signals in the network, and a *function unit* that evaluates logic functions. The instruction memory holds up to 8K functions (gate descriptions). The function unit is an eight-stage pipeline that completes one function evaluation every 80 nanoseconds.

During simulation, these PEs synchronously step through their instruction memories and use the fetched information to access and update values for signals stored in their data memories. There are no branches or conditional instructions, and hence the resulting execution model is much closer to VLIW than to full MIMD (see page 622). A further similarity to VLIW is the heavy dependence on the compiler, which not only partitions and distributes the original network but also schedules the sequence of function evaluations within each PE for efficient use of its pipeline and schedules the sequence of switch-routing configurations needed to accommodate the PE-PE communication introduced by the partitioning.

Note that each data item sent through the switch is only 2 bits, representing one of the signal states in four-valued logic, *e.g.*, 0, 1, undefined, or high-

---

[398] Separating the memory areas for instructions and data makes YSE a *Harvard architecture*, like the Harvard Mark I computer of the 1940s, and unlike von Neumann's *Princeton architecture* with both data and instructions in one memory. The program in a Harvard architecture can't modify itself, a restriction that makes instruction cache management and pipelining much easier.

impedance. The small data items allow the datapaths through the crossbar switch to be only 3 bits wide (2 data plus parity), which is what makes it possible to provide crossbar interconnection for so many PEs.[399]

The 256×256 network (including a 2-MB memory for switch settings) occupies a 24-inch-wide, air-cooled rack. Each group of 32 logic processors, with a total simulation capacity of 256,000 gates, occupies another such cabinet. Thus, the network represents one-ninth of the full YSE. A 16-PE prototype was running at the time the cited references were published (1982). Experiments showed an almost linear speedup with the number of PEs. It was estimated that a full YSE loaded with the logical description of the IBM 3081 processor (about 0.3 million gates) could run at about 1000 instructions per second, or about 10^4 times the actual 3081. Existing software simulators could not hold the entire design and would run about 5000 times slower even if they could. It is left as an exercise to show that this estimated YSE performance corresponds to about a 50% efficiency in usage of the pipeline and parallel hardware of this machine (i.e., that is how well the compiler handled the dependencies among the different parts of the design).[400] By mid-1986, eight 256-PE production versions of the YSE (called *EVE* for Engineering Verification Engine [56]) had been installed for use at various development sites within IBM.[401]

11.2   MSIMD Tree Machines

The main advantage of tree machines is that they are *buildable*—the interconnection of the processing cells is easy and fits particularly well with planar layouts and VLSI, as we illustrated in Figure 8.3 on page 387. We already described the embodiment of this idea in an MIMD design with medium-granularity parallelism and fairly substantial PEs, namely the DADO on page 505. A very early tree-machine proposal was put forth by Browning [76]. Here we discuss the Cellular Computer and the NON-VON, two tree machines

---

[399] The YSE's $(256 \times 3) \times (256 \times 3)$ crossbar is, by one measure, nine times larger than C.mmp's $(16 \times 16) \times (16 \times 16)$ crossbar (page 561).

[400] One very bad case would be a delay line, in which every input depended on the previous output and only one PE could be utilized. In the best case, all processors are utilized and all pipelines are always full.

[401] At the time, these special-purpose computers represented the largest-scale production use of highly parallel processing.

geared to more massive parallelism and designed with PEs too small for MIMD operation (i.e., not large enough to store their own programs).

11.2.1 UNC Cellular Computer

The Cellular Computer [328], [329] is a proposal by Gyula Mago at the University of North Carolina for a tree-connected ensemble of up to 10^6 simple processors, the whole machine being designed specifically for parallel execution of the expressions found in programs written in a reduction language such as Backus's FP (page 259). In terms of the computational models we discussed on page 136, this is a *string-reduction* machine.[402] The entire program, treated as a string of intermixed data and FP symbols, is loaded into the leaf cells of the tree. Executing this program consists of iteratively reducing this string to a sequence of simpler strings, the last of which is the answer. An iteration, or cycle, in this reduction process consists of a wave of activity that carries data from the leaves toward the root of the tree, followed by a downsweep that ends up modifying the leaf nodes. We illustrate the key ideas with a simple example from Mago's paper [328].

Consider the evaluation of the inner product (*dot product*) of two vectors [1 2 3 4] and [11 12 13 14]. The inner product's value is $(1 \times 11) + (2 \times 12) + (3 \times 13) + (4 \times 14) = 130$. Suppose the initial FP expression representing this program is written as

```
<IP, ( (1,2,3,4), (11,12,13,14) ) >
```

where < > is the application symbol (the first member of the enclosed order pair is *applied* to the second member) and IP (the inner product operator) is defined below. This string of symbols and data is loaded into the leaf cells (in shift-register fashion), to be replaced after each reduction cycle by a simpler expression string, the last one being the answer. Each simplified expression string is not necessarily *shorter* than its predecessor. For example, the first reduction cycle of the expression above replaces IP by its definition, resulting in the string

```
<(+,AA,*,TR), ( (1,2,3,4), (11,12,13,14) ) >
```

---

[402] To refresh readers' memories, *string reduction* means that an expression's definition is copied and evaluated each time its value is needed. In *graph reduction*, such an expression is evaluated only once; other references to this expression receive pointers to its value, as in Rediflow (page 498). Graph reduction is therefore faster and more space efficient but entails an extra overhead for the pointer mechanism.

Figure 11.3 Tree machine *(upper left), FP expression and its parse tree (upper right), and the expression mapped into the tree (bottom). Leaf cells perform computations; tree cells also provide communication. The four reducible applications (RAs) will be executed in cells A, B, C, and D* [328]. *Two RAs are shaded to make them easier to see. (Mago's paper treats this expression as part of a larger program, and his nesting levels are deeper by 3.)*

where AA (apply to all), TR (transpose), + (addition), and * (multiplication) are primitive operators of the language.

We wait several more cycles before explaining the machine's operation in more detail. At this point the expression in the leaf cells has become

```
<+,(  <*,(1,11)>,  <*,(2,12)>,  <*,(3,13)>,  <*,(4,14)> ) >.
```

The four multiplications represent the four innermost, or reducible, applications (RAs) that can be done in any order, or in parallel, by the Church-Rosser theorem (page 262). The parse tree of this expression is given at the upper right in Figure 11.3 on page 631. Each node of this tree shows one of the string's elements and its nesting level. (Some of the symbols in the original expression, such as trailing parentheses and commas, aid human understanding but are redundant, and hence they are dropped in the computer's internal representation of the string. We also omit them from the parse tree.) The bottom part of Figure 11.3 shows this expression's elements and their nesting levels stored in the leaf cells of the tree machine.

Each processing cycle of the machine consists of a sweep up the tree followed by a downsweep, and each cycle accomplishes three things:

1. *Partitioning.* In this phase, the machine is logically decomposed into a set of disjoint component binary tree machines such that each innermost FP application (RA) is contained in a separate component machine. Partitioning occurs during the upsweep, while all the cells are communicating with their parents. Whenever two application symbols (<) from the leaf cells meet in one of the tree cells, that tree cell becomes the root of a subtree dedicated to evaluating the left <'s RA during the rest of this cycle. The <s continue to propagate upward until they have met both their neighboring <s so that all the subroots can be determined. By the time the upward sweep completes, the root node of each active subtree is known, and each such root knows what microprogram is to be applied to its RA.

2. *Executing (or at least working on) each RA.* Each component tree machine attempts to replace its innermost application with its result expression. This attempt may involve requesting and receiving microprograms that correspond to the operations specified by the application. These microprograms are stored outside the machine and come in through the root,[403] finding their way to the proper tree cell by using trail markers left behind by the request. (Microprograms written so far take from several dozen to several hundred bits.)

3. *Storage management.* This phase is needed to preserve the linear representation, since the result may be *longer* than the original. Storage management involves a lot of work and also forces the current partitioning of the machine to be abandoned, but the next cycle begins with partitioning

---

[403] Or they may come in through a set of specialized tree cells at a level below the root in case the root is a bottleneck.

to adjust the machine to the changed expression now stored in the leaf cells.

Leaf cells and tree cells are different [328]. A leaf cell contains a "CPU", several dozen registers, and microprogram storage (the paper does not commit itself to details such as sizes and numbers). The CPU can execute segments of microprograms and performs processing related to storage management. A tree cell contains six groups of registers and four processors and can hold up to four nodes, each belonging to a different partition (subtree) of the machine (seven of the eight possible tree cell partitionings are shown in the example in Figure 11.3 on page 631). One layer of tree cells (different from the others) provides I/O ports for the machine.

Mago defines three types of processing. In type A, the result expression can be produced in the leaf cells that held the original RA; that is, *no additional cells are needed*. Types B and C are more complex and are implemented by executing suitable microprograms in the leaf cells, which, in turn, may initiate processing activities in tree cells. Type B still needs no additional cells, but some of the processing activities are data-dependent, creating a need for communication among some of the leaf cells. Type C is like Type B but needs additional leaf cells to hold the result. The AA (apply to all) operator is an example of type C processing—the result expression is longer than the starting expression. Reference [328] shows the microprogram involved.

The cellular nature of this processor results in reduced design time (only two cell designs are needed), and the tree topology improves the utilization of VLSI (whole subtrees can be put on a single chip using the planar layout of Figure 8.3 on page 387). The expected payoff is substantial speedup of an FP program obtained by evaluating a large number of its innermost expressions in parallel. To estimate the machine's performance, Mago uses the formula

$$\frac{D N}{14\, t \log N + K}$$

where

DN is the average number of RAs in the processor.

The number 14 comes from the processor's design.

t is the average time that state changes take to move from one level of the tree to another (not including time for bringing in microprograms or for storage management).

N is the number of leaf cells.

K is the average time used in one complete processor cycle to bring in all microprograms requested and to complete storage management.

As an example, if DN=20,000 RAs, t=100 nS, N=10^6, and K=120t, the performance is 500 MIPS (counting an RA as an instruction).

To achieve reasonable performance, the root of this tree machine must not be allowed to become a bottleneck for either the I/O involved in bringing in microprograms or the communication needed for managing storage and maintaining a linear representation for FP expressions. But the biggest challenge may well be the availability of substantial FP programs. There is a potential vicious cycle here in terms of getting started on such a machine, because one would like to test real programs on a small prototype first, but a small prototype does not offer enough speedup to encourage writing substantial applications in a new language.[404]

11.2.2 Columbia NON-VON

The NON-VON project [392] at Columbia University is a massively parallel, tree-connected design bearing some resemblance to Mago's Cellular Computer, but instead of FP programs, NON-VON's target is the rapid execution of large-scale data-manipulation tasks, including relational database operations. Most of the tree from the leaf nodes on up consists of simple, small processing elements (SPEs) not unlike those of the CM1 Connection Machine (page 446). With 3-micron linewidths, a custom-designed VLSI chip can hold between 8 and 16 of these SPEs, each with an 8-bit ALU (originally 1-bit), 16 registers, 64 bytes of local memory, and an I/O switch connecting to a parent and two children. The instruction cycle (equal to the inter-SPE communication time) is about 2 microseconds.

---

[404] This kind of problem is by no means unique to FP programs. An early IBM MIMD computer, the Wire Routing Machine (page 497) was not sufficiently more powerful than available serial computers to convince potential users to rewrite their programs from conventional high-level languages into machine language for the Z80 microprocessors so they could migrate to the WRM. Of course, the analogy is not perfect. FP is a high-level language (believed by some to be easier to program in than conventional languages). Nonetheless, converting a program into any new language is nonzero work and hence an impediment to rapid acceptance.

The SPE's local memory can store a tuple (row) from a relational database table, but it is far too small to hold meaningful programs, and so the SPE must import its instructions from one or more control processors. Control processors make up a second category called *LPEs* (large processing elements, expected to be off-the-shelf microprocessors) at the top of the tree.

The NON-VON 1 and NON-VON 3 prototypes (NON-VON 2 existed only on paper) are SPE trees with one LPE at the root controlling the SPEs in SIMD mode. NON-VON 4 was originally envisioned as one large tree, with the top few levels (9 or 10 levels in a 10^6-node design) being LPEs and the rest being SPEs. Later, the interconnection between the LPEs was changed to a shuffle-based, multistage network. Each LPE can be a control processor. Two additional modes of operation would thus be possible: MSIMD (multiple SIMD, with each LPE controlling a subtree, somewhat as in Mago's Cellular Computer) and MIMD (among the LPEs only, not the SPEs).

The paper by Hillyer, Shaw, and Nigam [233] compares the performance of a simulated 16-K SPE NON-VON on a set of relational database benchmarks against results from several earlier database machines (CASSM, RAP, INGRES, and DIRECT). NON-VON is found to be about 10 times faster on complex queries with joins. Shaw's parallel join algorithm is used, with the assumption that all the relevant data fit into NON-VON. As we pointed out on page 65, this is a strong assumption.

11.3   MSIMD Reconfigurable Designs

11.3.1   UT TRAC

The TRAC (Texas Reconfigurable Array Computer) research project [323] at the University of Texas uses a circuit-switched banyan network (pioneered by this group and described on page 403) to achieve a parallel computer whose resources can be dynamically reconfigured to fit the structure of (primarily scientific) problems. Programmers specified the desired machine configuration using a job-control language as well as declaration and dimension statements in the program.

The prototype consisted of four 8-bit processing elements (PEs) built from Intel 2910 bit-slice microprocessors and connected to nine 4-KB memory modules by a banyan network with 8-bit-wide data paths. The dashed lines in the network of the figure above show two *data trees*, each connecting a PE at the top to a number of (data-holding) memory modules at the bottom. The heavy lines in the same figure show an (upside-down) *instruction tree* that connects an (instruction-holding) memory module to two PEs that will work together (in SIMD mode) on the same task, for instance, inverting a matrix. Such a connection pattern can be created in less than one memory cycle and lasts for the duration of the task, say a few milliseconds. A larger machine could support an MSIMD mode in which a number of such SIMD *task trees* (instruction tree + data tree) operate in parallel on different tasks. Full MIMD operation requires the proposed TRAC 2.0 design, which capitalizes on memory capacity and price improvements to make the PEs full processors with up to 1 MB each.

Two mechanisms supplement the circuit-switched interconnection mode above, namely *shuttle-memory* and *packet switching*. In shuttle-memory mode, a PE loads data into a memory module, which is then connected to another PE instead. This mechanism avoids the bottleneck of tree creation. Packet switching is used when only one or a few words are to be sent and it is undesirable to dedicate a whole memory module to the "shuttle" transfer.

Another TRAC feature was *varistructure*. This used the data-tree mechanism to gang PEs together to tailor the word width to different precision needs. The supply of cheap, powerful 32-bit microprocessors has made this concept less useful.

The prototype was rich in architectural features and poor in hardware reliability. Operation at 1 MHz on small problems like Fibonacci numbers, histogramming, quicksort, and character-string search demonstrated the machine's dynamic partitioning capability, but substantial programs were not run. The book by Lipovsky and Malek [323] provides further discussion of the lessons learned[405] and plans for the future.

11.3.2   Purdue PASM

PASM is a Partitionable SIMD/MIMD system designed at Purdue University for parallel image understanding [398]. Like TRAC, PASM can be structured as one or more independent SIMD and/or MIMD machines of various sizes.

---

[405]   For example, TRAC was planned to be an *inductive* architecture (defined as one having an induction mechanism that can expand the architecture from N to $N+1$ PEs, something that a binary cube and numerous other designs cannot do), but this goal was made difficult to achieve by bottlenecks in setting up the trees in the banyan and also by the fact that as the number of levels in the banyan grows large, there will be too many memory modules.

However, its hardware solutions tend to be simpler and more straightforward than TRAC's [323]. (For example, TRAC time-slices a rather complex switch to provide both instruction sharing and I/O. PASM uses separate structures: a bus for instruction sharing and a crossbar for I/O.) PASM's SIMD clusters are created in a more direct way, too: a set of bus-connected microcontrollers, each acting as a control unit for a small number of PEs in SIMD mode or orchestrating PEs in MIMD mode.

A 16-PE prototype [397], [398] is a step toward the goal of a 1024-PE machine. The processing element uses a Motorola MC68010 coupled with 256 KB of local memory (expandable to 2 MB). The local-memory model is felt to be appropriate for many image- and speech-processing algorithms. Shared memory can be emulated by designating part of each PE's address space as shared. Sixteen PEs are controlled by four bus-connected microcontrollers (also MC68010-based). In addition, the PE memories are connected to a memory management system (for I/O), and the PEs are all interconnected by a circuit-switched, extra-stage cube network of the type shown in Figure 8.13 on page 408 (eight 2-input, 2-output switch boxes per stage, four stages, plus an extra stage for fault tolerance). Circuit switching was chosen because it is easy to implement and more suitable than packet switching for the large data transfers anticipated in the application. Establishing a path through the network is estimated to take 1 microsecond (assuming no conflicts in the network). Data transmission is expected to proceed from a network input to a network output at the rate of one 16-bit word every 400 nanoseconds. With the PEs operating at 10 MHz ($\approx$1/2 MIPS), the network should not be a computation bottleneck.

11.4 Exercises

1. Define the following terms: MSIMD, VLIW

2. Match each of the terms on the left with its attribute on the right:

   a. Cellular computer

   b. Multiflow

   c. NON-VON

   d. PASM

   e. TRAC

   f. YSE

   1) Banyan interconnect
   2) Massively parallel tree-connected design
   3) Partitionable SIMD/MIMD system
   4) String-reduction, demand-driven parallel processor
   5) VLIW processor emphasizing trace scheduling
   6) VLIW-like computer with large, narrow crossbar

3. The YSE contains a 256 by 256 crossbar. The complexity of a crossbar grows quadratically and normally a 16 by 16 crossbar is considered large. Explain the apparent contradiction. How is the intended application relevant?

4. What are the relative advantages of VLIW, SIMD, and MIMD architectures?

5. Describe how the Cellular Computer executes an FP program.

6. Explain the MSIMD nature of the Cellular Computer and of NON-VON.

7. Describe the levels of hardware parallelism available in CHoPP. How does the synchronization mechanism compare with the mechanism found in HEP?

Bibliography

[1]   Mike Accetta, Robert Baron, William Bolosky, David Golub, Richard Rashid, Avadis Tevanian and Michael Young, "Mach: A New Kernel Foundation for UNIX Development," *Summer Usenix Conference Proceedings*, pp. 93-112, 1986. Cited on page 369.

[2]   William B. Ackerman, "Data Flow Languages," *Computer*, vol. 15, pp. 15-25, February 1982. Cited on page 273.

[3]   George B. Adams, III and Howard Jay Siegel, "The Extra Stage Cube: A Fault-Tolerant Interconnection Network for Supersystems," *IEEE Transactions on Computers*, vol. 31, no. 5, pp. 443-454, May 1982. Cited on page 408.

[4]   Sanjaya Addanki, "Connectionism," in Stuart Shapiro, editor, *The Encyclopedia of Artificial Intelligence*, John Wiley, 1987. Cited on page 87.

[5]   Anant Agarwal, David Chaiken, Godfrey D'Souze, Kirk Johnson, David Kranz, John Kubiotowicz, Kiyoshi Kurihara, Beng-Hong Lim, Gino Maa, Dan Nussbaum, Mike Parkin and Donald Yeung, "The MIT Alewife Machine: A Large-Scale Distributed-Memory Multiprocessor," *Proceedings of Workshop on Scalable Shared Memory Multiprocessors*, Kluwer Academic Publishers, 1991. An expanded version appears as MIT/LCS Memo TM-454, June 1991. Cited on pages 555, 557, 557.

[6]   Anant Agarwal, John Kubiotowicz, David Kranz, Beng-Hong Lim, Donald Yeung, Godfrey D'Souze and Mike Parkin, "Sparcle: An Evolutionary Processor Design for Large-Scale Multiprocessors," *IEEE Micro*, vol. 13, no. 3, pp. 48-61, June 1993. Cited on page 556.

[7]   Anant Agarwal, Richard Simoni, John Hennessy and Mark Horowitz, "An Evaluation of Directory Schemes for Cache Coherence," *Proceedings of the 15th Annual International Symposium on Computer Architecture*, pp. 280-289, May-June 1988. Cited on pages 548, 548, 549.

[8]   Tilak Agerwala and Arvind, "Data Flow Systems: Guest Editor's Introduction," *Computer*, vol. 15, no. 2, pp. 10-13, February 1982. Cited on page 271.

[9]   Gul Agha, "Concurrent Object-Oriented Programming," *Communications of the ACM*, vol. 33, no. 9, pp. 125-141, September 1990. Cited on page 284.

[10]   Alfred V. Aho, John E. Hopcroft and Jeffrey D. Ullman, *The Design and Analysis of Computer Algorithms*, Addison-Wesley, 1974. Cited on pages 182, 186, 186, 186, 188.

[11]   Alfred V. Aho, Ravi Sethi and Jeffrey D. Ullman, *Compilers: Principles, Techniques, and Tools*, Addison-Wesley, 1986. Or Alfred V. Aho and Jeffrey D. Ullman, *Principles of Compiler Design*, Addison-Wesley, 1977. The newer book has more on code generation and interval analysis, but drops a very nice chapter on languages. Cited on pages 15, 236, 295, 298, 298, 300, 301, 301, 301.

[12]   M. Ajtai, J. Komlos and E. Szemeredi, "Sorting in c log n Steps," *Combinatorica*, vol. 3, no. 1, pp. 1-19, 1983. Cited on pages 203, 215.

[13]   S. K. Akl, "An Optimal Algorithm for Parallel Selection," *Information Processing Letters*, vol. 19, no. 1, pp. 47-50, 1984. Cited on page 215.

[14]   Khayri A. M. Ali and Roland Karlsson, "Full Prolog and Scheduling OR-parallelism in Muse," *International Journal of Parallel Programming*, vol. 19, no. 6, pp. 445-475, 1990. Cited on page 285.

[15]   Frances E. Allen, "Compiling for Parallelism," in George S. Almasi and George Paul, editors, *Proceedings of the 1986 IBM Europe Institute Course on Parallel Processing*, North-Holland, 1988. Cited on pages 296, 313, 313, 318, 609.

[16]   F. E. Allen and J. Cocke, "A Program Data Flow Analysis Procedure," *Communications of the ACM*, vol. 19, no. 3, pp. 137-147, March 1976. Cited on pages 300, 301.

[17]   John R. Allen and Ken Kennedy, "PSC: A Program to Convert FORTRAN to Parallel Form," in Kai Hwang, editor, *Supercomputers: Design and Application*, IEEE Computer Science Press, 1984. Cited on page 318.

[18]   Randy Allen and Ken Kennedy, "Programming Environments for Supercomputers," in F. A. Matsen and T. Tajima, editors, *Supercomputers*, pp. 21-38, University of Texas Press, 1986. Cited on page 308.

[19]   George S. Almasi, "Parallel Processing Overview," *Parallel Computing*, vol. 2, 1985. Cited on page 142.

[20]   G. S. Almasi, B. Alpern, C. L. Berman, J. L. Carter and D. Hale, "A Case-Study in Performance Programming: Seismic Migration," *Proceedings, 2nd Symposium on High Performance Computing*, Montpelier, France, October 1991. Also available as IBM Research Report RC 16951, June 1991. Cited on pages 51, 53, 53, 59.

[21]   G. S. Almasi, T. McLuckie, J. Bell, A. Gordon and D. Hale, "Parallel Distributed Seismic Migration," *Concurrency Practice and Experience*, vol. 5, no. 2, pp. 105-131, April 1993. Cited on pages 51, 56, 57, 59.

[22]   G. T. Almes, A. P. Black, E. D. Lazowska and J. D. Noe, "The Eden System: A Technical Review," *IEEE Transactions on Software Engineering*, vol. SE-11, pp. 43-59, 1985. Cited on page 343.

[23]   Robert Alverson, David Callahan, Daniel Cummings, Brian Koblenz, Allan Poterfield and Burton Smith, "The Tera Computer System," *Proceedings of the International Conference on Supercomputing*, Amsterdam, September 1990. Cited on page 571.

[24]   Makoto Amamiya, Masaru Takesue, Ryuzo Hasegawa and Hirohide Mikami, "Implementation and Evaluation of a List-Processing-Oriented Dataflow Machine," *Proceedings of the 13th Annual International Symposium on Computer Architecture*, pp. 10-19, 1986. Cited on page 537.

[25]   Thomas E. Anderson, Brian N. Bershad, Edward D. Lazowska and Henry M. Levy, "Scheduler Activations: Efficient Kernel Support for the User Level Management of Parallelism," *Proceedings of the Thirteenth ACM Symposium on Operating Systems Principles*, Oct. 1991. Cited on page 370.

[26]   Gregory R. Andrews, *Concurrent Programming – Principles and Practice*, Benjamin/Cummings, 1991. Cited on pages 163, 163, 163, 164.

[27]   G. R. Andrews and F. B. Schneider, "Concepts and Notations for Concurrent Processing," *ACM Computing Surveys*, vol. 15, pp. 3-43, March 1983. Cited on pages 148, 151, 152, 155, 155, 155, 161, 161, 239, 355.

[28]   Marco Annaratone, Emmanuel Arnould, Thomas Gross, H. T. Kung, Monica S. Lam, Ornat Mezilcioglu, Ken Sarocky and Jon A. Webb, "Warp Architecture and Implementation," *Proceedings of the 13th Annual International Symposium on Computer Architecture*, pp. 346-356, Computer Science Press, 1986. Cited on pages 296, 464, 465.

[29]   Anonymous, "Commercial Parallel-Computer Line Uses VLSI to Cut Number-Crunching Costs," *Computer Systems Equipment Design*, pp. 9-13, March 1985. Cited on page 488.

[30]   James Archibald and Jean-Loup Baer, "Cache Coherence Protocols: Evaluation Using a Multiprocessor," *ACM Transactions on Computer Systems*, vol. 4, no. 4, pp. 273-298, November 1986. Cited on page 548.

[31]   B. W. Arden, editor, *What Can Be Automated? (COSERS)*, MIT Press, 1980. Cited on pages 229, 231.

[32]   J. S. Arnold, D. P. Casey and R. H. McKinstry, "Design of Tightly-Coupled Multiprocessing Programming," *IBM Systems Journal*, vol. 13, no. 1, pp. 60-92, 1974. Cited on page 364.

[33]   Arvind; and David E. Culler, "Dataflow Architectures," *Annual Review of Computer Science*, vol. 1, pp. 225-253, 1986. Cited on pages 516, 516, 522, 522, 523, 523, 532, 537, 537, 538, 538.

[34]   Arvind; and Kim Gostelow, "The U-Interpreter," *Computer*, vol. 15, pp. 42-49, February 1982. Cited on page 332.

[35]   Arvind; and Robert A. Iannucci, "A Critique of Multiprocessing von Neumann Style," *Proceedings of the 10th Annual International Symposium on Computer Architecture*, pp. 426-436, Stockholm, 1983. Cited on pages 540, 560, 603.

[36]   Arvind; and Rishiyur S. Nikhil, "Executing a Program on the MIT Tagged-Token Dataflow Architecture," *Proceedings of the PARLE Conference, Eindhoven, June 1987; in Lecture Notes in Computer Science*, vol. 259, pp. 1-29, Springer-Verlag, 1987. Cited on page 537.

[37]   Arvind; Rishiyur S. Nikhil, and Keshav K. Pingali, "I-structures: Data Structures for Parallel Computing," *Proceedings of the Workshop on Graph Reduction*, Santa Fe, September 28 – October 1 1986. Also available as MIT LCS Computation Structures Group Memo 267, February 1987. Cited on pages 528, 529, 529, 530.

[38]   M. J. Atallah and U. Vishkin, "Finding Euler Tours in Parallel," *Journal of Computer and Systems Sciences*, vol. 29, no. 3, pp. 330-337, 1984. Cited on page 215.

[39]   Various Authors, "History of Programming Languages Conference Proceedings," *ACM SIGPLAN Notices*, vol. 13, no. 8, August 1978. Cited on page 229.

[40]   B. Awerbuch, A. Israeli and Y. Shiloach, "Finding Euler Circuits in Logarithmic Parallel Time," *Proceedings of the Sixteenth ACM Symposium on Theory of Computing*, pp. 249-257, 1984. Cited on page 215.

[41]   B. Awerbuch and Y. Shiloach, "New Connectivity and MSF ALgorithms for Ultracomputer and PRAM," *Proceedings of the 12th Annual International Conference on Parallel Processing*, pp. 175-179, 1983. Cited on pages 197, 215.

[42]   Robert G. Babb II, *Programming Parallel Processors*, Addison-Wesley, 1988. Cited on page 239.

[43]   Maurice J. Bach, *The Design of the UNIX Operating System*, Englewood Cliffs: Prentice-Hall, 1986. Cited on page 352.

[44]   Maurice J. Bach and S. J. Buroff, "Multiprocessor UNIX Systems," *Bell Laboratories Technical Journal*, vol. 63, no. 8, pp. 1733-1749, October 1984. Cited on page 368.

[45]   John Backus, at the ACM SIGPLAN Conference, 1-3 June, 1978. Cited in a letter by H. A. Hartung in *Physics Today,* p. 11, September 1984. Cited on page 234.

[46]   John Backus, "Can Programming be Liberated from the von Neumann Style? A Functional Style and its Algebra of Programs," *Communications of the ACM*, vol. 21, no. 8, pp. 613-641, August 1978. Cited on pages 233, 260, 271.

[47]   John Backus, "Is Computer Science Based on the Wrong Fundamental Concept of 'Program'?," in de Bakker and van Vliet, editors, *Algorithmic Languages*, pp. 133-165, North Holland, 1981. Cited on page 259.

[48]   John Backus, "Function-level computing," *IEEE SPECTRUM*, vol. 19, pp. 22-27, August 1982. Cited on pages 6, 257, 258, 260.

[49]   H. E. Bal, J. G. Steiner and A. S. Tanenbaum, "Programming Languages for Distributed Computing Systems," *ACM Computing Surveys*, vol. 21, no. 3, September 1989. Cited on page 248.

[50]   George H. Barnes, Richard M. Brown, Maso Kato, David J. Kuck, Daniel L. Slotnick and Richard A. Stokes, "The ILLIAC IV Computer," *IEEE Transactions on Computers*, vol. 17, no. 8, pp. 746-757, August 1968. Cited on page 431.

[51]   Ilan Bar-on and Uzi Vishkin, "Optimal Parallel Generation of a Computation Tree Form," *ACM Transactions on Programming Languages and Systems*, vol. 7, no. 2, pp. 348-355, 1985. Cited on page 215.

[52]   Joel F. Bartlett, "A NonStop Kernel," *Proceedings of the Eighth ACM Symposium on Operating Systems Principles*, pp. 22-29, Pacific Grove, California, December 1981. Cited on page 343.

[53]   K. Batcher, "Design of a Massively Parallel Processor," *IEEE Transactions on Computers*, vol. 29, no. 9, pp. 836-840, September 1980. Cited on page 459.

[54]   Bob Beck and Dave Olien, "A Parallel Programming Process Model," *Proceedings of the USENIX Conference*, pp. 83-102, Winter 1987. Cited on page 368.

[55]   G. R. Beck, D. W. L. Yen and T. L. Anderson, "The Cydra 5 Minisupercomputer: Architecture and Implementation," *The Journal of Supercomputing*, vol. 7, no. 1/2, pp. 143-180, 1992. Cited on page 624.

[56]   Daniel K. Beece, Georgina P. Papp and Frank Villante, "The IBM Engineering Verification Engine," *25th Design Automation Conference Proceedings*, June 1988. Cited on page 629.

[57]   J. Beetem, M. Denneau and D. Weingarten, "GF11 − A Supercomputer for Scientific Applications," *Proceedings of the 12th International Symposium on Computer Architecture*, Boston: IEEE Computer Society, 1985. Also see Journal of Statistical Physics, vol. 43, p. 1171, 1986. Cited on page 436.

[58]   J. Beetem, M. Denneau and D. Weingarten, "The GF11 Parallel Computer," in J. J. Dongarra, editor, *Experimental Parallel Computing Architectures*, Amsterdam: North-Holland, 1987. Cited on pages 436, 436, 440, 444, 445.

[59]   Adam Beguelin, Jack Dongarra, Al Geist, Robert Manchek and Vaidy Sunderam, "A User's Guide to PVM Parallel Virtual Machine," *Oak Ridge National Laboratory Report ORNL/TM-11826*, July 1990. To receive, send mail message "send userguide_shar from pvm" to netlib@ornl.gov. Cited on pages 251, 252.

[60]   V. E. Benes, *Mathematical Theory of Communication Networks and Telephone Traffic*, New York: Academic Press, 1965. Cited on page 398.

[61]   P. A. Bernstein, V. Hadzilacos and N. Goodman, *Concurrency Control and Recovery in Database Systems*, Addison-Wesley, 1987. Cited on pages 354, 355.

[62]   Brian N. Bershad, Thomas E. Anderson, Edward D. Lazowska and Henry M. Levy, "User-Level Interprocess Communication for Shared Memory Multiprocessors," *ACM Transactions on Computer Systems*, vol. 9, no. 2, pp. 175-198, May 1991. Cited on pages 62, 169.

[63]   Ronald Bianchini, Susan Dickey, Jan Edler, Gabriel Goodman, Allan Gottlieb, Richard Kenner and Jiarui Wang, "The Ultra III Prototype," *Proceedings of the Parallel Systems Fair at the 7th International Parallel Processing Symposium*, pp. 2-9, Newport Beach, California, April 13-16, 1993. Cited on pages 162, 407.

[64]   Lubomyr Bic and Robert L. Hartmann, "Hither Hundreds of Processors in a Database Machine," *Proceedings of the 4th International Workshop on Database Machines*, pp. 153-168, March 1985. Cited on page 68.

[65]   Andrew D. Birrell and Bruce Jay Nelson, "Implementing Remote Procedure Calls," *ACM Transactions on Computer Systems*, vol. 2, no. 1, pp. 39-59, February 1984. Cited on pages 166, 167.

[66]   D. Bitton, H. Boral, D. J. DeWitt, and K. Wilkinson, "Parallel Algorithms for the Execution of Relational Database Operations," *ACM Transactions on Database Systems*, vol. 8, pp. 324-353, September 1983. Cited on page 72.

[67]   Tom Blank, "The MasPar MP-1 Architecture," *COMPCON Proceedings*, pp. 20-24, 1990. Cited on page 459.

[68]   A. J. Blodgett and D. R. Barbour, "Thermal Conduction Module: A High-Performance Multilayer Ceramic Package," *IBM Journal of Research and Development*, vol. 26, pp. 31-36, January 1982. Cited on pages 110, 607.

[69]   Haran Boral and David J. DeWitt, "Database Machines: An Idea Whose Time has Passed? A Critique of the Future of Database Machines," in H.-O. Leilich and M. Misikoff, editors, *Database Machines*, pp. 166-187, Springer-Verlag, 1983. Cited on pages 71, 73, 73.

[70]   Alan Borodin and John. E. Hopcroft, "Routing, Merging, and Sorting on Parallel Models of Computation," *Proceedings of the Fourteenth ACM Symposium on Theory of Computing*, pp. 338-344, 1982. Cited on pages 189, 215.

[71]   Andrea J. Borr, "Transaction Monitoring in Encompass™: Reliable Distributed Transaction Processing," *Proceedings of the VLDB Conference*, pp. 155-165, 1981. Cited on page 504.

[72] Kenneth C. Bowler and G. Stuart Pawley, "Molecular Dynamics and Monte Carlo Simulation in Solid-State and Elementary Particle Physics," *Proceedings of the IEEE*, vol. 74, pp. 42-55, January 1984. Cited on page 460.

[73] Eugene D. Brooks III, "The Shared Memory Hypercube," *Parallel Computing*, vol. 6, no. 2, pp. 235-245, February 1988. Cited on page 470.

[74] Fred Brooks, *The Mythical Man Month*, Addison-Wesley, 1975. Cited on page 172.

[75] J. C. Browne, "Parallel Architectures for Computer Systems," *Physics Today*, vol. 37, no. 5, pp. 28-35, May 1984. (A version of this paper translated into computerese is in *Computer,* vol. 17, pp. 83-87, July 1984.). Cited on pages 8, 138, 140.

[76] Sally A. Browning, "Algorithms for the Tree Machine," in Carver Mead and Lynn Conway, editors, *Introduction to VLSI Systems*, pp. 295-312, Addison-Wesley, 1980. Cited on page 629.

[77] Ray Bryant, Hung-Yang Chang and Bryan Rosenburg, "Experience Developing the RP3 Operating System," *Computing Systems (The Journal of the USENIX Association)*, vol. 4, no. 2, pp. 183-216, Summer 1991. Cited on page 610.

[78] W. Buchholz, "The IBM System/370 Vector Architecture," *IBM Systems Journal*, vol. 25, pp. 51-62, 1986. In the same issue see related articles by Gibson et al and by Clark and Wilson. Cited on pages 415, 421, 425, 427.

[79] Michael Burke and Ron Cytron, "Interprocedural Dependence Analysis and Parallelization," *Proceedings of the Sigplan '86 Symposium on Compiler Construction*, vol. 21, no. 7, pp. 162-175, July 1986. Cited on page 309.

[80] Burroughs Corp., "Numerical Aerodynamics Simulation Facility Feasibility Study," *Report NAS2-9897*, March 1979. Cited on page 581.

[81] F. Butler, H. Chen, J. Sexton, A. Vaccarino and D. Weingarten, "Hadron Mass Predictions of the Valence Approximation to Lattice QCD," *Physical Review Letters*, vol. 70, pp. 2849-2852, 1993. Cited on page 445.

[82] Albert Cahana and Edith Schonberg, "How to Write Parallel Programs for the NYU Ultracomputer Prototype," *Ultracomputer Documentation Note #2*, March 20 1986. Cited on page 243.

[83] David Cann, "Retire Fortran? A Debate Rekindled," *Communications of the ACM*, vol. 35, no. 8, pp. 81-89, August 1992. Cited on page 333.

[84] H. L. Capron and Brian K. Williams, *Computers and Data Processing*, Benjamin/Cummings, 1984. Cited on page 236.

[85] Nicholas Carriero and David Gelernter, "Linda in Context," *Communications of the ACM*, vol. 32, no. 4, pp. 444-458, April 1989. Cited on pages 253, 255.

[86] Nicholas Carriero and David Gelernter, "How to Write Parallel Programs: A Guide to the Perplexed," *Journal of the ACM*, vol. 21, no. 3, pp. 323-357, September 1989. Cited on pages 239, 253.

[87] Nicholas Carriero and David Gelernter, "Coordination Languages and Their Significance," *Communications of the ACM*, vol. 35, no. 2, pp. 96-107, February 1992. Cited on page 253.

[88] Nicholas Carriero and David Gelerntner, "The S/Net's Linda Kernel," *ACM Transactions on Computer Systems*, vol. 4, no. 2, pp. 110-129, May 1986. Cited on page 596.

[89] Lucien M. Censier and Paul Feautrier, "A New Solution to Coherence Problems in Multicache Systems," *IEEE Trans. Computers*, vol. 27, no. 12, pp. 1112-1118, December 1978. Cited on page 548.

[90] David Chaiken, John Kubiotowicz and Anant Agarwal, "LimitLESS Directories: A Scalable Cache Coherence Scheme," *Proceedings Fourth International Conference on Architectural Support for Programming Languages and Operating Systems (ASPLOS IV)*, pp. 224-234, April 1991. Cited on pages 549, 549, 556.

[91] P-Y. Chen, D. H. Lawrie and P-C. Yew, "Interconnection Networks Using Shuffles," *Computer*, vol. 14, pp. 55-64, December 1981. Cited on page 398.

[92] D. R. Cheriton, "The V Kernel: A Software Base for Distributed Systems," *IEEE Software*, vol. 1, pp. 19-43, April 1984. Cited on page 343.

[93] F. Y. Chin, J. Lam and I. Chen, "Efficient Parallel Algorithms for Some Graph Problems," *Communications of the ACM*, vol. 25, no. 9, pp. 659-655, 1982. Cited on pages 197, 215.

[94] Wai-Mee Ching, "Program analysis and code generation in an APL/370 compiler," *IBM Journal of Research and Development*, vol. 30, no. 6, pp. 594-602, November 1986. Cited on pages 325, 325, 325.

[95] Wai-Mee Ching, "Evon: An Extended von Neumann Model for Parallel Processing," *Proceedings of the Fall Joint Computer Conference*, pp. 363 – 371, November 1986. Cited on page 326.

[96] Wai-Mee Ching and D. Ju, "Execution of automatically parallelized APL programs on RP3," *IBM Journal of Research and Development*, vol. 35, no. 5/6, pp. 767-778, September/November 1991. Cited on page 331.

[97] Wai-Mee Ching and Andrew Xu, "A Vector Code Back End of the APL370 Compiler on IBM 3090 and some Performance Comparisons," *Proceedings of the APL-88 Conference*, pp. 69-76, February 1988. Held in Sydney, Australia. Cited on page 329.

[98]   Norman H. Christ and Anthony E. Terrano, "A Very Fast Parallel Processor," *IEEE Transactions on Computers*, vol. 33, no. 4, pp. 344-349, April 1984. Cited on pages 444, 446.

[99]   Peter Christy, "Software to Support Massively Parallel Computing on the MasPar MP-1," *COMPCON Proceedings*, pp. 29-33, 1990. Cited on page 459.

[100]   Peter Christy, "Virtual Processors Considered Harmful," *Sixth Distributed Memory Computing Conference Proceedings*, 1991. Cited on page 459.

[101]   Andrzej Ciepielewski, "Scheduling in Or-Parallel Prolog Systems: Survey and Open Problems," *International Journal of Parallel Programming*, vol. 20, no. 6, pp. 421-451, 1991. Cited on page 285.

[102]   Leonard Allen Cohn, Theodore E. Mankovich and Herbert Sullivan, "Performance of CHoPP on the Livermore Loops," *Proceedings, 2nd International Supercomputer Conference*, pp. 11-19, May 1987. Cited on pages 625, 627.

[103]   Richard Cole and Uzi Vishkin, "Deterministic Coin Tossing and Accelerating Cascades: Micro and Macro Techniques for Designing Parallel Algorithms," *Proceedings of the Eighteenth ACM Symposium on Theory of Computing*, pp. 206-219, 1986. Cited on pages 198, 215.

[104]   M. E. Conway, "A Multiprocessor System Design," *Proceedings of the AFIPS 1963 Fall Joint Computer Conference*, vol. 24, pp. 139-146, New York: Spartan Books, 1963. Cited on pages 149, 344.

[105]   George F. Coulouris and Jean Dollimere, *Distributed Systems – Concepts and Design*, Addison-Wesley, 1988. Cited on pages 5, 166, 169, 169.

[106]   P. J. Courtois, F. Heymans and D. J. Parnas, "Concurrent Control with 'Readers' and 'Writers'," *Communications of the ACM*, vol. 14, pp. 667-668, October 1971. Cited on pages 358, 372.

[107]   Cray Research, Inc.., "Cray T3D: Technical Summary," September 1993. Cited on page 560.

[108]   W. Crowther, J. Goodhue, R. Gurwitz, R. Rettberg and R. Thomas, "The Butterfly (TM) Parallel Processor," *IEEE Computer Architecture Technical Committee Newsletter*, pp. 18-45, September-December 1985. This issue contains several other articles about the Butterfly. Cited on page 594.

[109]   W. Crowther, J. Goodhue, E. Starr, R. Thomas, W. Milliken and T. Blackadar, "Performance Measurements on a 128-Node Butterfly Parallel Processor," *Proceedings of the International Conference on Parallel Processing*, 1985. Cited on page 595.

[110]   Ron Cytron, "Useful Parallelism in a Multiprocessing Environment," *Proceedings of the International Conference on Parallel Processing*, pp. 450-457, 1985. Cited on pages 178, 178, 182.

[111]   Ron Cytron, "On the Implication of Parallel Languages for Compilers," *IBM Research Report RC 11723*, March 1986. Cited on page 309.

[112]   O.-J. Dahl, B. Myrhaug and K. Nygaard, "The SIMULA 67 Common Base Language," *Norwegian Computer Center Publication S-2*, 1968. Cited on page 232.

[113]   William J. Dally, "Performance Analysis of k-ary n-cube Interconnection Networks," *IEEE Transactions on Computers*, vol. 39, no. 6, pp. 775-785, June 1990. Cited on page 491.

[114]   William J. Dally, J.A. Stuart Fiske, John S. Keen, Richard A. Lethin, Michael D. Noakes, Peter R. Nuth, Roy E. Davison and Gregory A. Fyler, "The Message-Driven Processor: A Multicomputer Processing Node with Efficient Mechanisms," *IEEE Micro*, vol. 12, no. 2, pp. 23-39, April 1992. Cited on pages 557, 558.

[115]   William J. Dally and Charles L. Seitz, "The Torus Routing Chip," *Distributed Computing*, vol. 1, pp. 187-196, 1986. Cited on page 478.

[116]   William J. Dally and Charles L. Seitz, "Deadlock-free Message Routing in Multiprocessor Interconnection Networks," *IEEE Transactions on Computers*, vol. 36, no. 5, pp. 547-553, May 1987. Cited on page 396.

[117]   George B. Dantzig, *Linear Programming and Extensions*, Princeton University Press, 1963. Cited on page 203.

[118]   F. Darema, A. Karp and P. Teller, "Application Survey Reports – I," in F. Darema, editor, *IBM Research Report RC 12743*, May 6 1987. Cited on page 610.

[119]   F. Darema, S. Kirkpatrick and V. A. Norton, "Parallel algorithms for chip placement by simulated annealing," *IBM Journal of Research and Development*, vol. 31, no. 3, pp. 391-402, May 1987. Also available as IBM Research Report RC 12195. Cited on page 610.

[120]   Frederica Darema and Gregory F. Pfister, "Multipurpose Parallelism for VLSI CAD on the RP3," *IEEE Design & Test of Computers*, pp. 19-27, October 1987. An expanded version is available as IBM Research Report RC 12516. Cited on page 610.

[121]   F. Darema-Rogers, D. A. George, V. A. Norton and G. F. Pfister, "A VM Parallel Environment," *IBM Research Report RC 11225*, January 23 1985. Cited on page 609.

[122]   F. Darema-Rogers, V. A. Norton and G. F. Pfister, "Using a Single-Program-Multiple-Data Computational Model for Parallel Execution of Scientific Applications," *IBM Research Report RC 11552*, November 19 1985. Cited on page 609.

[123] F. Darema-Rogers, G. F. Pfister and K. So, "Memory Access Patterns of Parallel Scientific Programs," *Proceedings of the ACM SIGMETRICS Conference on Measuring and Modeling Computer Systems*, Banff, Canada, May 11-14 1987. Also available as IBM Research Report RC 12086, July 15, 1986. Cited on page 610.

[124] J. A. Darringer, W. A. Joyner, C. L. Berman and L. H. Trevillyan, "Logic Synthesis through Local Transformations," *IBM Journal of Research and Development*, vol. 25, pp. 272-280, July 1981. Cited on page 65.

[125] C. J. Date, *Introduction to Database Systems*, Addison-Wesley, 1981. Cited on pages 65, 67, 68.

[126] E. E. Davidson, P. W. Hardin, G. A. Katopis, M. G. Nealon and L. L. Wu, "Physical and electrical design features of the IBM Enterprise System/9000 circuit module," *IBM Journal of Research and Development*, vol. 36, no. 5, pp. 877-888, September 1992. Cited on pages 110, 110.

[127] Alan L. Davis and Robert M. Keller, "Data Flow Program Graphs," *Computer*, vol. 15, pp. 26-41, February 1982. Cited on page 273.

[128] Doug DeGroot, "Restricted AND-Parallelism and Side Effects in Logic Programming," in Kai Hwang and Doug DeGroot, editors, *Parallel Processing for Supercomputers and Artificial Intelligence*, McGraw-Hill, 1989. Cited on pages 279, 284, 285.

[129] D. DeGroot and J-H. Chang, "A Comparison of Two AND-Parallel Execution Models," *Proceedings, AFCET INFORMATIQUE Conference on Hardware and Software Components for the Fifth Generation, Paris*, March 5-7 1985. Cited on pages 84, 283.

[130] D. Degroot and G. Lindstrom, *Logic Programming—Functions, Relations, and Equations*, Prentice-Hall, 1986. Cited on page 282.

[131] J. C. Dehnert and R. A. Towle, "Compiling for the Cydra 5," *The Journal of Supercomputing*, vol. 7, no. 1/2, pp. 181-228, 1992. Cited on page 624.

[132] Robert H. Dennard, "Field-effect transistor memory," *U. S. Patent 3,387,286*, June 1968. Cited on page 125.

[133] Monty M. Denneau, "The Yorktown Simulation Engine," *ACM/IEEE 19th Design Automation Conference Proceedings*, pp. 55-59, 1982. Cited on page 627.

[134] Jack B. Dennis, "Data Flow Supercomputers," *Computer*, vol. 13, pp. 48-56, November 1980. Cited on page 272.

[135] Jack B. Dennis, Guang-Rong Gao and Kenneth W. Todd, "Modeling the Weather with a Data Flow Supercomputer," *IEEE Transactions on Computers*, vol. 33, no. 7, pp. 592-603, July 1984. Cited on pages 42, 523, 524, 529, 536.

[136]   Jack B. Dennis, Willie Y.-P. Lim and William B. Ackerman, "The MIT Data Flow Engineering Model," *Information Processing 83 (IFIPS)*, pp. 553-560, 1983. Cited on page 536.

[137]   J. B. Dennis and R. P. Misunas, "A preliminary architecture for a basic data flow processor," *Proceedings of the 2nd Annual Symposium on Computer Architecture*, pp. 126-132, 1973. Cited on page 516.

[138]   J. Dennis and E. C. Van Horn, "Programming Semantics For Multiprogrammed Computations," *Communications of the ACM*, vol. 9, no. 3, pp. 143-155, March 1966. Cited on page 366.

[139]   Robert B. K. Dewar and Matthew Smosna, *Microprocessors: A Programmer's View*, McGraw-Hill, 1990. Cited on pages 133, 248, 491, 495.

[140]   David DeWitt and Jim Gray, "Parallel Database Systems," *Communications of the ACM*, vol. 35, no. 6, pp. 85-98, June 1992. Cited on pages 67, 73.

[141]   Susan Dickey, *Systolic Combining Switch Designs*, Ph.D. thesis, NYU, January 1994. Cited on page 395.

[142]   Susan Dickey, Allan Gottlieb and Richard Kenner, "Using VLSI to Reduce Serialization and Memory Traffic in Shared Memory Parallel Computers," in Charles E. Leiserson, editor, *Advanced Research in VLSI: Proceedings of the of the Fourth MIT Conf.*, 1986. Cited on pages 580, 583.

[143]   Susan Dickey and Richard Kenner, "Hardware Combining and Scalability," *Proceedings of the 4th Annual ACM Symposium on Parallel Algorithms and Architectures*, pp. 296-305, San Diego, June 1992. Cited on page 162.

[144]   Digital Equipment Corporation, *Introduction to KL-10 Based Systems, Technical Description, EK-KL-TD-002*, Maynard MA, 1976. Cited on page 364.

[145]   E. W. Dijkstra, "Cooperating Sequential Processes," in F. Genuys, editor, *Programming Languages*, pp. 43-112, Academic Press, 1968. Cited on pages 155, 159.

[146]   E. W. Dijkstra, *A Discipline of Programming*, Prentice-Hall, 1976. Cited on pages 247, 284.

[147]   Isaac Dimitrikovsky, "A Short Note on Barrier Synchronization," *NYU Ultracomputer System Software Note #59*, January 1985. Cited on page 588.

[148]   Jack J. Dongarra, "Performance of Various Computers Using Standard Linear Equation Solvers," *Oak Ridge National Laboratory Report CS-89-85*, November 23 1993. Obtain via email to netlib@ornl.gov with header "send performance from benchmark" and no body. Cited on page 379.

[149]   Jack Dongarra, Joanne L. Martin and Jack Worlton, "Computer benchmarking: paths and pitfalls," *IEEE Spectrum*, vol. 24, no. 7, pp. 38-43, July 1987. Cited on pages 423, 493, 618.

[150]   Tim Johnson and Tony Durham, *Parallel Processing: The Challenge of New Computer Architectures*, Ovum Inc., 1986. Cited on pages 248, 392, 397.

[151]   J. Presper Eckert, Moore School Lecture, July 15, 1946. Cited on page 139.

[152]   Boleslaw K. Szymanski, editor, *Parallel Functional Languages and Compilers*, Addison-Wesley, 1991. Cited on pages 239, 261, 264, 266, 268, 269.

[153]   Jan Edler, Jim Lipkis and Edith Schonberg, "Memory Management in Symunix II: A Design for Large-Scale Shared Memory Multiprocessors," *NYU Ultracomputer Note #135*, April 1988. Cited on page 371.

[154]   Jan Edler, Jim Lipkis and Edith Schonberg, "Process Management for Highly Parallel Unix Systems," *NYU Ultracomputer Note #136*, April 1988. Cited on page 371.

[155]   P. Ein-Dor, "Grosch's law revisited," *Communications of the ACM*, vol. 28, no. 2, pp. 142-151, February 1985. Cited on page 6.

[156]   Susan Eisenbach, *Functional Programming – Languages, Tools, and Architectures*, Halsted Press/John Wiley, 1987. Cited on pages 267, 275.

[157]   Kattamuri Ekanadham, "A Perspective on Id," in Boleslaw K. Szymanski, editor, *Parallel Functional Languages and Compilers*, Addison-Wesley, 1991. Cited on pages 267, 332.

[158]   John Ellis, *Bulldog: A Compiler for VLIW Architectures*, MIT Press, 1985. Cited on pages 319, 321, 322.

[159]   Philip H. Enslow Jr., "Multiprocessor Organization—A Survey," *ACM Computing Surveys*, vol. 9, pp. 103-129, March 1977. Cited on pages 342, 363.

[160]   K. P. Eswaran, J. N. Gray, R. A. Lorie and I. L. Traiger, "The Notion of Consistency and Predicate Locks in a Database System," *Communications of the ACM*, vol. 19, no. 11, pp. 624-633, November 1976. Cited on pages 159, 189.

[161]   S. E. Fahlman, *NETL: A System for Representing and Using Real-World Knowledge*, MIT Press, 1979. Cited on pages 85, 85, 87.

[162]   S. E. Fahlman, "Three Flavors of Parallelism," *Proceedings AAAI-80*, 1980. Cited on pages 23, 169, 456.

[163]   Scott E. Fahlman and Geoffrey E. Hinton, "Connectionist Architectures for Artificial Intelligence," *Computer*, vol. 20, pp. 100-109, January 1987. Cited on page 87.

[164]   Tse-yun Feng, "A Survey of Interconnection Networks," *Computer*, vol. 14, pp. 12-27, December 1981. Cited on pages 380, 382, 392, 398.

[165]   Hohn T. Feo, David C. Cann and Rodney R. Oldehoft, "A Report on the Sisal Language Project," *Journal of Parallel and Distributed Computing*, vol. 10, pp. 349-366, 1990. Cited on pages 275, 332, 333, 334, 334.

[166] Alan R. Feuer and Narain H. Gehani, "A Comparison of the Programming Languages C and Pascal," *ACM Computing Surveys*, vol. 14, no. 1, pp. 73-92, March 1982. Cited on page 232.

[167] Raphael A. Finkel, *An Operating Systems Vade Mecum*, Prentice-Hall, 1986. Cited on pages 343, 344, 350.

[168] Charles N. Fischer and Richard J. LeBlanc Jr., *Crafting A Compiler*, Benjamin/Cummings, 1988. Cited on page 295.

[169] Joseph A. Fisher, *The Optimization of Horizontal Microcode within and beyond Basic Blocks*, Ph.D. thesis, NYU, October 1979. Cited on page 319.

[170] Joseph A. Fisher, "Very Long Instruction Word Architectures and the Eli-512," *Proceedings of the 10th Annual International Symposium on Computer Architecture*, pp. 140-150, 1983. Cited on pages 296, 319, 319, 323, 624.

[171] Joseph A. Fisher, John R. Ellis, John C. Ruttenberg and Alexandru Nicolau, "Parallel Processing: A Smart Compiler and a Dumb Machine," *Proceedings of the ACM SIGPLAN '84 Symposium on Compiler Construction, in SIGPLAN NOTICES*, vol. 19, no. 6, pp. 37-47, June 1984. Cited on pages 322, 323, 323, 332.

[172] Joseph A. Fisher and Stephen M. Freudenberger, "Predicting Conditional Branch Directions From Previous Runs of a Program," *Proceedings ASPLOS-V (Fifth International Conference on Architectural Support for Programming Languages and Operating Systems*, pp. 85-95, 1992. Cited on pages 323, 323.

[173] Joseph A. Fisher and John J. O'Donnel, "VLIW Machines: Multiprocessors We Can Actually Program," *COMPCON Proceedings*, pp. 299-305, 1984. Cited on page 622.

[174] Michael J. Flynn, "Some Computer Organizations and Their Effectiveness," *IEEE Transactions on Computers*, vol. C-21, pp. 948-960, 1972. Cited on pages 18, 142, 142, 561.

[175] C. L. Forgy, "Rete: A Fast Algorithm for the Many Pattern/Many Object Pattern Match Problem," *Artificial Intelligence*, vol. 19, pp. 17-37, 1982. Cited on pages 83, 507, 507.

[176] Jose A. B. Fortes and Benjamin W. Wah, "Guest Editors' Introduction: Systolic Arrays—From Concept to Implementation," *Computer*, vol. 20, pp. 12-17, July 1987. Cited on page 463.

[177] Steven Fortune and James Wyllie, "Parallelism in Random Access Machines," *Proceedings of the Tenth ACM Symposium on Theory of Computing*, pp. 114-118, 1978. Cited on page 189.

[178] Geoffrey C. Fox, "Concurrent Processing for Scientific Calculations," *COMPCON Proceedings*, pp. 70-73, 1984. Cited on pages 476, 476, 479.

[179] Geoffrey C. Fox and Steve W. Otto, "Algorithms for concurrent processors," *Physics Today*, vol. 37, no. 5, pp. 50-59, May 1984. Cited on page 479.

[180] Geoffrey Fox, "The Performance of the Caltech Hypercube in Scientific Calculations," in F. A. Matsen and T. Tajima, editors, *Supercomputers*, pp. 117-141, Berkeley, CA: Univ. of California Press, 1986. Cited on page 476.

[181] Geoffrey Fox, Semma Hiranadani, Ken Kennedy, Charles Koelbel, Uli Kemer, Chau-Wen Tseng and Min-You Wu, "FORTRAN D Language Specification," *Rice University Tech Report TR90-141*, April 1991. Cited on pages 241, 242, 242, 242, 243.

[182] Paul O. Fredrickson, Randall E. Jones and Brian T. Smith, "Synchronization and control of parallel algorithms," *Parallel Computing*, vol. 2, pp. 255-264, November 1985. Cited on page 152.

[183] M. Furtney, "Parallel Processing at Cray Research Inc," in R. H. Perrott, editor, *Software for Parallel Computers*, pp. 133-154, London: Chapman and Hall, 1992. Cited on pages 239, 244.

[184] D. D. Gajski, D. J. Kuck and D. A. Padua, "Dependence Driven Computation," *COMPCON Proceedings*, pp. 168-172, February 1981. Cited on page 616.

[185] D. D. Gajski, D. A. Padua, D. J. Kuck and R. H. Kuhn, "A Second Opinion on Data Flow Machines and Languages," *Computer*, vol. 15, pp. 58-69, February 1982. Cited on pages 273, 274, 275, 332, 516, 521, 525, 525, 525.

[186] Daniel D. Gajski and Jih-Kwon Peir, "Comparison of five multiprocessor systems," *Parallel Computing*, vol. 2, no. 3, pp. 265-282, November 1985. Cited on pages 143, 145, 294, 303.

[187] Zvi Galil, "Optimal Parallel Algorithms for String Matching," *Proceedings of the Sixteenth ACM Symposium on Theory of Computing*, pp. 240-248, 1984. Cited on page 215.

[188] Narain Gehani, *Ada Concurrent Programming*, Prentice-Hall, 1984. Cited on pages 153, 155, 165, 165.

[189] David A. George, "EPEX – Environment for Parallel Execution," in George S. Almasi and George Paul, editors, *Proceedings of the 1986 IBM Europe Institute Course on Parallel Processing*, North-Holland, 1988. Cited on page 609.

[190] William B. Gevarter, "An Overview of Artificial Intelligence and Robotics," *NASA Technical Memorandum 85836*, June 1983. Cited on page 74.

[191] Carlo Ghezzi, "Concurrency in programming languages: A survey," *Parallel Computing*, vol. 2, pp. 229-241, November 1985. Cited on pages 146, 166, 236, 239, 287.

[192] Carlo Ghezzi and Mehdi Jazayeri, *Programming Language Concepts*, John Wiley, 1982. Cited on pages 229, 236, 237, 237, 259.

[193] D. H. Gibson and G. S. Rao, "Design of the IBM System/390 computer family for numerically intensive applications," *IBM Journal of Research and Development*, vol. 36, no. 4, pp. 695-711, July 1992. Cited on page 427.

[194] George H. Gobel and Michael H. Marsh, "A Dual Processor VAX 11/780," *Purdue University Technical Report TR-EE 81-31*, September 1981. Cited on page 367.

[195] L. Rodney Goke and G. J. Lipovsky, "Banyan Networks for Partitioning Multiprocessor Systems," *Proceedings of the First Annual Symposium on Computer Architecture*, pp. 21-28, 1973. Cited on page 398.

[196] Andrew V. Goldberg and Robert E. Tarjan, "A New Approach to the Maximum Flow Problem," *Proceedings of the Eighteenth ACM Symposium on Theory of Computing*, pp. 136-146, May 86. Cited on page 215.

[197] J. R. Goodman, "Using Cache Memory to Reduce Processor-Memory Traffic," *Proceedings of the 10th Annual International Symposium on Computer Architecture*, pp. 124-131, 1983. Cited on page 547.

[198] Allan Gottlieb, "Avoiding Serial Bottlenecks in Ultraparallel MIMD Computers," *COMPCON Proceedings*, pp. 354-359, 1984. Cited on page 609.

[199] Allan Gottlieb, "An Overview of the NYU Ultracomputer Project," in J. J. Dongarra, editor, *Experimental Parallel Computing Architectures*, pp. 25-95, North-Holland, 1987. Cited on pages 464, 574, 584, 598.

[200] Allan Gottlieb, Ralph Grishman, Clyde P. Kruskal, Kevin P. McAuliffe, Larry Rudolph and Marc Snir, "The NYU Ultracomputer—Designing an MIMD Shared Memory Parallel Computer," *IEEE Transactions on Computers*, vol. C-32, no. 2, pp. 175-189, February 1983. An earlier version appeared in *Real-Time Signal Processing IV*, Tien F. Tao, Editor (Proceedings of SPIE), pp. 64-73, 1981. Cited on pages 584, 589.

[201] Allan Gottlieb and Clyde P. Kruskal, "Complexity Results for Permuting Data and other Computations on Parallel Processors," *Journal of the ACM*, vol. 31, pp. 193-209, April 1984. Cited on pages 24, 199, 209, 211, 212, 214, 215.

[202] Allan Gottlieb, Boris D. Lubachevsky and Larry Rudolph, "Basic Techniques for the Efficient Coordination of Very Large Numbers of Cooperating Sequential Processors," *ACM Transactions on Programming Languages and Systems*, vol. 5, no. 2, pp. 164-189, April 1983. Cited on pages 161, 162, 163, 572, 581, 586.

[203] Allan Gottlieb, Boris Lubachevsky and Larry Rudolph, "Coordinating Large Numbers of Processors," *Proceedings, International Conference on Parallel Processing*, 1981. Cited on page 577.

[204]   Ananth Y. Grama, Anshul Bupta and Vipin Kumar, "Isoefficiency: Measuring the Scalability of Parallel Algorithms and Architectures," *IEEE Parallel and Distributed Technology*, vol. 1, no. 3, pp. 12-20, August 1993. Cited on page 221.

[205]   Steve Gregory, *Parallel Logic Programming in PARLOG*, Addison-Wesley, 1987. Cited on pages 81, 225, 256, 279, 284, 285, 285, 285.

[206]   Leo J. Guibas and Frank M. Liang, "Systolic Stacks, Queues, and Counters," *Proceedings, 1982 Conf. Adv. Research in VLSI, MIT*, January 25-27 1982. Cited on page 463.

[207]   A. Gupta and C. L. Forgy, "Measurements on Production Systems," *Carnegie-Mellon University Technical Report*, 1983. Cited on page 23.

[208]   Anoop Gupta, Charles Forgy, Allen Newell and Robert Wedig, "Parallel Algorithms and Architectures for Rule-Based Systems," *Proceedings of the 13th Annual International Symposium on Computer Architecture*, pp. 28-37, Tokyo, 1986. Cited on pages 506, 507, 508, 508, 509.

[209]   J. R. Gurd, C. C. Kirkham and I. Watson, "The Manchester Prototype Dataflow Computer," *Communications of the ACM*, vol. 28, no. 1, pp. 34-52, January 1985. Cited on pages 516, 517, 519, 520.

[210]   J. Gurd, C. C. Kirkham and A. P. W. Boehm, "The Manchester Dataflow Computing System," in J. J. Dongarra, editor, *Experimental Parallel Computing Systems*, North-Holland, 1987. Cited on pages 516, 517, 519, 520, 529.

[211]   John L. Gustafson, "Reevaluating Amdahl's Law," *Communications of the ACM*, vol. 31, no. 5, pp. 532-533, May 1988. Cited on page 221.

[212]   John L. Gustafson, Stuart Hawkinson and Ken Scott, "Architecture of a Homogeneous Vector Supercomputer," *Proceedings, 1986 International Conference on Parallel Processing*, pp. 649-652, 1986. Cited on page 490.

[213]   John Gustafson, "The Consequences of Fixed Time Performance Measurement," *Proceedings of the 25th Hawaii International Conference on Systems Sciences*, vol. 3, Kauai, 1992. Cited on page 221.

[214]   E. Hagersten, S. Haridi and D.H.D. Warren, "The Cache-Coherent Protocol of the Data Diffusion Machine," in Michel Dubois and Shreekant Thakkar, editors, *Cache and Interconnect Architectures in Multiprocessors*, 1990. Cited on page 552.

[215]   Eric Hagersten, Anders Landin and Seif Haridi, "DDM—A Cache-Only Memory Architecture," *Computer*, vol. 25, no. 9, pp. 44-54, September 1992. Cited on page 552.

[216]   Dave Hale, "Stable explicit depth extrapolation of seismic wavefields," *Geophysics*, vol. 56, no. 11, pp. 1770-1777, November 1991. Cited on page 53.

[217]   Robert H. Halstead Jr., "Multilisp: A Language for Concurrent Symbolic Computation," *ACM Transactions on Programming Languages and Systems*, vol. 7, no. 4, pp. 501-538, October 1985. Cited on pages 239, 244, 246, 248, 287.

[218]   Per Brinch Hansen, "The Programming Language Concurrent Pascal," *IEEE Transactions on Software Engineering*, vol. SE-1, no. 2, pp. 199-207, June 1975. Cited on page 246.

[219]   Philip J. Hatcher and Michael J. Quinn, *Data-Parallel Programming on MIMD Computers*, Cambridge, Mass.: MIT Press, 1991. Cited on page 239.

[220]   John A. Hawley III and Walter B. Meyer, "MUNIX, A Multiprocessing Version of UNIX," *M.S. Thesis, Naval Postgraduate School Monterey, CA*, June 1975. Cited on page 367.

[221]   John P. Hayes, *Computer Architecture and Organization*, McGraw-Hill, 1978. Cited on pages 109, 431.

[222]   John P. Hayes, Trevor N. Mudge, Quentin F. Stout, Stephen Colley and John Palmer, "Architecture of a Hypercube Supercomputer," *Proceedings, 1986 International Conference on Parallel Processing*, pp. 653-660, 1986. Cited on page 490.

[223]   Leonard S. Haynes, Richard L. Lau, Daniel P. Siewiorek and David W. Mizell, "A Survey of Highly Parallel Computing," *Computer*, vol. 15, pp. 9-24, January 1982. Cited on pages 300, 562.

[224]   D. Heller, "A Survey of Parallel Algorithms in Numerical Linear Algebra," *SIAM Review*, vol. 20, pp. 740-777, 1978. Cited on pages 24, 38.

[225]   Peter Henderson, *Functional Programming – Application and Implementation*, MIT Press, 1980. Cited on page 266.

[226]   R. Henle, Irving T. Ho, William S. Johnson, W. David Pricer and James L. Walsh, "The Application of Transistor Technology to Computers," *IEEE Transactions on Computers*, vol. c-25, no. 12, December 1976. Cited on pages 104, 125.

[227]   John Hennessy and Mahadevan Ganapathi, "Advances in Compiler Technology," *Annual Review of Computer Science*, vol. 1, pp. 83-106, 1986. Cited on page 298.

[228]   John L. Hennesy and David A. Patterson, *Computer Architecture: A Quantitative Approach*, Morgan Kaufmann Publishers, Inc., 1990. Cited on page 374.

[229]   P. D. Hester, Richard O. Simpson and Albert Chang, "The IBM RT PC ROMP and Memory Management Unit Architecture," *IBM RT Personal Computer Technology, IBM Publication No. SA23-1057*, pp. 48-56, 1986. Reprinted in the IEEE tutorial *Reduced Instruction Set Computers,* edited by William Stallings, 1986. Cited on page 606.

[230]   P. Hibbard, A. Hisgen and T. Rodeheffer, "A Language Implementation Design for a Multiprocessor Computer System," *Proceedings of the 5th Annual Symposium on Computer Architecture*, pp. 66-72, 1978. Cited on pages 563, 563, 565, 565, 566.

[231]   W. Daniel Hillis, "The Connection Machine," *MIT Artificial Intelligence Laboratory Memo No. 646*, September 1981. Cited on page 447.

[232]   W. Daniel Hillis, *The Connection Machine*, MIT Press, 1985. Cited on pages 381, 392, 446, 448, 455, 455, 456, 456.

[233]   B. K. Hillyer, D. E. Shaw and A. Nigam, "NON-VON's Performance on Certain Database Benchmarks," *IEEE Transactions on Software Engineering*, pp. 577-583, April 1986. Cited on page 635.

[234]   Seema Hiranandani, Ken Kennedy and Chau-Wen Tseng, "Compiling Fortran-D for MIMD Distributed-Memory Machines," *Communications of the ACM*, vol. 35, no. 8, pp. 66-80, August 1992. Cited on page 318.

[235]   Seema Hirandani, Ken Kennedy and Chau-Wen Tseng, "Preliminary Experiences with the Fortran D Compiler," *Proceedings, Supercomputing '93*, pp. 338-350, Portland, November 1993. Cited on pages 243, 318.

[236]   Robert E. Hiromoto, Olaf M. Lubeck and James Moore, "Experiences with the Denelcor HEP," *Parallel Computing*, vol. 1, pp. 197-206, 1984. Cited on page 570.

[237]   C. A. R. Hoare, "Communicating Sequential Processes," *Communications of the ACM*, vol. 21, no. 8, pp. 666-677, August 1978. Cited on page 247.

[238]   Roger W. Hockney, "Measurements on the 2-CPU Cray X-MP," *Parallel Computing*, vol. 2, pp. 1-14, 1985. Cited on pages 421, 425.

[239]   R. W. Hockney and C. R. Jesshope, *Parallel Computers*, Adam Hilger Ltd., 1981. Cited on pages 415, 417, 418, 422, 423, 425, 425, 460.

[240]   R. C. Holt, *Concurrent Euclid, the UNIX System, and Tunis*, Addison-Wesley, 1983. Cited on page 367.

[241]   William C. Holton and Ralph K. Calvin, "A Perspective on CMOS Technology Trends," *Proceedings of the IEEE*, vol. 74, pp. 1646-1668, December 1986. Cited on page 104.

[242]   Se June Hong and Ravi Nair, "Wire-Routing Machines— New Tools for VLSI Physical Design," *Proceedings of the IEEE*, vol. 73, pp. 57-65, January 1983. Cited on page 497.

[243]   S. J. Hong, R. Nair and E. Shapiro, "A Physical Design Machine," in J. P. Gray, editor, *VLSI 81 Conference Proceedings*, Academic Press, 1981. Cited on page 65.

[244]   R. Michael Hord, *The Illiac-IV: The First Supercomputer*, Computer Science Press, 1982. Cited on pages 30, 431, 434, 435, 435.

[245] Tsutomu Hoshino, "An Invitation to the World of PAX," *Computer*, vol. 19, pp. 68-79, May 1986. Cited on pages 493, 494.

[246] Tsutomu Hoshino, Tomonori Shirakawa and Takeshi Kamimura, "Highly Parallel Processor Array 'PAX' for Wide Scientific Applications," *Proceedings of the International Conference on Parallel Processing*, pp. 95-105, 1983. Cited on page 493.

[247] D. K. Hsiao, "Database Machines are Coming, Database Machines are Coming!," *Computer*, vol. 12, pp. 7-9, March 1979. Cited on pages 71, 73.

[248] Paul Hudak, "Functional Programming Languages," *ACM Computing Surveys*, vol. 21, no. 3, pp. 359-411, September 1989. Cited on pages 225, 256, 261, 261, 262, 264, 267, 267, 278, 279, 331.

[249] Paul Hudak, "Para-Functional Programming Basics," in Boleslaw K. Szymanski, editor, *Parallel Functional Languages and Compilers*, Addison-Wesley, 1991. Cited on pages 267, 270.

[250] P. Hudak and A. Bloss, "The aggregate update problem in functional programming systems," *Proceedings of the 12th ACM Symposium on the Principles of Programming Languages*, pp. 300-313, January 1985. Copy elimination in functional language compilation.. Cited on page 334.

[251] Kai Hwang and Faye A. Briggs, *Computer Architecture and Parallel Processing*, McGraw-Hill, 1984. Cited on page 561.

[252] IBM Corporation, *Communications Programming Concepts*, 1990. Publication SC23-2206-00. Cited on pages 166, 167.

[253] IBM Corporation, *IBM VS FORTRAN Version 2 Language and Library Reference*, 1990. Publication SC26-4221-04. Cited on page 244.

[254] IBM Corporation, *IBM Power Visualization System Overview and Functional Characteristics*, 1991. Publication GA22-7137. Cited on page 611.

[255] IBM Corporation, *IBM Scalable POWERparallel Systems Reference Guide*, 1993. Publication G325-0648-00. Cited on page 512.

[256] Inmos Limited, *Occam Programming Manual*, 1985. Cited on page 248.

[257] Inmos Limited, *Occam2 Programming Manual*, Prentice Hall, 1988. Cited on page 248.

[258] Intel Corporation literature, November 1991. Cited on page 491.

[259] Noriyoshi Ito, Masatoshi Sato, Eiji Kuno and Kazuaki Rokusawa, "The Architecture and Preliminary Evaluation Results of the Experimental Parallel Inference Machine PIM-D," *Proceedings of the 13th Annual International Symposium on Computer Architecture*, pp. 149-156, 1986. Cited on page 538.

[260]   Y. Iwasaki, K. Kanaya, T. Yoshie, T. Hoshino, T. Shirakawa, Y Oyanagi, S. Ichii and T. Kawai, "QCDPAX – An MIMD Array of Vector Processors for the Numerical Simulation of Quantum Chromodynamics," *Proceedings, Supercomputing '89*, pp. 495-504, 1989. Cited on page 494.

[261]   George K. Jacob, A. Richard Newton and Donald O. Pederson, "An Empirical Analysis of the Performance of a Multiprocessor-based Circuit Simulator," *ACM/IEEE 23rd Design Automation Conference Proceedings*, pp. 588-593, 1986. Cited on page 62.

[262]   David V. James, Anthony T. Laundrie, Stein Gjessing and Gurindar S. Sohi, "Distributed-Directory Scheme: Scalable Coherent Interface," *Computer*, vol. 23, no. 6, pp. 74-77, June 1990. Cited on page 549.

[263]   Douglas Johnson and others, "Automatic Partitioning of Programs in Multiprocessor Systems," *COMPCON Proceedings*, pp. 175-178, 1980. Cited on page 536.

[264]   Anita K. Jones, "The Object Model: A Conceptual Tool for Structuring Software," in Rudolph Bayer, Robert M. Graham, and G. Seegmuller, editors, *Operating Systems: An Advanced Course — Lecture Notes in Computer Science*, pp. 7-16, Berlin: Springer-Verlag, 1978. :(Volume 60). Cited on page 366.

[265]   Anita K. Jones, Robert J. Chansler, Jr, Ivor Duram, Karsten Schwans and Steven R. Vegdahl, "StarOS, a Multiprocessor Operating System for the Support of Task Forces," *Proceedings of the Seventh Symposium on Operating Systems Principles*, pp. 117-127, December 1979. Cited on page 366.

[266]   A. K Jones and P. Schwarz, "Experience Using Multiprocessors," *ACM Computing Surveys*, vol. 12, pp. 121-165, June 1980. Cited on page 365.

[267]   Anita K. Jones and Brian T. Smith, "Programming issues raised by a multiprocessor," *Proceedings of the IEEE*, vol. 66, pp. 229-237, February 1978. Cited on page 366.

[268]   Geraint Jones, "Programming in Occam, A Tourist Guide to Parallel Programming," *Programming Research Group, Technical Monograph PRG-13, Oxford University Computing Laboratory*, 1985. Cited on page 248.

[269]   Harry F. Jordan, "A Special Purpose Architecture for Finite Element Analysis," *Proceedings of the 1978 International Conference on Parallel Processing*, pp. 263-266, 1978. Cited on pages 50, 160.

[270]   Gilles Kahn, "The Semantics of a Simple Language for Parallel Programming," *Information Processing 74 (IFIPS)*, pp. 471-475, 1974. Cited on page 500.

[271]   Eugenia Kalney-Rivas and David Hoitsma, "Documentation of the Fourth Order Band Model," *NASA Tech. Memorandum 80608*, December 1979. Cited on page 42.

[272] Narendra K. Karmarkar, "A New Polynomial-time Algorithm in Linear Programming," *Combinatorica*, vol. 4, pp. 373-379, 1984. Cited on page 203.

[273] Alan H. Karp, "Programming for Parallelism," *Computer*, vol. 20, pp. 43-57, May 1987. Cited on pages 239, 244, 486.

[274] David Katsuki, Eric S. Elsam, William F. Mann, Eric S. Roberts, John G. Robinson, F. Stanley Skowronski and Eric W. Wolf, "Pluribus—An Operational Fault-Tolerant Multiprocessor," in Daniel Siewiorek, C. Gordon Bell, and Alan Newell, editors, *Computer Structures: Principles and Examples*, pp. 371-386, New York: McGraw-Hill, 1982. Cited on page 365.

[275] James A. Katzman, "A Fault-Tolerant Computing System," *Proceedings of the 11th Hawaii International Conference on System Sciences*, pp. 85-117, 1978. Cited on page 503.

[276] Robert M. Keller, Frank C. H. Lin and Jiro Tanaka, "Rediflow Multiprocessing," *COMPCON Proceedings*, pp. 410-417, March 1984. Cited on pages 498, 500.

[277] P. Kermani and Leonard Kleinrock, "Virtual Cut-Through: A new Computer Communication Switching Technique," *Computer Networks*, vol. 3, pp. 267-286, 1979. Cited on page 396.

[278] L. G. I. Khachiyan, "A Polynomial Algorithm in Linear Programming," *Soviet Mathematika Doklady*, vol. 20, pp. 191-194, 1979. Cited on page 203.

[279] D. N. Kimelman and T. A. Ngo, "The RP3 Program Visualization Environment," *IBM Journal of Research and Development*, vol. 35, no. 5/6, pp. 635-652, September/November 1991. Cited on page 611.

[280] Masasuke Kishi, Hiroshi Yasuhara and Yasusuke Kawamura, "DDDP: A Distributed Data Driven Processor," *Proceedings of the 10th Annual International Symposium on Computer Architecture*, pp. 236-242, 1983. Cited on page 538.

[281] M. Kitsuregawa, H. Tanaka and T. Moto-oka, "GRACE:Relational Algebra Machine Based on Hash and Sort—Its Design Concepts," *Journal of Information Processing*, vol. 6, pp. 148-155, November 1983. Cited on page 71.

[282] Walter Kleinfelder, private communication. Cited on page 121.

[283] Leonard Kleinrock, *Queuing Theory, Volume 2: Computer Applications*, John Wiley & Sons, 1975. Cited on page 395.

[284] L. Kleinrock, "Distributed Systems," *Computer*, vol. 18, pp. 90-103, November 1985. Cited on page 5.

[285] K. Knowlton, "A Fast Storage Allocator," *Communications of the ACM*, vol. 8, no. 10, pp. 623-625, October 1965. Cited on page 372.

[286] Donald E. Knuth, *The Art of Computer Programming*, Addison-Wesley, 1968. Cited on page 372.

[287] Donald E. Knuth, "Big Omicron, big omega, and big theta," *SIGACT News (ACM)*, vol. 8, no. 2, pp. 18-24, 1976. Cited on page 185.

[288] Peter M. Kogge, *The Architecture of Pipelined Computers*, McGraw-Hill, 1981. Cited on pages 310, 415, 423, 424.

[289] Adam Kolawa, "Performance of iPSC and Mark II," *Caltech Concurrent Computation Program Technical Bulletin*, no. 3, pp. 7-8, March 1986. (Also see no. 1, January 6, 1986, p. 11.). Cited on page 488.

[290] David Korn and Norman Rushfield, "Washcloth Simulation of Three-Dimensional Weather Forecasting Code," *NYU Ultracomputer Note #55*, May 1983. Cited on pages 22, 39, 42.

[291] Janusz S. Kowalik, editor, *Parallel MIMD Computation: HEP Supercomputer & Its Applications, Scientific Computation Series*, MIT Press, 1985. See especially the sections by Harry F. Jordan and by Burton Smith. Cited on pages 417, 566, 569, 570.

[292] R. A. Kowalski, "Algorithm = Logic + Control," *Communications of the ACM*, vol. 22, no. 7, pp. 424-436, July 1979. Cited on page 279.

[293] David A Kranz, Robert H. Halstead Jr. and Eric Mohr, "Mul-T: A High-Performance Parallel Lisp," *ACM SIGPLAN Notices*, vol. 24, no. 7, pp. 81-90, July 1989. Cited on page 246.

[294] Nancy P. Kronenberg, Henry M. Levy and William D. Strecker, "VAXclusters: A Closely-Coupled Distributed System," *ACM Transactions on Computer Systems*, vol. 4, no. 2, pp. 130-146, 1986. Cited on page 343.

[295] E. Kronstadt and G. Pfister, "Software Support for the Yorktown Simulation Engine," *ACM/IEEE 19th Design Automation Conference Proceedings*, pp. 60-64, 1982. Cited on pages 64, 627.

[296] Clyde P. Kruskal, "Searching, Merging, and Sorting in Parallel Computation," *IEEE Transactions on Computers*, vol. C-32, pp. 942-946, 1983. Cited on page 215.

[297] Clyde P. Kruskal, Larry Rudolph and Marc Snir, "A Complexity Theory of Efficient Parallel Algorithms," *IBM Research Report RC 13572*, March 4 1988. Cited on page 199.

[298] Clyde P. Kruskal and Marc Snir, "Some Results on Interconnection Networks for Multiprocessors," *Proceedings of the Princeton Conference on Information Science Systems*, 1982. Cited on page 581.

[299] David J. Kuck, "ILLIAC IV Software and Application Programming," *IEEE Transactions on Computers*, vol. 17, no. 8, pp. 758-770, August 1968. Cited on page 431.

[300] D. J. Kuck, *The Structure of Computers and Computations*, John Wiley, 1978. Cited on pages 143, 143.

[301]   David J. Kuck, Edward S. Davidson, Duncan H. Lawrie and Ahmed H. Sameh, "Parallel Supercomputing Today and the Cedar Approach," *Science*, vol. 231, pp. 967-974, February 1986.   The book *Experimental Parallel Computer Architectures* (J. J. Dongarra, ed., North-Holland, 1987) contains a slightly updated version of this article.   Cited on pages 319, 606, 612, 612, 614, 615, 616, 618.

[302]   David J. Kuck, Robert H. Kuhn, Bruce Leasure and Michael Wolfe, "The Structure of an Advanced Retargetable Vectorizer," in   Kai Hwang, editor, *Tutorial on Supercomputers*, pp. 163-178, IEEE Press, 1984.   (Revised from The Proceedings of COMPSAC '80, 1980).   Cited on pages 243, 286, 310, 314.

[303]   J. T. Kuehn and Burton Smith, "The Horizon Supercomputer System: Architecture and Software," *Proceedings, Supercomputing '91*, Orlando, November 1988.   Cited on page 571.

[304]   Manoj Kumar and Yurij Baransky, "The GF11 Parallel Computer: Programming and Performance," *Proceedings of the InfoJapan'90 Computer Conference*, pp. 255-262, Tokyo, Oct. 2-5 1990.   (Also IBM Research Report RC 15494, 1990).   Cited on page 436.

[305]   Manoj Kumar and Kattamuri Ekanadham, private communication.   Cited on page 271.

[306]   Manoj Kumar and Gregory F. Pfister, "The Onset of Hot Spot Contention," *Proceedings of the 1986 International Conference on Parallel Processing*, pp. 28-34, 1986.   Cited on pages 598, 600.

[307]   H. T. Kung, "Synchronized and Asynchronous Parallel Algorithms for Multiprocessors," *Algorithms and Complexity*, pp. 153-200, Academic Press, 1976.   Reprinted in R. Kuhn and D. Padua, editors, *Tutorial on Parallel Processing,* IEEE, 1981.   Cited on page 24.

[308]   H. T. Kung, "Why Systolic Architectures?," *Computer*, vol. 15, pp. 37-46, January 1982.   Cited on pages 188, 464.

[309]   H. T. Kung and Charles E. Leiserson, "Systolic Arrays (for VLSI)," in Iain S. Duff and G. W. Stewart, editors, *Sparse Matrix Proceedings, 1978*, Knoxville: Academic Press, 1979.   Also in "Algorithms for VLSI Processor Arrays", which is Section 8.3 of *Introduction to VLSI Systems,* C. Mead and L. Conway, 1980, Addison-Wesley, pp. 271-292.   Cited on page 461.

[310]   Steve Kuo and Dan Moldovan, "The State of the Art in Parallel Production Systems," *Journal of Parallel and Distributed Computing*, vol. 15, pp. 1-26, 1992.   Cited on pages 74, 76, 80, 83, 285.

[311]   Duncan H. Lawrie, "Access and Alignment of Data in an Array Processor," *IEEE Transactions on Computers*, vol. 24, no. 12, pp. 1145-1155, December 1975.   Cited on page 398.

[312]   Bruce Leasure, private communication.   Cited on pages 310, 310.

[313]   Gyungho Lee, Clyde P. Kruskal and David J. Kuck, "The Effectiveness of Combining in Shared Memory Parallel Computers in the Presence of Hot Spots," *Proceedings of the 1986 International Conference on Parallel Processing*, pp. 35-41, 1986. Cited on page 600.

[314]   C. E. Leiserson, *Area-efficient VLSI Computation*, Ph.D. thesis, Computer Science Department, Carnegie-Mellon University, 1981. Cited on page 386.

[315]   Charles E. Leiserson, "Fat-trees: Universal Networks for Hardware-Efficient Supercomputing," *IEEE Transactions on Computers*, vol. C-34, no. 10, pp. 892-901, October 1985. Cited on page 405.

[316]   E. Lelarasmee, A. Ruehli and A. L. Sangiovanni-Vincentelli, "The Waveform Relaxation Method for Time-Domain Analysis of Large Scale Integrated Circuits," *IEEE Transactions on Computer-Aided Design*, vol. 1, pp. 131-145, July 1982. Cited on pages 64, 96.

[317]   Daniel Lenoski, James Landon, Kourosh Garachorloo, Wolf-Dietrich Weber, Anoop Gupta, John Hennessy, Mark Horowitz and Monica S. Lam, "The Stanford Dash Multiprocessor," *Computer*, vol. 25, no. 3, pp. 63-79, March 1992. Cited on pages 552, 553, 553, 555, 555.

[318]   Eric J. Lerner, "Data-flow Architecture," *IEEE Spectrum*, pp. 57-62, April 1984. Cited on page 516.

[319]   Nancy G. Leveson and Clark S. Turner, "An Investigation of the Therac-25 Accidents," *Computer*, vol. 26, no. 7, pp. 18-41, July 1993. Cited on page 355.

[320]   Ronald D. Levine, "Supercomputers," *Scientific American*, vol. 246, no. 1, pp. 118-135, January 1982. Cited on pages 425, 426, 435.

[321]   Peter Lewis in the New York Times, May 13, 1986. Cited on page 367.

[322]   G. J. Lipovsky and M. V. Hermenegildo, "EPILOG", private communication. Cited on page 80.

[323]   G. Jack Lipovsky and Miroslaw Malek, *Parallel Computing: Theory and Comparisons*, John Wiley & Sons, 1987. Cited on pages 635, 636, 636.

[324]   Ami Litman, "The DUNIX Distributed Operating System," *ACM SIGOPS Operating Systems Review*, vol. 22, no. 1, pp. 42-51, 1988. Cited on page 343.

[325]   Harold Lorin, *Parallelism in Hardware and Software: Real and Apparent Concurrency*, Prentice-Hall, 1972. Cited on page 33.

[326]   David B. Loveman, "High Performance Fortran," *IEEE Parallel & Distributed Technology*, vol. 1, no. 1, pp. 25-42, February 1993. Cited on page 241.

[327]   R. A. MacKinnon, "Advanced Function Extended with Tightly-Coupled Multiprocessing," *IBM Systems Journal*, vol. 13, no. 1, pp. 32-59, 1974. Cited on page 364.

[328] Gyula Mago, "A Network of Microprocessors to Execute Reduction Languages," *International Journal of Computer and Information Sciences*, vol. 8, no. 6, pp. 349-471 (123 pages), December 1979. Cited on pages 630, 630, 630, 633, 633.

[329] Gyula Mago, "A Cellular Computer Architecture for Functional Programming," *COMPCON Proceedings*, pp. 179-187, February 25-28 1980. Cited on page 630.

[330] Theodore E. Mankovich, Val Popescu and Herbert Sullivan, "CHoPP Principles of Operation," *Proceedings, 2nd International Supercomputer Conference*, pp. 2-10, May 1987. Cited on pages 625, 625.

[331] D. Marr, "Representing Visual Information," in A. R. Hanson and E. M. Riseman, editors, *Computer Vision Systems*, Academic Press, 1978. Cited on page 89.

[332] Brian D. Marsh, Michael L. Scott, Thomas J. Leblanc and Evangelos P. Markatos, "First Class User Level Threads," *Proceedings of the Thirteenth ACM Symposium on Operating Systems Principles*, Oct. 1991. Cited on page 370.

[333] MasPar Computer Corporation, *The MP-1 Family of Massively Parallel Computers*, 1991. Cited on page 459.

[334] James R. McGraw, "The VAL Language: Description and Analysis," *ACM Transactions on Programming Languages and Systems*, vol. 4, no. 1, pp. 44-82, January 1982. Cited on pages 274, 274.

[335] Carver Mead and Lynn Conway, *Introduction to VLSI Systems*, Addison-Wesley, 1980. Cited on page 100.

[336] Phillip C. Miller, Charles E. St. John and Stuart W. Hawkinson, "FPS T Series Parallel Processor," in Robert G. Babb II, editor, *Programming Parallel Processors*, Addison-Wesley, 1988. Cited on page 248.

[337] Tohru Moto-oka, "Overview to the Fifth Generation Computer Project," *Communications of the ACM*, vol. 26, pp. 417-422, 1983. Cited on pages 80, 282.

[338] Sape J. Mullender and Andrew S. Tanenbaum, "A Distributed File Service Based on Optimistic Concurrency Control," *Proceedings of the Tenth Symposium on Operating Systems Principles*, pp. 51-62, Orcas Island, Washington, December 1985. Cited on page 343.

[339] Jacek Myczkowski and Guy Steele, "Seismic Modeling at 14 Gigaflops on the Connection Machine," *Proceedings, Supercomputing '91*, Albuquerque, November 1991. Cited on page 491.

[340] NEC Corporation, *SX-3 Series: General Description*, 1991. Document number GAZ02A, Revision A. Cited on page 428.

[341]   John R. Nickolls, "The Design of the MasPar MP-1: A Cost Effective Massively Parallel Computer," *COMPCON Proceedings*, pp. 25-28, 1990. Cited on page 459.

[342]   Anil Nigam, private communication. Cited on page 66.

[343]   Nils J. Nilsson, *Principles of Artificial Intelligence*, Tioga, 1980. Cited on pages 74, 76, 77, 78, 79, 79, 87, 279.

[344]   Tak H. Ning and Denny D. Tang, "Bipolar Trends," *Proceedings of the IEEE*, vol. 74, no. 12, pp. 1669-1677, December 1986. This is a special issue on integrated circuit technology. Cited on page 102.

[345]   Michael D. Noakes, Debra A. Wallach and William J. Dally, "The J-Machine Multicomputer: An Architectural Evaluation," *Proceedings of the 20th Annual International Symposium on Computer Architecture*, pp. 224-235, May 1993. Cited on pages 558, 559.

[346]   R. Olson, "Parallel Processing in a Message-Based Operating System," *IEEE Software*, vol. 2, pp. 39-49, July 1985. Cited on page 366.

[347]   E. I. Organick, *The Multics System*, MIT Press, 1972. Cited on page 349.

[348]   E. I. Organick, *Computer System Organization: The B5700/B6700 Series*, New York: Academic Press, 1973. Cited on page 363.

[349]   Carlton M. Osburn and Arnold Reisman, "Challenges in Advanced Semiconductor Technology for High-Performance and Supercomputer Applications," *The Journal of Supercomputing*, vol. 1, pp. 149-189, 1987. Cited on page 102.

[350]   Anita Osterhaug, *Guide to Parallel Programming*, Sequent Computer Systems Inc., 1986. Cited on pages 151, 239, 344, 368.

[351]   John K. Ousterhout, Andrew R. Cherenson, Frederick Douglis, Michael N. Nelson and Brent. B. Welch, "The Sprite Network Operating System," *Computer*, vol. 21, no. 2, pp. 23-36, February 1988. Cited on page 343.

[352]   J. K. Ousterhout, D. A. Scelza and P. S. Sindhu, "Medusa: An Experiment in Distributed Operating System Structures," *Communications of the ACM*, vol. 23, pp. 92-105, February 1980. Cited on pages 366, 366.

[353]   David A. Padua and Michael J. Wolfe, "Advanced Compiler Optimizations for Supercomputers," *Communications of the ACM*, vol. 29, no. 12, pp. 1184-1201, December 1986. Also see Wolfe's Ph.D. thesis of the same title on which this article is based: University of Illinois Report No. UIUCDCS-R-82-1105, October 1982. Cited on pages 308, 309.

[354]   M.S. Papamarcos and J.H. Patel, "A Low Overhead Coherence Solution for Multiprocessors with Private Cache Memories," *Proceedings of the 11th Annual International Symposium on Computer Architecture*, pp. 348-354, 1984. Cited on page 554.

[355] ParaSoft Corporation, *Express C User's Guide (Version 3.0)*, 1990. Cited on pages 250, 250, 251.

[356] J. A. Patel, "Performance of Processor-Memory Interconnections for Multiprocessors," *IEEE Transactions on Computers*, vol. c-30, pp. 771-780, 1981. Cited on page 398.

[357] David A. Patterson, Garth Gibson and Randy H. Katz, "A Case for Redundant Arrays of Inexpensive Disks," *Proceedings of the SIGMOD Conference on Management of Data*, pp. 109-116, June 1-3 1988. "The" RAID reference. Cited on page 132.

[358] Simon L. Peyton-Jones, *The Implementation of Functional Programming Languages*, Prentice-Hall, 1987. Limited to graph reduction. Cited on pages 261, 264, 264, 267, 267, 267, 267, 268, 269, 270, 275.

[359] Gregory F. Pfister, private communication. Cited on pages 11, 25.

[360] G. F. Pfister, "Parallel Processing and Special-Purpose Hardware in Design Automation," *ACM Computer Science Conference Proceedings*, February 1983. Cited on pages 22, 62.

[361] Gregory F. Pfister, "An Introduction to RP3," in J. J. Dongarra, editor, *Experimental Parallel Computing Architectures*, North-Holland, 1987. Cited on page 597.

[362] Gregory F. Pfister and V. Alan Norton, "'Hot Spot' Contention and Combining in Multistage Interconnection Networks," *IEEE Transactions on Computers*, vol. c-34, pp. 943-948, October 1985. Cited on pages 405, 405, 406, 407, 484, 582, 598, 598, 600, 600, 600, 602.

[363] Andrew Pollack, "Fifth Generation Became Japan's Lost Generation," *New York Times*, p. D1, June 5 1992. Cited on page 80.

[364] C. D. Polychronopoulos, *Parallel Programming and Compilers*, Boston: Kluwer Academic, 1988. Cited on pages 295, 301, 317.

[365] James H. Pomerene, private communication. Cited on page 414.

[366] Michael L. Powell and Barton P. Miller, "Process Migration in DEMOS/MP," *Proceedings of the Ninth ACM Symposium on Operating Systems Principles*, pp. 110-119, Bretton Woods, New Hampshire, October 1983. Cited on page 343.

[367] Terrence W. Pratt, *Programming Languages – Design and Implementation*, Prentice-Hall, 1984. Cited on pages 147, 147, 149, 152, 153, 229, 234.

[368] F. Preparata and J. Vuillemin, "The Cube-Connected-Cycles: A Versatile Network for Parallel Computation," *Communications of the ACM*, vol. 24, no. 7, pp. 300-310, July 1981. Cited on pages 388, 391.

[369]   Richard F. Rashid and George G. Robertson, "Accent: A Communication Oriented Network Operating System Kernel," *Proceedings of the Eighth ACM Symposium on Operating Systems Principles*, pp. 64-75, Pacific Grove, California, December 1981. Cited on page 343.

[370]   B. D. Rathi, presentation charts (private communication). Cited on page 598.

[371]   B. R. Rau, D. W. L. Yen, W. Yen and R. A. Towle, "The Cydra 5 Departmental Supercomputer: Design Philosophies, Decisions and Tradeoffs," *Computer*, vol. 22, no. 1, pp. 12-35, 1989. Cited on page 624.

[372]   David P. Reed and Rajendra K. Kanodia, "Synchronization with Eventcounts and Sequencers," *Communications of the ACM*, vol. 22, pp. 115-123, 1979. Cited on page 373.

[373]   Anthony P. Reeves, "Parallel Pascal: An Extended Pascal for Parallel Computers," *Journal of Parallel and Distributed Computing*, vol. 1, pp. 64-80, 1984. Cited on pages 232, 460.

[374]   Randall Rettberg and Robert Thomas, "Contention is no obstacle to shared-memory multiprocessing," *Communications of the ACM*, vol. 29, no. 12, pp. 1202-1212, December 1986. Cited on page 595.

[375]   C. Rieger, J. Bane and R. Trigg, "ZMOB: a highly parallel multiprocessor," *Proceedings of the Workshop on Picture Data Description and Management*, August 27-28 1980. Asilomar, California. Cited on page 384.

[376]   Alfred A Rizzi, Louis L. Whitcomb and Daniel E. Koditschek, "Distributed Real-Time Control of a Spatial Robot Juggler," *Computer*, vol. 25, pp. 12-24, May 1992. Cited on page 249.

[377]   James Rothnie, "Overview of the KSR1 Computer System," *Kendall Square Research Report TR 9202001*, March 1992. Cited on page 550.

[378]   P. Roussel, "PROLOG: manuel de reference et d'utilisation," *Groupe d'Intelligence Artificielle, Universite d'Aix-Marseille, Luminy*, September 1975. Cited on page 279.

[379]   Daniel Sabbah, "Computing with Connections in Visual Recognition of Origami Objects," *Cognitive Science*, vol. 9, pp. 25-50, 1985. Cited on pages 88, 88, 91, 92.

[380]   Ahmed Sameh, "Numerical Parallel Algorithms—A Survey," *High Speed Computers and Algorithm Organization*, pp. 207-228, Academic Press, 1977. Reprinted in R. Kuhn and D. Padua, editors, *Tutorial on Parallel Processing*, IEEE, 1981. Cited on page 24.

[381]   Jean E. Sammet, "Programming Languages: History and Future," *Communications of the ACM*, vol. 15, no. 7, pp. 601-614, July 1972. Cited on page 229.

[382] Vivek Sarkar, "PTRAN—The IBM Parallel Translation System," in Boleslaw K. Szymanski, editor, *Parallel Functional Languages and Compilers*, Addison-Wesley, 1991. Cited on page 318.

[383] Edmond Schonberg, private communication. Cited on page 166.

[384] Edith Schonberg and Edmond Schonberg, "Highly Parallel Ada—Ada on an Ultracomputer," *Proceedings of the Ada International Conference*, pp. 58-71, May 1985. Also available as NYU Ultracomputer Note #81. Cited on page 233.

[385] Michael D. Schroeder and Michael Burrows, "Performance of Firefly RPC," *ACM Transactions on Computer Systems*, vol. 8, no. 1, pp. 1-17, February 1990. Cited on pages 169, 169.

[386] Jacob T. Schwartz, "Ultracomputers," *ACM Transactions on Programming Languages and Systems*, vol. 2, no. 4, pp. 484-521, October 1980. Cited on pages 189, 510.

[387] Charles L. Seitz, "The Cosmic Cube," *Communications of the ACM*, vol. 28, no. 1, pp. 22-33, January 1985. Cited on pages 476, 479, 482, 485.

[388] Ehud Y. Shapiro, "A subset of Concurrent Prolog and Its Interpreter," *New Generation Computing*, vol. 3, 1983. Cited on pages 233, 284.

[389] Ehud Shapiro, "The Family of Concurrent Programming Languages," *ACM Computing Surveys*, vol. 21, no. 3, pp. 413-510, September 1989. Cited on pages 284, 284, 284, 285, 285.

[390] A. C. Shaw, *Logical Design of Operating Systems*, Prentice-Hall, 1974. Cited on pages 155, 159, 239, 294.

[391] David E. Shaw, "A Hierarchical Associative Architecture for the Parallel Evaluation of Relational Algebraic Database Primitives," *Stanford Department of Computer Science Report STAN-CS-79-778*, October 1979. Cited on page 71.

[392] David Elliot Shaw, "SIMD and MSIMD Variants of the NON-VON Supercomputer," *COMPCON Proceedings*, pp. 360-363, March 1984. Cited on page 634.

[393] D. G. Shea, W. W. Wilcke, R. C. Booth, D. H. Brown,, Z. D. Christidis, M. E. Giampapa, G. B. Irwin, T. T. Murakami, and V. K. Naik, F. T. Tong, P. R. Varker, and D. J. Zukowski, "The IBM Victor V256 Partitionable Multiprocessor," *IBM Journal of Research and Development*, vol. 35, no. 5/6, pp. 573-590, September/November 1991. Cited on pages 495, 495.

[394] Y. Shiloach and U. Vishkin, "Finding the Maximum, Merging, and Sorting in a Parallel Computation Model," *Journal of Algorithms*, vol. 2, no. 1, pp. 88-102, 1981. Cited on page 215.

[395] Y. Shiloach and U. Vishkin, "An O(log n) Parallel Connectivity Algorithm," *Journal of Algorithms*, vol. 3, no. 1, pp. 57-67, 1982. Cited on pages 197, 215.

[396] Y. Shiloach and U. Vishkin, "An O(n² log n) Parallel Max-flow Algorithm," *Journal of Algorithms*, vol. 3, no. 2, pp. 128-146, 1982. Cited on page 215.

[397] Howard Jay Siegel, Thomas Schwederski, Nathaniel J. Davis IV and James T. Kuehn, "PASM: A Reconfigurable Parallel System for Image Processing," *Proceedings of the 1984 Workshop on Algorithm-guided Parallel Architectures for Automatic Target Recognition*, July 1984. Cited on page 637.

[398] Howard Jay Siegel, Thomas Schwederski, James T. Kuehn and Nathaniel J. Davis IX, "An Overview of the PASM Parallel Processing System," in D. D. Gajski, V. M. Milutinovic, H. J. Siegel, and B. P. Fuhrt, editors, *Tutorial – Computer Architecture*, pp. 387-407, IEEE, 1987. Cited on pages 636, 637.

[399] Jaswinder P. Singh, John L Hennessy and Anoop Gupta, "Scaling Parallel Programs for Multiprocessors," *Computer*, vol. 26, no. 7, pp. 42-50, July 1993. Cited on page 170.

[400] Stephen K. Skedzielewski, "Sisal," in Boleslaw K. Szymanski, editor, *Parallel Functional Languages and Compilers*, Addison-Wesley, 1991. Cited on page 267.

[401] D. L. Slotnick, "The Fastest Computer," *Scientific American*, vol. 224, no. 2, pp. 76-87, February 1971. Cited on pages 431, 431.

[402] D. L. Slotnick, "The Conception and Development of Parallel Processors—A Personal Memoir," *Annals of the History of Computing*, vol. 4, no. 1, pp. 20-30, January 1982. Cited on pages 431, 433, 434.

[403] Alan Jay Smith, "Cache Memories," *ACM Computing Surveys*, vol. 14, pp. 473-530, September 1982. Cited on page 545.

[404] Burton J. Smith, "Architecture and applications of the HEP multiprocessor computer system," in Tien F. Tao, editor, *SPIE (Real-Time Signal Processing IV)*, vol. 298, pp. 241-248, Bellingham, Washington: Society of Photo-Optical Instrumentation Engineers, August 1981. Reprinted in K. Hwang, editor, *Tutorial on Supercomputers,* IEEE, 1984. Cited on pages 566, 569.

[405] Marc Snir, "On Parallel Search," *Proceedings of the Principles of Distributed Computing Conference*, pp. 242-253, August 1982. Cited on page 189.

[406] Lawrence Snyder, "Introduction to the Configurable, Highly Parallel Computer," *Computer*, vol. 15, pp. 47-56, January 1982. Cited on pages 501, 502, 503.

[407] Lawrence Snyder, "Type Architectures, Shared Memory, and the Corollary of Modest Potential," *Annual Review of Computer Science*, vol. 1, pp. 289-317, 1986. Cited on page 193.

[408] Marvin H. Solomon and Raphael A. Finkel, "The Roscoe Distributed Operating System," *Proceedings of the Seventh Symposium on Operating Systems Principles*, pp. 108-114, December 1979. Cited on page 343.

[409]   Vason P. Srini, "An Architectural Comparison of Dataflow Systems," *Computer*, vol. 19, no. 3, pp. 68-88, March 1986. Cited on page 516.

[410]   Staff, "DADO System Suits Matching and Search Applications," *Computer*, vol. 20, no. 4, p. 94, April 1987. Cited on page 505.

[411]   Craig Stanfill and Brewster Kahle, "Parallel Free-Text Search on the Connection Machine System," *Communications of the ACM*, vol. 29, no. 12, pp. 1229-1239, December 1986. This issue contains several related articles on CM1. Cited on page 456.

[412]   Per Stenstrom, "A Cache Consistency Procol for Multiprocessors with Multistage Networks," *Proceedings of the 16th Annual International Symposium on Computer Architecture*, pp. 407-415, May 1989. Cited on page 548.

[413]   Per Stenstrom, "A Survey of Cache Coherience Schemes for Multiprocessors," *Computer*, vol. 23, no. 6, pp. 12-24, June 1990. Cited on pages 547, 547.

[414]   Per Stenstrom, Truman Joe and Anoop Gupta, "Comparative Performance Evaluation of Cache-Coherent NUMA and COMA Architectures," *Proceedings of the 19th Annual International Symposium on Computer Architecture*, 1992. Cited on page 552.

[415]   Salvatore J. Stolfo, "Initial Performance of the DADO2 Prototype," *Computer*, vol. 20, pp. 75-83, January 1987. Cited on pages 505, 505, 505, 509.

[416]   Salvatore J. Stolfo and Daniel P. Miranker, "The DADO Production System Machine," *Journal of Parallel and Distributed Computing*, vol. 3, pp. 269-296, 1986. Cited on pages 505, 508, 508.

[417]   H. S. Stone, "Parallel Processing with the Perfect Shuffle," *IEEE Transactions on Computers*, vol. 20, pp. 153-161, February 1971. Cited on page 402.

[418]   Wen-King Su, Reese Faucette and Chuck Seitz, "C Programmer's Guide to the COSMIC CUBE," *Computer Science Department Report 5203*, California Institute of Technology, 1985. Cited on page 485.

[419]   Herbert Sullivan, Theodore R. Bashkow and David Klappholz, "A Large Scale Homogeneous, Fully Distributed Parallel Machine," *Proceedings of the 4th Annual Symposium on Computer Architecture*, pp. 105-124, 1977. Cited on page 625.

[420]   Herbert Sullivan, Theodore R. Bashkow, David Klappholz and L. Cohn, "The Node Kernel: Resource Management in a Self Organizing Parallel Processor," *Proceedings, International Conference on Parallel Processing*, pp. 157-164, 1977. Cited on page 625.

[421]   V. S. Sunderam, "PVM: A Framework for Parallel Distributed Computing," *Concurrency: Practice & Experience*, vol. 2, no. 4, pp. 315-339, December 1990. Cited on pages 251, 252.

[422]   R. J. Swan, S. H. Fuller and D. P. Siewiorek, "Cm*—A modular, multi-microprocessor," *Proceedings of the AFIPS 1977 Fall Joint Computer Conference*, vol. 46, pp. 637-644, 1977. Cited on pages 365, 563, 563, 564.

[423]   J. C. Syre, D. Comte and N. Hifdi, "Pipelining, Parallelism, and Anachronism in the LAU System," *Proceedings of the 1977 International Conference on Parallel Processing*, pp. 87-92, 1977. Cited on page 536.

[424]   S. M. Sze, *Physics of Semiconductor Devices*, John Wiley, 1981. Cited on pages 102, 102.

[425]   N. Takahashi and M. Amamiya, "A Data Flow Processor Array System: Design and Analysis," *Proceedings of the 10th Annual International Symposium on Computer Architecture*, pp. 243-250, 1983. Cited on page 536.

[426]   Tandem Database Group, "NonStop SQL, a Distributed, High-Performance High-Availability Implementation of SQL," *Workshop on High-Performance Transaction Systems*, Asilomar, CA, September 1987. The Tandem Inc. internal report is dated April 1987. Cited on page 504.

[427]   Andrew S. Tanenbaum, *Structured Computer Organization*, Prentice-Hall, 1984. Cited on pages 23, 139.

[428]   Andrew S. Tanenbaum, *Operating Systems—Design and Implementation*, Prentice-Hall, 1987. Cited on pages 344, 349, 350.

[429]   C. K. Tang, "Cache system design in the tightly coupled multiprocessor system," *Proceedings of the AFIPS National Computer Conference*, vol. 45, pp. 749-753, 1976. Cited on page 548.

[430]   Robert E. Tarjan and Uzi Vishkin, "An Efficient Parallel Biconnectivity Algorithm," *SIAM Journal of Computing*, vol. 14, no. 4, pp. 862-874, 1985. Cited on page 215.

[431]   Teradata Corporation, "DBC/1012 Data Base Computer Concepts and Facilities," *Document CO2-0001-0111*, October 1984. Cited on page 504.

[432]   Avadis Tevanian, Jr., Richard F. Rahid, David B. Golub, David L. Black, Eric Cooper and Michael W. Young, "Mach Threads and the Unix Kernel: The Battle for Control," *Summer Usenix Conference Proceedings*, pp. 185-197, 1987. Cited on page 344.

[433]   C. P. Thacker, E. M. McCreight, B. W. Lampson, R. F. Sproull and D. R. Boggs, "Alto: A Personal Computer," in Daniel Siewiorek, C. Gordon Bell, and Alan Newell, editors, *Computer Structures: Principles and Examples*, pp. 549-572, New York: McGraw-Hill, 1982. Cited on page 343.

[434]   Thinking Machines Corporation, *Connection Machine Model CM-2 Technical Summary*, 1990. Cited on page 458.

[435]   Thinking Machines Corporation, *The Connection Machine CM-5 Technical Summary*, 1991. Cited on pages 239, 509.

[436] Robert H. Thomas, "Behavior of the Butterfly Parallel Processor in the Presence of Memory Hot Spots," *Proceedings of the 1986 International Conference on Parallel Processing*, pp. 46-50, 1986. Cited on pages 598, 598, 601.

[437] Evan Tick, *Parallel Logic Programming*, MIT Press, 1991. Cited on pages 281, 284, 285, 285.

[438] Kenneth R. Traub, *Implementation of Non-Strict Functional Programming Languages*, MIT Press, 1991. Cited on pages 263, 264, 264, 264, 267, 267, 268, 268, 269, 269, 270, 331.

[439] N. Tredennick, *Microprocessor Logic Design – The Flowchart Method*, Digital Press, 1987. Cited on page 236.

[440] Philip C. Treleaven, David R. Brownbridge and Richard P. Hopkins, "Data Driven and Demand-Driven Computer Architecture," *ACM Computing Surveys*, vol. 14, no. 1, pp. 95-143, March 1982. Cited on page 136.

[441] Philip Treleaven, "Control-Driven Data-Driven, and Demand-Driven Computer Architecture (Abstract)," *Parallel Computing*, vol. 2, 1985. Cited on pages 23, 143, 143.

[442] Arthur Trew and Greg Wilson, editors, *Past, Present, Parallel – A survey of Available Parallel Computing Systems*, Springer-Verlag, 1991. Cited on pages 249, 490, 495, 497, 624.

[443] Y. H. Tsin and F. Y. Chin, "Efficient Parallel Algorithms for a Class of Graph Theoretic Algorithms," *Computer Science Technical Report, University of Alberta, Edmonton*, 1982. Cited on page 215.

[444] Lewis W. Tucker and George G. Robertson, "Architecture and Applications of the Connection Machine," *Computer*, vol. 21, pp. 26-38, August 1988. Cited on page 458.

[445] Rao Tummala and Eugene Rymaszewski, *Microelectronics Packaging Handbook*, Van Nostrand, 1989. Cited on page 110.

[446] Leslie G. Valiant, "Parallelism in Comparison Problems," *SIAM Journal of Computing*, vol. 4, no. 3, pp. 348-355, 1975. Cited on page 215.

[447] Arthur H. Veen, "Dataflow Machine Architecture," *ACM Computing Surveys*, vol. 18, no. 4, pp. 365-396, December 1986. Cited on pages 332, 515, 516, 516, 519, 520, 521, 523, 524, 525, 529, 533, 535, 537, 538, 539, 539.

[448] Alexander Veidenbaum, *Compiler Optimization and Architecture Design Issues for Multiprocessors*, Ph.D. thesis, University of Illinois, 1985. Cited on page 312.

[449] Uzi Vishkin, "An Optimal Parallel Connectivity Algorithm," *Discrete Applied Mathematics*, vol. 9, pp. 197-207, 1984. Cited on page 215.

[450] Uzi Vishkin, "Optimal Parallel Pattern Matching in Strings," *Information and Control*, vol. 67, no. 1-3, pp. 91-113, 1985. Cited on page 215.

[451] Uzi Vishkin, "An Optimal Parallel Algorithm for Selection," *Advances in Computing Research*, vol. 4, pp. 79-86, 1987. Cited on page 215.

[452] Bruce Walker, Gerald Popek, Robert English, Charles Kline and Greg Thiel, "The LOCUS Distributed Operating System," *Proceedings of the Ninth ACM Symposium on Operating Systems Principles*, pp. 49-70, Bretton Woods, New Hampshire, October 1983. Cited on pages 343, 361.

[453] Paul Wallich, "Parallel architectures offer more bits for the buck," *The Institute (IEEE)*, p. 6, June 1987. Cited on page 624.

[454] Tadashi Watanabe, "Architecture and performance of NEC supercomputer SX system," *Parallel Computing*, vol. 5, pp. 247-255, 1987. Cited on page 428.

[455] David A. Watt, *Programming Language Concepts and Paradigms*, Prentice-Hall, 1990. Cited on pages 226, 229, 236, 268, 275, 279.

[456] Bayard Webster, "Do Animals Have the Capacity to Plan?," *The New York Times*, p. C1, March 6 1984. Cited on page 13.

[457] D. Weingarten, "Parallel QCD Machines," *Nuclear Physics B (Proc. Suppl.)*, vol. 26, pp. 126-136, 1992. Cited on pages 445, 446.

[458] Robert M. White, editor, *Introduction to Magnetic Recording*, IEEE Press, 1985. Cited on page 129.

[459] James M. Wilson, *Operating System Data Structures for Shared-Memory MIMD Machines with Fetch-and-Add*, Ph.D. thesis, New York University, June 1988. Cited on page 372.

[460] N. Wirth, *Algorithms + Data Structures = Programs*, Prentice-Hall, 1976. Cited on page 147.

[461] M. C. Woodward, "Coordination," in David J. Evans, editor, *Parallel Processing Systems*, Cambridge University Press, 1982. Cited on pages 156, 156, 239.

[462] Chuan-Lin Wu and Tse-Yun Feng, "On a class of multistage interconnection networks," *IEEE Transactions on Computers*, vol. 29, no. 8, pp. 694-702, August 1980. Cited on page 398.

[463] William A. Wulf and C. Gordon Bell, "C.mmp—A multi-mini-processor," *Proceedings of the AFIPS 1972 Fall Joint Computer Conference*, vol. 41, pp. 765-777, 1972. Cited on pages 365, 560, 562.

[464] W. A. Wulf, E. Cohen, W. Corwin, A. Jones, R. Levin, C. Pierson and F. Pollack, "Hydra: The Kernel of a Multiprocessor Operating System," *Communications of the ACM*, vol. 17, pp. 337-345, June 1974. Cited on page 365.

[465] W. A. Wulf, R. Levin and S. P. Harbison, *Hydra/C.mmp: An Experimental Computer System*, McGraw-Hill, 1981. Cited on pages 365, 365, 562.

[466]   William A. Wulf, R. Levin and C. Pierson, "Overview of the Hydra Operating System Development," *Proceedings of the Fifth Symposium on Operating Systems Principles*, pp. 122-131, Austin, Texas, November 1975. Cited on page 562.

[467]   Yoshinori Yamaguchi, Kenji Toda and Toshitsugu Yuba, "A Performance Evaluation of a Lisp-Based Data-Driven Machine (EM-3)," *Proceedings of the 10th Annual International Symposium on Computer Architecture*, pp. 363-369, 1983. Cited on page 537.

[468]   Shaula Yemini, G. Goldszmidt, A. Stoyenko, Y. Wei and L. Beeck, "Concert: A high-level language approach to heterogeneous distributed systems," *Proceedings, 9th International Conference on Distributed Computing Systems*, pp. 162-171, June 1989. Cited on pages 62, 169.

[469]   W. C. Yen, D. W. L. Yen and K.-S. Fu, "Data Coherence Problems in a Multi-cache System," *IEEE Transactions on Computers*, vol. c-34, no. 1, pp. 56-65, January 1985. Cited on pages 545, 547, 547.

[470]   Pen-Yung Yew, "Architecture of the Cedar Parallel Supercomputer," in George Paul and George S. Almasi, editors, *Parallel Systems and Computation: Proceedings of the 1986 IBM Europe Institute Seminar on Parallel Computing*, Amsterdam: North-Holland, 1988. Cited on page 612.

[471]   Michael Young, Avadis Tevanian, Richard Rashid, David Golub, Jeffrey Eppinger, Jonathan Chew, William Bolosky, David Black and Robert Baron, "The Duality of Memory and Communication in the Implementation of a Multiprocessor Operating System," *Proceedings of the Eleventh ACM Symposium on Operating Systems Principles*, pp. 63-76, Austin, Texas, November 1987. Cited on page 369.

[472]   H. Zima and B. Chapman, *Supercompilers for Parallel and Vector Computers*, New York: ACM Press, 1991. Cited on pages 151, 295, 318, 318.

Index